4

FOURTH EDITION

# Invitation to Critical Thinking

# Invitation to Critical Thinking

4

FOURTH EDITION

JOEL RUDINOW

SANTA ROSA JUNIOR COLLEGE

VINCENT E. BARRY

BAKERSFIELD COLLEGE

HARCOURT BRACE COLLEGE PUBLISHERS

FORT WORTH PHILADELPHIA SAN DIEGO NEW YORK AUSTIN ORLANDO SAN ANTONIO
TORONTO MONTREAL LONDON SYDNEY TOKYO

Publisher
Earl McPeek
Acquisitions Editor
David Tatom
Product Manager
Laura Brennan
Project Editor
Travis Tyre
Art Director
Linda Beaupré
Production Manager
Serena Barnett

ISBN: 0-15-505562-3
Library of Congress Catalog Card Number: 98-72953



*Address for orders:*
Harcourt Brace & Company
6277 Sea Harbor Drive
Orlando, FL 32887-6777
1-800-782-4479

*Address for editorial correspondence:*
Harcourt Brace College Publishers
301 Commerce Street, Suite 3700
Fort Worth, TX 76102

Web site address:
http://www.hbcollege.com



Printed in the United States of America

8 9 0 1 2 3 4 5 6 7 016 9 8 7 6 5 4

# PREFACE

Much has changed in the world since the first edition of *Invitation to Critical Thinking* was published fifteen years ago. Much about the book itself has had to change to remain in touch with its students and their world. Many illustrations and examples from previous editions have now disappeared into the "dustbin of history."

Times have changed in education as well. But at the same time, it is remarkable how much remains the same. Although there are ongoing discussions of revising general education requirements in colleges and universities around the country, and indeed around the world, courses in informal logic and critical thinking are by now well established as basic to all of education. These courses, designed to help students develop the ability to understand and assess ordinary, everyday arguments and thereby solve problems and make decisions, are clearly necessary in education. And so, while the examples continue to change, the instructional agenda of critical thinking remains just as important as ever.

In this text, the agenda remains substantially the same as in previous editions and continues to focus on the recognition, analysis, evaluation, and composition of arguments as discursive tools of rational persuasion.

Additions to the fourth edition of *Invitation to Critical Thinking* include:

- Units on paraphrasing arguments
- Units on constructing formal analogies as a strategy of argument evaluation
- An expanded section on categorical logic, including new material on translating statements into standard form for categorical logic, immediate inferences, and the traditional square of opposition
- An expanded chapter on inductive reasoning, including new material on margin of error, on "burden of proof" arguments, and on arguments by analogy

Much of the material in this new edition has been updated, overhauled, and streamlined.

Other changes in the text include the renaming of the four main parts, or divisions, of the book itself. They are now listed as The Basics, Analysis, Evaluation, and Applications. This reorganization has aided in consolidating and better arranging the conceptual core material, making the text considerably more suitable for use in courses taught on the quarter system, yet remaining equally suitable for semester-length presentations.

**PART ONE: THE BASICS** is intended to establish a few fundamental concepts and some shared terminology as the basic framework within which the text and the course can take shape. Chapter 1 begins by defining critical thinking and other basic terms and goes on to state a few basic assumptions, dispel a handful of common myths, and explore an array of common obstacles to critical thinking. In Chapter 2, the crucial interface between critical thinking and language is explored.

**PART TWO: ANALYSIS** presents and develops the core concept of an argument as a crucial tool of rational persuasion and as a composition in which ideas are arranged in relationships of rational support. Chapter 3 introduces relevant conceptual material and terminology and focuses on recognizing or identifying arguments as such. Chapter 4 presents techniques for paraphrasing arguments and breaking them down into their structural elements, as well as comprehending the structural relationships among these elements. Chapter 5 presents techniques for reconstructing arguments from their sometimes fragmentary expressions.

**PART THREE: EVALUATION** presents and develops standards and practices for evaluating arguments. Chapter 6 focuses on deductive reasoning and develops the concept of deductive validity in the context of categorical and truth functional logic. Chapter 7 focuses on inductive reasoning and develops criteria for evaluating inductive generalizations, analogies, and varieties of hypothetical and causal reasoning. Chapter 8 applies the concepts developed in Chapters 6 and 7 to evaluating the premises of arguments. Chapters 9 through 11 survey an array of common informal fallacies.

In previous editions of this book, the body was surrounded, supplemented, and interspersed with chapters on the mass media, reading and writing argumentative essays, and problem solving.

**PART FOUR: APPLICATIONS** retains these materials and collects them together in their own section. Chapter 12 on research and the media offers analysis and guidance for navigating through today's information environment. It applies the core material to the challenge of sifting reliable information out of the massive flow. The chapter consolidates material found in earlier editions on the news media, on journalism, and on advertising in mass communications. This chapter contains a new section on the Internet and the World Wide Web. Chapter 13 on reading for the argument also consolidates material from earlier editions and applies the core material to the reading of extended arguments. It includes both a model example and numerous practice examples. Chapter 14 applies the core material to the challenge of composing argumentative essays, and Chapter 15 applies the core material to the challenges of problem solving in general.

**ANCILLARY MATERIALS** Another major change to the fourth edition concerns the ancillary support materials that accompany the book. *Invitation to Critical Thinking, Fourth Edition,* now has an array of support resources on the

World Wide Web. Instructors using the printed text have access to an e-mail discussion group, a syllabus generator, and an array of teaching tools and resources available online at our Web site. Students using the book will have access to an interactive, self-paced, tutorial support program that is also available online. Within the chapters, Web tutorial exercises are identified by the "http://" icon (as shown). These hands-on exercises provide the student with immediate feedback and programmed instruction in key areas of the course content. To access the Web site for *Invitation to Critical Thinking, Fourth Edition,* first point your browser to **http://www.hbcollege.com.** Once there, access the Philosophy discipline where you will be directed to the Companion Web site for this book.

**ACKNOWLEDGMENTS** A project of this size owes a great deal to a lot of people. I must first thank my wife Dawn, who bore the brunt of the agonies of the tortured writer, and my parents Jack and Mattie Rudinow, who were there, as always, when the chips were down. I also wish to especially acknowledge the contributions of Michael Donovan, who rewrote the Instructor's Manual and co-wrote the Web tutorial; Craig Hermann and Katherine Sauceda, who contributed so much to the design of the Web site (writing much of the code for it and troubleshooting what we wrote); and Randy MacNally, Jay Field, Bill Stone, and all the folks at CATE (Center for Advanced Technology in Education) at Santa Rosa Junior College, where we did the programming.

Four reviewers of the third edition offered many helpful suggestions for improvement, which we took to heart and even used. They were Sylvia Culp, Western Michigan University; Joan Whitman Hoff, Lock Haven University of Pennsylvania; Sue Kataldi, Southern Illinois University; and George Rainbolt, Georgia State University.

I also wish to thank David Tatom at Harcourt Brace College Publishers for his understanding and for helping us realize our vision of something new and unprecedented in Internet-based pedagogy. Pam Hatley, Cathy Richard, Travis Tyre, Serena Barnett, Linda Beaupré, and Matt Ball managed to take a late manuscript and its accompanying materials through the labyrinth of editorial, graphic design, and production processes smoothly, painlessly, and on time!

Finally, I acknowledge with thanks the ongoing support and encouragement of my colleagues in the department of philosophy at Santa Rosa Junior College.

**JOEL RUDINOW**
*Sonoma, CA*

# CONTENTS

# LIST OF EXERCISES

# PART ONE The Basics

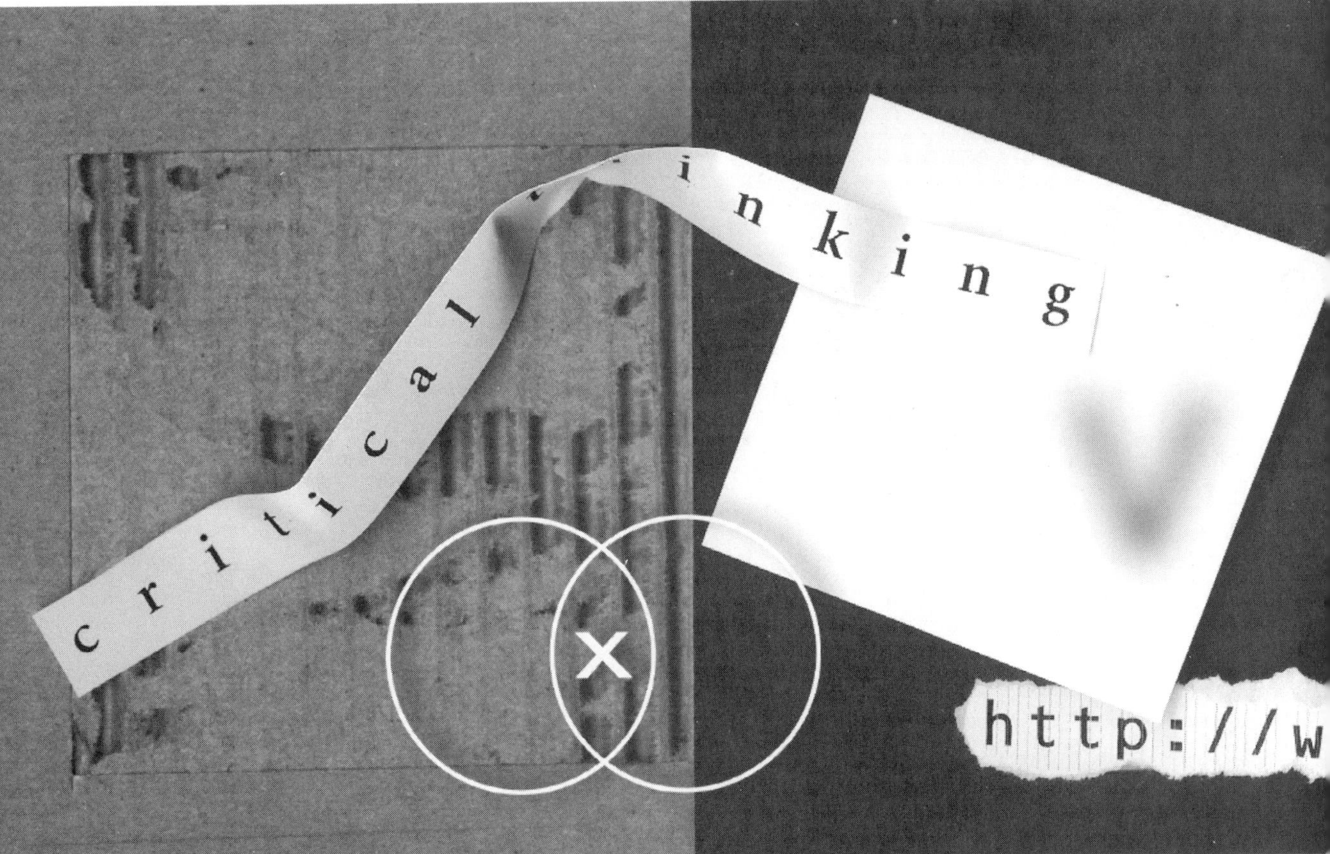

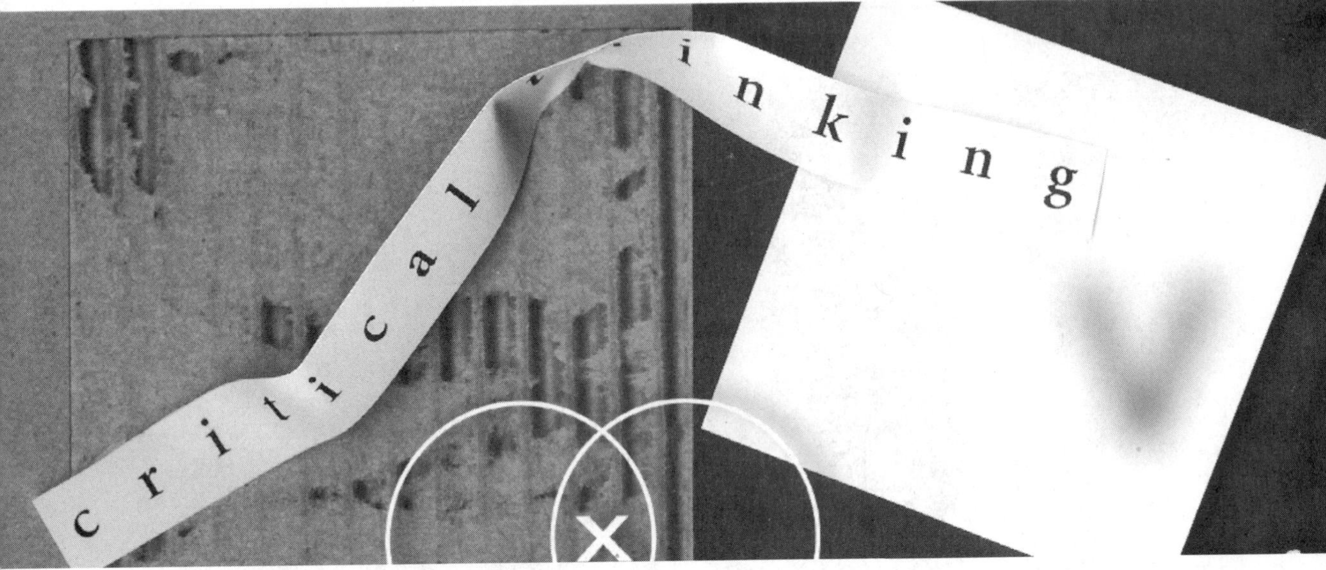


# CHAPTER 1 Critical Thinking

"Follow me." MARSHALL HERFF APPLEWHITE

In the early spring of 1997, Marshall Herff Applewhite, known by his followers as "Do," the leader of the doomsday cult Heaven's Gate—a group of people who believed many strange things including the idea that the appearance of the Hale-Bopp comet would be a divine sign of salvation and that a spaceship was cruising along in the tail of the comet waiting to pick them up and take them to the "next level," a level beyond this mortal, human world—led thirty-eight of his followers in a mass suicide. This event immediately became global front-page news attracting e-mails from as far away as Australia, Canada, Cyprus, New Zealand, Norway, and Scotland, where the story had been published on the front page. Here in the United States, the three major news weeklies, *Time, Newsweek,* and *U.S. News and World Report,* each ran extensive cover stories, complete with elaborate sidebars on UFOs, the Internet, comets, and cults. The *Time* and *Newsweek* covers were nearly identical, with captions that read: "Inside the Web of Death" and "'Follow Me': Inside the Heaven's Gate Mass Suicide."

These headlines seemed to acknowledge how bizarre the whole episode looked from the "outside," and at the same time appealed to the morbid curiosity of many readers who wanted a closer look, an "inside perspective." The statements attracted those who wanted to know "What makes such people tick?" The

cover caption on *U.S. News and World Report,* though aimed in the same general direction, had a slightly different spin: "Lost Souls: How Reasonable People Can Hold Unreasonable Beliefs."

Whether or not the members of Heaven's Gate were "reasonable people," and however "reasonable" or "unreasonable" their beliefs may have been, it certainly seems reasonable to suppose that from time to time perfectly "reasonable" people come to hold "unreasonable" beliefs about one thing or another. This is a pretty good point at which to begin talking about critical thinking. You probably know people whom you consider to be "reasonable," who nevertheless hold or have held beliefs that you consider to be "not entirely reasonable" and maybe even downright "unreasonable," beliefs that could get them into all kinds of avoidable difficulty. How does this happen? One answer is that there are many interfering urges, pressures, inducements, and distractions that make it relatively difficult, even for reasonable people, to reliably discriminate between reasonable and unreasonable beliefs. That fact is what makes critical thinking important.

For example, back in 1988 voters in the state of California were presented with not one but *six* separate ballot initiative measures, sponsored by a diverse array of interest groups, each of which claimed to provide the definitive answer to the question of insurance reform and regulation in the state. A consumer interest group proposed a measure that provided for an elected Insurance Commissioner, rate rollbacks, and other changes. The insurance industry countered with a barrage of

This poses an interesting question: "How is it that reasonable people come to hold unreasonable beliefs?" Notice how the question involves what in critical thinking we call "assumptions" or "presuppositions." In order to entertain this question in the context of this story, you have to assume that the thirty-nine members of the Heaven's Gate cult (or at least some of them) were "reasonable people," and you also have to assume that the beliefs that led them to commit mass suicide (or at least some of them) were "unreasonable beliefs." Are these "reasonable assumptions"? We'll come back to this shortly.

measures including a "No-Fault" proposal and a measure to limit lawyers' contingency fees. The lawyers countered with measures of their own, that included, with the collaboration of Mothers Against Drunk Driving, a "Good Driver" initiative.

During the heat of the campaign, we asked our students for their views on insurance reform. "After all," we said, "You're of voting age. Most of you drive, so the question of how insurance rate structures are regulated affects your lives in a direct way; and there's no shortage of information around at the moment. So, what do you think?"

The response oscillated between cynical indifference toward the entire issue to frustration that bordered on rage. The six measures were not circulated to the general public until the Voter's Manual was sent to all registered voters just prior to the election. They were also written in complicated legalese that many voters found completely unintelligible. Yet, voters were besieged for months leading up to the election by appeals for support from all sides. Some $75 million was spent on saturation television advertising, and literally tons of paper circulated throughout the state in the form of direct mail campaign literature that extolled the virtues of this measure and more typically decried the deficiencies of that one. "What do you want from me?" a typical student said. "One group says what the other denies. I don't know what to make of any of it! I think they're *all* lying."

Do you sense the anger in this response? We did. Now, let's consider the conclusion our "typical" student came to: "I think they're *all* lying." That was certainly among the possibilities. But, it was also possible that at least *some* of the arguments that we were all, as citizens, being called upon to consider were honest, legitimate, and truthful ones. Our "typical" student was closing her mind to this possibility. We didn't think that this was a very "reasonable" conclusion to reach. But, maybe this is not what our "typical" student actually had in mind.

*You may be wondering why we keep putting quotation marks (" ") around certain words (like "reasonable," "typical," "assumptions"). These are words that we think should be* "defined" *clearly so as to avoid misunderstandings. For example, when we called our student "typical," we don't mean that her response to our question was like that of all of our students, or even most of our students, but only that a fair number of students responded in pretty much the way she did. We'll come back to this shortly.*

Perhaps what our "typical" student actually had in mind was something more like this: "I don't know how to make up my mind here. All these arguments, counterarguments, rebuttals, accusations, counteraccusations, and denials have got me confused. And right now, I don't see how I can trust any of these sources." We think this *is* a pretty "reasonable" position to take. What it boils down to is the need for basic critical thinking skills and strategies to be applied in a situation like this. Then, maybe we and our students could figure out who's lying and who's telling the truth and who's got the better argument and which way we should vote.

## WHAT IS CRITICAL THINKING?

You're about to embark upon a course of study in critical thinking, and you have a right to know what you're getting into. *We think of critical thinking as a set of skills and strategies for making reasonable decisions about what to do or believe.* There's that word "reasonable" again. Maybe now would be a good time for us to clarify what we have in mind when we call something "reasonable."

The word "reasonable" has as its root the word "reason." So let's start there. "Reason" comes from the Latin word *ratio,* for "calculation or computation." *We think of reason as the capacity to use disciplined intelligence to solve problems.* On this basis, it is fairly easy to explain the meaning of other words in the same family. For example, "reasoning" can be understood as using disciplined intelligence to solve a problem or determine a course of action. A "reasonable decision" can be understood as one arrived at through the use of reason. A "reasonable person" can be understood as one who (at least ordinarily) uses reason to decide what to do or believe.

*Do you remember the question we started with about the members of Heaven's Gate? "How is it that reasonable people come to hold unreasonable beliefs?" Now, how would you answer the question we posed: "Is it reasonable to assume that at least some members of the Heaven's Gate cult were reasonable people and also that at least some of their beliefs were unreasonable beliefs?" We'll come back to this shortly.*

## EXERCISE | Freewriting

This first exercise is a "freewrite." Freewriting, like brainstorming, is a technique for liberating creative mental energy. When you freewrite, don't worry about parallel sentence structure, split infinitives, sentence fragments, or any of the other editorial problems your instructors will nag you about on a finished essay. When you freewrite, don't worry about anything—even spelling—which would simply interfere with the flow of your ideas onto paper.

Freewrite for ten minutes on what you hope and expect to get out of a course in critical thinking. Don't plan what you're going to write. Just start writing. And don't stop to reconsider, refine, edit, or correct what you've written. Just keep writing. If you can't think of a good way to begin, just complete this sentence: "What I hope and expect to get out of a course in critical thinking is . . . "

When you've written for this length of time, complete your final thought, and (if you're on a computer) save your freewrite. We'll be coming back to this later. Ready? Go.

Reason is a pretty special and important capacity. Some have held that it is a distinctively human capacity. An old tradition defines humans as the "rational animals," the only species with the capacity to reason. Other animals have intelligence. But only humans cultivate and develop their intelligence through discipline in order to solve problems. There are others who disagree with this and think that there is evidence of reason and reasoning capacity exhibited in the behavior of a few species of nonhuman animals. But, whether reason is a distinctively human characteristic or not, it has certainly proven to be an important survival trait in humans. Without reason, we humans would be severely handicapped in the struggle for the survival of our species. Notice also that reason pertains to *humanity.* As we understand it, reason is a *human* trait; it belongs to human beings, as human beings. It is not gender specific, nor is it restricted by age, race, or ethnicity. We presume that all members of the human species have the capacity to cultivate and develop their intelligence through discipline in order to solve problems. That's what education is all about.

In our definition of "reason," the word "disciplined" is crucial. Let us take a moment to reflect on the meaning of "discipline." There are two things that should be pointed out about this crucial concept right at the outset. First, any discipline has rules, or at least regularities of some kind. To master any discipline, you need to learn the rules and regularities. Secondly, discipline takes practice. Music is a good example of a "discipline." To become a musician, you need to learn a few of the rules and regularities by practicing. The same is true of critical thinking.

## THREE MYTHS ABOUT CRITICAL THINKING

In teaching critical thinking over the years, we have encountered a number of common myths and confusions about the subject. So, just in case you also have heard some of these ideas expressed, let us at least tell you what we think of them.

**Myth #1** *Critical Thinking and Negativity* Lots of people seem to think that the word "critical," almost by definition, involves negativity; that criticism is essentially fault finding, and that a critic is a fault-finder. And so, anything with the word "critical" in its name must be similarly concerned with finding faults and weaknesses and other negative things. This myth may spring primarily from a misunderstanding of the word "critical."

The word "critical" and its cognates "criticism," "critic," "critique," and so on, derive from the Greek word *kritikos,* meaning "discernment or the ability to judge," which in turn derives from the Greek word *krinein,* meaning "decision making." This is the way we prefer to understand critical thinking. This approach is concerned with decision making. So, yes, it is interested in finding faults and negative considerations, but not these alone. It is equally concerned with recognizing strengths and other positives. Critical thinking is interested in the "pros" as well as the "cons."

**Myth #2** *Critical Thinking and Personal Power* We often hear critical thinking discussed in terms of personal power. Sometimes, critical thinking is promoted as a means of "empowerment," which is considered to be a plus, something advantageous. On the other hand, we also often hear of concerns about critical thinking functioning as a means of domination, which is considered to be harmful, something to be avoided. So, what is the relationship between critical thinking and personal power?

In our view, critical thinking is indeed empowering and can significantly enhance one's chances of success in one's career as well as in the wide variety of social roles each of us is destined to play. This is because the strategies, skills, and dispositions of critical thinking are essential elements of something even more fundamental and basic: personal autonomy. "Autonomy" comes from the Greek words *auto* for "self" and *nomos* for "regulation." An autonomous person is self-regulating, or self-directing. Autonomy is empowering because it makes one less dependent upon—and so, less vulnerable to—the dictates, directions, and influence of others. Persons who can make up their own minds don't *need* others to tell them what to think or do, and so are less likely to be dominated by others.

But, let us at the same time be wary of the similar sounding idea that critical thinking will enable us to dominate or gain power over others, an unfortunate and dangerous way to conceive of critical thinking. We have seen some actual cases where people have tried to use some of the things they've learned in critical thinking to humiliate, control, or otherwise take advantage of people. We would say simply that to apply critical thinking toward such goals is to distort, misunderstand, and misuse it. Critical thinking should be thought of as liberating, not as a "power trip."

**Myth #3** *Critical Thinking and Creativity* Earlier, we said that critical thinking involves discipline, which is concerned with rules and regularities and requires practice. Sometimes people jump from this to the conclusion that critical thinking does not involve or encourage creativity. We think this stems in part from the mistaken idea that creativity is essentially a matter of *breaking* the rules. On the contrary, creativity is often very much involved in *following* the rules. Sometimes, an original creative insight is needed to know just how to interpret and apply the rules in a given situation. Such situations often call for "judgment" or "discretion." We hope and anticipate that you'll recognize such examples from time to time as you work your way through this book.

## BASIC ASSUMPTIONS

### ASSUMPTIONS

We said we'd come back to this. We described "assumption" as a word that needs to be defined clearly in order to avoid misunderstanding. *An assumption is a "claim" which is taken to be true without "argument."* In this definition, we use two terms, "claim" and "argument," which also need to be clarified. *A claim is a statement which is either true or false.* Argument is a concept which we're going to define and develop in detail later in this book. For the time being, just think of an argument as *support* for a *claim*. So, an *assumption* is an *unsupported claim*.

## HIDDEN ASSUMPTIONS

Sometimes assumptions are "hidden," which really means "unstated" or "implied." For example, suppose one of your sociology classmates says, "You know, as a society we really shouldn't be relying on computers as much as we do." And you wonder why, and she says, "Well, don't forget, computers are designed and built by human beings." Can you see intuitively that in this case there's an unstated assumption that human beings are unreliable, or at least that things designed and built by human beings are unreliable?

## EXPLICIT ASSUMPTIONS

Not all assumptions are hidden however. For example, when Thomas Jefferson wrote in the Declaration of Independence,

> We hold these truths to be self-evident, that all men are created equal, that they are endowed by their Creator with certain unalienable Rights, that among these are Life, Liberty and the pursuit of Happiness.

he was certainly not *hiding* these assumptions. There they are in black and white and in so many words (thirty-six to be exact). When Jefferson said "We hold these truths to be self-evident," he was saying that he thought it reasonable to assert these claims without support, in other words as assumptions.

## INFERENTIAL ASSUMPTIONS

Let's look once again at the example we used above to illustrate the category of hidden assumptions. Your classmate says, "As a society we really shouldn't be relying on computers as much as we do." You say, "Why?" and she says, "Well, computers are designed and built by human beings." Here the hidden assumption functions as added support linking the support your classmate *does* offer explicitly ("computers are designed and built by human beings") with the claim that you have called into question ("we shouldn't rely on computers so much"). Assumptions which play this sort of linking role are often called "inferential assumptions." We'll be developing this concept more fully in Chapter 5.

## PRESUPPOSITIONS

Other assumptions function in a different way. Sometimes in order to make any sense of what *is* stated or expressed explicitly, we are required to assume additional claims which are not stated explicitly. This is the way the *U.S. News and World Report* cover caption, "Lost Souls: How Reasonable People Can Hold Unreasonable Beliefs," works. Because you need to suppose that the thirty-nine members of the Heaven's Gate cult (or at least some of them) were "reasonable people," and that the beliefs that led them to commit mass suicide (or at least some of them) were "unreasonable beliefs," *in order to make sense of* the cover caption, we call these and other assumptions of this kind "*pre*suppositions."

## MAKING ASSUMPTIONS

Recognizing assumptions is an important part of critical thinking. But what then? What do we do once we've recognized that assumptions are being made? Perhaps you are familiar with a common usage according to which calling something an "assumption" is to say that it is suspect or dubious. Maybe you have heard the cliché, *'Assume' makes an 'ass' out of 'u' and 'me',* which is usually meant to counsel against making any assumptions at all. We hope you can tell from what we've said so far that we're not quite so heavily down on assumptions as this. We would prefer to say something slightly less drastic. Assumptions are generally *questionable.* In other words it is generally reasonable to ask for support for an unsupported claim. Maybe the assumptions *are* reasonable after all, in which case it ought to be possible to present a reasonable argument in support of them.

*Remember our earlier question about the members of Heaven's Gate: "Is it reasonable to assume that at least some members of the Heaven's Gate cult were reasonable people and also that at least some of their beliefs were unreasonable beliefs?" Well, how did you answer that question? Do you think it's reasonable to assume that at least some members of Heaven's Gate were reasonable people and that at least some of their beliefs were unreasonable beliefs? How would you support your answer?*

Like the editors of *U.S. News and World Report,* and like Thomas Jefferson in the Declaration of Independence, (and indeed like most thinking individuals in most situations—because it's *very* hard to avoid making any assumptions at all) we are basing this book on some assumptions. We of course think that the assumptions we're making, and asking you to make with us, are "reasonable" assumptions. But as we just admitted, all of this is open to question. And so we might be challenged to provide arguments in support of our assumptions. And of course we think we could do that, but first we should tell you what our assumptions are.

## ASSUMPTIONS ABOUT THE TRUTH

The concept of "the truth" is a tricky one. Philosophers have developed a number of competing "theories of truth" which could be debated at great length. However, for our purposes we are going to assume that "truth" is a relationship between ideas (or beliefs or statements) and whatever those ideas (or beliefs or statements) are about. The great American philosopher William James put it this way when he defined "truth":

> Truth is a property of certain of our ideas. It means their "agreement," as falsity means their disagreement, with "reality".[1]

A statement is true if (and only if) it reports an actual state of affairs (that is, some present, past, or future event, condition, or circumstance). Obviously there are many states of affairs in the world. If you're over five feet tall, that's a state of affairs; if the current air temperature is 60 degrees Fahrenheit, that's a state of affairs. And if you *are* over five feet tall, then the idea (or belief or statement) that you are over five feet tall is true—and of course the idea (or belief or statement) that you are not over five feet tall—is false.

Given this conception of truth, problems arise in determining which claims are actually true. Now this is not *always* difficult. We assume that you have no problem determining whether or not you are over five feet tall. (Unless you're approximately four feet, eleven and seven-eighths inches tall or something like that.) One reason we chose this particular example at this stage is because it is so straightforward and unproblematic. You just stand up in the door frame with the tape measure, no problem. But other claims are harder to decide. For example: Is it reasonable to assume that at least some members of the Heaven's Gate cult were reasonable people? Suppose you think it *is* reasonable to assume that some of the members of Heaven's Gate were reasonable people ("They just got 'brainwashed' by Applewhite into believing some unreasonable beliefs."). Suppose someone else thinks it's *not* reasonable to assume this ("Anyone who would let a weirdo like Applewhite 'brainwash' him into castrating and killing himself must have been not very tightly wrapped going in."). Which one of you is closer to the truth here? Hard to tell. And some claims are maybe even harder to decide. For example: Do you think it's reasonable to assume that there is extraterrestrial intelligent life? Suppose you think so. And somebody thinks not. Which one of you is closer to the truth here? Very hard to tell.

Please notice that what we're saying about the truth presupposes the existence of the truth. That is another one of our assumptions. We also assume that finding out what the truth is would be a reasonable thing to try to do *in any case*, however difficult or problematic the case may be. This again is why critical thinking is important.

## OBSTACLES TO CRITICAL THINKING

Throughout this chapter we've provided opportunities for you to wonder about how reasonable people come to hold unreasonable beliefs. Earlier, we suggested that a partial answer is that there are many interfering urges, pressures, inducements, and distractions that make it relatively difficult, even for reasonable people, to reliably discriminate between reasonable and unreasonable beliefs, which is why critical thinking is so important. This would suggest that critical thinking would be helpful to reasonable people who are trying to maintain a reasonable outlook. There's a very down-to-earth, commonsense dimension to critical thinking, as we understand the term. We've also thought about the extent to which people around us, and people in general, tend to think critically. And the impression we have is that a lot of pretty "normal" people generally don't think critically, or they think critically only about certain things in their lives but not at all about certain other things in their lives (sometimes the things that matter most). And this makes us wonder. Why isn't something as "down-to-earth" and "commonsense" as critical thinking more common? Why do so many people find

thinking critically so difficult? Why is it that so many otherwise intelligent people get taken in so regularly and easily by hucksters and confidence artists when just a little critical thinking would protect them from exploitation? Answering these questions calls for a look at some "obstacles" to critical thinking. An obstacle is something that stands in the way. Where do you suppose it would make sense to look for obstacles to critical thinking? Let's look at the thinking process itself.

Let's try a little thought experiment: Try saying the following sentence about yourself:

> Some of my beliefs are false.[2]

Some people have trouble with this. "After all," you might say, "part of believing something is believing that it's *true*." We agree. Part of believing something *is* believing that it's true.

"But then," someone might go on to argue, "if I were to do an inventory of my beliefs, they'd all seem true to me. In other words, if I found out that something was false, I wouldn't believe it. So, it doesn't really make sense for me to say that some of my own beliefs are false!"

Perhaps you experienced no such resistance. "After all," you might equally well say, "I've been mistaken in the past. I've learned on numerous occasions, and pretty much throughout my life, that things that I believed to be true were really false. Why should it be any different now? So, if I were to do an inventory of my beliefs, I probably wouldn't notice the false ones, but I'd still bet there are some in there somewhere."

There is some truth in both of these reactions. Also, there is some confusion and error in the first reaction particularly, which we'll get to shortly. But, for openers, let's just notice what together they tell us about critical thinking and why many people have such trouble with it. The second reaction expresses an attitude of maturity and "intellectual humility," a recognition of our natural human liability to error. Let's just say that this attitude is basic to thinking critically.

But, look what happens in the first reaction. Apparently, there are some equally deep-seated obstacles in each of us that stand in the way of developing this attitude. What *is* a belief, anyway? Try thinking of belief as though you were a kind of "investor." What you're investing is your trust or confidence. That's what we mean when we say "Part of believing something is believing that it's true."

Beliefs, like other investments, can be very difficult to walk away from, especially if you "live by your beliefs." This is true even when the evidence begins to mount that it was a bad investment. There's a natural inclination to cling to the investment and try one's best to salvage it and hope that it will turn out in the long run to be a good one. Holding on is common, even to the point of denying the evidence. And this, as we'll see shortly, explains quite a bit about obstacles to critical thinking.

## WHAT IS YOUR WORLDVIEW?

Let's try another little thought experiment: A moment ago, the idea came up of doing an inventory of our own beliefs. Now try to describe what this would actually be like. How long would it take? How would you start? What kind of procedure would you use? How would you keep track? . . . After you've struggled with this for a while, go ahead and start an inventory of your beliefs. Give yourself a measured five minutes and see what you come up with. Try this with somebody else and compare notes.

See if you don't notice that you've got more beliefs to keep track of than you might have thought at first and beliefs of more different kinds than you might have thought at first. Maybe you began to notice that you have beliefs about what beliefs are and about how many of them you have and so on.

And consequently, you may have begun to wonder about an "inventory control" problem. "Have these beliefs that I'm noticing been here all along? Or are they new ones that have now sprung up as a result of my paying this new and strange kind of attention to my beliefs?" Five minutes into your inventory, can you be sure that you still have all the beliefs you had when you started?

This, too, tells us something about obstacles to critical thinking. Each of us has a belief system into which we have incorporated a very large number of beliefs—so many, in fact, that trying to count them seems crazy. We routinely just assume most of these beliefs. In other words, we take them as true without questioning them or examining the adequacy of the support there may be for them. So, if you're like most people, a large part of your belief system is probably "subterranean," and it functions in a largely unexamined way, as a set of assumptions of which you may not even be fully aware. The sheer volume of a normal person's belief system, especially coupled with the largely unexamined status of most of its specific contents, greatly increases the likelihood of mistaken beliefs among them.

Secondly, our belief systems are not static or permanent. Rather, they undergo more or less constant change and revision as we deal with incoming information. Let's consider how this process normally works.

We live in what has come to be known as the "information age," a label which derives from the awesome volume of information constantly bombarding us on a daily basis. Just think of the amount of material contained in the average metropolitan daily newspaper. Now, multiply that by seven days a week, and then again by the number of metropolitan population centers you can think of in a few short minutes. That should be enough to make the point that there's far too much information to pay attention to, let alone absorb. And that's just daily newspapers. Then, there are weekly, monthly, quarterly, and annual publications, and books, not to mention radio and television, which together add up to literally hundreds of separate stations, channels, and cable services, many of which broadcast around the clock. And now, there's the advent of the Internet! Again, it's obvious that there's just no way to pay attention to or absorb all of the information we have access to.

Consequently, each of us has to be very selective about where we direct our attention in this overwhelming flow of information. Actually, this is nothing new or peculiar to our age. In fact, it's part of the human condition. There's always more to pay attention to than any of us has attention. And, if you're like most people, even within the narrow range of information you do become aware of, you continue to be selective. Some incoming information will be actively incorporated into your belief system; some will be rejected. What do you suppose are the main factors that govern this process? What do you suppose determines these selections?

Among the most important and influential of these factors is the existing content of our belief systems. The way we deal with incoming information is determined in large part by what we already believe. Your belief system is self-editing. This is what we mean by a person's "worldview." *We each have a tendency to view the world, including ourselves, according to a self-regulating system of assumptions and other beliefs.*

Don't forget, large portions of your worldview normally function unexamined below the threshold of your awareness, which makes it more likely that it contains mistaken beliefs. And, beliefs are inherently difficult to give up. So, the fact that your worldview functions also as a frame of reference against which new information is evaluated explains quite a bit about human fallibility. Such an arrangement, unavoidable and natural though it may be, makes it much more likely that mistaken beliefs will perpetuate themselves within our worldviews, if we don't make a special effort to guard against the invasion of these beliefs.

## EGOCENTRICITY

Let's explore further how difficult it can be to make such a special effort. One rather obvious thing about your worldview is that it's *yours.* You "identify with it." You probably favor it and are inclined to defend it in conflict with other worldviews. All of this is perfectly normal and natural. Not many people regularly read political journals that present views contrary to the ones they hold. Probably even fewer have ever seriously investigated religious views incompatible with their own, or have deeply considered alternatives to their views of right and wrong, good and bad. Indeed, many of us react to beliefs, values, and attitudes that challenge our own with self-righteous contempt. The fact is that many of us not only don't care to seriously consider alternative worldviews, we don't even want to know about them. Why? *In a word, we are naturally "egocentric." We are naturally inclined to favor and defend ourselves and the positions, values, traditions, and groups with which we identify ourselves.*

Even in science, one can find examples of egocentricity standing in the way of critical thinking. Galileo's astronomical treatise, *Dialogue on the Two Chief Systems of the World* (1632), was a thoughtful and devastating attack on the traditional geocentric view of the universe proposed by the ancient Greek Ptolemy (second century A.D.) and accepted by most scholars and scientists of Galileo's time. Galileo's treatise was therefore an attack not only on the views that these authorities held, as well as on the authoritative status that they were privileged to enjoy, but also on their self-images. Their reaction was to censor Galileo. Pope Urban, who was persuaded that Simplicio, the butt of the whole dialogue, was intended to represent himself, ordered Galileo to appear before the Inquisition. Although never formally imprisoned, Galileo was threatened with torture and forced to renounce what he had written. In 1633, he was banished to his country estate. His *Dialogue*, together with the works of Kepler and Copernicus, were placed on the Index of Forbidden Books, from which they were not withdrawn until 1835.

## WISHFUL THINKING AND SELF-DECEPTION

Not only is our belief structure so constituted as to harbor self-perpetuating falsehoods, which we sometimes try to hide from others, but we frequently engage in wishful thinking, and we are capable even of self-deception. "How can this be?" you might wonder. "How can a person know that something is false and continue to believe it? How can a person be both the successful deceiver and the victim of the deception at the same time?" These are very good questions. There is something deeply puzzling about self-deception. But, if you thought for a moment, you'd likely be able to come up with an example or two from your own experience of the sort of thing we're talking about. You probably know people who have on occasion talked themselves into believing things that they knew weren't true. For example, they may have said they were ready for the midterm exam when, in fact, they knew they weren't really prepared. If we were perfectly rational creatures, then we would no doubt recognize the inconsistency involved in self-deception, and so if we were perfectly rational creatures, then self-deception probably would never occur. But, there is little doubt that it does occur. We are rational creatures, but not perfectly so. We are also (in some ways and at some times) irrational creatures, and our wishes and desires often overwhelm our good sense. So, we often persist in believing what we want to believe or what we wish were true, in spite of what we know or have every reason to believe. And we do this sometimes at great peril to others and even ourselves.

"Why would we do something as irrational as deceive ourselves?" someone might ask. But this is not quite as good a question. It seems to be based on the assumption that self-deception is necessarily and always completely irrational. To be more fair, we should be prepared to admit that sometimes the truth is just too painful for people to watch or admit. Some people who identify with Nazism seem to find it impossible to believe that the Holocaust actually occurred. Some Jews find it too painful to confront the reality of the state of Israel supplying armaments to a white racist government in South Africa. Throughout the cold war period, many people found it too painful to confront the reality of a world poised constantly on the brink of nuclear winter. People go into what some psychologists call "denial." They simply refuse to believe it. They just say "No." The world contains such monstrous ugliness sometimes that we can't simply say that this kind of self-deception is always *completely* irrational. It *is* always irrational; but maybe not completely so. Can you think of a realistic scenario in which you'd be able to understand why a reasonable individual would refuse to recognize the truth? Of course, self-deception of any sort stands directly in the way of thinking critically.

## CULTURE AND ETHNOCENTRICITY

So far, we have been exploring obstacles to critical thinking from the point of view of individual human psychology. We should not overlook the social dimension of human nature. Humans are naturally social beings. We do not survive well or prosper in isolation. Rather, we collect together in groups, such as families, communities, nations, and cultures. Our welfare as individuals is largely determined by how well we do within our groups and how well our groups do. Being a successful member of a successful family in a successful community, nation, or culture is what human welfare is about. And this has an inevitable impact on our individual psychological lives and belief structures and on how and what we think, because to a large extent, we tend to think in terms shared by others in the groups with which we identify. Probably the two most basic social groupings are our families (kinship groupings) and our cultural groupings. Cultural groupings can be more or less formal, such as a nation or an organized religion, or they can be more or less informal, such as a generation or a circle of friends. However these groupings are defined, they tend to play an important role in the formation of our individual personal identities because we identify ourselves, to a large extent, in terms of them.

In recent years, cultural identity has gained recognition as a matter of political importance. Multiculturalism is high on the agenda of many educational institutions which are now sensitive to the importance of cultural diversity within the community and curriculum. Instructors now strive to reflect multicultural perspectives in their courses (as well as authors in their textbooks). In critical thinking, cultural diversity and an awareness of alternative cultural perspectives are especially useful because of the limitations inherent in any given cultural perspective. An appreciation of cultural diversity contributes to open-mindedness, an essential ingredient of critical thinking.

Ethnic consciousness, like self-awareness, and ethnic pride, like self-esteem, are important ingredients in a healthy personality and society. But they each have corresponding perversions that can stand as obstacles to critical thinking (and cause serious grief as well). The natural human tendency to be egocentric also can affect our attitudes regarding groups with which we identify. And so there arises a tendency to believe in the superiority of our family, our circle of friends, our age group, our religion, our nation, our race, our ethnicity, our gender, our sexual orientation, or our culture. Thus egocentricity, the view that mine is better—my ideas, my experience, my values, my agenda—becomes ethnocentricity, the view that ours is better—our ideas, our values, our ways. And this, besides closing a person's mind, can get Really Ugly.

## RELATIVISM

If open-mindedness and appreciation of diversity are essential ingredients of critical thinking, they nevertheless have their own related perversion. Sometimes, people seem to think that in order to remain "open-minded" they must avoid making up their mind about anything. To make up one's mind is to be "judgmental," and we wouldn't want to take responsibility for passing judgment on anyone else's beliefs. That would be intolerant of diversity of opinion. There's a cliché usage according to which identifying something as an "opinion" (as opposed to a "fact") means it can't be any closer to or further from the truth than any other opinion. Some people even go so far as to say that the truth is "relative," and varies from individual to individual. What's "true for me" may not be "true for you." This position is often referred to as "relativism" or "subjectivism."

Relativism seems to directly contradict two of our basic assumptions: that the truth exists, and that finding out what's true is a reasonable thing to attempt. We consider these assumptions basic to critical thinking, and so we consider relativism to be an obstacle to critical thinking. But since relativism does challenge our basic assumptions, we need to give them a little more support at this stage, or at least tell you what we think is confused and misleading about relativism. We think relativism starts out well enough by noting that opinions are inherently subject to error and challenge. Indeed, the word "opinion" (which comes from the Latin word for "belief") is conventionally used to indicate recognition that others may disagree with the opinion and that the opinion might be mistaken. Notice: "*might* be mistaken," not "*can't* be correct." Don't forget that part of believing something is believing that it's true. The truth may be elusive and hard to find, but that shouldn't stop us from trying to find it. And let's not get confused about what we're searching for. "True" means something different from "true-for-me." Truth is about what *is.* "Humans have visited the moon" reports an actual state of affairs. That state of affairs does not depend on what any one of us thinks or believes about it. Humans have either visited the moon or not. And as it turns out, they have. If someone has an opinion at odds with this, then that person just has a mistaken opinion. People have a right to hold mistaken opinions, but that doesn't make those opinions any less mistaken.

Sometimes the truth is not so easy to find. There are *some* questions for which there's no such thing as "*the* correct answer," all other answers being incorrect or mistaken—just as there's no such thing as "*the* correct way to make a pizza." But even in such areas as this we assume it is reasonable to persist in searching for the truth, because even if there's no such thing as "*the* correct answer," it's still true that some answers are better than others, just as some pizzas are better than others.

## CONFORMISM AND GROUP-THINK

Cooperation among the individual group members and group loyalty are each essential to the organization of the group, to the coordination of any group project, to the maintenance of the group as a stable entity. Thus there is a natural tendency in any group toward conformity and orthodoxy. We tend to incorporate into our own individual worldviews the ideas, attitudes, and values shared in our group. And there arises within any group a hierarchy of authority through which orthodoxy is established and conformity to it is reinforced.

All of this is perfectly natural and understandable in terms of its survival value for the individual, for the group, and for the species. However, it also contributes greatly to our human fallibility, because obviously nothing guarantees that the orthodox views within a given group will always be the correct ones or even the most advantageous ones for the group and its individual members. History provides a steady stream of examples of groups of people large and small (Heaven's Gate all the way up to entire populations) getting swept up and misled en masse. Both orthodoxy and conformism constitute obstacles to critical thinking.

## RELIANCE ON AUTHORITY

An authority is an expert source of information outside ourselves. The source can be a single individual (a parent, a teacher, a celebrity, a clergy member, the president), a group of individuals (doctors, educators, a peer group, a national consensus), or even an institution (a religion, a government agency, an educational establishment). Whatever its form, authority exerts considerable influence on our belief systems. And it's easy to see why. Consider how difficult it is to become an expert about anything. Nobody can ever hope to become an expert about *everything.* There's almost always going to be someone around who knows more about whatever it is that we're interested in than we do ourselves. And so it's almost always helpful to consult authorities for their expert opinions.

Now consider your own belief system. How many of the things that you believe can you trace back to your own immediate experience? If you're like most of the rest of us, chances are that a lot of the things you believe, you've gotten from other sources. Facts and opinions about world history, the state of your health, the direction of the economy, the events of the day, the existence of God and an afterlife—what are the sources of all of these beliefs? Chances are that many of them you got by relying on the words of others, sources you are in effect trusting as authorities. Again, all of this is perfectly normal and natural.

But there's a danger: How do we know that the authority we trust is in fact reliable? And there's a further danger: We can so rely on authority that we stop thinking for ourselves. Puzzled about something, we might invoke some authority to decide the answer for us. When dealing with a controversial issue, we might find out what the majority thinks and, looking no further, adopt the same position. Inside the Heaven's Gate cult a rigid authoritarian regime trained members to "purify" their "vehicles" (their bodies) through systematic self-denial and unquestioning obedience to authority. Listed offenses included knowingly breaking any instruction or procedure; trusting one's own judgment or using one's own mind; having private thoughts; curiosity; criticizing or finding fault with one's teacher or classmates. This blind acceptance of and obedience to authority is, of course, incompatible with intellectual autonomy and critical thinking. But, just how likely is it that an intelligent person would be susceptible to such a debilitating abuse of trust? How vulnerable are we to the dictates of authority?

To get some idea how influential authority can be, consider a series of experiments conducted by psychologist Stanley Milgram in the 1960s.[3] Milgram's famous experiment consisted of asking subjects to administer strong electrical shocks to people whom the subjects couldn't see. The subjects were told that they could control the shock's intensity by means of a shock generator with thirty clearly marked voltages, ranging from 15 to 450 volts and labeled from "Slight Shock (15)" to "XXX—Danger! Severe Shock (450)." We should point out that the entire experiment was a setup: No one was actually administering or receiving shocks. The subjects were led to believe that the "victims" were being shocked as part of an experiment to determine the effects of punishment on memory. The "victims," who were in fact confederates of the experimenters, were strapped in their seats with electrodes attached to their wrists "to avoid blistering and burning." They were told to make no noise until a "300-volt shock" was administered, at which point they were to make noise loud enough for the subjects to hear (for example, pounding on the walls as if in pain). The subjects were reassured that the shocks, though extremely painful, would cause no permanent tissue injury.

When asked, a number of psychologists predicted that no more than 10 percent of the subjects would follow the instruction to administer a 450-volt shock. In fact, well over half did—twenty-six out of forty. Even after hearing the "victims" pounding, 87.5 percent of the subjects (thirty-five out of forty) applied more voltage. The conclusion seems unmistakable: A significant number of people, when instructed by an authority, will hurt other people.

Authority not only influences the behavior of people, it also affects their judgment, perhaps even more so. For example, consider these three lines:

A ________

B ____________________

C _______

Which of the three matches this one?

____________________

Undoubtedly, B is the answer. Do you think you could ever be persuaded to choose A or C? Maybe not, but experiments indicate that some individuals can be persuaded to alter their judgments, even when their judgments are obviously correct. These experiments involved several hundred individuals, who were asked to match lines just as you just did. In each group, however, one and only one subject was naive; that is, unaware of the nature of the experiment. The others were confederates of the experimenter, who had instructed them to make incorrect judgments in about two-thirds of the cases and to pressure the dissenting naive subject to alter his or her correct judgment. The results: When subjects were not exposed to pressure, they inevitably judged correctly. But when the confederates pressured them, the naive subjects generally changed their responses to conform with the unanimous majority judgments. When one confederate always gave the correct answers, naive subjects maintained their positions three-fourths of the time. But when the honest confederate switched to the majority view in later trials, the errors made by naive subjects rose to about the same level as that of subjects who stood alone against a unanimous majority.[4] Make no mistake: Authority moves us. We are impressed, influenced and intimidated by authority, so much so that, under the right conditions, we will abandon our own values, beliefs, and judgments, even doubt our own immediate sensory experience.

Certainly none of this is intended to undermine the legitimacy of authority entirely as a source of information and guidance in developing and managing one's belief system. Indeed, as we said earlier, authorities are valuable sources of useful information which we need as critical thinkers. But we also need to know how to question authority, or authority can become a major obstacle to critical thinking.

## ADDITIONAL EXERCISES

Keep in mind as you work through the exercises in this book what we said earlier about relativism and the search for truth. There are some questions for which there's no such thing as *the* correct answer, and yet even in such cases, most likely some answers will be better than others. What matters most of all is how you reason your way to your answer, and whether your reasoning holds up under scrutiny. When you discuss these exercises don't be afraid to challenge answers that may be offered by your instructors, but you should also try to understand and appreciate the reasoning your instructors may have to offer in support of their preferred answers.

### Identifying assumptions

On June 24, 1997, the United States Air Force issued its official explanation of the Roswell Incident. The Roswell Incident is probably the most famous incident of an alleged earth landing of extraterrestrials, long thought by many UFO believers to involve a government cover-up, because the sightings occurred and the debris was collected on and around a government military reservation (Roswell Air Force Base in New Mexico), and because the government maintained an "official silence" about the incident for fifty years. The official explanation: An experimental high-altitude weather balloon and several humanoid "crash test dummies" fell to earth from very high altitudes. As you can imagine, this explanation didn't immediately convince many of the folks who believe that the government has been covering up real evidence of a UFO crash landing. And so there was a fairly big debate following the Air Force press conference. During this debate we heard the following argument offered in support of the government explanation:

> There's no government cover-up, and there were no aliens. Look, if you were an alien and you were scoping out the earthly terrain, the last place you'd go would be to one of the most highly fortified and tightly secured military installations in the United States.

We think there are a few interesting assumptions involved in this argument. How many can you identify? Write them down in the spaces below.

As a second step sort the list of assumptions you came up with using the categories we just discussed (Hidden Assumptions, Explicit Assumptions, Inferential Assumptions, Presuppositions).

| Assumption | Category |
|---|---|
| | |
| | |
| | |
| | |
| | |
| | |
| | |
| | |
| | |

## Critical thinking inventory

Based on your understanding of critical thinking as defined and explained in Chapter 1, now consider whether or not—or to what extent—the five people you know the best think critically. Who are the five people you know best? Do they include family members? Close friends? A roommate? A love interest? Did you consider yourself as a candidate? Do the people you have in mind think critically? Always? Often? Sometimes? Rarely? Never? Are there any patterns you can discern and describe?

| Name or Initials | Thinks Critically: Always | Often | Sometimes | Rarely | Never | Explanation |
|---|---|---|---|---|---|---|
| | | | | | | |
| | | | | | | |
| | | | | | | |
| | | | | | | |
| | | | | | | |

Now compose your thoughts in a short essay. Briefly describe the five people you know best and the extent to which, in your estimation, they think critically. (If you're concerned about anonymity, you might want to use initials or fictional names.) Then explain how you arrived at your estimates.

## Critical thinking on the Internet

Do you have access to the Internet? If so this exercise won't need much in the way of explanation. (If you don't have access to the Internet, ask your instructors where you can get access to the Internet on your campus.) Search the Internet under "Critical Thinking," and log what you find on the chart on the next page.

| Internet Address | Site Name | Brief Description |
|---|---|---|
| | | |
| | | |
| | | |
| | | |
| | | |
| | | |
| | | |
| | | |
| | | |
| | | |
| | | |
| | | |
| | | |
| | | |

## Cultural diversity

1. One of the most valuable things about the diversity of cultures you will find on most contemporary college campuses is what one can learn from cultures other than one's own about the limitations of one's own "worldview," the self-regulating system of assumptions and other beliefs according to which a person views the world or deals with incoming information. Here is a little exercise in self-awareness and appreciation of cultural diversity: Try to identify three items in your own worldview which are not shared by or which conflict with the worldview of a typical member of some identifiable culture other than your own. You may find it useful, perhaps even necessary, to approach one or more of your fellow students whose cultural heritages differ from your own, and learn a bit from them about the distinctive characteristics of their cultures.

2. Another of the valuable things about cultural diversity is what one can learn about common or shared humanity. Here is a follow-up exercise in cultural awareness: Try to identify three items in your own worldview which are or would be shared by a typical member of some identifiable culture other than your own.

### Self-deception

From your own experience, give an example of "self-deception" in which you or someone you know well persisted in maintaining a belief in the face of powerful contradictory evidence. As best you can, explain how this was possible for the person.

### Authority

Identify ten beliefs that you hold on the basis of some external authority. As best you can, identify the authoritative source of the belief in each case. Then evaluate the authority. Is the authority generally reliable? Is the authority an appropriate one for the belief in question?

### Freewrite rewrite

Now, with this introductory chapter under your belt, review what you wrote earlier in the freewrite exercise; that is, what you hope and expect to get out of a course of critical thinking. Have your hopes and expectations changed in any way as a result of your reading and experiences in the course so far? With the benefit of these experiences, edit your earlier thoughts into a short essay of one or two pages on the topic of what you hope and expect to get out of a course in critical thinking.

## GLOSSARY

**assumption** an unsupported claim
**authority** an expert or source of information outside ourselves
**claim** a statement which is either true or false
**egocentrism** favoritism for oneself and the beliefs, values, traditions, and groups with which one identifies
**ethnocentrism** favoritism for the beliefs, values, and traditions of one's ethnic group
**hidden assumption** an unstated or implied assumption
**inferential assumption** hidden assumption which functions as added support linking a stated premise with a conclusion
**presupposition** assumption required in order to make sense of what is explicitly stated
**reason** 1. the human capacity to use disciplined intelligence to solve problems
2. a claim used as a premise
3. a claim used as an explanation
**relativism** the view that the truth is "relative" and varies
**subjectivism** the view that the truth is "relative" or varies from individual to individual
**truth** the agreement of an idea with reality
**worldview** the self-regulating system of assumptions and other beliefs through which a person receives and interprets new information

## NOTES

[1] William James, preface to *The Meaning of Truth,* reprinted in *Pragmatism and Four Essays from the Meaning of Truth* (Cleveland: Meridian, 1955), p. 195.

[2] This thought experiment is derived from Jonathan Bennett's unpublished lectures on Descartes, given at the University of British Columbia, 1970–1972.

[3] Stanley Milgram, *Obedience to Authority: An Experimental View* (New York: Harper & Row, 1974).

[4] See S. E. Asch, "Effects of Group Pressure upon the Modification and Distortion of Judgment," in M. H. Guetskow, ed., *Groups, Leadership and Men* (Pittsburgh: Carnegie Press, 1951); S. E. Asch, "Opinions and Social Pressure, "*Scientific American* (September 1955): 31–35; S. E. Asch, "Studies of Individual and Conformity: A Minority of One against a Unanimous Majority," *Psychological Monographs* 70 (1956): 9.

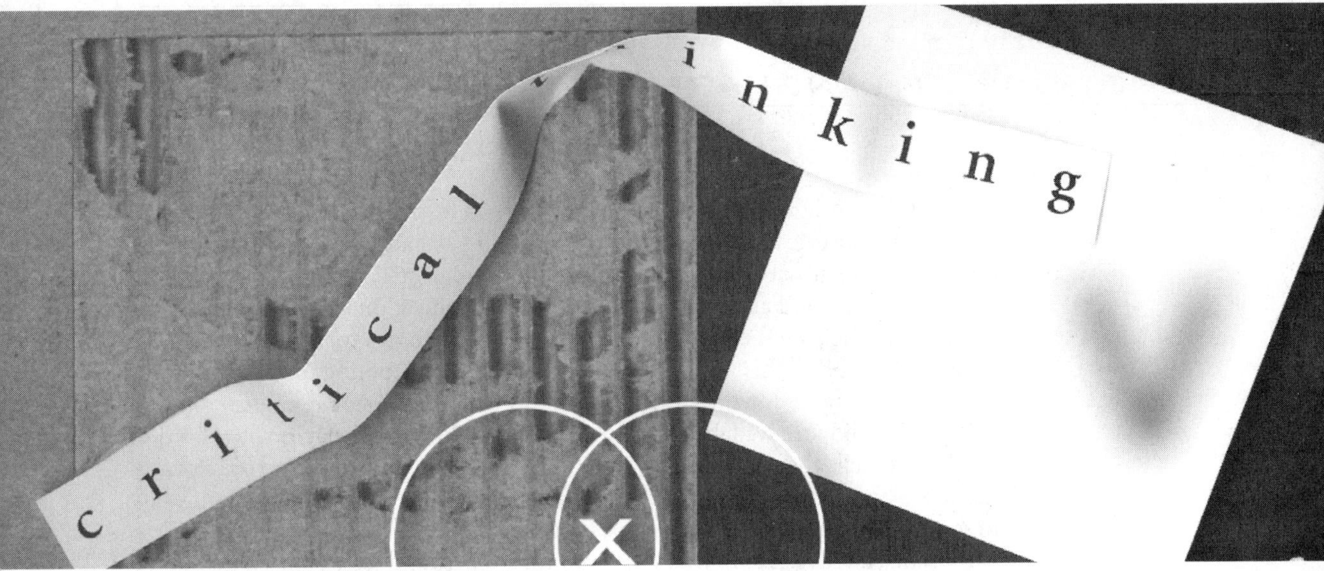


CHAPTER 2

# Language

"Some people have a way with words.
Some no have way." STEVE MARTIN

Try to imagine what thinking would be like without language. Hard to imagine, isn't it? In fact, the harder you try, the more you notice language creeping into the effort. The more you notice yourself trying to "put the ideas into words," so to speak, the more it becomes apparent that what we think, even how we think, can't be separated from language.

Language is the fundamental medium of our thinking, the fundamental medium within which our thoughts take form and gain expression. Two important consequences flow from this for our purposes in this text: Paying close attention to language is essential to finding out what and how people think. Language (narrowly conceived, as words) is, of course, not the only thing one pays close attention to in finding out what and how people think. Posture, gesture, vocal inflection, timing, context, and so on all are meaningful dimensions of human communication, and they frequently guide our interpretations of people's words. But it is language that is central and basic. Indeed, to say that posture, gesture, vocal inflection, timing, context, and so on are meaningful dimensions of human communication is as good as saying that they are linguistic dimensions of human communication—either part of language (more broadly conceived) or language-like.

# FUNCTIONS OF LANGUAGE

## LABELS

As important as language is in the formation and expression of our thoughts, it understandably exerts a powerful influence upon what and how we think. For example, let's begin with one common and basic linguistic function and activity: labels and labeling. Labels are essential for communication. To grasp things intellectually it helps to be able to generalize, to group things together. Labels help us to do this, and in this way give us "handles" to use in coming to grips with our world. Just imagine how hard it would be to talk about people, in general as a group, if we didn't have labels like "humanity" or "people." Imagine how hard it would be to talk about something like the functions of language if we didn't have the word "function." Labels also help us to point things out, or refer specifically to some particular part of a complex situation, as in "Please pass the *salt*." Labels help us orient ourselves in new and unfamiliar surroundings, as in "Where's the *restroom*?"

But as useful as labels are, they can also be pretty limiting. First, labels categorize things, in effect highlighting similarities and commonalities, but by the same token ignoring distinctive nuances and individual differences. Gloria Steinem is a feminist, but to label her as a "feminist" is to call attention to this single aspect of her identity and quite possibly to obscure other aspects of her identity which might in certain situations be as important as or more important than her identification with "feminism." Gloria Steinem is, like all of us, a complex and multifaceted individual. She is also a voter, a licensed driver, a taxpayer, a consumer, an author, and so on. Labeling her as a "feminist" or as an "author," or anything else, encourages us to see her just in terms of what she has in common with other members of a given category. Labels may distort not only our understanding and appreciation of individuals, but also our understanding of the category itself. The label "feminist," for instance, covers a wide variety of individuals and groups with a wide variety of distinct and even conflicting views. To assume otherwise or to overlook such differences, as labels sometimes encourage us to do, is what has come to be known as "stereotyping." Linguist Irvin Lee gives a graphic example:

> I knew a man who had lost the use of both eyes. He was called a "blind man." He could also be called an expert typist, a conscientious worker, a good student, a careful listener, a man who wanted a job. But he couldn't get a job in the department store order room where employees sat and typed orders which came over the telephone. The personnel man was impatient to get the interview over. "But you're a blind man," he kept saying, and one could almost feel his silent assumption that somehow the incapacity in one aspect made the man incapable in every other. So blinded by the label was the interviewer that he could not be persuaded to look beyond it.[1]

Stereotyping involves overgeneralization and oversimplification, both of which are naturally tempting to human intelligence. We look for simplicity in the answers and solutions we seek, and even more in the questions and problems we face. We find the suspense that inevitably attends doubt and uncertainty inherently uncomfortable and we're generally in a hurry to arrive at resolution and equilibrium. We often think that if we can manage to see things in simple terms, we stand a far better chance of escaping doubt quickly than if we try to consider a multitude of complexities. The danger in this is that we get trapped thinking in stark black-and-white terms of mutually exclusive dichotomies, like "Democrat/Republican" or "pro-life/pro-choice," and ignore other alternatives, such as compromise positions.

A living language is, of course, an immensely flexible medium, and a medium which is still evolving. So we are understandably only dimly aware, if we are aware at all, of the limitations language sets upon what we can meaningfully say, and indeed upon what we can think. But consider the fact that in Arabic there are more than 5,000 terms that pinpoint differences of age, sex, and bodily structure among camels, whereas we have only "camel." Consider how much more it must be possible to think and to say about camels in Arabic than in English.

Then, too, language embodies features like rhythm and rhyme, alliteration and onomatopoeia, emotional appeal, and so on. These are features which have subtle but deep and powerful psychological influence upon what we believe, what we agree and disagree with, what we remember or forget, in short upon what and how we think. For these reasons too, then, close attention to language is essential to deepening our awareness of what and how we think.

One very powerful thinking strategy, which we hinted at a moment ago, is to think in terms of *function*. Try in other words to understand things and their peculiar features in terms of their goals or purposes or uses.[2] For example, if we were trying to figure out or explain what a telephone is and why it has the peculiar features it has, a good place to begin would be to ask what a telephone is *for* and what its peculiar features contribute to that purpose or goal. For example it has a handset with that distinctive peculiar shape. And why does it have that shape? Well the shape functions so that you can easily hold the thing in one hand while you both talk into one end of it and listen to the other. And that's a pretty useful combination of features to have in a device designed to enable people to converse outside each other's physical presence. So now let's think about language in terms of function.

## EXERCISE | Functions of Language

Use your imagination. How many distinct uses of language can you think of in five minutes?

| Use or Function | Example |
|---|---|
| | |
| | |
| | |
| | |

(continued)

| Use or Function | Example |
|---|---|
| | |
| | |
| | |
| | |
| | |
| | |
| | |
| | |
| | |
| | |
| | |
| | |
| | |
| | |
| | |
| | |

We imagine that you will have noticed that language serves a large and wide variety of functions. Indeed the flexibility and power of language make it difficult to comprehend its many uses. Language can be used to describe the world or some part of it, pose problems, suggest solutions, issue orders, tell jokes, sing songs, exchange greetings, buy things, sell things, and the list goes on. And after what we just said about oversimplification, we'd better be careful here. If language can be said to serve any *single* function in essence, it would have to be communication. So let's say that the essential function of language is communication. Now beyond this it's very hard to say anything general about the functions of language without oversimplification, because there's an immense variety of kinds of communication too. Nevertheless, here are general categories into which many of the possible and actual uses of language can be sorted.

## INFORMATIVE

One main use of language is to communicate information. This is typically accomplished by formulating and then affirming (or denying) statements. *Language used to make claims is said to perform an informative function.*

The following statements are typical examples of the informative use of language:

Washington is the nation's capital.
Laetrile is not an effective treatment for cancer.
U.S. presidential elections are held quadrennially.
Business administration is currently the most popular college major.
One out of ten Americans has herpes.
The Democrats have never controlled the U.S. House of Representatives.

Notice that the last statement is false. "Information" as used here is taken to include *misinformation;* that is, false statements as well as true. Furthermore, statements whose truth is in doubt, such as "Extraterrestrial life exists" and "The next president will be a Republican," are still functionally informative.

## EXPRESSIVE

Besides conveying information about the world, language also serves to express feelings. *Whenever language is used to vent or arouse feelings, it is said to perform an expressive function.*

Poetry furnishes the best examples of the expressive function of language:

So fair, so sweet, withal so sensitive,
Would that the Little Flowers were to live,
Conscious of half the pleasures which they give. . .
—*William Wordsworth*

The poet did not compose these lines to report any information but to express certain emotions he felt and to evoke a similar response in the reader.

But expressive language need not be confined to poetry. We express sorrow by saying "What a pity" or "That's too bad" and enthusiasm by shouting "Wow!" or "Awesome!" And we express feelings of affection, passion, and love by murmuring "Darling" or "Honey" or like terms of endearment. None of these uses is intended to communicate information but rather feelings.

## DIRECTIVE

*Language serves a directive function when it is used in an attempt to influence the behavior of another person directly.* The clearest examples of directive discourse are commands and requests. When a teacher tells a class "Study for tomorrow's test," she doesn't intend to communicate information or express emotion but to bring about a specific action: studying. This sort of directive utterance depends upon the teacher's having some measure of authority and perhaps also power over those to whom the command is issued. Commands are not always appropriate as a means of getting people to do what we want. When the same teacher asks the audiovisual technician to set up a projector in her classroom, she is again using language directively; that is, to produce action. But here the directive is in the form of a request, rather than a command. Requests depend, for their effectiveness to elicit behavior, on the willingness to cooperate of the other party. If the teacher first asks the technician if there is a projector available, she is also using language directively, for questions typically are requests for answers.

## PERSUASIVE

*Language serves a persuasive function when it is used in an attempt to influence the beliefs or motivations of another person indirectly.* The persuasive function of language is close to the directive function. However, we recognize that other people, just like we ourselves, are free agents; and that we are rarely in a position of authority such that we can effectively *command* their behavior, much less their beliefs. Furthermore, we cannot always presume a willingness on the part of others to cooperate with our agenda. What do we do when we can neither command nor presuppose willingness to cooperate? We try to be persuasive. We try to influence the beliefs and motivations of people in less direct, more roundabout ways.

## PERFORMATIVE

Language can also be used in the performance of an action, for expressing certain words in a specific context can bring something about. For example, suppose that during a marriage ceremony, the bride says "I do." Or, in bumping into you, someone says, "I apologize." Or in christening a ship, a person says "I name this ship the *Nautilus*" and breaks a bottle of champagne across its hull. Or, after a heated discussion about the relative merits of baseball teams, a friend says to you "I bet you five bucks that the Dodgers make it to the World Series." Although all these utterances have the form of informative utterances, they are not simply reporting the performance of some action that has been done—the action of promising, apologizing, christening, betting. Rather, in saying what they do, the speakers are actually performing the action. When the bride says "I do," she is not describing or reporting the marriage ceremony, she is actually carrying it out; when a person says "I apologize," she is not describing or reporting an apology, but actually giving it. Utterances of this kind, which include verdicts and promises, are called "performative utterances." *Language serves the performative function, then, when it is used in certain contexts to make something so.*

## MULTIPLE FUNCTIONS

You don't have to be a linguist to realize that a given communication need not employ just a single language use. Indeed, most ordinary communication likely will exhibit multiple uses of language. Consider, for example, this poem:

> My heart leaps up when I behold
> A rainbow in the sky;
> So was it when my life began;
> So is it now I am a man;
> So be it when I should grow old;
> Or let me die!

The Child is father of the Man;
And I could wish my days to be
Bound each to each by natural piety.
—*William Wordsworth*

Although this poem, like most, is primarily expressive discourse, it can be said to be informative in the sense that the poet is stating that the adult can learn from the child and directive in the sense that the poet is urging us to get in touch with the feelings and intuitions of childhood. On the other hand, a classroom lecture, essentially informative, may express something of the professor's own enthusiasm, thus serving the expressive function, and of course it may include directions (e.g., reading assignments and the like).

The fact is that most ordinary language usage has mixed functions. This is an important point to remember when thinking critically about some discourse, for buried amid the rhetorical flourishes may lie the contentions that are the object of our critical inspection. We will say considerably more about this in later chapters when we discuss argument analysis and portrayal.

## EXERCISE | Language Functions

Identify the primary language function in each example.

| Example | Inf. | Ex. | Dir. | Pers. | Perf. |
|---|---|---|---|---|---|
| The suspect left the scene driving a green convertible with out-of-state plates. | | | | | |
| Follow Highway 12 west to Madrone Road, take Madrone to Arnold Drive, then turn left and drive 2 miles 'til you see the golf course. | | | | | |
| We must all hang together or most assuredly, we shall all hang separately. —Ben Franklin (to other signers of the Declaration of Independence) | | | | | |
| Baseball umpire: "You're out!" | | | | | |
| Teenage moviegoer after seeing *Star Wars:* "Awesome!" | | | | | |
| And God said, "Let there be light;" And there was light. —Genesis 1:3 | | | | | |
| Combine 2 cups water and 1 tablespoon butter and bring to a boil. Stir in rice and spice mix, reduce heat and simmer for 10 minutes. | | | | | |
| "How 'bout those Dallas Cowboys cheerleaders, ya know what I'm sayin'?!" | | | | | |
| Noticing that it was 5 minutes past bedtime, Mrs. Cleaver said, "Okay Beaver, let's close the book now and go to bed." | | | | | |
| For answers to these exercises and other similar exercises, click on the Language Functions button in the Critical Thinking tutorial. | | | | | |

## MEANING IN LANGUAGE

How do words get to mean what they mean? For example, how does the word "cat" come to stand for the creature? This is the sort of question that could easily lead to a lengthy and inconclusive debate, because it raises very deep and fundamental questions about what language and meaning are *in essence.* And these are by no means easy questions to answer.

### LANGUAGE AS CONVENTION

A primitive theory of meaning in language might answer such questions by supposing first that the relationship between the word "cat" and the creatures that the word refers to is *the* basic and essential meaning relation in language, that words are essentially labels for things; and second that the relationship between the word "cat" and the creature is somehow rooted in "the nature of things." Neither of these ideas, however plausible they might seem at first glance, goes very far or helps us very much to understand meaning in language. For one thing, it is not at all easy to see what kind of a "thing" the word "the" could be a label for. Then too, though some words, like "hiccup" and "splash," do seem to have some sort of identifiable natural connection to the things they stand for, most do not. For example, look at the last fifteen or so words in the last sentence. A more subtle and sophisticated account of meaning in language seems called for.

Let's try looking at things this way: Words are noises that human beings have assigned meaning to. Speakers of English use "cat" to refer to feline creatures, while speakers of French use "chat," speakers of Spanish use "gato," and speakers of German use "katze." There is nothing "required" or "natural" about such assignments of meaning to noises. Any other sound *could* have been made to stand for what "cat" stands for in English, and likewise in the other language communities. These assignments of meaning are merely "conventional," they are based on human conventions.

Other words, like "the," "and," "so," "on," and so on, have meanings in accordance with their conventional uses, with the roles they conventionally play in putting words together into meaningful sentences.

Much the same can be said of syntax as of word meaning. "Syntax" refers to the structural regularities in the ways words are put together to communicate thoughts and ideas. In English we put adjectives before nouns, as in "white house." In Spanish the adjective typically follows the noun: "casa blanca." The difference is a matter of convention.

Let's take a moment to explain more deeply what we mean by a "convention." *A convention is simply a behavioral regularity which humans maintain and follow in order to solve problems of coordination.* For example, suppose that you and your friend are cut off in the middle of a telephone conversation. Here you have what we might call a "coordination problem." What each of you should do depends on what the other person does. If you both pick up the phone and dial, you both get a busy signal. If you both hang up and wait, well, . . . you wait. You get back in contact if, and only if, one of you dials while the other hangs up and waits. What should you do? Well, suppose that in the past when this sort of thing has happened, you have always been the one to dial, and that has worked, and you know it has worked, and your friend knows it has worked, and you know that your friend knows it has worked, and you know that your friend knows that you know this, and so on. So, if you now pick up the phone and dial while your friend hangs up and waits, and you do these things because you are both thinking that this will solve the coordination problem, because both of you know that it has worked in the past, you are following a "convention."[3]

The basic problems of communication—understanding one another and making oneself understood—are coordination problems. Language can usefully be understood as a vast system of conventions which we learn to follow in order to solve the problems of communication.

A number of interesting and important consequences follow from this way of viewing language. First of all, linguistic conventions are, in one sense, arbitrary. This means that they could have been other than they are. And indeed, linguistic conventions evolve, sometimes quite rapidly and dramatically. But though linguistic conventions could have been other than they are and may well change, they nevertheless do regulate meaningful discourse. Linguistic conventions are thus a lot like the rules in a game.

Think of the rules governing organized sports like American football or basketball and you'll see what we mean. One rule in American football states that the length of the playing field between the end zones is 100 yards; another prescribes exactly eleven players per team. These rules are arbitrary; they could be other than what they are. For example, Canadian football is played on a 110-yard field with twelve players on each side. And the rules of a game can be changed by common consent. Thus, for example, the three-point field goal was recently instituted in professional and collegiate basketball. But the rules, whatever they are, do regulate the game. If you choose to play American football, then you must play by its rules. If you play Canadian football, you must observe its rules.

Similarly in playing the language game, we must generally abide by the conventions of the particular language in which we are attempting to communicate. And we can rightly expect others to do the same. Conventions in language are somewhat more flexible and informal than rules are in games. For one thing, you don't get thrown out of the game for committing five unconventional speech acts. Furthermore, sometimes violating a linguistic convention can be a very creative and effective way of communicating something unique and special. Nevertheless, meaningful departures from the conventions of our language presuppose those conventions as generally binding. If this were not the case, departing from our language's conventions would lead to hopeless confusion.

## THE RULE OF COMMON USAGE

In *Through the Looking Glass,* Alice and Humpty Dumpty have the following conversation:

> "There are 364 days when you might get un-birthday presents."
>
> "Certainly," said Alice.
>
> "And only *one* for birthday presents, you know. There's glory for you!"
>
> "I don't know what you mean by 'glory,'" Alice said.
>
> Humpty Dumpty smiled contemptuously. "Of course you don't—till I tell you. I meant, 'there's a nice knock-down argument for you!'"
>
> "But 'glory' doesn't mean 'a nice knock-down argument,'" Alice objected.
>
> "When I use a word," Humpty Dumpty said, in a rather scornful tone, "it means just what I choose it to mean—neither more nor less."[4]

Just imagine the confusion that would reign if, like Humpty Dumpty, each of us used words to mean exactly what we wanted them to mean, "neither more nor less." To avoid such chaos and inconvenience, we generally presuppose a conventional interpretation of what someone says. If a writer or speaker doesn't indicate a departure from common usage, we normally assume that the person is following common usage. Of course, this works both ways, which is why generally speaking it's best to *follow common usage* when we try to communicate. When we do use a word in an unconventional way, we need to give our audience extra guidance to our meaning. If we don't, we're likely to lose them. It should be obvious what happens if you and your audience are not coordinated regarding what you mean: communication breaks down.

## DENOTATION AND CONNOTATION

Critical thinking is concerned largely with informative statements. These statements are both the product and object of critical inspection. They of course consist of words in certain arrangements. Unless we know the meanings of these words, we cannot think critically about the statements that contain them, nor can we respond intelligently to the statements. Let us now look more closely at word meaning, and develop an important distinction between two of its dimensions: denotation and connotation. Though these dimensions of meaning apply to various of the parts of speech—nouns, verbs, adjectives, adverbs, pronouns, and so on—for the sake of simplicity we will confine our remarks to the meaning of general nouns that can apply to numerous particular items around us, for example, "bridge," "building," "school," "politician," "book," and the like.

Consider the word "bridge." What does the word "bridge" mean? In one sense, the word means what it serves to refer or point to. It points to a group of objects: bridges. This pointing-to relationship between the word and its objects is called *denotation.* The group of objects denoted by a term is called the term's *extension.* For example, the extension of the word "bridge" includes the Golden Gate Bridge; the extension of the word "building" includes the Empire State Building. And so we could also say that at least part of what the word "bridge" means is the whole set of things it denotes (in other words its extension), including the Golden Gate Bridge; and part of what the word "building" means is its extension, including the Empire State Building.

The word "building" has a very large and relatively diverse extension which includes the Empire State Building, the Sydney Opera House, the Pentagon, the lighthouse at Point Reyes, and the outhouse behind the barn. They're all buildings. But not everything is a building. This book is not a building. Nor is every structure a building, nor even everything built; the Golden Gate Bridge is a structure, but not a building. Why is this and how do we know? In many cases this is so and we know it to be so because there are criteria governing the extension of the term. Bridges and buildings are bridges or buildings because they satisfy criteria that make them bridges or buildings rather than, say, tunnels or microchips. *These criteria, which define the extension of the term, are called the term's intension.* And so we could also say that part of what the word "bridge" means is its intension, this set of criteria which define its extension. If the intension of a term is part of its meaning, we don't want to confuse it with what the term denotes. So we'll say that it is part of what the term *"connotes." The connotative meaning of a word includes the word's intension, or the set of characteristics which defines the term's extension.*

The extension and the intension of a word add up to the word's *literal* meaning. But many words have additional dimensions of meaning, which are included among its connotations. Quite often a word has special meaning for an individual or group of individuals because it evokes an emotional response. *The emotional connotation of a word refers to its emotional impact.* For example, the literal intension of "prima donna" is "the principal female singer in an opera company." But, because the term has come by convention to carry the added connotation of "a vain, temperamental person," no woman or man would want to be called a "prima donna." Consequently, using the term "prima donna," especially outside of the specialized context of opera, is an effective way of putting someone down. Similarly, the word "tabloid" literally means a newspaper whose format is about half the size of a standard-size newspaper page. But most tabloid newspapers tend toward sensationalism. As a result "tabloid" conventionally carries an additional negative or pejorative connotation. And so, similarly, to call a newspaper a "tabloid" is to put it down. Of course, emotional connotations need not be derogatory. Many are complimentary. Terms such as "statesperson" (as opposed to the negative "politician"), "moderate" (as opposed to the negative "wishy-washy"), and "professor" (as opposed to the negative "pedagogue") all carry a positive emotional charge.

These nonliteral connotations of words are particularly important to the persuasive function of language. They make it possible, by the careful selection of terminology, to color a statement emotionally and to communicate a bias.

## AMBIGUITY AND VAGUENESS

Pianist—and comedian (he'd probably call himself a "sit-down comic")—Victor Borge tells a story about a hotel clerk who once inquired whether he had

"Found anything missing?" Borge says this got him to wonder: How, if he had *found* it, was he going to know it was *missing?* To really appreciate this joke, it helps to know that Borge, who is Danish, hears English as a second language. From the vantage point of fluent speakers of other languages, some of the conventions of our language, and of its many dialects, can seem pretty comical. Borge's tag line (after the laugh): "It's *your* language. I'm just trying to *use* it."

Let us now distinguish and define two important concepts having to do with the clarification of meaning and which will prove increasingly useful as we proceed: ambiguity and vagueness. Each corresponds to a source of confusion in communication (which may help explain why they so often get confused with each other).

By permission of Johnny Hart and Creators Syndicate, Inc.

*An ambiguous term or expression is one with more than one conventional meaning.* In other words it can be understood and defined in more than one way. For example, the word "bank" can mean:

1. any piled up mass, such as snow or clouds
2. the slope of land adjoining a body of water
3. the cushion of a billiard or pool table
4. to strike a billiard shot off the cushion
5. to tilt an aircraft in flight
6. a business establishment authorized to receive and safeguard money, lend money at interest, etc.

*A vague term or expression is one that has an indefinite extension.* In other words it is not entirely clear what it does and does not apply to. For example, the term "bald" clearly applies to Paul Shaffer (David Letterman's TV sidekick and music director) or basketball commentator Dick Vitale. It clearly does not apply to Michael J. Fox. But there is an indefinite area in between where it isn't clear whether a person is bald or not. Vagueness admits of degrees according to how clearly cases fall within and without its extension and how large the indefinite area is. Thus "bald" is less vague than "happy," and "vague" is itself pretty vague.

## EXERCISE | Ambiguity and Vagueness

Identify and explain any ambiguity and/or vagueness you can find in the examples.

| Example | Vague Term(s) | Ambiguous Term(s) | Explanation |
|---|---|---|---|
| Rappers continue to get a bad rap in the press. | | | |
| How do reasonable people come to hold unreasonable beliefs? | | | |
| Headline: "Drunk Gets Nine Months in Violin Case" | | | |
| The streets are perfectly safe here in New York City. It's the muggers you have to watch out for. | | | |
| Random urinalysis for drugs in safety-sensitive job categories does not constitute an unreasonable search. | | | |
| A man walks up to the Zen Buddhist hot dog vendor and says, "Make me one with everything." | | | |
| Nuclear energy is just as natural as any other fuel, and cleaner than many already in use. | | | |
| Can you explain the humor in Victor Borge's remark about "finding something missing"? | | | |
| According to the Supreme Court, flag burning is protected under the First Amendment as an instance of political speech. | | | |
| For answers to these and other similar exercises, click on the Ambiguity/Vagueness button in the Critical Thinking tutorial. | | | |

## DEFINITIONS

Do you remember in Chapter 1 how we began to define certain words (like "reasonable," "typical," and "assumptions")? Then you probably also remember that one of the words we said we'd get around to defining was "define." Suppose we now said, "to 'define' is to give a 'definition.' " That wouldn't be much help, would it? Not unless you already knew what a "definition" was, in which case you'd probably already know what "define" meant and so you wouldn't need the definition. *A definition is an "explanation" of the meaning of a term.* The word "definition" and its cognates "define," "definite," "definitive," and so on, come from the Latin *definire,* for "setting boundaries or limits." This source contributes something very important to an understanding of certain kinds of definition, as we'll explain shortly.

Notice that the definition we finally got around to toward the end of the last paragraph—the sentence in *italics*—is a functional one. That is, we have defined "definition" in terms of its essential explanatory *function.* The function of a definition is to explain something—the meaning of a term. (The term "explanation" can also be defined functionally. The function of an explanation is to help somebody understand something better. *An "explanation" is language used to help somebody understand something better.*) This illustrates one of the ways that definitions can be sorted into different kinds: by the way they go about explaining the meanings of terms.

Another way to sort definitions into different kinds would be by function, because definitions are used for a variety of purposes. One of the most common and basic purposes of definitions is to help someone understand new or unfamiliar terms. This might well be the most basic function of definitions: teaching people the language, something even fluent speakers of any language need regularly. Definitions are constantly needed for the purpose of orienting people to new and unfamiliar terminology because there are so many words and because language is dynamic and evolving constantly. For example, we didn't know what "vaporware" meant the first time we saw it used ("vaporware" is software that is announced as forthcoming, usually with great promotional fanfare, but never actually comes out). Some years before that we didn't know what "software" meant either.

## OSTENSIVE DEFINITION

One simple sort of definition often used for the purpose of teaching the language consists of indicating examples of the term being defined. For example, if someone didn't know what "reptile" meant, you could help that person by giving a definition like this one: "Snakes, lizards, turtles, and crocodiles are reptiles." Here you are explaining the meaning of the general term by giving examples of the kinds of things included in its extension. This kind of definition is called *ostensive definition* from the Latin word for "show," as in "show me what it means." A special case—in fact we could say the basic prototype—of ostensive definition consists of pointing while saying the word.

## SYNONYMY

Another basic strategy of definition, also useful for the purpose of teaching new or unfamiliar vocabulary, is through "synonyms." "Synonyms" are words or expressions that have the same meaning. "Synonym" comes from the Greek for "same name." For example, suppose we run across the word "poltroon" in a line of verse about pirates (rhymes with "dubloon"). The poet's meaning might easily elude us. If we didn't know that "poltroon" means "coward," we might easily wind up thinking that the line was about a parrot or a drunken sailor or something.

## ETYMOLOGIES

A lot of words have fascinating histories. Here is a brief history of the word "etymology." It comes through Middle English and old French, from the Medieval Latin *ethimologia,* which is derived from the Latin *etymologia*, which came from the Greek *etumologia*, which is based on the Greek word *etumon*, which means "true sense of the word." OK? Knowing where a word comes from can tell you a lot about what it means, as this example shows perfectly. So definition by etymology is often a very useful strategy for explaining unfamiliar terms.

## WHAT DICTIONARIES DO

Once again let's think in terms of function. Functionally, a dictionary is an interesting kind of a book. It's a guidebook which tells you how to use and understand words in the language. A dictionary gives you the spelling so that you can recognize the word in print and clearly and correctly indicate it in writing; it gives you a pronunciation key so that you can recognize the word when you hear it and pronounce it correctly in conversation; and then it gives you the definitions, many of which are ostensive, synonymous, or etymological (as defined above).

What dictionaries do is try to accurately report the conventional usage of words in the language. That's why using a dictionary is so helpful in following the "rule of common usage" we mentioned earlier in the chapter. This focus on common or conventional usage flows directly from the function of teaching the language. Teaching and learning in any language always start with conventional usage.

## WHAT DICTIONARIES DON'T DO

A dictionary won't tell you the meaning of a word that is being used in an unconventional way, though knowing what the word conventionally means is often very helpful and maybe even essential for figuring out the unconventional meaning. And a dictionary won't ordinarily tell you a word's intension. And so there are certain kinds of definition that you won't ordinarily find in a dictionary:

### STIPULATIVE DEFINITIONS

Suppose a writer or speaker wants to communicate an idea for which no conventionally understood term is exactly right. Maybe there's some new invention or category to deal with (like "vaporware"). Maybe conventional usage isn't precise enough for what the writer or speaker wants to accomplish. Often it seems we need to depart from conventional usage and use words in unconventional ways in order to get our meanings across. In specialized or technical disciplines, it frequently becomes necessary to set up terminology with specialized technical meanings. In geometry, for example, the words "point," "line," and "plane" are given quite specific meanings much more precise than their conventional ones. In legal and other policy contexts it is often necessary to make distinctions and classifications more precisely than conventional vocabulary will express; for example, "In this contract for purposes of eligibility for benefits a 'full-time employee' shall be defined as an 'employee working twenty-five hours or more per week.' " *A stipulative definition is one that specifies an unconventional meaning for a term in a particular context.* The word "stipulate," which comes from the Latin word for "bargaining," means to specify in an agreement. In effect what we're doing when we stipulate a definition is negotiating an agreement about how a word is to be used and understood in the context of some discourse, where conventional usage and understanding are inadequate or unsuitable in some way.

### ESSENTIAL DEFINITIONS

Here's a list of words we'd be willing to bet you all know and understand. If you ran across any of the words on this list, you wouldn't need to go look it up. And you'd be able to use any of these words quite comfortably and correctly in your own conversation and writing. And you'd be able to teach any of these words to another person ostensively. You'd be able to point to examples in order to indicate what any of these words means. Ready for the list?

| | |
|---|---|
| Art | Beauty |
| Chair | Desk |
| Information | Jazz |
| Love | Music |
| News | Obscenity |
| Pornography | Religion |
| Sign | Time |

OK. Now here's a challenge: Take any of the words on this list and explain its intension.

Remember what "intension" means. The intension of a word is the set of criteria which define the word's extension, which is the set of examples it conventionally applies to. Maybe we should explain the word "criteria" a little bit. "Criteria" is the plural form of "criterion," which derives from the same Greek root as "critical," which you remember from Chapter 1 is about "decision making." *Criteria are rules or standards for decision making.* So the criteria which define a word's extension would be the rules or standards according to which decisions are made about whether something is in the extension of the word or not.

Take "music" for example. Remember, this is a word you are quite familiar with. It's in your working vocabulary. You don't need a dictionary to help you understand a question like, "Do you want to listen to some music?" And you can easily identify examples of music. Now try to state the criteria according to which you decide whether something is music or not. This is not as easy as one might think, or as easy as one might think it should be. What you're trying to state here is a kind of definition which we're going to refer to as an "essential definition." People have often described what we're challenging you to try to do here as "stating the *essence* or *essential nature* of" (in this case) music.

Another way to describe what you're trying to do is this. Think of the extension of the word "music" as though it were a bounded territory. The things which the word "music" conventionally applies to, all the things in its extension, are "inside the boundaries of the territory"; things to which the word "music" does *not* apply are "outside the boundaries." And what you're trying to do is produce a verbal map of the territory, or describe its boundaries in words. (Remember the word "definition" comes from the Latin for "setting boundaries or limits.")

## FUNCTION OF ESSENTIAL DEFINITIONS

Now you might wonder what essential definitions are good for. What special purpose or purposes do they serve? Assuming that people are familiar with the word we're defining, there's no need to teach it as a new vocabulary item. And in that case why would we need *any* sort of definition, especially a hard-to-formulate one that we can't simply look up in a dictionary? Well, sometimes it's not immediately clear whether or not a given example is in the extension of the word. And sometimes deciding whether or not a given example is in the extension of the word is a matter of practical importance. Suppose the local city government has just passed an ordinance regulating the sale and distribution of "obscene" and "pornographic" materials to minors, and now the local purveyor of recorded entertainment (CDs, tapes, videos) is brought up on charges of violating the ordinance in connection with the sale of an En Vogue music video to a sixteen-year-old. The case turns partly on whether or not the En Vogue video is "obscene" and/or "pornographic," and that turns on the essential definitions of "obscenity" and "pornography." The function of an essential definition is to make the criteria which define the extension of the word clear. "Getting to the essence" is difficult, sometimes crucial to what's up, and also sometimes just plain interesting in its own right.

**NECESSARY AND SUFFICIENT CONDITIONS** In order to fulfill its function, an essential definition must allow you to do two things: rule things in and rule things out. In the example we just mentioned we need a ruling as to whether the En Vogue video is "obscene" or not. An essential definition of "obscenity" should tell us what to look for in the video to see if it satisfies or fails to satisfy the criteria for "obscenity." We are now going to stipulate the definitions of two important ingredients of essential definitions: "sufficient conditions" and "necessary conditions." They are the parts of an essential definition that enable you to rule things in and rule things out.

*A necessary condition is a characteristic or set of characteristics* required *for membership in the word's extension.* To illustrate we will use an example that's quite a bit easier to define essentially than any of the words on the foregoing list. Let us define the word "square" as used in plane geometry. The essential definition can be stated in two words: "equilateral rectangle." A square is defined essentially as an equilateral rectangle. In this definition both "equilateral" and "rectangle" indicate necessary conditions. In other words both equilaterality and rectangularity are required for membership in the extension of the word "square." If you find out that something is not rectangular, or is not equilateral, you don't need to know anything more about it. You already know enough to rule it out.

*A sufficient condition is a characteristic or set of characteristics which is* by itself adequate *for membership in the word's extension.* Again, in the essential definition of "square" as an equilateral rectangle, the set of characteristics "equilateral and rectangle" constitutes a sufficient condition. In other words, if you find out that something is both equilateral and rectangular, you don't need to know anything more about it. You don't have to know its size, its age, its color, its value, or its molecular structure. You already know enough to rule it in.

As we said, providing an essential definition of a word like "square" is relatively simple and straightforward. "Obscenity" is harder to define. "Music" is *much* harder to define. In fact, words like "music," "art," "information," "jazz," "love," and others like "justice," "liberty," and "equality" are so hard to define in this way that many people give up the attempt. People who persist in the attempt to formulate essential definitions of words like these are often called "philosophers," and their attempted essential definitions are often called "philosophies" or "theories," and take a whole book to present and explain, as in "Kant's philosophy of art" or John Rawls's *A Theory of Justice.*

## A DIALECTICAL STRATEGY FOR ESSENTIAL DEFINITION

Earlier we tried to answer the question "Why would we need an essential definition (of a word we already understand), especially a hard to formulate one that we couldn't simply look up in a dictionary?" Now we'll try to answer the question "How are we supposed to figure out a hard-to-formulate definition that we can't simply look up in a dictionary?" Here are a couple of strategic hints and a strategic approach. They're all helpful. We've tried them and they do work. But you've also got to do some (guess what!) critical thinking.

**Strategic Hint #1** Look the word up in the dictionary. We know, . . . we know, . . . we just got through saying you can't simply look the essential definition up in the dictionary. But you *can* look up the word and find out about its etymology and synonyms and so on. There you may find very useful information to work with.

**Strategic Hint #2** Use what you know. This will almost certainly include familiarity with examples both inside and outside the extension of the word whose essential definition you are trying to formulate.

**Strategic Approach** We call this a "dialectical" approach because it goes back and forth in dialogue form. To illustrate it we'll continue with the example we used earlier to explain what necessary and sufficient conditions are.

**Step #1** Formulate a definition. Just go for it. Write it down (so that it stays put and doesn't start changing and evolving before you get to Step #2). When we gave the essential definition of "square" earlier, we were able to do it in two words, and we got to it in one step, without any of this back and forth business. Squareness is a pretty simple essence to capture in words, but that's pretty rare. We can't expect to get to the essence in one step of two words very often. In most of the interesting cases we're more likely going to need to try something and then tinker with it, refine it, and adjust it. This dialectical approach is designed to help the tinkering process stay on a productive track. So for purposes of illustration let's imagine that we had initially defined the word "square" as an "equilateral shape."

### Three Things to Try to Avoid in Step #1

**Circularity** A definition is circular if it defines a word in terms of itself. The problem with circularity is that it defeats the purposes of definitions. This is what we were hinting at when we said earlier that to define "define" as "give a definition" wouldn't be very helpful. Once when we were learning Spanish we ran across a conjugated form of the verb "fructificar." Having no idea what this meant, we referred to the Spanish/English dictionary in the back of the book, where we learned that "fructificar" is Spanish for "to fructify." What we really needed to know was what "to fructify" means ("to fructify" is "to bear fruit"). The rest we had already figured out. The purposes of the definition will be defeated by circularity whether what you are trying to do is teach the conventional meaning of a new or unfamiliar word, or stipulate an unconventional meaning, or give an essential definition.

**Obscurity** A similar problem results from obscurity. If the terminology in which the definition is formulated is even less familiar than the word being defined, or more difficult to grasp and understand, then the definition will be harder to understand than the word whose meaning it is supposed to explain. Now it's not always possible to avoid obscurity, especially in formulating an essential definition, because people are not all familiar with the same words. What is obscure to one reader may be quite familiar to another. Even more important, sometimes the ideas you will need to capture in words are themselves out of the ordinary and only relatively obscure words will do the trick. Basically you should try to keep the words as simple and familiar as the ideas you're working with will permit.

**Negativity** A definition should explain what a word means, not what it doesn't mean. Of course, some words defy affirmative definition. "Orphan" means a child whose parents are not living; "bald" means the state of not having hair on one's head. Unless negativity is an essential element in the meaning of the word, try to formulate the definition in the affirmative.

**Step #2** Critique Step #1 by example. This is where Strategic Hint #2 applies. Using what you know about shapes, you can see that something's not entirely right about the definition of "square" as an "equilateral shape." And you can demonstrate this by example:

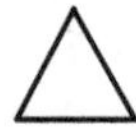

The example does two important things. First, it exposes a flaw in the definition as formulated in Step #1, because the example fits all the criteria specified in the definition but it's not a legitimate member of the extension of the word "square." In other words the example *refutes* the definition. An example used for this purpose, or which accomplishes this purpose, we will call a "counterexample." There are two kinds of counterexample: counterexamples that show that the definition is "too broad" or "overly inclusive" or "lets in too much" (this is how the triangle example above works); and counterexamples that show that the definition is "too narrow" or "overly restrictive" or "leaves out too much." An example which *is* a legitimate member of the extension of a word but does not satisfy all of the criteria specified in a proposed definition would show that definition to be too narrow. The second thing the counterexample does is point the way in Step #3.

**Step #3** Revise the original definition. What was wrong with the definition of "square" as an "equilateral shape"? Our first definition was too broad, as demonstrated by our counterexample in Step #2, so we know we need to make the definition more restrictive. That means adding another necessary condition. How shall we formulate it? The counterexample in Step #2 gives us good guidance here: not enough sides. So that's what we want to add to our definition in Step #3. So let's revise our definition to say that "square" means "equilateral quadrilateral." ("Quadrilateral" of course means "four-sided figure".)

**Step #4** Repeat Step #2. Critique Step #3 by example. Once again, using what you know about shapes, you can see that something's still not entirely right about the definition of "square" as an "equilateral quadrilateral." And you can demonstrate this by example:

**Step #5** Repeat Step #3. Revise the revised definition. What was wrong with the definition of "square" as an "equilateral quadrilateral"? Once again our definition was too broad, as demonstrated by our counterexample in Step #4, so we know we need to make the definition even more restrictive. That means adding another necessary condition. How shall we formulate it? The counterexample in Step #4 again gives us good guidance: The angles are not 90-degree angles. So that's what we want to add to our definition at this point. And so we arrive at "square" meaning "equilateral rectangle." ("Rectangle" of course means "four-sided figure with 90-degree angles.")

**Step #6** Keep going as needed. At this point the process is complete for the essential definition of the word "square," because it isn't possible to refute our current definition by example. Anything that fits all the criteria specified in our current definition will turn out to be a legitimate member of the extension of the word, and vice versa: Any member of the extension will turn out to satisfy all the criteria in our definition. The word and our definition are "coextensive," which means they have the same extension. That's how we know we're done.

### ESSENTIAL DEFINITION BY GENUS AND DIFFERENTIA

A related strategic approach involves a two-step procedure and the concept of categories:

**Step #1** Locate the extension of the term you are defining within some larger category (called the "genus"). So for example squares are part of the larger category of plane geometric figures.

**Step #2** Now specify the feature or set of features (called the "differentia") that distinguishes the extension you are defining from the rest of the larger category. In this case you want to specify the feature or set of features that distinguishes squares from the rest of the plane geometric figures.

| Term | Larger Category | Distinguishing Characteristics |
|---|---|---|
| square | plane geometric figure | with 4 equal sides and 90-degree angles |

Similarly

| Term | Class | Distinguishing Characteristics |
|---|---|---|
| spoon | utensil | consisting of a small, shallow bowl with a handle, used in eating or stirring |
| watch | machine | portable or wearable for telling time |
| Ethics | branch of Philosophy | concerned with morality |

Notice that the definition of "square" which we arrived at by using the dialectical approach is worded differently from the one we arrived at by genus and differentia. But the two definitions "equilateral rectangle" and "plane geometric figure with four equal sides and 90-degree angles" are synonymous. They express the same criteria. These two strategic approaches can also be effectively combined. If you're stuck you can use the genus/differentia approach to formulate an initial definition, and you can use the dialectical approach to critique and refine a definition by genus and differentia.

## PSEUDO-DEFINITIONS

Before we leave the subject of definitions we should briefly mention a couple of things which resemble definitions, and are often called by that name, but which are probably better separated off into other categories.

### METAPHORICAL DEFINITIONS

Occasionally people will try to get to the essence of some word or concept without specifying the criteria that define the extension of the word. For example Bob Dylan once defined a "song" as a "poem that walks by itself." Speaking strictly it would probably be better to call this something other than a "definition," because it doesn't really fulfill the function of explaining the intension, although it does get at something essential about songs in an insightful and interesting way. Statements like this often involve highly unconventional, even poetic, uses of words (called "metaphors") to suggest ways of conceptualizing or thinking about things which might not otherwise occur to us.

## PERSUASIVE DEFINITIONS

Occasionally something looking more or less like a definition is offered for what turn out to be ulterior purposes or motives having to do with somebody's persuasive agenda. Typically this will involve some relatively subtle (or perhaps not so subtle) alteration or shift in the meaning of the word or words being "defined." Portions of the conventional meaning will be preserved, but changes will be introduced in order to serve the persuasive purposes that are at work behind the scenes. These changes are typically not meant to be noticed, because that would tend to undermine the persuasive strategy. A device which is frequently used to cover up such changes is the introduction of an adjective like "real" or "genuine" or "true" as a qualifier of the word being "defined" for persuasive purposes, as in "True democracy means uniform proportional representation in the primary process, instead of the present hodgepodge of caucuses and winner-take-all primaries."

### EXERCISE | Definitions

http://www

1. Make up one example of definition by synonymy.

| Word Defined | Definition |
|---|---|
| | |

2. Find an example of definition by synonymy in a dictionary.

| Word Defined | Definition | Source |
|---|---|---|
| | | |

3. How many examples of definition by etymology can you find in this book so far? List them below.

| Word Defined | Page Number |
|---|---|
| | |
| | |
| | |
| | |
| | |

(continued)

| Word Defined | Page Number |
| --- | --- |
| | |
| | |
| | |
| | |
| | |
| | |
| | |
| | |
| | |
| | |
| | |
| | |
| | |
| | |

4. How many definitions can you find in this book so far? List them below, and then sort them using the categories you've just learned.

| Word Defined | Page Number | Type of Definition |
| --- | --- | --- |
| | | |
| | | |
| | | |
| | | |
| | | |
| | | |
| | | |
| | | |
| | | |

| Word Defined | Page Number | Type of Definition |
|---|---|---|
| | | |
| | | |
| | | |
| | | |
| | | |
| | | |
| | | |
| | | |
| | | |
| | | |
| | | |

5. Give an example of stipulative definition.

| Word Defined | Definition |
|---|---|
| | |

6. Find one example of stipulative definition in this book.

| Word Defined | Definition |
|---|---|
| | |

7. Classify the following definitions.

| Example | Func. | Osten. | Syn. | Etym. | Stip. | Pers. | Ess. | Meta. |
|---|---|---|---|---|---|---|---|---|
| For purposes of financial aid eligibility, a "full-time student" shall be defined as a student enrolled in twelve or more units per semester. | | | | | | | | |
| Octad: a group or sequence of eight, from the Greek word *okto* for "eight." | | | | | | | | |

(continued)

| Example | Func. | Osten. | Syn. | Etym. | Stip. | Pers. | Ess. | Meta. |
|---|---|---|---|---|---|---|---|---|
| Philosophy? Oh yeah, that's the stuff written by Plato and Aristotle and Descartes and those guys. | | | | | | | | |
| Floppy disk: A small magnetically coated piece of plastic used to store electronic information. | | | | | | | | |
| The blues ain't nothin' but a good man feelin' bad. | | | | | | | | |
| That's not music. Real music by definition has rhythm *and* melody. | | | | | | | | |
| Art is anything that humans do or make for reasons other than survival or reproduction. | | | | | | | | |
| "Augur" means "predict." | | | | | | | | |

8. Critique the following "essential definitions."

| Example | Broad | Narrow | Neg. | Figrtv. | Circ. | Expl. |
|---|---|---|---|---|---|---|
| "Pornography" is any pictorial display of human sexuality or nudity. | | | | | | |
| "Philosophy" is the study of the classical Greek works of Plato and Aristotle. | | | | | | |
| "Rape" is forcing a woman to have sex against her will. | | | | | | |
| "Circular": Of or pertaining to a circle; the property of circularity. | | | | | | |
| "Alimony" is when two people make a mistake and one of them continues to pay for it. | | | | | | |
| A "definition" is an explanation of the meaning of a term. | | | | | | |
| Jazz: "The music of unemployment." —Frank Zappa | | | | | | |
| Economics is the science which treats of the phenomena arising out of the economic activities of men in society. — J. M. Keynes | | | | | | |

## CATEGORIES OF ISSUES AND DISPUTES

With the previous discussion of language, meaning, and definition as a background, let us now look ahead to the next chapter of this book, which will introduce the central concept of an "argument."

Should there be a law against abortion? Should animals be used in medical experimentation? Does extraterrestrial intelligent life exist? What is the average temperature of the water in Lake Tahoe? Do recent leadership changes in China indicate a fundamental shift in its foreign policy? Is there a global environmental crisis? These are all questions to which a number of significant and conflicting alternative responses are both genuinely open and defensible. They are good examples of what we call an "issue." You may have heard the expression "Reasonable people may differ . . ." An issue is what we call a topic about which reasonable people may differ. *An issue is a genuinely disputable topic.* And a dispute is a disagreement or controversy over an issue. It is what happens when one of several opposed positions on a particular issue gets challenged from the point of view of another.

Sometimes it seems as though reasonable people can disagree about anything, everything, even nothing at all. It would help if we could dispense with disputes over nothing at all. So before we begin to categorize issues, let us explain more deeply what we mean by "genuinely disputable," by pointing out and setting aside another kind of thing which frequently *passes for* an issue.

### VERBAL DISPUTES

Philosopher William James tells the story about how on a camping trip everyone got into a dispute over the following puzzle:

> The corpus of the dispute was a squirrel—a live squirrel supposed to be clinging to one side of a tree-trunk; while over against the tree's opposite side a human being was imagined to stand. This human witness tries to get sight of the squirrel by moving rapidly round the tree, but no matter how fast he goes, the squirrel moves just as fast in the opposite direction, and always keeps the tree between himself and the man, so that never a glimpse of him is caught. The resultant problem now is this: *Does the man go round the squirrel or not?* He goes round the tree, sure enough, and the squirrel is on the tree; but does he go round the squirrel?[5]

James's idea was that although you can easily imagine people going round and round in an endless dispute over such a puzzle, you can just as easily dissolve the puzzle by drawing a simple terminological distinction: It all depends upon what you mean by "going round" the squirrel.

If you mean passing from the north of him to the east, then to the south, then to the west, then to the north again, obviously the man does go round him, for he occupies these successive positions. But if on the contrary you mean being first in front of him, then on the right of him, then behind him, then on the left, and finally in front again, it is quite as obvious that the man fails to go round him, for by the compensating movements the squirrel makes, he keeps his belly turned towards the man all the time, and his back turned away.[6]

Since it hardly matters which meaning of "going round" the squirrel applies, this could be called a "purely verbal" dispute. To put it another way, there's no real issue here; the dispute arises out of a simple ambiguity in the way the puzzle is worded. A similar example is the old dispute "If a tree falls in the forest and nobody is there to hear it, is there a sound?" Clarifying the meaning of "sound" dissolves the dispute. If you're talking about sound *waves*, then presumably there are sounds whether or not anyone is there to hear the tree fall. But if you mean sound *sensations*—the experience of sound—then the falling tree makes no sound, for no one is there to experience the sound sensations.

Perhaps it would be nice if all issues were as trivial as these. Perhaps it would be nice if all disputes arose out of simple ambiguities and could be dismissed as mere "matters of semantics." On the other hand, perhaps it would be boring if all disputes were idle and there were no real, serious, and urgent issues to argue about. Reasonable people may differ about this, possibly leading to another kind of idle dispute. But in any case, most genuinely important disputes are concerned with genuine issues of one sort or another. The rest of this book will be devoted to developing and refining strategies and procedures for resolving serious disputes about real and important issues, which comprise a variety as wide as all of human interest and concern.

## ISSUE ANALYSIS

Among the immediate challenges that most issues present is their inherent complexity. Take one of the issues we mentioned earlier as an example. The question whether there should be law against abortion, even though it is worded as a simple "yes-or-no" question, is hardly a simple issue. The moment we begin to confront it seriously and address it, we recognize a multitude of points over which reasonable people may differ. Reasonable people will disagree over not just whether the law should restrict abortion. Reasonable people will disagree over whether abortion is in the same moral category as murder, or homicide, or elective surgery, or birth control. Reasonable people will disagree over whether a woman's reproductive processes are private and over whether the government can or should interfere with her choices. Reasonable people will disagree over whether the fetus is a person or only a potential person. Reasonable people will disagree over whether potential persons have rights. Reasonable people will disagree over whether the right to life includes the right to use another person's body as a life support system. Even among those who agree that the law should restrict abortion, reasonable people will disagree, for example over whether the restriction should be total or partial, rigid or flexible, and if partial and flexible, over what the exceptions should be, and so on. So what we have is not just one issue, but more like a whole nest of them, resembling a can of worms. The challenge this poses for human intelligence is obvious: This much complexity is confusing.

*Confusion: another one of the things that make it difficult even for reasonable people, even when they're not distracted by external pressures and enticements or internal longings and fears, to discriminate between reasonable and unreasonable beliefs.*

Most interesting issues are deep and complex enough to present this challenge and the trick is to find an approach to the issue which brings its complexity under intellectual control rather than allowing its complexity to confuse and overwhelm us. We want an approach that is likely to result in illuminating the issue and moving in an orderly way toward its resolution. What we need is an orderly agenda of inquiry. An "agenda" is a list of things to do. The function of an agenda is to monitor progress, especially when there are a lot of things to keep track of. An agenda of inquiry would be a list of things to find or figure out, and its function would be so that you can know whether you are making progress toward resolving the issue rather than wandering around aimlessly and getting lost in it or going round and round in circles.

For this purpose, and because appropriate strategies and procedures for addressing and resolving issues vary from situation to situation depending largely on the nature of the issue, we now propose to sort issues into three general categories for which we will later develop general strategies and procedures: factual issues, evaluative issues, and interpretive issues. These categories are neither mutually exclusive nor exhaustive. This means that a given issue may belong to more than one of these categories or fall outside all of them. Bear in mind that the purpose of this categorical scheme has little to do with labeling issues or sorting them "correctly." It's more about figuring out what questions to ask in what order.

We are going to be using the terms "factual," "evaluative," and "interpretive" in a way that departs slightly but significantly from what we believe is current popular usage. Our impression is that people generally draw a very sharp distinction between "factual" matters on the one hand and "evaluative and interpretive" matters on the other, but also that people generally do not draw any very sharp and clear distinction at all between "evaluative" and "interpretive" matters. Popular usage seems to go something like this: "Factual matters" are matters which pertain to the "facts." The "facts" are everything which is proven or known beyond doubt or question. Everything else (values, interpretations, whatever) is a "matter of opinion" and as such unprovable and unknowable.[7] This usage is not going to work very well for our purposes, first because it doesn't recognize the need for strategies and procedures for the resolution of issues about what the facts actually are, and second because it doesn't open up any useful strategic or procedural options for the resolution of evaluative and interpretive issues. We are therefore going to stipulate meanings with somewhat greater precision and utility than popular conventional usage has for the words "factual," "evaluative," and "interpretive." We will use "factual" to refer to "matters which can be investigated by either the methods of empirical science or documentary research." We will use "evaluative" to refer to "matters which concern the merits of things." And we will use "interpretive" to refer to "matters which concern the meanings of things."

Categorizing an issue is a way of setting the agenda of inquiry. To approach an issue as a factual issue is to raise questions of evidence. What sort of evidence would be relevant and decisive? What evidence is there already available which bears on the issue? What additional evidence is required? What sorts of experiment or research would be needed in order to obtain that additional evidence? To approach an issue as an evaluative issue is to raise questions of standards. To approach an issue as an interpretive issue is to raise the question of interpretive hypotheses. There may be several ways to get into a given issue, each of which is reasonable. Let's not assume that there is one and only one "correct" approach, or even that among the many available avenues of approach there is one that is clearly superior to all the others. But something's got to come first in the order of investigation and inquiry and then something's got to come next and so on.

## FACTUAL ISSUES AND DISPUTES

In modern Olympic history which nation has won the most medals in weight lifting? What city is the world's coldest national capital? What is the average temperature of the water in Lake Tahoe? All of these are factual questions. They illustrate what we mean by saying that factual matters can be investigated by doing empirical science or documentary research. If a dispute were to arise about any of these questions, say for example during a game of Jeopardy or Trivial Pursuit, there are already well-established procedures available for settling it. We might look the information up in a reliable source (documentary research). Or if the information is not already recorded, we could easily imagine the sort of scientific investigation by which the information could be gathered.

Having said that, we should also note right away that things are not always so simple with factual issues. Suppose that for some reason we needed to figure out how many feral cats are living in the city of San Francisco? In this case the question is not "theoretically" difficult to answer. It's a simple factual matter of counting the cats. But in practice how in the world is anyone ever going to count all the feral (wild) cats in the city of San Francisco?! They run away. They hide. They breed like, uh, feral cats. So we would need to "estimate" the number in some way. In fact things might not be very simple even with the simple (or simple sounding) examples we mentioned above. Suppose we were asked to determine the average temperature of the water in the Pacific Ocean. You can begin to appreciate the difficulty of determining matters of fact. Doing good science involves both evaluation and interpretation, as does doing good documentary research.

The question of whether or not there is a global environmental crisis is a good example. Suppose we approach it initially as a factual question. What sort of evidence would be relevant? Well, suppose there were hard empirical evidence of significant changes in weather patterns on a global scale. That would be relevant evidence. Notice that evaluation (of the evidence) is already involved. "Hard" evidence *has merit,* "significant" changes *merit attention.* And supposing for the moment that we do have "hard" evidence of significant global weather anomalies, we would still need some understanding of their causes in order to answer our original question. And this will involve interpreting the evidence we already have as well as additional evidence which we may seek concerning for example extraordinary fluctuations in the average temperature in the Pacific Ocean and so on. We will discuss all of this further in Chapters 7 and 8.

## EVALUATIVE ISSUES AND DISPUTES

Now let's reconsider two issues we mentioned earlier. Should there be a law against abortion? Should animals be used in medical experimentation? One thing is clear right away: Neither can be resolved *simply* as a matter of fact. We could not possibly hope to settle a dispute over the right and proper legal status of abortion by documentary research alone. Nor could we hope to settle a dispute over the use of animals in experimental medicine on the basis of empirical science alone. Not that documentation and empirical evidence are irrelevant to these issues. Just as evaluation and interpretation are important parts of any good factual inquiry, so good science and good documentary research often play a crucial role in evaluation and interpretation. But no amount of empirical evidence and/or documentation could possibly be *by itself decisive* in either of these issues. So it would make sense to approach them initially not as factual issues, and the word "should" is a clue that they are each fundamentally evaluative issues, which raises the question of standards. What standards of evaluation are we concerned with? In each of these issues it is apparent that moral or ethical standards are central. So they will need to be clarified in the course of the inquiry. Interpretive and factual questions will take their place in the agenda of inquiry as they arise in the process of clarifying and applying these moral or ethical standards. We will discuss this further in Chapter 8.

## INTERPRETIVE ISSUES AND DISPUTES

Suppose that in her first speech before the United Nations General Assembly the newly appointed U.S. ambassador makes five explicit references to human rights, free trade, opium, democracy, and Hong Kong. Is the United States "sending a message" to Beijing? And if so, what is the message? Or take this example from our earlier list of issues:

> Do recent changes in Chinese leadership and internal policy indicate a fundamental shift in philosophy and direction?

These questions indicate issues concerning what things mean, or how they should be understood. Such issues frequently arise in our attempts to understand things whose meanings may be flexible, complicated, multilayered, obscure, or even deliberately veiled. Issues of this sort are probably the most complex and difficult issues procedurally that we are likely to encounter in everyday discourse. Yet they are also absolutely fundamental to the process of communication, since they have to do with the discernment of meaning. Indeed, many, perhaps most, of the activities you will be performing throughout this book involve interpretation. Deciding whether a particular passage is an argument or not involves interpretation. Deciding whether a passage is intended to serve an expressive or persuasive or informative function involves interpretation. There is no single simple procedure for resolving interpretive issues or settling interpretive disputes. Rather there are a number of kinds of information relevant to interpretation, some of which have already been mentioned, and some of which we will be discussing further in Chapter 8.

For example, the conventions governing the use of a term or expression are relevant to its interpretation. Similarly, there are what are known as "diplomatic conventions," which would be relevant to the interpretation of communications between one government, for example through its UN ambassador, and another. In addition to conventions, information about the context surrounding a passage is relevant to its interpretation. Knowing that a particular speech was delivered before the UN General Assembly, rather than for example by confidential communiqué to the Chinese ambassador, is an important piece of information which can guide us closer to an accurate understanding of what was meant. Contextual information in the case of oral communication, as well as in film and video, includes facial expression, vocal inflection, bodily posture, timing, and so on.

It should be apparent already that gathering and sifting evidence of such a wide variety, especially in living contexts, where time is of the essence, is a process of considerable complexity and subtlety. And there is a good deal of disagreement among theorists about what the proper procedures are for doing interpretive work, and how they should be applied in different sorts of interpretive controversy. Nevertheless, interpretation is something you are probably pretty good at by now. So you no doubt already recognize that some interpretive issues can be resolved relatively firmly and easily, whereas others are more difficult and may be quite resistant to resolution. In disputed cases, perhaps the most useful procedural strategy is the use of hypothetical reasoning. This involves formulating and testing interpretive hypotheses. An hypothesis is an idea which we *suppose* to be true, though we do not yet *know* it to be true. This is a procedure which also has important applications in dealing with factual issues. We will be discussing it in greater detail in Chapter 8.

## EXERCISE **Issues and Disputes**

Sort the following issues using the categories discussed so far in this chapter.

| Example | Verbal | Factual | Eval. | Interp. |
|---|---|---|---|---|
| Don King: Boxing is a great sport! It requires excellent physical skills and conditioning and mental toughness.<br>Larry King: Come on, Don. Boxing is nothing but a barbaric spectacle: two brutes beating each other senseless. | | | | |

| Example | Verbal | Factual | Eval. | Interp. |
|---|---|---|---|---|
| Newt: Nuclear weapons have been effective in keeping the peace ever since World War II.<br>Noam: Not if you count the wars in Korea, Vietnam, Nicaragua, the Middle East, and the Persian Gulf. | | | | |
| Tommy and Timmy are identical twins. Tommy says, "I'm Timmy's older brother." Timmy says, "No, we're the same age." | | | | |
| Did O. J. Simpson kill Ronald Goldman and Nicole Brown Simpson? | | | | |
| Did the prosecution in the criminal trial establish O. J. Simpson's guilt "beyond a reasonable doubt"? | | | | |
| Were the verdicts in the O. J. Simpson criminal and civil trials "just"? | | | | |
| Brad has an old car. One day he replaces one of its defective parts. The next day he replaces another. Before the year is out, Brad has replaced every part in the entire car. Is Brad's car the same car he had before he began changing parts? | | | | |
| A bad peace is even worse than war. —Tacitus<br>The most disadvantageous peace is better than the most just war. —Erasmus | | | | |
| Gene: That example where Tacitus and Erasmus seem to be disagreeing about peace is just a verbal dispute. They just mean different things by the word "peace."<br>Jean: No I think they have a factual dispute. They really disagree about history. | | | | |
| Phil told his brother Fred, "When I die I'll leave you all my money." A week later he changed his mind and decided to leave all his money to his wife instead. So Phil wrote in his will, "I leave all my money to my next of kin" (his wife). Unknown to Phil, his wife had just died in a car accident. The day after he made out his will Phil himself died, and his money went to his next of kin—his brother Fred. Did Phil keep his promise to his brother Fred or didn't he? | | | | |

## ADDITIONAL EXERCISES

1. Spend five to ten minutes observing what happens in some open public area, like a busy intersection, the campus quadrangle, or a shopping mall. Write a paragraph that contains a strictly factual descriptive account of what you observed. Next write a paragraph that, besides being informative, is also entertaining. Next write a paragraph that uses the information in a persuasive way.

Informative

Entertaining

Persuasive

2. Explain both the conventional meaning and the current emotional connotations of the following terms: "New Democrat," "New Right," "liberal," "welfare queen," "Barbie," "high technology," "higher learning," "ivory tower," "free trade," "free market," "drug-free zone," "gay" (as opposed to "homosexual"), "big government," "big business," "family entertainment," "adult entertainment," "urbane," "urban," "inner city."

3. The same thing can be called by different names, depending on whether one is for it or against it. For example, if you're for a proposal to outlaw retail discounts on certain merchandise, you might call it the "fair trade practices act"; if you're against it you might call it a "price-fixing law." Take a current issue or piece of legislation and give it a favorable and an unfavorable name by which it could be designated.

**4.** Imagine yourself as the creator of a successful national consulting firm specializing in political slogans. Your clients cover the spectrum of issues and interest groups. This month the following groups have scheduled rallies in major cities for the causes listed below. Your job is to come up with a set of five catchy slogans to successfully communicate each group's message. You're also scheduled to address a national radio audience at the end of the month on the topic of "Successful Strategies for Political Communication." You plan to use your work for your current roster of clients to explain the secrets of your success.

| Group | Cause |
|---|---|
| Mothers Against Drunk Driving | demanding tougher penalties for drunk driving |
| PETA (People for the Ethical Treatment of Animals) | opposing the use of animal subjects in AIDS research at the state university medical center |
| ACT-UP | counterdemonstration in support of accelerating the pace of AIDS research |
| NORML (National Organization for the Reform of Marijuana Laws) | supporting national legislation to permit medical use of marijuana |
| DARE | counterdemonstration to keep marijuana classified as an illegal substance |
| EarthFirst | supporting a moratorium on logging in old-growth redwood forests |
| National Wise Use Coalition | counterdemonstration supporting the rights of private interests to harvest timber resources on private lands |
| AFA (American Family Association) | opposing a permit for a Marilyn Manson concert |
| ACLU (American Civil Liberties Union) | counterdemonstration against censorship |
| San Francisco Historical Preservation Society | supporting a citywide ordinance banning skateboarding on all sidewalks and public spaces |
| *Thrasher Magazine* | counterdemonstration in support of skateboard right of way |

**5.** Identify and explain the ambiguity(ies) and/or vagueness in the following examples.

a.

By permission of Johnny Hart and Creators Syndicate, Inc.

b. When asked why he robbed banks, notorious bank robber Willy Sutton replied, "Because that's where the money is."

c. He was thrown from the car as it left the road. Later he was found in the ditch by some stray cows.

d. As the great escape artist Harry Houdini drove south along Jefferson Boulevard he suddenly turned into a side street.

e. Baseball pitcher Tug McGraw, asked if he preferred Astroturf to grass, said, "I don't know. I never smoked Astroturf."

f. Sexual harassment is defined as unwelcome sexual advances, requests for sexual favors, and other verbal or physical conduct of a sexual nature when:

> submission to such conduct is made either explicitly or implicitly a term or condition of an individual's employment, appointment, admission, or academic evaluation;
>
> submission to such conduct is used as a basis for evaluation in personnel decisions or academic evaluations affecting an individual;
>
> such conduct has the purpose or effect of unreasonably interfering with an individual's performance or of creating an intimidating, hostile, offensive or otherwise adverse working or educational environment; or

the conduct has the purpose or effect of interfering with a student's academic performance, creating an intimidating, hostile, offensive, or otherwise adverse learning environment or adversely affecting any student.

**6.** For each of the following sets of related issues or questions, identify the one that you consider to be the most basic or fundamental—the one which the other related questions presuppose an answer to—and explain your decision.

a. Should there be a law against "hate speech" on the Internet?
What is "hate speech"?
Should the service provider or the government be responsible for the enforcement of regulations prohibiting "hate speech" over the Internet?
What kinds of penalties should be imposed on people who post "hate speech" on the Internet?

b. Is time travel possible?
Is time travel technically feasible?
Is the technical feasibility of time travel worth investigating?
What is meant by "time travel"?

c. What are the defining criteria for being a person?
Should abortion be prohibited under criminal law as a form of homicide?
Is abortion a form of homicide?
Is the human fetus a person?

d. Should same-sex couples be allowed to join in legally sanctioned marriages?
Will the recognition of same-sex marriages undermine the institution of the family?
What purposes are served by the institution of legally sanctioned marriage?
Could civilization survive the collapse of the family as an institution?

## GLOSSARY

**ambiguous** describes a term or expression with more than one conventional meaning
**analysis** the process of breaking things down into their constituent elements
**connotation** the intension plus the emotional impact of a term
**convention** a behavioral regularity followed in order to solve interpersonal coordination problems
**definition** an explanation of the meaning of a term or expression
**definition, essential** definition which gives a term's intension
**definition, ostensive** definition by example
**definition, persuasive** an apparent definition which alters the conventional meaning of the term defined for persuasive purposes
**definition, stipulative** definition which specifies an unconventional meaning of a term for use in a specific context of discourse
**denotation** the relationship between a word and the objects it "points to"
**etymology** the history of a word
**explanation** language used to facilitate understanding
**extension** the set of objects denoted by a term

**intension** the criteria which define the extension of a term
**issue** a topic about which reasonable people may disagree
**issue, evaluative** an issue concerning the merits of things
**issue, factual** an issue to be resolved by either the methods of empirical science or documentary research
**issue, interpretive** an issue concerning the meanings of things
**necessary condition** a characteristic or set of characteristics required for membership in the word's extension
**sufficient condition** a characteristic or set of characteristics which is by itself adequate qualification for membership in the word's extension
**synonymy** sameness of meaning
**vague** a term or expression with an indefinite extension
**verbal dispute** a dispute arising out of overlooked verbal ambiguity

## NOTES

[1] Quoted in Gordon Allport, *The Nature of Prejudice* (Reading, Mass.: Addison Wesley, 1954).

[2] The Greek philosopher Aristotle was an early developer of this concept. For a more recent treatment of this concept as a general strategy, see David N. Perkins, *Knowledge as Design* (Hillsdale, N.J.: Erlbaum, 1986).

[3] This account of linguistic convention is derived from Jonathan Bennett, *Linguistic Behavior* (London: Cambridge University Press, 1976), and David Lewis, *Convention* (Cambridge, Mass.: Harvard University Press, 1969).

[4] Lewis Carroll, *Through the Looking Glass*, in *The Complete Works of Lewis Carroll* (New York: Random House, 1936), p. 214.

[5] William James, *Pragmatism*, Lecture II (Cambridge, Mass.: Harvard University Press, 1975).

[6] Ibid.

[7] This is a version of "relativism." See the section on "Relativism" in Chapter 1.

# PART TWO Analysis

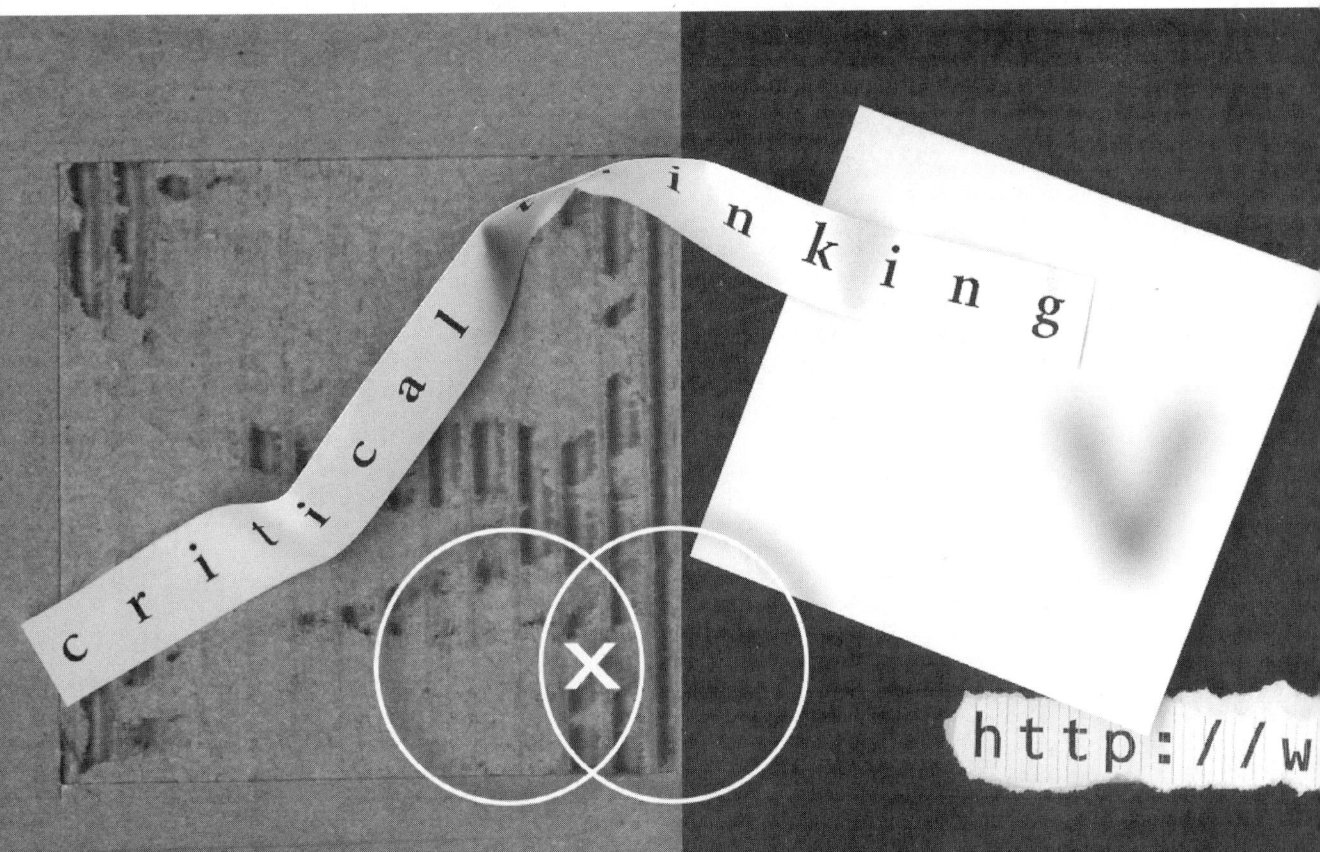

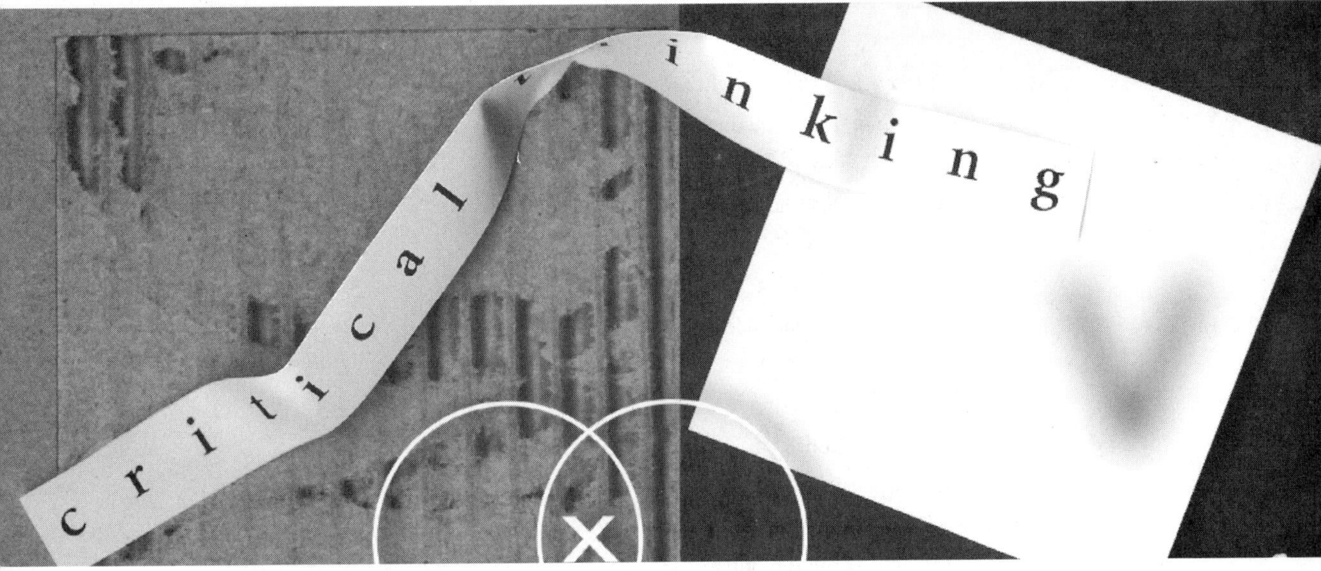


CHAPTER 3

# Argument

We concluded Chapter 2 with a discussion of issues and disputes. Let us now suppose that you and some other reasonable person find yourselves divided over an issue, say for example whether or not we are in the midst of a global environmental crisis. One of you is of the opinion that we are, while the other thinks that we are not. What do reasonable people do when they recognize they are divided over an issue? They argue. In this chapter we will introduce and develop the concept of an "argument," as at once a product of critical thinking and an object to which critical thinking is applied.

The word "argument" is ambiguous. For clarity let us center on one of its conventional meanings and set aside the other as outside our focus of primary concern. In this book we are primarily concerned with the sense of the word "argument" in which an individual person *makes* or *offers* an argument, not the sense in which two people *have* an argument. In the sense of the word with which we're primarily concerned, an "argument" can be defined as *a composition whose primary purpose is to persuade a person by appealing to the person's reasoning capacity.* To reinforce this distinction, consider the following portion of the Monty Python's Flying Circus "Argument Clinic" sketch. A "customer," played by Michael Palin, enters the reception area requesting an argument and is sent down the hall to Room 12A, where he finds an attendant, played by John Cleese.

*Customer:* Is this the right room for an argument?
*Attendant:* I told you once.
*C:* No you haven't.
*A:* Yes I have.
*C:* When?
*A:* Just now.
*C:* No you didn't.
*A:* I did.
*C:* Didn't!
*A:* Did!
*C:* Didn't!
*A:* I'm telling you I did.
*C:* You did not!
*A:* Oh, I'm sorry. Just one moment. Is this the five minute argument or the full half hour?
*C:* Oh, just the five minutes.
*A:* Ah, thank you. Anyway, I did.
*C:* You most certainly did not.
*A:* Look, let's get this thing clear. I quite definitely told you.
*C:* No, you did not.
*A:* Yes I did.
*C:* No you didn't.
*A:* Yes I did!
*C:* No you didn't!
*A:* Yes I *did!*
*C:* No you *didn't!*
*A:* Yes I *DID!*
*C:* No you *DIDN'T!*
*A:* *DID!*
*C:* Oh now look. This isn't an argument.
*A:* Yes it is.
*C:* No it isn't. It's just contradiction.
*A:* No it isn't.
*C:* It IS!
*A:* It is NOT!
*C:* Look. You just contradicted me.
*A:* I did not.

*C:* Oh, you did.

*A:* No, no, no.

*C:* You did just then!

*A:* Nonsense.

*C:* Oh, this is futile . . .

*A:* No it isn't.

*C:* I came here for a good argument.

*A:* No, you didn't. No, you came here for an *argument.*

*C:* Well, an argument isn't just contradiction.

*A:* Can be.

*C:* No it can't. An argument is a connected series of statements intended to establish a proposition.

*A:* No it isn't.

*C:* Yes it is. It's not just contradiction.

*A:* Look if I'm going to argue with you I must take up a contrary position.

*C:* Yes, but that's not just saying "No it isn't."

*A:* Yes it is.

*C:* No it *ISN'T!*[1]

The humor here depends on both senses of the term "argument." What the attendant is offering is a perverse trivialization of the kind of argument that two people "have." In this sense "argument" is synonymous with "dispute" as we used that term in Chapter 2: argument = verbal conflict, which Cleese's character has reduced in this scene to mere mechanical contradiction of whatever Palin's character says. Palin's character is interested in something more substantial, and he gives a definition:

"An argument is a connected series of statements intended to establish a proposition."

This is an alternative to the functional definition given at the beginning of the chapter. It also gives the intension of the word "argument" in the sense with which we are primarily concerned, but it does so by reference to structural features rather than function. In other words, *an argument is a composition consisting of a set of assertions, one of which, called the "thesis" or "conclusion," is understood or intended to be supported by the others, called the "premises."* The two definitions, functional and structural, are closely linked, because the structure suits the function. To persuade someone by appeal to her reasoning capacity, typically one presents a composition consisting of claims or assertions, some of which support others. In what follows we will be using both definitions. The functional definition will serve as a basis for argument identification. The structural definition will serve as a basis for argument analysis.

Our study of argument can be divided into four main skill areas: argument identification, argument analysis, argument evaluation, and argument construction. Argument identification is about recognizing arguments and telling them apart from other sorts of material. Argument analysis is about taking arguments apart, understanding how they are put together and designed to work. Argument evaluation involves criticizing them and appraising their strengths and weaknesses. And argument construction is simply the generation of original arguments of our own.

Here is a simple example of an argument: "Mothers are females. Pat's a mother. Therefore Pat's a female." "Pat is a female" is the statement which the others are intended to establish. If we wanted we could combine all three statements into a single sentence and still have an argument. "Since (1) mothers are female and (2) Pat is a mother, (3) Pat is a female." So an argument can take the form either of individual assertions or of a single sentence that embodies those assertions.

## ARGUMENT IDENTIFICATION

Arguments are compositions in language, which as you know is an immensely flexible medium of expression. Open any magazine or daily newspaper and you will find a wide variety of material composed in language, including some arguments. Listen in on any conversation and you will hear many things going on, including argumentation. It is not so difficult to identify cases of verbal conflict, especially when one is involved. But identifying arguments, in the sense relevant to our purposes, can be much more difficult, especially when they are embedded in larger contexts. This is due in part to the fact that recognizing arguments involves recognizing the speaker's or the writer's intentions, and the fact is that speakers and writers can have complex intentions and that they do not always make their intentions perfectly clear in what they write and say.

Distinguishing arguments from explanations, or jokes, or greetings, or narratives, or instructions is a matter of discerning the author's intentions to persuade by appeal to reason. Sometimes, it is clear that what the author is trying to do is to persuade by appeal to reason. In that case, what the author has put forward is clearly an argument. Sometimes, it is clear that the author is trying to do something other than persuade by appeal to reason. In that case, what the author has put forward is clearly not an argument. Sometimes, an author may be trying to do two or more things at once (e.g., persuade by appeal to reason and amuse the reader). Sometimes, it is simply just not clear what the author is trying to do.

We often assert things without arguing for them: "Baseball is a popular sport in the United States. Football is generally played in the winter. Hockey is a popular sport in Canada. Basketball can be played inside or outside. Soccer is played throughout the world." These statements are nonargumentative. None of them is intended to support or establish any of the others; so, taken as a group, they do not constitute an argument.

We also use statements to explain things: "The class on the history of music has been canceled for lack of enrollment." "The horse was frightened by a snake in the grass." "Last night's rain made the streets wet." These are explanatory statements. They help explain something: the cancellation of the class, the fright of the horse, the wet pavement. They are, in other words, presumably intended to help someone understand something more deeply.

The basic difference between such nonargumentative statements and arguments is one of intent or purpose. If people are interested in establishing the truth of a claim and offer evidence intended to do that, then they are arguing, and what they are offering is an argument. But if they regard the truth of a claim as nonproblematic, or as already having been established, and are trying to help us understand *why* it is the case (rather than establish that it is the case), then they are explaining. Thus, when we say, "The streets are wet because it rained last night," we are not trying to establish that the streets are wet. We are taking that as an established truth and are offering an explanation of how they got that way. But if we say, "You should take your umbrella today, because the forecast calls for rain," we are trying to persuade you that you should take your umbrella by offering the weather forecast as a reason. We are not taking the statement that you should take your umbrella as an established truth, rather we are trying to show how it follows from the other statement. Thus we are setting forth an argument.

## EXERCISE | Argument Identification

Which of the following passages express or contain arguments? You can use either the functional or the structural definition of "argument" or both to make your determination.

| Example | Arg. | Not. | Undec. |
|---|---|---|---|
| ". . . a principle I established for myself early in the game: I wanted to get paid for my work, but I didn't want to work for pay." —Leonard Cohen, poet | | | |
| I object to lotteries, because they're biased in favor of lucky people. | | | |
| The most serious issue facing journalism education today is the blurring of the distinctions between advertising, public relations, and journalism itself. | | | |
| "Even the most productive writers are expert dawdlers, doers of unnecessary errands, seekers of interruptions—trials to their wives and husbands, associates, and themselves. They sharpen well-pointed pencils and go out to buy more blank paper, rearrange their office, wander through libraries and bookstores, change words, walk, drive, make unnecessary calls, nap, day dream, and try not 'consciously' to think about what they are going to write so they can think subconsciously about it." —Donald M. Murray, in "Write before Writing" | | | |

(continued)

| Example | Arg. | Not. | Undec. |
|---|---|---|---|
| "They're going to feed you," said Roosta, "into the Total Perspective Vortex!" Zaphod had never heard of this. He believed that he had heard of all the fun things in the Galaxy, so he assumed that the Total Perspective Vortex was not fun." —Douglas Adams, in *The Restaurant at the End of the Universe.* | | | |
| "Willy Loman never made a lot of money. His name was never in the paper. He's not the finest character that ever lived. But he's a human being, and a terrible thing is happening to him. So attention must be paid. He's not to be allowed to fall into his grave like an old dog. Attention, attention must be paid to such a person . . ." —Arthur Miller, in *Death of a Salesman* | | | |

## ARGUMENT ANALYSIS

As we indicated earlier, argument analysis involves taking arguments apart into their structural elements and seeing how they are intended to work. Argument analysis is a natural extension of argument identification, because argument identification already involves recognizing a set of claims as constructed for a certain intended purpose.

### PREMISES AND CONCLUSIONS

If an argument is a set of assertions one of which is understood or intended to be supported by the others, then we may proceed to define two important basic concepts for both argument identification and argument analysis: the concepts of premise and conclusion. *The premises of arguments are the claims offered in support of the conclusion. The conclusion is the claim that the premises are offered to support.*

Thus far we have considered two simple arguments:

(1) All mothers are females.

Pat is a mother.

---

Pat is a female.

(2) The weather forecast calls for rain.

---

You should take your umbrella today.

The solid line indicates the transition from supporting material to what the material supports, or from premises to conclusion. Statements above the line are the premises; statements below the line are conclusions.

## SIGNAL WORDS

As we mentioned earlier, identifying arguments can be difficult, especially when they are embedded in larger contexts, due to the fact that recognizing arguments involves recognizing the author's intentions. Similarly, identifying the premises and conclusion of an argument can be difficult, especially when we find them embedded in longer passages. If you read and listen carefully, however, you can pick up clues to the presence of arguments and to the identity of premises and conclusions in written or spoken discourse.

One of the most important clues is the *signal word,* or *signal expression.* Authors frequently use signal words or expressions to signal their intentions. *A signal word or expression is a word or expression that indicates the presence of a premise or conclusion.* There are three main kinds of signal words: (1) words or phrases that signal conclusions, (2) words or phrases that help locate the general area where premises are to be found, and (3) words or phrases that help locate particular premises.

### CONCLUSION SIGNALS

The English language has a rich store of signal words and phrases that often indicate conclusions; that is, what is being argued for. They include the following:

so
thus
therefore
consequently
it follows that
as a result
hence
finally
in conclusion
we see, then, that
one can conclude that
shows that

On first reading a passage, it is often useful to underline its conclusion indicators. You will thereby alert yourself to an important part of the argument's structure: the conclusion. Consider for example the following passage:

> Capital punishment deters crime. It also ensures that a killer can never strike again. It follows that capital punishment should be permitted.

"It follows that" in the last sentence helps locate the argument's conclusion: "Capital punishment should be permitted." The first two claims are reasons or premises used to support that conclusion.

Here's another example, followed by a comment:

**Example:** "A teacher who asks a question is tuned to the right answer, ready to hear it, eager to hear it. . . . He will assume that anything that sounds close to the right answer is meant to be the right answer. So, for a student who is not sure of the answer, a mumble may be the best bet."[2]

**Comment:** The word "so" in the last sentence helps locate the conclusion: "For a student who is not sure of the answer, a mumble may be the best bet." The author offers two reasons to support this conclusion: (1) "a teacher who asks a question is tuned to the right answer, ready to hear it, eager to hear it" and (2) the teacher "will assume that anything that sounds close to the right answer is meant to be the right answer."

## GENERAL AREA PREMISE SIGNALS

General area premise signals are words or phrases that indicate the general area of the passage within which you will likely find a premise. Conclusion signals function as general area premise signals, since they not only indicate that conclusions follow but that premises likely precede. But there are other general area premise signals, and premises typically are found after them. Such expressions include the following:

since
because
for
for the reason that
this follows from
consider the following
after all
the following reasons
inasmuch as
insofar as

Again, in reading a passage, underline such expressions in order to discover another important part of an argument's anatomy: its premises. Consider the following example:

> Capital punishment should not be permitted because it allows the possibility of executing an innocent person. Indeed, people have been executed who have been proved innocent later.

In this passage the word "because" indicates that what follows it are the reasons for the arguer's opposition to capital punishment. It helps locate the general area in which the premises are to be found.

Here is another example, followed by a comment:

**Example:** "It is worth saying something about the social position of beggars, for when one has consorted with them, and found that they are ordinary human beings, one cannot help being struck by the curious attitude that society takes toward them."[3]
**Comment:** In this passage the word "for" indicates the general area in which the premise can be found. It signals the author's reasons for asserting "It is worth saying something about the social position of beggars."

## SPECIFIC PREMISE SIGNALS

Besides expressions that indicate generally where premises or conclusions are likely to be found, there are words and phrases that help point out specific individual premises in a passage. Such expressions may be termed specific premise signals. They include:

1. Devices for numbering premises, such as "first . . . , second . . . , third . . ."; "in the first place . . . , in the second place . . . , finally . . ."
2. Devices used for indicating the accumulation of different considerations related to the same conclusion, such as "for one thing . . . for another . . ."; ". . . furthermore . . ."; "moreover . . ."; "in addition . . ."; "also . . ."; "consider this . . . and this . . . and finally this . . ."
3. Devices used to contrast considerations related to the same conclusion, such as "however . . ."; "despite this . . ."; "nevertheless . . ."; "but . . ."; "on the other hand . . ."

Underlining such expressions will help you focus on the premises of an argument, as illustrated in this passage:

> Prisons in the United States are an abysmal failure. First, they don't rehabilitate anyone. Second, they don't so much punish as provide free room and board. Third, they further alienate those with well-established antisocial tendencies. Fourth, they bring criminals together, thereby allowing them to swap information and refine their unseemly crafts. Finally, those who do time are far more likely to commit additional crimes than those who have never been in prison.

In this passage the arguer uses "first . . . second . . . third . . . fourth . . . finally . . ." to indicate the accumulation of reasons that support the conclusion that prisons in the United States are an abysmal failure. Here's an additional example followed by a comment:

**Example:** "There is nothing in the biorhythm theory that contradicts scientific knowledge. Biorhythm theory is totally consistent with the fundamental thesis of biology, which holds that all life consists of discharge and creation of energy, or, in biorhythmic terms, an alternation of positive and negative phases. In addition, given that we are subject to a host of smaller but nonetheless finely regulated biological rhythms, it seems reasonable that longer rhythms will also come into play."[4]

**Comment:** In this passage the arguer uses "in addition" to indicate the accumulation of the premises: (1) "biorhythm theory is totally consistent with the fundamental thesis of biology" and (2) "given that we are subject to a host of smaller but nonetheless finely regulated rhythms, it seems reasonable that longer rhythms will come into play." These premises support the conclusion stated in the opening sentence: "There is nothing in the biorhythm theory that contradicts scientific knowledge."

## A CAUTION CONCERNING AMBIGUITY

We should caution you to distinguish between argumentative and nonargumentative functions of some signal words and expressions. For example if we compare

> You should take your umbrella *because* the forecast calls for rain.

with

> The streets are wet *because* it rained last night.

we see that the first is an argument in which the word "because" indicates a premise but that the second is not an argument at all. In the second, "because" has an explanatory, not a logical, function: It indicates that the assertion is intended merely to explain the wetness of the streets. "Because" and other such terms (like "since" and "for") are ambiguous. That is, they can be understood in more than one way. Sometimes they function to indicate the presence of an argument, and sometimes not.

The point is this: Because some signal words are ambiguous, the presence of signal words cannot be relied on mechanically as an absolutely foolproof indication of the presence of an argument. Like most interpretive tasks, identifying arguments—and even recognizing an expression as an argument signal—is in large measure context dependent.

## ARGUMENTS WITHOUT SIGNALS

Though authors who are putting forward arguments frequently do signal their intentions by means of devices such as we've just discussed, frequently they do not. Many of the arguments we encounter and express contain no signals. Rather the author's intention is left implicit, or "for the reader to figure out." Take this one, for example:

> When we cheat impersonal corporations, we indirectly cheat our friends—and ourselves. Department of Commerce data show that marketplace theft raises the cost of what we buy by more than 2 percent. Doctors who collect Medicare and Medicaid money for unnecessary treatments cost the average taxpayer several hundred dollars a year. The same applies to veterans who collect education money but who do not attend school.

This passage contains four sentences but no explicit verbal clues to its status as an argument. Yet evidently the passage is an argument, because one of the claims contained in it is evidently supported by the others. How can we tell this?

The passage opens with the general claim that when we cheat impersonal corporations we are really cheating our friends and ourselves. This claim is what the arguer is advancing; it is the conclusion. How can we tell *this?*

Well, if we ask the natural next question—"Why should we believe this claim?" or "What reasons support it?"—the next three sentences in the passage are evidently responsive to our question. They cite several pieces of evidence: (1) Department of Commerce data that show that marketplace theft raises the cost of what we buy by more than 2 percent; (2) federal estimates that indicate that doctors who collect Medicare and Medicaid money for unnecessary treatments cost the average taxpayer several hundred dollars a year; and (3) veterans who collect education money but who do not attend school further inflate the taxpayer's bill. In effect, the author has anticipated the challenge, the demand for support for a controversial claim, that naturally arises in the reader's mind, and has supplied evidence to meet it. These three claims are therefore the argument's premises.

In dealing with passages which contain no signal words, an effective first question is "What, if anything, is being advocated? What claim is the arguer attempting to establish as true? What is the arguer trying to convince me of or get me to do?" This helps you determine whether the passage expresses or contains an argument, and if so, it helps you locate the argument's conclusion.

Having done that, you can then locate the premises by asking questions like "What reasons, data, or evidence does the arguer offer in support of the conclusion?" Arguments with no signal words require close contextual analysis. Contextual analysis is a set of skills that take considerable time and much exercise and practice to develop and refine. But they are well worth mastering.

Here are some additional arguments without signals to get you started:

**Example:** "Names are far more than mere identity tags. They are charged with hidden meanings and unspoken overtones that profoundly help or hinder you in your relationships and your life."[5]

**Comment:** The first claim is the conclusion. The second sentence helps establish the conclusion by anticipating and responding to the predictable challenge: "What functions, other than identity tags, do names perform?" Thus the second claim supports the first.

**Example:** " 'An unhappy alternative is before you Elizabeth. Your mother will never see you again if you do *not* marry Mr. Collins, and I will never see you again if you *do*.' "[6]

**Comment:** The speaker is attempting to show Elizabeth that an unhappy alternative faces her. The alternative is unhappy because should Elizabeth not marry Mr. Collins, her mother will never see her again; if she does marry Mr. Collins, then the speaker, who happens to be her father, will never see her again. Thus the first sentence is the conclusion, the second the premise.

## EXERCISE | Signals

Highlight the signals in the following passages:

1. Two out of three people interviewed preferred Zest to another soap. Therefore Zest is the best soap available.
2. In the next century more and more people will turn to solar energy to heat their homes because the price of gas and oil will become prohibitive for most consumers and the price of installing solar panels will decline.
3. People who smoke cigarettes should be forced to pay for their own health insurance since they know smoking is bad for their health, and they have no right to expect others to pay for their addictions.
4. It's no wonder that government aid to the poor fails. Poor people can't manage their money.
5. Even though spanking has immediate punitive and (for the parent) anger releasing effects, parents should not spank their children, for spanking gives children the message that inflicting pain on others is an appropriate means of changing their behavior. Furthermore, spanking trains children to submit to the arbitrary rules of authority figures who have the power to harm them. We ought not to give our children those messages. Rather, we should train them to either make appropriate behavioral choices or to expect to deal with the related natural and logical consequences of their behavior.
6. Public schools generally avoid investigation of debatable issues and instead stress rote recall of isolated facts, which teaches students to unquestioningly absorb given information on demand so that they can regurgitate it in its entirety during testing situations. Although students are generally not allowed to question it, much of what is presented as accurate information is indeed controversial. But citizens need to develop decision-making skills regarding debatable issues in order to truly participate in a democracy. It follows then that public schools ought to change their educational priorities in order to better prepare students to become informed, responsible members of our democracy.
7. Ever since the injury to Jerry Rice, the 49er running game has been under pressure to produce. But since their won/lost record is best in the NFL West, we must conclude that the loss of Rice, while damaging to their overall offense, has not been devastating.
8. Latenight radio talk show host: "I've heard more heart attacks happen on Monday than on any other day of the week, probably because Mondays mark a return to those stressful work situations for so many of you. So let's all call in sick this Monday, OK, folks, because we don't want any of you to check out on us."
9. The answers to these exercises are programmed into our Critical Thinking tutorial. So if you want to check and see how you're doing, you should click on the Argument Identification button.

## INCOMPLETELY STATED ARGUMENTS

Just as authors sometimes put forward arguments without signals, leaving it up to the listener or reader to recognize their implicit intentions, so they frequently put forward arguments which are not completely stated, leaving it up to the listener or reader to fill in the missing element(s). Sometimes the conclusion of an argument is left implicit. Sometimes a portion of the support in an argument is implied but not stated. But implicit conclusions and premises are nevertheless important elements in the logical structure of arguments, and need to be taken into account in their analysis and evaluation.

### UNEXPRESSED CONCLUSIONS

Suppose that you are standing in line at the polling place on election day, waiting to have your registration verified and receive your official ballot, and you overhear the official say to the person in front of you:

> I'm sorry, sir, but only those citizens whose names appear on my roster are eligible to vote, and your name does not appear.

Clearly there is something further implied here. The implied conclusion, which is evidently intended to follow from the two claims explicitly made, is that the person in front of you is not eligible to vote. This example, then, does express an argument. And recognizing it as such depends upon recognizing that the two claims which are explicitly stated are intended to support the unstated conclusion.

Here are three more arguments whose conclusions are unexpressed:

> **Argument:** "Yond Cassius has a lean and hungry look. . . . Such men are dangerous."[7]
> **Unexpressed Conclusion:** Cassius is a dangerous man.

> **Argument:** "Only demonstrative proof should be able to make you abandon the theory of Creation; but such a proof does not exist in nature."[8]
> **Unexpressed Conclusion:** Nothing in nature should be able to make you abandon the theory of Creation.

> **Argument:** "When we regard a man as morally responsible for an act, we regard him as a legitimate object of moral praise or blame in respect of it. But it seems plain that a man cannot be a legitimate object of moral praise or blame for an act unless in willing the act he is in some important sense a 'free' agent."[9]
> **Unexpressed Conclusion:** Free will is a precondition of moral responsibility.

### UNEXPRESSED PREMISES

Just as conclusions can be implied but unstated, so when we argue we frequently leave premises unexpressed. Yet unexpressed premises are just as important as the explicit premises to the structure of arguments. Suppose once more that you are standing in line at the polling place on election day, and you overhear the official say to the person in front of you:

> I'm sorry sir, but only those citizens whose names appear on my roster are eligible to vote.

Here again the context makes clear that the official is offering support for the claim that the person in front of you is not eligible to vote. But in addition to the unstated conclusion, there is an unstated premise:

> Your name does not appear on my roster.

How can we determine this? Consider the argument from the stated premise to the unstated conclusion:

> Only those citizens whose names appear on my roster are eligible to vote.
> ___
> Therefore you are not eligible to vote.

The missing premise "Your name does not appear on my roster" is clearly implied here, because only if it is also assumed as a premise does the stated premise count as a reason for the person's ineligibility to vote. Therefore it is reasonable to suppose that it is intended as a premise in the argument.

Here are three additional examples of arguments with unexpressed premises:

**Argument:** Bill must be a poor student, for he spends most of his time watching television.
**Unexpressed Premise:** Any student who spends most of his time watching television must be a poor student.
**Expressed Premise:** Bill spends most of his time watching television.
**Conclusion:** Bill must be a poor student.

**Argument:** It's hard to appreciate Jackson Pollock's painting "Convergence," for it's a work of modern art.
**Unexpressed Premise:** It's hard to appreciate modern art.
**Expressed Premise:** Jackson Pollock's painting "Convergence" is a work of modern art.
**Conclusion:** It's hard to appreciate Jackson Pollock's painting "Convergence."

**Argument:** Since Smith married largely for sexual reasons, his marriage won't last long.
**Unexpressed Premise:** Marriages entered into largely for sexual reasons don't last long.
**Expressed Premise:** Smith married largely for sexual reasons.
**Conclusion:** Smith's marriage won't last long.

We have intentionally kept these examples simple. But filling in the missing premises of an argument can be a very difficult part of the process of argument analysis, and it raises some tricky interpretive problems. We will say more about this subject in Chapter 5. Suffice it here to point out that unexpressed premises are part of the structure of many arguments.

## EXERCISE | Incompletely Stated Arguments

Each of the following arguments has an unstated conclusion. Formulate the conclusion.

1. I'm sorry, but you may stay in the country only if you have a current visa; and your visa has expired.
   Therefore,

2. God has all the virtues, and benevolence is certainly a virtue.
   Therefore,

3. Either the battery in the remote control is dead or the set's unplugged, but the set is plugged in.
   Therefore,

4. All mammals suckle their young, and all primates are mammals, and orangutans are primates.
   Therefore,

5. Software is written by humans, and humans make mistakes.
   Therefore,

6. Legislation that can't be enforced is useless, and there's no way to enforce censorship over the Internet.
   Therefore,

Each of the following arguments has an unstated premise. Formulate the missing premise.

7. All propaganda is dangerous. Therefore network news is dangerous
   because

8. UCLA will play in the Rose Bowl, because the Pac 10 champion always plays in the Rose Bowl,
   and

9. Everything with any commercial potential eventually gets absorbed into the corporate world, so the Internet will eventually get absorbed into the corporate world
   because

10. Hip-hop is a fad, so it will surely fade,
    because

## PREMISE SUPPORT

When we set forth an argument, we recognize that people generally require reasons to persuade them to accept a claim. But the premises of an argument, like its conclusion, are also claims; so people may well require reasons to accept them. Recognizing this, authors frequently anticipate the need to supply further support for the premises of their arguments—in other words, to build in arguments for the premises of their arguments. Consider the structural features of these two arguments, which deal with censorship:

> **Argument 1:** Censorship is acceptable only if it can be easily enforced. *But* censorship cannot easily be enforced. *Therefore* censorship is not acceptable.
>
> **Argument 2:** Censorship is acceptable only if it can be easily enforced. *But* censorship cannot be easily enforced. The main problem with enforcement is determining which works will not be censored. *Therefore* censorship is not acceptable.

The main argument contained in the two examples is identical:

> **Premise:** Censorship is acceptable only if it can be easily enforced.
> **Premise:** Censorship cannot be easily enforced.
> **Conclusion:** Censorship is not acceptable.

However Argument 2 differs from Argument 1 in offering some support for the second premise. The argument states that if we consider the problems of identifying which works need not be censored, there is good reason to think that censorship cannot be easily enforced. In effect, there is a third premise expressed in the second argument:

> The main problem of enforcement is determining which works will not be censored.

This premise, like the first two premises, supports the conclusion. But unlike the first two premises, this one supports it indirectly, by supporting the second premise. How do we determine this? Well, consider the natural question which arises in response to the second premise: "What reason is there to suppose that censorship cannot easily be enforced?" or "What's the problem with enforcing censorship?" The third premise is responsive to this question. Evidently the author has anticipated the challenge to the second premise and supplied a reason to meet it. Thus it is reasonable to interpret the third sentence in the second argument as support for the second premise, which, together with the first premise, is intended to support the conclusion.

Of course the reason supplied to support the premise can itself be challenged. Recognizing this, authors sometimes provide support for the support for the premises of an argument, and so on, occasionally at considerable length and with considerable complexity.

For example, consider the same argument with more developed support, as represented by the italicized portion of the following passage:

> Censorship is acceptable only if it can be easily enforced. But censorship cannot be easily enforced. The main problem is determining which works will not be censored. *For example, some have said that the "classics" will and should be exempt from censorship. But what is a "classic"? Any traditional definition probably would exclude new works, since a work usually cannot be recognized as a classic until some time after its release. That means that the censor must determine which works will become classics, surely an impossible task. As a result censors will have little choice but to ban those "nonclassics" that smack of smut. If you think this is an idle fear, recall that plenty of works of art and literature that today are considered classics were once banned. Works by Chaucer, Shakespeare, Swift, and Twain are just a few. More recently William Faulkner, Ernest Hemingway, and James Joyce found their works banned. There is no question, then, that determining which works will not be censored is a major, perhaps insurmountable, problem in enforcing censorship.* Therefore censorship is not acceptable.

There is no simple way to determine how much support is needed to substantiate a premise and by implication an argument's conclusion. But surely the more controversial the conclusion, the more support it needs. The same goes for premises. The more controversial a premise, the more likely it is to be challenged. Thus, the more important it becomes to the argument that the premise be supported.

The importance of premise support becomes most apparent in extended arguments; that is, in the multiparagraph arguments that we commonly encounter in editorials, reviews, and the like, and in the essays we are called on to write. Since the following chapters deal with refining analytical and evaluative skills, they take up the challenge of determining adequate premise support. It's enough here, therefore, simply to acknowledge premise support as an integral part of the structure of many arguments.

## ADDITIONAL EXERCISES

### Argument identification and analysis

**1.** Which of the following passages express or contain arguments? You can use either the functional or the structural definition of "argument" or both to make your determination.

| Example | Arg. | Not | Undecidable |
|---|---|---|---|
| "While taking my noon walk today, I had more morbid thoughts. What *is* it about death that bothers me so much? Probably the hours. Melnick says the soul is immortal and lives on after the body drops away, but if my soul exists without my body I am convinced all my clothes will be loose fitting." —Woody Allen, *Without Feathers* | | | |

| Example | Arg. | Not | Undecidable |
|---|---|---|---|
| "Gentlemen of the jury, surely you will not send to his death a decent, hard-working young man, because for one tragic moment he lost his self-control? Is he not sufficiently punished by the lifelong remorse that is to be his lot? I confidently await your verdict, the only verdict possible: that of homicide with extenuating circumstances." —Albert Camus, *The Stranger* | | | |
| I've heard more heart attacks happen on Monday than on any other day of the week, probably because Mondays mark a return to stressful work situations for so many. | | | |
| I knew a guy once who was so influenced by statistics, numbers ruled his entire life! One time he found out that over 80 percent of all automobile accidents happen within five miles of the driver's home. So he moved! | | | |
| "It seems that mercy cannot be attributed to God. For mercy is a kind of sorrow, as Damascene says. But there is no sorrow in God; and therefore there is no mercy in him." —Thomas Aquinas | | | |
| Look for answers to these exercises in the Critical Thinking tutorial under Argument Identification | | | |

**2.** Decide which passages are arguments and which are not. Analyze the arguments by: (1) underlining any and all signal words; (2) highlighting the conclusion; and (3) highlighting the premises. (This exercise will be more rewarding and instructive obviously if you use one highlighter color consistently for conclusions and another consistently for premises.)

a. The game has been delayed because of rain.

b. We must maintain a strong defense; otherwise we will invite war.

c. Most teachers want better pay. It follows that most teachers are in favor of unions.

d. Anyone who criticizes and disrupts society is a threat to social stability. That's why civil disobedience should have no place in society.

e. Because students come to school to learn, they should have no say in curriculum decisions.

f. "The shad, perhaps, or any fish that runs upriver [would be ideal for sea ranching]. . . . They range out to sea, using their own energies, grow, and then come back."[10]

g. "In bureaucratic logic, bad judgment is any decision that can lead to embarrassing questions, even if the decision was itself right. Therefore . . . no man with an eye on a career can afford to be right when he can manage to be safe."[11]

h. "An arctic mirage is caused by a temperature inversion created when the air immediately above the earth's surface is cooler than air at a higher elevation. Under these conditions, light rays are bent around the curvature of the earth. The stronger the inversion, the more bending. With a high degree of bending, the earth's surface looks like a saucer, and the landscape and ship normally out of sight below the horizon are raised into view on the saucer's rim. The effect can last for days and cover thousands of kilometers."[12]
i. "And the tragic history of human thought is simply the history of a struggle between reason and life . . . reason bent on rationalizing life and forcing it to submit to the inevitable, to mortality; life bent on vitalizing reason and forcing it to serve as a support for its own vital desires."[13]
j. "Vitamin E is an essential part of the whole circulation mechanism of the body, since it affects our use of oxygen."[14]
k. "Why are youngsters rediscovering booze? One reason is pressure from other kids to be one of the gang. Another is the ever-present urge to act grown up. . . . Perhaps the main reason is that parents don't seem to mind."[15]

**3.** Identify the unexpressed premises in Exercise 2 b, c, d, and e.

## Argument analysis: Premise support

Identify the conclusions, premises, and premise support in the following arguments. Use highlighters as you did in the previous Exercise 2. But this time use three colors: one for conclusions, a second for premises that support the conclusions *directly,* and a third color for premises which support other premises.

**1.** Part of believing something is believing that it's true. So if I were to do an inventory of my beliefs, they'd all seem true to me. Or, to put it another way, if I knew something was false, I wouldn't believe it. So it doesn't really make sense for me to say that some of my own beliefs are false.

**2.** I've been mistaken in the past. I've learned on numerous occasions, and pretty much throughout my life, that things that I believed to be true were really false. Why should it be any different now? So if I were to do an inventory of my beliefs, I probably wouldn't notice the false ones, but I'd still bet there are some in there somewhere.

**3.** "Nor is there anything smart about smoking. A woman who smokes is far more likely than her nonsmoking counterpart to suffer from a host of disabling conditions, any of which can interfere with her ability to perform at home or on the job. . . . Women who smoke have more spontaneous abortions, stillbirths, and premature babies than do nonsmokers, and their children's later health may be affected."[16]

**4.** "Since the mid '50's, for example, scientists have observed the same characteristics in what they thought were different cancer cells and concluded that these traits must be common to all cancers. All cancer cells had certain nutritional needs, all could grow in soft agar cultures, all could seed new solid tumors when transplanted into experimental animals, and all contained drastically abnormal chromosomes—the 'mark cancer.' "[17]

5. "One woman told me that brown spots, a bugaboo to older women, were twice as numerous on the left side of her face and arm due to daily use of her car. The right, or interior, side of her face and right arm showed far fewer brown spots. Since these unattractive marks seem to be promoted by exposure to the sun, either cover up or use a good sunscreen."[18]
6. "It also appears that suicide no longer repels us. The suicide rate is climbing, especially among blacks and young people. What's more, suicide has been appearing in an increasingly favorable light in the nation's press. When Paul Cameron surveyed all articles on suicide indexed over the past 50 years in the *Reader's Guide to Periodical Literature,* he found that voluntary death, once portrayed as a brutal waste, now generally appears in a neutral light. Some recent articles even present suicide as a good thing to do and are written in a manner that might encourage the reader to take his own life under certain circumstances. Last year, a majority of Americans under 30 told Gallup pollsters that incurable disease or continual pain confer on a person the moral right to end his life."[19]
7. "If there were clear boundaries between the animals and people, each side having its own territory, friction would be minimized. But that is not the case. Although some of the 5000 square miles of ecosystem that lie outside the park are protected areas—including neighboring Ngorongoro Conservation Unit and Masai Mara Game Reserve in Kenya—sizable sectors have no conservation status. Consequently, the migratory herds spend a good part of their annual cycle competing with humans for food."[20]
8. President Bush promised no new taxes. But in his first term of office he compromised with the Congress over tax hikes. But since such behavior clearly amounts to a betrayal of the public trust, President Bush did not deserve to be reelected for a second term.

## GLOSSARY

**analysis** the process of breaking complex things down into their constituent elements
**argument** (defined functionally) a composition whose primary function is to persuade a person by appealing to the person's reasoning capacity; (defined structurally) a composition consisting of a set of claims one of which, called the "thesis" or "conclusion," is supported by the others, called the "premises."
**conclusion** the claim in an argument supported by the premises
**premises** the claims in an argument that support the conclusion
**signal word** word indicating the presence of an argument or argument part
**thesis** conclusion, especially in an extended argument

## NOTES

1 "The Argument Clinic," in *Monty Python's Flying Circus—Just the Words,* vol. 2, Roger Wilmut, ed. (New York: Random House, 1989), p. 86.

[2] John Holt, *Why Children Fail* (New York: Delacorte, 1982), p. 82; underscore added.

[3] George Orwell, *Down and Out in Paris and London* (New York: Berkley, 1967), p. 125; underscore added.

[4] Bernard Gittelson, *Biorhythms: A Personal Science,* (New York: Basic Books, 1977), p. 146; underscore added.

[5] Christopher A. Anderson, *The Name Game* (New York: Simon & Schuster, 1977), p. 1.

[6] Jane Austen, *Pride and Prejudice.*

[7] Wm. Shakespeare, *Julius Ceasar.*

[8] Moses Maimonides, *The Guide for the Perplexed.*

[9] C. Arthur Campbell, "Is 'Freewill' a Pseudo-Problem?" *Mind,* 60, no. 240 (1951): 447.

[10] John D. Isaacs, "Interview," *Omni,* August 1979, p. 122.

[11] John Ciardi, "Bureaucracy and Frank Ellis," in *Manner of Speaking* (New Brunswick, N.J.: Rutgers University Press, 1972), p. 250.

[12] Barbara Ford, "Mirage," *Omni,* August 1979, p. 38.

[13] Miguel de Unamuno, *The Tragic Sense of Life* (New York: Dover, 1921), p. 63.

[14] Ruth Adams and Frank Murray, *Vitamin E: Wonder Worker of the 70's* (New York: Larchmont Books, 1972), p. 17.

[15] Carl T. Rowan, "Teenagers and Booze," in *Just Between Us Blacks* (New York: Random House, 1974), pp. 95–96.

[16] Jane E. Brody and Richard Engquist, "Women and Smoking," *Public Affairs Pamphlet* 475 (New York: Public Affairs Committee, 1972), p. 2.

[17] Michael Gold, "The Cells That Would Not Die" in "This World," *San Francisco Chronicle,* May 17, 1981, p. 9.

[18] Virginia Castleton, "Bring Out Your Beauty," *Prevention,* September 1981, p. 108.

[19] Elizabeth Hall with Paul Cameron, "Our Failing Reverence for Life," *Psychology Today,* April 1976, p. 108.

[20] Norman Myers, "The Canning of Africa," *Science Digest,* August 1981, p. 74.

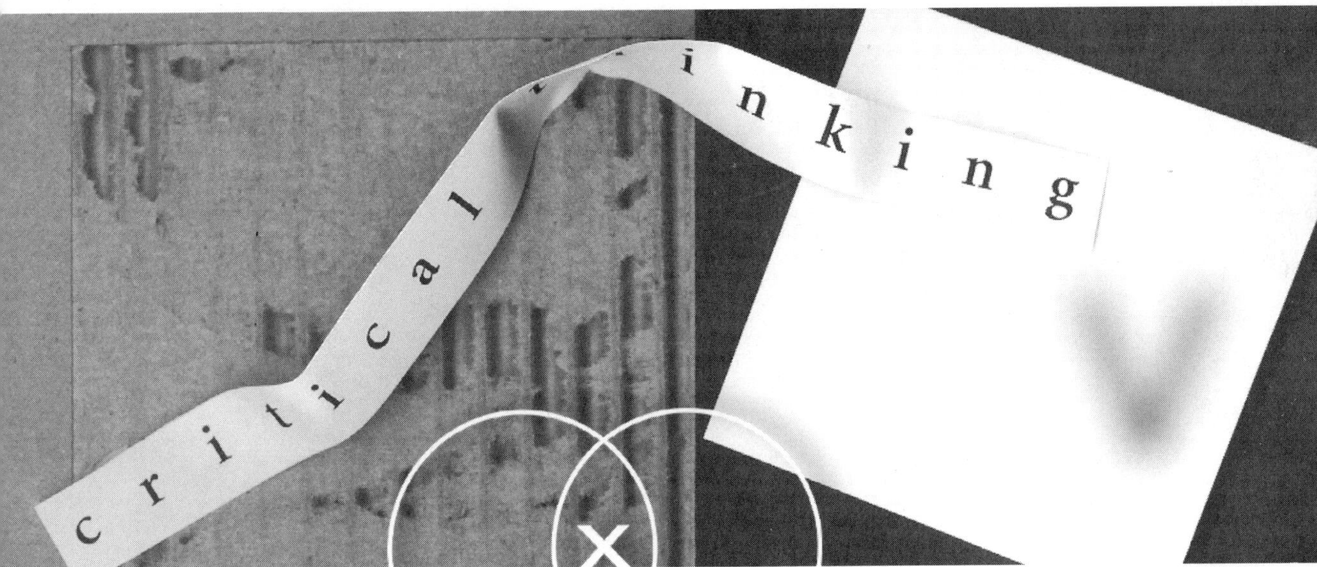


CHAPTER 4

# Argument Analysis I: Paraphrasing and Casting Arguments

Analysis is the process of breaking things down (or taking them apart) into their constituent elements. Argument analysis is important in critical thinking as a preliminary step toward argument evaluation. Before we pass judgment as to the merits of an argument, we need to make sure that we have understood the argument accurately, fairly, and in detail. That is the goal of argument analysis.

In Chapter 3 we defined an "argument" as (a) *a composition whose primary function is to persuade a person by appealing to the person's reasoning capacity,* and (b) *a composition consisting of a set of claims one of which, called the "thesis" or "conclusion," is supported by the others, called the "premises."* Just as the functional definition (a) is a good basis for argument identification, the structural definition (b) will now serve as a basis for argument analysis. Breaking an argument down into its constituent elements is a matter of taking it apart structurally. The crucial structural relationships in arguments, as you can see clearly in the structural definition, are relationships of support. So argument analysis really boils

*"But I see you're having difficulty following my argument."*



down to figuring out what supports what. With short and simple arguments, this can be a relatively easy thing to do, especially if the argument is fully expressed, with signal words clearly indicating which claim is the conclusion and which claims support it. But many of the arguments you will encounter in real life are more challenging and difficult to deal with. An argument may be long and complex. It may be less than fully expressed. Parts of the argument may be veiled or implied, or perhaps just not worded clearly. Material which is extraneous to the argument may surround or be mixed in with it. In this chapter, we offer you strategies and suggestions for analyzing arguments that present these challenges.

## PARAPHRASING ARGUMENTS

A good place to begin would be with the goal of argument analysis: a fair and accurate understanding of the argument in detail. How would we know if we had achieved this goal? How could we tell whether our understanding of someone else's argument is fair and accurate? Well, one obvious way to proceed would be to compare our understanding of the argument to the author's understanding of it. If we could talk directly to the author of the argument, we might say something like:

> If I understand your argument correctly, your point is . . .

or

> Are you saying . . .

and then we would restate the argument to the author in our own words. The author might then tell us whether she thinks we got it right or whether our understanding is mistaken in any way. Obviously we can't *always* do this. We can't expect to be able to check the accuracy of our grasp of *every* argument directly with its author. Nevertheless, this is a good way to understand the goal of argument analysis and a good basis for an overall approach to it: *Can we take the argument apart and reassemble it in our own words without changing what it means, or how it is designed to work as a tool of rational persuasion? In a word, can we "paraphrase" the argument?* This is a very good test, perhaps the best test, of the adequacy of one's grasp of another person's argument.

Many arguments come in multiparagraph form and are commonly termed "argumentative essays" or "extended arguments." An extended argument ordinarily will contain all the elements of a short argument: a thesis, premises, signal words, unexpressed premises, and premise support. In many cases, the extended argument can be viewed as a collection of shorter arguments, all of which support some main or central thesis.

So analyzing an extended argument is essentially the same sort of thing as analyzing a short one. In either case argument analysis involves grasping and appreciating the relationships of support which exist between individual structural elements, the most important of which is the conclusion or thesis. And just as the conclusion of a short argument can appear at any point from the beginning to the middle to the end, so can the thesis of an extended argument. Typically though, one can expect to find the thesis at or near the beginning of the essay, in its opening few paragraphs. These paragraphs are then followed by paragraphs that provide supporting materials. Occasionally however, a writer may present her supporting materials first, especially in dealing with highly controversial topics where she understands the thesis to be especially provocative. In such cases the bulk of the essay may be intended to pave the way for the thesis, which is stated or implied in the closing paragraphs.

## FIND THE THESIS FIRST

*The thesis is a statement of the main idea of the essay.* The word "thesis" comes from Greek, where it means "proposed idea," an idea being presented for consideration. In an argumentative essay, the thesis is presented along with other supporting ideas, ideas presented in order to encourage the reader to consider the thesis favorably. Thus identifying the thesis of an argumentative essay is crucial to both the analysis and the evaluation of the argument that the essay presents. The thesis is the single most important landmark for argument analysis.

Sometimes an author will announce the thesis directly by providing a clearly indicated thesis statement in the essay. But more often the thesis will be woven into the fabric of the composition so that simply scanning for it is going to be pretty discouraging. Nevertheless, even when the thesis is not explicitly stated, but only implied, there are ways to zero in on it. If the essay is written in response to a particular issue, a very good way to identify the thesis is to orient yourself to the issue. Remember, an issue is simply a genuinely disputable topic. Issues can usually be conveniently captured in the form of a question:

> Should the human fetus be considered a person from the moment of conception?
>
> Is the publication of racist material subject to First Amendment protection?
>
> Under what circumstances, if any, should the government in a democracy be permitted to conduct covert operations?

The thesis of an essay addressed to an issue should be understandable as a direct response to the question.

> The human fetus should (should not) be considered a person from the moment of conception.
>
> The publication of racist material is (is not) subject to First Amendment protection.

Notice, by the way, that some questions admit of more answers than "Yes" or No"; accordingly, sometimes there are more than two positions available on a given issue. But here too finding (and paraphrasing) the thesis will be a matter of discerning the author's position on the issue under consideration, the author's answer to the question being addressed.

> A democratic government should not under any circumstances be permitted to conduct covert operations.
>
> A democratic government should be permitted to conduct covert operations at the discretion of duly elected constitutional officers.
>
> A democratic government should be permitted to conduct covert operations only to protect national security and only in such a way as is ultimately subject to strict procedures of public accountability.
>
> A democratic government should be permitted to conduct covert operations whenever national security is at risk.

Another important clue to the thesis is the essay's title. Ordinarily the main function of an essay's title is to identify the topic, perhaps the issue under discussion, and occasionally even the thesis itself. Titles also have other functions—such as to intrigue, or entertain—which can sometimes obstruct access to the topic or the thesis. But once you have identified the essay's main topic, finding out what the author is interested in telling you about it or figuring out the author's attitude or viewpoint on it will point the way to the main idea, the thesis.

## EXERCISE | Thesis Identification

These passages are excerpts from essays. For each, identify the topic and the author's attitude, then write an appropriate thesis statement in your own words, but faithful to the author's intended meaning.

1. Capital punishment is meted out to some groups in society more than to others. Minority groups are hit hardest by this imbalance of justice. In addition, wealthy people seldom receive the death penalty because they can afford better counsel. All the people executed in the United States in 1964 were represented by court-appointed attorneys. Finally, the death penalty can wrongfully execute an innocent person. There are documented cases of this happening.

| Topic | |
|---|---|
| Author Attitude | |
| Thesis | |

2. We have seen "hunting" rifles used to kill a president, Martin Luther King, and numerous others. It is said that these and other guns would not kill if there were not people to shoot them. By the same token, people would rarely kill if they lacked the weapons to do so. There exists, however, an even more pressing threat to our lives than the sniper or assassin. African Americans, after centuries of exploitation, are openly rebellious. Given the weapons, young African Americans could ignite the bloodiest revolution in this country since the Civil War. The Los Angeles riots may have been merely a glimpse of what's ahead. On the other side are white racists arming in fear. And don't forget the militant right-wingers, survivalists, and even religious cults storing up arsenals in anticipation of Armageddon.

| Topic | |
|---|---|
| Author Attitude | |
| Thesis | |

3. This weekend, the city of Indianapolis is hosting approximately 500,000 people to create a two-day saturnalia out of the annual celebration of grease, gasoline, and death. . . .

   The stands inside the Indy Speedway will be filled on Monday with hundreds or thousands of real racing fans. I can't help but think of them as vultures who come to watch the 500-mile race on the highway of death to nowhere, hoping that the monotony of watching cars flick by at speeds in excess of 190 mph will be relieved by mechanical—and human—catastrophe.

The beltway around Indianapolis is staked with grim white crosses, mute reminders to travelers of the fatal consequences of a too-heavy foot on the accelerator.

Watching the race from the Indy grandstand is a little like watching hyperactive hamsters tread a cage wheel. The cars fly by like brightly painted berserk vacuum cleaners sucking the ground.[1]

| | |
|---|---|
| Topic | |
| Author Attitude | |
| Thesis | |

4. Feminists have long complained that playing with dolls is one way of convincing impressionable little girls that they may only be mothers or housewives. . . . But doll playing may have even more serious consequences for little girls than that. Do girls find out about gravity and distance and shapes and sizes playing with dolls? Probably not.

   A curious boy, if his parents are tolerant, will have taken apart a number of house-hold and play objects by the time he is ten, and, if his parents are lucky, he may even have put them back together again. In all this he is learning things that will be useful in physics and math.

   Sports is another source of math-related concepts for children which tends to favor boys. Getting to first base on a not very well hit grounder is a lesson in line, speed and distance. Intercepting a football thrown through the air requires some rapid intuitive eye calculations based on the ball's direction, speed and trajectory.[2]

| | |
|---|---|
| Topic | |
| Author Attitude | |
| Thesis | |

## MACRO-ANALYSIS

In an argumentative essay a great many points typically will be made, some will be offered as direct support for the thesis, others will be offered in support of these main points, and still others offered in support of these. A considerable number of sub-arguments may typically be found embedded in a given argumentative essay. Thus understanding the organization or logical structure of an argumentative essay typically involves analysis at several levels or layers of detail. It's best to start with the most basic—what might be called the "macro-structure" of the essay—the essay's main argument. The main argument consists of the essay's thesis and main premises, or those points which are offered to support the thesis *directly*. When you have sketched out the main argument, you'll find it easier to proceed with "micro-analysis," focusing more closely on the details of the embedded sub-arguments.

Once we have identified the thesis of an extended argument, the next step in argument analysis is to identify the argument's main premises, the principal claims offered in support of the thesis of an extended argument. These main premises are themselves usually argued for, often at considerable length. So, in practice, isolating them can be a challenge. But there is an intuitively simple strategy for finding them, if we bear in mind the special relationship between the main premises and the thesis: The main premises are those points that are offered as *direct* support for the thesis. They are the points which will seem to respond *most directly* to the question "Why should I, the reader, agree with the writer's thesis?" Thus an effective strategy for identifying the main premises of an extended argument is simply to challenge the thesis. Once you have identified the thesis, simply adopt the posture of a skeptical reader. Ask, "Why should I agree with the thesis?" An extended argument will contain answers. You'll want to zero in first on the answers that are most directly responsive to your skeptical challenge. They will be the argument's main premises. That's argument analysis at the macro-level in a nutshell.

### MICRO-ANALYSIS

In evaluating an extended argument you will have to determine how well each of the main premises is justified. That in turn requires a close and critical inspection of the paragraphs in which the main points are made. Having sketched out the main argument, you can now proceed with "micro-analysis," focusing more closely on the details of the embedded sub-arguments.

Since a well-constructed argumentative paragraph is really a microcosm of a well-constructed extended argument, macro-analysis and micro-analysis are essentially identical, only applied at different levels of depth and detail. Your main difficulty in moving from one to the other is likely to be one of keeping your bearings. Use the thesis as your landmark. Periodically it's a good idea to see if you can trace your way from where you are in your micro-analysis back to the thesis, by asking questions like "How is this point relevant to the thesis?"

## CASTING ARGUMENTS

A chart or graphic map of the structure of the argument as a whole can also help you to stay oriented within the argument's overall macro-structure as you focus more and more closely in your micro-analysis. We devote the rest of this chapter to developing a system, called "casting," for this purpose. What a casting of an argument should do for us is what an organizational flowchart does for understanding any complex system. We need to be able to keep track of a large number of claims and of the relationships between them. We have adopted a system developed by Michael Scriven, which does three things: It isolates the constituent claims in the argument; it marks the claims for identification; and it arranges them spatially so as to portray relationships of support among them.[3] Accordingly, the procedure consists of three steps:

1. Putting brackets at the beginning and end of each claim.
2. Numbering the claims consecutively in their order of appearance in the passage.
3. Arranging the numbers spatially on the page according to relationships of support among the claims they stand for.

A word of caution before we begin: You will soon discover that portraying an argument's micro-structure demands careful judgment. Casting involves interpretation. And you know what that means: Interpretive issues can and will arise. When people are casting an argument, they won't always agree. You might consider a sentence to be merely a single claim, someone else might see two claims in it; you might consider an example integral to an argument, someone else might see it as a tangent. Though it is possible for people to be mistaken in their interpretations, and in their castings, it is also possible for several conflicting interpretations, or several alternative castings, each to have some reasonable basis in the text of an argument. So keep in mind that, except for the very simplest arguments, there will almost always be room for alternative castings. Don't be unduly concerned or confused by this. Casting is a means to an end, not an end in itself. You are learning to cast arguments so that you are better able to assess them critically. Keep in mind the ultimate goal of argument analysis: demonstrating that we can take the argument apart and reassemble it *in our own words without changing what it means.*

## ARGUMENT ORGANIZATION: SERIES AND CHAIN

As a first step in learning to cast, let's distinguish two ways in which premises may support their conclusions: (1) in some cases the premises comprise a set of *separate* reasons each independently supportive of the conclusion; (2) in other cases the premises function together as an *interdependent team* in support of the conclusion. Consider, for example, the following argument concerning the legalization of voluntary euthanasia, which (as you probably know) refers to the practice of allowing terminally ill patients to elect to die:

> Our traditional religious and cultural opposition to euthanasia is a good reason for not liberalizing euthanasia laws. *Also,* permitting a patient to make a death decision would greatly add to the person's suffering and anguish. *Additionally,* once a death decision has been carried out, there is no chance of correcting a mistaken diagnosis. *Therefore* voluntary euthanasia should not be legalized.

This passage presents three *separate and mutually independent* reasons in support of the view that voluntary euthanasia should not be legalized. Although each of these reasons is related to the conclusion, they do not depend on one another as support. Any of them could be deleted without undermining the status of the others as support, although the argument itself as a whole probably would be weakened. Each is a separate reason for opposing the legalization of voluntary euthanasia. We will refer to a set of premises which are separate and independent of each other, as they are in this example, as a simple *series* of premises, and we will diagram their supporting roles in the argument as follows:

**Steps 1 & 2** [Our traditional religious and cultural opposition to euthanasia is a good reason for not liberalizing euthanasia laws. ① ] *Also* [permitting a patient to make a death decision would greatly add to the person's suffering and anguish. ② ] *Additionally,* [once a death decision is carried out, there is no chance of correcting a mistaken diagnosis. ③ ] *Therefore* [voluntary euthanasia should not be legalized. ④ ]

**Step 3**

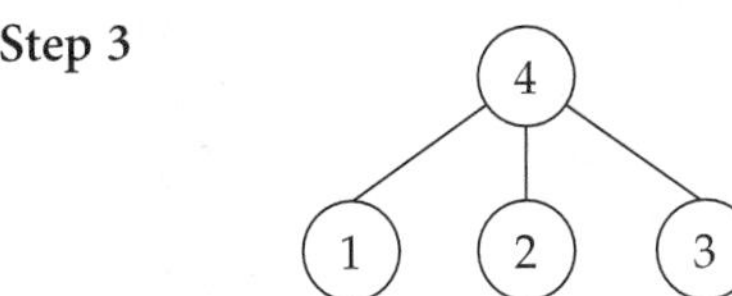


The diagram shows (a) the number of claims in the argument, (b) the order of their appearance, and (c) which are the premises and which the conclusion. The solid lines from each premise to the conclusion also indicate that each of the premises functions independently as a reason in support of the conclusion.

By way of contrast, now let us consider the following argument on the same subject:

> Voluntary decisions about death by definition presuppose freedom of choice. *But* freedom of choice entails the absence of freedom-limiting constraints. Such constraints almost always are present in cases of the terminally ill. *Therefore* terminally ill patients cannot make a voluntary decision about death.

The premises in this passage are *interdependent.* The elimination of any one of them not only weakens the argument as a whole but also undermines the status of the others as supporting premises. For example, the claim that freedom of choice entails the absence of freedom-limiting constraints does not by itself support the conclusion that the terminally ill cannot make a voluntary death decision. Only when it is linked together with the claims that a voluntary decision presupposes freedom of choice and that freedom-limiting constraints are almost always present in cases of terminal illness does it begin to function clearly in support of the conclusion. We will refer to a set of premises which are linked together interdependently, as they are in this example, as a *chain* of premises, and we will diagram their relationships as follows:

**Steps 1 & 2** [Voluntary decisions about death by definition presuppose freedom of choice. ① ] *But* [freedom of choice entails the absence of freedom-limiting constraints. ② ] [Such constraints almost always are present in cases of the terminally ill. ③ ] *Therefore* [terminally ill patients cannot make a voluntary decision about death. ④ ]

**Step 3**

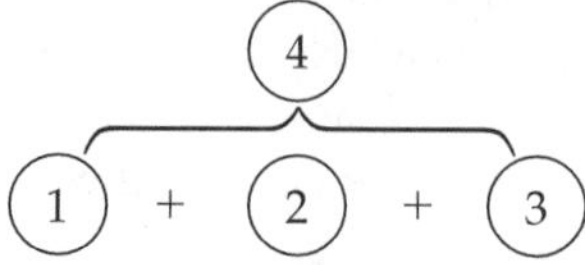

Again the diagram shows the number of claims in the argument, their order of appearance, and which are the premises and which the conclusion. The bracket and plus signs indicate that the premises are linked together interdependently in support of the conclusion.

Here are a couple of additional examples with our comments:

**Example:** A college education makes you aware of interests you didn't know you had. This helps you choose a satisfying job. Job satisfaction is itself your best assurance of personal well-being. Certainly personal well-being is a goal worth pursuing. *Therefore* a college education is a worthy goal.

**Comment:** The points of this argument are arranged in a chain. The first point would support the conclusion independently, but the second point makes little sense without the first. Similarly the third point depends on the second, and fourth on the third. So it is really only when they are taken together, in their logical sequence, that the four points hang together in support of the claim that a college education is valuable.

The argument can be cast as follows:

**Steps 1 & 2** [A college education makes you aware of interests you didn't know you had. ① ] [This helps you choose a satisfying job. ② ] [Job satisfaction is itself your best assurance of personal well-being. ③ ] [Certainly personal well-being is a goal worth pursuing. ④ ] *Therefore* [a college education is a worthy goal. ⑤ ]

**Step 3**

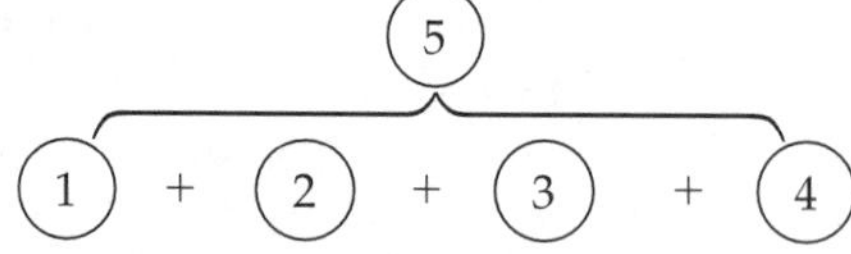

**Example:** That cell-phone we looked at yesterday stores a half-hour's worth of messages, as opposed to this one's twenty minutes. It also has better automated dialing features than this one; and this one's $30 more expensive. I think we should get that other one.

**Comment:** This argument is based on a simple series of premises. Even though they might be said to "add up to" a good case for the conclusion, each and every one of the three premises would remain standing as support for the conclusion even if the other two were eliminated.

The argument can be cast as follows:

**Steps 1 & 2** [That cell-phone we looked at yesterday stores a half-hour's worth of messages, as opposed to this one's twenty minutes; ① ]

[It also has better automated dialing features than this one; ②] [and this one's $30 more expensive. ③] [I think we should get that other one. ④]

**Step 3**

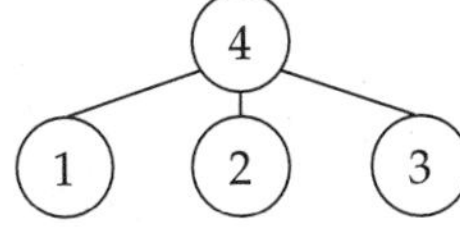


## SOME SIMPLE VARIATIONS

In each of the arguments we have worked through as examples so far in this chapter, the conclusion happened to appear at the end of the passage. But, as you know, a conclusion can appear at the beginning of a passage:

Capital punishment should not be permitted *because* it in fact consists of killing human beings, *and* killing human beings should never be permitted by society.

Bracketing and numbering this version of the argument, we get:

[Capital punishment should not be permitted ①] *because* [it in fact consists of killing human beings, ②] *and* [killing human beings should never be permitted by society. ③]

The diagram for this argument would be:

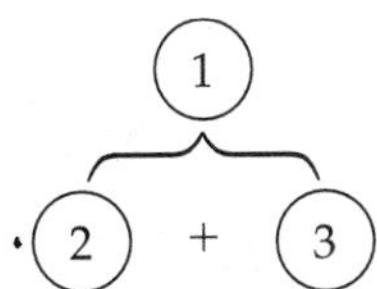


Of course, conclusions also can come sandwiched between premises, as in the following version of the same argument:

*Because* killing human beings should never be permitted by society, capital punishment should not be permitted, *for* it in fact consists of killing human beings.

Bracketing and numbering this version we get:

*Because* [killing human beings should never be permitted by society, ①] [capital punishment should not be permitted, ②] *for* [it in fact consists of killing human beings. ③]

Diagrammed:

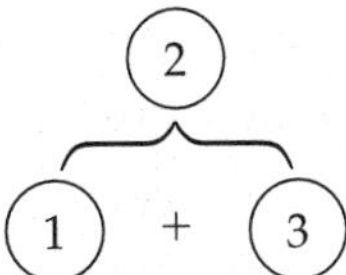

## EXERCISE | Basic Casting

Complete the castings of the following arguments:

| | |
|---|---|
| *Since* [it is only a matter of time before space-based missile defense technology becomes obsolete ① ], *and since* [the funds earmarked for the development of such technology are sorely needed elsewhere ② ], [we should abandon the Star Wars program ③ ]. | |
| [The Star Wars program is our only realistic option for national defense in the nuclear age ① ]. [Any defense program which relies on nuclear deterrence raises the risk of nuclear war ② ], and [that is not a realistic option for national defense ③ ]. [The Star Wars program is the only option yet proposed which does not rely on nuclear deterrence ④ ]. | |
| [President Bush promised no new taxes ① ]. *But* [in his first term of office, he compromised with the Congress over tax hikes ② ]. But *since* [such behavior clearly amounts to a betrayal of the public trust ③ ], [President Bush did not deserve to be re-elected for a second term ④ ]. | |

## CASTING SUB-ARGUMENTS

So far we have cast arguments involving only one level or layer of support between premises and conclusions. But, as you know, many arguments also contain support for premises. Authors often recognize that the claims they are using as premises are themselves controversial and open to debate, and so we may find sub-arguments embedded in a passage, and perhaps sub-arguments in support of premises used in sub-arguments, and so on to several levels or layers of depth. Dealing with layers of support is one of the most challenging dimensions of argument analysis, but fortunately this is one area in which our casting system can be most useful. Let us demonstrate this with a couple of relatively simple examples:

**Example 1:** Censorship is acceptable only if it could be easily enforced. *But* censorship cannot be easily enforced. *Therefore* censorship is not acceptable.

**Example 2:** Censorship is acceptable only if it could be easily enforced. *But* censorship cannot be easily enforced. The main problem with enforcement is determining which works will not be censored. *Therefore* censorship is not acceptable.

Following the three-step procedure, we can cast the first example as follows:

**Steps 1 & 2** [Censorship is acceptable only if it could be easily enforced. ① ] *But* [censorship cannot be easily enforced. ② ] *Therefore* [censorship is not acceptable. ③ ]

**Step 3**

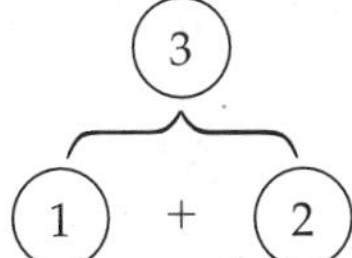


The second example differs from the first in providing support for its second premise. The claim "The main problem with enforcement is determining which works will not be censored" presumably supports the premise "But censorship cannot be easily enforced." It's intuitively easy to reflect this relationship in our casting as follows:

**Steps 1 & 2** [Censorship is acceptable only if it can be easily enforced. ① ] *But* [censorship cannot be easily enforced. ② ] [The main problem with enforcement is determining which works will not be censored. ③ ] *Therefore* [censorship is not acceptable. ④ ]

**Step 3**

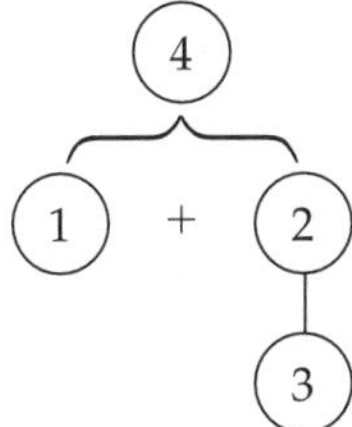


Since claim 3 stands alone in support of claim 2, we treat it as an independent premise, indicated by the solid line. Now let's suppose that the same argument contained additional support material, as in the following passage:

> **Example 3:** [Censorship is acceptable only if it can be easily enforced. ① ] *But* [censorship cannot be easily enforced. ② ] [The main problem with enforcement is determining which works will not be censored. ③ ] [*Another* problem concerns who will do the censoring. ④ ] [*Still another* problem pertains to the standards that will be used. ⑤ ] *Therefore* [censorship is not acceptable. ⑥ ]

In this passage claims 3, 4, and 5 are offered as support for claim 2 and can be diagrammed as follows:

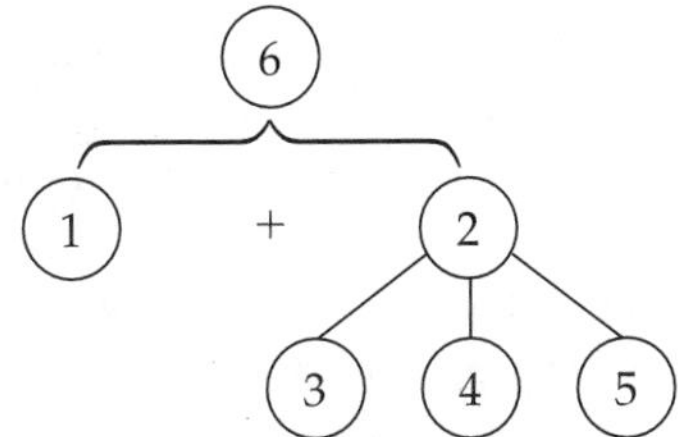

The diagram indicates that claims 3, 4, and 5 are intended to function independently in support of claim 2.

Here are some further examples of passages with embedded sub-arguments.

**Example:** [Most marriages between people under twenty end in divorce.①] [This should be enough to discourage teenage marriages.②] *But there is also the fact that* [marrying young reduces one's life options.③] [Married teenagers must forget about adventure and play.④] [They can't afford to spend time "finding themselves."⑤] [They must concentrate almost exclusively on earning a living.⑥] *What's more,* [early marriages can make parents out of young people, who can hardly take care of themselves, let alone an infant.⑦]

**Comment:** This passage offers three claims—1, 3, and 7—in opposition to teenage marriages (claim 2). Claims 1, 3, and 7 thus function as premises in the main argument. In addition, claim 3 is further supported by reasons given in claims 4, 5, and 6. Taken together, assertions 3, 4, 5, and 6 form a sub-argument that can be diagrammed as follows:

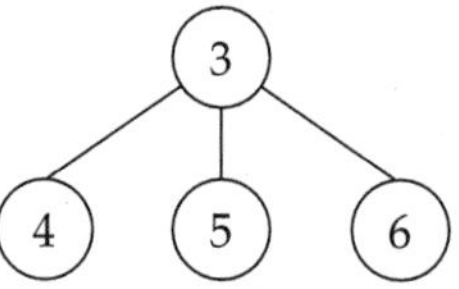


The entire argument in turn can be diagrammed as follows:

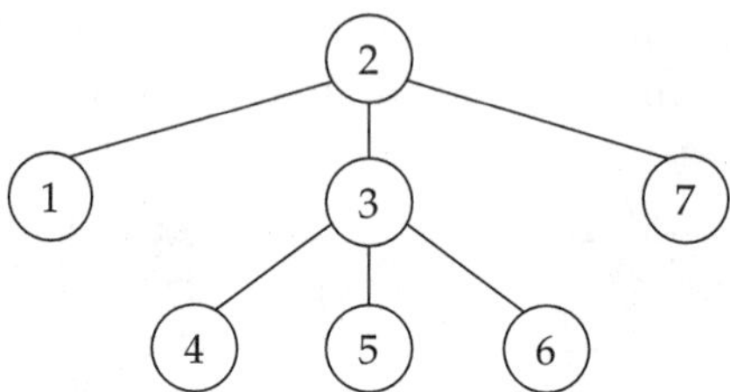


**Example:** ["Suicide no longer repels us.①] [The suicide rate is climbing, especially among blacks and young people.②] *What's more,* [suicide has been appearing in an increasingly favorable light in the nation's press.③] [When Paul Cameron surveyed all articles on suicide indexed over the past 50 years in the *Reader's Guide to Periodical Literature*, he found that voluntary deaths . . . generally appear in a neutral light.④] [Some recent articles even present suicide as a good thing to do. . . .⑤] [They are written in a manner that might encourage the reader to take his own life under certain circumstances."⑥][4]

**Comment:** This passage offers claims 2 and 3 as premises for the conclusion that suicide no longer repels us (claim 1). In support of claim 3, the arguer offers claim 4 and claim 5, which is supported by 6. Therefore claims 5 and 6 make up a sub-argument within a larger sub-argument consisting of claims 3, 4, 5, and 6, and can be diagrammed as follows:

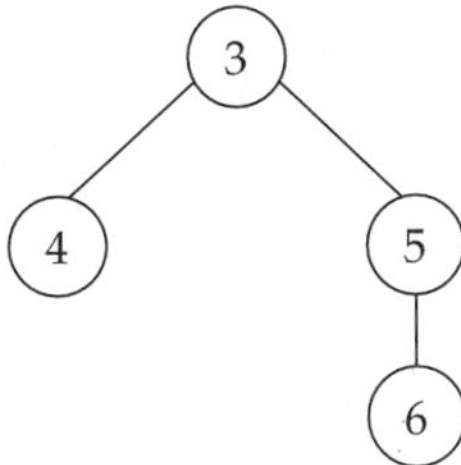

The entire argument can be diagrammed this way:

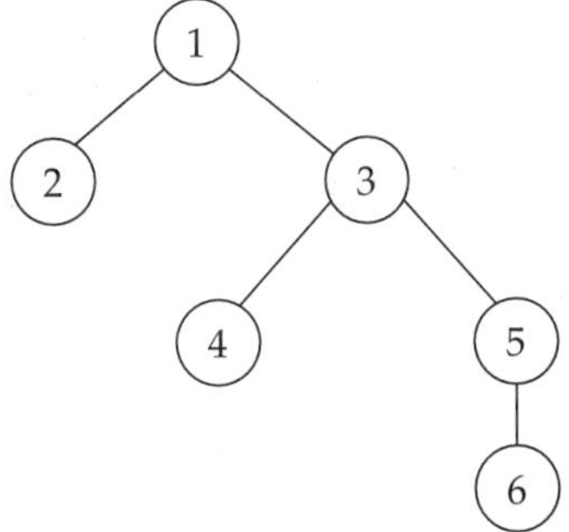

**Example:** ["More and more silent evidence is being turned into loudly damning testimony. ①] [Over the past ten years, no area has developed faster than the examination of blood stains. ②] [Before we used to be satisfied with identifying a blood sample as type A, B, AB or O. ③] [Now we have three or more different antigen and enzyme systems. ④] . . . [The probability that any two people will share the same assessment of their blood variables is 1 percent or less. ⑤] . . . [The size, shape, and distribution of blood spatters tells much about the location and position of a person involved in a crime. ⑥] . . . [The use of bite-mark evidence has skyrocketed. ⑦] . . . [Even anthropology is making a courtroom contribution. ⑧] [Some anthropologists can identify barefoot prints as well as match a shoe to its wearer." ⑨ ][5]

**Comment:** In this passage claims 2, 7, and 8 are the premises of the main argument in support of the claim that "more and more silent evidence is being turned into loudly damning testimony" (claim 1). Taken together, the chain of premises 3, 4, and 5 provides one piece of evidence for claim 2. So one sub-argument in the passage consists of the relationship between claims 3, 4, 5, and 2. This relationship can be diagrammed as follows:

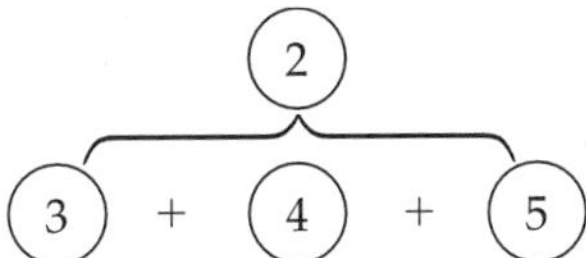

Claim 6 provides additional support for claim 2, thus yielding a second sub-argument:

Claim 9 supports claim 8, yielding a third sub-argument:

We can represent the relationships among these various claims in the argument by means of the following diagram:

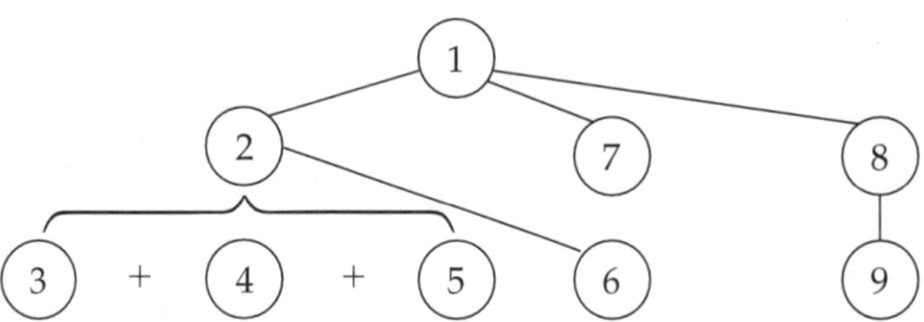


## EXERCISE | Casting Sub-Arguments

Cast the following arguments, all of which contain embedded sub-arguments:

| | |
|---|---|
| [President Bush promised no new taxes ①]. [But in his first term of office he compromised with the Congress over tax hikes ②]. But *since* [such behavior clearly amounts to a betrayal of the public trust ③], [President Bush did not deserve to be re-elected for a second term ④]. | |
| A recent five-year study at a major electronics company indicates that getting fired may have a lot to do with overreaching ①]. [Among 2,000 technical, sales and management employees who were followed during their first five years with the company, the 173 people who eventually were fired | |

| | |
|---|---|
| started out with much higher expectations of advancement than either the 200 people who left voluntarily or the people who remained ② ]. [On a questionnaire given during their first week on the job, more than half of the people who were fired within the first two years ranked themselves among the top 5% of typical people in their job category ③ ]. [Only 38% of those who stayed with the company ranked themselves that highly ④ ].<br>—Berkeley Rice[6] | |
| [We must stop treating juveniles differently from adult offenders ① ]. [Justice demands it ② ]. [Justice implies that people should be treated equally ③ ]. *Besides,* [the social effects of pampering juvenile offenders has sinister social consequences ④ ]. [The record shows that juveniles who have been treated leniently for offenses have subsequently committed serious crimes ⑤ ]. | |

## CASTING UNEXPRESSED PREMISES AND CONCLUSIONS

As you remember, in many arguments not all of the crucial elements are explicitly stated. Sometimes the conclusion is implied. Sometimes one or more premises are implied. A thorough and detailed argument analysis requires that we take account of all of an argument's elements whether they are explicitly presented or implied. Our casting system can accommodate unstated premises and conclusions relatively easily and simply. In order to indicate implied premises or conclusions, and to distinguish them from explicitly stated elements, we will use letters of the alphabet rather than numerals. Here is an example:

> *I'm convinced that* [textbooks contain mistakes ① ], *because* [they are written by humans ② ].

The stated premise, claim 2, does not by itself secure the conclusion, claim 1, and it is intuitively reasonable to suppose that the arguer is assuming something else which together with the stated premise would secure the conclusion. Let's suppose the missing premise is "Humans make mistakes." We may represent this premise as an element in the argument by assigning it the letter *a:*

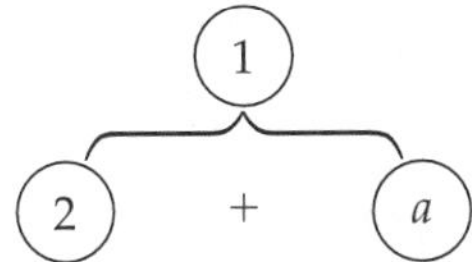

Here's another simple example:

> [Phyllis must be a college graduate ①], *for* [she's a member of the American Association of University Women (AAUW). ②]

This argument has a single stated premise, claim 2, and an explicitly stated conclusion, claim 1. But there is a considerable gap in the inference from the premise to the conclusion. It is reasonable to suppose that the inference depends upon an additional premise covering conditions for membership in the AAUW: something like "Membership in the AAUW is restricted to college graduates." Again we may represent this as a premise in the argument by assigning it the letter *a:*

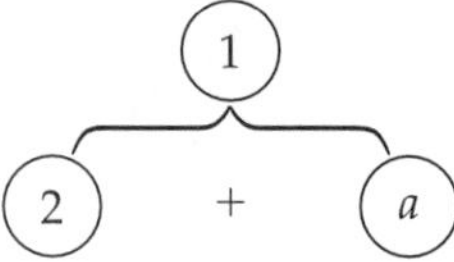


Unstated conclusions can be handled in a similar way. For example, recall this argument from *Julius Caesar:*

> [Yond Cassius has a lean and hungry look. . . . ①] [Such men are dangerous. ②]

The conclusion of this argument, even though it's not explicitly stated, is obvious: "Cassius is dangerous." We may represent it as a crucial element in the argument by assigning it the letter *a:*

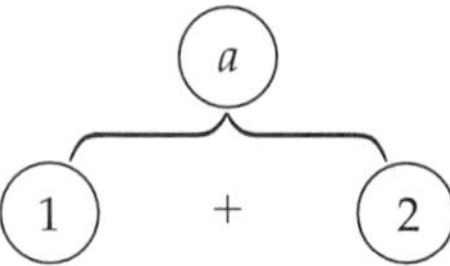


A slightly more complicated example: Imagine that you are waiting to be seated at a busy beachfront restaurant immediately behind an attractive couple who happen to be barefoot. The hostess says not one word, but points to a sign which reads "No shirt, no shoes, no service." In this context it is reasonable to understand the hostess's gesture as a justification for refusing to seat the couple; in other words, it functions as an argument in support of her refusal to seat them. So we might represent her refusal to seat them by assigning it the letter *a.* So far, the argument looks like this:

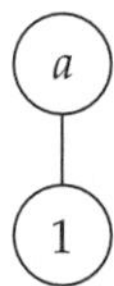


where 1 stands for "If you are not wearing a shirt and shoes, you will be refused service" (what the sign means); and where *a* stands for "you are being refused service" (addressed to the barefoot couple). There is also an unstated premise, and you can easily understand why it's not stated: It's obvious. The couple are not wearing shoes. If we want our casting to reflect this as a part of the justification for the refusal of service (which it obviously is), we need to represent it in the diagram, and we may do so by assigning it the letter *b*. So the fully analyzed argument looks like this:

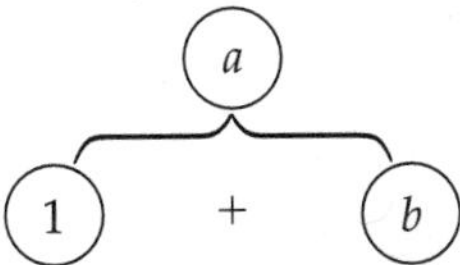


where *b* stands for "you are not wearing shoes" (addressed to the barefoot couple).

## EXERCISE | Casting Unexpressed Premises and Conclusions

Formulate the missing elements (compare with the Incompletely Stated Arguments exercise in Chapter 3) and complete the casting for each of the following arguments:

| | |
|---|---|
| I'm sorry, but [you may stay in the country only if you have a current visa ①], *and* [your visa has expired ②]. | |
| [God has all the virtues ①], *and* [benevolence is certainly a virtue ②]. | |
| [Either the battery in the remote control is dead or the set's unplugged ①], *but* [the set is plugged in ②]. | |
| [All mammals suckle their young ①], *and* [all primates are mammals ②], *and* [orangutans are primates ③]. | |

## CASTING "CONCESSION CLAIMS"

Occasionally we encounter passages in which the author draws and defends a conclusion while at the same time conceding a point to the opposition. If we want our casting to serve as a basis for a thorough and systematic evaluation of the author's argument we may wish to keep track of such claims (we'll call them "concession claims"), even though they do not function as premises in support of the conclusion. Our casting system affords this option. Simply number all the relevant claims *including* concession claims in their order of appearance. Then set the number of any concession claim off to one side using a minus (−) sign to indicate its status.

**Example:** Capital punishment does ensure that a killer can never strike again. *But* it consists of killing human beings, *and* killing human beings should never be allowed. *Therefore* capital punishment should not be permitted.

**Comment:** In this argument two interdependent points are offered in support of the conclusion that capital punishment should not be permitted. These points are thought to be convincing despite the fact that capital punishment does ensure that a killer can never strike again (first assertion), which points to an opposite conclusion.

The argument can be cast as follows:

**Steps 1 & 2** [Capital punishment does ensure that a killer can never strike again. ① ] *But* [it consists of killing human beings ② ] *and* [killing human beings should never be allowed. ③ ] *Therefore* [capital punishment should not be permitted. ④ ]

**Step 3**

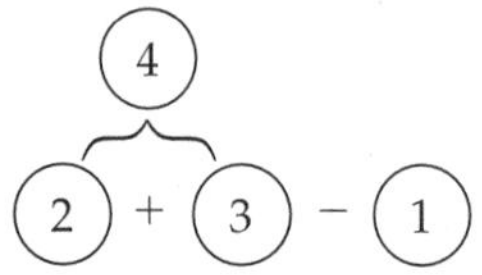

④
︵
② + ③ − ①

Here is another example:

**Example:** A college education increases your earning potential. *In addition,* it makes you aware of interests you didn't know you had. *Most important,* it teaches you the inherent value of knowledge. It is true, of course, that a college education is very expensive. *Nevertheless,* a college education will be worth every penny it costs.

**Comment:** This argument presents a series of reasons, each of which taken independently offers support for the conclusion that a college education is worthwhile. At the same time, the arguer concedes a claim that conflicts with this conclusion: "A college education is very expensive." The word "nevertheless," which indicates the conclusion, functions also to indicate the conflict between the conclusion and the claim which is conceded.

The argument can be cast as follows:

**Steps 1 & 2** [A college education increases your earning potential. ① ] *In addition,* [it makes you aware of interests you didn't know you had. ② ] *Most important,* [it teaches you the inherent value of knowledge. ③ ] [It is true, of course, that a college education is very expensive. ④ ] *Nevertheless,* [a college education will be worth every penny it costs. ⑤ ]

**Step 3**

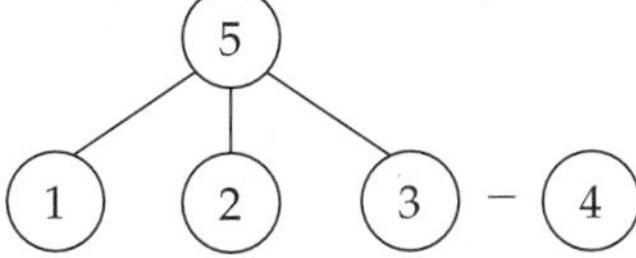


## GENERAL GUIDELINES AND HELPFUL HINTS

At least we hope they'll be helpful. Argument analysis is challenging in large measure because arguments are composed in language and language is an amazingly flexible multipurpose medium of expression. This means that the argument will very often be found woven into the fabric of an essay or speech which is also meant to serve other purposes, like entertaining or amusing the reader, or arousing passionate anger in the audience. Disentangling the argument from the other ingredients in the composition—the jokes, the suspenseful descriptions, the rousing rhetoric, and so on—often involves extensive paraphrasing and interpretation. To help you keep the process focused in a productive direction, here are a couple of pointers.

It is important not to confuse the organizational structure of the composition, the order of presentation of its ideas, with the structure of the argument. It should already be quite clear from the variety of examples we have considered so far in this chapter how widely the relationships of support among the claims in the argument may differ from the order in which they are presented in the essay.

Similarly, it is important not to confuse the grammatical structure of a passage in a composition with the structure of the argument it conveys. In some cases, with very carefully and clearly written passages of argumentation, the grammar and the structure of the argument may coincide. The author may construct the passage so that the grammar can be used as a guide to the argument. But in many cases not. Sometimes a single sentence makes a single claim:

> Roses are red.

Sometimes a single sentence contains several distinct claims:

> Roses are red, and violets are blue, and sugar is sweet, and so are you.

And sometimes the several distinct claims are not even distinguished from each other grammatically as independent clauses or separated grammatically by punctuation:

> All cancer cells have drastic chromosomal abnormalities as well as distinct nutritional needs in order to grow in soft agar cultures as well as in animal tissue where they are capable of seeding new solid tumors.

On the other hand, you will sometimes find that several distinct grammatical sentences are used to make one claim in an argument. For example, maybe the same claim gets repeated several times. For instance, perhaps the same point is reiterated more than once. In other words, . . . well, you get the idea.

What matters most for argument analysis is not the grammar of the composition but what supports what. A general rule of thumb is: Break a grammatical unit down when and only when different parts of the grammatical unit play separate and distinct roles in the argument in terms of support relationships. And, by the same token, disregard grammatically distinct repetitions of the same claim.

Finally, remember to stay focused on the argument. In many cases the composition that you're analyzing will contain material that is extraneous to the argument: tangential asides, background information, entertaining embellishments, rhetorical flourishes, and so on. A general rule of thumb is: Be thorough but stay relevant. If you think you understand and can explain the distinct contribution a given claim makes to the argument, include it in your analysis. Otherwise leave it out.

For example, in the following argument the first sentence is the conclusion, while the second, fourth, and fifth sentences are premises. But the third sentence and the clause beginning with "which" in the fourth sentence are irrelevant. The argument, then, can be cast as follows:

> [Women still don't get a fair shake in the workplace. ①] *For one thing* [they're not paid the same as their male counterparts. ②] This, by the way, is also true of black males in relation to white males. *For another thing* [women are not as often promoted to upper-level executive positions as men are, ③] which is really unfortunate because women have qualities desperately needed by American business. *But beyond this* [women continue to be plagued by stereotyping. ④]

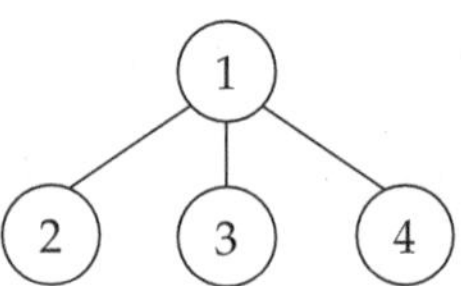


In the following example the first two sentences provide background information. While informative, they are not part of the argument, which is to be found in the last two sentences. Accordingly the argument may be cast as follows:

> The most fundamental question involved in the long history of thought on abortion is: When is the unborn a human? To phrase the question that way is to put in comprehensive humanistic terms what theologians either dealt with as an explicitly theological question under the heading of "ensoulment" or dealt with implicitly in their treatment of abortion. [The answer to the question of when the unborn is a human is simple: at conception. ①] *The reason is that* [at conception the new being receives the genetic code. ②]

One more example, followed by a comment:

**Example:** "In recent years government policies intended to ensure fairer employment and educational opportunities for women and minority groups have engendered alarm. Although I shall in this paper argue in support of enlightened versions of these policies, I nevertheless think there is much to be said for the opposition arguments. In general I would argue that the world of business is now overregulated by federal government, and I therefore hesitate to support an extension of the regulative arm of government into the arena of hiring and firing. Moreover, policies that would eventuate in reverse discrimination in present North American society have a heavy presumption against them, for both justice-regarding and utilitarian reasons."[7]

**Comment:** The first two sentences of this paragraph provide background information. The author's argument is contained in the third and fourth sentences, in which he provides support for his reluctance to extend further the "regulative arm of government into the arena of hiring and firing." Thus the argument can be cast as follows:

In general *I would argue that* [the world of business is now overregulated by federal government, ①] *and* [I *therefore* hesitate to support an extension of the regulative arm of government into the arena of hiring and firing. ②] *Moreover,* [policies that would eventuate in reverse discrimination in present North American society have a heavy presumption against them, for both justice-regarding ③] *and* [utilitarian reasons. ④]

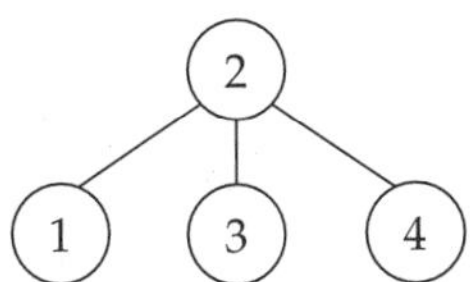


## ADDITIONAL EXERCISES

### Casting arguments

**1.** Cast the following arguments, all of which contain embedded sub-arguments:

The development of a human being from conception through birth into childhood is continuous ①. . . .] To [draw a line, to choose a point in this development and say "before this point the thing is not a person, after this point it is a person" is to make an arbitrary choice ②]. [This is] [a choice for which in the nature of things no good reason can be given ③]. *It is concluded that* [the fetus is . . . a person from

the moment of conception ④].
—Judith Jarvis Thomson[8]

[It's high time we seriously investigated the impact of television on children ①]. [Children spend much of their free time watching television ②]. [The average American child by age eighteen has watched thousands of hours of television ③]. [The same average viewer has watched thousands of hours of inane situation comedy, fantasy, soap operas, and acts of violence ④].

[It isn't likely that managed competition [the Clinton health care reform concept] can be counted on to save money ①]. *For one thing,* [at least two managed-care setups must be present in a community if there is to be competition ②], *and* [each of them needs a potential market of roughly 250,000 people to achieve economies of scale ③]. [Only about half of all Americans, it turns out, live in places densely populated enough to support two or more such programs ④]. *What's more,* [insurers would constantly hustle to win and retain business ⑤], *because* [employers would constantly be shopping for better deals, just as they do now ⑥]. [The sales staff, recruiters, advertising personnel, and clerical staff that such "marketing" entails contribute nothing to the provision of health care ⑦]. . . . [And the physicians, nurses, and others whom insurers and HMOs [health maintenance organizations] hire to oversee—that is, second-guess—the decisions individual doctors make with individual patients—an essential feature of managed care—have to be paid too . . . adding to the overhead cost ⑧]. [Administrative costs already soak up about $225 billion a year—25 cents of every dollar spent on health care in this country ⑨]. [Under managed competition, such costs would, at best, stay the same ⑩]. [More probably, they would increase ⑪]. —Judith Randal[9]

[To the extent that it is working at all, the press is always a participant [in, rather than a pure observer of, the events it reports] ①]. [Our

| | |
|---|---|
| decisions on where (and where not) to be and what (and what not) to report have enormous impact on the political and governmental life we cover ② ]. [We are obliged to be selective ③ ]. [We cannot publish the Daily Everything ④ ]. And so long as this is true—so long as we are making choices that 1) affect what people see concerning their leaders and 2) inevitably cause those leaders to behave in particular ways—we cannot pretend we are not participants. —Meg Greenfield[10] | |

**2.** Formulate the missing elements (compare with the Incompletely Stated Arguments exercise in Chapter 3) and complete the casting for each of the following arguments:

| | |
|---|---|
| [Software is written by humans ① ], *and* [humans make mistakes ② ]. | |
| [All propaganda is dangerous ① ]. *Therefore* [network news is dangerous ② ]. | |
| [Everything with any commercial potential eventually gets absorbed into the corporate world ① ], *so* [the Internet will eventually get absorbed into the corporate world ② ]. | |
| [UCLA will play in the Rose Bowl ① ], *because* [the Pac 10 champion always plays in the Rose Bowl ② ]. | |

(continued)

| | |
|---|---|
| [Legislation that can't be enforced is useless ① ], *and* [there's no way to enforce censorship over the Internet ② ]. | |
| [Hip-hop is a fad ① ], *so* [it will surely fade ② ]. | |

**3.** More arguments to practice on:

a. Evolution is a scientific fairy-tale just as the "flat earth theory" was in the 12th century. Evolution directly contradicts the Second Law of Thermodynamics, which states that unless an intelligent planner is directing a system, it will always go in the direction of disorder and deterioration. . . . Evolution requires a faith that is incomprehensible![11]

b. Contrary to popular assumption, volcanoes are anything but rare. The Smithsonian Scientific Event Alert Network often reports several dozen [volcanic eruptions] per quarter. America's slice of the volcanic "ring of fire" includes the Cascades, a mountain range that arcs across the Pacific Northwest. When peaceful, shimmering Mt. St. Helens exploded this past spring, blasting 1.3 billion cubic yards of rock into powder, the people of Washington state received a rude lesson about nature's penchant for change. Bathed in ash every few weeks over the summer, the Washingtonians queasily came to the realization that the mountain might stay belligerent for years, that they had, in a sense, been living on borrowed time between inevitable eruptions. "There are potential volcanoes all over the Cascade Range where Mt. St. Helens stands," says geologist Alfred Anderson of the University of Washington. "There's still a lot of change, a lot of formations, going on in that area of the world." [12]

c. A scientific colleague of mine, who holds a professorial post in the department of sociology and anthropology at one of our leading universities, recently asked me about my stand on the question of human beings having sex relations without love. Although I have taken something of a position on this issue in my book, *The American Sexual Tragedy,* I have never quite considered the problem in sufficient detail. So here goes. . . . In general, I feel that affectional, as against non-affectional, sex relations are *desirable*. . . . It is usually desirable that an association between coitus and affection exist—particularly in marriage, because it is often difficult for two individuals to keep finely tuned to each other over a period of years.[13]

d. Scientists are human beings with their full complement of emotions and prejudices, and their emotions and prejudices often influence the way they do their science. This was first clearly brought out in a study by Professor Nicholas Pastore . . . in 1949. In this study Professor Pastore showed that the scientist's political beliefs were highly correlated with what he believed about the roles played by nature and nurture in the development of the person. Those holding conservative political views strongly tended to believe in the power of genes over environment. Those subscribing to more liberal views tended to believe in the power of environment over genes. One distinguished scientist (who happened to be a teacher of mine) when young was a socialist and environmentalist, but toward middle age he became politically conservative and a firm believer in the supremacy of genes![14]
e. Many a reader will raise the question whether findings won by the observation of individuals can be applied to the psychological understanding of groups. Our answer to this question is an emphatic affirmation. Any group consists of individuals and nothing but individuals, and psychological mechanisms which we find operating in a group can therefore only be mechanisms that operate in individuals. In studying individual psychology as a basis for the understanding of social psychology, we do something which might be compared with studying an object under the microscope. This enables us to discover the very details of psychological mechanisms which we find operating on a large scale in the social process. If our analysis of socio-psychological phenomena is not based on the detailed study of human behavior, it lacks empirical character and, therefore, validity.[15]
f. Flextime (Flexible Working Hours) often makes workers more productive because being treated as responsible adults gives them greater commitment to their jobs. As a result it decreases absenteeism, sick leave, tardiness and overtime, and generally produces significant increases in productivity for the work group as a whole. For example, in trial periods in three different departments, the U.S. Social Security Administration measured productivity increases averaging about 20%. None has reported a decline.[16]
g. The medical community has long debated the effects of tobacco smoke on non-smokers. Now recent studies have bolstered the contention of many physicians that, apart from the clear health hazard to smokers, tobacco smoke has harmful effects on non-smokers as well. In fact, in 1972 the U.S. Surgeon General devoted fully a quarter of his 226-page report, "The Health Consequences of Smoking," to the other effects of smoke on non-smokers. Other people's smoking, says the report, is retarding fetal growth and increasing the incidence of premature birth; is exacerbating respiratory allergies in children and adults; and is causing acute irritation and taxing hearts and lungs of non-smokers by filling the air in smoky rooms with carbon monoxide, the deadly poison found in automobile exhaust.[17]
h. Government control of ideas or personal preferences is alien to a democracy. And the yearning to use governmental censorship of any kind is infectious. It may spread insidiously. Commencing with suppression of books as obscene,

it is not unlikely to develop into official lust for the power of thought-control in the areas of religion, politics, and elsewhere. Milton observed that "licensing of books . . . necessarily pulls along with it so many other kinds of licensing." Mill notes that the "bounds of what may be called moral police" may easily extend "until it encroaches on the most unquestionably legitimate liberty of the individual." We should beware of a recrudescence of the undemocratic doctrine uttered in the seventeenth century by Berkeley, Governor of Virginia: "Thank God there are no free schools or preaching, for learning has brought disobedience into the world, and printing has divulged them. God keep us from both."[18]

i. While the networks are among the staunchest defenders of free expression . . . they will compromise principles in order to enhance their audience ratings. In an astonishing article *The New York Times* described how ABC subordinated its news division's integrity to an outside influence. Soviet officials were permitted to censor and monitor ABC news stories about life in Russia. Some Soviet officials actually sat in ABC's New York offices reviewing its network reporting. The *Times* article contended that these startling concessions to the Russians were part of the network's effort to secure coverage rights for the 1980 Olympics.[19]

j. Well, is it true that the black community is edging into the middle class? Let's look at income, the handiest guide and certainly the most generally agreed-upon measurement. What income level amounts to middle-class status? Median family income is often used, since that places a family at the exact midpoint in our society. In 1972 the median family income of whites amounted to $11,549, but black median family income was a mere $6,864.

   That won't work. Let's take another guide. The Bureau of Labor Statistics says it takes an urban family of four $12,600 to maintain an "intermediate" living standard. Using that measure, the average black family not only is *not* middle class, but it earns far less than the "lower, non-poverty" level of $8,200. Four out of five black families earn less than the "intermediate" standard.[20]

k. American institutions were fashioned in an era of vast unoccupied spaces and preindustrial technology. In those days, collisions between public needs and individual rights may have been minimal. But increased density, scarcity of resources, and interlocking technologies have now heightened the concern for "public goods," which belong to no one in particular but to all of us jointly. Polluting a lake or river or the air may not directly damage any one person's private property or living space. But it destroys a good that all of us—including future generations—benefit from and have a title to. Our public goods are entitled to a measure of protection.[21]

l. What, after all, is the foundation of the nurse's obligation to follow the physician's orders? Presumably, the nurse's obligation is to act in the medical interest of the patient. The point is that the nurse has an obligation to follow physician's orders because, ordinarily, patient welfare (interest) thereby is ensured. Thus when a nurse's obligation to follow a physician's order comes into *direct* conflict with the nurse's obligation to act in the medical interest of the patient, it would seem to follow that the patient's interests should always take precedence.[22]

m. Even though spanking has immediate punitive and (for the parent) anger-releasing effects, parents should not spank their children, for spanking gives children the message that inflicting pain on others is an appropriate means of changing their behavior. Furthermore, spanking trains children to submit to the arbitrary rules of authority figures who have the power to harm them. We ought not to give our children those messages. Rather, we should train them to either make appropriate behavioral choices or to expect to deal with the related natural and logical consequences of their behavior.

n. Such crises [of employees departing with a firm's trade secrets] are not surprising. . . . The highly educated employees of R & D [research and development] organizations place primary emphasis on their own development, interests and satisfaction. Graduates of major scientific and technological institutions readily admit that they accept their first jobs primarily for money. [They also want] the early and brief experience they feel is a prerequisite for seeking more satisfying futures with smaller companies. . . . Employee mobility and high personnel turnover rates are also due to the placement of new large federal contracts and the termination of others. One need only look to the Sunday newspaper employment advertisements for evidence as to the manner in which such programs are used to attract highly educated R & D personnel.[23]

## GLOSSARY

**chain** premises which function interdependently as support for a conclusion
**concession claims** claims introduced into the text of an argument which count against the thesis
**main premises** the premises offered as direct support for the thesis
**paraphrase** a reformulation intended to capture the same meaning
**series** premises which function separately and independently of each other as support for a conclusion
**sub-argument** an argument supporting a premise
**thesis** conclusion, especially of an extended argument

## NOTES

1 Joan Ryan, "Grease, Gasoline and Death," *Washington Post,* May, 1979.

2 Sheila Tobias, "Who's Afraid of Math, and Why?" *Atlantic Monthly,* November 1970.

3 Michael Scriven, *Reasoning* (New York: McGraw-Hill, 1976). People who know Scriven's book will recognize that we have inverted our castings. We think this more closely reflects the vocabulary of premises as "support for" their conclusions, and therefore also will be closer to students' intuitive spacializations of arguments.

[4] Elizabeth Hall with Paul Cameron, "Our Failing Reverence for Life," *Psychology Today,* April 1976, p. 108.

[5] Bennett H. Beach, "Mr. Wizard Comes to Court," *Time,* March 1, 1982, p. 90.

[6] Berkeley Rice, "Aspiring to a Fall," *Psychology Today,* March 1980, p. 25.

[7] Tom Beauchamp, "The Justification of Reverse Discrimination," in William T. Blackstone and Robert Heslep, eds., *Social Justice and Preferential Treatment* (Athens: University of Georgia Press, 1977).

[8] Judith Jarvis Thomson, "A Defense of Abortion," *Philosophy and Public Affairs* 1 (Fall 1971).

[9] Judith Randal, "Wrong Prescription: Why Managed Competition Is No Cure," *The Progressive,* May 1993, pp. 23–24.

[10] Meg Greenfield, "When the Press Becomes a Participant," in *Washington Post Company Annual Report,* 1984, p. 21.

[11] Edward Blic, *21 Scientists Who Believe in Creation* (Harrisonburg, Va.: Christian Light Publications, 1977).

[12] Edward M. Hart, "The Shape of Things to Come," *Next: A Look into the Future,* December 1980, pp. 69–70.

[13] Albert Ellis, *Sex without Guilt* (New York: Lyle Stuart, 1966).

[14] Ashley Montagu, *Sociobiology Examined* (Oxford: Oxford University Press, 1980), p. 4.

[15] Eric Fromm, *Escape from Freedom* (New York: Avon Books, 1965), p. 158.

[16] Barry Stein et al., "Flextime," *Psychology Today,* June 1976, p. 43.

[17] *Reader's Digest,* July 1974, pp. 102, 104.

[18] Jerome Frank, dissenting opinion in *United States* v. *Roth,* 354 U.S. 476 (1957).

[19] Marvin Maurer, in Herbert M. Levine, ed., *Point–Counterpoint: Readings in American Government* (Glenview, Ill.: Scott, Foresman, 1977).

[20] Vernon E. Jordan Jr., "The Truth about the Black Middle Class," *Newsweek,* July 8, 1974.

[21] Amitai Etzioni, "When Rights Collide," *Psychology Today,* October 1977.

[22] E. Joy Kroeger Mappes, "Ethical Dilemmas for Nurses: Physicians' Orders versus Patients' Rights," in T. A. Mappes and J. S. Zembatty, eds., *Biomedical Ethics* (New York: McGraw-Hill, 1981), p. 100.

[23] Michael S. Baram, "Trade Secrets: What Price Loyalty?" *Harvard Business Review,* November–December 1968.

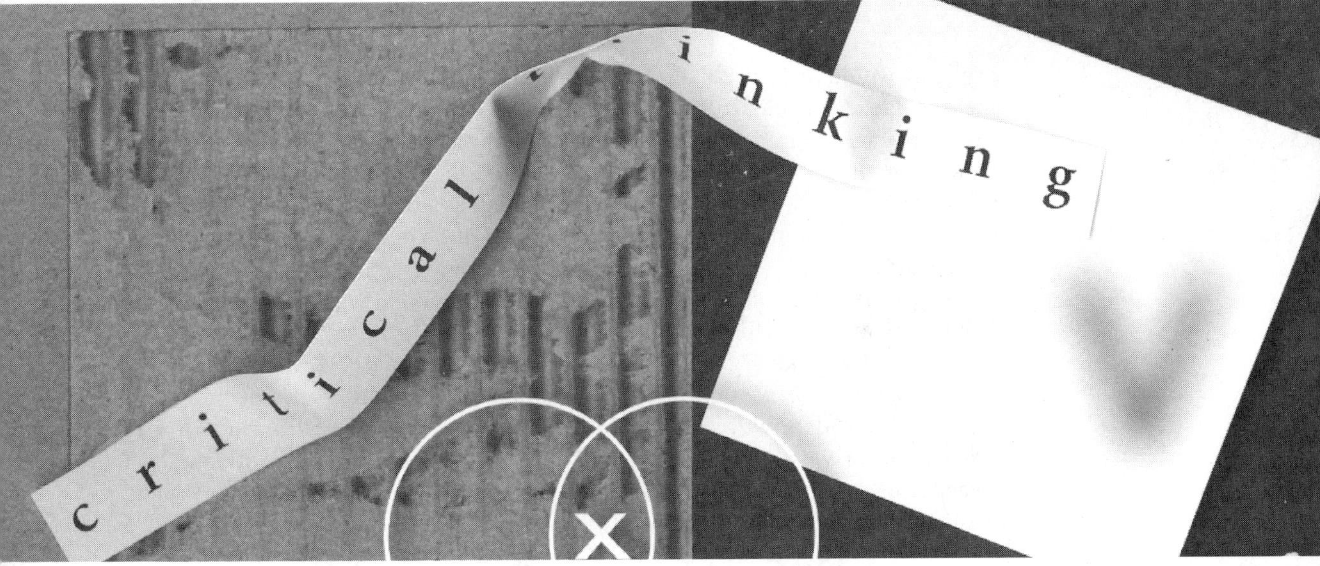


# CHAPTER 5 Argument Analysis II: Reconstructing Argument Fragments

**If you want to complain about Marilyn Manson, start from the beginning. Start with Shakespeare. What was *Romeo and Juliet* about? Suicide!** Ozzy Osbourne

In Chapter 4 we discussed briefly several examples of argument analysis in which the arguments were incompletely stated. We noted that for example in this argument:

> I'm convinced that textbooks contain mistakes because they are written by human beings.

there is an additional unstated premise to the effect that "human beings make mistakes." In Chapter 4 we discussed such examples simply to indicate the features of our casting system which are designed to accommodate them. In this chapter we will concentrate on such incompletely stated arguments, or as we will refer to them here, argument "fragments." The main reason for devoting a whole chapter to reconstructing argument fragments is that most, by far the vast majority, of "real world" arguments, the kind you encounter in the media and in everyday conversation, are presented as fragments.

This happens for several reasons, some good, some not so good. Here is a good reason. Sometimes things are so obvious that spelling them out completely and explicitly would be unnecessary, needlessly time-consuming, or even insulting to the intelligence of one's audience. So we often leave things out of our presentation of the argument as a matter of economy or common courtesy. On the other hand, sometimes people leave things out because they aren't completely aware of all of the assumptions that their reasoning depends on, or they gloss over elements in their reasoning that they'd just as soon not have exposed to careful critical consideration.

In any case, a fair and comprehensive evaluation of *any* argument depends on a thorough and detailed analysis, again for more or less obvious reasons. First, if we find fault with an argument one or more of whose parts we haven't noticed or taken account of, we may be guilty of unfairly dismissing a genuinely worthy argument, and depriving ourselves of an opportunity to learn from it. On the other hand, if we allow ourselves to be swayed by an argument with hidden weaknesses, . . . well, spelling this out any more completely and explicitly would be unnecessary.

## THE ESSENCE OF RECONSTRUCTION

Let's return for a moment to the example we used earlier. When someone says

> I'm convinced that textbooks contain mistakes because they are written by human beings.

we said that what is assumed as an unexpressed premise is obvious:

> Human beings make mistakes.

How did we know this? How did we know that the unexpressed premise was not something entirely different? Or suppose someone says

> Healthful outdoor exercise is the best therapy. That's why I recommend cycling.

We would say that it's obvious that what is assumed as an unexpressed premise is

> Cycling is healthful outdoor exercise.

How do we know this? How do we know that the arguer is not assuming

> Cycling is a great way to meet other single people.

Suppose you now respond, "The unexpressed premises we filled in are the right ones because they are the ones that make the most sense of what the arguer *did* say." That is a good answer for a couple of reasons.

First of all, it's true. The unexpressed premises we filled in *do* make sense of what the arguer did say—better sense, no doubt, than anything else we could have come up with. "Human beings make mistakes" does make sense of "I'm convinced that textbooks contain mistakes because they're written by human beings." And "Cycling is healthful outdoor exercise" does, where "Cycling is a great way to meet other single people" does not, make sense of "Healthful outdoor exercise is the best therapy. That's why I recommend cycling."

Second, it captures the essence of the whole business of reconstructing argument fragments: When we reconstruct argument fragments, we are trying to make sense of what people say (and *don't* say). Remember the example of the barefoot couple at the beachfront restaurant. The hostess says not one word, but the context helps us to make sense of her gesture as an argument fragment and to reconstruct the entire argument.

These examples are all relatively simple and straightforward. They are examples of what logicians traditionally refer to as "enthymemes" or "enthymematic," which means essentially that parts of the reasoning are left for members of the audience to recognize on their own, which they can do easily because of the logic of the argument (see Chapter 6). Though they are each fragments, they each embody a sufficient measure of guidance so that it's not very difficult to identify their unexpressed elements. This is part of what we mean when we say that the unexpressed elements are "obvious."

But many cases are much more difficult. Frequently there are *several different ways* of "making sense" of what someone says. Then too, sometimes what people say just doesn't make very much sense. It won't always be possible to know, with certainty, which of several different statements should be cast in the role of missing premise, or whether one should be bothering to look for missing premises at all.

Some of the problems that arise in connection with reconstructing argument fragments can be traced to the obvious fact that the missing elements are missing. And some of the problems can be traced to an inevitable fact about human communication: Making sense of what people say is *non-algorithmic.* This means that it is not governed by any absolute, mechanical, foolproof decision procedures. Rather, it involves the application of multiple criteria which sometimes conflict with one another. Hence it tends to yield multiple solutions each with advantages and liabilities. The most one can expect by way of systematic guidance to this sort of process is a set of guidelines—"rules of thumb," which is what we will present in this chapter. But as you work with these guidelines, building experience and cultivating sensitivity and judgment, keep in mind that there will be exceptions.

## WHEN TO RECONSTRUCT

Consider the following example. Suppose you and a friend are solving a puzzle in which you are supposed to match the names and brief biographies of twenty people from a set of clues, and your friend says, "Pat must be a man because here in the fifth clue it says that Pat is Jason's father." Of course it follows from the fact that Pat is Jason's father that Pat is a man. But this also depends on the facts that by definition (1) a father is a male parent, and (2) a parent is presumably an adult, and (3) a man is an adult human male. Ordinarily it would not be necessary to spell these three premises out explicitly in order to fully appreciate the reasoning, any more than it was necessary to spell them out in the original presentation of the reasoning.

In general, reconstruction is appropriate where the hidden or missing elements are both crucial and controversial, or where spelling out the hidden elements explicitly will help in isolating the crucial and controversial ones. Take this argument, for example: "You say textbooks don't contain mistakes? Here, I'll prove it to you that they do. My science book says that whales are mammals. But everybody knows that whales live in the sea, which is what a fish is, an animal that lives in the sea."[1] We will reconstruct this argument fragment shortly. For now, it will be sufficient to note that the reasoning evidently has some weaknesses in it somewhere. Spelling out all of its elements, even the ones that are obvious, becomes useful when we attempt to pinpoint those weaknesses.

## GUIDELINES FOR RECONSTRUCTING PREMISES

In reconstructing an argument fragment we are essentially trying to make sense of what someone has said so that we can assess its merits as a piece of reasoning. Naturally therefore we will want the outcome of our reconstruction to be as *fair* and as *logical* as we can make it. From these two general values flow several more specific guidelines. Logic, a subject which we will explore more deeply in Chapter 6, calls for a *complete* and *relevant* reconstruction. Fairness to the person whose reasoning we are considering requires *fidelity* to the person's actual position and that we select the most *plausible* available reconstruction.

### COMPLETENESS AND THE "WHAT IF" STRATEGY

Consider the argument "Since Smith is a police officer, he's probably in favor of gun-control legislation." If you wanted to determine whether this argument was completely stated, you could ask "*What if* it's true that Smith is a police officer? Must it follow that he's probably in favor of gun-control legislation?" Not necessarily, for it may well be that most police officers are opposed to such legislation. Nothing in the stated premise disallows that possibility. If in fact most police officers are not in favor of such laws, then the conclusion would not follow from this premise. Something is missing; the argument is not completely stated. Here we are using an important and fundamental logical concept called "validity," (which we will discuss more thoroughly in Chapter 6) to determine whether the statement of the argument we have before us is complete or enthymematic. Notice that in applying this "what if" strategy we needn't know whether the expressed premise is actually true. All we have to do is ask "*What if* it were true? Would the conclusion then have to be true?" Thus the "what if" strategy consists of *assuming* that the expressed premise or premises are true and asking whether the conclusion therefore would *have to be* true. If the answer is yes, the argument is completely stated; if it is no, the argument is enthymematic. If the argument is enthymematic we then try to identify the additional unstated premises that the argument is assuming until we arrive at the point that the argument is completely stated.

## EXERCISE | Completeness and the "What If" Strategy

http://www

Using the "what if" strategy, determine which of the following arguments are enthymemes:

| | Enth. | Complete |
|---|---|---|
| Because prisons do not rehabilitate inmates, they are an ineffective form of punishment for criminal behavior. | | |
| The United States should develop solar energy on a widespread basis because it must become energy-independent. | | |
| Abortion involves the taking of a life. Therefore it should be discouraged. | | |
| Jane's probably married. She's wearing a wedding ring. | | |
| God has all the virtues. Therefore, God is benevolent. | | |
| Men are not innately superior to women. If they were they wouldn't establish caste systems to ensure their preferred positions, and they wouldn't work so hard to maintain these systems. But obviously men do both. | | |

## RELEVANCE AND THE TOPIC COVERAGE STRATEGY

Let's now return to another of our earlier examples:

> Healthful outdoor exercise is the best therapy. That's why I recommend cycling.

We considered two alternative missing premises for this argument:

1. Cycling is healthful outdoor exercise.
2. Cycling is a great way to meet other single people.

and we said that "Cycling is healthful outdoor exercise" does, where "Cycling is a great way to meet other single people" does not, make sense of "Healthful outdoor exercise is the best therapy. That's why I recommend cycling." This was based on the fact that the first alternative is relevant to the argument, whereas the second is not. The first alternative connects the expressed premise to the conclusion, whereas the second alternative, though it may be true, and though it may count as a reason for recommending cycling, does not link the conclusion to the reason given in the expressed premise. Here is a strategy you can use to determine the relevance of candidates for the role of missing premise.

When we identify an argument as an enthymeme, we in effect sense a gap or hole in it. But we can be more specific than this. The hole has a more or less definite shape which we can discern, to some extent at least, by paying close attention to what surrounds it—to the argument's conclusion and its expressed premises. Think of this as similar to searching for a missing piece in a jigsaw puzzle. You study closely the shapes and colors of the pieces which surround the one you're searching for. This helps you find the missing piece. When the puzzle is an incomplete argument and what we're searching for is a missing premise, we can guide ourselves by close attention to the topics covered in the conclusion and expressed premises of the argument. This helps us get a better sense of the "shape" of the hole or gap we're trying to fill in, and of the missing premise which can fill it. So, for example, in the argument we've been discussing, the topics covered in the conclusion and the expressed premise are:

1. Reasons why the arguer recommends cycling
2. The arguer's notion that healthful outdoor exercise is the best therapy

The gap or hole in the argument, then, is something which relates these to each other. The second alternative we considered, "Cycling is a great way to meet other single people," doesn't do this. Though it might fit with topic 1, reasons why the arguer might recommend cycling, it doesn't fit with topic 2, the arguer's notion that healthful outdoor exercise is the best therapy. The first alternative, however, fits with both in such a way that we can see the "missing link" in the chain of reasoning.

## EXERCISE | Relevance and the Topic Coverage Strategy

The following arguments are incomplete. Each is followed by a list of possible missing premises. Use the topic coverage strategy to select from each list the missing premise most relevant to the argument.

1. People who were born at exactly the same time often have vastly different life histories and personalities. Therefore astrology is not a reliable predictive system.

| | |
|---|---|
| | People who believe in astrology are superstitious. |
| | If astrology were a reliable predictive system, people born at exactly the same time would not have vastly different life histories and personalities. |
| | No two people are born at exactly the same time. |

2. Since no human system of justice is infallible and capital punishment imposes an irreversible penalty, capital punishment is an unacceptable form of punishment.

| | |
|---|---|
| | No form of punishment which imposes an irreversible penalty is acceptable. |
| | If we could perfect a system of justice so that no mistaken convictions could possibly occur, then capital punishment would be acceptable. |
| | No form of punishment which imposes an irreversible penalty is acceptable within a fallible system of justice. |

## PLAUSIBILITY

In reconstructing argument fragments we generally try to avoid implausible assertions, because we want to give an argument a fair run for its money. To reconstruct an argument on the basis of an implausible premise when a more plausible alternative is available does no service either to the argument or to any criticism of it. So, in assessing candidates for the role of missing premise, preference generally goes to the more plausible of two alternatives. This derives from a general principle of fairness which ought to govern our attempts to make sense of or critique what people say.

Plausibility literally means deserving of applause. But it has a more precise technical meaning relating to credibility or believability. In technical terms plausibility is a measure of how well we think an idea is likely to survive critical scrutiny. If we were to devise strenuous tests designed to falsify the idea, how well would the idea survive such tests? A plausible idea is one which we think would survive relatively well. An implausible idea is one which we think would not.

Neither plausibility nor implausibility are "absolute." Rather, they both admit of degrees. This means that some ideas are more plausible than others. A good place to look for examples to illustrate this point (implausible though this may sound) is in tabloids like the *National Enquirer.* In these publications you will find a steady diet of highly implausible ideas, like: "Confederate Flag Sighted on Bottom of UFO," and "Elvis Presley Planning Return to United States from Seclusion in Brazil to Expose his Death as Hoax"; and a good many ideas which are somewhat less implausible, like: "Hypnosis Cures Urge to Smoke"; alongside a few ideas which might be quite a bit more plausible, like: "Madonna Has New Love Interest," or "Royal Family Locked in Power Struggle Over Engagement of Prince William."

Moreover, our estimates of an idea's plausibility or implausibility are not static. Rather, they are subject to adjustment in accordance with new incoming information. What may appear initially to be a plausible idea may, on further investigation, seem more and more or less and less plausible. And plausibility is only loosely correlated with truth. A plausible idea may well turn out not to be the case. And there are a good many cases throughout history of initially implausible ideas which have nonetheless been confirmed as true. Plausibility, in other words, is a *preliminary* measure of an idea's worth. This is one reason why it is appropriate as a criterion for filling in missing premises.

Now let's reconsider this example:

> Since Smith is a police officer, he's probably in favor of gun-control legislation.

There are a number of distinct alternatives we might consider casting in the role of missing premise. Take, for example, these two:

1. All police officers favor gun-control legislation.
2. Most police officers favor gun-control legislation.

Either of these alternatives will complete the argument. But the first alternative is somewhat less plausible than the second. Remember, this means simply that if we were to devise strenuous tests designed to falsify them, the first would be less likely to survive than the second. This is because the first alternative makes a stronger claim than the second.

### EXERCISE | Plausibility

Rank the following statement pairs in terms of plausibility. Compare your rankings with those of someone else in the class. Wherever your rankings conflict, explain your initial ranking. Compare notes and see whether your ranking is affected.

| | |
|---|---|
| | 1. a. There is intelligent life in outer space. |
| | b. Some nonhuman animals have the capacity for language. |
| | 2. a. The use of computer technology in weapons systems increases the risk of a nuclear accident. |
| | b. The perfection of a space-based missile defense system is feasible. |
| | 3. a. Some of the assassins of President Kennedy are still alive. |
| | b. Some of the assassins of President Kennedy presently hold high office in Washington. |
| | 4. a. Human adults generally use less than 10 percent of the capacity of their minds. |
| | b. The universe is finite. |

## FIDELITY TO THE ARGUER'S POSITION

Probably the trickiest part of filling in missing premises is remaining faithful to the arguer's actual position. If, in reconstructing an incomplete argument, we wind up with something which no longer reflects the views of the arguer, our efforts have obviously gone astray. In saying this, we remember that, as we said earlier, sometimes arguers are unaware of all of the premises they may be assuming in their arguments. They may even be unwilling to learn or admit that they are assuming a particular premise in an argument. That's part of what makes this tricky. When we say that in filling in missing premises we should try to remain faithful to the arguer's position, we don't merely mean that we should remain faithful to what the arguer is aware of or is willing to admit to. On the other hand, we don't mean that we can attribute any statement or view we want to the arguer. We mean rather that the missing premise should be something that the arguer would accept as part of her view if she were aware of it, or which she *must* be committed to in order for her reasoning to make sense. Another thing that makes this tricky is the obvious point once again that in filling in missing premises, we are interpreting beyond what the arguer actually says. You can see what the difficulty is here by considering the difference between oral and written discourse. In oral contexts, when we are listening to someone present an argument, we at least have the opportunity to question the person if we think she is relying on an unexpressed premise. With written arguments we generally cannot do this. We must guide our efforts on the basis of information which is of necessity incomplete. As you can tell, there is a delicate balance to achieve in reconstructing an argument fragment. One reasonably good approach to this balancing act is through a general principle of charity to the argument. In a choice between the argument and a criticism of it, in other words where two otherwise equally acceptable alternative reconstructions are such that one favors the argument while the other favors the criticism, give the benefit of the doubt to the argument.

Consider once again this argument: "Since Smith is a police officer, he's probably in favor of gun-control legislation." The "what if" strategy tells us that the argument is incomplete as it stands. Using the topic coverage strategy we can see that the missing premise will need to link the category of police officers with favoring gun-control legislation in some way. But this still leaves the field open to several candidates:

**Reconstruction 1** Some police officers favor gun-control legislation.

**Reconstruction 2** Most police officers favor gun-control legislation.

**Reconstruction 3** All police officers favor gun-control legislation.

Let's first consider reconstruction 1: "Some police officers favor gun-control legislation." If "some" is taken to mean at least one, then we can be quite certain that the arguer would accept this premise as part of her position. After all, the argument explicitly commits her to the claim that Smith is a police officer and to the claim that Smith is for that reason probably in favor of gun-control legislation. The arguer must be committed at least to the view that some police officers are in favor of gun-control legislation. But the arguer must be committed to something stronger than reconstruction 1, because the arguer concludes that Smith is *probably* in favor of gun-control legislation and if reconstruction 1 were all that the arguer were committed to, then she would lack an adequate basis for that conclusion. In other words, even with the addition of reconstruction 1 as a missing premise, the argument would remain incomplete.

Reconstruction 3 is the strongest of the three. Certainly if "All police officers favor gun-control legislation," then the conclusion can be inferred: "Smith is probably in favor of gun-control legislation." In fact, reconstruction 3 would allow the even stronger conclusion "Smith *must be* in favor of gun-control legislation." That the arguer qualifies her conclusion with the word "probably" gives us pretty convincing evidence that reconstruction 3 would not be in keeping with the arguer's position. As we earlier said, if we insisted on reconstruction 3, then, we'd be saddling the arguer with a needlessly implausible premise, thereby turning her argument into a sitting duck. All you'd have to do to discredit the argument would be to cite a single example of a police officer opposed to gun-control legislation. That single example would disprove the claim that all police officers favor gun-control legislation, which in turn would prove the argument faulty.

Reconstruction 2 falls between these extremes. In referring to the position of *most* police officers, it avoids the overstatement of reconstruction 3 and the understatement of reconstruction 1. It is strong enough to complete the argument but not so strong as to overstate the arguer's position.

As tricky as it is to faithfully extrapolate an arguer's position from an incomplete expression of it, there is also a risk that we will wind up merely restating the original incomplete argument as our reconstruction of a missing premise. Take this example:

> Most working women don't complain of sexual harassment on the job. *Therefore* sexual harassment on the job must not be a widespread problem.

First of all, the "what if" strategy tells us that this argument is enthymematic. Suppose it's true that most working women don't complain of sexual harassment on the job. Must it be true therefore that sexual harassment on the job is not a widespread problem? Not necessarily. What is the missing premise? The topic coverage strategy indicates that the missing premise will need to link the incidence of sexual harassment on the job (the topic of the conclusion) with the incidence of complaints from working women concerning sexual harassment on the job (the topic of the expressed premise). One way to do this would be with the addition of the premise that

> If most working women don't complain about sexual harassment on the job, then it's not a widespread problem.

This premise does complete the argument. Check this with the "what if" strategy. Suppose that this new premise and the original expressed premise are both true. Must it necessarily be true then that sexual harassment on the job is not a widespread problem? Yes. Furthermore we can be quite sure that the arguer is committed to this assertion. This is because it merely restates the original argument in a single sentence. Indeed, that's what's wrong with this as a candidate for the role of missing premise. To suppose that the arguer had nothing more in mind than a mere restatement of what she did say in the form of a general principle—so as to plug a logical gap in her argument—is neither fair nor reasonable. Such a reconstruction, were the arguer herself to supply it, would be dismissed as ad hoc. The term *ad hoc,* which derives from Latin, means roughly "without independent reason." We should be wondering if the arguer didn't have some deeper, more independent basis for her conclusion, something like:

> Only those things that are widely protested are widespread problems.

If there is a plausible and relevant alternative which would complete the argument and which goes beyond what is already present in the incomplete original to a broader principle on which the arguer may reasonably be supposed to have based her reasoning, that alternative is preferable.

## PUTTING IT ALL TOGETHER

Earlier in this chapter, to illustrate both the essence and essential function of argument reconstruction, we used an example which we said we would return to and reconstruct. Let's do that now. Here is the example once again:

> You say textbooks don't contain mistakes? Here, I'll prove it to you that they do. My science book says that whales are mammals. But everybody knows that whales live in the sea, which is what a fish is, an animal that lives in the sea.

Let's begin by numbering the claims, for our casting:

> [You say textbooks don't contain mistakes? Here, I'll prove it to you that they do. ①] [My science book says that whales are mammals. ②] But everybody knows that [whales live in the sea, ③], which is what [a fish is, an animal that lives in the sea. ④]

Notice that we have bracketed the first two sentences as claim 1. This is a good example of the grammatical structure and the logical structure of the passage diverging from each other. Claim 1 is evidently the thesis of the passage, and we can easily capture it in a single sentence: "Textbooks contain mistakes." You may also have noticed that we ignored the (bad) grammar of the sentence in bracketing claim 4. But claim 4 presents bigger problems than mere "grammatico-logical divergence." Claim 4 really needs to be reworded in order to accurately reflect the argument. What the arguer is really trying to say is "Any animal that lives in the sea is a fish," and this is the way we'll represent claim 4 from now on.

Now that we have identified the thesis, let us see if we can identify the premises which directly support it. Claim 2 is offered as direct support for the thesis. But what about claims 3 and 4? They both seem intended to contribute support for the thesis, but the support is not direct. To bring this out clearly, we can use the "what if" and topic coverage strategies. What if it's true that the arguer's science book says that whales are mammals? That would not, by itself, show that textbooks contain mistakes. What then, do we need to add in order to link the topics covered in the premise with the topics covered in the thesis? One additional implied claim is that the arguer's science book is a textbook. A second additional implied claim is that the statement that whales are mammals is mistaken. The first of these claims pretty obvious, and also pretty obviously part of the arguer's position. The second is implausible (to say the least), but it is part of the arguer's position, as we can see quite clearly from claims 3 and 4, which are offered in support of it. So let us assign the letter *a* to the first and the letter *b* to the second of these hidden premises.

Now let us consider the relationship between claims 3 and 4 and hidden premise *b*. Again using the "what if" and topic coverage strategies we can see that the support is not direct. What if it is true that whales live in the sea and that animals that live in the sea are fish? That would not, by itself, show that whales are not mammals. In order to link the topics covered in claims 3 and 4 with the topics covered in hidden premise *b* we need to add the claim that whales are fish, which *does* follow directly from claims 3 and 4, and the claim that no fish are mammals, which is both highly plausible (to say the least) and again obviously part of the arguer's position. So let us assign the letter *c* to the claim that whales are fish and the letter *d* to the claim that no fish are mammals. And now we can complete the casting:

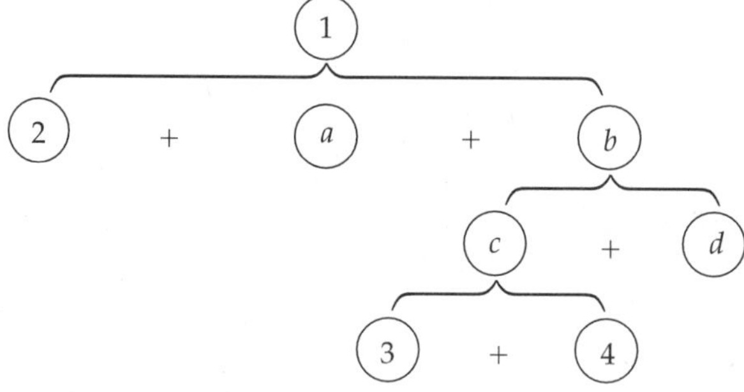

## EXERCISE | Filling in Missing Premises

1. For this exercise, you'll need a study partner, preferably someone who is also taking critical thinking. Formulate and evaluate possible missing premises for the incomplete arguments in the exercise on completeness and the "what if" strategy. As you examine possible reconstructions, consider the questions of plausibility and relevance and fidelity to the arguer's position. Compile a list of alternatives for each along with your assessments of relative advantages and liabilities, for class discussion.

2. Select the best reconstructed premise from the alternatives offered for each of the following arguments:
   a. Some of these people can't be golfers. They're not carrying clubs.

| | |
|---|---|
| | Some golfers are carrying clubs. |
| | Everyone carrying clubs is a golfer. |
| | All golfers carry clubs. |

b. If capital punishment isn't a deterrent to crime, then why has the rate of violent crimes increased since capital punishment was outlawed?

| | |
|---|---|
| | Because the rate of violent crime has increased since capital punishment was outlawed, it must be a deterrent to crime. |
| | An increase in the rate of crime following the abolition of a punishment proves that the punishment is a crime deterrent. |
| | An increase in the rate of crime following the abolition of a punishment usually indicates that the punishment is a crime deterrent. |

c. Constitutionally only the House of Representatives may initiate a money-raising bill. Thus when the Senate drafted the recent tax bill, it acted unconstitutionally. Therefore the proposed tax bill should not be made law.

| | |
|---|---|
| | Any bill the Senate drafts should not be made law. |
| | Any bill that originates unconstitutionally should not be made law. |
| | Any tax bill originating in the Senate should not be made law. |

3. Fill in the missing premises of the following incomplete arguments, and cast them. Some may have *more than one* premise missing.
   a. All successful politicians are self-serving, for only ambitious people succeed in politics.
   b. Whatever invades privacy threatens justice. That's why subjecting people to polygraph tests as a condition of employment is so serious.
   c. Resident reacting against a mobile home park's becoming part of the neighborhood: "I have nothing against mobile homes as a way of living, but it's unthinkable to put a mobile home park right in the middle of a residential area. After all they're usually in outlying areas."

## LONGER ARGUMENTS

So far we have restricted our discussion of missing premises to short arguments. Longer arguments will present additional challenges due to their relative size and complexity. A given extended argument may contain many sub-arguments which may themselves individually require reconstruction. Let's work our way up the scale of length and complexity slowly, starting with an example only slightly longer and more complex than that fishy argument about whales:

> [President Reagan promised to balance the federal budget by 1984.①] *But* [in his first term of office he succeeded in multiplying the budget deficit by over 250 percent.②] *And* [he refused to seriously address the issue of the budget deficit throughout the 1984 reelection campaign.③] *But since* [such behavior evidently amounts to a betrayal of the public trust,④] [President Reagan was unworthy of reelection.⑤]

This argument contains five explicit claims, the last of which is the argument's main conclusion. The first three claims together support number 4, which, in turn supports the main conclusion. On the face of it, the argument could be cast as follows:

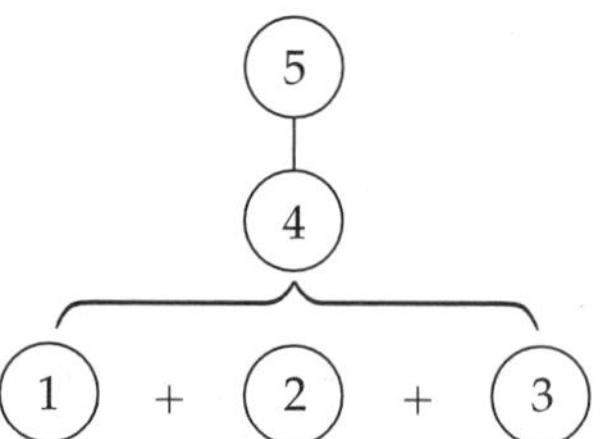


Does this argument involve any enthymemes? It does if *either* of its conclusions, claim 4 or claim 5 is not fully warranted by the support expressed, which we can tell by using the "what if" strategy.

Both the inference from claims 1, 2, and 3 to claim 4 and the inference from claim 4 to claim 5 are enthymemes. What if claims 1, 2, and 3 are all true? Does that guarantee that claim 4 is true? Suppose that President Reagan did make a campaign promise to balance the federal budget but instead multiplied the budget deficit by over 250 percent during his first term in office, and suppose also that he refused to seriously address this issue during the 1984 reelection campaign. It does not necessarily follow that this adds up to a betrayal of the public trust. It is possible that the rise in the deficit was due to factors beyond the president's control and that a frank public discussion of the issue during the 1984 campaign would have jeopardized a fragile economic balance. So claim 4 is still debatable. It is, however, worded somewhat cautiously. It says the president's record *evidently* adds up to a betrayal of the public trust. This gives us some guidance as to possible additional premises which the arguer may be appealing to:

**a.** In the absence of evidence to the contrary, such a record in office would add up to a betrayal of the public trust.

**b.** There is little or no evidence to the contrary.

Now let's consider the inference from claim 4 to claim 5. Again, the inference is an enthymeme. Even if it's true that President Reagan betrayed the public trust the question remains open as to whether he was worthy of reelection. That is, unless the arguer is also appealing to a general principle to the effect that

**c.** Any elected officer of the public trust who betrays that trust while in office is unworthy of reelection.

This would complete the sub-argument. It fits in well with both claim 4 and the argument's conclusion. As a principle, it is highly idealistic, though that doesn't make it implausible in the least. It does, however, raise a certain question concerning fidelity to the arguer's actual position. Many people would question the wisdom of claim *c* from the point of view of political pragmatism. But people who find the claim that betraying the public trust makes one unworthy of re-election to public office "too idealistic" or "impractical" or "unworkable" would be unlikely to make the sort of argument we're presently considering. It therefore remains reasonable to suppose that the arguer is committed to *c*, or to something very close to it, in arguing from claim 4 to claim 5. Thus the argument might be cast as follows:

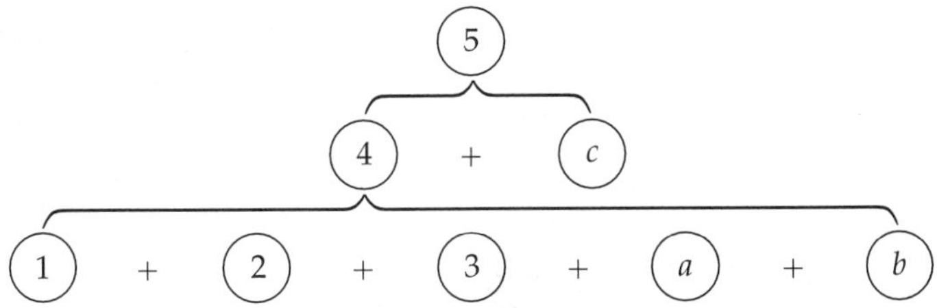


Now let us consider an even longer argument, which connects the increase in premarital sex with a reduction in teenage marriages and a subsequent reduction in the divorce rate:

> [Premarital sex is on the rise.①] [One study shows that sexual intercourse is initiated at a younger age②] *and that* [its occurrence among teenagers is increasing.③] *Another shows that* [the percent of married persons between the age of eighteen and twenty-four who had sexual experience prior to marriage was 95 percent for males and 81 percent for females.④] *Still another* [survey shows that of the sampled adolescents between ages thirteen and nineteen, 52 percent had had some premarital intercourse.⑤] [This increase in the prevalence of premarital sex is bound to reduce the number of teenage marriages.⑥] *Thus* [there will probably be a substantial decline in the divorce rate.⑦]

This argument consists of seven explicit assertions. (The second sentence offers two separate statements, each of which plays an important supporting role in the argument.) The main conclusion is claim 7, which the arguer feels is implied by claim 6. This claim is supported by claim 1, which in turn is supported by claims 2, 3, 4, and 5. The argument, then, has two sub-arguments, which can be cast as follows:

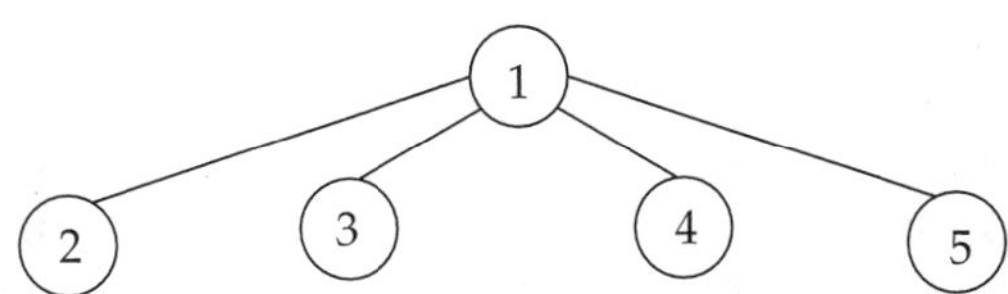

and

Taken on face, the entire argument may be cast:

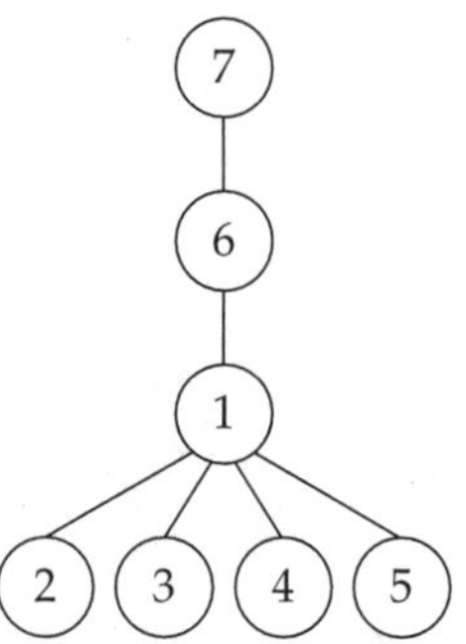

Does this argument involve any enthymemes? It does if *any* of its conclusions, claim 1, claim 6, or claim 7 is not warranted by the support expressed. To see if there are any unwarranted inferences, we can apply the "what if" strategy.

Claim 1 is inferred from a series of independent statistical references expressed in claims 2, 3, 4, and 5. What if these data are true? Must it then be true that "Premarital sex is on the rise"? If we concede that the data are up-to-date and typify the results of research in the field, then they do entail the inference. There is no point in reconstructing these concessions as assumptions because they merely repeat the argument. After all, the arguer presumably believes that these data are typical and current and that they support the mini-conclusion about the increased incidence of premarital sex. So we can take the data presented in mini-premises 2, 3, 4, and 5 as providing conclusive support for mini-conclusion 1. (Obviously, if we have reason to dispute the data as atypical or dated, then in evaluating the argument, we'd criticize them.)

Let's now turn to the second sub-argument, in which claim 6 is inferred from claim 1. *What if* it's true that premarital sex is on the rise? Must it then be true that teenage marriages will be reduced; that is, that the age of the average couple at marriage will be older than it was, say, in the immediately preceding generation? Not necessarily. Why couldn't premarital sex just as likely encourage teenagers to marry *earlier?* It's possible that, having satisfied themselves that they are sexually compatible, a couple might be more inclined to marry than if they hadn't. Or because they are having premarital sex, a couple might be inclined to marry rather than risk having a baby or facing an abortion decision outside marriage. Thus the premise that premarital sex is on the rise doesn't by itself warrant the conclusion that teenage marriages will decline. What, then, gets us from claim 1 to claim 6? What must the arguer be assuming that will complete the sub-argument "Premarital sex is on the rise. . . . This . . . is bound to reduce the number of teenage marriages"?

The reconstruction should link premarital sex with a reduction in the number of teenage marriages. It should be strong enough to support the conclusion but not so strong that it overstates the case. And it should not merely repeat the argument in an ad hoc fashion.

Here are three possible reconstructions:

**Reconstruction 1** Whenever premarital sex is on the rise, marriages are bound to be delayed.

**Reconstruction 2** Premarital sex discourages people from marrying.

**Reconstruction 3** Premarital sex discourages teenagers from marrying.

Reconstruction 1 merely repeats the argument. We are still left wondering why premarital sex is bound to delay marriage. Reconstruction 2 looks better, but it's too strong. Taken together with claim 1, it would yield the conclusion that there will be fewer marriages, or something to that effect. But the arguer infers only that *teenage* marriages will be reduced. Young people may marry later; they won't stop marrying altogether. Reconstruction 3 expresses what needs to be covered. It connects premarital sex and teenage marriages. It is strong enough to help produce the conclusion without overstating the case. And, unlike reconstruction 1, it illuminates rather than repeats. With the help of reconstruction 3, we see how the arguer was led to claim 6 from the expressed premise 1. The second sub-argument, therefore, can be diagrammed as follows:

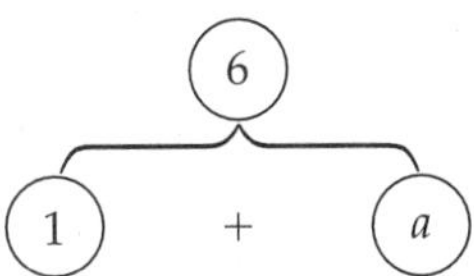


where "a" is taken to mean reconstruction 3 in our list of candidates.

The arguer then moves from claim 6 that "the prevalence of premarital sex is bound to reduce the number of teenage marriages" to the argument's main conclusion, claim 7, that "there will be a substantial decline in the divorce rate."

You needn't be a professional logician to sense a considerable leap of logic between claims 6 and 7. The conclusion covers a decline in the divorce rate but the premise mentions nothing of this. Why will a reduction in teenage marriages produce a substantial reduction in the number of divorces? Clearly the arguer must be making at least one other assumption *b*, which together with claim 6, helps provide support for the conclusion, claim 7. Here are four possible reconstructions for the missing premise *b:*

Reconstruction 1: If the number of teenage marriages is reduced the divorce rate likely will decline substantially.

**Reconstruction 2** Teenage marriages end in divorce.

**Reconstruction 3** A substantial number of teenage marriages end in divorce.

**Reconstruction 4** A substantial number of divorces involve teenage marriages.

Reconstruction 1 merely repeats the argument; it doesn't illuminate it. We're still left wondering "But why will a reduction in teenage marriages likely lead to a substantial decline in divorce?" Reconstruction 2 supplies an answer: Teenage marriages result in divorce. The problem, however, is that this reconstruction is a sweeping generalization. It's not very plausible and it overstates the case. Not all teenage marriages end in divorce. And even if they did, a reduction in teenage marriages wouldn't necessarily produce a *substantial* decline in the number of divorces. This last observation applies equally to reconstruction 3, though 3 is somewhat more plausible than 2.

To illustrate this point, let's say that 75 percent of teenage marriages fail; that is, a substantial number of teenage marriages end in divorce (reconstruction 3). Let's further say that these divorces account for only 2 percent of the total number of divorces; the other 98 percent involves nonteenage marriages. If this were the case, then reducing the number of teenage marriages would not produce a *substantial* decline in the divorce rate. But the conclusion of this argument implies that a substantial percentage of the total divorce rate involves teenage marriages. Reconstruction 3 misses this point; it merely asserts that a lot of teenage marriages end in divorce. Thus, if the number of such marriages can be reduced, then the number of divorces will decline, assuming that everything else remains constant. But will they decline *substantially?* They will do so only if teenage marriages contribute *substantially* to the total number of divorces.

Reconstruction 4 covers this point. It rightly focuses on the contribution teenage marriages make to the total divorce picture and not on the number of teenage marriages ending in divorce, as reconstructions 2 and 3 do. In addition it is strong enough to help support the conclusion but not so strong that it overstates the case, as does reconstruction 3. If it's true that a substantial number of divorces involve teenage marriages (reconstruction 4) and that the number of teenage marriages will decline (claim 6), it must be true that the divorce rate probably will decline (claim 7). The diagram for this sub-argument, therefore, would be:

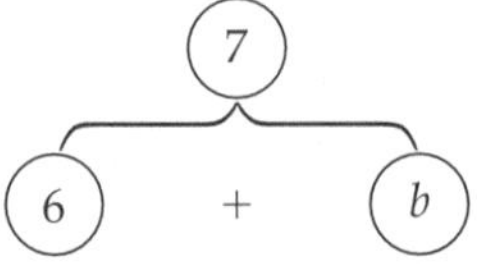

where *b* is now taken to mean reconstruction 4 in our list of candidates. The diagram for the entire argument would be:

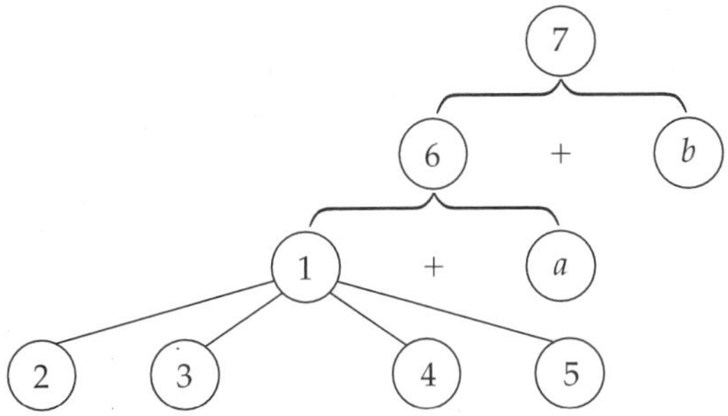


## ADDITIONAL EXERCISES

The following arguments contain at least one missing premise and possibly more. Fill in the missing premise (or premises) and cast the argument.

1. God has all the virtues. Therefore, God is benevolent.
2. Prime-time television encourages sexism because it reinforces gender stereotypes.
3. It's little wonder that many ads are misleading. They are geared primarily to selling us something.
4. *X-Files* director Kim Manners: I feel that since we are doing a science fiction show, morals don't enter into it—because none of it is true.
5. Abortion is legal. It's also a way of preventing unwanted, unloved babies from being born. Abortion is therefore morally acceptable.
6. There's no evidence that capital punishment deters crime. So it should be outlawed. Besides, capital punishment is barbaric.
7. Add naught to MacNaughton—because you don't dilute a great Canadian Whisky.
8. Inasmuch as a college education increases one's earning potential, it's wise to get that degree. A degree provides uncommon social opportunities and testifies to one's persistence and self-discipline, two time-honored character qualities.
9. Because they see it as a hedge against malpractice suits, doctors typically welcome a patient's informed consent.

**10.** Imperialist is a dirty word, all right, but it hardly fits a nation like the United States which, with all our faults, is ready to give millions of dollars to help starving and dying Cambodians. —William Randolph Hearst Jr.[2]

**11.** Former Michigan Governor George Romney, in describing the Equal Rights Amendment as a "moral perversion": Surely this resolution and its supporting statements are designed to legitimize sex and social relationships other than those that form the basis of divinely ordained marriage, parenthood and home.[3]

**12.** The Roman Catholic Diocese of Phoenix has refused to marry a couple because the man is a quadriplegic unable to consummate the union. He retains some use of his arms and hands, but is paralyzed from the chest down.[4]

**13.** Studies indicate that sexual harassment is increasing, not abating, on the job. So even though we fancy ourselves "enlightened," we have a long way to travel down the road to sexual equality. Employers need to sensitize workers to the many subtle, even unconscious, forms of sexual harassment in order to ensure that we start practicing as individuals what we preach as a nation: fair play in the workplace.

**14.** If you want to complain about Marilyn Manson, start from the beginning. Start with Shakespeare. What was *Romeo and Juliet* about? Suicide! —Ozzy Osbourne[5]

**15.** Murphy's law of [computer] programming states that no nontrivial program is free of bugs. A corollary states that any program with more than ten lines is by definition nontrivial. The bottom line—your program will have bugs. —Daniel Appleman[6]

**16.** Even though they'll rarely admit it, little boys do like little girls. . . . A little boy, the acknowledged "tough guy" in the class, found a dead snake on the playground. To the accompaniment of cheers and jeers from the other boys, he picked it up and slung it carelessly around his neck. Then he marched purposefully across the playground to where the girls were huddled, shrieking and squealing. Unerringly he sought her out, the loudest squealer of them all, and stopped in front of her. In the silence that followed, the young lover cast his trophy at the feet of his beloved. Secure in the knowledge that he had bestowed a gift of inestimable value, he turned and strode away, while behind him the shrieks and squeals of outraged femininity broke out anew. —Joan C. Roloff and Virginia Brosseit[7]

**17.** After thirteen years in universities, trying to teach writing and literature, I am convinced it is impossible to teach anyone to write, compose, paint, sculpt, or innovate creatively. With luck, you might get across minor techniques, or perhaps elementary craftsmanship suitable for low skill level commercial production. And, of course, you can teach about art and creativity and perhaps inspire self-confidence in individuals who already possess innate creative abilities. You can also teach individuals to recognize and appreciate perceptual innovation and significance. And, of course, you can teach about the importance of creativity in our cultural heritage. But no one can be taught to create a significant human experience in any media form. —Wilson Bryan Key[8]

**18.** In spite of the menacing developments (nuclear weapons, overpopulation, biological and psycho-pharmacological engineering, hibernation, changes in the environment), we remain unable to forecast the social consequences of technology. . . . Scientists are aware of the technological possibilities but are not sufficiently sensitive to their social implications. Some of the scientists care only about the success of their favorite projects. Some apply to these problems a personal pseudo-sociology made useless by its arrogance or naiveté. And still others dodge responsibility by arguing that technology itself is neither good nor bad, that its virtues are determined by its uses. —D. N. Michael[9]

**19.** The medical professional undoubtedly has special skills for determining and applying the specific criteria that measure whether particular body functions have irreversibly ceased. Whether the Harvard criteria [i.e., criteria that define death largely in terms of the absence of brain activity] taken together accurately divide those who are in irreversible coma from those who are not is clearly an empirical question (although the important consideration of just how sure we want to be takes us once again into matters that cannot be answered scientifically). But the crucial policy question is at the conceptual level: should the individual in irreversible coma be treated as dead? . . . If I am to be pronounced dead by the use of a philosophical or theological concept that I do not share, I at least have a right to careful due process. Physicians in the states that do not authorize brain-oriented criteria for pronouncing death who take it upon themselves to use those criteria . . . should be . . . prosecuted. —Robert M. Veatch[10]

**20.** At its heart, the question of whether the sane can be distinguished from the insane (and whether degrees of insanity can be distinguished from each other) is a simple matter: do the salient characteristics that lead to diagnoses reside in the patients themselves or in the environments and contexts in which observers find them? . . . Gains can be made in deciding which of these is more nearly accurate by getting normal people (that is, people who do not have, and have never suffered, symptoms of serious psychiatric disorders) admitted to psychiatric hospitals and then determining whether they were discovered to be sane and, if so, how. If the sanity of such pseudo-patients were always detected, there would be prima facie evidence that a sane individual can be distinguished from the insane context in which he is found. . . . If, on the other hand, the sanity of the pseudo-patients were never discovered, . . . this would support the view that psychiatric diagnosis betrays little about the patient but much about the environment in which an observer finds him. —D. L. Rosenhan[11]

**21.** No matter what my conviction may be as to the advisability of abortion for a given patient, it is overruled by my adherence to the principle of autonomy. By this I mean that we should support the adolescent patient in her autonomous decision making. [We must ask] questions in an unbiased fashion. (If we can't do this, our obligation is to refer the patient to someone else.) This approach may increase the anxiety and suffering of the patient. . . . The increased anxiety . . . may lead to further exploration, reading of material on abortion, talking to people who agree or disagree with her, etc. She will then make a decision with more understanding. . . . By guiding the adolescent not to avoid stressful questions, . . . a counselor also is preparing her for a better future. The tragedy of the adolescent facing the abortion decision is that she has to choose between the "sin of aborting" and the "sin of harming one's life." In her dilemma the adolescent might have to "sin boldly." —Thomas Silber[12]

**22.** Let us now examine the Golden Rule ["Do unto others as you would have them do unto you"] in terms of its clarity. . . . We might begin by asking about the unit of action. Are the actions implied by the rule [those of] a person or persons, groups or some larger social [unit]? Are you and the others in the Golden Rule to be seen as representatives of various social units or as independent citizens or persons in their own right, or does it make a difference? Of course the word "do" in the Golden Rule can mean many things too, and as usually interpreted all behaviors are included. Another thing which is not too clear has to do with the adequacy of resources. In most human situations there is a scarcity of resources. . . . We know from the research in psychology that emotional and situational factors, among others, can alter and distort what is perceived to be done to oneself, this seemingly inviting considerable distortion and error. And of course the Golden Rule is not very clear as to how one measures the consequences which arise by using it. Do we look at both mental and physical consequences, how does the time dimension come in, and so on? . . . I believe that we have demonstrated that the Golden Rule cannot be taken as a categorical imperative. —Craig C. Lundberg[13]

**23.** The photograph shows a strange cloud of dust billowing up from the surface of Io, one of the moons of Jupiter. At first thought to be debris thrown up by an impacting meteor, further computer enhancement and analysis showed that it was in fact the result of a volcanic eruption. Jupiter, then, has at least one moon which is still geologically active.[14]

**24.** In policy debates one party sometimes charges that his or her opponents are embracing a Nazi-like position. . . . Meanwhile, sympathizers nod in agreement with the charge, seeing it as the ultimate blow to their opponents. . . . The problem with using the Nazi analogy in public policy debates is that in the Western world there is a form of anti-Nazi "bigotry" that sees Nazis as almost mythically evil beings. . . . Firsthand knowledge of our own culture makes it virtually impossible to equate Nazi society with our own. The official racism of Germany, its military mentality, the stresses of war, and the presence of a dictator instead of a democratic system make Nazi Germany in the 1940s obviously different from America in the 1980s. —Gary E. Crum[15]

## GLOSSARY

**enthymeme** an argument containing an inferential assumption
**paraphrase** a reformulation intended to capture the same meaning
**plausibility** the credibility or believability of an idea which we estimate as likely to survive critical scrutiny
**relevant** related to the topics under discussion

## NOTES

[1] This example is adapted from Howard Kahane, *Logic and Contemporary Rhetoric,* 4th ed., (Belmont, Calif.: Wadsworth, 1984), p. 6.

[2] William Randolph Hearst Jr., *Los Angeles Herald Examiner,* November 4, 1979, p. F3.

[3] Associated Press release, January 2, 1980.

[4] "Church Refuses to Marry Couple," *Birmingham Post-Herald,* July 5, 1982.

[5] Ozzy Osbourne, *Rolling Stone Magazine,* no. 763, p. 28.

[6] Daniel Appleman, *How Computer Programming Works,* (Emeryville, Calif.: Ziff-Davis Press, 1994).

[7] Joan C. Roloff and Virginia Brosseit, *Paragraphs* (Encino, Calif.: Glencoe, 1979), pp. 109–110.

[8] Wilson Bryan Key, *The Clam-Plate Orgy and Other Subliminal Techniques for Manipulating Your Behavior* (New York: New American Library, 1980), p. 69.

[9] D. N. Michael, "Science, Scientists, and Politics," in Willis H. Truitt and T. W. Graham Solomons, eds., *Science, Technology and Freedom* (Boston: Houghton Mifflin, 1974), p. 180.

[10] Robert M. Veatch, *Death, Dying and the Biological Revolution* (Englewood Cliffs, N.J.: Prentice-Hall, 1978), p. 75.

[11] D. L. Rosenhan, "On Being Sane in Insane Places," *Science* 179 (January 19, 1973): 251.

[12] Thomas Silber, "Abortion in Adolescence: The Ethical Dimension," *Adolescence* 15 (Summer 1980): 467.

[13] Craig C. Lundberg, "The Golden Rule and Business Management: Quo Vadis?" *Economic and Business Bulletin* 20 (January 1968): 39–40.

[14] "Update on Space Exploration," *Theorist,* Fall, 1983.

[15] Gary E. Crum, "Disputed Territory" *Hastings Center Report,* August–September 1988, p. 31.

# PART THREE Evaluation

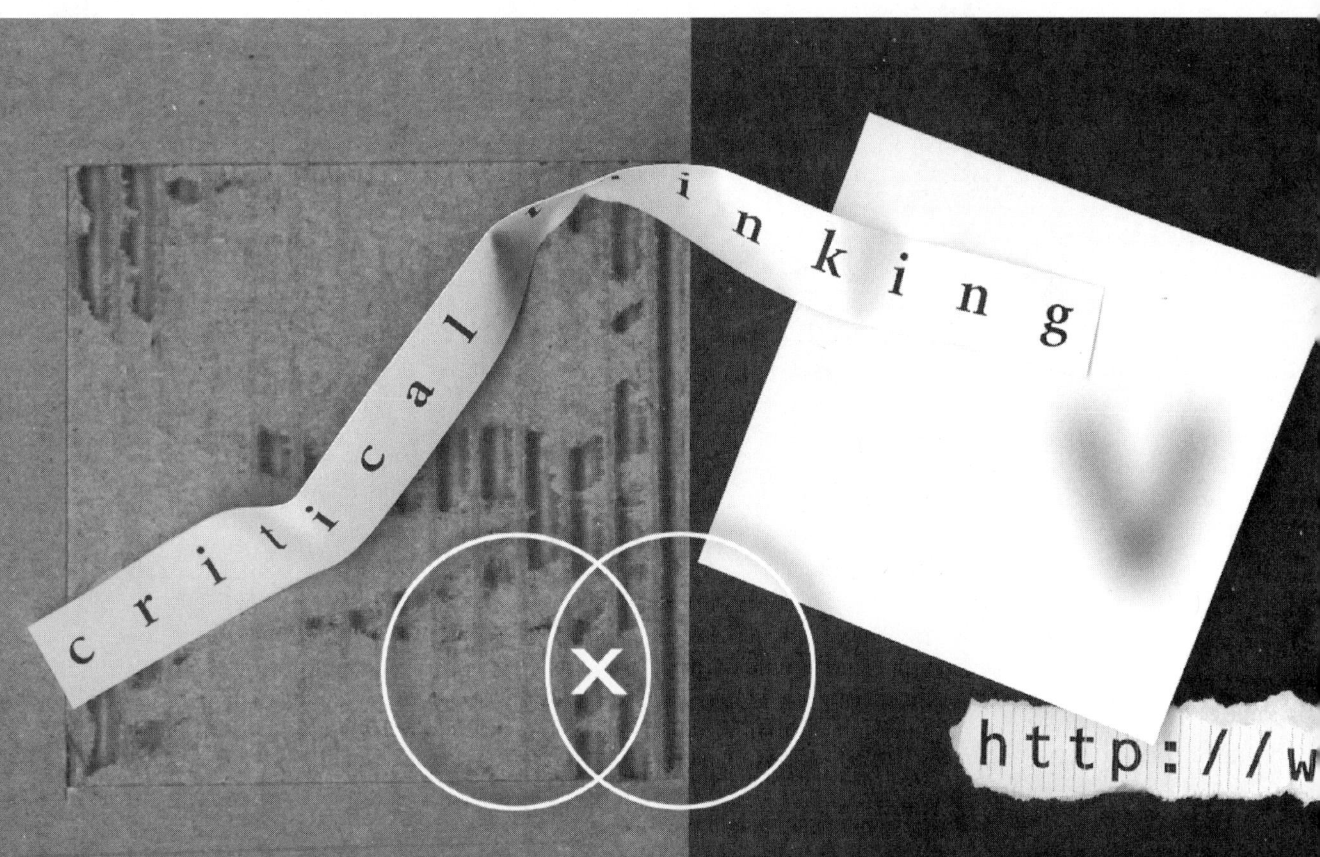

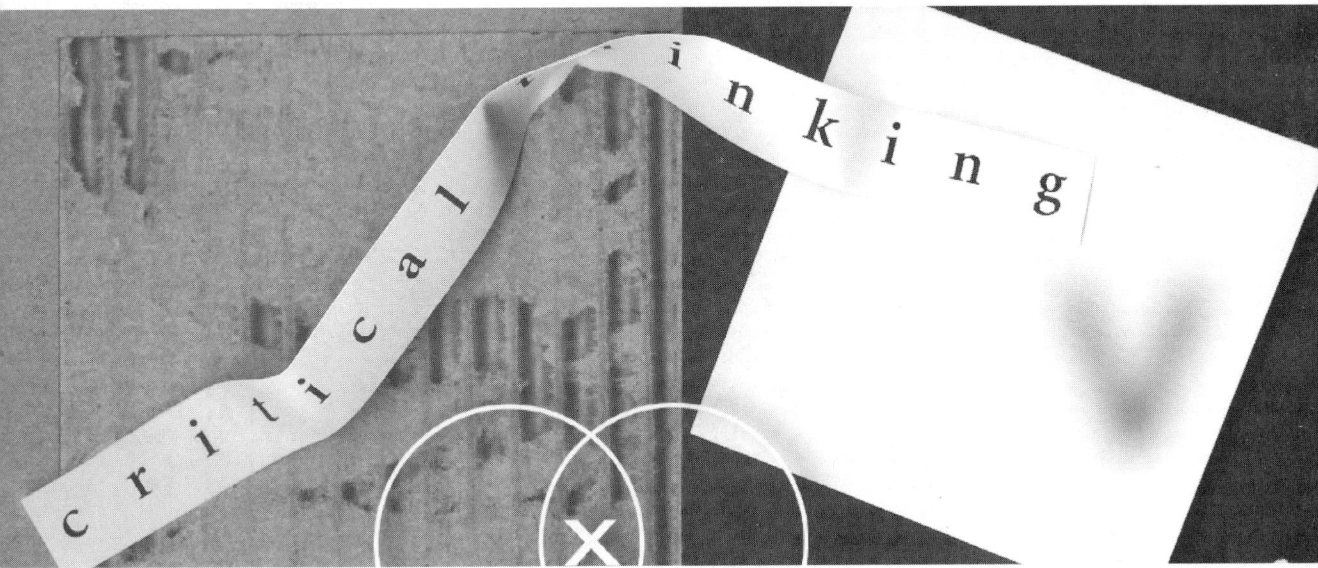


# CHAPTER 6 Evaluating Arguments I: Deduction

Now that we have covered argument identification and analysis, we are ready to address the evaluation of arguments. Most of us intuitively recognize qualitative differences between arguments, especially where the differences are relatively great. That is to say, we have little difficulty in intuitively recognizing the superiority of an excellent argument to one that is extremely weak. But our intuitions may fail to guide us where competing arguments are more closely matched. Different people often have conflicting intuitions about which of two closely matched competing arguments is superior, and we may even experience conflicting intuitions ourselves individually. Nor do our intuitions help us explain our evaluative judgments. So, we need a bit of theory to support, to guide, and to explain our evaluative intuitions.

So, for theoretical purposes we'll make a basic distinction between the structural features of an argument and the materials used in its construction. One way to understand this distinction is to think of an argument as a building. Now suppose we are evaluating buildings; for example, suppose we're buying a house. Some houses are obviously and intuitively better built than others. We can tell "intuitively" that the White House is a stronger building than an outhouse. But

*"I shall now punch a huge hole in your argument."*



we need a more systematic set of criteria to make reasonable decisions where houses are more closely matched. Buildings are complicated, so there are many criteria relevant to evaluating buildings. That's why we would want to make the set of criteria "systematic." The system gives us organization. One way to organize is to divide. And with buildings, a reasonable and powerful first distinction for purposes of evaluation would be between the materials used and the construction, which would include the design or blueprint and the assembly. So also in evaluating arguments we will sort things into "materials factors" and "construction/design factors." In this comparison (or analogy) the "materials" are the premises of the argument, the "design" is the plan according to which the premises are assembled in support of the conclusion, and of course the "construction" is the execution of the design.

## SOUNDNESS AND COGENCY

Now let us suppose further that there are two basic design strategies for arguments. This would enable us to further systematize our evaluative theory. We would need a set of criteria for evaluating argument design and construction in each of the two main design categories and a set of criteria for evaluating materials. There you have it: a preview of Chapters 6, 7, and 8. In Chapter 6 we will develop a set of criteria for evaluating the design and construction of deductive arguments. *We will use the term "sound" to indicate well designed and constructed ("valid") deductive arguments based on true or acceptable premises.* A deductive argument which is either "invalid" (faulty in design and/or construction) or based on false or dubious premises we will call "unsound." In Chapter 7 we will develop a set of criteria for evaluating the design and construction of inductive arguments. *We will use the term "cogent" to describe well designed and constructed ("strong") inductive arguments based on true or acceptable premises.* An inductive argument which is either "weak" (faulty in design and/or construction) or based on false or dubious premises we will call "not cogent." In Chapter 8 we will discuss criteria for evaluating premises.

## DEDUCTIVE AND INDUCTIVE REASONING

First we need to distinguish between the two main argument design categories: deductive and inductive. Consider the following two examples:

1. Your neighbor, Jones, is a member of the American Association of University Professors. Only members of the faculties of accredited colleges and universities are eligible for membership in the American Association of University Professors. Therefore your neighbor, Jones, is a college professor.
2. Your neighbor, Jones, wears a tweed sport coat with patches on the elbows; and he carries a battered briefcase; and he rides his bicycle to the college campus every day. Therefore your neighbor, Jones, is a college professor.

Deductive reasoning is designed and intended to secure its conclusion with the kind and degree of certainty illustrated by example 1 above. Inductive reasoning is designed to lend to its conclusion the kind of support illustrated in example 2 above. Notice how much stronger the connection is between the premises and conclusion in the first example as compared with the second example. In the first example we could say that anyone who fully understands what the statements in the argument mean must recognize that the premises cannot both be true without the conclusion also being true. But that is not the case with the second argument. In the second example we could say at most that the premises, if true, make the conclusion reasonable or likely. As we'll go on to explain more fully in the next two chapters, deductive reasoning, when it is well designed and constructed ("valid"), completely eliminates all risk of error in the inferential move from the premises to the conclusion, whereas in inductive reasoning, the truth of the premises makes the conclusion reasonable, probable, or likely, but not certain. This difference between deduction and induction will be reflected in different sets of evaluative criteria. Accordingly, an early step in the process of evaluating arguments is deciding which set of criteria should be applied, or in other words, whether the argument should be evaluated as a deduction or as an induction.

Before we address this question, we'd better clear up an old and widespread misunderstanding about what the essential difference is between induction and deduction. It is often said that deduction moves from general premises to particular conclusions, while induction moves in the opposite direction from particular premises to general conclusions. It is true of *some* deductive inferences that they move from general premises to particular conclusions. But it's not an essential distinguishing feature of all deductions. For example:

> Ford Motor Company has reported record profits for last year. General Motors has reported record profits for last year. And Chrysler has reported record profits for last year. Therefore all of the major U.S. auto manufacturers made money last year.

is a deductive argument with particular premises and a general conclusion. Similarly, it is true of *some* inductive inferences that they move from particular premises to general conclusions. But it's not an essential distinguishing feature of all inductions. For example:

> All United States presidents have so far been men. Therefore it is likely that the next United States president will be a man.

is an inductive argument with a general premise and a particular conclusion.

## DEDUCTIVE AND INDUCTIVE SIGNAL WORDS

Just as the presence of arguments, premises and conclusions are frequently indicated by means of signal words, so the modality of the inference, that is, whether it is intended as a deductive or an inductive one, is often indicated by signal words. Deductive signals include:

certainly
necessarily
must

For example:

> Your neighbor, Jones, is a member of the American Association of University Professors. Only members of the faculties of accredited colleges and universities are eligible for membership in the American Association of University Professors. Therefore your neighbor, Jones, *must be* a college professor.

Inductive signals include:

probably
in all likelihood
chances are
it is reasonable to suppose that
it's a good bet that

For example:

> Your neighbor, Jones, wears a tweed sport coat with patches on the elbows; and he carries a battered briefcase; and he rides his bicycle to the college campus every day. *I'd be willing to bet* your neighbor, Jones, is a college professor.

But just as with argument indicator words discussed so far, you need to be aware of the ambiguities and other nuances of meaning in context, in order to avoid overly mechanical readings of things. For example, even if someone said:

> Your neighbor, Jones, wears a tweed sport coat with patches on the elbows; and he carries a battered briefcase; and he rides his bicycle to the college campus every day. Therefore your neighbor, Jones, *must be* a college professor.

it would still be appropriate to evaluate the argument as an induction. A reasonable and charitable reading would interpret the speaker as having "overstated" the certainty of the conclusion relative to the premises. And similarly, if someone were to say:

> Your neighbor, Jones, is a member of the American Association of University Professors. Only members of the faculties of accredited colleges and universities are eligible for membership in the American Association of University Professors. *I'd be willing to bet* your neighbor, Jones, is a college professor.

it would be appropriate to evaluate the argument as a deduction. A reasonable and charitable reading would interpret the speaker as having "understated" the certainty of the conclusion relative to the premises.

## EXERCISE | Deductive and Inductive Arguments

For each of the following passages, indicate whether it is a deductive argument, an inductive argument, or not an argument.

| | Ded. | Ind. |
|---|---|---|
| Since tests proved that it took at least 2.3 seconds to operate the bolt of the rifle, Oswald obviously could not have fired three times—hitting Kennedy twice and Connally once—in 5.6 seconds or less. | | |
| At bottom, I did not believe I had touched that man. The law of probabilities decreed me guiltless of his blood. For in all my small experience with guns, I had never hit anything I had tried to hit, and I knew I had done my best to hit him. —Mark Twain | | |
| All of the leading economic indicators point toward further improvement in the economy. You can count on an improved third quarter. | | |
| During an interview with the school paper, Coach Danforth was quoted as saying, "I think it's safe to assume that Jason Israel will be our starting point guard next year. Both of our starting guards are graduating this spring and no one else on the team has Jason's speed and ball-handling skills." | | |

(continued)

| | Ded. | Ind. |
|---|---|---|
| The answers to many of the exercise sets in this book so far have been in the Critical Thinking tutorial. Chances are, the answers to this exercise set will be in the Critical Thinking tutorial as well. | | |

## ARGUMENT FORM

We turn now to the first of these two argument design categories, deduction, and the main criterion of design evaluation, validity. As a first step we must introduce the important notion of argument form. Consider the following argument:

> *Because* [all Americans are human ①] *and* [all humans are mortal, ②] *it follows that* [all Americans are mortal ③].

Casting the argument shows that premises 1 and 2 together support conclusion 3. But now we want to look more closely at the *way* in which the premises relate to the conclusion. Let us first represent the argument according to a conventional format:

(1) All Americans are humans.
(2) All humans are mortal.
_______________
∴ (3) All Americans are mortal.

In this format the premises are listed in order of their appearance above the solid line and the conclusion is listed below it. The symbol (∴) can be read as shorthand for "therefore." Notice that in this particular argument there appears to be a very strong connection between the conclusion and the premises: It is impossible to deny the conclusion without also denying at least one of the premises (or contradicting yourself). Try it.

Now consider a second example:

> [Rubies are corundum. ①] *And* [all corundum has a high refractive index. ②] *So* [all rubies have a high refractive index. ③]

Represented in the same conventional format, the argument looks like this:

(1) All rubies are corundum.
(2) All corundum has a high refractive index.
_______________
∴ (3) All rubies have a high refractive index.

Notice that here too the same very strong connection appears to exist between the conclusion and the premises. You might be less well acquainted with the optical properties and gemological classification of precious stones, but if you found out that all corundum has a high refractive index and all rubies are corundum, you would then *know* that all rubies have a high refractive index. (So if a particular stone has a low refractive index it *can't be* a ruby.) It would be impossible to deny this conclusion without also denying at least one of the premises (or contradicting yourself). Try it.

Now consider the following two statements:

(1) All primates are mammals.

(2) All mammals suckle their young.

Suppose these two statements are true. What conclusion could you draw from these two statements as premises?

(1) All primates are mammals.

(2) All mammals suckle their young.

---

∴ (a) ?

If you said, "All primates suckle their young," then notice once again that the same very strong connection appears to exist between your conclusion and the two premises.

Finally, suppose someone argues as follows:

[All propaganda is dangerous. ①] *That's why* [all network news is dangerous. ②]

From what you learned in previous chapters you can see that this argument depends on a missing premise, *a*.

(a) ?

(1) All propaganda is dangerous.

---

∴ (2) All network news is dangerous.

What is missing premise *a* ? (Use the topic coverage strategy if you need to.) No doubt you can see that the missing premise is "All network news is propaganda." Notice once again the very strong connection between the conclusion and the two premises. If you suppose that both premises are true you cannot deny the conclusion without contradicting yourself. Try it. You may have some doubt about the conclusion in this case. But if you doubt the truth of the conclusion, you must also doubt the truth of at least one of the premises.

Now let's reconsider the four examples we have just examined:

(1) All Americans are humans.
(2) All humans are mortal.
∴(3) All Americans are mortal.

(1) All rubies are corundum.
(2) All corundum has a high refractive index.
∴(3) All rubies have a high refractive index.

(1) All primates are mammals.
(2) All mammals suckle their young.
∴(a) ?

(a) ?
(1) All propaganda is dangerous.
∴(2) All network news is dangerous.

These four examples have something important in common. It is a single and simple common feature which explains not only how we can arrive at the conclusion in the third example that "All primates suckle their young" and how we can fill in the missing premise in the fourth example that "All network news is propaganda"; but most important it explains the very strong connection which holds between the conclusion of each of the four arguments and its premises. All four arguments follow the same pattern or form. Here is what the form looks like schematically:

(1) All A's are B's
(2) All B's are C's
∴ (3) All A's are C's

or

(1) All ______ are ______.
(2) All ______ are ______.
∴ (3) All ______ are ______.

## DEDUCTIVE VALIDITY

Deductive validity is another name for the kind of connection which holds between the conclusion and premises of arguments which follow this (or any other deductively valid) form. The essential property of a deductively valid argument form is this: If the premises of an argument which follows the form are taken to be true, then the conclusion of the argument (no matter what it is) must also be true. Because this is a feature of the form (or pattern) which an argument follows rather than of the argument's specific content, deductive validity is sometimes referred to as "formal validity."

Of course there are very many forms that arguments can follow. Some of them are so commonly used and well known that they have been given names. You just met a variation of Barbara. Barbara is a deductively valid form. This means that for any argument whatsoever, as long as it follows the form, accepting the premises forces you to accept the conclusion. Try it. Make some up. Even something as absurd as this:

(1) All snakes are fish.

(2) All fish can fly.

∴ (3) All snakes can fly.

## EXERCISE | Concept of Deductive Validity

| True | False | |
|---|---|---|
| | | A deductively valid argument can have a false conclusion. |

Explain or give an example.

| True | False | |
|---|---|---|
| | | A deductively valid argument can have false premises. |

Explain or give an example.

| True | False | |
|---|---|---|
| | | One cannot tell whether a deductive argument is valid without knowing whether its premises are actually true. |

Explain or give an example.

| True | False | |
|---|---|---|
| | | A deductively valid argument can have false premises and a true conclusion. |

Explain or give an example.

| True | False | |
|---|---|---|
| | | If a deductive argument is cogent, it may still be invalid. Explain or give an example. |

Explain or give an example.

## INVALIDITY

Deductively valid argument forms are important because they provide a guarantee that if the premises of the argument are true the conclusion must be as well. But not every form or pattern is deductively valid. Consider the following example:

(1) All Americans are human.

(2) All Californians are human.

∴ (3) All Californians are Americans.

Many people initially see nothing deficient in this as a piece of reasoning. This is probably because (1) they can see that the claims are in some way related to each other, and (2) they think that all three claims are true. But notice what happens if you ask whether the truth of the premises *guarantees* that the conclusion is true. Try the "what if" strategy here. Suppose the premises are true. Could the conclusion not still be false? For example, suppose that some Californians are not Americans. This possibility conflicts in no way with either premise 1 or premise 2. So accepting both premises does not *force* you to accept the conclusion.

If this is difficult to take in, consider this next example:

(1) All men are human.

(2) All women are human.

∴ (3) All women are men.

The falsity of this conclusion is obviously compatible with the truth of these two premises. But this argument follows the same form as the argument about Californians. Here is what the form looks like schematically:

| | | |
|---|---|---|
| (1) All A's are B's | | (1) All _______ are _______ . |
| (2) All C's are B's | or | (2) All _______ are _______ . |
| ∴ (3) All C's are A's | | ∴ (3) All _______ are _______ . |

Because it is possible for an argument following this form to move from true premises to a false conclusion, it is easy to see that this form is unreliable. The general name for an unreliable inference is "fallacy." An inference that is unreliable because it follows an unreliable form or pattern is said to be formally fallacious or to commit a formal fallacy.

## AN INTUITIVE TEST FOR DEDUCTIVE VALIDITY

The two argument forms we've just been studying resemble each other closely, yet one is deductively valid while the other is formally fallacious, and this is a crucial difference for the purposes of argument evaluation. It is therefore important to be able to reliably distinguish between deductively valid arguments and formally fallacious ones though they may look very much alike. One way to do this would be to memorize argument forms. But this proves to be an endless and unmanageable undertaking. Fortunately there is a relatively simple and reliable intuitive procedure for determining whether a particular argument is deductively valid, which derives from the essential property of deductively valid forms mentioned above. The procedure consists of asking:

> Can I assert the premises and deny the conclusion without contradicting myself?

If you cannot, if asserting the premises and denying the conclusion results in a contradiction, then the inference is deductively valid. If you can assert the premises and deny the conclusion without contradiction, the inference is not deductively valid.

## EXERCISE | Testing for Deductive Validity

Which of the following passages express or contain arguments? You can use either the functional or the structural definition of "argument" or both to make your determination.

| | V | Inv |
|---|---|---|
| Some entertainers abuse drugs, and all comedians are entertainers, so it stands to reason that some comedians are drug abusers. | | |
| Some college professors support the idea of a faculty union, an idea supported by many socialists. So at least some college professors must be socialists. | | |
| Everyone knows that whales live in the sea, and anything that lives in the sea is a fish. Therefore whales must be fish. | | |
| All artists are creative people. Some artists live in poverty. Therefore, some creative people live in poverty. | | |
| All of the justices on the Supreme Court are lawyers, and all members of the prestigious Washington Law Club are lawyers, so at least some of the Supreme Court justices are members of the Washington Law Club. | | |

## THE SCENARIO METHOD

Some people find the validity testing method just described difficult to conceptualize and tricky to keep straight. Here is a slightly weaker variation which may be easier to grasp intuitively. Try to imagine a scenario in which the premises are all true and the conclusion is false. If you can imagine such a scenario, then the inference is not deductively valid. For example, we can imagine a scenario in which the conclusion of the argument about Americans, Californians, and humans is false. Simply imagine that there are some Californians who are not also Americans. Imagine for example that there are some legal residents of the state of California who are not American citizens, let's say because they are foreigners married to Americans. Notice that both premises would still be true. Thus the scenario method shows that the argument is invalid. But be careful. If you can't imagine such a scenario, it doesn't necessarily mean that the inference is deductively valid. It may simply mean that you haven't been imaginative enough.

## EXERCISE | The Scenario Method

Use the scenario method to test the validity of the five arguments in the exercise on Testing for Deductive Validity.

| | V. | Inv. |
|---|---|---|
| Some entertainers abuse drugs, and all comedians are entertainers, so it stands to reason that some comedians are drug abusers. | | |
| Some college professors support the idea of a faculty union, an idea supported by many socialists. So at least some college professors must be socialists. | | |
| Everyone knows that whales live in the sea, and anything that lives in the sea is a fish. Therefore whales must be fish. | | |
| All artists are creative people. Some artists live in poverty. Therefore some creative people live in poverty. | | |
| All of the justices on the Supreme Court are lawyers, and all members of the prestigious Washington Law Club are lawyers, so at least some of the Supreme Court justices are members of the Washington Law Club. | | |

## CONSTRUCTING FORMAL ANALOGIES

One of the best procedures for demonstrating that an inference is unreliable, or fallacious, is to compose an inference which is analogous to it and which moves from premises which are obviously true to a conclusion which is obviously false. The example that concludes "All women are men," is formally analagous to, or follows the same pattern as, the example about Californians and Americans, but it moves from two premises each of which is obviously true to a conclusion which is just as obviously false. By means of this analogy we prove that the original argument—indeed any argument following this pattern—is fallacious.

Let's try these procedures on a couple of examples:

(1) Some entertainers abuse drugs.

(2) All comedians are entertainers.

---

∴ (3) Some comedians are drug abusers.

Is this a deductively valid argument? In other words, if we assert both of the premises and deny the conclusion does a contradiction result? Now it may well be true that some comedians abuse drugs, but does it follow from these two premises? No. It is possible for both of the premises to be true and the conclusion false. Let's try to imagine a scenario in which the premises are both true and the conclusion is false. Let's suppose it's true that some entertainers abuse drugs and that all comedians are entertainers. What kind of situation would be compatible with these two assumptions and yet incompatible with the conclusion? Well, suppose that all of the drug abusing entertainers just happen to be accordion players, while the rest of the entertainment industry is totally clean and sober. This may be hard to imagine because it is so at odds with what you may have heard. But it is *possible* to imagine it. Try it. Now notice that what you are imagining rules out the conclusion but is perfectly compatible with each of the premises. This shows that the conclusion does not *follow from* the premises.

Let's now try to demonstrate that this inference is fallacious by producing a formally analogous inference which moves from obviously true premises to an obviously false conclusion. Step one is to reveal the form of the argument. Using the letter "C" (or ______) to represent the category of comedians, the letter "A" (or ______) to represent the category of drug abusers, and the letter "E" (or ______) to represent the category of entertainers, we get from this:

(1) Some entertainers abuse drugs.
(2) All comedians are entertainers.

∴ (3) Some comedians are drug abusers.

to this:

| | | |
|---|---|---|
| (1) Some E's are A's | | (1) Some ______ are ______. |
| (2) All C's are E's | or | (2) All ______ are ______. |
| ∴ (3) Some C's are A's | | ∴ (3) Some ______ are ______. |

Now, starting with the conclusion, we substitute terms for the abstract placeholders in the formula. We want to pick terms which result in an obviously false conclusion. For example, let "C" (or ______) now stand for the category of fathers and let "A" (or ______) now stand for the category of women. That results in the obviously false conclusion that some fathers are women. Now simply substitute the same terms wherever the abstract placeholders "C" (or ______) and "A" (or ______) occur in the formula. This gives us:

| | |
|---|---|
| (1) Some E's are women. | (1) Some ______ are women. |
| (2) All fathers are E's | (2) All fathers are ______. |
| ∴ (3) Some fathers are women. | ∴ (3) Some fathers are women. |

Now all we need is a value for "E" (or ______) which would make both premises 1 and 2 true. Suppose we let "E" stand for the category of parents. That would give us:

(1) Some parents are women.
(2) All fathers are parents.

∴ (3) Some fathers are women.

Here's another example:

(1) Some books are mysteries.

(2) Some mysteries are entertaining.

---

∴ (3) Some books are entertaining.

Is this a deductively valid argument? In other words, if we assert both of the premises and deny the conclusion does a contradiction result? No, it is possible for both of the premises to be true and the conclusion false. This may be hard to appreciate especially if you think just about the conclusion and your actual experience. The conclusion is no doubt true as a matter of fact. But it does not *follow from* these two premises. It is possible to imagine a scenario in which both premises are true and the conclusion is false. Imagine, for example that no books are entertaining (in other words, imagine that the conclusion is false). This does not conflict with the first premise. It could easily be the case that some books are mysteries and that no books are entertaining. Nor does it conflict with the second premise. Suppose that all of the entertaining mysteries are movies.

Now let us demonstrate that this inference is fallacious by producing a formally analogous inference which moves from obviously true premises to an obviously false conclusion. First we reveal the form of the argument. Using the letter "B" (or ______) to represent the category of books, the letter "M" (or ______) to represent the category of mysteries, and the letter "E" (or ______) to represent the category of things which are entertaining, we get from this:

(1) Some books are mysteries.

(2) Some mysteries are entertaining.

---

∴ (3) Some books are entertaining.

to this:

(1) Some B's are M's

(2) Some M's are E's

---

∴ (3) Some B's are E's

or

(1) Some ______ are ______.

(2) Some ______ are ______.

---

∴ (3) Some ______ are ______.

Again, starting with the conclusion, we substitute terms for the abstract placeholders in the formula. We want to pick terms which result in an obviously false conclusion. For example, let "B" (or ______) now stand for the category of females, and let "E" (or ______) now stand for the category of males. That results in the obviously false conclusion that some females are male. Now simply substitute the same terms wherever the abstract placeholders "B" (or ______) and "E" (or ______) occur in the formula. This gives us:

| | | | |
|---|---|---|---|
| (1) | Some females are M's. | (1) | Some females are ______. |
| (2) | All M's are male. | (2) | All ______ are male. |
| ∴ (3) | Some females are male. | ∴ (3) | Some females are male. |

Now all we need is a value for "M" (or ______) which would make both premises 1 and 2 true. Again suppose we let the remaining term "M" stand for the category of parents. That would give us:

(1) Some females are parents.

(2) Some parents are male.

∴ (3) Some females are male.

## EXERCISE | Formal Analogies

For each of the *invalid* arguments in the Scenario Method exercise, construct a formally analogous argument which moves from obviously true premises to an obviously false conclusion.

| | Invalid Argument | Formally Analogous Argument |
|---|---|---|
| Premise | | |
| Premise | | |
| Conclusion | | |

| | Invalid Argument | Formally Analogous Argument |
|---|---|---|
| Premise | | |
| Premise | | |
| Conclusion | | |

| | Invalid Argument | Formally Analogous Argument |
|---|---|---|
| Premise | | |
| Premise | | |
| Conclusion | | |

| | Invalid Argument | Formally Analogous Argument |
|---|---|---|
| Premise | | |
| Premise | | |
| Conclusion | | |

## CATEGORICAL LOGIC

A "syllogism" is defined as a deductive inference from two premises. The argument forms we have been studying so far in this chapter are called "categorical syllogisms" because they are made up of "categorical statements" (statements about relationships between categories of things). The Greek philosopher Aristotle developed a relatively simple but very powerful system of logic based on categorical syllogisms. One of his insights was that anything one might want to say about the relationships between any two categories can be said in one of four ways. In other words, all categorical statements can be reduced to one of the four following standard forms:

| | Affirmative | | Negative |
|---|---|---|---|
| A: | Universal Affirmative | E: | Universal Negative |
| e.g. | All mothers are female. | e.g. | No fathers are female. |
| I: | Particular Affirmative | O: | Particular Negative |
| e.g. | Some women are mothers. | e.g. | Some women are not mothers. |

These forms are arranged above in a matrix which reflects two major distinctions cutting across each other.

The categorical statements in the left-hand column *affirm* an *inclusive* relationship between two categories. The categorical statements in the right-hand column each *deny* such a relationship between the two categories; the relationships they indicate are *exclusive*. This is traditionally understood as a "qualitative" distinction and is designated by the terms "affirmative" and "negative." The conventional designation of these statement forms by the letters "A," "E," "I" and "O" derives from this qualitative distinction via the Latin words ***A***ff***I***rmo ("I affirm") and n***E***g***O***, ("I deny").

The statements on the top line of the matrix assert the *total* inclusion or exclusion of an entire category in or from another. The statements on the bottom line of the matrix assert the *partial* inclusion or exclusion of one category in or from another. This is traditionally understood as a "quantitative" distinction and is designated by the terms "universal" and "particular."

A way to measure the "theoretical power" of a system would be to divide the number of cases that the system effectively covers by the size of the theoretical apparatus. By this measure, Aristotle's system of categorical logic is extremely powerful. Look at how elemental the theoretical apparatus is: two major distinctions—All (or None)/Some and Affirmative/Negative—yield four statement forms, which together cover pretty close to the entire range of statements about category relationships. This is bound to score way up on the scale of theoretical power.

### TRANSLATING INTO STANDARD FORM

However, there is a catch. Understandably the power of the system depends heavily on being able to translate the wide variety of things that people actually say about categories in their actual arguments into one or another of the four standard forms. But because language is so flexible and rich in possibilities, and because people are so imaginative and innovative—or is it rebellious and imprecise?—in their use of language, translation into standard form is a matter of some complexity and uncertainty, governed by a few general rules, which come complete with exceptions, and an indefinitely large set of interpretive guidelines, of which we will give you a short sample.

The general rules are:

1. Categorical statements begin with a "quantity indicator" ("all," "some," or "no").
2. There is a verb in the middle (either "are" or "are not") to indicate the "quality" of the statement (whether it is affirmative or negative).
3. There are two terms, each denoting a category. The term before the verb is called the "subject term," and the term after the verb is called the "predicate term." Subject and predicate terms must be nouns or noun phrases. For convenience below we will use angle brackets < > to set off the subject and predicate terms from the quantity and quality indicators in standard formulations of categorical statements.

The exceptions are:

1. You can't say "All <xxx's> are not <yyy's>" as in "All the computers on campus aren't IBM compatible." This formulation is unavailable because it is ambiguous. It could mean "Not all the computers on campus are IBM compatible" (which would be the same as saying, "*Some* of the computers on campus are *not* IBM compatible"); or it could mean "None of the computers on campus are IBM compatible." You have to decide whether the statement is supposed to say "Not *all* xxx's are yyy's" or "Not *any* xxx's are yyy's."

   If the meaning is "Not all xxx's are yyy's," use the "O" form: "Some <yyy's> are not <xxx's>."

   If the meaning is "Not any xxx's are yyy's," use the "E" form: "No <xxx's> are <yyy's>."
2. There are categorical statements about individuals. For example, "David Letterman is a talk show host"; or "The Artist Formerly Known as 'Prince' is a musician"; or "The World Series is an annual event." For all practical purposes (and especially because we are at the very beginning of the study of formal logic), it will work best for now to treat any statement like these as though it were a universal affirmative (or "A") categorical statement, even though there is only one real "category" involved. Categorical logic can handle such statements quite effectively if we pretend that we're talking for example about *all members of the category* "The Artist Formerly Known as 'Prince' " (a category of which there is only one member) when we say that he's in the category "musicians."

Interpretive guidelines include:

1. Turn adjectives into nouns or noun phrases. In some cases this is pretty straightforward and intuitive. For example,

   Bill Gates is wealthy.

   becomes

   <Bill Gates> is a <wealthy man>.

   Use the context to help determine how to formulate the noun phrase. For example, consider this context:

   Wealthy individuals enjoy disproportionate access to power. Bill Gates is wealthy. So he must have disproportionate access to power.

   The premise expressed in the second sentence makes the most sense if we interpret it to mean that Bill Gates is in precisely the category indicated by the subject term in the first sentence, <wealthy individuals>. Otherwise the logic of the inference is undermined. So here:

   Bill Gates is wealthy.

   becomes

   <Bill Gates> is a <wealthy individual>.

2. Turn verbs into nouns or noun phrases. Again, in some cases this is pretty straightforward and intuitive. For example:

   Deciduous plants shed their leaves.

   becomes

   All <deciduous plants> are <things which shed their leaves>.

   Use the context to help determine how to formulate the noun phrase. For example, consider this context:

   All dancing bears are performing animals. Smokey the Bear is dancing the tango. Therefore Smokey the Bear is a performing animal.

   The logic of the premise expressed in the second sentence only makes sense if we render it thus:

   <Smokey> is a <dancing bear>.

3. Use the grammar as a guide, but bear in mind that grammatical structure and logical structure often diverge. For example, in the sentence

   Happy is the man who finds work doing what he loves.

   the subject term <the man who finds work doing what he loves> is contained in the grammatical predicate. Also notice that although the subject term is grammatically singular, the meaning for the purposes of categorical logic is plural; "the man who finds work doing what he loves" is meant to stand for the whole category of people who find work doing what they love. So the standard formulation of this statement would be:

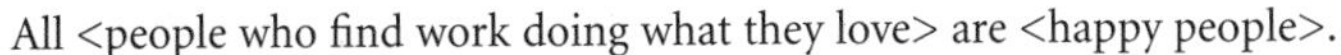
All <people who find work doing what they love> are <happy people>.

## EXERCISE | Translating Categorical Statements into Standard Form

For each example, use the scheme of abbreviation to translate into standard form.

| | | | |
|---|---|---|---|
| All computer hardware has a short shelf life. | C = Computer hardware | S = Things with short shelf life | |
| Some of my beliefs are false. | B = My beliefs | F = Things which are false | |
| One major corporation is Microsoft. | C = Major corporations | M = Microsoft | |
| Some of the members of Heaven's Gate were reasonable people. | M = Members of Heaven's Gate | R = Reasonable people | |
| Any discipline has rules, or at least regularities of some kind. | D = Disciplines | R = Things with rules or regularities | |
| El Niño is the cause of some of these abnormal weather patterns. | A = These abnormal weather patterns | N = Things caused by El Niño | |
| I like action movies. | A = Action movies | L = Things I like | |
| San Francisco is a city in California. | S = San Francisco | C = Cities in California | |
| My favorite actress is a Gemini. | F = My favorite actress | G = Geminis | |
| Answers to these exercises can be found in the Critical Thinking tutorial under Categorical Logic. | A = Answers to these exercises | C = Things that can be found in the Critical Thinking tutorial under Categorical Logic | |
| Dogs love trucks. | D = Dogs | L = Lovers of trucks | |

## IMMEDIATE INFERENCES AND THE SQUARE OF OPPOSITION

Let us now return to the matrix which we used earlier to introduce the four standard forms of categorical statements.

| | | | |
|---|---|---|---|
| A: | Universal Affirmative | E: | Universal Negative |
| e.g. | All <bonds> are <secure investments>. | e.g. | No <bonds> are <secure investments>. |
| I: | Particular Affirmative | O: | Particular Negative |
| e.g. | Some <bonds> are <secure investments>. | e.g. | Some <bonds> are not <secure investments>. |

This time we've used the same subject and predicate terms in all four examples so that we can concentrate entirely on differences in quality and quantity. Traditionally in categorical logic two categorical statements which differ from each other in quality or in quantity or both but which are otherwise the same are said to stand in "opposition" to each other. There are several kinds of "opposition," depending on whether the difference is one of quality or quantity or both. Let's start with what might be described as the "strongest" form of opposition.

Look at the "A" statement and the "O" statement together. Notice that they can't both be true, *and* they can't both be false. This kind of opposition is traditionally called "contradiction." Now look at the "E" and "I" statements together. Like the "A" and "O" statement pair, if either "E" or the "I" statement is true, the other one must be false; they also "contradict" each other.

Now look at the "A" statement and the "E" statement together. Notice that they can't both be true, but they *might* both be false. This is a somewhat weaker form of opposition than contradiction. This kind of opposition is traditionally called "contrariety." Two categorical statements which stand in this kind of opposition to each other are called "contraries" of each other.

Now look at the "I" statement and the "O" statement together. Notice that they *could* both be true, but they *can't* both be false. This kind of opposition is traditionally called "sub-contrariety." Two categorical statements which stand in this kind of opposition to each other are called "subcontraries" of each other.

There is something a little peculiar about the technical way in which logicians use the word "opposition." So far all of the different kinds of opposition we have discussed seem to involve some sort of "disagreement." But now if you look at the "A" and the "I" statements together you'll see that they seem to agree with each other. In fact, it seems reasonable to say that if the "A" statement is true, the "I" statement is also true, "by implication." For example, if it *is* true that all bonds are secure investments, it must surely be true that *some* bonds are secure investments as well. The same relationship also holds between "E" and "O" statements. For example, if it is true that no bonds are secure investments, it must surely be true as well that some bonds are *not* secure investments. Traditionally this kind of opposition is called "subalternation." If two categorical statements with the same subject and predicate terms agree in quality (are both affirmative or both negative) but differ in quantity, the universal statement implies its subalternate particular statement. Notice that this is a one-way relationship. The particular statement does not imply the universal statement. Even if it is true that some bonds are secure investments, that does not, all by itself, imply that *all* bonds are secure investments. Similarly, even if it is true that some bonds are *not* secure investments, that doesn't by itself imply that *no* bonds are secure investments.

We may summarize the above relationships in the following chart:

**SQUARE OF OPPOSITION**

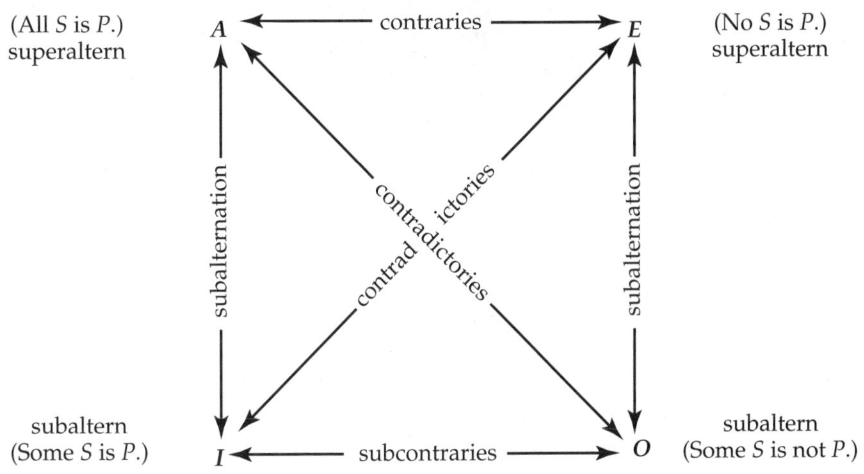

(All *S* is *P*.) superaltern — *A* ← contraries → *E* — (No *S* is *P*.) superaltern

*A* ↔ *I*: subalternation

*E* ↔ *O*: subalternation

*A* ↔ *O*: contradictories

*E* ↔ *I*: contradictories

subaltern (Some *S* is *P*.) — *I* ← subcontraries → *O* — subaltern (Some *S* is not *P*.)

Based on these relationships logic has traditionally recognized certain inferences as deductively valid:

> Assuming that a given "A" statement is true: its contradictory "O" statement is false; its contrary "E" statement is false; its subalternate "I" statement is true.
>
> Assuming that a given "E" statement is true: its contradictory "I" statement is false; its contrary "A" statement is false; its subalternate "O" statement is true.
>
> Assuming that a given "I" statement is true: its contradictory "E" statement is false.
>
> Assuming that a given "O" statement is true: its contradictory "A" statement is false.

Inferences such as these are traditionally referred to as "immediate," meaning that they proceed directly from a single categorical statement as a premise to a conclusion. Beyond such immediate inferences as these, categorical logic is concerned with categorical syllogisms, that is, inferences based on combinations of two categorical statements as premises, some of which, as we illustrated earlier in this chapter, are deductively valid, and some of which are not.

## VENN DIAGRAMS

British logician John Venn invented a graphic system for representing categorical statements and testing the validity of categorical syllogisms. The system consists of intersecting circles, each of which represents a category. A shaded area represents an area or category in which there are no particular examples or members. An X represents the existence of some particular examples or members of a category. The membership of an unmarked area is undetermined. This means that an area in a circle without any mark (without any shading or an X) may or may not have any members. Using two intersecting circles and these simple symbols we can represent any of the above four standard forms of categorical statements.

In the following Venn diagram, the circle on the left represents the category of Mothers and the circle on the right represents the category of Females. The shaded area indicates that there are no members of the category Mothers who are not also members of the category Females.

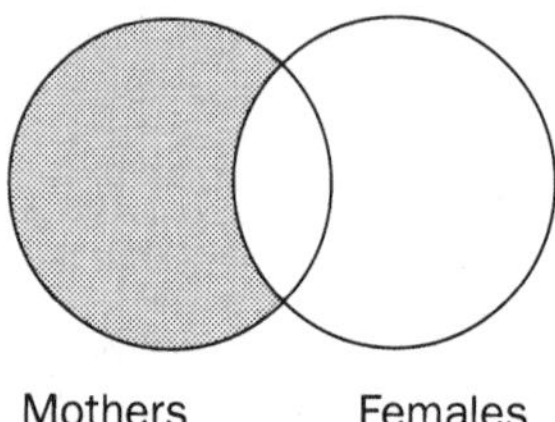


In the following diagram, the circle on the left represents the category of Fathers and the circle on the right represents the category of Females. The shaded area indicates that there are no members of the category Fathers who are also members of the category Females.

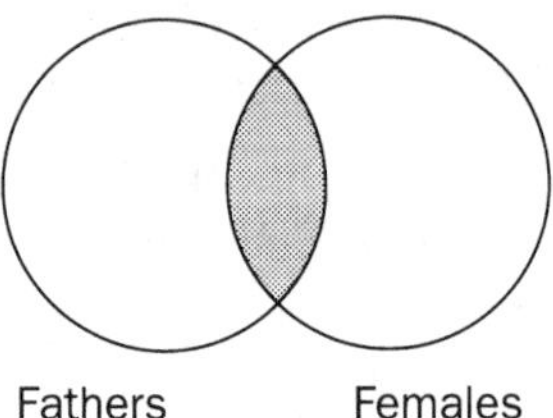


In each of the next two diagrams, the circle on the left represents the category of Women and the circle on the right represents the category of Mothers. In the first one, the X indicates that there are some members of the category Women who are also members of the category Mothers. Thus, it diagrams the statement that some women are mothers. In the second, the X indicates that there are some members of the category Women who are not also members of the category Mothers. Thus, it diagrams the statement that some women are not mothers.

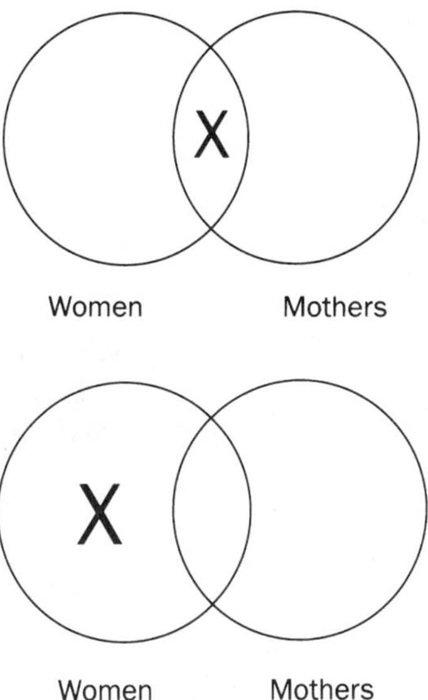


In a categorical syllogism there are three terms, corresponding to three categories, two of which appear in the conclusion. In a categorical syllogism each of the premises states a relationship between one of these two categories which appear in the conclusion and a common third (or "middle") category. Thus in order to diagram a categorical syllogism we need three intersecting circles, one for each of the categories in the conclusion and a third for the middle category, like this:

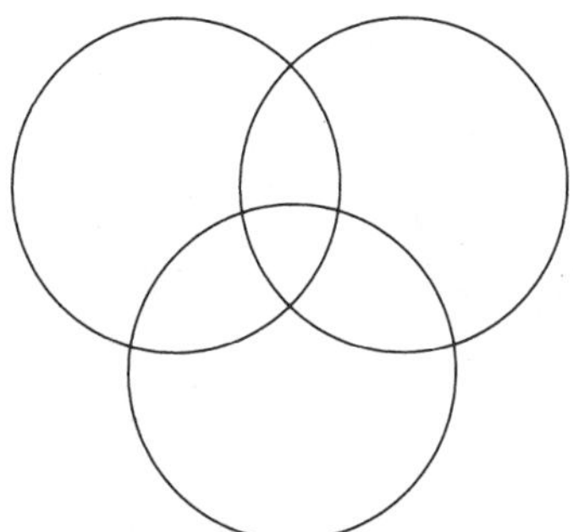

In using the diagram to test for the validity of categorical syllogisms we should remember what the essential characteristic of deductively valid arguments is: If the premises of an argument which follows the form are taken to be true, then the conclusion of the argument (no matter what it is) must also be true. In a certain important sense, the conclusion of a deductively valid inference is already "contained in" its premises. Thus, if we represent the information contained in the two premises in the diagram, the conclusion should automatically be represented as well, *if* the argument is a valid one. Let's try this with the first of the examples we considered in this chapter:

(1) All Americans are human.

(2) All humans are mortal.

∴ (3) All Americans are mortal.

In the following diagram, the circle on the left will represent the category of Americans, the circle on the right will represent the category of Mortals and the lower circle will represent the middle category of Humans.

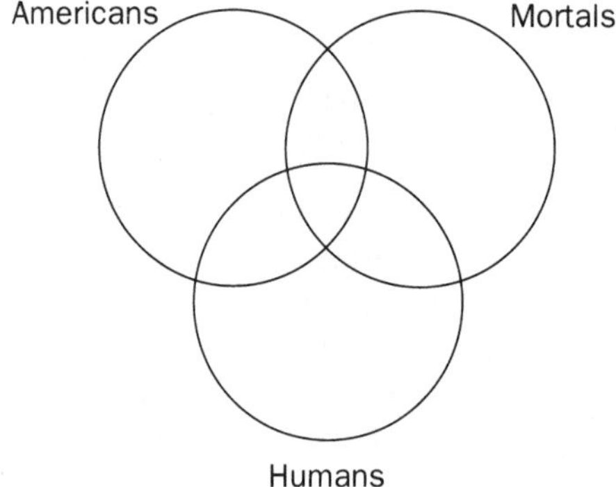


To represent premise 1 in the diagram, we shade in all of the Human circle except where it intersects with the Mortal circle:

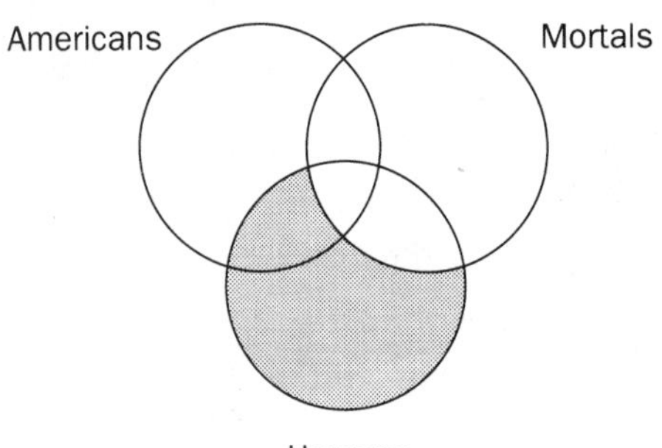


This indicates that there are no members of the category Humans who are not also members of the category Mortals. Similarly, we represent premise 2 in the diagram by shading in all of the American circle except where it intersects with the Human circle:

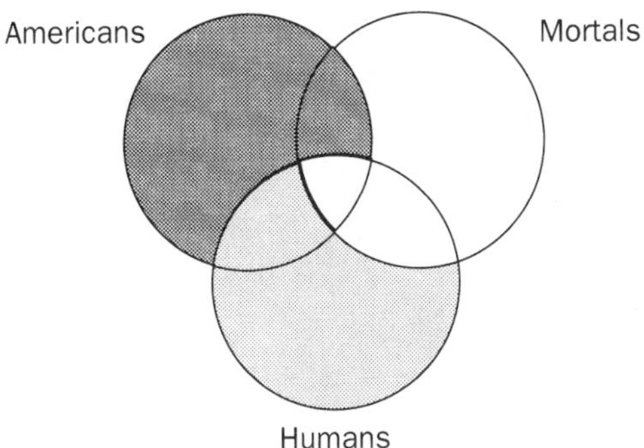


This indicates that there are no members of the category Americans who are not also members of the category Humans. Lo and behold, our diagram already represents the conclusion, because the area inside the American circle but outside its intersection with the Mortal circle is shaded in, which indicates that there are no members of the category Americans who are not also members of the category Mortals. Thus, our diagram demonstrates the validity of the inference.

Now let's try the same procedure with the first formally fallacious example we previously considered:

(1) All Americans are human.

(2) All Californians are human.

∴ (3) All Californians are Americans.

In the following diagram, we'll let the circle on the left represent the category of Californians, the circle on the right will represent the category of Americans and the lower circle will represent the middle category of Humans.

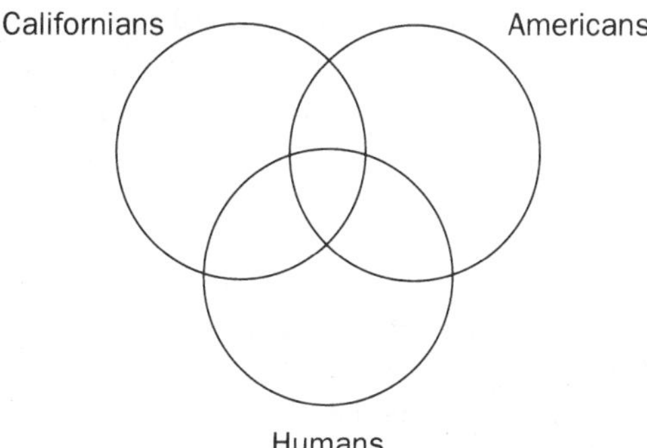


To represent premise 1, we shade in the entire area in the American circle except where it intersects with the circle of Humans, indicating that there are no members of the category Americans who are not also members of the category Humans.

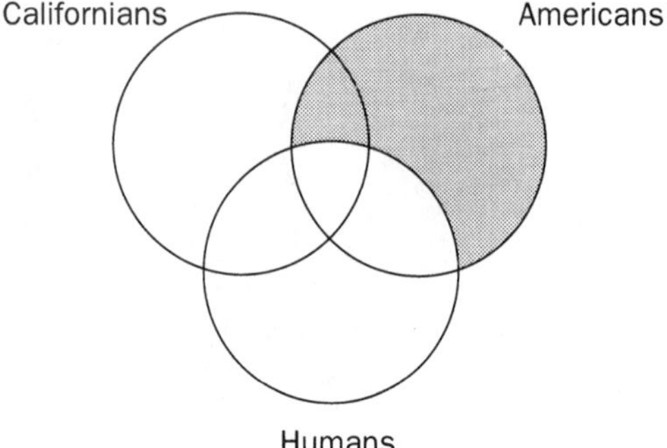


To represent premise 2 we shade in the entire Californian circle except where it intersects with the circle of Humans indicating that there are no members of the category Californians who are not also members of the category Humans.

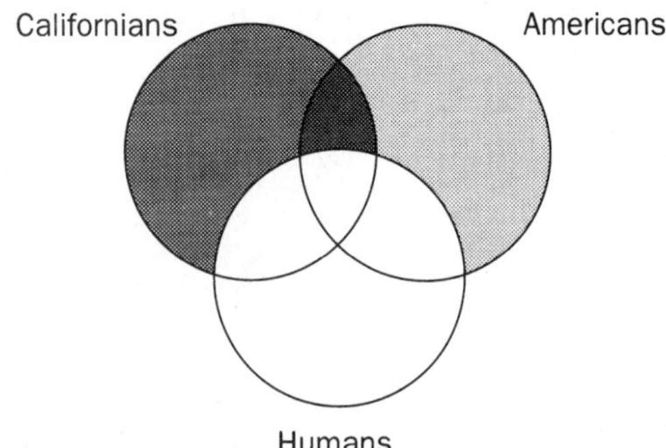


Does our diagram represent the conclusion that all Californians are American? It would if the entire area within the Californian circle were shaded in except where it intersects with the American circle. But there remains an unshaded area inside the Californian circle but outside the American circle, indicating that there *may be* some Californians who are not American. This shows that even if premises 1 and 2 are both true the possibility that the conclusion is false is still open. In other words the inference is not valid.

Some of you may still wonder *why* this is an invalid inference. This may be due to your awareness that California is part of the United States of America. So, you may be thinking, it's not possible to be a Californian without also being an American. But it *is* possible to be a Californian without being an American. One can be a legal, taxpaying, permanent resident of the state of California without being an American citizen. Suppose an American woman who resides in California marries a Frenchman and the couple chooses to reside in California but the husband retains his French citizenship. One can even be a *native-born,* legal, taxpaying, permanent resident of the state of California without being an American citizen. The main point here, however, is that these possibilities don't conflict with either of the premises of the inference. In other words, it's possible for the premises both to be true and the conclusion still to be false, which again, is what the Venn diagram shows.

We've now diagrammed two syllogisms involving universal categorical statements. Let's try a couple of examples involving particular categorical statements as well. First consider this:

(1) All entertainers love attention.

(2) Some drug abusers are entertainers.

∴ (3) Some drug abusers love attention.

In the next diagram, we'll let the circle on the left represent the category of Drug Abusers, the circle on the right will represent the category of Attention Lovers, and the lower circle will represent the middle category of Entertainers.

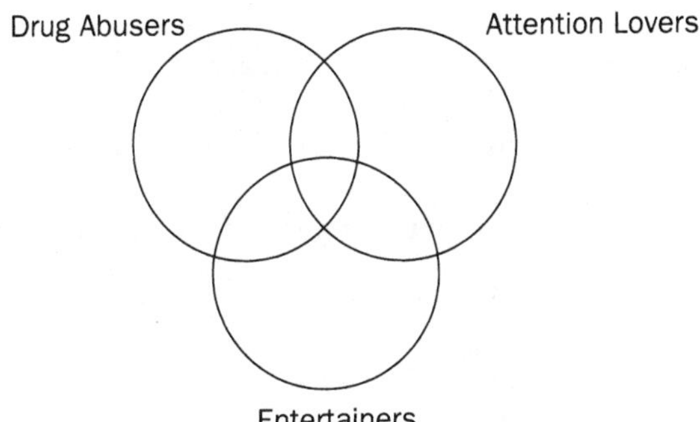


To represent premise 1, we shade in the entire area in the Entertainers circle except where it intersects with the circle representing those who love attention (see next diagram), indicating that there are no entertainers who do not also love attention. (Note: To avoid confusion, if one of the premises is universal and the other is particular, always diagram the universal premise first.)

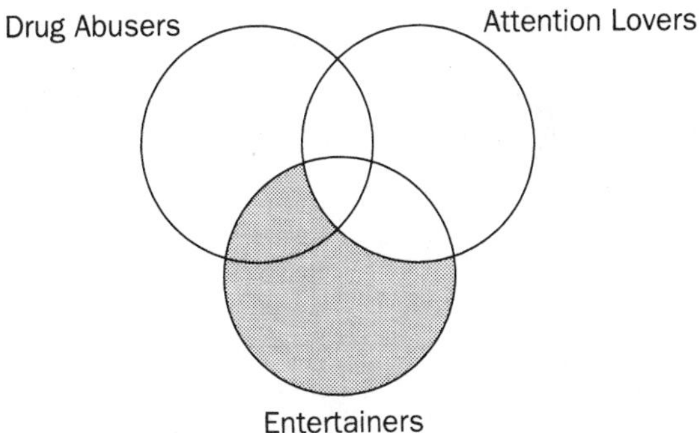

To represent premise 2, we must place an X somewhere in the intersection of the Drug Abusers and Entertainers circles:

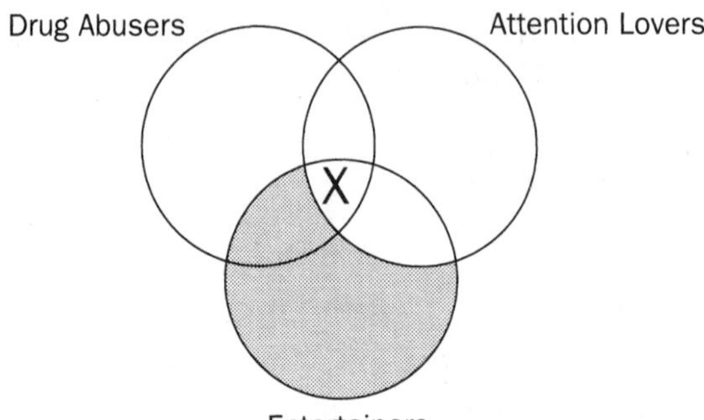


Does our diagram represent the conclusion that some drug abusers love attention? Yes, it does. An X already appears in the intersection of the circles representing drug abusers and those who love attention. This shows the inference to be valid.

Compare this last example with the similar one we discussed earlier:

(1) Some entertainers abuse drugs.

(2) All comedians are entertainers.

∴ (3) Some comedians are drug abusers.

In our next diagram, we'll let the circle on the left represent the category of Comedians, the circle on the right will represent the category of Drug Abusers and the lower circle will represent the middle category of Entertainers.

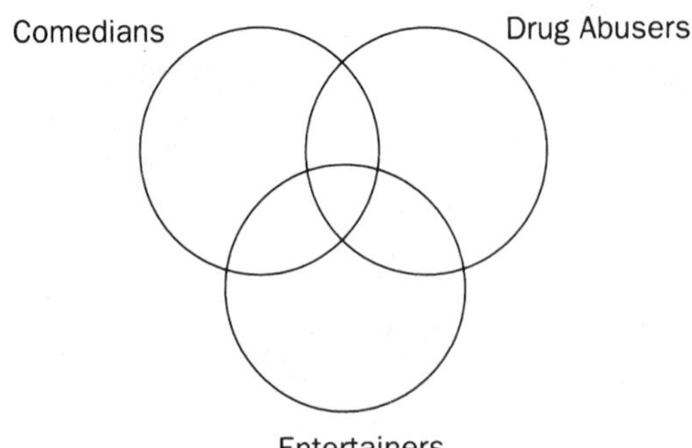

This time we'll start with premise 2 following the guideline to diagram a universal premise before a particular one. To represent premise 2 we shade in the entire area in the Comedians circle except where it intersects with the Entertainers circle, indicating that there are no comedians who are not also entertainers.

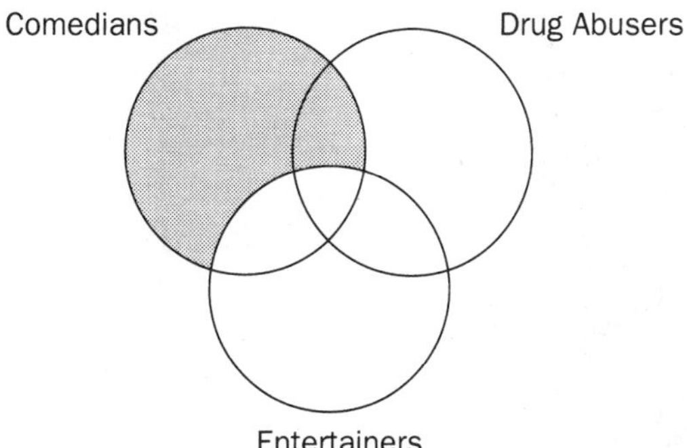


To represent premise 1 we must place an X somewhere in the intersection of the Drug Abusers and Entertainers circles. But do we place it inside or outside the circle of Comedians? Since we don't know, the X goes on the line:

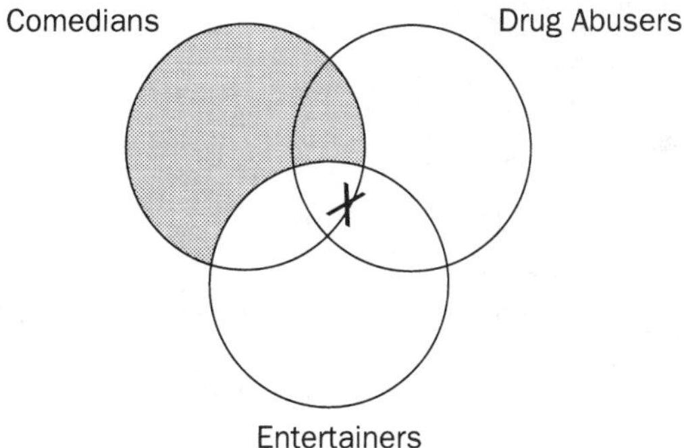


Now, does our diagram represent the conclusion that some comedians are drug abusers? It would if the X appeared clearly within the intersection of the Comedians and Drug Abusers circles. But it does not. It appears on the line, indicating that on the basis of our two premises it is not yet clear whether the conclusion is true, and thus that the inference is not valid.

## EXERCISE | Venn Diagrams

Using Venn diagrams, test the following arguments for validity.

1. Some college professors support the idea of a faculty union, an idea supported by many socialists. So at least some college professors must be socialists.

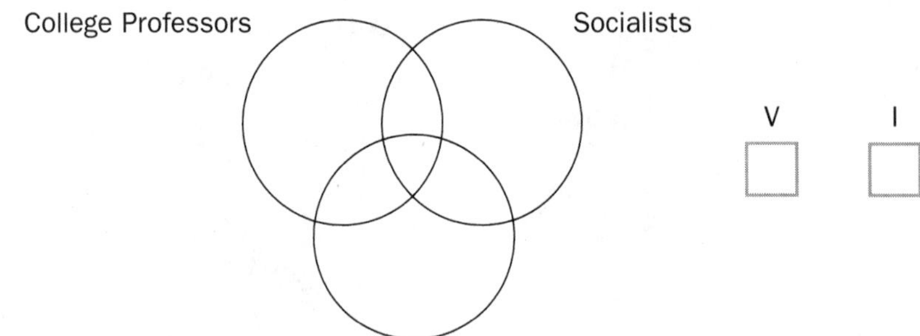


2. Everyone knows that whales live in the sea, and anything that lives in the sea is a fish. Therefore whales must be fish.

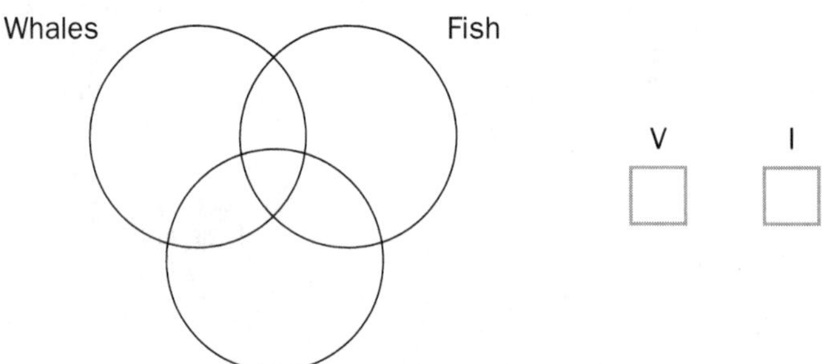


3. All artists are creative people. Some artists live in poverty. Therefore some creative people live in poverty.

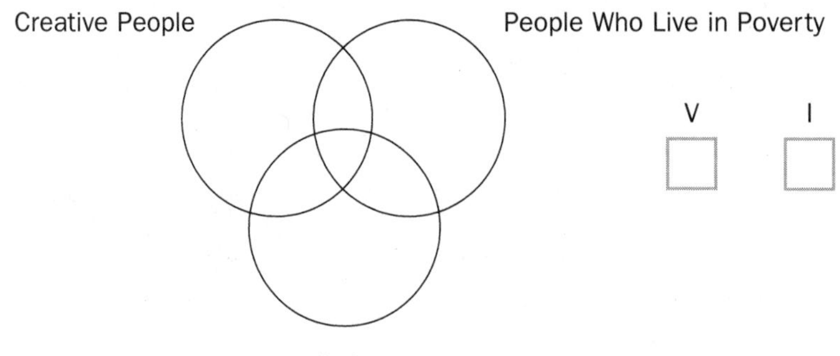

4. All of the justices on the Supreme Court are lawyers, and all members of the prestigious Washington Law Club are lawyers, so at least some of the Supreme Court justices are members of the Washington Law Club.

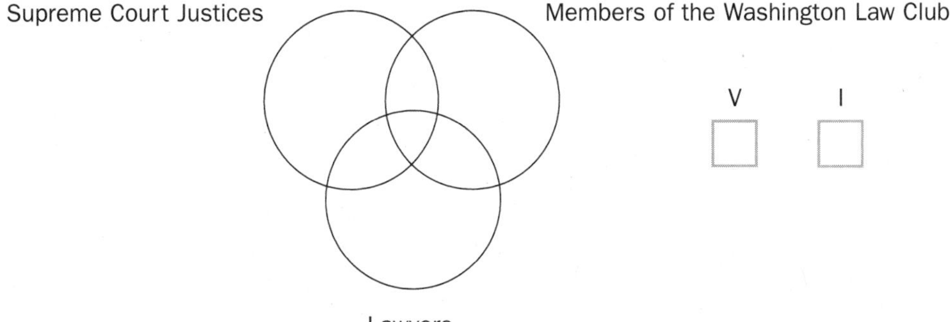


## TRUTH FUNCTIONAL LOGIC

The argument forms we have been studying so far have been composed entirely out of categorical statements. But as you are no doubt aware, there are many more kinds of statement in our language out of which arguments can be composed. Some of these play a particularly prominent and important role in argumentation. We will consider two of these: hypothetical statements and disjunctive statements. From the point of view of grammar, hypothetical statements are "if . . . then . . ." statements, and disjunctive statements are "either . . . or . . ." statements. However, in studying the role they each play in argumentation, we will need to understand not only their grammatical structure, but also their logical structure. And in order to do this we will need to introduce a bit more of the apparatus of modern logic: truth functional analysis of logical operators.

### TRUTH FUNCTIONAL ANALYSIS OF LOGICAL OPERATORS

What in the world is a logical operator? As a first step, let us distinguish between simple and compound statements. A simple statement is one that does not contain another statement as a component part. A compound statement is one that does contain at least one other statement as a component part. For example, "The weather is great" and "I wish you were here" are each simple statements, but "The weather is great and I wish you were here" is a compound statement. Think of logical operators as devices for making compound statements out of simpler ones. In this example, the word "and" is used to express the logical operator known as conjunction.

Logical operators are defined and distinguished from each other according to how they affect the "truth values" of the compound sentences we make with them. And truth functional analysis is simply a way of keeping track of this. The simplest of the logical operators and the easiest to understand truth functionally is negation. For example, the compound statement "The weather is not great" is produced by negating the simple statement "The weather is great." In this example the word "not" is used to express the logical operator negation. How does the logical operator negation affect the truth value of the compound statement "The weather is not great"? Well, if the simple statement "The weather is great" is true, then the compound statement "The weather is not great" is false, and if the simple statement "The weather is great" is false, then the compound statement "The weather is not great" is true. In other words, negation simply reverses the truth value of the component statement to which it is applied.

Here is a simple graphic representation. Let the letter "P" represent any statement. The symbol "~" will be used to represent the logical operator negation. Thus "~P" represents the negation of P.

| **P** | **~P** |
|---|---|
| T | F |
| F | T |

This sort of graphic representation is called a "truth table." We use it here to define the logical operator negation by showing what the truth value of the compound statement produced by negation would be for each of the possible truth values of its component statement.

A truth table needs to have as many lines as there are possible combinations of truth value for the number of distinct components involved. Negation operates on a single component statement, P. Since P is either true or false (not true), our truth table for negation required only two lines. But most logical operators connect two component statements, each of which might be either true or false. So a truth table defining any such operator will require four lines to represent each of the four possible combinations of truth value for the components. To illustrate, let us use the example of conjunction mentioned earlier: "The weather is great and I wish you were here." This once again is composed of the two simple statements "The weather is great" and "I wish you were here." The components of a conjunction are called "conjuncts." Let "P" stand for the first conjunct and the letter "Q" stand for the second. The symbol "&" will be used to represent the logical operator conjunction. Thus "P & Q" represents the conjunction of P and Q. It is fairly easy to see intuitively that the conjunction "P & Q" is true only if both of its conjuncts are true. "The weather is great and I wish you were here" is true only if the weather really is great and I really do wish you were here. If either conjunct or both were not true then the conjunction "P & Q" would also not be true, as indicated in the following truth table:

| **P** | **Q** | **P & Q** |
|---|---|---|
| T | T | T |
| T | F | F |
| F | T | F |
| F | F | F |

## HYPOTHETICAL STATEMENTS

We're now ready to examine the logical structure of hypothetical statements. First of all, hypothetical statements are compound statements. And what they assert is that a peculiar kind of relationship (a "truth-dependency" relationship) holds between their component parts. For example, the hypothetical statement

If love is blind, then fools rush in.

is composed of the two simple component statements "Love is blind" and "Fools rush in." What it asserts is—not that either of them is true—only that the truth of the second one depends on the truth of the first. It asserts that the statement "Love is blind" implies the statement "Fools rush in." We call both this relationship and the logical operator involved in making hypothetical statements implication.

Because this is not a reciprocal relationship—because it only goes in one direction—we'll need terms to keep track of which statement depends on which. In a hypothetical statement, the component introduced by the word "if" is called the *antecedent* and the component introduced by the word "then" is called the *consequent.* In this example "Love is blind" is the antecedent and "Fools rush in" is the consequent.

Sometimes hypothetical statements are used to say more than just that one statement implies another. For example, the statement

If abortion is homicide then by definition it involves the killing of human beings.

expresses also that the consequent follows (by definition) from the antecedent. For another example, the statement

If the economy doesn't improve then the president will have a hard time getting reelected.

expresses also that the antecedent is causally connected to the consequent. And the following statement

If the Congress overrides the president's last veto, then I'll eat my hat.

expresses also that the speaker is committed to do something on a certain condition. In each of these cases though, the statement expresses at a minimum that the truth of the consequent depends on the truth of the antecedent. This is the logical structure at the core of hypothetical statements, represented in the following truth table. Let "P" represent the antecedent and "Q" represent the consequent. The symbol "$\supset$" will be used to represent the logical operator implication. Thus "$P \supset Q$" represents the hypothetical statement "If P then Q."

| **P** | **Q** | **$P \supset Q$** |
|---|---|---|
| T | T | T |
| T | F | F |
| F | T | T |
| F | F | T |

You'll notice that according to our truth table the hypothetical statement "If P then Q" comes out false *only* when the antecedent is true and the consequent is false. In all other cases logic treats hypothetical statements as true. It is intuitively reasonable to suppose that a hypothetical statement with a true antecedent and a false consequent is false. Generally this is how hypothetical statements are tested for truth. Take the following example:

> If the economy does not improve then the president will lose his bid for a second term.

We could be certain that this hypothetical statement is false only if the economy does not improve (i.e., the antecedent is true) and the president nevertheless wins reelection (i.e., the consequent is false). But you might wonder why we would want to call a hypothetical statement true whose antecedent and consequent are both false? Well, suppose you and your friend are scanning the radio dial for something new and you happen to tune into a station broadcasting the very latest in avant garde electronic music which sounds to both of you something like the dishwasher full of bone china falling down a flight of stairs. And so your friend says:

> If this is music then I'm the king of Peru.

The point of such a statement is to assert the falsity of the antecedent, to claim that this isn't *(can't possibly be)* music. Here's how the hypothetical statement is being used to make this point: In effect, your friend is saying: "Since the consequent is obviously false (I'm not the king of Peru), if the antecedent *were* true the hypothetical statement itself would be false. But what I am now saying is true, so the antecedent has to be false too."

## FIVE ARGUMENT FORMS WITH HYPOTHETICAL PREMISES

Because of their unique structure hypothetical statements are extremely powerful reasoning tools and so they play a crucial role in a great many arguments and argument forms. Let's suppose, for example, that an experimental space probe begins with the following hypothetical first premise:

(1) If there is life on Mars, then there is adequate life support on Mars.

Now suppose that the space probe establishes that in fact:

(2) There is life on Mars.

From this as an additional premise together with the first premise we can conclude that:

(3) There is adequate life support on Mars.

Notice first that premise 2 is identical with the antecedent of the hypothetical premise 1, and that the conclusion is identical with its consequent. Notice also that it is impossible to assert 1 and 2 and deny 3 without contradicting yourself. Try it. Thus this is a deductively valid argument. It follows a form which can be represented schematically as follows:

(1) $P \supset Q$
(2) P

---

∴ (3) Q

Logicians traditionally refer to this argument form by the Latin label *Modus Ponens* which means "affirmative mood." Because Modus Ponens, like Barbara, is deductively valid, for any argument whatsoever, as long as it follows the form of Modus Ponens, accepting the premises forces you to accept the conclusion. Try it. Make some up.

Now let us suppose that our space probe turns up another kind of evidence. Suppose the space probe establishes that:

(2a) There is adequate life support on Mars.

Suppose we drew the conclusion from this together with premise 1 that:

(3a) There is life on Mars.

Perhaps conclusion 3a is correct. But do our two premises really guarantee it? No, they don't. It is possible to deny 3a without contradicting the assertion either of 1 or 2a. Try it (using the scenario method).

If you're having trouble with this, consider the following formally analogous argument:

If a figure is square, then it has four sides.

This rhombus has four sides.

---

∴ This rhombus is square.

Thus this argument is not deductively valid. And the form it follows, which can be schematically represented as follows, is unreliable, or formally fallacious:

(1) $P \supset Q$
(2a) Q

---

∴ (3a) P

Logicians traditionally refer to this form as the *Fallacy of Asserting the Consequent*, because that's what the second premise does. It asserts the consequent of the hypothetical first premise.

Now let us suppose that our space probe turns up yet another kind of evidence. Suppose the space probe establishes that:

(2b) There is no adequate life support on Mars.

From this together with our first premise it is possible to conclude that:

(**3b**) There is no life on Mars.

Notice here that premise 2b is the denial of the consequent of premise 1, whereas 3b is the denial of its antecedent. And notice that here again it is impossible to assert 1 and 2b and deny 3b without contradicting yourself. Try it. Thus this inference is deductively valid. It follows a pattern which can be represented schematically as follows:

(1) $P \supset Q$
(2b) $\sim Q$

---

∴ (3b) $\sim P$

Logicians traditionally refer to this argument form by the Latin label *Modus Tollens*, which means "denying mood." Because Modus Tollens, like Barbara and Modus Ponens, is deductively valid, for any argument whatsoever, as long as it follows the form of Modus Tollens, accepting the premises forces you to accept the conclusion. Try it. Make some up.

Next let's suppose our space probe establishes that:

(**2c**) There is no life on Mars.

Suppose we drew from this and our first premise the conclusion that:

(**3c**) There isn't adequate life support on Mars.

Again, perhaps 3c is correct, but do premises 1 and 2c guarantee it? No they don't. It is possible to assert both 1 and 2c and deny 3c without contradicting yourself. Try it (again using the scenario method).

Recall the earlier example. You can demonstrate the invalidity of this inference by means of a formally analogous argument thus:

If a figure is square then it has four sides.

This figure (a rhombus) is not a square.

---

∴ This figure (a rhombus) does not have four sides.

Thus this argument is not deductively valid. And the form it follows, which can be schematically represented as follows, is unreliable, or formally fallacious:

(1) $P \supset Q$
(2c) $\sim P$

---

∴ (3c) $\sim Q$

Logicians traditionally refer to this form as the *Fallacy of Denying the Antecedent*, because that's what the second premise does. It denies the antecedent of the hypothetical first premise.

This Valid/Invalid chart summarizes what we've said about these four hypothetical forms:

| Valid | | Invalid | |
|---|---|---|---|
| Modus Ponens | (1) $P \supset Q$<br>(2) $P$<br>∴(3) $Q$ | Asserting the Consequent | (1) $P \supset Q$<br>(2a) $Q$<br>∴(3a) $P$ |
| Modus Tollens | (1) $P \supset Q$<br>(2b) $\sim Q$<br>∴(3b) $\sim P$ | Denying the Antecedent | (1) $P \supset Q$<br>(2c) $\sim P$<br>∴(3c) $\sim Q$ |

Another commonly used and important argument form involves two hypothetical premises. Let's suppose once again, for example, that an experimental space probe begins with the following hypothetical first premise:

(1) If there is life on Mars, then there is adequate life support on Mars.

This time, however, let's add a second hypothetical premise:

(2d) If there is adequate life support on Mars, then a manned mission to Mars is feasible.

From this, together with our premise 1, it is possible to conclude that:

(3d) If there is life on Mars, then a manned mission to Mars is feasible.

Notice here that premise 2d is an hypothetical statement whose antecedent is identical with the consequent of premise 1, whereas the conclusion 3d is another hypothetical statement, whose antecedent is identical with the antecedent of premise 1 and whose consequent is identical with the consequent of premise 2d. And notice that here again it is impossible to assert 1 and 2d and deny 3d without contradicting yourself. Try it. Thus this inference is deductively valid. It follows a pattern which can be represented schematically as follows:

(1) $P \supset Q$
(2d) $Q \supset R$
―――――
(3d) $P \supset R$

Logicians traditionally refer to this argument form as *Hypothetical Syllogism.* Because Hypothetical Syllogism, like Barbara, Modus Ponens, and Modus Tollens, is deductively valid, for any argument whatsoever, as long as it follows the form of Hypothetical Syllogism, accepting the premises forces you to accept the conclusion. Try it. Make some up.

But now compare the last example with this one:

(1) If there is life on Mars, then there is adequate life support on Mars.

(2e) A manned mission to Mars is feasible only if there is adequate life support on Mars.

---

∴ (3d) If there is life on Mars, then a manned mission to Mars is feasible.

This inference is not deductively valid. You can see why if you use the scenario method, and your imagination. Suppose that it's true that the existence of life on Mars presupposes adequate life support on Mars (premise 1). Suppose also that a manned mission to Mars is feasible *only* if there is adequate life support on Mars (premise 2e). Now let us also suppose that there is indeed life on Mars, and so also adequate life support on Mars. And yet intuitively it's pretty clear that the feasibility of a manned mission to Mars is still an open question. So the conclusion 3d does not follow logically from these two premises.

## USING TRUTH TABLES TO TEST FOR VALIDITY

Earlier we found the system of Venn diagrams useful as a graphic means of testing the validity of categorical syllogisms. Venn diagrams don't accommodate the kind of argument forms we've just been considering very well. But we can use truth tables for this purpose. For example, we can use the truth table for implication to demonstrate both the validity of Modus Ponens and the invalidity of the Fallacy of Asserting the Consequent.

So far we have used truth tables to define and explain logical operators. If we divide the truth table for implication vertically (see following diagram), the left side of the table represents all of the possible combinations of truth value for all of the components involved in any hypothetical statement, while the right side of the table represents the truth value of the compound statement for any of these possible combinations:

| **Components** | | **Compound** |
|---|---|---|
| P | Q | P ⊃ Q |
| ***(premise 2)*** | ***(conclusion)*** | ***(premise 1)*** |
| T | T | T |
| T | F | F |
| F | T | T |
| F | F | T |

It so happens that the truth table also represents all of the possible truth value combinations of the premises and conclusion of the argument form Modus

Ponens. The column on the right corresponds to premise 1, the column on the left corresponds to premise 2, and the column in the middle corresponds to the conclusion. So we should also be able to tell from the truth table whether or not it's possible for both of the premises to be true while the conclusion is false. As always, if so, the argument form is not deductively valid, but if not, the argument form is deductively valid. There is only one line (line 1) of the truth table on which both premises are true, and on that line the conclusion is also true. So the argument form is a valid one:

| **Components** | | **Compound** |
|---|---|---|
| P | Q | P ⊃ Q |
| *(premise 2)* | *(conclusion)* | *(premise 1)* |
| T | T | T |
| T | F | F |
| F | T | T |
| F | F | T |

It also turns out that the truth table for implication also represents all of the possible truth value combinations of the premises and conclusion of the Fallacy of Asserting the Consequent. In this case the column on the right corresponds to premise 1, the column in the middle corresponds to premise 2, and the column on the left corresponds to the conclusion. So again we should also be able to tell from the truth table whether or not it's possible for both of the premises to be true while the conclusion is false. This time, there are two lines (lines 1 and 3) of the truth table on which both premises are true, and on line 3 the conclusion is false. In other words, the following truth table shows that it is possible for an argument of this form to have true premises and a false conclusion, and therefore that the argument is not valid:

| **Components** | | **Compound** |
|---|---|---|
| P | Q | P ⊃ Q |
| *(conclusion)* | *(premise 2)* | *(premise 1)* |
| T | T | T |
| T | F | F |
| Ⓕ | T | T |
| F | F | T |

To test the validity of Modus Tollens and the Fallacy of Denying the Antecedent is only slightly more complicated. This is because none of the truth tables we have generated so far happens to represent all of the possible truth value combinations for the premises and conclusions of either of these two argument forms. However we need merely add a couple of columns to the truth table for implication to get this accomplished. These two columns are to represent the truth values of ~P and ~Q, which according to the truth table for negation are simply the reverse of the truth values for P and Q respectively:

| **Components** | | **Compounds** | | |
|---|---|---|---|---|
| P | Q | P ⊃ Q | ~P | ~Q |
| T | T | T | F | F |
| T | F | F | F | T |
| F | T | T | T | F |
| F | F | T | T | T |

To test the validity of Modus Tollens we simply need to locate the columns representing the premises and conclusion and check to see whether or not it's possible for both of the premises to be true while the conclusion is false. In our truth table the third column now represents premise 1, the column on the far right represents premise 2 and the column between them represents the conclusion, and there is only one line (line 4) on which both premises are true. Since the conclusion is also true on this line, the argument form is a valid one:

| **Components** | | **Compounds** | | |
|---|---|---|---|---|
| P | Q | P ⊃ Q | ~P | ~Q |
| | | *(premise 1)* | *(conclusion)* | *(premise 2)* |
| T | T | T | F | F |
| T | F | F | F | T |
| F | T | T | T | F |
| F | F | T | T | T |

Similarly, to test the Fallacy of Denying the Antecedent we simply need to locate the columns representing the premises and conclusion and check to see whether or not it's possible for both of the premises to be true while the conclusion is false. In our truth table the third column now represents premise 1, the column immediately to the right of it represents premise 2 and the column on the far right represents the conclusion. But this time, there are two lines (lines 3 and 4) of the truth table on which both premises are true, and on line 3 the conclusion is false. In other words, the truth table shows that it is possible for an argument of this form to have true premises and a false conclusion, and therefore that the argument is not valid:

| Components | | Compounds | | |
|---|---|---|---|---|
| P | Q | P ⊃ Q | ~P | ~Q |
| | | *(premise 1)* | *(premise 2)* | *(conclusion)* |
| T | T | T | F | F |
| T | F | F | F | T |
| F | T | T | T | Ⓕ |
| F | F | T | T | T |

## AN ARGUMENT FORM INVOLVING DISJUNCTION

Like hypothetical statements, disjunctions are extremely powerful reasoning tools and so they play a crucial role in a great many arguments and argument forms.

Like hypothetical statements, disjunctive statements assert a "truth-functional relationship" between the two component statements of which they are made up. These component statements are called disjuncts. Normally the relationship asserted by a disjunction can be expressed as follows: At least one of the disjuncts is true (possibly both). For example, the statement

Either the battery is dead or there is a short in the ignition switch.

asserts that at least one of the two statements "The battery is dead" and "There is a short in the ignition switch" is true. This relationship and the logical operator used to make compound statements which assert it we call disjunction , and we can represent it by means of the following truth table. Let the letters "P" and "Q" represent the two disjuncts and the symbol "v" represent the operator disjunction. Thus "P v Q" represents the statement "Either P or Q."

| P | Q | P v Q |
|---|---|---|
| T | T | T |
| T | F | T |
| F | T | T |
| F | F | F |

Let's suppose, for example, that we've been trying to diagnose a mechanical problem with the car, and we have eliminated all possible problems but two: the battery and the ignition switch. So we now have good reason to believe that

(1) Either the battery is dead or there is a short in the ignition switch.

Now suppose we check the battery and find that it's fully charged and functioning properly. We now know that

(2) The battery is not dead.

From this together with our first premise it is possible to conclude that

(3) There is a short in the ignition switch.

Notice here that premise 2 is the denial of one of the disjuncts of premise 1, whereas 3 is identical with the other disjunct. And notice that here again it is impossible to assert 1 and 2 and deny 3 without contradicting yourself. Try it. Thus this inference is deductively valid. It follows a pattern which can be represented schematically as follows:

(1) P v Q
(2) ~P
_______
∴ (3) Q

Logicians traditionally refer to this argument form as *Disjunctive Syllogism.*

## AN ARGUMENT FORM WITH BOTH HYPOTHETICAL AND DISJUNCTIVE PREMISES

One of the oldest and most powerful argumentative strategies combines hypothetical and disjunctive premises. The strategy aims at proving a point by showing that it is implied by each of two alternatives, at least one of which must be true. The strategy and the argument form which embodies it are called dilemma. For example, suppose that during the Monday Night Football pre-game commentary you hear Frank Gifford say:

> If the Saints beat the Rams tonight, then the Forty-niners are in the playoffs as Division champs. But if the Rams beat the Saints, then the 'Niners are in the playoffs as a wild card.

This is actually an incompletely stated argument. Two of its elements, the thesis and one of the premises, are implied (*). When these elements are filled in, the argument goes like this:

(1)* Either the Saints will beat the Rams or the Rams will beat the Saints.

(2) If the Saints beat the Rams, then the 'Niners are in the playoffs (as Division champs).

(3) If the Rams beat the Saints, then the 'Niners are in the playoffs (as a wild card).
_______
∴ (4)* The 'Niners are in the playoffs.

Notice here that the antecedent of premise 2 is one of the disjuncts of premise 1, and the antecedent of premise 3 is the other disjunct, while the consequent of each hypothetical premise is the argument's conclusion. And notice that here again it is impossible to assert 1, 2, and 3, and deny the conclusion without contradicting yourself. Try it. Thus this inference is deductively valid. It follows a pattern which can be represented schematically as follows:

(1) P v Q
(2) P ⊃ R
(3) Q ⊃ R

∴ (4) R

And again we can demonstrate its validity by means of a truth table. This time we are dealing with three distinct components: P, Q, and R. So our truth table will need eight lines in order to represent all the possible combinations of truth value for the number of distinct components involved:

| **Components** | | | **Compounds** | | |
|---|---|---|---|---|---|
| P | Q | R | P ⊃ R | Q ⊃ R | P v Q |
| | | *(conclusion)* | *(premise 2)* | *(premise 3)* | *(premise 1)* |
| T | T | T | T | T | T |
| T | T | F | F | F | T |
| T | F | T | T | T | T |
| T | F | F | F | F | T |
| F | T | T | T | T | T |
| F | T | F | T | T | T |
| F | F | T | T | T | F |
| F | F | F | T | T | F |

This time, there are three lines (lines 1, 3, and 5) of the truth table on which all of the premises are true. Since the conclusion is also true on each of these lines, the argument form is a valid one.

## EXERCISE | Using Truth Tables to Test for Validity

1. Analyze and evaluate the following two arguments:
   a. If astrology is correct, then all people born at the same time would have the same sort of personalities, experiences, and opportunities, yet this is not the case.
      i. What is the thesis of this argument?
      ii. The argument is an example of which argument form?
      iii. Is the argument deductively valid or not?
      iv. Use a truth table to explain how you arrived at your answer.

b. If astrology has been refuted, then we should not depend on the predictions in the horoscope. But since astrology has not been refuted, we *should* depend on them.

i. What is the thesis of this argument?

ii. The argument is an example of which argument form?

iii. Is the argument deductively valid or not?

iv. Use a truth table to explain how you arrived at your answer.

2. Demonstrate the validity of the argument form Hypothetical Syllogism by means of a truth table.

## ADDITIONAL EXERCISES

**1.** For each of the following passages, indicate whether it is a deductive argument, an inductive argument, or not an argument:

| | Ded. | Ind. | N/A |
|---|---|---|---|
| We can't lose. They've got no offense and they've got no one to stop our leading scorer. They've lost their last four games, and it'll be on our court. | | | |
| In a democracy, the poor have more power than the rich, because there are more of them. —Aristotle | | | |
| I've been eating corn on the cob for years, and I always count the number of rows. I have never found an ear of corn with an odd number of rows. I'm convinced that ears of corn *always* have even numbers of rows. | | | |
| Even God makes mistakes. In the Bible, God says, "It repenteth me that I have made man." Now either the Bible is not the word of God, or we must believe that God did say, "It repenteth me that I have made man." But then, if we are to believe the word of God, we must further conclude that He really did repent making man, in which case, either God made a mistake in making man, or He made a mistake in repenting making man. | | | |
| The theory of the unreality of evil now seems to me untenable. Suppose that it can be proved that all that we think evil was in reality good. The fact would still remain that we think it evil. This may be called a delusion or mistake. But a delusion or mistake is as real as anything else. The delusion that evil exists is therefore real. But then it seems certain that a delusion which hid from us the goodness of the universe would itself be evil. And so there would be real evil after all. —J. M. E. McTaggart | | | |

| | | | |
|---|---|---|---|
| First of all, as the eighteenth century Scottish philosopher David Hume pointed out, we never directly observe causal relationships. We have to infer them. Next, we can never infer them with deductive certainty. Since the evidence for a causal relationship is always indirect, there will always be some room for doubt when we infer a cause. In other words, we must reason inductively about them. | | | |
| In the entire history of the stock market, every bull market has been followed by a bear market, and vice versa. Therefore the stock market behaves cyclically. | | | |
| Grumble County has voted for the loser in every State Senate contest since 1876. Grumble County polls show incumbent Senator Press Fleshman running 27 points behind challenger Mary Kay Weedemout. But I'm tired of always voting for losers and lost causes. I'm going to vote for Fleshman, since it looks like he's going to win anyway. | | | |

**2.** Using a combination of any two of the procedures discussed in this chapter (the intuitive test, the scenario method, Venn diagrams, truth tables) determine which of the following are valid deductive arguments. (Be sure to fill in any missing premises.) Then cast the valid ones. For each of the invalid ones compose a formally analogous argument that moves from obviously true premises to an obviously false conclusion.

a. All crooks deserve to be punished. But some politicians are not crooks. So some politicians do not deserve to be punished.

b. I must necessarily exist, for in order to think one must exist, and to doubt is to think. And here I am doubting that I exist, so I must really exist after all.

c. In our society the right to life is our most basic human right, and it is considered irrevocable. The revocation of this irrevocable right is illegal. Suicide is the voluntary revocation of one's right to life. It follows, then, that suicide is indeed illegal.

d. Since all birds eat worms, and chickens are birds, chickens must eat worms.

e. Marty must be a real male chauvinist. After all, he's an athlete, isn't he?

f. Some reference books are textbooks, for all textbooks are books intended for careful study and some reference books are intended for the same purpose.

g. Most poets drink to excess, and some poets are women. So, some women drink to excess.

h. Everyone who smokes marijuana goes on to try heroin. Everyone who tries heroin becomes a junkie. So everyone who smokes marijuana becomes a junkie.

i. The argument must be sound because its premises are true and its conclusion is true and all arguments with true premises and conclusions are sound.

j. The argument must be sound because its premises are true and it's valid and all valid arguments with true premises are sound.

**3.** Demonstrate the formal fallaciousness of Asserting the Consequent and Denying the Antecedent by composing arguments of each form that move from intuitively acceptable or obviously true premises to intuitively unacceptable or obviously false conclusions.

**4.** What is the formal structure of the following argument?

(1) If there is life on Mars, then there is adequate life support on Mars.

(2e) A manned mission to Mars is feasible only if there is adequate life support on Mars.

---

∴ (3d) If there is life on Mars, then a manned mission to Mars is feasible.-169

Demonstrate its invalidity by means of a truth table.

**5.** If you want somebody to go up there to Washington and just *talk* about it, don't vote for me. —Independent presidential candidate H. Ross Perot

a. What is the thesis of this argument?
b. The argument is an example of which argument form?
c. Is the argument deductively valid or not? Explain how you arrive at your answer.
d. How cogent is this argument? Explain how you arrive at your answer.

**6.** Try the following puzzle, from Raymond Smullyan's book *To Mock a Mockingbird:* "Suppose I offer you two prizes—Prize 1 and Prize 2. You are to make a statement. If the statement is true, then I am to give you one of the two prizes (not saying which one). If your statement is false, then you get no prize. Obviously you can be sure of winning one of the two prizes by saying 'Two plus two is four,' but suppose you have your heart set on Prize 1; what statement could you make that would guarantee that you will get Prize 1?"

**7.** Now test the validity of the following solution to Smullyan's puzzle (Exercise 6 above) using truth tables: "You say, 'You will not give me Prize 2.' If the statement is false, then what it says is not the case, which means that I *will* give you Prize 2. But I can't give you a prize for making a false statement, and so the statement can't be false. Therefore it must be true. Since it is true, then what it says *is* the case, which means that you will not get Prize 2. But since your statement was true, I must give you one of the two prizes, and since it is not Prize 2, it must be Prize 1."

**8.** A variation on Smullyan's puzzle, this one from Smullyan's book *Forever Undecided:* "Again I offer two prizes—Prize 1 and Prize 2. If you make a true statement, I will give you at least one of the two prizes and possibly both. If you make a false statement, you get no prize. Suppose you are ambitious and wish to win both prizes. What statement would you make?"

**9.** Now test the validity of the following solution to Smullyan's puzzle variation (Exercise 8 above) using truth tables: "[You say], 'I will either get both prizes or no prize.' If the statement is false, then what it says is not the case, which means that you will get exactly one prize. But you can't get a prize for a false statement. Therefore the statement must be true, and you really will get either both prizes or no prize. Since you did not make a false statement, which would result in no prize, you must get both prizes."

## GLOSSARY

**antecedent** in a hypothetical statement, the component introduced by the word "if"
**categorical statement** a statement about a relationship between categories
**categorical syllogism** a syllogism made up of categorical statements
**cogent** a strong inductive argument based on true or acceptable premises
**conjunction** a compound statement which is true only when both of its components are true; the logical operator "and" used to make such a statement
**consequent** in a hypothetical statement, the component introduced by the word "then"
**contradiction** 1. a conflict between a statement and its negation
2. in categorical logic, a form of opposition between categorical statements; two categorical statements which cannot both be true and also cannot both be false are contradictories
**contrariety** a form of opposition between categorical statements; two categorical statements which cannot both be true but which might both be false are contraries
**deductive** reasoning designed and intended to secure its conclusion with certainty so that anyone who fully understands what the statements in the argument mean must recognize that the premises cannot both be true without the conclusion also being true
**dilemma** an argument form or strategy combining hypothetical and disjunctive premises which seeks to prove its point by showing that it is implied by each of two alternatives, at least one of which must be true
**disjunct** component of a disjunction
**disjunction** a compound statement which is true when either one or both of its components are true; the logical operator "or" used to make such a statement
**disjunctive syllogism** a deductively valid argument form based on a disjunction and the denial of one of its disjuncts
**fallacy** an unreliable inference
**fallacy of asserting the consequent** a deductively invalid argument form based on a hypothetical statement and the affirmation of its consequent
**fallacy of denying the antecedent** a deductively invalid argument form based on a hypothetical statement and the denial of its antecedent
**formal fallacy** an inference that is unreliable because it follows an unreliable form or pattern
**hypothetical syllogism** a deductively valid argument form based on two hypothetical statements as premises, where the consequent of the first is the antecedent of the second

**inductive** reasoning designed and intended to make the conclusion reasonable, probable, or likely, but not certain
**logical operator** in truth functional logic, a device for making a compound statement out of simpler ones
**modus ponens** a deductively valid argument form based on a hypothetical statement and the affirmation of its antecedent
**modus tollens** a deductively valid argument form based on a hypothetical statement and the denial of its consequent
**negation** the logical operator which reverses the truth value of the component statement to which it is applied; a statement formed by applying this logical operator
**sound** a valid deductive argument based on true or acceptable premises
**square of opposition** in categorical logic, the array of relationships between the four statement forms showing the immediate inferences which may be drawn on the basis of differences of quality and quantity
**sub-alternation** in categorical logic, the relationship between statements with the same subject and predicate terms which agree in quality (both affirmative or both negative) but differ in quality (not both universal)
**sub-contrariety** a form of opposition between categorical statements; two categorical statements which might both be true but which can't both be false are sub-contraries
**syllogism** a deductive inference from two premises
**truth functional analysis** system for keeping track of how logical operators affect the truth values of compound sentences made with them
**truth functional logic** system of logic based on truth functional analysis
**truth table** chart used in truth functional logic for listing variable truth values
**truth value** the truth or falsity of a statement
**validity** the essential characteristic of a successful deductive argument, or deductive argument form; if the premises are taken to be true, then the conclusion must also be true

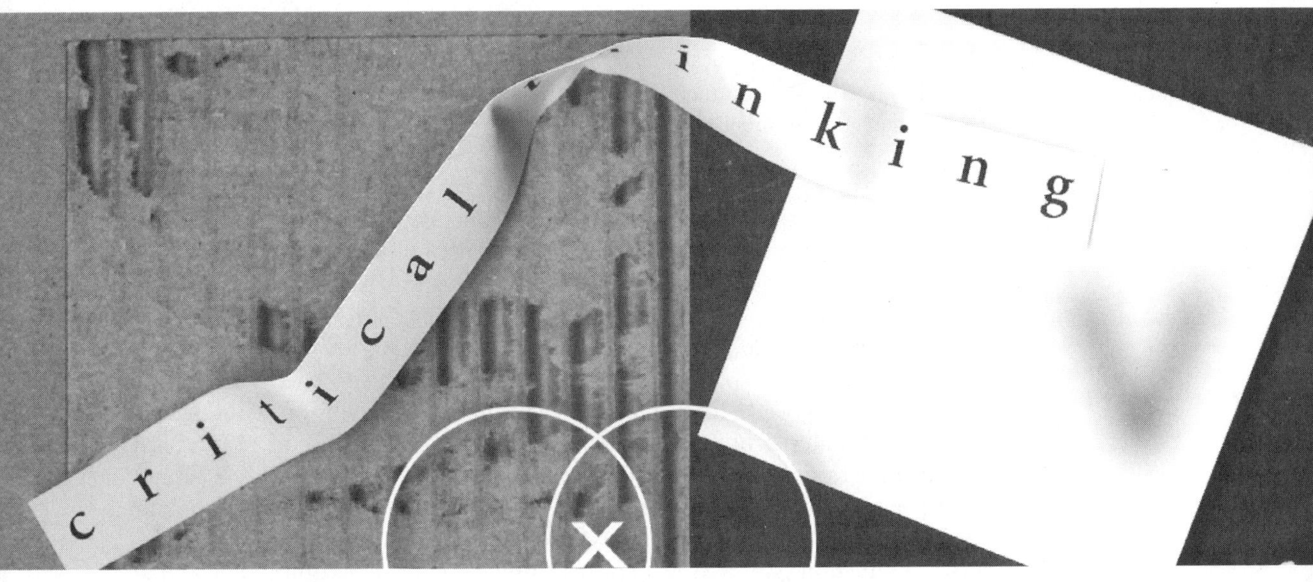


# CHAPTER 7 Evaluating Arguments II: Induction

We have just seen how deductively valid arguments guarantee their conclusions. If the truth of the premises of a deductively valid argument can be established, that leaves no more room for doubt about the argument's conclusion. But many arguments that do not provide deductively valid grounds for the acceptance of their conclusions nevertheless provide some substantial support for their conclusions and are therefore not to be dismissed simply on the grounds that they are not deductively valid. There are some arguments whose premises, though they do not guarantee the conclusion, nevertheless make the conclusion more reasonable or probable or likely. Here is an example of such an argument:

[Professor Jones has never missed a class. ①] So [chances are she'll be in class today. ②]

If the premise (claim 1) is accepted as true, then it would be reasonable to accept the argument's conclusion (claim 2). Of course, even if the premise is true the conclusion may prove to be false: Professor Jones may not show up for class. She may not even be *likely* to show up for class. Perhaps she's ill or has had an accident or been arrested or has an important conflicting appointment. Nevertheless, the premise does provide reasonable support for the conclusion. Here is another example:

> [It's highly unlikely that any female will play football in the National Football League in the near future,① ] for [none has so far.② ]

Again, if the premise (claim 2) is accepted as true, it provides good—though not deductively valid—grounds for accepting the conclusion (claim 1).

Such arguments are called *inductive.* The essential difference between deductive and inductive reasoning is once again that valid deductions provide absolutely reliable grounds for their conclusions, where well designed and constructed inductions do not. Because the conclusion of a valid deduction is logically implied by—or contained within—its premises, the truth of its premises leaves no room for doubt as to the truth of its conclusion. Thus deduction eliminates all risk of error when we move from premises to conclusions. But for much the same reason, deduction has a very important limitation. It cannot take us beyond what is logically entailed by our premises. If we are to reason our way beyond what we already know, we often need additional reasoning strategies beyond deduction. We need ways of reasoning which will accommodate and at the same time help us to manage some risk of error, as in the above examples. That is what inductive reasoning is for.

## ASSESSING INDUCTIVE STRENGTH

Let's now turn to the evaluation of inductive arguments. A deductive argument is either valid or not valid. But inductive strength is relative, by which we mean it admits of degrees. Some valid inductive arguments are stronger than others. Because the conclusion of an induction "goes beyond" what is contained within its premises, an inductive argument always contains an element of doubt. And when we critique inductive arguments, we are essentially interested in weighing this element of doubt. In evaluating inductive inferences, the question is: How much doubt? Consider the following two arguments:

(1) The last three cars we have owned have been Chrysler products and they've all been trouble free. So we're probably safe to assume that a new Dodge will be reliable.

(2) In Consumers' Union nationwide studies of new cars purchased over the last ten years, Chrysler had a 30 percent lower frequency of repair rate than the other manufacturers. So we're probably safe to assume that a new Dodge will be reliable.

In each argument the premise does provide some reason for accepting the conclusion. But the first argument leaves more room for doubt than the second. So the second argument is that much stronger than the first.

If inductive strength is a matter of degree, then the essential question in evaluating an inductive inference or argument is: How much doubt does it leave room for? The answer to this question is: It depends. Inductive strength depends on a number of variables, including the type of inductive reasoning involved. Let's begin with the simplest and most common of the varieties of inductive reasoning: projecting general conclusions from a number of particular instances. This variety of inductive reasoning is called "inductive generalization." Its relative simplicity, widespread use, and commonsense appeal help to explain why it is often mistaken for the essence of induction.

## INDUCTIVE GENERALIZATIONS

Suppose that you work with computers and you have just opened a new shipment of computer diskettes. It will make things easier if we imagine that computer diskettes are delivered in shipments of 100. The first diskette you try is defective. So you try a second one and it's defective too. So you try a third diskette. Also defective. At some point you begin to wonder whether the whole shipment might be defective. So far you've only tried three diskettes. They've all been defective, but still you can't be very sure that the entire shipment is defective. In fact, at this point you merely suspect that the entire shipment might be defective. That's because you've barely sampled the shipment. Suppose you keep going. You try a fourth diskette and a fifth diskette. Both defective. This confirms your suspicion. Obviously the more diskettes you try (assuming each one is defective) the more certain you become that the entire shipment is defective. By the time you get to the thirty-fifth diskette (assuming each one is defective) you're going to be much more certain—though still not absolutely certain—that the entire shipment is defective. This highlights two of the variables that affect the strength of an inductive generalization. From now on, let's refer to the number of diskettes you've tried as "the sample" and the entire shipment (the general class you're wondering about) as "the population." The size of the sample and the size of the population each affect the strength of the induction. *As the size of the sample increases relative to the population, so does the strength of the induction.*

There are other variables which affect inductive strength. If the only variables affecting inductive strength were the size of the sample and the size of the population, then the only way to increase inductive strength—or reduce doubt—would be to keep on plodding along—testing the diskettes one by one until the sample coincides with the population. But you don't need to test each and every diskette in order to be reasonably certain about the entire population. A commonsense shortcut would be, after the first three or so diskettes have been identified as defective, to dig down deeper into the shipment and try a diskette from the middle and another one from near the bottom. If they too turn out to be defective you can be more certain—though still not entirely certain—that the entire shipment is defective. But notice also that if you followed this procedure and got these results you would be more certain than if you had just tried the next two diskettes. Why? Because it is much more *unlikely* that by sampling in this more "random" way you would end up picking just those diskettes which are defective (see figure on next page). This highlights another of the variables that affect the strength of an inductive inference: the degree to which the sample is representative of the population as a whole. *The more representative the sample is of the population as a whole, the stronger the induction.*

How do we determine the degree to which the sample is representative of the population as a whole? This is a really a matter of variety. In this example, our "expanded for variety" sample" (Figure 7.1c) is equal in size to our "keep on plodding along sample" (Figure 7.1b), but covers more variables.

Suppose the diskettes are (naturally) packed in order, and you began by sampling them in (reverse) order. In sampling the middle and both ends of the shipment, rather than just sampling the beginning, what you're doing is adding to the variety of the sample, by including within it particular examples representing the entire population, whether packed first, middle, or last. You've added to the variety of the sample in the *dimension* of "numerical order within the shipment." And this is significant because numerical order within the shipment—numerical position in the "packing order"—could have something to do with whether a given diskette is defective. Maybe there was a short run of thirty consecutive defective diskettes. By varying the sample through the dimension of numerical order you have a way of ruling this out as a possible source of error—a way to reduce the risk of error. Because numerical order within the shipment might have something to do with whether a diskette is defective or not, numerical order within the shipment is a *relevant* dimension here. *Generally, you should try to vary the sample as widely and in as many different relevant dimensions as you can think of.* In science this is called "controlling the variables."

These two factors, sample size relative to population size and representativeness of the sample, help explain why the first of our two examples of induction

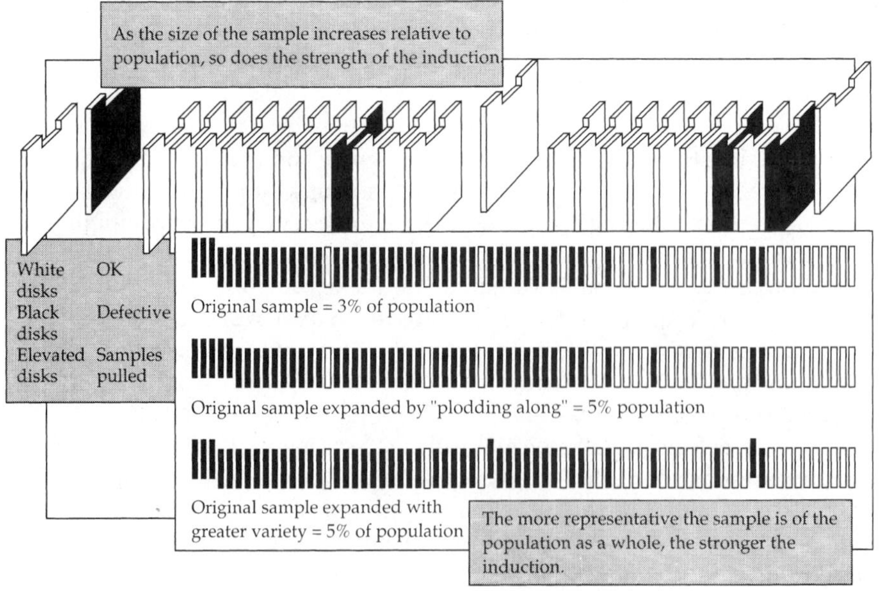

was weaker than the second. A nationwide comparative study of frequency of repair rates involving not just Chrysler products but those of other manufacturers as well constitutes both a larger and more representative sample than the tiny and highly selective "the last three cars we have owned."

## STATISTICAL GENERALIZATIONS

In our example of the defective computer diskettes notice that *all* of the members of the sample turned out to be one way: defective. Life is rarely as simple as that. More often, some members of the sample will be one way, and some another. So a variation on simple inductive generalization involves projecting trends or percentages observed in the sample onto other instances or onto the population as a whole. This is commonly called statistical generalization. For instance, suppose we're interested in how likely college students with different majors are to gain admission to law school. We might survey law school admissions for a certain period of time. Suppose our survey showed that 20 percent more of the applicants with philosophy majors were admitted than were admitted from the next most successful major. We might then project inductively that philosophy majors are 20 percent more likely to gain admission to law school than other college students.

The same principles used to evaluate the strength of simple inductive generalizations also apply in evaluating the strength of statistical generalizations. In both simple inductive generalization and statistical induction the strength of the inference increases with the size of the sample relative to the population and with the degree to which the sample is representative of the population as a whole. Suppose our survey of law school admissions was only one year long, or was confined to the state of California. Then we might be overlooking variables which might otherwise show up in a ten-year nationwide survey. Perhaps in a particular year more students with law school aptitude happened to elect philosophy as a major. Perhaps the state of California has particularly strong instructional programs in philosophy. In any case, the smaller and more selective the sample the weaker the induction.

Another variable which affects the strength of statistical generalizations is the degree of precision and certainty attached to the conclusion relative to the evidence contained in the premises. A statistical generalization can generally be strengthened by hedging the conclusion with appropriate qualifications, essentially by toning down the language with which the conclusion is presented. This is one reason why statistical arguments often sound so "wishy washy" in spite of all the numbers in them. Similarly the degree of precision with which the figures in the conclusion are stated can affect the strength of a statistical generalization. We may lack sufficient evidence to conclude with very much certainty that precisely 73.86 percent of the electorate favors the president's new economic program. However the very same data might well be sufficient to conclude with a good deal of confidence that *more than two-thirds* or *most* of the electorate favors it.

## MARGIN OF ERROR

Often we hear the results of some inductive research, like a public opinion poll, announced as having a certain margin of error, as in

> The exit polling predicts that Proposition X will pass by a 62 percent majority, with a 3 percent margin of error.

Margin of error is an estimate of the likelihood of error in the conclusion of an inductive inference. You may wonder how it would be possible to estimate such a thing so precisely—especially given the size of the sample relative to the population in most public opinion polling. To give a detailed and systematic answer to this perfectly reasonable question would require a course in statistics. Statistics is the branch of mathematics having to do with collecting and interpreting numerical data. Nevertheless, here's a way to begin to think about the problem conceptually: Margin of error is an estimate of how well you think the research has controlled the variables. Notice how closely this relates to both the degree of precision and the certainty with which the results of the polling are presented and understood.

### EXERCISE | Inductive Generalizations

1. Rank the following inductive arguments in order of strength. Explain your ranking.
   a. Contrary to current media claims, our schools appear to be doing a superb job of teaching our children to read. A leading news magazine recently tabulated the results of the thousands of responses it received to the survey it published in its May issue. Readers from every state in the Union responded. Ninety percent of the respondents believed that their school-aged children's reading skills were good to excellent. Eight percent more believed that their children's reading skills were at least adequate. Less than one percent felt that their children were developing less than adequate reading skills. (One percent of the respondents failed to answer this question.)
   b. In all of the studies that have been done over the past thirty years concerning the relationship between standardized test performance and success in school—involving several hundred thousand school-age subjects from a variety of ethnic, regional, and socioeconomic backgrounds—I.Q. (Intelligence Quotient) tests have been shown to be the single most reliable predictor of success in school. Therefore, if one scores highly on I.Q. tests, one will probably perform well in school.
   c. An hour in a hot tub will probably impair a man's fertility for up to six weeks. According to one study, three men who sat in a hot tub with water heated to 102.4° F—most health clubs heat theirs to 104° F—showed reductions in the number and penetrating capacity of their sperm cells. In samples taken thirty-six hours later, the damage was present, but the most dramatic effects did not show up until four weeks later. This indicated that even immature sperm cells had been harmed by the high heat. (It takes about seven weeks for a newly created sperm cell to mature and pass through a system of storage ducts.) Seven weeks after their dip in the hot tub, their sperm returned to normal.

2. List and explain two different ways in which each of the following inferences might be strengthened.
   a. The last three cars we have owned have been Chrysler products and they've all been trouble free. So we're probably safe to assume that a new Dodge will be reliable.
   b. In Consumers' Union nationwide studies of new cars purchased over the last ten years, Chrysler had a 30 percent lower frequency of repair rate than the other manufacturers. So we're probably safe to assume that a new Dodge will be reliable.
   c. My English teacher has recommended three novels and they've all been wonderful. I think I'm going to enjoy this book of poetry because she just recommended it too.

## ARGUMENT BY ANALOGY

One of the most widely used varieties of inductive inference is based on analogies. An analogy is a comparison. Things which are alike in some respect are said to be "analogous." Analogies are similarities which have been noticed and are being applied to some intellectual purpose. There are many such purposes, because similarity is a basis for recognition. Here, for example, musician Wynton Marsalis uses an analogy to explain the usefulness of analogies in explaining some of the fascinating dimensions of music:

> As we explore the world of music, we'll be looking for similarities. It's kind of like when you try to begin a conversation with someone you don't know. It's better to talk about what you have in common, rather than be stifled by your obvious differences. We want to have fun with music, not fight it.[1]

Analogies can be used very effectively to explain new and unfamiliar or abstract and intangible things by comparing them to more familiar and tangible ones. Here, for example, mathematician John Allen Paulos uses two analogies to explain an instance of mathematical understatement which most of us might otherwise find very difficult to grasp:

> In a *Scientific American* column on innumeracy, the computer scientist Douglas Hofstadter cites the case of the Ideal Toy Company, which stated on the package of the original Rubik cube that there were more than three billion possible states the cube could attain. Calculations show that there are more than $4 \times 10^{19}$ possible states, 4 with 19 zeroes after it. What the package says isn't wrong; there are more than three billion possible states. The understatement, however, is symptomatic of a pervasive innumeracy which ill suits a technologically based society. It's analogous to a sign at the entrance to the Lincoln Tunnel stating: New York, population more than 6; or McDonald's proudly announces that they have sold more than 120 hamburgers.[2]

"Innumeracy" itself is quite possibly an unfamiliar concept, which Paulos introduces by means of an analogy with the more familiar concept of illiteracy. This analogy is compressed into his book's title, *Innumeracy: Mathematical Illiteracy and Its Consequences.* Analogies can be used simply to give a vivid description or to spice up a narrative. Imagine a recent divorcee telling her sister the story of how she fended off unwanted advances at the office, ". . . and I need a date like a fish needs a bicycle." An analogy can be used as the basis for a joke, as Lily Tomlin does when she notes that we get olive oil by squeezing olives and corn oil by squeezing kernels of corn and sesame oil by pressing sesame seeds and peanut oil by mashing peanuts, and then wonders how we get baby oil.

Analogies can also be used inferentially or argumentatively, that is, to infer conclusions and to support or defend controversial positions. We call this reasoning by analogy or argument by analogy. Here is an example in which the eighteenth century Scottish philosopher Thomas Reid argues for the probability of there being extraterrestrial organic life in our solar system:

> We may observe a very great similitude between this earth which we inhabit, and the other planets, Saturn, Jupiter, Mars, Venus and Mercury. They all revolve round the sun, as the earth does, although at different distances and in different periods. They borrow all their light from the sun, as the earth does. Several of them are known to revolve round their axis like the earth, and by that means, must have a like succession of day and night. Some of them have moons, that serve to give them light in the absence of the sun, as our moon does to us. They are all, in their motions, subject to the same law of gravitation, as the earth is. From all this similitude, it is not unreasonable to think that those planets may, like our earth, be the habitation of various orders of living creatures. There is some probability in this conclusion from analogy.[3]

Notice that Reid recognized that the inference is not deductively valid, in other words, that this is a form of inductive inference in which there is room for doubt and error. Nevertheless, he expressed cautious confidence in it as an inference. Now by the turn of the twenty-first century we have accumulated enough additional evidence to be pretty sure that the conclusion Reid was cautiously drawing is not true, though we may yet find evidence of organic life having at some earlier time inhabited one or more of the other planets in our solar system. But he was not essentially misguided in placing confidence in the argument. Indeed he was following a familiar and generally reliable line of reasoning, which a great many of our everyday inferences follow as well. If you try to enroll in Professor Smith's section of the upper division poetry course because you have taken three of her lower division courses and found her to be a knowledgeable and stimulating instructor, you are following the same analogical reasoning strategy as Reid was. In effect, you are reasoning as follows:

> I have observed several items: a, b, and c, each of which has the important characteristic 1 in common with target item d. [*I have taken three courses taught by the instructor of the course I'm contemplating.*]
>
> The observed items a, b, and c also have characteristics 2 and 3. [*The three courses I've taken were stimulating and imparted knowledge.*]
>
> Therefore, it is likely that target item d will have characteristics 2 and 3 as well. [*The course I'm contemplating is likely to be stimulating and to impart knowledge.*]

The basic inferential strategy of an argument by analogy, as illustrated in these examples, is to infer that if things are alike in some respects, they are probably alike in other ways as well. In the process of analysis and evaluation of arguments by analogy it is useful to distinguish the items compared by the roles they play in the comparison. For this purpose we will call the item used as the basis of the comparison the *analogue* and we will refer to the item about which conclusions are drawn or explanations are offered as the *target.* So, for example, in Thomas Reid's argument about extraterrestrial life, the planet earth is the analogue and the other planets in our solar system are the target. In the example about Professor Smith's poetry class, the three lower division courses you have taken are the analogues and the target is her upper division class.

## EXERCISE | Argument by Analogy

Identify the analogues and targets in each of the following analogies. Which analogies are used inferentially or argumentatively, and which are used for explanatory purposes, or narrative enhancement or entertainment?

1. If we were to repeat the same note without accents, it would be like our pulse. But what happens if we accent the first of every four **beats**—*one,* two, three, four, *one,* two, three, four? Accenting that first note sets up a rhythm we can count. Each note becomes part of a four-beat rhythm, and every four beats is one unit. This could get confusing if we didn't have a way to organize these units. But other things are that way, too. For example, if I ask you how far from home to school, you might say 5 blocks, but you wouldn't say 6,737 steps. Or you might say 10 minutes, not 600 seconds. You divide the distance or organize the time into convenient units. —Wynton Marsalis[4]

| Analogue | Target | Arg. | Exp. | Other |
|---|---|---|---|---|
| | | | | |

Explain your answer:

2. Suppose that someone tells me that he has had a tooth extracted without an anesthetic, and I express my sympathy, and suppose that I am then asked, "How do you know that it hurt him?" I might reasonably reply, "Well, I know that it would hurt me. I have been to the dentist and know how painful it is to have a tooth stopped [filled] without an anesthetic, let alone taken out. And he has the same sort of nervous system as I have. I infer, therefore, that in these conditions he felt considerable pain, just as I should have. —Alfred J. Ayer[5]

| Analogue | Target | Arg. | Exp. | Other |
|---|---|---|---|---|
| | | | | |

Explain your answer:

3. Social Security has given a bunch of money to old people. That's not terrible. But Social Security is a pyramid scheme. People who get in early make out like bandits. People who get in late are screwed. And Social Security is a very sophisticated pyramid scheme. The people who are going to get screwed weren't even born when Social Security was set up. But they have been now. And they're you. —P. J. O'Rourke[6]

| Analogue | Target | Arg. | Exp. | Other |
|---|---|---|---|---|
| | | | | |

Explain your answer:

4. What grounds have we for attributing suffering to other animals[?] It is best to begin by asking what grounds any individual human has for supposing that other humans feel pain. Since pain is a state of consciousness, a "mental event," it can never be directly observed. No observations, whether of behavioral signs such as writhing or screaming or physiological or neurological recordings, are observations of pain itself. Pain is something one feels, and one can only infer that others are feeling it from various external indications. The fact that only philosophers are ever skeptical about whether other humans feel pain shows that we regard such inferences as justifiable in the case of humans. Is there any reason why the same inference should be unjustifiable for other animals? Nearly all the external signs that lead us to infer pain in other humans can be seen in other species, especially "higher" animals such as mammals and birds. Behavioral signs—writhing, yelping, or other forms of calling, attempts to avoid the source of pain, and many others—are present. We know, too, that these animals are biologically similar in the relevant respects, having nervous systems like ours which can be observed to function as ours do. So the grounds for inferring that these animals can feel pain are nearly as good as the grounds for inferring other humans do.
—Peter Singer[7]

| Analogue | Target | Arg. | Exp. | Other |
|---|---|---|---|---|
| | | | | |

Explain your answer:

## EVALUATING ARGUMENTS BY ANALOGY

The variables that affect the strength of inductive inferences generally also pertain in evaluating arguments by analogy. For example the number of analogues relevant to the number of targets affects the strength of an argument by analogy in the same way as the size of the sample relative to the size of the population affects the strength of an inductive generalization. An argument based on a comparison to a large series of analogous cases will tend to be stronger than one based on a comparison to a single analogue, just as an inductive generalization based on many instances will be stronger than one based on a tiny sample. Similarly the number of observed similarities between analogue and target affects the strength of the analogy just as the representativeness of the sample relative to the population affects the strength of an inductive generalization. This is intuitively fairly obvious. In general the more similar things are observed to be the more likely they are to be similar in additional ways as well. Another variable which affects the strength of both inductive inferences generally and arguments by analogy is the strength of the conclusion relative to the evidence contained in the premises. An argument by analogy can be strengthened by hedging the conclusion with appropriate qualifications, as Thomas Reid did in the example about extraterrestrial life. Had he expressed the conclusion with greater certainty than he did, his argument would have been weaker than it was.

An important point about analogies in general: Analogies are always possible. That is, there are no two items in the universe that are so completely different from each other that they can't be compared in *some* way. Pick any two items you can think of. Use your imagination. Choose items as different from each other as you possibly can, like the moon and your left thumb. Now start thinking of ways in which they are similar to each other. This may not be *easy*, but it *is* possible. For example, both the moon and your left thumb take up space. Now, the flip side of this coin is important too: Analogies are always limited. That is, no two items in the universe are so completely alike that they cannot be distinguished in some way. In evaluating arguments by analogy we need to take account not only of similarities but also of differences. And the same general considerations that apply to similarities in the evaluation of analogical inferences apply to differences too, only in reverse. The more differences there are between analogue and target the weaker the analogy tends to be.

But there is another factor to consider in the evaluation of arguments by analogy, a factor which affects both similarities and differences, and which is more important than either similarities or differences by themselves. This is the factor of *relevance.* In our earlier example of the defective computer diskettes we noted that numerical order within the shipment might have something to do with whether a diskette is defective or not. Thus numerical order within the shipment is a *relevant* variable. Similarly in evaluating arguments or inferences by analogy we are most interested in similarities and differences which might reasonably be thought to have something to do with the conclusion being inferred about the target. In general the more relevant the observed similarities between analogue and target are to the conclusion being inferred, the stronger the analogy, and by the same token the more relevant the differences between analogue and target are to the conclusion being inferred, the weaker the analogy. For example, suppose you are shopping for a new car, and you decide that the new Honda Accord is likely to be a reliable low-maintenance vehicle because Hondas you have owned in the past have been reliable and required minimal maintenance, your inference is based on a relevant similarity, the identity of the manufacturer. But suppose someone drew the same conclusion about a car because it was blue, and the blue cars she had owned in the past had been reliable and required minimal maintenance. This inference would be based on an irrelevant similarity. There are good reasons for thinking that in general cars made by the same manufacturer will meet similar standards of reliability, but no similarly good reason to suppose that the color of a car makes a difference as to its reliability.

The most straightforward approach to evaluating an argument or inference by analogy is to add up the relevant similarities and differences. This can be accomplished fairly easily by means of a simple form (see following table).

For purposes of illustration we will use two examples from the Exercises you just completed: Alfred J. Ayer's inference to the conclusion that another person besides himself feels pain, and Peter Singer's very similar argument to the conclusion that nonhuman animals suffer pain. Ayer uses himself as the analogue. The target is some other person. There is one basic similarity used as a premise: similar nervous system. And of course the conclusion is that the other person would have the same sort of pain that Ayer would. Thus:

| ***Ayer's Argument*** | **Analogue** Ayer | **Target** Other humans | **Comment** |
|---|---|---|---|
| **Basic points of similarity used as premises** | Central nervous system basic to physiology of sensory experience of pain | Central nervous system basic to physiology of sensory experience of pain | |
| **Conclusion** | Ayer experiences pain when undergoing dental work w/o anesthetic | **Other people experience pain when undergoing dental work w/o anesthetic** | |
| **Differences** | | | |

To evaluate this as an argument by analogy we would first want to know whether the similarity Ayer asserts in fact exists. Is it really the case that people have similar neurophysiology? And they do. Next we want to determine whether this similarity is relevant to the conclusion Ayer is trying to draw. And it is. Because we have good theoretical grounds and empirical evidence to suppose that a body's neurophysiology is the central mechanism involved in the person's sensory experience. So, we might add the following in the Comment column:

| ***Ayer's Argument*** | **Analogue**<br>Ayer | **Target**<br>Other humans | **Comment** |
|---|---|---|---|
| **Basic points of similarity used as premises** | Central nervous system basic to physiology of sensory experience of pain | Central nervous system basic to physiology of sensory experience of pain | High degree of similarity<br>Highly relevant to conclusion |
| **Conclusion** | Ayer experiences pain when undergoing dental work w/o anesthetic | **Other people experience pain when undergoing dental work w/o anesthetic** | |
| **Differences** | | | |

At this point, we would want to determine whether there are significant relevant differences between the analogue and the target. In the case of this particular argument, since the analogy is between Ayer himself and *any* other human being, the differences would have to relate to characteristics unique to Ayer which would distinguish him from *any* other human being. And, of course, there are many such characteristics, as there are with all human individuals. For example, Ayer was the author of an important work of philosophy published in 1936 titled *Language, Truth and Logic.* This is true of no other human being. But, we can't think of any such differences which would be relevant to Ayer's conclusion. So, we might complete the evaluation as follows:

| ***Ayer's Argument*** | **Analogue**<br>Ayer | **Target**<br>Other humans | **Comment** |
|---|---|---|---|
| **Basic points of similarity used as premises** | Central nervous system basic to physiology of sensory experience of pain | Central nervous system basic to physiology of sensory experience of pain | High degree of similarity<br>Highly relevant to conclusion |
| **Conclusion** | Ayer experiences pain when undergoing dental work w/o anesthetic | **Other people experience pain when undergoing dental work w/o anesthetic** | |
| **Differences** | Ayer was the author of *Language, Truth and Logic* published in 1936 | No other human being was the author of *Languge Truth and Logic* published in 1936 | True but irrevelant |

So, Ayer's argument appears to be quite strong, in spite of the fact that it is based on one lone similarity. Let us now look at Singer's closely similar argument about nonhuman animals. In this case the analogue is human beings and the target is nonhuman animals. The conclusion is that nonhuman animals have experiences of pain similar to those of humans. This inference rests on two basic points of similarity: similarity of neurophysiology, and similarity in behavioral responses to stimuli. Thus:

| ***Singer's Argument*** | **Analogue** Human beings | **Target** Nonhuman animals | **Comment** |
|---|---|---|---|
| **Basic points of similarity used as premises** | Central nervous system basic to physiology of sensory experience of pain | Central nervous system basic to physiology of sensory experience of pain | |
| | Expressive behavioral responses to sensory stimuli | Expressive behavioral responses to sensory stimuli | |
| **Conclusion** | Humans enjoy pleasure and suffer pain | **Nonhuman animals enjoy pleasure and suffer pain** | |
| **Differences** | | | |

To evaluate this as an argument by analogy, we would first want to know whether the similarities Singer asserts in fact exist. Is it really the case that humans and nonhuman animals have similar neurophysiology? They do. And how similar are human and nonhuman animal neurophysiology? In some cases the similarity is extremely high in complex and sophisticated detail. And do humans and nonhuman animals exhibit similar behavioral responses to stimuli? Again, the answer is yes, to a remarkably high and complex degree of similarity in many cases. Next, we want to determine whether these similarities are relevant to the conclusion Singer is trying to draw. And they are. Because we have good theoretical grounds and empirical evidence to suppose that a body's neurophysiology is central mechanism involved in an organism's sensory experience, and similarly good theoretical and evidentiary grounds to connect behavioral manifestations to inner experience. So, we might add the following comments:

| ***Singer's Argument*** | **Analogue** Human beings | **Target** Nonhuman animals | **Comment** |
|---|---|---|---|
| **Basic points of similarity used as premises** | Central nervous system basic to physiology of sensory experience of pain | Central nervous system basic to physiology of sensory experience of pain | High degree of similarity<br>Highly relevant to conclusion |
| | Expressive behavioral responses to sensory stimuli | Expressive behavioral responses to sensory stimuli | High degree of similarity<br>Highly relevant to conclusion |
| **Conclusion** | Humans enjoy pleasure and suffer pain | **Nonhuman animals enjoy pleasure and suffer pain** | |
| **Differences** | | | |

At this point, we would want to determine whether there are significant relevant differences between the analogue and the target. And, of course, there are many differences between humans and animals of other species (and several perhaps that people might think relevant to Singer's conclusion). For example, Singer goes on in the essay from which the example was taken to consider the issue of language. Now there may be some controversy over the question of whether humans are the only species of animal with the capacity to develop and use languages. But for the sake of the argument let's suppose that this difference genuinely does exist. Now the question is whether this is a relevant difference. Singer argues that it is not because we do not attribute pain to human beings on the basis of their linguistic behavior, but more so on the basis of the sorts of behavior exhibited by other species of animal. So, on this basis, we might go on toward completing the evaluation of the argument as follows:

| *Singer's Argument* | **Analogue** Human beings | **Target** Nonhuman animals | **Comment** |
|---|---|---|---|
| **Basic points of similarity used as premises** | Central nervous system basic to physiology of sensory experience of pain | Central nervous system basic to physiology of sensory experience of pain | High degree of similarity<br>Highly relevant to conclusion |
| | Expressive behavioral responses to sensory stimuli | Expressive behavioral responses to sensory stimuli | High degree of similarity<br>Highly relevant to conclusion |
| **Conclusion** | Humans enjoy pleasure and suffer pain | **Nonhuman animals enjoy pleasure and suffer pain** | |
| **Differences** | Human beings have linguistic capacity | Nonhuman animals do not have linguistic capacity | Plausible, although open to question<br>Irrelevant to conclusion |

So far, Singer's argument, like Ayer's, appears to be quite strong.

## REFUTATION BY ANALOGY

An argumentative use of analogy which deserves special mention is the refutation of arguments by comparison. In this strategy the target is usually an argument (occasionally the thesis of an argument) and the goal is to discredit the target by showing that it is analogous to some other argument (or thesis) which is obviously weak or objectionable. In the following passage from *Alice's Adventures in Wonderland,* Alice gets refuted by the Mad Hatter and the March Hare. The Mad Hatter has told Alice, who has just said something illogical, that she should "say what she means."

> "I do," Alice hastily replied; "at least—at least I mean what I say—that's the same thing, you know."
>
> "Not the same thing a bit!" said the Hatter. "Why, you might just as well say that 'I see what I eat' is the same thing as 'I eat what I see'!"
>
> "You might just as well say," added the March Hare, "that 'I like what I get' is the same thing as 'I get what I like'!"[8]

In Chapter 6 we used an example of refutation by logical analogy in presenting and explaining the concept of a formal fallacy when we compared the two arguments below:

| | |
|---|---|
| (1) All Americans are human. | (1) All men are human. |
| (2) All Californians are human. | (2) All women are human. |
| ∴ (3) All Californians are Americans. | ∴ (3) All women are men. |

And we presented a strategy for demonstrating an argument to be formally fallacious by constructing a formally analogous argument, that is, one which follows an identical formal pattern but has obviously true premises and an obviously false conclusion.

## PRESUMPTION AND THE BURDEN OF PROOF

Another variety of inductive inference consists of "burden of proof" arguments—arguments based on presumption. The most obvious and familiar example of this sort of reasoning is the "presumption of innocence" in many legal traditions. For example, in the American system of jurisprudence the accused is presumed innocent unless and until the prosecution meets its "burden of proof." "Burden of proof" means the obligation to produce the argument. The party with the burden of proof is the party that has to produce the argument. If the party with the burden of proof fails to meet its burden of proof, the issue is decided in favor of the other party.

A legitimate question concerning burden of proof is how we decide where, on which side of an issue, the burden of proof belongs. Why, for example, does the prosecution have the burden of proof in American criminal law? Why not the defense? Why shouldn't the accused have to prove his or her innocence? Another legitimate question concerns the size of that burden. How heavy is the burden of proof? For example the burden of proof in a criminal trial is heavier than in a civil trial. In a criminal trial the prosecution must prove guilt "beyond a reasonable doubt" (a deliberately vague, but nevertheless very high standard of proof). In a civil trial, the plaintiff (the one who is bringing the lawsuit, the one making the complaint) has only the obligation of making a *prima facie* case, which then shifts the burden of proof onto the defense. Why is this?

Let us approach these questions at the more general theoretical level. In general, the placement of the burden of proof on one or another side of an issue and the weight of that burden are governed by a number of general rules of thumb (remember, this is the kind of rule which will have exceptions). One such rule is based on the concept of plausibility as explained in Chapter 5. In general, the less plausible the arguer's position, the heavier the burden of proof. Another general rule, derived from the discipline and traditions of rhetoric, has to do with the distinction between the "affirmative" and "negative" positions in a debate. In general, the affirmative side in a debate has the burden of proof. The reason for this is that it is in general so much harder to "prove the negative." For example, if someone believes in the healing power of the mind, or the therapeutic efficacy of marijuana, or the existence of intelligent extraterrestrial life, they are expected to produce the evidence. All the affirmative side would need to do to prove conclusively that extraterrestrial intelligent life exists would be to bring forward one specimen. You can see how much harder it would be to prove *conclusively* that extraterrestrial intelligent life does *not* exist. So, in fairness, the general rule is to place the burden of proof on the affirmative position in a dispute. Fairness is also behind the placement of the burden of proof on the prosecution in American criminal and civil law. In civil law it seems fair to place the burden of proof initially on the party making the complaint, but then to have it shift to the other party if there's enough evidence to support reasonable suspicion. In criminal law the accused is (usually) an individual, whereas the prosecution is the "people" acting collectively through the agency of the government, and the stakes are almost always some form of punishment. Fairness seems to call for the prosecution to produce conclusive proof of guilt. There is another rationale for placing the burden of proof on the prosecution. Consider the question of how justice could be miscarried. It seems that there are only two kinds of miscarriage of justice: where a guilty party gets off without penalty; and where an innocent party gets penalized. Which of these two kinds of miscarriage of justice is worse? Some legal traditions, the American system for example, are based on the idea that it's worse to punish an innocent person than to let a guilty person go unpunished.

*Not everyone agrees with this idea. Question: Is it worse to punish an innocent person than to let a guilty person go unpunished? Or is it the other way around? Or are the two equally bad? An interesting exercise would be to consider the arguments that might be made on all sides.*

This idea about possible outcomes and their costs and benefits points to another general rule of thumb governing the placement of the burden of proof. In general the greater the risk of error and the higher the cost associated with being wrong the heavier the burden of proof. For example, if someone suggested that you invest a small sum of money in a mutual fund you might want some evidence that the fund is well and profitably managed, but you'd want even more stringent proof of the security of your investment if it represented your entire life savings. In general then, the burden of proof is placed and the standard of proof is set where they "reasonably belong," which is to say where reasonable explanation and argument will support.

Burden of proof arguments then consist in first locating the burden of proof, establishing the standard of proof and then arguing that the standard of proof has not been met by whoever has that burden. In situations involving the burden of proof there is almost always room for doubt regarding the truth of either side's case. The burden of proof establishes which side gets the benefit of the doubt. So, for example, the defense in a criminal trial can argue not that the defendant didn't do it, but that the evidence submitted by the prosecution does not prove beyond a reasonable doubt that he did. The benefit of the doubt goes to the defense.

## REASONING HYPOTHETICALLY

A subtle and complex, but crucial variety of inductive reasoning consists in reasoning from facts or observations to explanatory hypotheses. An explanation is an idea or set of ideas which succeeds in reducing or eliminating puzzlement. An "explanatory hypothesis" is an idea or set of ideas put forward for that purpose. The word "hypothesis" means supposition or conjecture. It comes originally from the Greek word *thesis,* which means "idea proposed or laid down for consideration" and the Greek root *hypo-*, which means "under." Here the "under" is meant to indicate that the idea which has been proposed is "under investigation."

As the terms suggest, this variety of inductive reasoning, "hypothetical reasoning," is used primarily in trying to better understand the many puzzling things there are in life—the many things that prompt the question "Why?" Why is the water salty in the Pacific Ocean but not in Lake Tahoe? Why do so many incumbents continue to win reelection in spite of overwhelming anti-incumbent sentiment in the polls? Why does the Dow Jones index continue rising while fundamental economic indicators such as the unemployment rate indicate a recession? Why does the sound of an approaching train whistle appear to drop in pitch as the train passes by? We draw inferences to explanations constantly in all sorts of situations, and when we do, just as when we generalize, we risk error—that is, we reason inductively.

A simple example will illustrate the general structure of inferences to explanatory hypotheses. A customs inspector is examining the contents of a crate. In it she finds several plastic bags of white powder. What is it? Heroin? Cocaine? Flour? She tests it by tasting it, and finds that it is sweet, identifying it as powdered sugar. We might represent her reasoning in the form of the argument or inference:

This tastes sweet.

---

∴ This is sugar.

In identifying the powder as sugar the customs inspector has not reasoned deductively. The conclusion does not follow deductively from the premise. But the inference from the taste of the substance to its classification is a reasonable induction. Though there remains room for doubt about the truth of the conclusion, the premise does make it *reasonable to suppose* that the conclusion is true. What makes the inference reasonable? How does the premise make it reasonable to suppose that the conclusion is true? What makes the inference reasonable is the idea that *if the conclusion were true, that would explain the truth of the premise*—or—*if the conclusion were not true, that would make the premise much more puzzling.* In other words, the observed fact that the substance tastes sweet *can be best explained* by assuming that it is sugar. This is the general structure of inferences to explanatory hypotheses, or hypothetical reasoning.

The importance of hypothetical reasoning lies in its capacity to extend or expand our knowledge of the world. Since hypothetical reasoning always takes us beyond what we already know it always involves the risk of error. Just as with inductive generalizations, the strength of an inference to an explanatory hypothesis is essentially a matter of how well the risk of error is managed or controlled. There really is no way to manage the risk of error in hypothetical reasoning on an individual inference-by-inference basis. In order to manage the risk of error in hypothetical reasoning we must engage in more and more of it—in effect, using hypothetical reasoning to evaluate hypothetical reasoning. More precisely, the risk of error is measured and managed in terms of the relative plausibility of competing explanatory hypotheses, their relative explanatory power, and the degree to which a given hypothesis can be supported by experimental evidence.

## PLAUSIBILITY

In Chapter 5 we introduced the idea of plausibility as a measure of how well we think an idea is likely to survive critical scrutiny. How well would the idea hold up were we to devise strenuous tests designed to expose any falsity in the idea? A plausible idea is one which we think would hold up well. An implausible idea is one which we think would not hold up so well.

From our earlier discussion in Chapter 5 you'll remember that neither plausibility nor implausibility is "absolute." Rather, they admit of degrees. This means that some ideas are more plausible than others. Moreover, our estimates of an idea's plausibility or implausibility are not static. Rather, they are subject to adjustment in accordance with new incoming information. What may appear initially to be a plausible idea may, on further investigation, seem more and more or less and less plausible. And plausibility is only loosely correlated with truth. A plausible idea may well turn out not to be true. And there are a good many cases throughout history of initially implausible ideas which have nonetheless been confirmed as true. Plausibility, in other words, is a preliminary estimate of an idea's worth. *In general, the more plausible the explanatory hypothesis, the stronger the inference.* Here we are interested in *relative* plausibility. We need to know how the explanatory hypothesis under investigation compares with others. Is there another hypothesis which is just as or even more likely to survive critical scrutiny? If not, that strengthens the inference.

For example, remember the customs inspector. As soon as she tastes the powder, she has occasion to consider the explanatory hypothesis that the powder is sugar. This is of course not the only hypothesis which might account for the observed fact that the powder tastes sweet. It could possibly be a new derivative of coca, genetically engineered to have a taste indistinguishable from powdered sugar, so as to escape detection as a variety of cocaine. This hypothesis, if true, would account for the observed fact that the powder tastes sweet, and it is certainly within the realm of the "possible," but it is much less plausible than the simple powdered sugar hypothesis.

Here's another hypothesis which might account for the observed fact that the powder tastes sweet. Perhaps the powder is cocaine and the customs inspector has suddenly developed a "taste blindness," so that cocaine and powdered sugar taste identical to her. Again, this hypothesis, if true, would account for the observed fact that the powder tastes sweet. This hypothesis too is within the realm of the "possible." But like the "sweet cocaine hypothesis" also much less plausible than the simple powdered sugar hypothesis.

An interesting theoretical problem arises when you compare the taste blindness hypothesis and the sweet cocaine hypothesis against each other. Is one of them more plausible than the other? If so, which one? Or are they equally implausible? How do we tell? In this case it doesn't matter a whole lot since there's a much more plausible option available in the simple powdered sugar hypothesis. But what if we had to choose between competing hypotheses which seemed about equally plausible—or equally implausible? Or what if we couldn't agree which of several competing hypotheses was the most plausible—or the least plausible? Fortunately plausibility is not the only standard we have to appeal to.

## EXPLANATORY POWER

Remember that an explanatory hypothesis is an idea or set of ideas put forward to reduce or eliminate puzzlement. And a good explanation is one that succeeds in reducing or eliminating puzzlement. The "explanatory power" of a given hypothesis is the capacity it has to reduce or eliminate puzzlement. *In general, the greater the explanatory power of a given hypothesis, the stronger the inference.* Here, as with plausibility, we are interested in *relative* explanatory power. We need to know how the explanatory hypothesis under investigation compares with others. Is there another hypothesis which would explain the observed facts in the premises equally well or better? If not, that strengthens the inference. Are there other observed facts besides the ones in the premises which the hypothesis explains better than competing hypotheses? If so, that too strengthens the inference.

For example, consider the following case: The neighbors have discovered the body of a well known but reclusive novelist. The homicide inspector arrives at the scene. The body of the deceased is slumped over the typewriter in which there is a sheet of paper with what appears to be an unfinished suicide note. Beside the body is a hypodermic syringe. Traces of white powder are recovered from the table beside the typewriter. The autopsy establishes the cause of death as heroin overdose, and fixes the time of death at around 3 A.M. A psychiatric history of the deceased reveals several bouts of depression over a ten-year period and two previous suicide attempts. One plausible hypothesis, the obvious one, is that the novelist committed suicide by injecting himself with heroin and lost consciousness while at the typewriter composing the suicide note. Still the inspector is puzzled. She cannot account for the fact that the typewriter, an IBM electric, is switched off. Nor can she account for the fact that neither the reading lamp nor the overhead light was on in the room at the time the body was discovered. If the novelist died at 3 A.M. while typing, how did he manage to turn off the typewriter and all of the lights?

What the inspector needs now is an explanatory hypothesis with greater explanatory power. Perhaps the novelist was murdered by someone who tried to make the murder look like a suicide. Perhaps the murderer was surprised at the scene of the crime by approaching footsteps, and, in order to discourage the approaching party from intruding upon the scene and discovering the crime, turned off the lights and the typewriter. This hypothesis, though not nearly as plausible as the suicide hypothesis, nevertheless has greater explanatory power, because it accounts for everything that the suicide hypothesis accounts for plus the fact that the typewriter and lights were switched off.

Just as with plausibility, a theoretical problem arises in connection with explanatory power, when we have to compare competing hypotheses which seem about equally powerful, or when we can't agree which of several competing hypotheses is the most powerful. Just as with the earlier problem, we can appeal to the plausibility standard when the explanatory power standard is not decisive. But we're still left with the problem of what to do when competing hypotheses seem to measure up roughly equally in both areas. And there is another theoretical problem. In our present example, the murder hypothesis is less plausible but more powerful as an explanatory hypothesis. This raises the question: How do we determine the strength of a hypothetical inference when our standards conflict? Does explanatory power outweigh plausibility? Or is it the other way around? Or does it depend? Maybe explanatory power outweighs plausibility when the explanatory-power gap is bigger than the plausibility gap, and vice versa. It would be nice if there were a good answer to this question which is both simple and straightforward. But as far as we know, the best approach to resolving any of these problems is just to test hypotheses experimentally.

## EXERCISE | Plausibility and Explanatory Power

Several theories have arisen since the assassination of President Kennedy, an event which remains shrouded in mystery and controversy more than thirty years after the fact. Rank the following theories in descending order of plausibility. Then rank them in descending order of explanatory power.

| Plausibility | Explanatory Power | |
|---|---|---|
| | | Lee Harvey Oswald, acting alone, assassinated the president. |
| | | The assassination was planned and executed by the Mafia. |
| | | The assassination was planned and executed by officials of the United States government. |
| | | The assassination was planned and executed by officials of the United States government, in collaboration with the Mafia. |
| | | The assassination was planned and executed by officials of a foreign government. |

(continued)

| Plausibility | Explanatory Power | |
|---|---|---|
| | | The assassination was planned and executed by officials of a foreign government in collaboration with officials of the United States government. |
| | | The assassination was carried out by aliens from outer space. |

Compare your rankings with those of your classmates. Try to resolve any points of disagreement by explaining your answers to each other.

## TESTING HYPOTHESES

Remember that the word "hypothesis" means an idea or set of ideas which is "under investigation." To investigate hypotheses is to search for experimental evidence relevant to their truth or falsity. And the "scientific method" for doing this boils down to first using the hypothesis under investigation to predict things, and then seeing whether or not the predictions turn out to be true. *If what the hypothesis predicts turns out to be true that counts in favor of, or "confirms," the hypothesis. If what the hypothesis predicts turns out not to be true that counts against, or "disconfirms," the hypothesis.*

For example, let's go back to the customs inspector's first hypothesis, that the white powder is sugar. What else do we know about sugar that we could use to test this hypothesis? We know that sugar is soluble in water. So, using the hypothesis, along with this knowledge, we might predict that the powder will dissolve in water. Now if we place the powder in water, and it does dissolve, this counts as evidence confirming the hypothesis that the powder is indeed sugar. If we place the powder in water, and it does not dissolve, this counts as evidence disconfirming the hypothesis that the powder is sugar. Confirming and disconfirming evidence each vary in strength according to the strength of the prediction involved. *The more certain the prediction, the stronger the evidence. In testing hypotheses we should search for both confirming and disconfirming evidence.*

In quite a few cases we may expect to find evidence of both kinds. For example, in the case of the deceased novelist there is some evidence which confirms the suicide hypothesis and some evidence which disconfirms it. Naturally we would be interested in the relative weight of the evidence for and against a given hypothesis. At first there seems to be more evidence in favor of the hypothesis than there is against it. But when the disconfirming evidence first emerges the homicide inspector quite correctly becomes suspicious. She not only begins to consider other hypotheses, but she also begins to focus her investigation in search specifically of more evidence disconfirming the suicide hypothesis. Why does she proceed in this way, instead of simply concluding that the suicide hypothesis is correct because there is more confirming evidence than disconfirming evidence? The homicide inspector is following the general principle that *disconfirming evidence weighs more heavily than confirming evidence.*

Why does disconfirming evidence outweigh confirming evidence? Again, let's consider the customs inspector and the white powder. To test the sugar hypothesis, we derived the prediction that the powder will dissolve in water. And so, if it does we have confirming evidence, otherwise disconfirming evidence. Confirming evidence does not completely verify the hypothesis. But notice that disconfirming evidence completely refutes it. Here's why.

Our prediction that the powder will dissolve takes the form of this hypothetical statement:

> If our hypothesis that the powder is sugar is correct, then the powder will dissolve in water.

When our test confirms the hypothesis, what we observe is, in effect, the consequent of this hypothetical statement coming true:

> The powder does dissolve in water.

You'll remember that from these two statements we cannot validly deduce the conclusion that the powder is sugar. If we simply inferred this as a conclusion we would be committing the fallacy of asserting the consequent. This makes sense, when you consider that there may well be other white powdered substances (like artificial sweeteners) which taste sweet and dissolve in water. Nevertheless, the combination of the two statements does, in this sort of situation, provide relevant though not absolutely conclusive evidence in support of the hypothesis under investigation.

On the other hand, when our test disconfirms the hypothesis, what we observe is, in effect, the negation of the consequent coming true:

> The powder does not dissolve in water.

You'll remember that from these two statements we can validly deduce the conclusion that the powder is not sugar by Modus Tollens. This is why disconfirming evidence is stronger than confirming evidence, and also why this inferential method is often referred to as the "hypothetical deductive" method.

An interesting application of the principle that disconfirming evidence outweighs confirming evidence generates an additional form of confirming evidence. If we search thoroughly for disconfirming evidence, and find none, that in itself constitutes a kind of confirming evidence. This is sometimes referred to as "indirect confirmation."

## EXERCISE | Testing Hypotheses

The following is an argument from businessman (and former presidential candidate) H. Ross Perot:

> We have unfairly blamed the American worker for the poor quality of our products. The unsatisfactory quality is the result of poor design and engineering—not poor assembly. If

> you take a car made in Japan by Japanese workers and place it alongside a Japanese car made in a U.S. plant by U.S. workers (led by Japanese executives), there is no difference in quality. The Honda cars made in this country by U.S. workers are of such high quality that Honda intends to export them. Obviously, the American worker is not the problem. The problem is failure of leadership.

Write a short essay in which you explain Perot's argument using the concepts discussed above. What hypotheses is Perot considering? What evidence does he present? Explain how the evidence is being used by Perot to confirm or disconfirm the hypotheses he's considering.

## CAUSAL REASONING

One of the most widespread and important applications of hypothetical inductive reasoning has to do with figuring out how things work—determining the causes and effects of things. Why is the left channel of the stereo intermittently fuzzy and distorted? What is causing that little clicking noise at 40 miles per hour? What will the environmental, psychological, and social consequences of the development of virtual reality technology be? These are typical of the kind of causal reasoning problems we encounter so frequently in so many aspects of our lives. But reasoning about causes and effects is tricky. First of all, as the eighteenth century Scottish philosopher David Hume pointed out, we never directly observe causal relationships. We have to infer them. Next, we can never infer them with deductive certainty. Since the evidence for a causal relationship is always indirect, there will always be some room for doubt when we infer a cause. In other words, we must reason inductively about them. Finally, reasoning about causes by means of simple inductive generalization turns out not to be very reliable, due to the fact that inductive generalization by itself provides no basis for distinguishing between a causal relationship and a mere coincidence.

### MILL'S METHODS

The nineteenth century English philosopher John Stuart Mill, best known for his work in moral and political philosophy, also made significant contributions to inductive logic, particularly in its applications to causal reasoning. Mill spelled out a number of guidelines—extensions of the above evaluative principles for inductive generalization—designed to make reasoning about causes and effects more reliable. These guidelines, often referred to as "Mill's methods" are widely respected and followed as part of what we now call the "scientific method."

#### METHOD OF AGREEMENT

Mill's method of agreement is a variation of simple inductive generalization. It consists of seeking out some common antecedent condition in all cases of the effect whose cause we are trying to determine. It is based on the (reasonable) assumption that *the cause will be present in every instance in which the effect occurs.* Thus if we can identify some such common antecedent condition, it is a likely candidate for the cause. For example, suppose that certain people start showing a strange new set of debilitating symptoms in several major cities at around the same time. What is the cause of the strange new disease? Right away we would want to know what these people have in common that might account for their symptoms. We know they live in different parts of the world. Let's suppose that no two individuals live within five hundred miles of each other, that they range in age from five to seventy-five years old, that some of them are male, some female, that they have no common occupation, and so on. Now if we were to discover that all of the people suffering from these symptoms had traveled during the month of June to a particular vacation spot (let's call it Fantasy Island), then we might suppose that the cause of the symptoms is related in some way to vacationing on Fantasy Island in June.

The following table illustrates the method of agreement. Let the ten instances represent the ten individual cases under investigation, the letter "s" represent the effect of suffering from the symptoms, and the letters "A," "B," "C," "D," "E," "F," and "G" represent a range of antecedent conditions, "F" representing having vacationed on Fantasy Island in June.

### METHOD OF AGREEMENT

| Instance | Antecedent Conditions | | | | | | | Effect |
|---|---|---|---|---|---|---|---|---|
| 1 | A | B | | D | E | F | | s |
| 2 | A | | C | | E | F | G | s |
| 3 | | B | | D | E | F | G | s |
| 4 | | | C | D | E | F | | s |
| 5 | A | B | | | | F | | s |
| 6 | | | | D | | F | G | s |
| 7 | | | | | | F | | s |
| 8 | A | B | C | D | E | F | G | s |
| 9 | A | B | | | | F | | s |
| 10 | | | C | | | F | G | s |

Of course, the fact that all of the symptom sufferers vacationed on Fantasy Island in June does not *prove* (deductively) a causal connection. But it does make it *reasonable to suppose* that such a causal relationship exists, and that is all we can expect from an inductive inference. If having vacationed on Fantasy Island were the *only* common factor we could find among all of the symptom sufferers, we could be even more confident of a causal connection. *In general, the more isolated the common antecedent condition, the more likely it is to be causally related to the effect.*

## METHOD OF DIFFERENCE

The problem, of course, is that any collection of individuals will have not one but very many different antecedent conditions in common, most of which will turn out not to have any causal connection with the effect we are seeking to understand. In this example, having been on Fantasy Island in June together means having not just one but many things in common: exposure to common sources of food and water, exposure to the full range of substances and organisms present in the environment, including the other vacationers, and so on. So we need a way of narrowing the field—eliminating some of the many candidates we're likely to identify by means of the method of agreement.

For this purpose, Mill formulated the method of difference. The method of difference is based on the reasonable assumption that *the cause will be absent from every instance in which the effect does not occur.* To continue with our example, let us suppose that we get a list of all of the people who traveled to Fantasy Island in June and it turns out that some of them have not suffered any of the symptoms we're investigating. So next we would want to know what differences there are between these people and the symptom sufferers. Now suppose we discover that the Fantasy Island vacationers who did not get sick also did not go swimming. This would suggest that the cause of the symptoms has something to do with swimming.

The following table illustrates the method of difference. Let the twelve instances represent the twelve individuals who vacationed on Fantasy Island in June, the letter "s" represent the effect of suffering from the symptoms, and the letters "L," "M," "N," "O," "P," "R," and "S" represent a range of activities like attending the luau, beach volleyball, cycling, drinking rum, and so on, "S" representing swimming.

### METHOD OF DIFFERENCE

| Instance | Antecedent Conditions | | | | | | | Effect |
|---|---|---|---|---|---|---|---|---|
| 1 | L | M | N | O | P | R | S | s |
| 2 | L | | N | O | P | | S | s |
| 3 | L | M | N | O | P | | S | s |
| 4 | | M | | O | P | R | S | s |
| 5 | L | M | N | | P | R | S | s |
| 6 | L | M | N | O | P | R | S | s |
| 7 | L | M | | O | | R | S | s |
| 8 | | | N | O | P | | S | s |
| 9 | L | | N | O | P | R | S | s |
| 10 | L | M | | O | P | R | S | s |
| 11 | L | M | N | O | P | R | – | – |
| 12 | L | M | N | O | P | | – | – |

Like the method of agreement, the method of difference is a variation of simple inductive generalization. Instead of looking for a correlation between instances of the effect and some common antecedent condition, here we are looking for a correlation between the *absence* of the effect and the *absence* of an antecedent condition. Like the method of agreement, the method of difference is not absolutely conclusive. The discovery of such a correlation, in this example between not having gone swimming and not suffering the symptoms, does not *prove* (deductively) that the symptoms and swimming are causally related, but it does make it reasonable to suppose that they are. If having gone swimming were the *only* difference we could find between the symptom sufferers and the vacationers who did not get sick, we could be even more confident of a causal connection. *In general, the more isolated the difference, the more likely it is to be causally related to the effect.*

## JOINT METHOD OF AGREEMENT AND DIFFERENCE

Since the method of agreement and the method of difference each enhance the reliability of inductive inferences about causal relationships when used separately, it is reasonable to suppose that using them together in the same investigation (as in our example) would strengthen the inductive inference to a causal relationship even further. In other words, if some antecedent condition is *both* common to all instances of the effect whose cause is under investigation *and* absent from instances where the effect is also absent, that makes a causal connection even more likely.

## METHOD OF CONCOMITANT VARIATION

Now, suppose we turn up a Fantasy Island vacationer who went swimming but didn't get sick or a Fantasy Island vacationer who got sick but didn't go swimming.

We saw earlier how the method of agreement is limited by the fact that any collection of individuals will have not one but many common antecedent conditions, most of which will have no causal connection with the effect we are seeking to understand. For this reason the method of agreement, by itself, is rarely adequate to identify the cause of any phenomenon. And we have now seen how the method of difference helps to identify the cause by a process of elimination. But the method of difference has a limitation of its own, which in turn limits the joint method of agreement and difference. The method of difference—and therefore also the joint method of agreement and difference—depends upon being able to observe instances from which a suspected cause is *absent.* To apply the method of difference we need to find, or experimentally bring about, an instance in which an antecedent condition which is suspected as a cause is out of the picture. Let's suppose that by the method of agreement we have discovered that there are five antecedent conditions common to all instances in which the effect we're investigating has been observed. To apply the method of difference thoroughly we would need to be able to observe what happens when each of these five antecedent conditions is missing. And this is not always easy to do. Sometimes it's practically impossible. Mill's own example of isolating the cause of tides shows this. When it was suspected that one of the many antecedent conditions which accompanies the ebb and flow of the tides—the position of the moon—was the actual cause of tidal motion, it was nevertheless impossible to confirm this suspicion by the method of difference. As Mill said, "We cannot try an experiment in the absence of the moon, so as to observe what terrestrial phenomena her annihilation would put an end to."[9] To overcome this limitation Mill formulated the method of concomitant variation. When it is difficult or impossible to eliminate a suspected cause it may nevertheless still be possible to *vary* it, or to observe its natural variations, and see whether these variations are accompanied by corresponding variations in the effect under investigation. In the case of the moon and the tides it turns out that the closer the moon is to a particular coastal region the higher the tide, and the further the moon is from a particular coastal region the lower the tide, which makes it reasonable to suppose that there is a causal connection.

The following table illustrates the joint method of agreement and difference supplemented by the method of concomitant variation for three instances of some effect "s." The letters "L," "M," "N," "O," "P," "R," and "S" represent a range of antecedent conditions. By the method of agreement we determine that five of these conditions—"L," "N," "O," "P," and "S"—are present in all cases where "s" is observed. So these are our causal candidates. But there are no cases where any of these conditions, or the effect "s," is absent. So we cannot isolate a cause by the method of difference. But each of the antecedent conditions varies in degree (represented by the plus and minus signs). And only one of them varies in a way which corresponds to variations in the effect. So that condition, "O," is most likely to be causally connected to "s."

### JOINT METHOD OF AGREEMENT AND DIFFERENCE WITH CONCOMITANT VARIATION

| Instance | Antecedent Conditions | | | | | | | Effect |
|---|---|---|---|---|---|---|---|---|
| 1 | L+ | M | N− | O | P− | R | S+ | s |
| 2 | L | | N+ | O+ | P | | S− | s+ |
| 3 | L− | M | N | O− | P+ | | S | s− |

The method of concomitant variation is a widely used experimental strategy in the sciences. For example, in pharmacology researchers routinely study the efficacy of experimental drugs by varying the dosage. If the observed effects on the alleviation of symptoms vary with the dosage, going up when the dosage is increased and going down when the dosage is decreased, that counts as confirmation of the causal efficacy of the drug. If the alleviation of symptoms does not vary with the dosage—if for example the symptoms are alleviated slightly with small doses, and slightly more with slightly larger doses, but not at all with large doses—that would raise doubts about the causal efficacy of the drug (see the following figure).

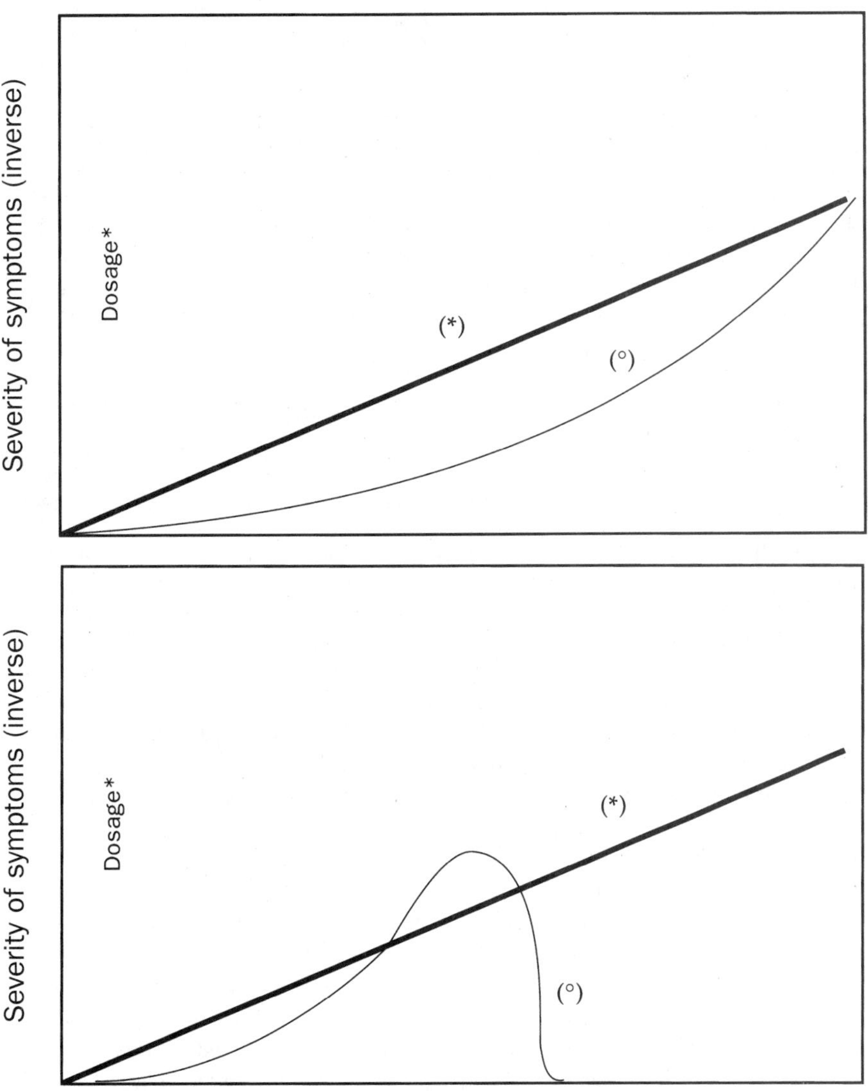

## ADDITIONAL EXERCISES

1. "In Consumers' Union nationwide studies of new cars purchased over the last ten years, Chrysler had a 30 percent lower frequency of repair rate than the other manufacturers. So we're probably safe to assume that a new Dodge will be reliable."

   Suppose we wanted to evaluate the sample in the above inference more deeply for representativeness. Which of the following dimensions would be relevant and which would not?

   | | |
   |---|---|
   | the color of the car | the age of the principle driver of the car |
   | the price paid for the car | the number of miles driven annually |
   | the size of the car | the size of the owner's family |
   | the trim package | the brand of gasoline used in the car |

2. "Look! The first ten people to come out of the theater are all smiling and laughing. I guess this is going to be a good show!"

   Suppose we wanted to evaluate the sample in the above inference more deeply for representativeness. Which of the following dimensions would be relevant and which would not?

   | | |
   |---|---|
   | the ages of the people | the gender identities of the people |
   | the racial identities of the people | the ethnic identities of the people |
   | the religious affiliations of the people | the economic status of the people |
   | the political affiliations of the people | the class status of the people |

   Compare your answers with those of your classmates. Try to resolve any and all points of disagreement rationally, by explaining your answers to each other.

3. "My English teacher has recommended three novels and they've all been wonderful. I'll bet you round-trip plane fare to Hawaii that you'll enjoy this book of poetry because she just recommended it too."

   Is the degree of confidence expressed reasonable? Why? or why not?

4. Identify the analogues and targets in each of the following analogies. Which analogies are used inferentially or argumentatively, and which are used for explanatory purposes, or narrative enhancement or entertainment?

   a. Up to this point we've talked about accents and rests of the same length. But what do musicians like to do most with rhythms? Well, we like to do what everybody likes to do. We like to play. That's right. In basketball, when we first learned how to dribble, it was an achievement just to bounce the ball in a steady motion. You know, you could spend a long time just learning to bounce the ball in one unchanging rhythm. It might take two weeks to learn how to do that comfortably, or a month. But in order to have fun playing, we have to vary the bounces with accents and rests. In a game you would want to fake out an opponent. You wouldn't dribble only at one speed, or in the same predictable rhythm. Sometimes you would go fast, sometimes a little slower, and then maybe real quick between your legs or behind your back. And then sometimes you'd stop dribbling and pass the ball. In a basketball game we dribble the ball to go from one point on the court to another, we hope closer to the basket, and of course we always want to dribble with imagination and style. If you're not going to have imagination and some type of style, it doesn't make sense to play. In music we play with rhythms from tiny fast ones to long slow ones, just like dribbling the ball. —Wynton Marsalis[10]

| Analogue | Target | Arg. | Exp. | Other |
|---|---|---|---|---|
| | | | | |

Explain your answer:

b. Well, thish-yer Smiley had rat-tarriers, and chicken cocks, and tom-cats, and all them kind of things, till you couldn't rest, and you couldn't fetch nothing for him to bet on but he'd match you. He ketched a frog one day, and took him home, and said he calculated to educate him; and so he never done nothing for three months but set in his back yard and learn that frog to jump. And you bet yet he *did* learn him, too. He'd give him a little punch behind, and the next minute you'd see that frog whirling in the air like a doughnut. —Mark Twain[11]

| Analogue | Target | Arg. | Exp. | Other |
|---|---|---|---|---|
| | | | | |

Explain your answer:

(continued)

c. When someone writes a piece of music, what he or she puts on the paper is roughly the equivalent of a recipe—in the sense that the recipe is not the food, only instructions for the preparation of the food. Unless you are very weird, you don't eat the recipe. If I write something on a piece of paper, I can't actually "hear" it. I can conjure up visions of what the symbols on the page mean, and imagine a piece of music as it might sound in performance, but that sensation is nontransferable; it can't be shared or transmitted. It doesn't become a "musical experience" in normal terms until "the recipe" has been converted into wiggling air molecules. Music, in performance, is a type of sculpture. The air in the performance space is sculpted into something. This "molecule-sculpture-over-time" is then "looked at" by the ears of the listeners—or a microphone.
—Frank Zappa[12]

| Analogue | Target | Arg. | Exp. | Other |
|---|---|---|---|---|
| | | | | |

Explain your answer:

**5.** Use the argument by analogy evaluation form to assess the following examples:

a. Putting up a traffic light after last week's deadly accident is like locking the barn door after the horse has been stolen.

| | Analogue | Target | Comment |
|---|---|---|---|
| **Basic points of similarity used as premises** | | | |
| | | | |
| **Conclusion** | | | |
| **Differences** | | | |

b. Last spring, when Arsenio Hall's new sitcom was yanked from the lineup after a handful of showings, the comic appeared on *The Late Show With Tom Snyder* and told the host that the show was being "retooled." This did not mean that *Arsenio* had been canceled, he insisted, but only sent back to the shop for more work. Hall ingeniously explained that a flawed sitcom was like an aircraft, which was much easier to repair while parked on the ground than in mid-flight. —Joe Queenan[13]

| | Analogue | Target | Comment |
|---|---|---|---|
| **Basic points of similarity used as premises** | | | |
| | | | |
| **Conclusion** | | | |
| **Differences** | | | |

c. One of the most well known instances of argument by analogy is the famous Teleological Argument for the existence of God. As formulated by the eighteenth century theologian William Paley, the argument goes something like this:

Suppose we happened to find a watch lying on the ground in the woods, or on the moon. How could we explain it? Unlike a rock, which we could easily imagine to have just been lying there indefinitely, a watch, we would be forced to conclude, was the product of some intelligent designer, because no other explanation would be adequate to account for the marvelous degree to which the parts and features of the watch seem to be designed, adapted, and coordinated for the purpose of telling time. But now compare the watch to the natural universe or to organic phenomena in the natural universe such as the human eye. The human eye, like the watch, is a complex organ whose parts, like the parts of a watch, seem marvelously well adapted and coordinated for the purpose of enabling visual experience. So it is reasonable to suppose that the human eye, and other similar phenomena in nature, and indeed the entire natural universe, are the products of an intelligent designer: God.

| | **Analogue** | **Target** | **Comment** |
|---|---|---|---|
| **Basic points of similarity used as premises** | | | |
| | | | |
| **Conclusion** | | | |
| **Differences** | | | |

**6.** According to Paul and Nathalie Silver, of the Carnegie Institute, California's "Old Faithful" geyser can predict large earthquakes within a radius of 150 miles. They argue for this conclusion on the basis of a twenty-year record of geyser eruptions. Ordinarily the geyser erupts at very regular intervals (which is why it came to be known as "Old Faithful"). On the day before the Oroville earthquake of August 1, 1975, the interval between geyser eruptions suddenly changed from 50 minutes to 120 minutes. In 1984 the geyser was erupting every 40 minutes. But the day before the April 24 Morgan Hill tremor, the pattern became irregular, fluctuating between 25-, 40-, and 50-minute intervals. A change was also noted before the 1989 Loma Prieta quake in the San Francisco area. Two and a half days before the quake, eruption intervals at the geyser suddenly shifted from 90 minutes to 150 minutes. The researchers noted that a number of things, including rainfall, can affect the regularity of eruptions in geysers. However, an analysis of rainfall amounts in the Calistoga area rules this out as an explanation of the abrupt pattern changes preceding each of these earthquakes. Evaluate the evidence and the reasoning involved here. What strengths can you identify? What weaknesses? What kinds of further evidence would confirm the hypothesis that Old Faithful is an effective earthquake predictor? What kinds of further evidence would disconfirm the hypothesis? What kinds of experiments can you think of to discover such evidence?

**7.** A few years ago the upstart Fox television network surprised a lot of people in the television industry by running a rather primitively drawn cartoon about a dysfunctional family at the same time as the nation's consistently top-rated prime-time television program, *The Bill Cosby Show. The Simpsons* knocked *The Cosby Show* out of first place and went on to several successful seasons, establishing the Fox network as a force to be reckoned with. What accounts for the success of *The Simpsons?* Consider the following list of explanatory hypotheses in terms of plausibility and explanatory power. On this basis narrow the list down to two leading hypotheses. Describe the kinds of experimental evidence that would then be needed in order to choose between the two finalists.

a. *The Simpsons* was more daring in its humor than the safe and mainstream *Cosby Show.*
b. It was racism. *The Simpsons* is about a white family and *The Cosby Show* was about a black family.
c. It was just a fluke.
d. It was novelty appeal. *The Cosby Show* was getting old. People were looking for something new.
e. *The Simpsons* was more challenging and rewarding intellectually than *The Cosby Show.*

**8.** Using the concepts and terminology of Mill's methods explain how, in the following story from the history of medicine, nineteenth century medical researcher Ignaz Semmelweis discovered and demonstrated the importance of physician hygiene in patient care:

Between 1844 and 1846, the death rate from a mysterious disease termed "childbed fever" in the First Maternity Division of the Vienna General Hospital averaged an alarming 10 percent. But the rate in the Second Division, where midwives rather than doctors attended the mothers, was only about 2 percent. For some time no one could explain why. Then one day a colleague accidentally cut himself on the finger with a student's scalpel while performing an autopsy. Although the cut seemed harmless enough, the man died shortly thereafter, exhibiting symptoms identical to those of childbed fever. Semmelweis formed the hypothesis that doctors and medical students, who spent their mornings doing autopsies before making their divisional rounds, were unwittingly transmitting to the women something they picked up from the cadavers. Semmelweis tested this hypothesis by requiring the doctors and students to clean their hands before examining patients. Doctors and students were forbidden to examine patients without first washing their hands in a solution of chlorinated lime. The death rate in the First Division fell to less than 2 percent.

## GLOSSARY

**analogue** an item used as a basis of comparison in an explanation or argument by analogy
**analogy** a comparison
**burden of proof** obligation to produce the argument in a dispute over an issue; failure to meet the burden of proof settles the issue in favor of the other side
**confirming evidence** evidence consistent with what an hypothesis predicts
**disconfirming evidence** evidence inconsistent with what an hypothesis predicts
**explanatory power** an idea's capacity to reduce or reduce puzzlement
**hypothesis** an idea or set of ideas under investigation
**hypothetical deductive method** a method of scientific investigation involving both hypothetical inductive reasoning and deductive reasoning
**inductive generalization** a variety of inductive reasoning in which general conclusions are projected from a number of particular instances
**joint method of agreement and difference** a principle of causal reasoning which combines the method of agreement with the method of difference
**method of agreement** a principle of causal reasoning which consists of seeking out some common antecedent condition in all cases of the effect whose cause we are trying to determine
**method of concomitant variation** a principle of causal reasoning which consists of varying a suspected cause and checking for corresponding variations in the effect, useful for situations where it is difficult or impossible to eliminate a suspected cause
**method of difference** a principle of causal reasoning which consists of looking for a correlation between the *absence* of the effect and the *absence* of an antecedent condition
**Mill's methods** guidelines for reliable causal reasoning formulated by philosopher John Stuart Mill
**plausibility** a measure of an idea's likelihood of surviving critical scrutiny
**population** the set of instances about which general conclusions are projected in an inductive or statistical generalization
**relevance** in inductive reasoning, refers to factors which might reasonably be thought to have something to do with the conclusion being inferred
**sample** particular observed instances used in inductive or statistical generalizations
**sample size** a measure of the number of particular observed instances relative to the population in an inductive or statistical generalization

**statistical generalization** a variety of inductive reasoning in which trends or percentages observed in the sample are projected onto other instances or onto the population as a whole

**target** an item about which conclusions are drawn or explanations are offered by analogy

## NOTES

[1] Wynton Marsalis, *Marsalis on Music* (New York: Norton, 1995), p. 20.

[2] John Allen Paulos, *Innumeracy: Mathematical Illiteracy and Its Consequences* (New York: Hill and Wang, 1988), pp. 9–10.

[3] Thomas Reid, Vol. 1, *Philosophical Works,* edited by Sir William Hamilton (G. O. Berlagesbuchen: Herstellung, 1967), p. 36.

[4] Wynton Marsalis, *Marsalis on Music,* p. 26.

[5] Alfred J. Ayer, "One's Knowledge of Other Minds," *Theoria,* 19 (1953)

[6] P. J. O'Rourke, "Why I Believe What I Believe," *Rolling Stone,* July 13–27, 1995.

[7] Peter Singer, "Animal Rights: Is a Human-Centered Ethics Just Another Prejudice," *Current Issues and Enduring Questions* 4th Ed., Sylvan Barney and Hugo Bedau, eds. (Boston: Bedford Books, 1996) pp. 235–238.

[8] Lewis Carroll, "A Mad Tea-Party," chap 7 in *Alice's Adventures in Wonderland* (New York: Macmillan, 1950), p. 71. Originally published in 1865.

[9] John Stuart Mill, chap. 8, sec. 6 in *A System of Logic,* book 3 (London: Longmans, Green, and Co., 1884), pp. 253–267.

[10] Wynton Marsalis, *Marsalis on Music,* p. 26–27.

[11] Mark Twain, "The Celebrated Jumping Frog of Calaveras County."

[12] Frank Zappa, "All About Music," *The Real Frank Zappa Book* (New York: Poseidon Press, 1989), p. 161.

[13] Joe Queenan, "The Retooling Channel," *TV Guide,* July 26–August 1, 1997.

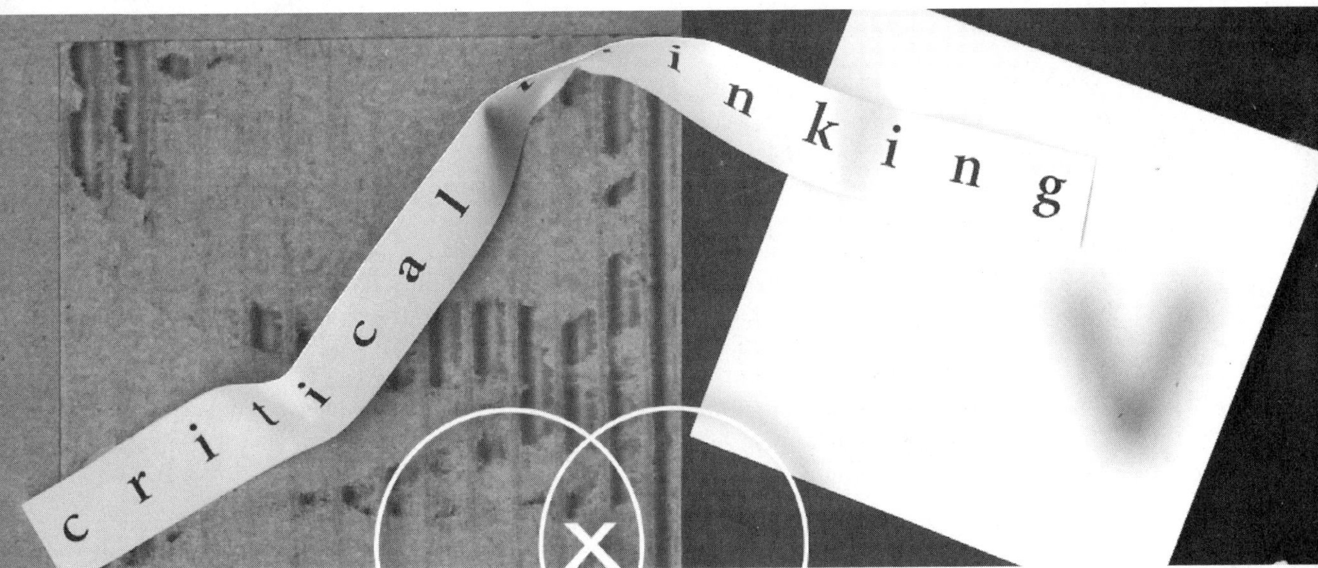


# CHAPTER 8 Evaluating Arguments III: Premises

In Chapter 6, we distinguished between the structural features of arguments and the premises out of which they are constructed, and we indicated that evaluating arguments involves assessing both. A sound deductive argument is both valid and based on true or at least defensible premises. A deductive argument which is either invalid (faulty in design and/or construction) or based on false or dubious premises is unsound. A strong inductive argument based on true or at least defensible premises is cogent. An inductive argument which is either weak (faulty in design and/or construction) or based on false or dubious premises is not cogent. In Chapter 6, you learned how to evaluate deductive arguments for validity. In Chapter 7, you learned how to assess the strength of inductive arguments. Now that you have studied the structural features of arguments in both of these two main argument design categories, it's time to look at the standards and practices of evaluating premises. You'll be happy (we imagine) to know that there's not much new for you to learn at this stage about evaluating the premises of an argument. Because the premises of any argument are themselves each conclusions of sub-arguments—or potential conclusions of potential sub-arguments—evaluating the premises of an argument turns out to be more or less simply a matter of applying what you've already learned about issues and arguments. If there is support for a particular premise offered in the text of the argument itself, then in effect what we have is a sub-argument whose conclusion is the premise we're interested in evaluating, and so we can evaluate the sub-argument. But eventually you will run into premises that aren't supported in the text of the argument itself. All arguments have to start somewhere, and this means that every argument will have unsupported premises in it.

Experienced arguers usually try to use as their most "basic" premises claims which are as invulnerable to challenge as possible. For example, when Thomas Jefferson wrote in the Declaration of Independence "We hold these truths to be self-evident," he meant "Here are some basic premises which we don't think we *need* to argue for. These are claims (for example that all people are equal when it comes to basic human rights) which can and should be accepted at face value by any rational human being."

*Notice, however, that even if you agree that this doesn't (or shouldn't) need to be argued for it's still an interesting question: Why not? And, we still hold, as a basic assumption of critical thinking, that in general it's perfectly reasonable to ask for support for an unsupported claim. Even a claim like:*

*All people are equal when it comes to basic human rights.*

*Another interesting question is how one might "prove" something as basic as this claim. We'll come back to this question shortly.*

## NECESSARY TRUTHS

But first, are there any claims which are *really* invulnerable to criticism, which are truly "self-evident"? If all arguments have to start somewhere, aren't there claims available for use as premises which don't need any additional support of their own? Are there any places for an argument to start where it can move forward without having to back up? There are a few kinds of claim which some consider to be "necessarily true," meaning that the claims are impossible to deny in a coherent way.

For example, here is a statement which you might say must *necessarily* be true, because to deny it would be self-contradictory:

Either the president knew of the arms-for-hostages deal or he didn't.

In fact, you might say that *any* statement whose formal structure is "Either X or not X" must necessarily be true, because to deny it would be self-contradictory (and therefore necessarily false).

*As an exercise, see if you can demonstrate that any statement of the form "Either X or not X" is necessarily true by means of a truth table.*

Statements which you can't deny without contradicting yourself are traditionally called *tautologies* and are traditionally considered to be necessarily true. It's also worth noting that tautologies don't tell you much, or to put it a little more technically, they don't convey very much information. For this reason, tautologies are often referred to as "trivially true," as in "That's true, but so what?" Nevertheless, they can occasionally play a crucial role in an argument. For example:

> Either the president knew of the arms-for-hostages deal or he didn't.
>
> If he did know of the arms-for-hostages deal, then he's involved in the cover-up and is therefore unworthy of his office.
>
> If he didn't know of the arms-for-hostages deal, then he's not in control of his own administration, and is therefore unworthy of his office.
>
> In any case, he is definitely unworthy of his office.

Another kind of statement is traditionally considered to be necessarily true not because of formal structure but because of the meanings of its terms. For example, consider the statements "All humans are vertebrates" and "No circle is square." The meaning of "vertebrates" is included in the meaning of "humans," and the statement "All humans are vertebrates" merely asserts this inclusion. Similarly, the meanings of "circle" and "square" are mutually exclusive, and the statement "No circle is square" merely asserts this mutual exclusion. Such statements are sometimes said to be true "by definition." Or one might say that such statements will be understood and recognized as true by anyone who understands the meanings of the terms involved in them. Here, by the way, is an interesting variation:

> This sentence has seven words in it.

Sometimes tautologies are funny, sometimes not, and sometimes unintentional, and sometimes all three at once, as for example when outgoing Dallas Cowboys coach Tom Landry answered the question about how he felt on learning he was losing his job, "I felt empty and exhausted and older than I'd ever been in my life."

Most statements are neither self-contradictory nor necessarily true. Statements that are neither self-contradictory nor necessarily true are called *contingent statements,* meaning that their truth or falsity is contingent (or *depends*) upon something outside of them, beyond their formal structures and the meanings of their terms.

## EXERCISE | Necessary Truths and Contingent Statements

Sort the following statements into three groups: (1) those that are necessarily true (NT); (2) those that are self-contradictory (SC); (3) those that are contingent (CON).

| | NT | SC | CON |
|---|---|---|---|
| A rectangle has four sides. | | | |
| Abortion is murder. | | | |
| Murder is wrong. | | | |

(continued)

| | NT | SC | CON |
|---|---|---|---|
| Either we go out for burgers, or we order a pizza. | | | |
| Either she's married, or she's not married. | | | |
| She's either married or engaged. | | | |
| Wherever you go, there you are. | | | |
| White is a color. | | | |
| The White House is white. | | | |
| All arguments have to start somewhere. | | | |

## CONTINGENT STATEMENTS

Now, what about Jefferson's "self-evident truth" that all men are created equal? Is it a tautology? Is it necessarily true? Is it "self-evident" in that way? It seems to actually say something important. In other words, if it's true, it's not just "trivially true," such as a tautology would tend to be. So, let's suppose that it is a contingent statement. That would mean that its truth depends on something outside its formal structure and the meanings of its terms. What does its truth depend on? And let us also suppose that someone were to challenge it.

The first question to ask, when we come to the evaluation of an unsupported premise, is: What kind of claim does the premise make? Does the premise make a factual claim? An evaluative claim? Does it offer an interpretation? Does it offer a definition? What kind of definition? A closely related question is: If someone were to challenge the premise, what sort of issue would that raise? A factual issue, an evaluative issue, an interpretive issue, a complex issue involving more than one of these categories? Thinking about these questions helps to determine what sorts of support may be needed in order to establish a given contingent claim as a premise in an argument.

*We highly recommend at this point that you review the section in Chapter 2 on issues and disputes. It's especially relevant at this stage, and it'll make even better sense now than it did at the beginning.*

### CONTINGENT STATEMENTS OF FACT

As we pointed out in Chapter 2, most issues are complex and involve elements from all three issue categories. Factual issues, those which are to be resolved by either the methods of empirical science or documentary research, often give rise to both evaluative and interpretive issues as well. Similarly for both evaluative and interpretive issues. Thus establishing a particular premise as a "matter of fact" can turn out to be a tall and complicated order, for example, if we're trying to determine as a matter of fact what has caused the stock market to suddenly lose five hundred points. Here we are deep into the realm of hypothetical reasoning with all of its nuances and complexities as described in Chapter 7, and we're a long way from anything that might be considered to be "self-evident."

However, some factual statements seem to be so basic that they might be considered "self-evident." These would be statements of basic empirical observation, or "observation statements" for short. Suppose for example you were to say,

> My best friend is more than five feet tall.

Whether this is true or not depends upon the height of your best friend, something "out there in the world" which can be tested empirically, that is by reference to sense experience, or to what scientists call "observations." Whenever scientists weigh, measure, or take the temperature of something and then record their findings, they are making observations. When can you accept an observation statement as correct? Suppose someone now challenges your claim that your best friend is over five feet tall. How do you respond? Well, suppose you say, "I'm five feet, two inches tall and my best friend is taller than I am, so my best friend is over five feet tall." Now suppose you are challenged to defend these two premises. How do you know you are five feet, two inches tall? The truth of this sort of observation statement in general depends on the conditions under which the observation was made and the ability of the observer. In this rather basic and simple instance it would be sufficient to know that you had been measured, when standing erect, using an accurate standard instrument of measurement, by someone who knew how to use it, in circumstances that didn't impair the user's performance. OK, so how do you know you were standing erect when your height was being measured? And how do you know your best friend is taller than you are? At some point, you wind up saying something like, "Look. There isn't anything more basic for me to appeal to here in support of this claim. We stand next to each other, and I look up and she looks down. That's all there is to it! It's a basic observation!! It's self-evident!!!" Notice that if you say something like this, you're also admitting that there *are indeed* further claims that you could appeal to in support of the observation that your best friend is taller than you are. You've even specified a little empirical experiment, standing next to each other, whose results support the claim. "Self-evident" in this connection seems to mean something like this: The supporting claims are no more basic or evident than what they support. This may well be close to what Jefferson meant when he called the claim that all men are created equal "self-evident," but it is also pretty clearly evident that "all men are created equal" is neither a basic observation statement nor any other sort of statement of fact.

## VALUE JUDGMENTS

Probably the best short answer as to what sort of claim "all men are created equal" is making is this: It states a basic moral principle, which would put it in the category of value judgments. Evaluative disputes are differences of opinion about matters of value, and they concern what we call "value judgments."

Ordinarily, we think of these as expressing our values in ethics, the arts, social and political philosophy, lifestyle choice, and so on. Thus, regarding ethics someone might claim "You *shouldn't* lie" or "Murder is *immoral*" or "Abortion is *wrong*." Regarding art: "Beethoven's Fifth Symphony is his *best*"; "Neil Simon's latest plays are *flawed*"; "Steven Spielberg is a *great* film director." Regarding social and political philosophy: "Democracy is the *best* form of government"; "Capital punishment *should* be legalized"; "The United States *should* redistribute its wealth *more equitably* among its citizenry"; or "All men are created equal." And of course, sometimes a value judgment turns up as a premise in an argument. For example:

> JJ's Uptown Liquors sells cigarettes to children, and this city should not be licensing such socially irresponsible business practices. JJ's business license should be immediately revoked.

## VALUES RELATIVISM

Let's consider the kind of issue which arises when a premise which happens to express a value judgment is challenged. In the example above, the first premise:

> JJ's Uptown Liquors sells cigarettes to children.

is a contingent statement of fact, and as such is subject to verification by normal empirical means (in this case eyewitness testimony, or video surveillance, or something similar). But the second premise:

> This city should not be licensing such socially irresponsible business practices.

is a value judgment—actually two value judgments: It states both that selling cigarettes to children is socially *irresponsible,* and that the city *should not* license such business practices. If either of these two claims were challenged the issue which would then have arisen would be not a factual issue but an issue of values. As such it would not be subject to the same sort of verification procedures as the factual claim about the liquor store selling cigarettes to children. So how does one go about establishing a value judgment as a premise in an argument? Well, some people seem to think you can't. In fact some people seem to think that the difference between these two kinds of issue is that factual disputes can be easily settled empirically, whereas evaluative disputes can't be settled at all. Facts are "objective," values are "subjective."

What we have to say about this view is pretty much the same as what we said about "relativism" in Chapter 1, namely that it is a confusion which stands as an obstacle to thinking critically about values issues. Indeed this view that value judgments are "subjective" could be fairly characterized as a variety of relativism: "values relativism." Values relativism is a somewhat more understandable position than relativism is in its most sweeping and general form, because values issues are in general harder to settle than factual issues generally are. By definition they cannot be resolved by the methods of empirical science or simple appeal to the documentary record. But it doesn't follow, from the fact that value judgments can't be *empirically* verified, that they can't be established at all. In fact some evaluative issues are much more firmly settled than some factual ones—and some value judgments better established than some factual ones. For example, the statement:

> Gandhi's leadership of his people was morally more admirable than Hitler's.

clearly expresses a value judgment. Yet, clearly it is also much more firmly justified than the factual statement:

> There is extraterrestrial intelligent life out there somewhere.

How can this be? Of course it is not *absolutely certain* that Gandhi's leadership of his people was morally more admirable than Hitler's. But even though this is a value judgment and even though it may yet be open to challenge and debate, it is nevertheless quite firmly established because the arguments that can be made in favor of it are so obvious, so powerful and so persuasive:

> Gandhi led his people out of the bondage of colonial rule. He also guided the struggle away from violence. To do this required great courage and wisdom and saved a great many human lives. Human life is precious. Freedom is better than colonial bondage as a way of life. Therefore, Gandhi was a great leader.
>
> By contrast, Hitler led his people into World War II. He directed his people to invade and forcibly occupy the territory of neighboring states. He directed his people to exterminate several million civilian noncombatants. He led the world to develop nuclear weapons. Human life is precious. Peace is precious. Therefore Hitler was a terrible leader.

whereas the arguments that might possibly be made against it are, well, . . . what are they? Can you think of any even remotely comparable counterargument? This example illustrates how it is in general that value issues are resolved and value judgments established as true—by considering and evaluating competing arguments.

Some of you may be thinking, "Wait a minute. We're going around in circles here! In order to evaluate an argument with a value judgment as a premise, we have to evaluate the truth of the premise. But in order to do that we have to evaluate arguments. Does one ever get to the bottom of this?"

This is not a bad question, but remember that much the same sort of question arose about contingent statements of fact, and remember how we "got to the bottom" of that. At some point, you encounter observation statements that are so "basic" that, even if you could go on to support or defend them with further observation statements, the supporting statements are no more basic or evident than what they support. And so, unless there is some evidence or good reason to the contrary, these are taken as "self-evident." Similarly, with value judgments; at some point, you encounter statements of moral principle—the Golden Rule would be a good example—that are so basic that, even if you could go on to support or defend them with further arguments, the arguments would be hardly more convincing than the principles they uphold.

This is probably what Jefferson meant by calling the claim that all men are created equal "self-evident." Not that it's impossible to produce an argument in support of it. Here, for example, is an argument in support of the claim that all people are equal when it comes to basic human rights:

> Morality presumes consistency. In other words, in the absence of a justification for differential treatment, all moral rules and considerations apply equally to all parties, and this would include basic human rights. There is no justification for differential treatment among people with respect to basic human rights. So all people are equal when it comes to basic human rights.

Now compare the argument to the claim that it supports. As a whole this is a burden of proof argument, and as such not absolutely conclusive. Some of the argument's premises reach a higher level of generality and abstraction perhaps than the conclusion does, but does that make them any *more* evidently true? Now what about the challenged claim itself. Does it not seem evidently true on its face?

## INTERPRETATIONS

Interpretive issues are about how something should be understood. For example, reporters on the progress of German reunification have noted occasionally that the fall of the Berlin Wall occurred on the anniversary of Kristallnacht.[1] An interesting interpretive question is: What should we make of this coincidence? This is not an easy or simple question. In fact, it's more like a Pandora's Box of questions: Is the coincidence significant or not? If it is significant, what significance does it have? Does it have political implications or not? If so, what are these implications? These are all examples of interpretive questions. Obviously it's easy for reasonable people to differ in response to these questions. So they each indicate an interpretive issue. As we mentioned in Chapter 2, issues of this sort are probably the most complex and difficult issues we're likely to encounter in everyday discourse. There is no single simple procedure for resolving interpretive issues or settling interpretive disputes. And so there is no single simple procedure for establishing interpretive claims as premises in an argument. Information of various kinds is relevant to interpretation. Establishing an interpretive premise is therefore a matter of gathering relevant information and, as with value judgments, weighing relevant reasons and arguments.

Some of this information will be of a relatively straightforward factual nature. For example, a detailed chronology of events leading up to the fall of the Berlin Wall would be relevant to the issue of the significance of its timing on the anniversary of Kristallnacht. But factual information alone is rarely adequate to resolving an interpretive issue. Often the issue will turn also on some point of principle or value or on some further point of interpretation. In such cases establishing an interpretive premise will eventually require us to consider and evaluate value judgments or further interpretive claims.

Perhaps the most useful procedural strategy is to treat interpretive claims as hypotheses and to apply the procedures of hypothetical reasoning. Again from the discussion in Chapter 7 you already know what these procedures are. Establishing interpretive hypotheses is done inductively, by assessing their relative plausibility, and their relative explanatory power. With interpretive hypotheses, as opposed to empirical ones, it is often difficult to construct empirical experiments. Once again, premises offered in support of an interpretive premise may themselves be called into question and so may in turn need to be supported. Once again we must recognize and accept that evaluating premises leads us into areas where knowing how to construct and evaluate arguments is essential.

## ADDITIONAL EXERCISES

**1.** One of the principles on which the American system of criminal justice is theoretically based is that it's worse to punish innocent people than to let guilty people escape punishment. This principle can be understood to express a value judgment. Do you agree with this principle and the value judgment it expresses? If so, formulate three distinct justifications for them. If not, construct three distinct justifications for rejecting them. Write a short essay in which you explain your position.

**2.** Here are several justifications for the principle mentioned in Exercise 1 above. For each justification, identify the elements which appeal to consequences and those which appeal to principle. (Don't forget to consider missing premises.) Can you identify any elements which appeal to both or which appeal neither to consequences or to principle?

a. When a society punishes an innocent person, it inevitably increases the unwarranted suffering in the world. It is always wrong to increase the unwarranted suffering in the world.

b. When you punish an innocent person, you turn that person against society, and this leads to an increase in antisocial behavior.

c. Punishing the innocent is inherently wrong because they've done nothing to deserve punishment. Letting the guilty escape punishment is inherently wrong because they don't get what they deserve. But punishing the innocent is worse because when you punish an innocent person, you are also letting a guilty person escape punishment.

What are the most "basic" premises of each of the above arguments? If these premises were challenged how might they be defended? Which of the above arguments, a, b, or c, do you find most firmly persuasive? Explain why.

**3.** Analyze and evaluate the following argument, which we used in this chapter to illustrate our criticism of "values relativism." Which of the premises are factual ones? Which of the premises express value judgments? Which of the premises are interpretive statements? Discuss how you would go about verifying, justifying or challenging each of the premises in this argument.

Gandhi led his people out of the bondage of colonial rule. He also guided the struggle away from violence. To do this required great courage and wisdom and saved a great many human lives. Human life is precious. Freedom is better than colonial bondage as a way of life. Therefore, Gandhi was a great leader.

Hitler led his people into World War II. He directed his people to invade and forcibly occupy the territory of neighboring states. He directed his people to exterminate several million civilian noncombatants. He led the world to develop nuclear weapons. Human life is precious. Peace is precious. Therefore, Hitler was a terrible leader.

**4.** What are the most "basic" premises of each of the following arguments? Include in your analysis any hidden inferential assumptions. If these premises were challenged how might they be defended?

a. According to modern physics, radio is our only hope of picking up an intelligent signal from space. Sending an interstellar probe would take too long—roughly 50 years even for nearby Alpha Centauri—even if we had the technology and funds to accomplish it. But radio is too slow for much dialogue. The most we can hope from it is to establish the existence (or, more accurately, the former existence) of another civilization. —Patrick Moore[2]

b. How important are professional athletes to society? Not very. They're mere entertainers. They often present bad role models for children—for every Dave Dravecky there's a Pete Rose, or a Steve Garvey, or a Jose Canseco; for every Michael Jordan or Grant Hill there's a Dennis Rodman. And, given the attention they get, they tend to distract us from serious social concerns. At the very least then, the salaries of these prima donnas should be drastically reduced to reflect their social insignificance.

c. If a being suffers, there can be no moral justification for refusing to take that suffering into consideration, and, indeed, to count it equally with the like suffering (if rough comparisons can be made) of another being. So the only question is: Do animals other than man suffer? Most people agree unhesitatingly that animals like cats and dogs can and do suffer, and this seems also to be assumed by those laws that prohibit wanton cruelty to such animals. —Peter Singer[3]

d. Proposition 215 will allow seriously and terminally ill patients to legally use marijuana, if, and only if, they have the approval of a licensed physician. We are physicians and nurses who have witnessed firsthand the medical benefits of marijuana. Yet today in California, medical use of marijuana is illegal. Doctors cannot prescribe marijuana, and terminally ill patients must break the law to use it. Marijuana is not a cure, but it can help cancer patients. Most have severe reactions to the disease and chemotherapy—commonly severe nausea and vomiting. One in three patients discontinues treatment despite a 50 percent chance of improvement. When standard anti-nausea drugs fail, marijuana often eases patients' nausea and permits continued treatment. . . . University doctors and researchers have found that marijuana is also effective in: lowering internal eye pressure associated with glaucoma, slowing the onset of blindness; reducing the pain of AIDS patients, and stimulating the appetites of those suffering malnutrition because of AIDS "wasting syndrome"; and alleviating muscle spasticity and chronic pain due to multiple sclerosis, epilepsy, and spinal cord injuries. When one in five Americans will have cancer, and 20 million may develop glaucoma, shouldn't our government let physicians prescribe any medicine capable of relieving suffering? . . . Today, physicians are allowed to prescribe powerful drugs like morphine and codeine. It doesn't make sense that they cannot prescribe marijuana, too.[4]

e. There are an estimated 2 billion children (persons under age eighteen) in the world. Since Santa Claus is apparently not responsible for visiting the Muslim, Hindu, Jewish, and Buddhist children, that reduces his workload to 15 percent of the total, or 378 million children, according to the Population Reference Bureau. Assuming an average of 3.5 children per household, that means 91.8 million homes (assuming at least one good child per household). Assuming Santa travels from east to west, and factoring in the earth's rotation and the different time zones, Santa has thirty-one hours of Christmas to work with. This works out to 823 visits per second, which means that Santa has a little more than 1/1000th of a second to park, get out of the sleigh, get down the chimney, fill stockings, distribute presents under the tree, eat the snacks left for him, get back up the chimney and into the sleigh, and fly to the next house. Assuming each of the 91.8 million stops to be evenly distributed geographically, each stop would be .78 miles apart, which means that Santa's sleigh will be traveling at 650 miles per second, thousands of times the speed of sound. Assuming that each child gets nothing more than a medium-sized Lego set (approximately two pounds), the payload of the sleigh, not counting Santa, would be 321,300 tons. On land, conventional reindeer can pull about three hundred pounds. Assuming even that "flying reindeer" could pull ten times that amount, the team required to pull Santa's payload would be 214,200 reindeer, which increases the weight of the loaded sleigh and team to 353,430 tons (four times the weight of the *Queen Elizabeth*). An object weighing 350,000 tons traveling at 650 miles per second creates enormous air resistance, with resultant friction and heat, enough to vaporize a reindeer in about 4/1000ths of a second. In conclusion, if Santa ever did deliver presents on Christmas Eve, he's dead now.

## GLOSSARY

**contingent statement** a claim whose truth value depends on something outside itself
**necessary truth** a claim that is impossible to deny in a coherent way
**tautology** a claim that is necessarily true because to deny it would be self-contradictory

## NOTES

[1] On the night of November 9–10, 1938, a riot organized and directed by the German Nazi Party took place in which Jewish shops and synagogues were firebombed and Jews were attacked and taken away to concentration camps. The night is remembered by many Jews as "the Night of Broken Glass" and the beginning of the Holocaust.

[2] Patrick Moore, "Speaking English in Space: Stars," *Omni*, November 1979, p. 26.

[3] Peter Singer, "Animal Liberation," in James Rachels, ed., *Moral Problems*, 2nd ed. (New York: Harper & Row, 1975), p. 166.

[4] Excerpt from the Argument in Favor of Proposition 215, *State of California Voter Manual*, 1996.

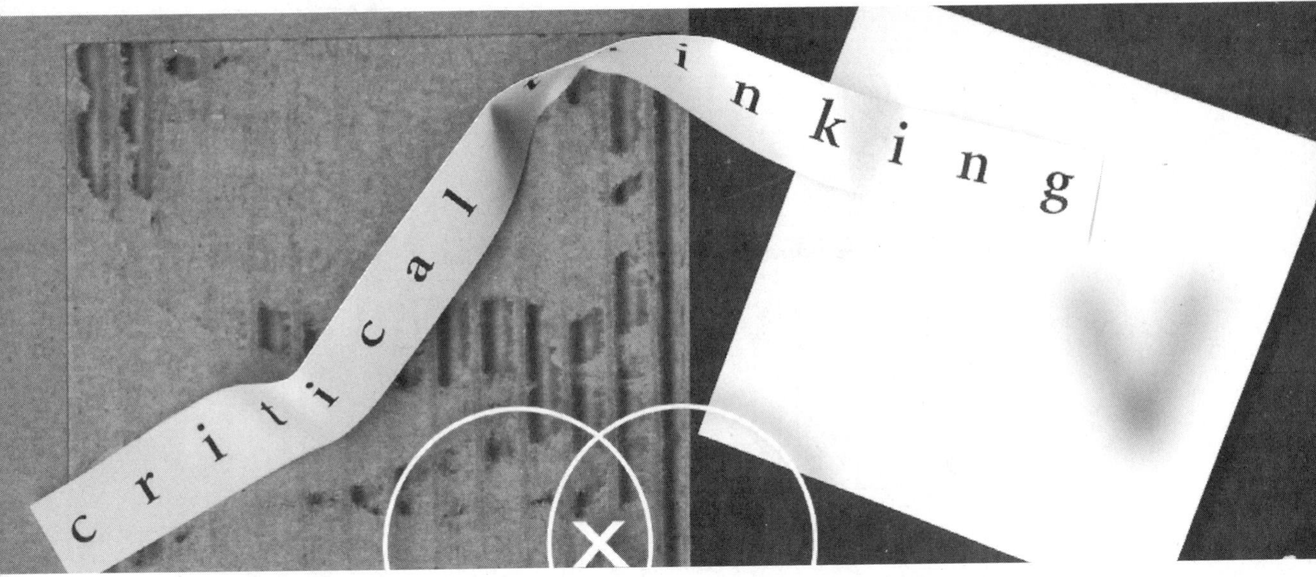


CHAPTER 9

# Fallacies I: Informal Fallacies of Language

In Chapter 6, we introduced the concept of a fallacy, as an unreliable inference. This is an extremely important concept for argument criticism. Why? First of all, fallacies are inferences. So they appear to be reasonable. Secondly, their unreliability is not always evident on the surface. In fact, they can be very persuasive. Finally, as a result, they're quite widespread and prevalent in all sorts of everyday discourse, both public and private. So knowing how to spot them and understanding how they work are useful tools for the critical thinker.

## INFORMAL FALLACIES

In Chapter 6, we discussed formal fallacies, which, as you'll remember, are inferences whose unreliability is due to their formal structure. But, there are many more things that can go wrong with an argument besides formal structure. *Thus, an informal fallacy is an inference whose unreliability is due to something other than its formal structure.* In this and the next two chapters, we will survey a fairly wide range of common informal fallacies. Before we begin, a few general comments and words of caution are in order.

"Rose is Rose" by Pat Brady. Reprinted by permission of UFS, Inc.

The informal fallacies constitute a large and very mixed bag. The author of one critical thinking textbook estimates that several hundred informal fallacies are covered in one or another logic text. One such text distinguishes over ninety informal fallacies, far too many for us to cover completely here. In fact there are so many ways to argue badly that some of them haven't even been given names yet. Moreover, there is no standard classification system for the informal fallacies, nor any generally applicable and mechanically reliable procedure for identifying informal fallacies (as there is for formal fallacies). For the sake of simplicity we have divided the informal fallacies into three groups. In this chapter, we will survey fallacies of linguistic confusion, fallacies which can be understood and explained in terms of the peculiarities of language. In Chapter 10, we'll look at fallacies of relevance, and in Chapter 11 we'll look at fallacies of evidence.

For the reasons just mentioned many students find the array of informal fallacies bewildering and even intimidating. But don't make the mistake of approaching the informal fallacies as a list of labels to be memorized along with a capsule definition and mechanical application procedure for each. The results of this approach are almost always disastrous.

Here is a much better approach. Think of the informal fallacy categories as tools for doing a certain kind of work. Just as a carpenter has a kit of carpentry tools, you are assembling a set of tools for criticizing arguments. Your goal should be to attain mastery in their employment, and the best way to pursue this goal is by working with the tools. The work of the carpenter is to construct things out of wood. In the course of this work a carpenter will perform a wide variety of tasks including measuring, cutting, fitting, fastening, finishing, and so on. A good deal of the carpenter's mastery has to do with selecting the right tool for the specific task at hand. The product that argument criticism is aimed at producing is a form of understanding. Just as the carpenter's mastery is evident in the product of the work, so the mastery of argument criticism shows in the understanding it achieves. Your emphasis should be not on labeling fallacies correctly but rather on how well you are able to understand and explain what is wrong with the faulty arguments you encounter, bearing in mind that a given argument can have more than one thing wrong with it. Remember also that it is possible to drive a nail with a screwdriver or a screw with a hammer. In other words, some tools will perform tasks for which they were not designed and which other, more suitable tools will perform much more effectively. Thus the greater the number of tools you have at your command and the more discriminating you are in their employment, the more complete your mastery becomes.

One final word of caution: The informal fallacy categories you will be working with are fault-finding tools. An important liability is inherent in using them. Special care needs to be taken not to find fault where there isn't any. An embarrassing, but revealing, example of this pitfall was reported recently by newspaper columnist Jack Smith. In a column entitled "Critique of an Ironic Writer's Critical Thought" Smith recounts how an earlier column of his, in which he poked fun at transcendental meditation as taught at Maharishi International University, was critiqued in a critical thinking class:

> These [devotees of transcendental meditation] believe, as you may remember, that if enough people meditate together, achieving a state of pure consciousness and connecting with the Unified Field, the basis of all life, they can actually alter events—lowering crime rates, quelling riots, easing international tension and even causing the Dow Jones average to rise.
>
> The theme of my essay was that I did not believe this. However, my tone was irony, which, as we have often seen, is a risky tone to effect. . . .
>
> Pinpointing my first fallacy, [the student] quotes a paragraph:
>
> "The meditators held a mass meditation . . . thereby raising the temperature and saving the Florida orange crop, lowering drunken driving arrests in Des Moines, influencing Fidel Castro to give up cigars, and causing the stock market to rally."
>
> Obviously, I hope, I am being ironic. I do not for a moment believe that the meditation had any effect whatever on the events cited.
>
> But [the student] comments:
>
> "This is the fallacy of False Cause, or thinking that because someone did one thing, something else happened as a result. The meditators may have believed that they were the reason for the temperature rise in Florida, but were probably wrongly justified."

This is precisely the point Smith was himself trying to make! The moral of this story for our present purposes is that a prerequisite to good argument criticism is a fair and accurate understanding of the argument you are criticizing.

It's also important to recognize that an informally fallacious argument may very closely resemble an argument which is perfectly reasonable, and that the difference between the two often depends on the context within which each is offered. So criticisms of arguments themselves need to be critically examined. Don't overlook the possibility that the argument you find fault with might be reasonably and persuasively defended against your criticism. Therefore be especially careful not to condemn an argument too hastily. Be prepared to defend your criticism, to argue for it, in other words. And in arguing for your criticism you'll want, of course, to avoid committing any fallacies, formal or informal.

## FALLACIES OF AMBIGUITY

In Chapter 2 we encountered the important notion of ambiguity. An ambiguous expression is one that can be understood in more than one way. Here are a number of common informal fallacies that depend on one or another sort of ambiguity.

### EQUIVOCATION

If someone were to offer you a choice between eternally increasing ecstatic bliss and a three-day-old Big Mac, which would you choose? Well, consider the following argument:

> Nothing is better than eternally increasing ecstatic bliss, and a three-day-old Big Mac is better than nothing, so a three-day-old Big Mac is better than eternally increasing ecstatic bliss.

Obviously there's *something* wrong with this argument. But what can it be? It *looks* so logical. The problem here is that the word "nothing," on which the apparently logical comparison hinges, actually changes meaning from the first premise to the second. The first premise can be paraphrased as follows:

> *There isn't anything* better than eternally increasing ecstatic bliss.

And the second premise can be paraphrased as follows:

> *Having* a three-day-old Big Mac is better than not having anything at all.

When the premises have been paraphrased in this way, we're no longer tempted to think that eternally increasing ecstatic bliss and a three-day-old Big Mac are both being compared to the same thing, and the apparent logic of the inference falls away. When an argument depends on switching the meanings of an ambiguous crucial term or expression, as in this example, the argument commits the fallacy of equivocation.

A more serious instance of equivocation is seen in this sometimes-invoked argument for the existence of a Supreme Being:

> The laws of gravitation and motion must have a lawmaker for the simple reason that they are laws, and all laws have a lawmaker.

Here the word "law" is given various meanings. In one sense laws are "artificial" (which means "made by humans") statutes to *proscribe*, or "rule out" certain behavior. This is the sense of "laws" in which the premise "All laws have a lawmaker" is true. But the laws of gravitation and motion are "scientific laws" intended to *describe* regularities in the behavior of the physical universe. Such laws are "discovered" more than "made" and as such do not presuppose lawmakers. Therefore the conclusion is unwarranted.

In criticizing an argument as an equivocation, you should be able to identify the term or expression that is being used equivocally, and demonstrate its equivocal employment by clarifying the distinct senses in which it is employed. A convenient and effective way to do this is to paraphrase the assertions in which it occurs, as we did in the Big Mac example.

## AMPHIBOLY

A close cousin of equivocation is amphiboly. Equivocation results from verbal or "lexical" ambiguity, or the capacity of an individual word or expression to support more than one interpretation. By way of contrast, some expressions are "syntactically" ambiguous. They can be understood in more than one way due to their grammatical structure or word order. For example:

> The loot and the car were listed as stolen by the Los Angeles Police Department.

Here there is an ambiguity of reference. The expression is presumably intended to indicate that the police listed the loot and car as stolen, not that the listed property was stolen by the police. An expression whose ambiguity is due to its grammatical structure or word order is called an amphiboly. An argument which exploits or depends on this sort of ambiguity commits the fallacy of amphiboly.

Occasionally this device finds employment in certain sales gimmicks which verge on fraud. For instance, at the end of a direct mail sales offer appears the following guarantee:

> We're convinced that you will love your new Acme widget even more than you could begin to imagine. But rest assured. If for any reason you are the least bit dissatisfied, just send it back. We'll give you a prompt and a full refund.

Does this mean that you get a full refund promptly? When a dissatisfied customer applies for the refund and receives a nominal reimbursement along with a statement of "service charges," it becomes evident that this is not what the guarantee meant. Should the customer insist upon a full refund it may take an indefinitely long time to receive it.

Just as with equivocation, the strategy for exposing amphiboly consists in pointing out the grammatical ambiguity and explicating the several interpretations of the passage.

## ACCENT

Ambiguity can also result from the placement of emphasis, or "accent," on certain words or phrases in an expression. The fallacy of accent consists of drawing an unwarranted conclusion, or suggesting one, by the use of improper emphasis. For example:

> *Tom:* I'm not going to contribute any more to your charity.
>
> *Liz:* Great! I'll just put you down for the same amount as last year.

Here Liz draws the faulty conclusion that Tom is willing to contribute the same as he did the year before because she erroneously accents "more." Without the accent, the colloquial expression "any more" means "any longer."

The news media and ad writers commonly use accent to get our attention. **"PRESIDENT DECLARES WAR,"** a headline screams in bold print. Concerned that the country is embroiled in combat somewhere, you buy the paper and anxiously read the article. The "war," you discover, is a "war on inflation." Accent is one of the main devices exploited in the promotion of the tabloids or "scandal sheets." Not to be outdone, television has begun using this tactic ad nauseam. In order to heighten viewer anticipation, talk shows and even the newscasts are routinely promoted by means of ten-, twenty-, and thirty-second "teases," as they are called in the television industry. The tease accents the most sensational, titillating, or alarming aspect of a story or topic and promises "Details at eleven!" or "on the next *Geraldo!*"

An important variation of the accent fallacy is the out-of-context quote, a device frequently used by candidates for political office to discredit each other. A vivid example of the out-of-context accent fallacy occurred in a statement in which former President Ronald Reagan defended his controversial visit to Germany's Bitburg cemetery in 1985. The visit was controversial because Nazi SS officers are buried there, and an official visit by the American head of state was interpreted by many as a gesture of tribute to those officers, and by extension to the Nazi regime. In explaining and defending his visit Reagan said:

> One of the many who wrote me about this visit was a young woman who had recently been bas mitzvahed. She urged me to lay the wreath at Bitburg cemetery in honor of the future of Germany, and that is what we have done.

As the president was later forced to admit, he was here distorting a letter unequivocally opposed to the visit, in which the writer had said that *if* he went to Bitburg, Reagan should do so *not* to honor the soldiers of the German army and SS buried there, but in honor of the future of Germany.

A more recent example occurred during the 1992 presidential campaign and in the immediate wake of the Los Angeles riots following the acquittal of four police officers in the beating of Rodney King. Candidate Bill Clinton took a comment by rapper Sister Souljah out of context and criticized it as an incitement to violence against whites. In an article published in the May 13 *Washington Post,* Sister Souljah was quoted as saying, "I mean, if black people kill black people every day, why not have a week and kill white people?" Out of context such a statement certainly is susceptible to Clinton's interpretation, but as Sister Souljah attempted—largely without effect—to explain in a series of press conferences in subsequent days, her point had been to *explain* the mob psychology which had led to violence against white truck driver Reginald Dennie during the rioting and the roots of this mob psychology in a prevailing social climate of violence in the community of South Central Los Angeles. Attention to the full text of her statement and the context in which it was given would have made this more clear.

A caution: Not every instance of the use of ambiguous expressions is fallacious. Ambiguity is an especially valuable feature of language. It gives language a lot of its remarkable flexibility and adaptability. Without ambiguity poetry, and comedy, and lots of other delightful and insightful things would be impossible. The deliberate use of ambiguity, even in an argument, may be perfectly legitimate as an intentional pun or play on words or double entendre.

## FALSE IMPLICATION

However, understanding how fallacies of ambiguity work is useful in arming oneself against some genuinely deceptive persuasive strategies, many of which play a crucial role in advertising. For example there is a widely used advertising strategy known as "false implication," which consists in stating something true while implying something else that is false. As you might suspect, the implied falsehood is likely to be more relevant to motivating the purchase than the stated truth.

Examples of this strategy are not hard to find. Recently we spotted a candy bar wrapper imprinted in bold type with the words BIGGEST EVER! The implication is clearly that the candy bar used to be smaller than it is now, that it has been *increased in size.* The truth of the matter is that the candy bar is as big as it's ever been—and also as small as it's ever been—because it's the same size as it's always been. This example illustrates a particularly common variety of false implication based on the use of superlative adjectives. This strategy is standard in the promotion of parity products. Parity products are products which are identical regardless of brand name. Aspirin is a good example of a parity product. Aspirin is aspirin is aspirin. It doesn't matter whether you buy it in the bottle which says "Bayer" on it or in the bottle with the regional brand name or the bottle with the generic label. You get the same number of milligrams of the same chemical formula per tablet. Understandably, producers of parity products work very hard in their ads to promote name recognition and brand loyalty, and frequently use superlatives such as "best," "strongest," "most powerful," and so on to describe their products. "How can this be!" you may ask. "If all of the products are identical, they must all be equally good, equally strong, equally powerful, and so on." Quite right. If you have this doubt, it's probably because you recognize that normally a superlative implies a comparison. For example, consider the following sets of adjectives:

| | | |
|---|---|---|
| Superlative: | best | strongest |
| Comparative: | better | stronger |
| Descriptive: | good | strong |

Normally, as you read down the list, each adjective implies the one below. If something is better than something else, this implies that it is good. If something is best, this implies it is better than the rest. Not so in parity ads. In parity ads you almost never encounter explicit comparisons between one parity product and another, because to say that one parity product is better than another would be false. Yet they almost all describe themselves in superlative terms. In the context of this sort of employment the superlative "best" is taken to mean "there are none better"; the superlative "strongest" is taken to mean "there are none stronger"; and so on. Thus, if an over-the-counter pain reliever is described as "the strongest pain reliever you can buy without a prescription," this should not be interpreted to mean "stronger than the other over-the-counter pain relievers," though that is what the advertiser expects you to think because that is what would normally be implied by such a claim. The truth of the matter is that the pain reliever is "as strong as any of the other over-the-counter pain relievers"; in other words, you are simply getting the maximum dosage which may legally be dispensed without a doctor's prescription, the same as with all of the other over-the-counter pain pills.

## AMBIGUOUS COMPARISONS

Advertisers frequently make comparisons which can be interpreted in more than one way, again, in order to effectively suggest what cannot truthfully be said explicitly. The most common device is simply to leave the comparison unfinished. For example, in one famous ad we are told, "Anacin: Twice as much of the pain reliever doctors recommend most." Compared to what? And what exactly is the pain reliever doctors recommend most? Well, as you might guess, the pain reliever doctors recommend most is aspirin. Can it be then that what the ad is really saying is that one tablet of Anacin contains twice as much aspirin as one aspirin tablet? In unfinished comparisons some advertisers think they have found the greatest thing since sliced bread. The Continental Baking Company, in promoting Profile Bread as a weight loss product, said that a slice of Profile contained seven fewer calories than other breads. When challenged by the Federal Trade Commission (FTC), Continental was forced to reveal that this was merely because Profile was sliced thinner than most other breads. Here's one from Detroit: "Ford LTD—700% quieter!" Compared to what? Viewers of this ad are understandably prone to fill out the comparison for themselves in one or another of several ways relevant to selecting a new car. So, for example, many viewers naturally assume that the ad means that this year's model is 700% quieter than last year's model, or that the Ford LTD is 700% quieter than the competitors in its price category. When the FTC challenged the claim, Ford admitted that the real basis of the comparison was exterior noise. The inside of the car was 700% quieter than the outside.

## EXERCISE | Fallacies of Ambiguity

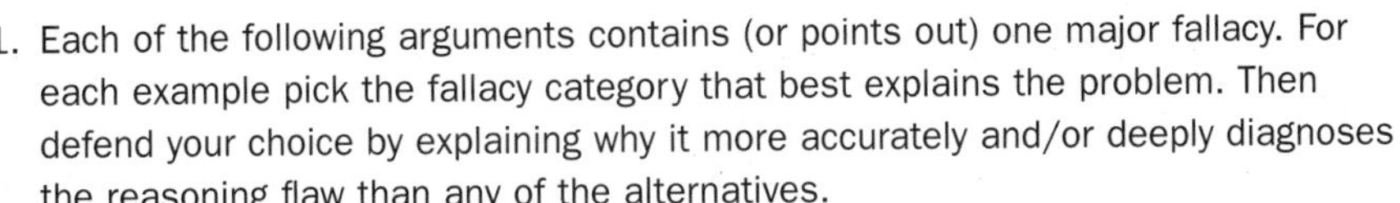

1. Each of the following arguments contains (or points out) one major fallacy. For each example pick the fallacy category that best explains the problem. Then defend your choice by explaining why it more accurately and/or deeply diagnoses the reasoning flaw than any of the alternatives.
   a. Airplanes are used for getting high. And airplanes are perfectly legal. Drugs are used for getting high. So they should be legal too.

| | |
|---|---|
| | Equivocation |
| | Amphiboly |
| | Accent |
| | Ambiguous Comparison |

Explain your answer:

_______________________________________________

_______________________________________________

_______________________________________________

_______________________________________________

   b. I passed nobody on the road. Therefore nobody is slower than I am.
   —Lewis Carroll

| | |
|---|---|
| | Equivocation |
| | Amphiboly |
| | Accent |
| | False Implication |

Explain your answer:

_______________________________________________

_______________________________________________

_______________________________________________

_______________________________________________

c. Look! The notice on his office door says "Back Soon." But I've been waiting here for over an hour and a half!

| | |
|---|---|
| | Equivocation |
| | Amphiboly |
| | Accent |
| | False Implication |

Explain your answer:

## RHETORICAL FALLACIES

In Chapter 2, we distinguished persuasion as an important function of language. There are a number of common informal fallacies which can best be understood as improper applications of the numerous persuasive capacities of language.

### ABUSE OF VAGUENESS

In Chapter 2, we also developed the notion of vagueness as lack of clarity in the extensional meaning of an expression. The persuasive power of vague expressions has to do with the fact that they allow one to project into them meanings determined by one's desires. This helps explain why they have become literally the stock in trade of the modern sophists that populate the so-called "human potential" industry. For example, just as we were composing this chapter, there arrived through the mail an unsolicited flyer which read in part:

> This two-day weekend seminar will open you to the wonders of the contemporary experience of modern High-Tech Serendipity Meditation, as your seminar leader and originator of the High-Tech Serendipity Meditation Experience personally conducts this expansive program, demonstrating the power and potential of this contemporary meditative technology. The weekend includes four power-packed sessions of Holodynamic Serendipity material presented in such a way as to enable each participant to personally experience the contemporary ease and the full potential of High-Tech Meditation.

Sounds exciting, intriguing, beneficial, attractive, but what does all this mean? It is virtually impossible to tell. The terminology, though it sounds very positive and indeed technically precise, is hopelessly vague. That's the important thing to notice here. Because it is so vague, it invites the reader to project onto it whatever meanings are most closely connected with the reader's own search and longings. Of course, if you want to find out in detail what High-Tech Holodynamic Serendipity Meditation is all about, you can sign up for the two-day weekend seminar for a fee of $250, which, assuming you can afford it, might not be such a bad deal for two full days of whatever you want to believe you're hearing. The overuse of vague expressions for their persuasive power and as a substitute for argument constitutes the fallacy of abuse of vagueness.

*Incidentally, the thought crossed our minds that the timing of the arrival of this flyer, to coincide with the writing of this chapter, might itself have been a case of serendipity. But see the fallacy category of post hoc in Chapter 11.*

## ASSUMPTION-LOADED LABELS

A similar fallacy consists in simply labeling things in such a way that hasty conclusions are strongly suggested by the labels rather than supported with reasons. As we discussed in Chapter 2, labels can be dangerous when they conceal assumptions that may be questionable, leading us to accept uncritically a doubtful or contestable view of things. When Hitler referred to "the Jewish problem" and Nazi propaganda systematically repeated the phrase this implied a host of questionable assumptions, not the least of which was that a nation's economic problems were caused by individuals of a particular religion or ethnic background. The persuasive power of labeling (and of sheer repetition) is evident from the way in which Nazi Germany was eventually led to consider and even implement brutal "solutions" to "the Jewish problem."

More recently we speak of the "welfare problem," even the "welfare mess." "Welfare" means organized efforts to improve the living conditions of needy persons. In what sense, then, is welfare a "problem"? In fact, welfare is the result of many problems: unemployment, age, infirmity, racial prejudice, broken homes, limited resources, and so forth. These in turn are likely the results of fundamental problems in our political, social, and economic institutions and philosophies. The label "welfare problem" obscures the complexity of the issue. It is loaded with the assumption that welfare is the disease, not the symptom. As a result, it encourages us not only to consider welfare in isolation from its underlying causes but to blame welfare and its recipients for various social ills—for "infecting" the nation, to extend the medical metaphor.

Certain vague words have become particular favorites of advertisers, apparently because they carry a positive emotional charge. "Homemade," "fun," and "pleasure," immediately come to mind. In recent times "natural" has surfaced as a special favorite of advertisers, as in

"It's natural for fresh breath." (Ad for Wrigley's Doublemint gum)

"It's only natural." (Ad for Winston cigarettes)

and

> "Welcome to the pure and natural world of feminine care." (Ad for a feminine deodorant spray)

Though the word "natural" has extremely positive connotations today, it is hopelessly vague as it is most frequently used in advertising. What does it mean in these ads? That the use of the product has become rather commonplace? That using the product is as natural as, say, eating or sleeping? In what sense are gum chewing, smoking, and using feminine deodorant sprays "natural"?

In contrast with these vague uses, notice that the word "natural" has also a quite specific meaning in some advertising contexts. As applied to a product's ingredients, "natural" means "not artificial," where "artificial" means "human-made." This is the sense in which, for example, Tree Sweet Products Company was challenged to defend its claim that its grape drink contained only "natural color." When the company was unable to defend this claim, it was forced to pay a consumer-plaintiff $250,000 in punitive damages and an estimated 75-cent refund to everybody who purchased the grape drink between 1973 and 1976.

With growing public awareness and concern over environmental degradation has come a parallel boom in environmental public relations. "Environmentally friendly" has become an advertising favorite for the nineties. Like the preface "eco-," "environmentally friendly" terminology functions presently as a potent motivator. But like green labeling and such related terms as "recycled" and "recyclable," it is just as vague as "natural," and probably winds up subverting a good deal of the environmental concern it so effectively appeals to.

Another current favorite is "light," intended to appeal to the body-conscious among us by suggesting reduced fat, cholesterol, calories, and the like. But as with "natural" and "eco-friendly," it never gets clearly enough defined to make intelligent consumer decisions possible. Even less so its even vaguer surrogate "lite."

## WEASEL WORDS

Already we have seen a number of devices and strategies whose function is to enable the advertiser to suggest what cannot truthfully be said in an explicit and straightforward way. Another such device is known as the "weasel word." This expression is derived from the egg-eating habits of weasels. A weasel will bite into the eggshell and suck out the contents, leaving what appears to the casual observer to be an intact egg. Similarly, *a weasel word or phrase is a device whose function is to evacuate the substance from what appears on the surface to be a substantial claim.* In effect, what the weasel word does is to make the claim in which it is used a vague claim, while, at the same time, at least partially concealing the vagueness.

"Help" functions in advertising as a weasel. "Help" means "aid" or "assist" and nothing more. Yet as one author has observed, "'Help' is the one single word which, in all the annals of advertising, has done the most to say something that couldn't be said."[1] Once "help" is used to qualify a claim, almost anything can be said after it. Accordingly we are exposed to ads for products that "*help* keep us young," "*help* prevent cavities," and "*help* keep our houses germ free." Just think of how many times a day you hear or read pitches that say "*helps* stop," "*helps* prevent," "*helps* fight," "*helps* overcome," "*helps* you feel," and "*helps* you look." But don't think "help" is the only weasel in the advertiser's arsenal.

"Like (as in "makes your floor look *like* new"), "virtual" or "virtually" (as in "*virtually* no cavities"), "up to" (as in "provides relief *up to* eight hours"), "as much as" (as in "saves *as much as* one gallon of gas"), and other weasels say what cannot be said. Studies indicate that on hearing or reading a claim containing a weasel word, we tend to screen out the weasel and take the assertion as an unqualified statement. Thus, on hearing that a medicine "can provide up to eight hours' relief," we screen out the "can" and the "up to" and infer that the product will give us eight hours' relief. In fact, according to a strict reading of the wording of the ad, the product may give no relief at all; and if it does give relief, the relief could vary in length from a moment to just under eight hours.

## EUPHEMISM

When certain words are considered too blunt, harsh, painful, or offensive, people sometimes substitute a more acceptable term, a term with fewer negative and/or more positive connotations. Such a term is called a euphemism. The term "euphemism" comes from the Greek for "good speech" or "good word." The tendency to favor euphemisms is a natural and understandable defense mechanism in many cases, but it is also a dangerous tendency in some ways. The dangers inherent in euphemism were almost prophetically envisioned by the writer George Orwell in his famous novel *1984* and a lesser known but very illuminating essay "Politics of the English Language." Orwell put forward the idea that an effective mechanism of political control is control of the terms of public discussion. Thus for example, rather than "fight a war," we "engage in a conflict" (as in the "Vietnam conflict") or a "police action" (as in the "Korean police action"). Rather than "spy" we "gather intelligence." Rather than "assassinate" people, the Central Intelligence Agency "terminates them with prejudice."

Rather than "firing" employees, bureaucrats speak of "selecting out," and instead of "rationing" gasoline, they talk of "end-use allocation." Today in some political circles it is fashionable to speak of a "tax" as a "revenue enhancement."

To be sure, euphemism sometimes is an appropriate adjustment of the language to a situation. We may be better able to deal with the death of a loved one by thinking of the person as having "passed away" rather than having "died." But euphemism can also be used to gloss over unpleasant realities that need attention or to divert us from giving an issue or event the critical inspection it warrants. Worse yet, euphemism is frequently used in place of genuine argument to "settle" controversial issues by controlling the terms of debate.

In recent history the rhetoric of Vietnam is one of the preeminent examples of this use of euphemism. Here are just a few examples with "translations":

| Euphemism | Word Replaced |
|---|---|
| pacification center | concentration camp |
| protective reaction strike | bombing |
| incontinent ordnance | off-target bombs (usually when civilians are killed) |
| friendly fire | shelling friendly villages or troops by mistake |
| specified strike zone | area where soldiers could fire at anything—replaced "free fire zone" when that became notorious |
| strategic withdrawal | retreat (when the U.S. and its allies did it) |
| advisor | military officer (before the U.S. admitted involvement) |
| terminate | kill |
| infiltrators | enemy troops moving into battle area |
| reinforcements | friendly troops moving into battle area[2] |

Military operations are often given euphemistic names. "Operation Just Cause" was the name the Bush administration gave to what was essentially the invasion of Panama. "Operation Desert Shield" was the name given to the massive military airlift in preparation for "Operation Desert Storm" which was selected over "Operation Desert Sword" for its more natural and less warlike connotations as the name for the war against Iraq. Just as in the Vietnam period euphemisms were used to soften the language used to describe what we were doing in the Persian Gulf so as to lend credibility to the benevolence of our intentions and rationale. Here again are a few examples with "translations":

| Euphemism | Word Replaced |
| --- | --- |
| operation | deployment of military forces on foreign soil |
| exercise the military option | wage (undeclared) war |
| authorize the use of force | declare (undeclared) war |
| servicing the target | bombing |
| visiting the site | bombing |
| revisiting the site | more bombing |
| force packages | bombs |
| sanitize | destroy by bombing |
| degrade | destroy by bombing |
| attrition | destruction by bombing |
| suppression | destruction by bombing |
| damage assessment | estimate of destruction caused by our side (excluding civilian casualties) |
| collateral damage | civilian casualties caused by our side |
| terrorism | casualties (civilian or otherwise) caused by their side |
| press pool | Pentagon censorship |

In President Bill Clinton's second term in office, issues were raised in Congress about the integrity of his campaign fund-raising practices. During a press conference Clinton offered the following response, carefully worded in the passive voice:

> No one is blameless here. At the edges errors are made, and when they're made they need to be confessed.[3]

Commenting on the cultural struggles over "political correctness" which erupted as the 1980s gave way to the 1990s, one commentator remarked:

> We think in language, and so the quality and clarity of our thoughts depend on the integrity of our language. Language is a natural weapon, then, for corrupt governments, oily salespeople, or anyone else who sets out to delude us. Sadder still is the American determination to delude ourselves, to protect ourselves from discomfort by burying reality in euphemisms and roundabout language that circumvents the truth. Politically correct language is just excessive politeness. It is simply an extreme effort to accord everybody the utmost respect in every conceivable context. As for this "people of color" business: there isn't a human being on this earth who isn't "of color." Even albinos have a "color."[4]

Nor are euphemisms confined to the political sphere. Euphemism is a strategy of first resort throughout public relations, for instance where "human resource managers" (i.e., the boss) devise more and more artful and evasive ways of saying "you're fired," like "your functions have been outsourced" (huh?), or "you've been made redundant." Or here's one from the wonderful world of customer service. It seems that Blockbuster Video has stopped charging a "late fee" for videos returned after they're due. Instead they assess "extended viewing fees." Sounds much more agreeable. Euphemism as a means of controlling discourse and thought is clearly an equal-opportunity and multipurpose strategy.

Think of euphemism as exaggeration in the "positive" direction. An equally powerful strategy consists in exaggerating the negative. This strategy is extensively employed in the political sphere of discourse. It is particularly useful in the demonization of "official enemies" of the state, as for example in virtually all mainstream descriptions of Iraqi leader Saddam Hussein throughout the 1980s and 1990s in the United States. Such language is called "dysphemistic," from the Greek for "bad speech" or "bad word."

## EXTREME QUANTIFIERS AND INTENSIFIERS

Another way writers load language, and thereby communicate bias, is by using extreme quantifiers—terms like "all" or "every"—and extreme intensifiers—terms like "absolutely" or "certainly." When these devices are used in place of reasons in support of controversial claims, the result can be criticized as informally fallacious. The fallacy of extreme quantifiers or intensifiers consists in using extreme quantifiers or intensifiers to strongly suggest a conclusion rather than support it with reasons. Of course we need not qualify everything we say or write. But it is important to frame our assertions with as much accuracy and fairness as possible and to expect the same of others. Such framing is not only conducive to precise and fruitful thinking but precludes needless disagreement, for frequently controversy is kindled through the use of an immoderate term, an intensifier.

Unfortunately, natural human indolence and intellectual limitations make us eager to view questions in the simplest terms possible, and as we saw in Chapter 1, cultural conditioning encourages this tendency to oversimplify. These factors show up in our approaches to practical problems but even more so in questions of human conduct or social policy. One cannot say with easy assurance, "The environment *certainly* must be cleaned up, even if that means plant shutdowns, unemployment, and a reduced standard of living," or "*Surely* the best way to ensure domestic tranquillity is to erect the strongest military defense possible," or "Abortion should *never* be permitted," or "Drafting young men in peacetime *simply* isn't justifiable." Perhaps each or some of these assertions are warranted, perhaps none is. But before any are adopted as settled conviction, the thinking person must consider their full implications. When the implications are explored, it may be found that these unqualified generalizations don't hold up; that their extreme quantifiers and intensifiers need to be diluted. But the writer who employs these devices ordinarily wants to shut off debate precisely where it needs to be opened up.

## HYPE

A common intensification device in advertising is the use of hyperbolic language, or "hype." This terminology derives from "hyperbole," which refers to an exaggeration or extravagant language used as a figure of speech. For example, someone may say "I could sleep for a week!" as an extravagant way of saying "I'm very tired"; or "I could eat a horse!" as an exaggerated way of saying "I'm very hungry." In advertising, such extravagance is intended not to inform but to *excite* the consumer. Here are just a few of literally hundreds of exaggerations you come across daily in reading and watching television:

"Spectacular Two-Day Fur Sale"

"Waterford: The Ultimate Gift!"

"Diamonds are forever!"

"Whirlpool at sizzling low prices!"

"The amazing 'Face-Lift-in-a-Jar'—Used by Hollywood stars who didn't want plastic surgery."

"You won't believe your eyes!" (Ad for Medical curiosities)

"Incredible! $3.25 worth of E-A-D cream FREE!"

"Wipe away stretch marks instantly!" (Ad for Fade-Out)

"Shampoo, Wave & Curls! No Permanent! No Nitely Curlers! No Teasing! No Blow Driers! Chic Salon look for pennies!" (Ad for Wave & Curl)

"A most incredible achievement in cosmetic science! Remove skin discolorations forever!" (Ad for Dermacure)

"Amazing new 'computerized' forehead thermometer makes oral, rectal thermometers obsolete!" (Ad for Tel-A-Fever)

It is true that the FTC and the Food and Drug Administration (FDA) sometimes make advertisers defend their boasts, and censures them if they are unable to. In the tire industry, the FTC has questioned Goodyear's claim that its Double-Eagle Polysteel Radials can be driven over ax blades without suffering damage. The FTC has sued American Enviro Products for claiming that its Bunnies disposable diapers are "degradable" or "biodegradable," and First Brands for claiming that its Glad trashbags would break down in landfills. But before you conclude that government regulators are protecting you from the onslaught of exaggeration in advertising, remember that of the huge number of claims and implied claims made by advertisers the vast majority are never questioned. More important, the law permits what in the trade is termed "puffery."

## PUFFERY

Puffery is defined in law as advertising or other sales representations that praise an item with vague subjective opinions, superlatives, or exaggerations. In his book *The Great American Blowup,* Ivan L. Preston gives a long list of examples, among which are these:

"When you say Budweiser, you've said it all."

"When you're out of Schlitz, you're out of beer."

"You can be sure if it's Westinghouse."

"Toshiba—in touch with tomorrow."

"With a name like Smucker's, it's got to be good."

"Come to where the flavor is." (Marlboro cigarettes)

"Prudential is the strength of Gibraltar."

"The rock of Prudential—Above and Beyond!"

"You'll love it at Levitz"

Lawmakers permit puffery because they have decided, on the basis of actual cases, that most puffery is not deceptive. Certainly, in some cases puffery is not deceptive. When an oil company says that you'll have a tiger in your tank when you use its gasoline, no one expects a tiger. But are most puffs so outlandish that no one takes them seriously? If puffery were not deceptive, it wouldn't sell products. But advertising experts agree that puffs sell. What's more, a survey conducted in 1971 by R. H. Bruskin Associates supports the view that puffery deceives. In that survey a sample of citizens was asked whether they felt that various advertising claims were "completely true," "partly true," or "not true at all." Although puffery was not identified by name, a number of claims fell into that category and were rated as follows:

"State Farm is all you need to know about life insurance." (22 percent said completely true, 36 percent said partly true)

"The world's most experienced airline." (Pan AM) (23 percent said completely true, 47 percent said partly true)

"Ford has a better idea." (26 percent said completely true, 42 percent said partly true)

"You can trust your car to the man who wears the star." (Texaco) (21 percent said completely true, 47 percent said partly true)

"It's the real thing" (Coca-Cola) (35 percent said completely true, 29 percent said partly true)

"Perfect rice every time." (Minute Rice) (43 percent said completely true, 30 percent said partly true)

"Today aluminum is something else." (Alcoa) (47 percent said completely true, 36 percent said partly true)[5]

The conclusion seems unmistakable: Puffery does work. Evidently it does deceive at least some people, even though our lawmakers think otherwise. And, even where it doesn't actually deceive, it excites, and this probably accounts even more deeply for its effectiveness as an advertising strategy. Since the law doesn't restrict the use of puffery, we must guard against being victimized by it.

## MINIMIZERS

A closely related device works in the opposite direction to downplay potential controversy, or to minimize the need for substantial support for a claim. Expressions like "Needless to say," "It goes without saying that," "Obviously," and the like lend themselves to this application. They are generally intended and taken to mean that the claims they introduce are so uncontroversial or universally accepted as to require no argument or evidence. To be sure, there are such claims, and it goes without saying that claims which require no argument or evidence need not be argued for or supported with evidence. But when a speaker or writer attempts to slip a controversial assertion by as though it were "self-evident," it is time to raise an objection. The fallacy of minimizers, consists in using minimizers to mask the absence of reasons in support of a conclusion.

## RHETORICAL QUESTIONS

A rhetorical question is a question with a built-in answer. Rhetorical questions seem to leave the conclusion up to the reader but are worded in such a way that only one answer is possible. "Would you recommend that the United States not spend every penny necessary to ensure national security?" "Can a law that is opposed to the wishes of millions of honest citizens be fair and just?" "Since students don't know which courses will contribute to their education, should they have a strong voice in curriculum decisions?" It's hard to answer "Yes" to these questions. That's the point: The rhetorical question is intended to elicit a predetermined response. The beauty of the rhetorical question is that it makes you think that you are drawing the inference yourself. The implication of the writer's rhetorical setup is that if we took the time and made the effort to discover the answer, we would arrive at the same conclusion as the writer. Although this device is occasionally used effectively to dramatize an important point for which the supporting evidence has already been laid out, more often it is used to cover up a lack of good arguments.

In a 1983 television address intended to justify the continued presence of the U.S. Marines in Lebanon, former President Reagan asked rhetorically:

> Can the United States, or the free world for that matter, stand by and see the Middle East incorporated into the Soviet bloc? What of Western Europe's and Japan's dependence on Middle East oil for the energy to fuel their industries?

Here the audience is expected to draw several conclusions—(1) that the incorporation of the Middle East into the Soviet sphere of influence is unacceptable to the free world; (2) that it would curtail the supply of oil to Western Europe and Japan; (3) and that the withdrawal of the Marines would bring all of this about—all without any argument whatsoever. Incidentally, several months after this address the Marines were withdrawn from Lebanon, and to this date none of the dire consequences Reagan predicted has come about. (See the *slippery slope fallacy* and *false cause* sections in Chapter 11.)

## INNUENDO

Innuendo consists of drawing or implying a judgment, usually derogatory, on the basis of words that suggest but don't assert a conclusion. "Has Jones been fired?" someone asks you. You may reply directly "No." Or you may say "Not yet." By innuendo, the second response numbers Jones's days. Jones may in fact be on the proverbial block, but you have given no logical grounds for so inferring. Innuendo, then, is dangerous to critical thinking because it encourages us to imply things or draw inferences that we are unable or unwilling to defend. Innuendo needn't be as obvious as in the preceding example. The person who says "Most physicians are competent and altruistic health care professionals" probably isn't prepared to substantiate the charge made against the minority of physicians who by implication are incompetent and/or self-serving. The political candidate who distributes a brochure in which she promises to restore honesty and integrity to an office seldom is prepared to prove that her opponent is by implication a crook. Indeed, sometimes merely by calling attention to something, we provide enough innuendo to sandbag somebody. Consider this amusing episode—amusing, that is, for everyone except the captain in question:

> Captain L had a first mate who was at times addicted to the use of strong drink, and occasionally, as the slang has it, "got full." The ship was lying in port in China, and the mate had been on shore and had there indulged rather freely in some of the vile compounds common in Chinese ports. He came on board, "drunk as a lord," and thought he had a mortgage on the whole world. The captain, who rarely ever touched liquor himself, was greatly disturbed by the disgraceful conduct of his officer, particularly as the crew had all observed his condition. One of the duties of the first officer [i.e., the first mate] is to write up the log each day, but as that worthy was not able to do it, the captain made the proper entry, but added: "The mate was drunk all day." The ship left port the next day and the mate got "sobered off." He attended to his writing at the proper time, but was appalled when he saw what the captain had done. He went back on deck, and soon after the following colloquy took place:
>
> "Cap'n, why did you write in the log yesterday that I was drunk all day?"
>
> "It was true, wasn't it?"
>
> "Yes, but what will the shipowners say if they see it? It will hurt me with them."
>
> But the mate could get nothing more from the Captain than, "It was true, wasn't it?"
>
> The next day, when the Captain was examining the book, he found at the bottom of the mate's entry of observation, course, winds, and tides: "The captain was sober all day."[6]

Obviously the mate is hoping that the ship's owners will interpret his entry about the captain as more than the literal truth. Probably they will infer that the mate recorded the captain's sobriety because it was the exception, not the rule. When they do the mate will gain his revenge.

## COMPLEX QUESTION

Sometimes a question is so worded that you can't answer it without granting a particular answer to some other question. Such a construction is called a complex question, sometimes called a "loaded question" or "leading question." A well known example is the old vaudeville line "Have you stopped beating your wife (or husband) yet?" Such a question boxes you in because either way you answer it presupposes that you are or were beating your spouse. Another example:

> Why is it that most men prefer beauty to intelligence in women?

This complex question asks for an explanation of a phenomenon which may or may not be the case but which is presupposed as having already been established.

## THE PHANTOM DISTINCTION

Drawing distinctions is often essential to avoiding confusion and consequently it is often of central importance to arguing about an issue. Moreover some important distinctions are quite subtle and difficult to make clear. However, when the linguistic devices useful in drawing and indicating differences are used to suggest differences which do not in fact exist the fallacy of phantom distinction is committed. Suppose your next door neighbor makes some subtle and suggestive threatening gesture towards you in an attempt to get you to move your car from the curb in front of his house. You challenge the unfriendly tone: "Are you threatening me?" And the neighbor responds, "It's not a threat, it's a promise."

Sometimes this rhetorical device is employed with deliberate intent to mislead a discussion, by baffling an essentially accurate description or understanding of some controversial action, or policy, or what have you—often in combination with a more euphemistic description of the same controversial item. For example, suppose that at the annual stockholders' meeting the corporate public relations officer responds to a pointed question about the firm's new tactical approach to labor relations, saying, "We're not talking about union busting here. We're simply reasserting management prerogative in the area of determining compensation."

## MOB APPEAL

All of the rhetorical devices and fallacies discussed so far are powerful persuasive tools, and as such they are all useful to the orator, the persuasive public speaker. Often they are employed together and compound each other into a sort of "super-fallacy" of mob appeal. The fallacy of mob appeal consists in the attempt to win assent to a view by arousing the emotions of a group en masse. One could say that the fallacy of mob appeal is what happens when the skills of oratory run amok. Oratory is the art of public eloquence, of moving an audience as a body with words. A skillful public speaker will usually understand the common needs and drives likely to be shared by the overwhelming majority of the members of a given audience: the drive for emotional security, for self esteem, for acceptance, status, and so on, and will naturally couch her argument in terms chosen to appeal to and gratify these needs. But when a public speaker succeeds in stampeding an audience by means of such methods and in the absence of good reason, a fallacious mob appeal has been committed.

Perhaps the best classical example of mob appeal is Mark Antony's famous funeral oration in Shakespeare's *Julius Caesar* (Act 3, Scene 2). Antony is called upon by Brutus to address the crowd assembled at Caesar's funeral. He is introduced by Brutus, who with other conspirators had assassinated Caesar and who has already convinced the crowd that the assassination was in the best interests of Rome. Antony's speech, which begins with the famous line "Friends, Romans, Countrymen . . .," immediately gains the crowd's sympathy and gradually and imperceptibly, but very quickly, subverts Brutus's bid to succeed Caesar and in the end incites the mob against Brutus and his fellow conspirators. The speech is of course a work of art, but it accomplishes its goal by a combination of flattery, innuendo, staging, timing, and repetition, and with a notable lack of real argument. The main engine of its effectiveness, though, is the momentum of the emotional energy generated within the crowd. To the extent that the speech is deliberately designed to fuel, direct, and exploit the crowd's reaction, rather than present an argument in support of rising up against Brutus, it is a case of mob appeal.[7]

## EXERCISE | Fallacies of Language

1. Each of the following arguments contains (or points out) one (or more) major fallacies. For each example check any fallacy category that you think would help explain the problem. Then give your explanation.
   a. Look! The notice on his office door says "Back Soon." But I've been waiting here for over an hour and a half!

| | |
|---|---|
| | Equivocation |
| | Accent |
| | Amphiboly |
| | Abuse of Vagueness |

Explain your answer:

________________________________________

________________________________________

________________________________________

________________________________________

b. It's not a pay raise. It is a pay equalization concept. —U. S. Senator Ted Stevens explaining a congressional measure to increase the compensation of members of the U. S. Congress

| | |
|---|---|
| | Phantom Distinction |
| | Equivocation |
| | Euphemism |
| | Minimizer |

Explain your answer:

c. Have you just lost your mind, or were you born nuts?

| | |
|---|---|
| | Phantom Distinction |
| | Accent |
| | Complex Question |
| | Rhetorical Question |

Explain your answer:

## ADDITIONAL EXERCISES

**1.** a. At the beginning of this chapter there is a cartoon in which a mother (Rose) is negotiating with her toddler about ice pops. What is the fallacy illustrated by the cartoon?

b. For comparison, consider the following passage from Lewis Carroll's *Through the Looking Glass.* Can you explain what's wrong with the Queen's reasoning?

> "You couldn't have it if you did want it," the Queen said. "The rule is jam tomorrow and jam yesterday—but never jam today."
>
> "It must sometimes come to jam today," Alice objected.
>
> "No it can't," said the Queen. "It's jam every other day: today isn't any other day, you know."

**2.** Cartoonists sometimes provide the most "artful" examples of fallacious reasoning. Here's a wonderful example drawn by the great satirist Jules Feiffer, in which the politically ambitious leader of the Christian right, Reverend Jerry Falwell, arrives by a suspect line of argument at the seemingly contradictory conclusion that in order to remain part of the free world South Africa must continue to enslave its black population. Can you explain what is wrong with Falwell's reasoning?

**3.** Consider the following more or less well known advertising slogans and brand names. Using the concepts and terminology covered in this chapter, explain how you imagine these slogans are designed to work.

a. "Fleischmann's—made from 100 percent corn oil"
b. "Coffee-mate gives you more body, more flavor"
c. "Free gifts with every new deposit"
d. "With Real Blueberry Buds and Other Natural Flavors" (front of the package of Aunt Jemima frozen Jumbo Blueberry Waffles)
e. "Most Colgate kids got fewer cavities"
f. "In today's Army, you can earn good money, while learning a skill to make even more money. . . . If you qualify [for a number of jobs], you can enlist for one of hundreds of exciting Army skills. Or you can choose the initial area or

unit you'd like to serve in, near home in the continental United States or someplace new. Your choice will be guaranteed in writing before you enlist."

g. "We try harder" (Avis)
h. "Pleasure is where you find it" (Viceroy cigarettes)
i. "When you can't take five, take three! Anacin Three"
j. "Listerine Antiseptic! It says what it does! It does what it says!"
k. Top-Flite Golf Balls
l. Super Shell
m. Wonder Bread
n. "Take the road to flavor in a low-tar cigarette" (Raleigh Lights)
o. "Ahhhhhh! Anusol"
p. "Bud—the King of beers!"
q. "Anything else is just a light" (Bud Lite beer)

**4.** Sometimes it's hard to tell whether what we're hearing is a fallacy or not. Consider:

a. "It's not a lie. It's just an exaggeration."
Is this an instance of the fallacy of phantom distinction (with a little euphemism thrown in) or not? Well, now consider:
b. "That's not just an exaggeration. It's a lie."
Could this be an instance of the fallacious use of intensifiers? Perhaps the best answer here is "It depends." Compose a scenario in which you would consider a falsehood to be an exaggeration rather than a lie. Now change the scenario in such a way that you would no longer consider the falsehood to be a mere exaggeration but instead a lie. Now write a short essay in which you explain the two scenarios and the variables which influenced your judgment.

**5.** For this exercise you'll need a partner, preferably someone who is taking the critical thinking course with you. One of you can play the role of finding and explaining the flaw in the argument or rhetorical appeal, while the other challenges and tests the diagnosis by trying to defend the argument against the proposed criticism. Take turns as you work your way through the following examples. Don't forget, a given argument can have more than one thing wrong with it. If you arrive at a consensus criticism, move on to the next example.

a. Having missed Veterans Administration deadlines for application for college benefits, two men sued the VA, arguing that under VA guidelines "disabled veterans" had longer to apply, and that their disability—alcoholism—qualified them for the extended deadline.
b. Todd: Why do you dislike Frank so much, when the Bible says, "Love thy neighbor"?
Ted: But Frank's not my neighbor. He doesn't live anywhere near me.
c. Pushy father-in-law to new bride: "So, when are you kids planning to make us grandparents?"
d. From a political campaign brochure: Candidate X has resorted to "name-calling." She says that our candidate is a "professional politician." That's not

fair. It is coloring the truth. The truth in black and white is that our candidate was a deputy sheriff up until he nearly lost his life in the line of duty. Hardly a "professional politician." Our candidate has run for office only once in his life and that was four years ago. Hardly a "professional politician."

e. From another political campaign brochure: What would you call a politician who didn't pay his property taxes on time? We'd call him a little forgetful. What would you call a politician who owned a business but never paid his local business taxes? We'd call him more than a little forgetful. What would you call a politician who owned property but refused to pay his property taxes from 1981 until 1984? We'd call him a lot of the same things you'd call him. But none of us would call him our next assemblyman.

f. God is love.
Love is blind.
———
∴ God is blind.

g. How can you deny that abortion is murder? The fetus is certainly alive, isn't it? And it certainly is human, isn't it? And it hasn't done anything wrong, has it? So you're talking about taking an innocent human life. What else is there to say?

h. People object to sexism and racism on the ground that they involve discrimination. But what is objectionable about discrimination? We discriminate all the time—in the cars we buy, the foods we eat, the books we read, the friends we choose. The fact is there's nothing wrong with discrimination as such.

i. Most Calvinists were theological determinists. Most New England Puritans were Calvinists. Therefore, most New England Puritans were theological determinists. . . . The fortunes of the Federalists decayed after 1800. Joseph Dennie was a Federalist. Therefore, the fortunes of Joseph Dennie decayed after 1800.[8]

j. The end of anything is its perfection. Therefore, since death is the end of life, death must be the perfection of life.

k. Letter to the editor: "Question for today: How can the federal budget deficits ever be brought under control as long as conservative superpatriots insist that the Defense Department is a sacred cow, despite endless examples of waste and mismanagement? Put another way, how many over-priced ash trays and toilet seats must Congress learn about before it realizes that the Pentagon brass hats are bemedaled equivalents of Imelda Marcos?"

l. On the eve of the 1992 election Vice President Dan Quayle made a last frantic dash through the swing state of Ohio. Speaking to reporters at one airport, Quayle said that what the American people want "is a president who has been faithful to his country, faithful to his principles, faithful to his family. And George Bush certainly is that man." Asked if he specifically was calling challenger Bill Clinton unfaithful, Quayle replied, "I'll let others answer that."

m. "Nuclear Energy Means Cleaner Air. For a free booklet on nuclear energy, write to the U.S. Council on Energy Awareness."

n. A term I use to describe the mess that surrounds most issues in the world today and prevents us from getting at what is really so about the world's problems is "pea soup." The pea soup is a mass of confusion, controversy, argument, conflict, and opinions. As long as you are asking what more can you do, what better solution have you got, what have you come up with that's different, you cannot see that the confusion, controversy, conflict, doubt, lack of trust, and opinions surrounding the problem of hunger and starvation result inevitably from any position you take. Once you are clear that you cannot take any position that will contribute in any way to the end of hunger and starvation, that any position you take will only contribute to the pea soup that engulfs the problem of hunger and starvation, then hope dies. And when hope dies, hopelessness dies with it: Without hope you can't have hopelessness. You are now close to the source of the problem of hunger and starvation on the planet. If you can see that the problem is without hope, you are no longer hopeless and frustrated. You are just there with whatever is so. —Werner Erhard[9]

**6.** Find examples of your own in the public media of the informal fallacies discussed in this chapter. For each example, give a brief but careful explanation of the fallacies you find in it.

## GLOSSARY

**amphiboly** grammatical ambiguity, or a fallacy based on grammatical ambiguity
**complex question** question presupposing a particular answer to some further question, or a fallacy based upon such a presupposition
**dysphemism** negative exaggeration
**equivocation** inconsistent use of an ambiguous expression, or a fallacy based on such usage
**euphemism** positive exaggeration
**false implication** advertising strategy in which important claims are strongly implied but remain literally unstated, often because they are known to be false
**hype** advertising and public relations strategy in which exaggerated (hyperbolic) terminology is used to promote excitement
**informal fallacy** unreliable inference whose flaw or weakness is attributable to something other than its formal structure
**innuendo** public relations strategy in which important claims are strongly implied or suggested but left unstated, often because they cannot be proven
**phantom distinction** use of language to suggest a difference which doesn't exist
**puffery** advertising strategy in which vague terminology is used to promote enthusiasm
**rhetorical question** question used to mask a claim, or a fallacy based on such usage
**weasel word** advertising and public relations strategy based on the use of a vague word or expression in order to evade responsibility for an implied claim

## NOTES

[1] Paul Stevens, "Weasel Words: God's Little Helpers," in Paul A. Eschol, Alfred A. Rosa, and Virginia P. Clark (eds.), *Language Awareness* (New York: St. Martins, 1974).

[2] See William Lutz, *Doublespeak: From "Revenue Enhancement" to "Terminal Living"—How Government, Business, Advertisers, and Others Use Language to Deceive You* (New York, Harper & Row, 1989).

[3] Reported in *The Weekly Standard,* February 10, 1997.

[4] Algernon D'Ammassa, "A Race by Any Other Name," *Quarterly Review of Doublespeak,* 18, no. 4 (July 1992).

[5] From Ivan L. Preston, *The Great American Blowup* (Madison: University of Wisconsin Press, 1975), reported in Howard Kahane, *Logic and Contemporary Rhetoric* (Belmont, Calif.: Wadsworth, 1980), p. 186.

[6] Charles E. Trow, *The Old Shipmasters of Salem* (New York: Macmillan, 1905), pp. 14–15.

[7] For a more extensive analysis of this rhetorical classic, see S. Morris Engel, *With Good Reason: An Introduction to Informal Fallacies,* 2nd ed. (New York: St. Martin's, 1982), pp. 176–180.

[8] Paraphrase of historian Vernon Parrington, "Main Currents of American Thought," in David Hackett Fischer, ed., *Historians' Fallacies* (New York: Harper & Row, 1970), p. 222.

[9] Werner Erhard, *The End of Starvation: Creating an Idea Whose Time Has Come,* (San Francisco: The Hunger Project, 1982), pp. 10–11.

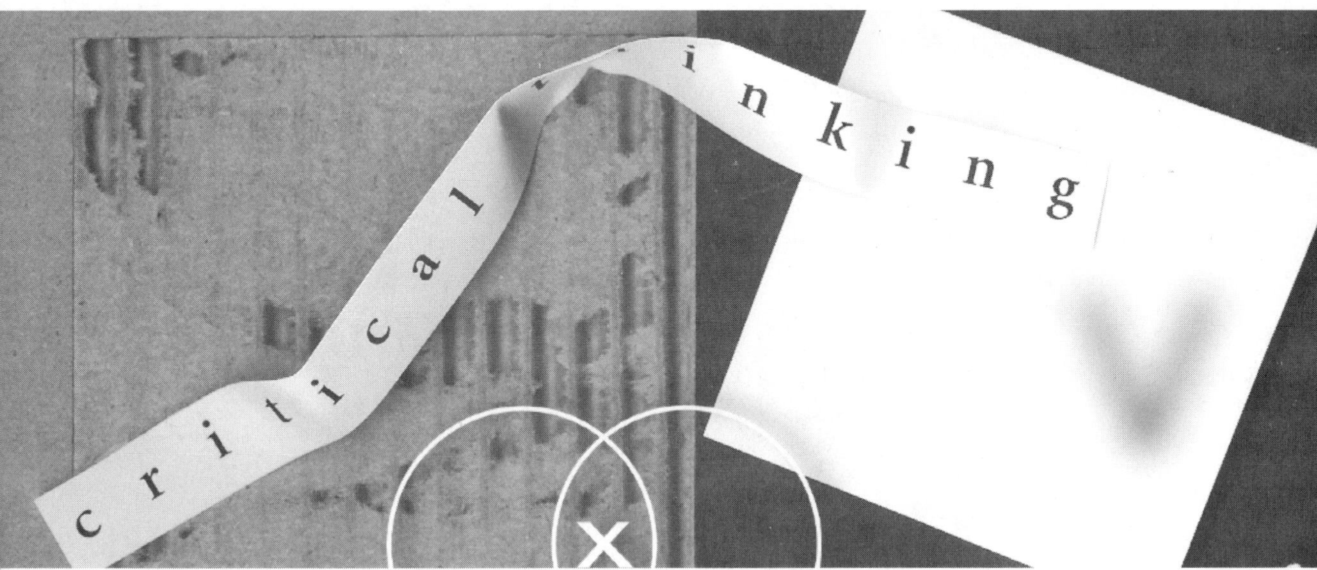


# CHAPTER 10 Fallacies II: Informal Fallacies of Relevance

Suppose that someone said to you, "Now that I know how to construct a deductively valid argument I can finally settle the abortion issue once and for all!" Here's the person's argument:

If "abortion" is an eight-letter word, then abortion should be against the law.

"Abortion" is an eight-letter word.

---

∴ Abortion should be against the law.

Are you convinced? Since the argument is in the form Modus Ponens it can't be faulted formally. So what's wrong with it? Are the premises false? The second one is true. Count the letters. That verifies that. Which leaves premise 1. Is premise 1 false? Before you answer this question just suppose for a moment that the conclusion of the argument is true. Now, is premise 1 false? Hard to tell, isn't it? You don't know yet whether the conclusion is true, but it might be, and in that case you can't really be sure that premise 1 is false. (See section on using truth tables to test for deductive validity in Chapter 6.)

So what's wrong with the argument? The problem here is that both premises are irrelevant to the issue. Why? Because the number of letters in the

*"Let me tell you, folks—I've been around long enough to develop an instinct for these things, and my client is innocent or I'm very much mistaken."*



word "abortion" is irrelevant to the moral status of abortion and therefore also to the question of abortion law.

Here you can see the concept of relevance in bold relief. An important informal consideration in evaluating arguments is whether the premises appealed to are relevant to what is at issue. If they are, so much the better for the argument. If not, some kind of fallacy of relevance, or "irrelevant appeal," has been committed.

A general strategy for exposing irrelevant appeals is to challenge the relevance of the premise to the conclusion of the argument or to the issue under discussion. Bear in mind, however, that to challenge the relevance of a premise is not the same as establishing that it *is* irrelevant. Relevance is not always obvious on the surface. So it remains open to the arguer to meet the challenge by explaining how the premise bears on the conclusion or issue. But if a premise *is* relevant, it should be possible to explain the connection.

## IRRELEVANT APPEALS

A more pointed strategy for exposing irrelevant appeals is to assimilate an argument to one or another of the common categories of irrelevant appeal which we will survey in this chapter. To keep your criticisms as sharp and clear as possible, remember that there is considerable overlap between many of these categories, and that a given argument can also have more than one thing wrong with it. Most important, take care not to dismiss, as irrelevant, considerations whose relevance is just not apparent on the surface.

## AD HOMINEM

Perhaps the most common and certainly one of the most objectionable of the informal fallacies of relevance is the ad hominem argument. *Ad hominem* is the Latin phrase for "to the man." When people argue ad hominem, they attack the person, not the person's position or argument, a special case, in other words of irrelevant reasoning. A most persuasive way of diverting attention from the real issue, ad hominem commonly takes two forms: abusive, which consists of attacking characteristics of the person; and circumstantial, which consists of trying to persuade someone to accept a position based upon the special facts or circumstances of the person's life.

### ABUSIVE AD HOMINEM

The abusive ad hominem fallacy is committed when, instead of trying to disprove the truth of what is asserted, one attacks the person making the assertion. Those employing abusive ad hominems attempt to discredit ideas by discrediting the persons who hold them. It's as if they were saying: "Since so-and-so is (*some abusive term*), anything so-and-so says is without merit."

A talk-radio favorite, abusive ad hominem takes two principal forms:

1. *Raising suspicions about the motives or character of a person or group:* For example, here is ad hominem arguer extraordinaire Rush Limbaugh commenting on the animal rights movement:

   > The animal rights movement, like so many others in this country, is being used by leftists as another way to attack the American way of life. They have adopted two constituencies who cannot speak and complain about the political uses to which they are put. One of them is trees and other plant life; the other is the animal kingdom. People for the Ethical Treatment of Animals (PETA) takes in over $10 million every year by preying on people's concern for animals. Most of its contributors think most of the money goes to making sure animals are treated kindly . . . but PETA's real mission is destroying capitalism, not saving animals.[1]

   Besides distorting the actual positions and arguments of those who believe that nonhuman animals have rights (see straw person and provincialism later in this chapter), this comment amounts to an irrelevant attack on their character and motives.

2. *Showing outright contempt for a person:* Here's Rush Limbaugh again on the same subject:

> I have spoken extensively in this book about the various fringe movements and the spiritual tie that binds them: radical liberalism. Two groups that are particularly close, to the point of being nearly indistinguishable, are the environmentalists and the animal rights activists. Because I devoted a chapter to the environmentalists I thought it only fair to include one about animal rights activism. I certainly do not want to be accused of discrimination. Every wacko movement must have its day in my book.[2]

   And later in the same chapter:

> The basic right to life of an animal—which is the source of energy for many animal rights wackos—must be inferred from the anticruelty laws humans have written, not from any divine source. Our laws do not prevent us from killing animals for food or sport, so the right to life of an animal is nonexistent.[3]

   These are truly lousy arguments, in several ways. But here we may focus on the expression "fringe movements" and the even more obvious "wacko."

A special kind of ad hominem has grown increasingly common in the television age: dismissing a person's argument or position because of the person's image or appearance. Consider, for example, the way in which many viewers and even some television commentators assessed the candidacy of Paul Simon for the 1988 Democratic presidential nomination, or Paul Tsongas in 1992, or the way in which many commentators on the O. J. Simpson murder trial focused on the appearance, dress, and hairstyle of prosecutor Marcia Clark.

And as you might imagine, ad hominem is quite often accomplished by innuendo. That is, by *merely suggesting* something unflattering about an individual, arguers frequently hope in addition to discredit the person's positions.

You should be aware, though, that not every argument that introduces the character or motives of the parties to the dispute is fallacious. In the political context, for instance, attacking one's opponent is not necessarily ad hominem. If one's attack is on one's opponent's record in office, that is not irrelevant to the issue of the campaign. Personal considerations are certainly relevant when deciding whether a person is reliable or conscientious. If people have proven themselves unreliable, we surely have a basis for holding what they say suspect. But suspecting their words is different from rejecting them. Weighing the reliability of a witness differs from assuming that personalities dispose of issues.

## CIRCUMSTANTIAL AD HOMINEM

The circumstantial ad hominem consists of attempting to persuade someone to accept or reject a position based upon the special facts or circumstances of the person's life, rather than on the merits of the position itself. For example, rather than show why a proposed tax bill is a bad piece of legislation and therefore unworthy of support, someone argues, "You're a businesswoman. Don't you realize that the U.S. Chamber of Commerce opposes this measure?" Similarly, Dr. Henry can't understand how a fellow physician can support the new Massachusetts health plan. "Don't you worry about how this will affect your income?" she warns her colleague. In these cases the arguers fail to address the issues, preferring to argue that the measures they oppose cannot be consistently supported by their opponents owing to their opponents' special circumstances. Although such arguments might succeed in placing one's opponent on the defensive, they are quite beside the point.

## GUILT BY ASSOCIATION

The fallacy of guilt by association, a special case of circumstantial ad hominem, consists of making negative judgments about people, or their positions and arguments, solely on the basis of their relationships with others. For example, during the congressional campaigns of 1982 and 1986, many Democratic candidates tried to defeat their Republican opponents by identifying them with President Reagan's economic programs, which in part had contributed to widespread unemployment, farm foreclosures, and homelessness, even though many of the Republican candidates were trying to dissociate themselves from Reagan's policies, and many of these same Democratic candidates had supported Reagan's policies in Congress.

The abuse of this fallacy reached epic proportions in the 1986 California races, as numerous candidates sought successfully to tar the images of their opponents by linking their campaigns to State Supreme Court Chief Justice Rose Bird, already the target of a massive negative campaign waged by advocates of stiffer criminal penalties and more liberal procedures for the execution of the death penalty. The campaign to unseat Chief Justice Bird reached such a pitch of hysteria that the question of association with Bird became, in terms of public campaigning and most of all in advertising, the top priority issue in many a legislative district and the *only* issue in some. In some 30-second television spots it was thought sufficient merely to suggest such an association by far-fetched innuendo.

## GENETIC APPEAL

A similar fallacy consists in evaluating something strictly in terms of its origin, sources, or genesis. For example, it is sometimes argued by religious fundamentalists that dancing be forbidden because it originated as a form of pagan worship, or that day care centers are insidious because of their socialist origins.

Another kind of example, closer to guilt by association and ad hominem, involves either endorsing or dismissing an idea simply on grounds of who its originators or supporters are. For example, in 1988 a struggle was waged through the ballot initiative process over the regulation of the insurance industry in the state of California. One measure which qualified for the election made the insurance industry publicly accountable for rate changes. The insurance industry countered by promoting a measure of its own, called the No-Fault Initiative. Voters were understandably confused. In their confusion, many voters were swayed to "consider the source." It was argued that the No-Fault Initiative could not be good for the consumer because the insurance industry had cooked it up and was supporting it. Strictly speaking, this argument commits the fallacy of genetic appeal.

But we should be careful here. Speaking equally strictly, the identity of the source is not entirely irrelevant to the issue, in that one could make a reasonably solid inductive case for conflict of interest between consumer protection (the advertised aim of the No-Fault Initiative) and protection of a profitable business climate in which no substantial consumer protection existed. The fallacy consists in closing the issue on the basis solely of the identity of the source, or treating the identity of the source as decisive. At most, the identity of the source constitutes a reason for looking more closely at the measure itself and at the arguments made for and against it. In this case, these are the factors which should be regarded as decisive.

## POISONING THE WELL

A similar fallacious argumentative strategy consists of attempting to discredit a position, or its advocate, before the argument for the position has had a chance to get a hearing. This strategy of attempting to arouse prejudice against an argument which should be allowed to stand on its own merits or fall of its own weight is described metaphorically as "poisoning the well" (before anyone can drink from it). In effect the arguer tries to maneuver an opponent into a position from which he or she cannot reply. For example: "You're not a woman, so it doesn't matter what you have to say about the question of abortion."

Another example: Nineteenth century philosopher and theologian John Henry Cardinal Newman engaged in frequent disagreements with clergyman and novelist Charles Kingsley. During the course of one of these disputes, Kingsley suggested that Newman could not place the highest value on truth because of his Catholicism. Newman rightly objected that this was poisoning the well, since it made it impossible for him (or any Catholic) to state his case. No matter what reasons or arguments Newman might offer to show that he did value the truth and that this value was basic to his faith, Kingsley would have already ruled out because they had come from a Catholic.

Poisoning the well is a favorite government tactic for managing domestic public opinion about foreign policy, as is evident from the history of "official enemies" over many years. For example, the Reagan administration worked very hard at—and, with the general cooperation of the American press, largely succeeded in—painting a portrait of Nicaraguan leader Daniel Ortega as basically unworthy of trust regardless of whatever he had to say. This strategy effectively prevented any independent assessment of the Nicaraguan perspective on Central American affairs on the part of the American people. The Bush and Clinton administrations pursued a similar strategy to similar effect with a series of official enemies, most notably Manuel Noriega (Panama) and Saddam Hussein (Iraq), despite the fact that both of these figures had earlier enjoyed preferential treatment as clients and instruments of U.S. foreign policy.

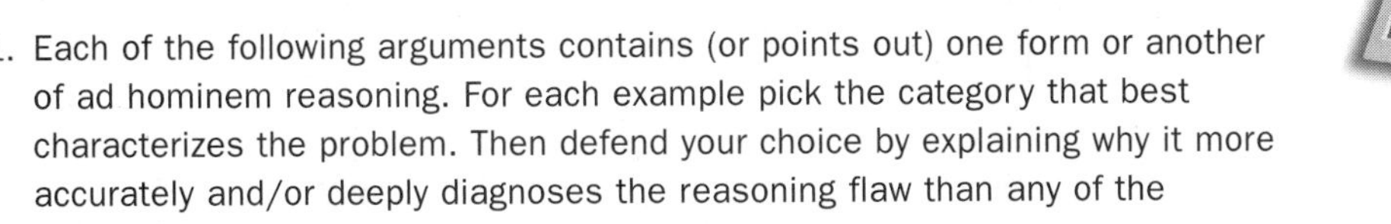

## EXERCISE | Ad Hominem Appeals

1. Each of the following arguments contains (or points out) one form or another of ad hominem reasoning. For each example pick the category that best characterizes the problem. Then defend your choice by explaining why it more accurately and/or deeply diagnoses the reasoning flaw than any of the alternatives.
   a. No man can know anything about pregnancy and childbirth, because no man can ever go through the experience. So no man is qualified to render an opinion about abortion.

| | |
|---|---|
| | Abusive Ad Hominem |
| | Circumstantial Ad Hominem |
| | Guilt by Association |
| | Genetic Appeal |
| | Poisoning the Well |

Explain your answer:

________________________________________

________________________________________

________________________________________

   b. How can you believe anything that this bimbo has to say? Can't you see that she has everything to gain by implicating the president in this scandal? Look, she's sold her story to *Hard Copy!*

| | |
|---|---|
| | Abusive Ad Hominem |
| | Circumstantial Ad Hominem |
| | Guilt by Association |
| | Genetic Appeal |
| | Poisoning the Well |

Explain your answer:

________________________________________

________________________________________

________________________________________

c. Letter to the Editor: I was profoundly dismayed by the badgering of witnesses during the hearings by Senator D. "Mo" Cratic. Doesn't he realize that such criticism reflects badly on the president? If we can't expect the members of our own party to support the president in a time of crisis, just who can we turn to?

| | |
|---|---|
| | Abusive Ad Hominem |
| | Circumstantial Ad Hominem |
| | Guilt by Association |
| | Genetic Appeal |
| | Poisoning the Well |

Explain your answer:

d. I can't vote for the man, because I remember some years ago in his law practice he defended that wacko Unabomber guy.

| | |
|---|---|
| | Abusive Ad Hominem |
| | Circumstantial Ad Hominem |
| | Guilt by Association |
| | Genetic Appeal |
| | Poisoning the Well |

Explain your answer:

## APPEALS TO AUTHORITY

As we discussed in Chapter 1, we are understandably reliant upon authority in many areas of our lives. Much of what we learn, we are taught by authorities. And since we never arrive at the stage of knowing everything, of being experts in every field, we continue to rely on authority from time to time throughout our lives. But this can lead to error. The risk is that we might rely too heavily on authority or rely on authority when we shouldn't. If we arrive at conclusions by an improper appeal to authority we commit a fallacy. When is an appeal to authority improper? When the appeal is considered absolutely decisive on its own, when the authority appealed to is not genuinely expert in the relevant field, is not to be trusted, or when the genuine experts in the field are divided on the issue, the fallacy of false or questionable authority is committed. From this list of considerations we may distinguish several specific varieties of this fallacy: appeal to invincible authority, appeal to authorities with irrelevant expertise, testimonials, appeal to unidentified experts, appeal to experts with axes to grind, and appeal to partisan experts when expert opinion is divided.

### INVINCIBLE AUTHORITY

When an appeal to authority wipes out all other considerations it constitutes a fallacious appeal to authority. Such appeals to invincible authority have a notorious kind of currency within cults, or groups whose organization depends upon subordinating all personal autonomy. The Heaven's Gate mass suicide discussed in Chapter 1 presents a particularly chilling example of overreliance on authority, but by no means the only such example: A number of vivid and scary accounts have emerged in recent years of cults such as Scientology, the Moonies, the Rajneeshees, Jonestown (where several hundred followers of Reverend Jim Jones were led to commit mass suicide), and David Koresh's Branch Davidians. All of these accounts illustrate the danger of allowing reality to be defined by appeal to the unassailable pronouncements of some "spiritual leader." But such appeals are not confined to the dark and sinister world of spiritual fascism. We find fallacious appeals to invincible authority of all places in the history of science, where, for example, Galileo's colleagues refused to look into his telescope because they were convinced that no evidence whatsoever could possibly contradict Aristotle's account of astronomy. This is no isolated aberration, by the way. Galileo himself made a similar argument in his *Dialogues Concerning Two New Sciences,* when he said:

> But can you doubt that air has weight when you have the clear testimony of Aristotle affirming that all the elements have weight including air, and excepting only fire?

### IRRELEVANT EXPERTISE

When the appeal is to an authority whose expertise is in some field other than the one at issue, the appeal is again fallacious. For example, quoting the political or economic opinions of a distinguished physicist like Oppenheimer or Einstein is fallacious because the massive weight of Einstein's opinion in the field of physics may not transfer to other fields. Of course it is entirely possible that a brilliant and distinguished thinker in one specialty might be quite well informed and insightful in other areas as well. But to accept such a person's judgments outside of the established area of expertise and on the basis solely of the person's reputation is to commit a fallacious appeal to authority.

## TESTIMONIALS

A common variety of appeal to irrelevant expertise is the celebrity testimonial. Examples of testimonials abound in advertising, where celebrities are used to endorse everything from aspirin to presidential candidates. Here are just a few:

> "Take it from Bruce Jenner [former Olympic decathlon champ]: 'You need a good start to get in shape. And I can't think of a better start than a complete breakfast with Wheaties.'"
>
> "Take it from me, Tommy Lasorda [manager of the Los Angeles Dodgers]. Ultra Slim-Fast will take off the weight."
>
> "Want to be a 'Super-Model'? Don't Dream it; just do it." (Supermodel Rachel Hunter for Cover Girl)
>
> "I think it's important that we take care of ourselves. That's why doctors have advised millions of caffeine-concerned Americans, like me, to drink delicious Sanka Decaffeinated Coffee." (Robert Young, actor who played TV doctor Marcus Welby, M.D., for Sanka)

That last ad, with its reference to doctors, illustrates not only how the prestige of a profession , but also how *fictionalized* expertise, can take on authoritative significance. This particular variety of fallacious testimonial hit a new low in the still-famous ad for an over-the-counter pain reliever which began:

> "I'm not a doctor, but I play one on TV . . ."

Even cartoon characters have started getting into the act:

> "Get Met. It pays." (Charlie Brown for Met Life Insurance)
>
> "Don't touch my Butterfinger!" (Bart Simpson for Butterfinger candy bars)

Celebrity endorsements effectively short-circuit the reasoning process: They are meant to substitute for the scrutiny you should give a product before purchasing, a candidate before voting, or a cause before supporting it.

## UNIDENTIFIED EXPERTS

Frequently expert opinion is merely alluded to, or is identified in such a vague or incomplete way that its reliability, accuracy, and weight are impossible to verify. This is a favorite device of tabloids such as the *National Enquirer,* who use phrases like "experts agree," "university studies show," or "a Russian scientist has discovered," to lend the weight of authority to all sorts of quackery. Here's an interesting one from Anacin:

Doctors recommend one pain reliever most: the one you get in Anacin.

Of course you get the same pain reliever, aspirin, in a smorgasbord of other analgesics. But consumers are unlikely to notice this, which is exactly how this sort of testimonial is designed to work. Thus, this example can also be understood as a case of false implication of uniqueness (see Chapter 9).

## CONFLICT OF INTEREST—OR "EXPERTS WITH AXES TO GRIND"

Sometimes claims are advanced by appeal to experts who do have impressive and genuinely relevant credentials, but whose testimony may legitimately be suspected due to a demonstrable conflict of interest. Suppose our attention is directed to an inconclusive study of the effects of secondhand tobacco smoke conducted at a reputable institution under the direction of someone with genuine scientific credentials. Now suppose we learn that the study was underwritten by a research grant supplied by the Tobacco Institute. We should at least look for other studies to compare this one with.

Now you might wonder, "What's the difference between this example and poisoning the well or guilt by association?" Notice that we are not simply dismissing the evidence on an automatic basis by considering its source, which would amount to well poisoning. We are not refusing to consider the evidence nor are we automatically assuming that it is false. Rather, we are not treating the evidence as decisive; we are suspending judgment and discounting the weight of the authority with which the evidence is introduced pending additional evidence from sources more likely to be objective and impartial.

## DIVISION OF EXPERT OPINION

Issues often arise within specialized fields of expertise so that expert opinion is divided. When experts disagree, citing the authority of representatives of one side or the other constitutes a fallacy because it fails to settle the issue. This type of fallacy can be called division of expert opinion. A good example of controversy among the experts recently occurred within the medical profession. A widely known research team, Masters, Johnson, and Kolodny, challenged the prevailing medical estimates of the rate and risk of the spread of AIDS in the heterosexual population. They went further to claim that there is a significant risk of contracting the virus through mosquito bites and exchange of saliva and other kinds of "casual contact." Their findings were in turn challenged by researchers at the Centers for Disease Control (CDC) and other recognized experts in epidemiology. In such a climate of controversy it would be inadequate simply to quote Masters, Johnson, and Kolodny, or their critics, in support of an assessment of these risks. What one needs to do, when there is no consensus among the experts, is to look more closely at their evidence and evaluate their competing arguments.

As you can see, there are quite a few pitfalls to watch out for in appealing to authority. However, bear in mind that appealing to authority is not always fallacious. So long as (1) the authority is truly an expert in the field, (2) the authority is trustworthy, (3) there is a consensus of expert opinion to corroborate the claim, and (4) one could in theory verify the claim for oneself, then an appeal to authority may be perfectly legitimate. For example, suppose someone claimed that smoking was harmful and based that judgment on the opinion of the surgeon general. The appeal here is presumably legitimate because (1) the surgeon general is an expert witness, (2) in the absence of any specific evidence to the contrary, the surgeon general may be presumed trustworthy in this matter, (3) there is agreement among medical experts that smoking is indeed harmful, and (4) in theory one could verify the claim for oneself if one took the time to conduct scientifically valid experiments.

## APPEALS TO PSEUDO-AUTHORITY

In addition to the six ways of appealing to false or questionable authority just discussed, there are a number of other fallacies closely enough related to authority to deserve mention here: popularity, positioning, tradition, novelty, and provincialism.

### POPULARITY

Closely related to the fallacious appeal to authority is the appeal to popular opinion. "Five million people have already seen this movie. Shouldn't you?"; "Why do I think that the president's program is sound? Because the polls indicate that the vast majority supports it"; "By a margin of two to one, shoppers prefer Brand X to any other of the leading competitors. Reason enough to buy Brand X." In the appeal to popularity sheer numbers are substituted for individual testimonial. Popular opinion in effect takes on the weight of authority. But since it is possible for a large population to be mistaken or misled, as history has amply demonstrated time and again, such an appeal is not a reliable guide to the truth.

### POSITIONING

Just as people sometimes attempt to discredit others through associations, they can just as effectively promote themselves and others by positioning, by capitalizing on the reputation of a leader in a field to sell a product, candidate, or idea. Here's how it works.

Suppose a car rental agency such as Avis advertises "We're the world's second-largest car rental agency. Since we're second, we must try harder." Avis successfully positions itself next to the leader, Hertz, thereby creating through transference a position in the consumer's mind. Goodrich has used this technique masterfully when it reminds us "We're the ones without the blimp."

In advertising, positioning creates a spot for a company in the prospective buyer's mind by invoking not only the company's image but that of its leading competitor as well. The assumption here is that the consumer's mind has become an advertising battleground. So a successful advertising strategy involves relating to what has already been established in the consumer's mind. Thus, although RCA and General Electric tried in vain to buck IBM directly in the early years of the mainframe computer market, the smaller Honeywell succeeded using the theme of "the other computer company."

Positioning is hardly confined to advertising. During presidential election years, many a congressional campaign is based almost entirely on party affiliation with the incumbent president, or the front-runner. This is called "riding in on the coat-tails," a much discussed phenomenon in the 1992 election of President Clinton. In politics, part of waging a successful campaign often means trading on the reputation of another well-known, popular political figure. Thus candidates of both parties are forever attempting to appropriate the mantle of a Lincoln or a Kennedy, by invoking lines from their famous speeches and forging all sorts of tenuous connections. In a rather striking case in 1988, televangelist and Republican presidential hopeful Pat Robertson attempted, unsuccessfully, to overcome public skepticism based on his background as a televangelist, by pointing out that JFK had had to overcome anti-Catholic prejudice in his first campaign. One of the most famous attempts at positioning was Dan Quayle's attempt to link himself with JFK in the 1988 vice presidential debate, saying that he was as seasoned and experienced a potential leader as Kennedy had been prior to his election as president. The attempt backfired when Democratic candidate Lloyd Bentson positioned himself even closer to Kennedy, saying "I served with Jack Kennedy in the Senate. Jack Kennedy was a friend of mine. Senator, you're no Jack Kennedy." Bentson's response to Quayle was and still is considered by many commentators as the "knock-out punch" of the entire campaign. Yet it was no less an instance of the fallacy of positioning than Quayle's.

## APPEAL TO TRADITION

The appeal to tradition consists of assuming or arguing that something is good or desirable simply because it is old or traditional. Jane's friend tells her, "I don't think you should keep your maiden name after marrying. In this culture the woman always takes her husband's name. That's what distinguishes a married woman from a single one." Although there may be good reasons for a woman's not keeping her maiden name after marrying, this isn't one of them. Jane is trying to link her opinion to a long-standing custom; that is, to what has been historically approved by society. But why must custom necessarily dictate present behavior? It needn't, and that's the point.

During the Watergate scandal in 1974 there were frequent appeals to tradition surrounding the attempt to impeach President Richard Nixon. Many insisted that Nixon should not be impeached because never before had a U.S. president been successfully impeached and removed from office. In a word, they tried to protect Nixon by invoking a tradition of reluctance to impeach presidents, urging that the future be fashioned in the image of the past. But the mere fact that a president had never before been removed from office following impeachment was no good reason to conclude that Nixon, or any subsequent president for that matter, should not be impeached. Indeed the fact was irrelevant to the issue of whether or not to impeach Nixon.

Certain phrases often signal an attempt to summon tradition to the support of a claim. Among them are "tried and true," "the lessons of history," "from time immemorial," "the Founding Fathers," "the earliest settlers," and so on. Of course the appeal to tradition is not always fallacious. The question of whether or not something is in line with tradition is not always irrelevant to the issue. For example, if you are trying to decide whether such and such a costume is suitable for the Founder's Day parade, appeal to tradition may be legitimate. But most issues are such that tradition in and of itself is irrelevant.

## APPEAL TO NOVELTY

In contrast to the appeal to tradition, but just as deadly to correct reasoning, is the appeal to novelty, which consists of assuming or arguing that something is good or desirable simply because it is new. In the elections of 1980, 1984, 1988, and 1992 a number of candidates argued or used slogans like "Leadership for a change," which, besides suggesting by innuendo that the incumbent was providing no leadership, meant to many people a change in economic and social philosophy. There may be solid reasons for so altering the nation's course, but change for the sake of change is not one of them. Every policy, law, idea, program, or action requires justification independent of its novel character. That a politician represents "new ideas" or a proposal offers a "new approach" is not a logical defense, though it sometimes is an appealing one.

## PROVINCIALISM

Provincialism occurs when our thinking is dominated by considerations of group loyalty. To appeal to considerations of group loyalty in support of a claim, or to arrive at a conclusion simply on the basis of such considerations, is to commit the fallacy of provincialism. During the heated debate in 1980 over the treaty that would transfer responsibility for maintaining the Panama Canal from the United States to Panama, provincialism resounded throughout the land. Most of the arguments against the treaty assumed that (1) the United States had some kind of proprietary claim over the canal, or (2) Americans were uniquely qualified to run the canal. The provincialism came in when it was suggested, as it was frequently, that to question either of these assumptions was unpatriotic and disloyal. The fallacy of provincialism need not be confined to examples of national loyalty. Sometimes the group identified with is considerably smaller, perhaps a professional, occupational, or religious group, or a school, or team. Sometimes the group is even larger than a nation: a gender, for example.

## EXERCISE | Appeals to Authority/Pseudo-Authority

1. Each of the following arguments contains (or points out) one type of fallacious appeal to authority. For each example pick the fallacy category that best explains the problem. Then defend your choice by explaining why it more accurately and/or deeply diagnoses the reasoning flaw than any of the alternatives.
   a. We are, quite bluntly, broke. We don't have the money to sustain the dreams and experiments of liberalism any longer. We have a $400 billion a year budget deficit and a $4 trillion debt. The economist Walter Williams points out that with the money we've spent on poverty programs since the 1960s we could have bought the entire assets of every Fortune 500 company and virtually every acre of U.S. farmland. —Rush Limbaugh[4]

| | |
|---|---|
| | Invincible Authority |
| | Irrelevant Expertise |
| | Unidentified Experts |
| | Conflict of Interest |
| | Division of Expert Opinion |

Explain your answer:

   b. Letter to the Editor responding to the question "Do you care about preserving the local July 4th fireworks display?": Not celebrate the 4th of July with fireworks? What would John Adams say?—having been the very first to advocate the very day after independence was declared, that the birth of our nation ought to be "celebrated by succeeding generations as the great anniversary festival"? What would our founding fathers say?—who planted the seeds of liberty and Christianity on a wilderness shore, not for themselves only, but for their children and their children's children?

| | |
|---|---|
| | Appeal to Popularity |
| | Positioning |
| | Appeal to Tradition |
| | Appeal to Novelty |
| | Provincialism |

(continued)

Explain your answer:

c. Turns out roughing up punks ain't really necessary. On account of most guys and gals hurt *themselves* by not getting enough calcium. So reach out for 3 glasses of milk a day. Your body will thank you. Especially if we don't have to tell you again. (Ad sponsored by the National Fluid Milk Processor Promotion Board, featuring actors Jimmy Smits and Dennis Franz of *NYPD Blue* posed menacingly with glasses of milk and milk mustaches)

| | |
|---|---|
| | Invincible Authority |
| | Irrelevant Expertise |
| | Unidentified Experts |
| | Conflict of Interest |
| | Division of Expert Opinion |

Explain your answer:

d. Owner of a San Francisco restaurant, reacting against a proposed truth-in-advertising ordinance requiring restaurant owners to identify food prepared off the premises and then frozen: "Three-quarters or seven-eighths of the people who come into my place . . . don't give a good goddamn."[5]

| | |
|---|---|
| | Appeal to Popularity |
| | Positioning |
| | Appeal to Tradition |
| | Appeal to Novelty |
| | Provincialism |

Explain your answer:

e. Letter to the Editor: "I was profoundly dismayed by the badgering of witnesses during the hearings by Senator D. "Mo" Cratic. Doesn't he realize that such criticism reflects badly on the president? If we can't expect the members of our own party to support the president in a time of crisis, just who can we turn to?"

| | |
|---|---|
| | Invincible Authority |
| | Irrelevant Expertise |
| | Unidentified Experts |
| | Conflict of Interest |
| | Division of Expert Opinion |

Explain your answer:

## EMOTIONAL APPEALS

A special category of irrelevant appeal involves the invocation of emotion in support of a claim. Emotions can exert a powerful influence over our thinking, but they are not always relevant to the issue at hand. Three of the most common informal fallacies that make irrelevant appeal to emotion are appeal to anger, appeal to fear, and appeal to pity.

### APPEAL TO ANGER

One of the most powerful emotions is anger. Often anger is powerful enough to overwhelm reason and good common sense, as we recognize for example when we speak of crimes of passion and distinguish them from premeditated crimes.

Thus a very powerful persuasive strategy consists of arousing and mobilizing anger in support of a position. When this strategy is pursued in place of reasoning the fallacy of appeal to anger is being committed. Like so many other fallacies we've discussed, the appeal to anger is a favorite of political campaign strategists, especially where the electorate is relatively poorly informed. The congressional "check kiting scandal" of 1992 provided many a campaign with fuel to feed the growing anger of an electorate frustrated with government generally. Quite a few campaign slogans in 1992—for certain candidates and also for "term limits"—took the following form: "Are you tired of fat-cat insiders voting themselves pay raises, riding around in limos, and bouncing checks while you bust your hump trying to make ends meet? Throw the bums out! Vote for an outsider for a change!" To be sure, there is often good cause to be angry, and anger, when it's justified, is not at all inappropriate. But when little or no specific reason is presented for being angry, and instead a vague and rhetorical appeal to general frustration is used to arouse anger, watch out. This is the sort of urging that often leads people to "shoot themselves in the foot."

## APPEAL TO FEAR OR FORCE

A similar strategy involves attempting to intimidate people into accepting a position. The strategy takes the basic form, "Believe this (or do this), or else!" For example, in the late 1980s, as the public policy issue over secondhand smoke swung more and more in the direction of segregating smokers and restricting them to designated smoking areas, the Philip Morris corporation launched what became quite a controversial campaign, based on full-page ads in major newspapers such as the one in the *New York Times* which read as follows:

> **$1 trillion is too much financial power to ignore**
>
> America's 55.8 million smokers are a powerful economic force. If their household income of $1 trillion were a Gross National Product, it would be the third largest in the world. The plain truth is that smokers are one of the most economically powerful groups in this country. They help fuel the engine of the largest economy on the globe.
>
> **The American Smoker—an economic force**

The implication was pretty clear. Municipalities and private businesses (such as restaurants and airline companies) that might be considering the adoption of policies restricting or banning smoking have something to fear: a possible trillion dollar boycott.

## APPEAL TO PITY

A device frequently exploited in sales presentations and in attempts to secure special dispensation or exemption from deadlines and penalties, this fallacious but often effective strategy consists of attempting to persuade people by making them feel sorrow, sympathy, or anguish, where such feelings, however understandable and genuine, are not relevant to the issue at stake.

For example, the student who deserves a C in history might try to persuade his teacher to raise his grade for a variety of lamentable reasons: It's the first grade below a B he's ever received; it spoils a 3.85 GPA; he needs a higher grade to qualify for law school and his family has taken a third mortgage to finance his pre-law education.

A word of caution. Invoking sympathy is not always irrelevant to the issue. For example, when an attorney asks a judge to take into consideration the squalid upbringing of a client in determining a criminal sentence, this is probably not a fallacious appeal to pity. Although such an appeal would be irrelevant and fallacious in arguing for the person's innocence, it may be perfectly germane to the question of the severity of the sentence. Think of the German youth who in the summer of 1987 flew a small plane into the middle of Red Square in Moscow. That he may have been acting out of simple youthful exuberance rather than some motive more threatening to Soviet national security is irrelevant to whether he acted illegally, but it's not irrelevant to how severely he should be punished.

## DIVERSION

A common argumentative strategy consists of attempting to divert attention from an issue, especially where one lacks effective arguments relevant to it. This is a particular favorite of public figures when they find themselves called upon to address delicate or controversial topics and are not well enough prepared. Caught in such a bind, officials (and office seekers) frequently respond to an embarrassing question by answering some other question, usually without explicitly indicating that this is what they are doing. Sometimes a speaker will give explicit indication of a shift in focus: "Before I answer this question, Ted, let me make a few things clear . . ." This sort of thing, followed by a long and winding excursion through a number of relatively complicated points, may effectively leave the original topic buried in obscurity.

A caution: As we've already discussed, sometimes a question may itself be loaded or slanted or otherwise objectionable, so that an exposé of the assumptions and so on underlying it, in place of a direct answer to it, would be perfectly appropriate. However, if a diversionary tactic is employed simply as a means of evading a perfectly reasonable question, this too is worth pointing out as a fallacious move. There are a number of common diversionary strategies worth individual mention.

### APPEAL TO HUMOR OR RIDICULE

A common variety of the diversionary strategy is the appeal to humor and ridicule. When one is stuck for a good argument, and sometimes even when one isn't, getting a laugh out of one's audience can be an effective substitute. For example, a member of the British Parliament named Thomas Massey-Massey once introduced a bill to change the name of "Christmas" to "Christide." He reasoned as follows: Since "mass" is a Catholic term and since Britons are largely Protestant, they should avoid the suffix "mass" in "Christ*mas*." On hearing the proposal another member suggested that Christmas might not want its name changed.

"How would you like it," he asked Thomas Massey-Massey, "if we changed your name to Thotide Tidey-Tidey?" The bill died in the ensuing laughter.

Similarly, a story is told of an incident that occurred at the Yalta meeting of the Allied leaders Franklin D. Roosevelt, Winston Churchill, and Joseph Stalin. Churchill reportedly mentioned that the Pope had suggested a particular course of action as the right one, whereupon Stalin is said to have replied "And how many divisions did you say the Pope had available for combat duty?" thus diverting attention from the issues through a form of ridicule.

## TWO WRONGS

A particularly common fallacy of diversion where moral blameworthiness is at issue involves introducing an irrelevant comparison to other instances of wrongdoing. For example, a police officer stops a speeding motorist. "Why stop me?" the driver asks. "Didn't you see that Jaguar fly by at 80 mph?" The motorist is trying to divert attention from his own infraction, and perhaps to excuse it, by pointing out the wrongdoing of another. But what other motorists are doing is irrelevant to whether this motorist has exceeded the speed limit. The two wrongs fallacy takes two general forms:

1. *Tu Quoque* Tu quoque is Latin for "You also," or "You too," or more colloquially, "Look who's talking!" In its tu quoque form, the two wrongs fallacy consists of accusing one's critic of what he is criticizing. For example, Brad advises Beth to get more exercise. Beth reminds Brad that, being the world's greatest couch potato, he's in no position to give such advice. Again, a mother cautions her teenage son against using drugs. "That's a laugh coming from you," he replies. "You smoke, drink, and use caffeine." Even if Brad is sedentary and mom is addicted to alcohol, nicotine, and caffeine, that doesn't make their advice any less sage. And it is the advice that's at issue, not whether or not those who preach it practice it.
2. *Common Practice* Sometimes, rather than appealing to single instances of similar wrongdoing, people appeal to a widely accepted or long-standing practice to divert attention from and excuse their behavior. Caught using company stationery for personal use, a worker may say "Everybody else does it." In other words, since helping themselves to company stationery is a common practice of workers in this office, it's OK for me to do it.

## STRAW PERSON

The fallacy of straw person consists of so altering a position that the new version is easier to attack than the original, or of setting up a position to attack so that one's alternative position will appear stronger by comparison. The name of this fallacy says what it accomplishes: It sets up a "straw" that's easy to "blow over." Of course, the straw version is not the original, but that's precisely the point: The altered version makes an easier, though irrelevant target.

A common device for erecting straws is *exaggeration*. For example, suppose a mother objects to her son's going out on a school night before a test. The son responds: "What! You're telling me that I can't ever go out on weeknights? That's unreasonable." The *real* issue concerns going out on *this particular* weeknight before a test. The straw issue is not *ever* going out on a school night.

Exaggeration is one form of *distortion*, which indicates a broader and more general strategy for setting up a straw person. Wanting to engage students in the electoral process, a school board votes to give students released time during an election to campaign for the candidates and issues of their choice. An angry citizen accuses the board of conspiring to get liberals elected and conservatives thrown out of office. The real issue: political involvement through released time; the straw issue: partisan politics.

Notice how much easier it is in each case to assail the straw issue than the real issue. This is what makes the straw person such an effective and insidious diversion and attack ploy.

A common species of this sort of thing involves the assumption that proponents of the interests of one group are antagonistic to the interests of some other group, as for instance when supporters of the Equal Rights Amendment were characterized as antimale, or when critics of United States foreign policy are characterized as unpatriotic, or when defenders of the First Amendment who oppose antipornography legislation are labeled as supporters of pornography. One can be in favor of a constitutional amendment guaranteeing against gender discrimination without being antimale. One can be critical of United States foreign policy on perfectly patriotic grounds. One can be opposed to antipornography legislation on grounds that it would compromise the principle of freedom of speech, and one might be interested in preserving this principle simply as a crucial hedge against tyranny. When the American Civil Liberties Union took the case of the American Nazi Party in its attempt to obtain a parade permit in Skokie, Illinois, they did so not because they were pro-Nazi, but in order to defend the First Amendment from what they argued would be a serious erosion in principle. To attack their position as pro-Nazi, as some did, would have been to attack a straw person.

Because of the predictable and general human tendency to want to understand one's opponent's position in a way one feels confident to dispute, it is generally wise not to accept, without question, the account or description of a position or an argument given by someone opposed to it. Sometimes opponents do give a fair account of positions they oppose, but not certainly not always. The best technique we're aware of for detecting straw person arguments, and for avoiding them in one's own reasoning, is to pretend you're the person whose position is being criticized and ask if the criticism does justice to the position you imagine yourself now to be defending.

## RED HERRING

A common diversionary tactic consists of presenting facts that do not support the position at issue but some other position which vaguely resembles it. This tactic has come to be known as the red herring, a colorful name which derives from an old ruse used by prison escapees to throw dogs off their trails. The escapees would smear themselves with herring (which turns red when it spoils) to cover their scent.

For example, in charging an executive with embezzlement, a prosecutor quotes harrowing statistics about white-collar crime. Although her statistical evidence may influence the jury, it is irrelevant to establishing the guilt of the defendant. The alarming statistics only support the assertion that white-collar crime is a serious social problem. They give no support to the charge that the defendant is guilty of embezzlement and in fact divert attention from it.

## EXERCISE | Diversions and Emotional Appeals

1. Each of the following examples contains (or points out) at least one major diversionary or emotional fallacy. For each example pick the fallacy category or categories that best explain the problem. Then use your choices to explain your diagnosis of the flaws in the reasoning.
   a. And the Lord God commanded man, saying, "You may eat freely of every tree of the garden; but the tree of the knowledge of good and evil you shall not eat, for in the day that you eat of it you shall die." —Genesis 2:16–17

| | |
|---|---|
| | Appeal to Anger |
| | Appeal to Fear or Force |
| | Appeal to Pity |
| | Humor or Ridicule |
| | Two Wrongs |
| | Straw Person |
| | Red Herring |

Explain your answer:

b. Precisely what is Nixon accused of doing . . . that his predecessors didn't do many times over? The break-in and wire-tapping at the Watergate? Just how different was that from the bugging of Barry Goldwater's apartment during the 1964 presidential campaign? —Victor Lasky[6]

| | |
|---|---|
| | Appeal to Anger |
| | Appeal to Fear or Force |
| | Appeal to Pity |
| | Humor or Ridicule |
| | Two Wrongs |
| | Straw Person |
| | Red Herring |

Explain your answer:

c. [The fight for the Equal Rights Amendment in Iowa] is about a socialist, antifamily political movement that encourages women to leave their husbands, kill their children, practice witchcraft, destroy capitalism, and become lesbians. —Televangelist (and former candidate for president) Pat Robertson

| | |
|---|---|
| | Appeal to Anger |
| | Appeal to Fear or Force |
| | Appeal to Pity |
| | Humor or Ridicule |
| | Two Wrongs |
| | Straw Person |
| | Red Herring |

(continued)

Explain your answer:

d. Turns out roughing up punks ain't really necessary. On account of most guys and gals hurt *themselves* by not getting enough calcium. So reach out for 3 glasses of milk a day. Your body will thank you. Especially if we don't have to tell you again. (Ad sponsored by the National Fluid Milk Processor Promotion Board, featuring actors Jimmy Smits and Dennis Franz of *NYPD Blue* posed menacingly with glasses of milk and milk mustaches)

| | |
|---|---|
| | Appeal to Anger |
| | Appeal to Fear or Force |
| | Appeal to Pity |
| | Humor or Ridicule |
| | Two Wrongs |
| | Straw Person |
| | Red Herring |

Explain your answer:

## ADDITIONAL EXERCISES

**1.** At the beginning of this chapter there is a cartoon in which a lawyer offers a dubious argument for his client's innocence. What is the fallacy illustrated by the cartoon?

**2.** Is gender relevant? Perhaps a better question is: *When* is gender relevant? Do you think Susie commits a fallacy in the following Calvin and Hobbes cartoon? Write a short essay in which you explain why. Are there any circumstances in which you think gender is relevant? Which circumstances and why?

**Calvin and Hobbes** **by Bill Watterson**

**3.** The following notice was published on the inside of a carton of cigarettes as part of a campaign to defeat a tobacco products tax measure in the state of California. Comment on the legitimacy of the argument's strategy.

**4.** The 1990 general election in the state of California included two measures concerning liquor taxation. Proposition 134, the "Nickel-a-Drink" initiative supported by a coalition led by Mothers Against Drunk Driving (MADD), competed with Proposition 126, which was lobbied through the state legislature. Supporters of Proposition 134 argued against Proposition 126 in part as follows:

> Proposition 126 is sponsored by the liquor industry. The reason they say Proposition 126 is a better approach to taking on the liquor industry than Proposition 134, the "Nickel-a-Drink" proposal, is that Proposition 126 taxes them less.
>
> The only reason Proposition 126 is on the ballot is that the liquor industry spends $1,000,000 each year lobbying the Legislature and has contributed over $1,600,000 to politicians since 1988. What the liquor industry wants, the Legislature gives. That's why the Legislature has not changed the wine tax from 1 cent per gallon since 1937.
>
> The sole purpose of Proposition 126 is to defeat Proposition 134, the "Nickel-a-Drink" Alcohol Tax Initiative. When reading the argument in favor of Proposition 126, CONSIDER THE SOURCE—IT IS THE LIQUOR INDUSTRY!

Is this argument an instance of the fallacy of genetic appeal or not? Explain.

**5.** Once again, with your study partner, take turns critically examining the following examples in terms of the informal fallacy categories you have learned so far, including those covered in the previous chapter, and testing your critical assessments for clarity and fairness. One of you can play the role of finding and explaining the flaw in the argument, while the other challenges and tests the diagnosis by trying to defend the argument against the proposed criticism. Take turns as you work your way through the following examples. Don't forget, a given argument can have more than one thing wrong with it. If you arrive at a consensus criticism, move on to the next example.

a. Republican presidential candidate Jack Kemp in a 1988 televised presidential primary debate, attacking the eventual Republican nominee George Bush (who was supporting the ratification of the INF Treaty with the Soviet Union): "I can't believe I'm hearing a Republican say 'Let's give peace a chance'!"

b. Philip Morris vice president for corporate affairs, Guy L. Smith, defending the Philip Morris ad campaign mentioned in this chapter against the criticism that it was designed to appeal to fear, said the ads were "an attempt to raise the level of awareness, but certainly not to scare anybody."

c. From an editorial: "Because of the unique position of Justice Lewis F. Powell, Jr., at the ideological center of a divided Supreme Court, the person who replaces him will have a major hand in determining the next generation of constitutional law. Judge Robert H. Bork of the D.C. Circuit Court of Appeals, who was nominated by President Reagan, is a rock-solid right-winger in the mold of Chief Justice William H. Rehnquist and Associate Justice Antonin Scalia."

d. Many of my colleagues in the press are upset about the growing practice of paying newsmakers for news. The auction principle seems to them to strike somehow at the freedom of the press, or at least the freedom of the poor press to compete with the rich press. But I find their objections pious and, in an economy where everything and everybody has its price, absurd. —Shana Alexander[7]

e. Repressive environmentalists and population and economic zero-growthers have requested President Reagan to oust James G. Watt as Secretary of the Interior. Those stop-all-progress destructionists have thick-skinned craniums. They lack the intelligence to realize that the United States of America is no longer a subsidiary of the baby-and-people hating and business-repressive do-gooders. President Reagan and Secretary Watt have done what should have been done long ago. Their critics can go to blazes on a one-way ticket.[8]

f. For three decades ('60s, '70s, '80s) the environmentalists, Greens, tree huggers—choose any epithet that suits your fancy but mainly descriptions of those who've ranted and railed against growth—have managed to defeat every attempt to modernize Sonoma County transportation to handle the growing load. I would like to point out that sticking your head in the sand and saying you're against growth simply won't cut the mustard. You cannot pass a law (urban growth boundaries) against growth; stupid even to think of it. If you can manage to come up with an elixir that can be delivered in the water system a la Big Brother, which will prevent human sexuality, then you can slow growth.[9]

g. A Soviet official, commenting on the Reagan administration's unwillingness to negotiate key issues, such as the location of the Soviet Union's SS-20 missiles and a new Strategic Arms Limitation Treaty: "We shall continue to urge real negotiations but our patience is not unlimited. This does not mean, of course, that we would start a war, but ultimately if there is not change we will have to counter measures being taken by your administration with measures of our own. We don't want to do this. It can only result in a dangerous spiral. This would be a very dangerous development."[10]

h. When the Senate Judiciary Committee, headed by Senator Joseph Biden, began to challenge the nomination of Robert Bork to the Supreme Court, Vice President George Bush said, "I find it ironic that Senator Biden would take issue with Judge Bork's judicial philosophy. That philosophy is one of judicial restraint, and what that means above all else is that Congress should make the laws, not the court."

i. From the San Francisco Chronicle: "Everybody complains about the U.S. mail these days—prices going up and service down. But our Postal Service seems like a winner compared with the Canadian one. In fact, our neighbors to the north have elevated post-office bashing into a national sport." (The article goes on to catalogue deficiencies in the Canadian postal system.)[11]

j. President Reagan suggesting a way to pacify those who object to the sight of oil rigs off their beaches: "Maybe we ought to take some of those liberty ships out of mothballs and anchor one at each one of the oil platforms between that and onshore, because people never objected to seeing a ship at sea."[12]

k. Televangelist Pat Robertson in a 1986 *Conservative Digest* interview: "It's amazing that the Constitution of the United States says nothing about the separation of church and state. That phrase does appear, however, in the Soviet constitution. . . . People in the education Establishment, and in our judicial establishment, have attempted to impose soviet strictures on the United States."

l. Bill Clinton has ceased promising that the missus will play a key role in his White House. The reason is clear from [a recent] profile of Hillary in *American Spectator.* Since her Yale days, Hillary has been enthusiastically engaged with the radical Left. While she headed the New World Foundation, it gave grants to such leftist organizations as the fellow-traveling National Lawyers Guild and CISPES (the Committee in Support of the People of El Salvador).[13]

m. Lt. Colonel Oliver North campaigning in 1992 against Senator Barbara Boxer: "[She's a] check-kiting, pay-raising, self-promoting, defense-cutting, tax-raising, free-spending permanent political potentate of pork. Who are Barbara Boxer's buddies? They are environmental radicals, people who believe in lifestyles we wouldn't even talk about, much less embrace. She believes spotted owls are higher on the food chain than we are, and that's not how I read Genesis."

n. Former President George Bush, during his 1992 speech accepting his party's nomination for reelection: "And I'm heartened by the polls. The ones which say I look better in my jogging shorts than Governor Clinton."

o. Former President George Bush, in the final days of his unsuccessful run for reelection: "My dog Millie knows more about foreign policy than these two Bozos (Democratic running mates Bill Clinton and Albert Gore)." In the same speech, this time about Gore in particular: "You know why I call him Ozone Man? This guy is so far out in the environmental extreme, we'll be up to our neck in owls and outta work for every American. He is way out, far out, man."

p. Independent presidential candidate Ross Perot: "Bill Clinton's on MTV playin' the saxophone [gets laugh]. Meanwhile Dan Quayle's tryin' to figure out how to spell 'potato' [gets really big laugh]."

q. First Lady Hillary Rodham Clinton arguing in support of "managed competition" (and against the "Canadian style single-payer system" of health care delivery): "It's an American solution to an American problem."

r. A fire inspector faced dismissal for accepting free meals at the elegant Fairmont Hotel, which he was inspecting. In defense of this particular fire inspector (who happens to be black), the local fire employees' union introduced a 1991 confidential city report detailing widespread abuse and corruption throughout the department, including the use of 911 emergency operators to place illegal bets on horseraces and other sporting events. The union argued that rule-breaking is not only widespread but tolerated and condoned by top officials in the department, who have themselves accepted illegal gratuities. Every Christmas, building contractors shower the department with cases of liquor that are distributed throughout the department. The union went on to argue that the Fire Department, which has been resisting implementation of racial and sexual integration, had singled out a black man for punishment.

s. "The picture of reliability. To Magnavox it's the idea that every time you turn on one of our color television sets you know it's going to do what you bought it to do. Our Star® System color television sets combine advanced design concepts, high technology and new manufacturing systems to deliver the highest level of reliability in Magnavox history. Magnavox. For a picture as reliable as it is bright and clear. Time after time. Magnavox. The bright ideas in the world are here today."

t. It's impossible for somebody who doesn't live it to understand it. . . . If you ain't really been fucked over by the police, you can't have the same hatred, and if you're looking to understand the anger in the voice of the rapper, you never will unless you live it. And then if you live it, it doesn't seem as angry. My real anger sounds much madder than the voice I put on that record. . . . The government has a check and balance game: Do wrong, consequences; do wrong, consequences. This is how they play. You speed, you go to jail. You're drunk, you go to jail. The people cannot issue a consequence against the government. When they do wrong, what do we do? How many people have filed civil suits against the police and won? So what L.A. did was say, "You all been bad. Check this out," and we issued a consequence. The riots are the consequence. —Ice-T[14]

u. From a Ku Klux Klan circular: "Every criminal, every gambler, every thug, every libertine, every girl ruiner, every home wrecker, every wife beater, every dope peddler, every moonshiner, every crooked politician, every pagan Papist priest, every shyster lawyer, every K. of C. [Knights of Columbus, a Roman Catholic lay organization], every white slaver, every brothel madam, every Rome controlled newspaper, every black spider—is fighting the Klan. Think it over. Which side are you on?"

v. Mr. North, a fascist flunky, wishes by means of his semantics to make meaningless not only the sacred deed of heroism of the fighters against fascism, but the whole past and future struggle for liberty. But he only exposes his reactionary guts, his hatred for liberty and social progress. . . . Stuart Chase, the petty bourgeois American economist, who writes prescriptions for the disease of capitalism, having read the writing of semantics has lost the last remnants of common sense and has come forward with a fanatical sermon of the new faith, a belief in the magical power of words. —Bernard Emmanuilovich Bykhovsky[15]

w. Name calling, derogatory articles, and adverse propaganda are other methods used to belittle persons refusing to recommend refined foods. We have long been called crackpots and faddists regardless of training or of accuracy in reporting research. The words "quack" and "quackery" are now such favorites that any one using them is receiving benefits from the food processors. —Adele Davis[16]

x. Speaking in 1983 in front of the Brandenburg Gate, which divided Berlin into East and West sectors, President Reagan struck a chord reminiscent of President Kennedy's famous declaration *"Ich bin ein Berliner"* ("I am a Berliner"). Said Reagan: "I join you as I join our belief: *Es gibt nur ein Berlin* (There is only one Berlin). . . . Like so many Presidents before me, I come here today because wherever I go, whatever I do: *Ich habe noch einen Koffer in Berlin* (I still have a suitcase in Berlin [a line from a popular song])."

6. Find examples of your own in the public media of the informal fallacies discussed in this chapter. For each example, give a brief but careful explanation of the fallacies you find in it.

7. Remember that a given argument can have more than one thing wrong with it. With that in mind, go back and review the examples in the Additional Exercises section of Chapter 9. Give a brief and careful explanation of any additional fallacies you can find using the fallacy categories developed in this chapter.

## GLOSSARY

**abusive ad hominem** fallacy consisting of irrelevant attacks on the characteristics of the person making the assertion
**ad hominem** fallacy consisting of irrelevant personal references or attacks
**appeal to anger** fallacious strategy of arousing irrelevant anger in support of a position
**appeal to authority** fallacious use of authority in support of a claim
**appeal to fear or force** fallacy of attempting to intimidate people into accepting a position
**appeal to humor or ridicule** fallacious strategy of substituting humor or ridicule for argument
**appeal to novelty** fallacy of assuming or arguing that something is good or desirable simply because it is novel or new
**appeal to pity** fallacious strategy of arousing irrelevant pity in support of a position
**appeal to popularity** fallacy of assuming or arguing that something is true, good, or desirable simply because it is popularly believed or esteemed
**appeal to tradition** fallacy of assuming or arguing that something is good or desirable simply because it is old or traditional
**circumstantial ad hominem** fallacy consisting of irrelevant references to the circumstances of a person's life
**common practice** variety of the two wrongs fallacy in which one's own wrongdoing is excused by assimilation to widespread practice
**conflict of interest** any combination of interests that interferes with impartiality, hence a variety of fallacious appeal to authority where the authority cited has such a combination of interests
**division of expert opinion** variety of fallacious appeal to authority where the authorities with relevant expertise are divided over the question at issue
**genetic appeal** fallacy of assessment simply in terms of origin, sources, or genesis
**guilt by association** fallacy of supporting negative claims about people or their views or positions solely on the basis of their relationships with others
**invincible authority** variety of fallacious appeal to authority where the authority is taken to outweigh any conflicting consideration
**irrelevant expertise** variety of fallacious appeal to authority where the authority cited lacks expertise relevant to the question at issue

**poisoning the well** fallacious strategy of attempting to discredit a position, or its advocate, before the argument for the position can be considered
**positioning** fallacy of supporting positive claims about people or their views or positions solely on the basis of their relationships with others
**provincialism** fallacy of appealing to considerations of group loyalty in support of a claim
**red herring** fallacious argument strategy of diverting attention from the real issue to another one
**straw person** fallacious argument strategy of attacking a weak or distorted representation of an opponent's position
**testimonial** advertising and public relations strategy based on testimony of a celebrity, often an instance of the fallacy of irrelevant expertise
**tu quoque** means "You're another," a variety of the two wrongs fallacy
**two wrongs** fallacy of excusing one's own wrong by comparing it to others'
**unidentified experts** variety of fallacious appeal to authority where the authority is not identified sufficiently to make assessments of expertise, impartiality or other relevant variables

## NOTES

[1] Rush Limbaugh, *The Way Things Ought to Be* (New York: Pocket Books, 1992), p. 107.

[2] Limbaugh, *The Way Things Ought to Be,* p. 102.

[3] Limbaugh, *The Way Things Ought to Be,* p. 113.

[4] Limbaugh, *The Way Things Ought to Be,* p. 302.

[5] *Los Angeles Times,* July 4, 1974, Part 1, p. 11.

[6] Victor Lasky, "It Didn't Start with Watergate," *Book Digest,* November 1977, p. 47.

[7] Shana Alexander, "Loew's Common Denominator," *Newsweek,* April 14, 1975, p. 96.

[8] From the *Los Angeles Times,* July 24, 1981, Part 2, p. 6.

[9] From the *Sonoma County Independent,* February 12, 1998, p.3.

[10] Quoted in Fred Warner Neal, "America Frustrates Soviets—And That's Dangerous," *Los Angeles Times,* July 31, 1981, Part 2, p. 7.

[11] From "The World," *San Francisco Chronicle,* July 26, 1982, p. 5.

[12] Quoted in "Reagan Backs Watt Stand," *Santa Barbara Evening News Press,* August 5, 1981, p. A4.

[13] From an editorial in the *National Review,* August 1992.

[14] Ice-T, "The Rolling Stone Interview," *Rolling Stone,* no. 637, August 20, 1992.

[15] Bernard Emmanuilovich Bykhovsky, *The Decay of Bourgeois Philosophy* (Moscow: Mysl, 1947), p. 173.

[16] Adele Davis, *Let's Eat Right to Keep Fit* (Los Angeles: Cancer Control Society, 1970), p. 21.

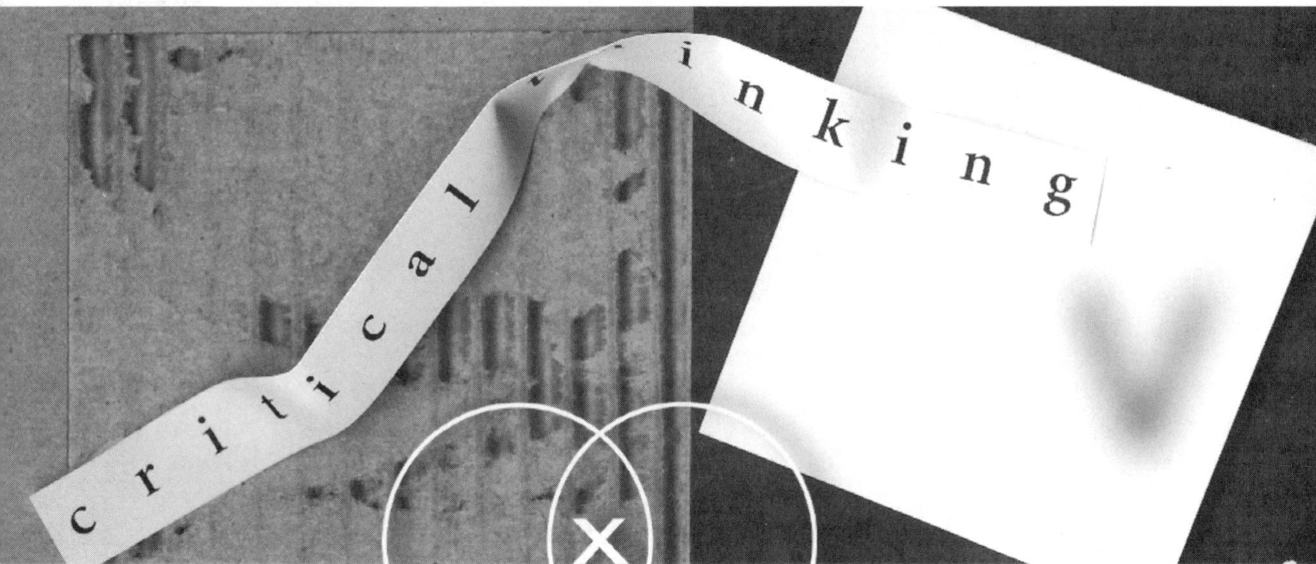


# CHAPTER 11 Fallacies III: Informal Fallacies of Evidence

Evidence is information that is relevant to an inference. Thus, a great deal of importance attaches to how evidence is evaluated and handled in the process of drawing inferences. The discussion in Chapters 7 and 8 of inductive and hypothetical reasoning provides a basic introduction to reliable procedures for gathering, evaluating, and handling evidence. In addition, though, you should be aware of some of the more common pitfalls in this area. In this chapter, we will survey a number of common informal fallacies which have to do with the gathering, evaluation, and handling of evidence in inferential contexts.

It's probably worth mentioning jumping to conclusions at the outset as a useful general fallacy category, simply because it corresponds to such a widespread tendency in human reasoning. The tendency, which results from the longing for closure, the discomfort associated with suspended judgment mentioned in Chapter 1, is to accept a conclusion as settled before all of the relevant evidence is in.

In the most obvious and extreme cases conclusions are hastily arrived at on the basis of single, if striking, instances. For example, on the basis of one sour

"Irrefutable Evidence." Drawing by R. Chast; © 1988 The New Yorker Magazine, Inc.

romance, a man concludes "No woman can be trusted." Or, having been disappointed in one Madonna movie, the viewer concludes "Obviously, the woman can't act."

Several of the more specific fallacies to be discussed in this chapter fall into this general category. But, if you find an inference which doesn't seem to fall neatly into any one of these more specific categories yet seems questionable, it may be that "jumping to conclusions" is the most accurate way to describe what has gone wrong. In criticizing an inference as a case of jumping to conclusions, it is helpful to be able to identify one or more factors that were left out in making the inference but which ought to have been taken into account. Let's now turn to a group of informal fallacies which plague inductive inferences in general and statistical studies more specifically.

## FALLACIES OF STATISTICAL INFERENCE

You'll remember that an inductive inference is one in which the premises leave room for doubt as to the truth of the conclusion, though they do lend support to it as probable or likely. The main question, then, in assessing inductive arguments is: "Given the evidence presented in the premises, how probable or likely is the conclusion?" Accordingly, some of the most common pitfalls to inductive reasoning can conveniently be understood in terms of overestimating the strength of an inductive inference.

In Chapter 7 you learned that the strength of an inductive inference depends most heavily on two factors: the size and representativeness of the sample from which the evidence was taken. We can distinguish several informal fallacies of induction, each of which relates in some way to the size and representativeness of the sample.

## SMALL SAMPLE

Sometimes what appears to be a significant pattern in a small number of cases disappears altogether when we investigate a larger number of cases. For example, suppose we are taking a poll to determine political preferences and of the first ten responses seven favor the challenger over the incumbent. But by the time we have interviewed a hundred people we may find the incumbent ahead seventy-five to twenty-one with four undecided. The fallacy of small sample consists in overestimating the statistical significance of evidence drawn from a small number of cases. But one must be careful in applying this as a criticism. The size of the sample relative to the target population is not the only factor involved in determining the reliability of the inductive inference. Even a relatively small sample can be used to reliably project trends on a massive scale, if the study is carefully controlled and based on a representative sample. Thus, it would be insufficient basis for criticism merely to point out, for example, that a national political preference poll had been conducted on the basis of five thousand responses. In fact, a poll of just fifteen hundred, adhering to all the criteria of a scientifically respectable sample, can yield accurate information about the nation as a whole with a margin of error of only ± 3 percent. And doubling the sample would only reduce the margin of error by about 1 percent.

## UNREPRESENTATIVE SAMPLE

But suppose the aforementioned five thousand responses were all taken from one geographical region. This regional bias would greatly increase the inference's liability to error. Fundamentally, the representativeness of a sample is even more important than sample size, since what one is trying to do by means of induction is to project conclusions which are affected by many variables. If one can control all of the relevant variables in a relatively small sample, so much the better for the economy of the study. The important thing is to control all of the variables. But this can be very difficult to accomplish in an area such as political preference which is affected by such a wide range of variables. The problem is made greater by the fact that not all of the relevant variables may be known. The fallacy of unrepresentative sample consists in overestimating the statistical significance of evidence drawn from a sample of a particular kind.

Perhaps the most famous example of a genuine, but failed, attempt to avoid this fallacy is the 1936 *Literary Digest* poll, which incorrectly predicted that Alf Landon would defeat Franklin Delano Roosevelt in the presidential race, on the basis of two million respondents selected at random from telephone directories and auto registration lists. The relevant variable which the poll overlooked was that in 1936 (during the Great Depression) those who could afford a car or even a phone were relatively few and far between, and of course enjoyed a much higher than average standard of living. So, because the sample was far from random it failed to truly represent the target population.

Randomness means that each member of the target population has an equal chance of appearing among the sample. If, for example, pollsters wish to find out what adult U.S. Catholics think about their church's official teaching on abortion, they must ensure that every U.S. Catholic is equally likely to be among those polled. Notice that this doesn't mean that every Catholic needs to be polled—only that they have an equal chance of being asked. If pollsters ask only California Catholics or New York Catholics, they violate randomness, and thus representativeness. We needn't detail here the techniques pollsters use to ensure randomness. Suffice it to say that professional polling organizations—Harris, Roper, Gallup, and the like—do work hard to ensure randomness in sampling. Informal poll taking often violates this critical criterion of a sound poll.

## BIASED METHODOLOGY

A statistical study is slanted when the methodology determines its outcome in some particular predetermined direction. An unrepresentative sample can slant a study. But a study can also be misleading if even a perfectly representative sample is asked to respond to leading questions, or questions which restrict the range of available responses. For example, suppose that you live in a community where rapid growth has stretched the existing waste management resources to the breaking point, resulting in environmental pollution serious enough to have raised public concern. Now suppose the local newspaper conducts a readers' poll asking:

> Which of the following policy options would you prefer?
>
> 1. A municipal bond issue to construct new sewage treatment facilities.
> 2. A regional bond issue to construct a pipeline to transport excess sewage to the ocean.
> 3. An increase in property tax to pay for improvement and expansion of existing facilities.

Does this exhaust the range of available options? Hardly. Notice that each of the options mentioned presupposes acceptance of the present rate of growth. What about a tax on new development? What about a stiffer zoning policy or a statutory limit on growth? A poll which effectively excludes options from consideration is methodologically slanted against them.

By the same token, a question can be ambiguous or vague. For example, "Do you think it's a good practice for employers to seek out minority members and women for jobs?" Precisely what does "good practice" mean? Or the question can be loaded. For example, "*Given that the future of the free world depends on U.S. military strength,* do you think it's wise to reduce defense spending?"

Respondents can also slant a poll or study, because people often report not what they really think but what they think appropriate. Some years ago interviewers asked respondents: "What magazines does your household read?" A large percentage of households apparently read *Harper's* but not many read *True Story.* This was odd, since publisher's figures clearly showed that *True Story* tremendously outsold *Harper's.* After eliminating other possible explanations, pollsters finally concluded that a good many respondents had not responded truthfully.

Here's an interesting case of slanted study, as well as suppressed evidence (courtesy of *Consumer Reports*):

> Dodge dealers in the New York City area recently aired a series of TV commercials boasting that more than 70 percent of the owners of *Toyota Corollas, Honda Civics, Ford Escorts* and *Chevrolet Cavaliers* actually preferred the new *Dodge Shadow,* according to "100 [people] surveyed." Since our own surveys of subscribers have shown that owners of *Civics* and *Corollas* are more satisfied with their cars than are owners of *Dodge Shadows,* the commercial piqued our interest. The reasons for the difference between our survey results and those reported in the Dodge commercial became clear after Chrysler described the survey's methodology to us.
>
> A survey firm retained by Chrysler chose owners of 1988 to 1991 *Civics, Corollas, Cavaliers,* and *Escorts* to participate in an experiment. The willing respondents—about 25 for each competitor—were given an opportunity to inspect a '92 *Dodge Shadow* and a '92 version of the car they already owned. They were also allowed to take the *Dodge*—but not the other car—out for a spin. After the look-see, the 100 people were asked if they thought the Dodge was better or worse than their current car. 73 percent reportedly said the *Dodge* was better.
>
> Does this mean that most *Civic* and *Corolla* owners would prefer a new *Dodge Shadow* to a new *Civic* or *Corolla,* as the commercial implied? Probably not. Here's why:
>
> First, of course, since the respondents were allowed to test-drive only the *Dodge,* not a new version of the model they owned, they were actually comparing a new car with a used one. For balance, we would like to have seen what owners of an older *Dodge Shadow* thought of their car after driving a new *Corolla, Civic, Escort,* and *Cavalier.*
>
> Second, combining the opinions of owners of four different cars hides any distinctions among them. *Civic* and *Corolla* owners, for example, might have preferred their own car to the *Dodge Shadow,* while *Escort* and *Cavalier* owners might have strongly opted for the *Dodge.* One can't know from the reported result.
>
> Finally, it's hard to believe that the respondents couldn't have guessed what the test was all about (and perhaps have wanted to please the sponsor), since they'd been promised $60 apiece to do a test that involved driving just one manufacturer's car.

## BAD BASE LINE

Statistics often invite misinterpretation, particularly in the direction of overestimating the significance of some trend. The fallacy of bad base line consists of deriving an interpretation of statistical results on an inappropriate basis of comparison. For example, suppose that in some small town the number of car thefts rises from three in one year to four in the next. This represents a 33 percent rise in the incidence of car theft in one year, but indicating it in these terms exaggerates the significance of the increase. Suppose, for example, that over the same period the town's population has doubled. In that case, the incidence of car theft *per capita* (that is, relative to population) has significantly dropped.

Or suppose that studies indicate that the number of teenage drunk driving arrests has risen in three decades from one out of twenty to one out of five of all such arrests. Do such figures indicate that teenagers are drinking and driving more frequently now than they were thirty years ago? Not necessarily. It depends upon what is being used as the base line for comparison. Such figures could result equally from an overall reduction in drunk driving arrests, while the incidence of teenage drunk driving remained constant.

## SUPPRESSED EVIDENCE

Sometimes relevant evidence is deliberately kept from view because it conflicts with the arguer's intended interpretation of the evidence which is presented, or because it would detract from the arguer's thesis. This constitutes the fallacy of suppressed evidence. A common political foible and a particular favorite in the field of advertising, particularly where statistical data are used, this is an obviously disreputable argumentative strategy. For example, advertisers are forever referring to "scientific" studies which "demonstrate" the superiority of their products, but strategically neglecting to mention that they have commissioned the studies themselves, a crucial piece of information relevant to assessing the objectivity of the studies.

Arguably even more sinister are certain common political manipulations of statistics, such as the deliberate understatement of unemployment by obscuring or changing the base line for comparison, for example by tightening eligibility requirements for unemployment benefits or reducing the length of eligibility. Either of these adjustments if implemented on a national scale would predictably result in disallowing claims and eliminating benefits for tens of thousands of unemployed people. But then to report this result as a drop in unemployment would be quite misleading.

It's worth noting that the fallacy of suppressed evidence is not confined to statistical inference. It occurs any time significant information or evidence—information or evidence that makes a difference to the conclusion—is omitted. For example, in 1996 opponents of California's Proposition 215, the ballot initiative measure which made marijuana legally available as a prescription drug, argued correctly that marijuana's safety and effectiveness compared to the already legal synthetic substitute Marinol had not been scientifically established. What they conveniently neglected to mention was that this lack of scientific evidence was due to the fact that the Food and Drug Administration had up to that point refused to investigate the matter.

Suppressed evidence is a relatively common advertising ploy. If the primary goal of advertising is to motivate the purchase, it is hardly to be expected that advertisers would feature the weaknesses and shortcomings of their products. And in fact advertisers do regularly conceal unfavorable information about their products. As a result consumers who rely heavily on advertising for product information rarely have the complete information they need to make a fully informed choice about product price and quality. A well known example from the history of advertising is the old Colgate-Palmolive ad showing Rapid Shave cream being used to shave "sandpaper." We were told: "Apply, soak, and off in a stroke." Certainly this was an impressive ad for any man who had ever scraped his way awake. But Colgate failed to mention that the "sandpaper" in the demonstration was actually Plexiglas and that actual sandpaper had to be soaked in Rapid Shave for about eighty minutes before it came off in a stroke.[1] More recently Campbell's vegetable soup ads showed pictures of a thick, rich brew calculated to whet even a gourmet's appetite. What Campbell's didn't mention was that clear glass marbles had been deposited in the bowl to give the appearance of solidity.

## GAMBLERS' FALLACIES

Lately it seems that more and more large governmental entities have instituted some form of gambling as a means of raising revenue. There is no doubt that a state lottery can produce an enormous cash flow, and enormous jackpots, particularly in a state the size of California. But when the jackpot goes over the moon, cogent reasoning tends to go out the window. The lottery craze is both producing and feeding on a rising tide of "lottery logic," a family of fallacies about "luck" and "beating the odds."

The most obvious and common fallacy to which gamblers seem prone is superstition about "luck." Lucky days, lucky numbers, lucky socks, lucky hunches, all essentially amount to impotent attempts to predict the unpredictable. (For more on this particular sort of fallacious thinking, see the section on fallacies of causal reasoning, later in this chapter.) Gamblers would do well, however, to bear in mind that the stock market is, like a horse race, in many ways unpredictable and therefore risky. Yet there are a number of responsible ways of gathering evidence relevant to managing and controlling the risks of investment—none of which reduce to occult numerology.

There are also a couple of common gamblers' mistakes which can be assimilated to fallacies of induction, since they have to do with the estimation of probabilities. One such fallacy consists of thinking that the probability of a certain outcome of a future chance event is affected by past outcomes. For example, suppose we are gambling on coin flips and the last ten flips have come up heads. Many people are tempted to think that tails are therefore more likely to come up than heads on the next flip. The problem here is failure to recognize that the chances of heads or tails coming up are the same for each flip (50/50), because each flip is an independent chance event. The chances of a run of eleven heads in a row are of course much lower than 50/50, but the odds against such a run have no bearing whatsoever on the outcome of the next flip. And yet people persist in the belief to the contrary. Watch people play the slots in Nevada. Again and again you will see people pumping coins into a machine which hasn't paid off for hours, thinking that this fact alone makes it more likely that the machine will pay off soon.

Just as unreliable is the inference to continue playing because one has been winning. The idea of "riding a streak" involves the same mistake as thinking that the odds against you eventually have to "even out." If chance determines the outcome of the next play, past outcomes have no bearing whatsoever.

Gamblers also tend to be (sometimes pathologically) attracted to "systems" designed to "beat the odds," most of which are completely fallacious products of wishful thinking and don't work at all. (The occasional exception, such as card-counting in blackjack, is very quickly found out and one gets escorted from the premises of gaming establishments.) One such system consists of "doubling the bet." Suppose you put $2 on red at even money and lose. Following this system you would put $4 on red on the next play. If you win, you're up $2. If you lose, you're down $6, but you bet $8 on the next play. If you win, you're up $10. The idea is, that eventually you win, and when you do, you're ahead of the game. The main trouble with this system is that the odds remain uniformly stacked against you throughout the game as you continue to raise your stake, which has the effect primarily of digging you more deeply and quickly into a hole. In other words, if you follow this "system" the only probability that you raise is the probability that you will run out of scratch before you win.

There is really only one rule of thumb which we can confidently recommend as having any useful validity at all for the person who finds games of chance appealing: Quit while you're ahead—(or cut your losses).

## EXERCISE | Fallacies of Statistical Inference

1. Each of the following examples contains (or points out) at least one major statistical fallacy. For each example pick the fallacy category or categories that best explain the problem. Then use your choices to explain your diagnosis of the flaws in the reasoning.
   a. "My last three blind dates have been bombs. This one's bound to be better!"

| | |
|---|---|
| | Small Sample |
| | Unrepresentative Sample |
| | Biased Methodology |
| | Bad Base Line |
| | Suppressed Evidence |
| | Gambler's Fallacy |

Explain your answer:

______

______

______

b. A poll is being conducted to find out what students think of their college newspaper. A sample is taken in the cafeteria on a Tuesday between 8 A.M. and noon. Every fifth person who enters the cafeteria is asked his or her opinion. The results find that 72 percent of the students are highly critical of the newspaper. The student government decides to use these results to revamp the editorial board.

| | |
|---|---|
| | Small Sample |
| | Unrepresentative Sample |
| | Biased Methodology |
| | Bad Base Line |
| | Suppressed Evidence |
| | Gambler's Fallacy |

Explain your answer:

c. Professor Smith, wishing to improve his teaching, decides to poll his physics class. He commissions a questionnaire from one of his colleagues in statistics which satisfies all the criteria of a sound polling instrument. He calls each member of his class individually into his office and asks them to complete the questionnaire. What is wrong with his polling methods?

| | |
|---|---|
| | Small Sample |
| | Unrepresentative Sample |
| | Biased Methodology |
| | Bad Base Line |
| | Suppressed Evidence |
| | Gambler's Fallacy |

Explain your answer:

d. Survey question: "Whom do you think the U.S. should support in the Middle East: The Israelis or the Arab states?"

| | |
|---|---|
| | Small Sample |
| | Unrepresentative Sample |
| | Biased Methodology |
| | Bad Base Line |
| | Suppressed Evidence |
| | Gambler's Fallacy |

Explain your answer:

e. In 1997 the small town of Sulphur Springs experienced a 200 percent increase in felony auto theft, according to the *Sulphur Springs Weekly Standard.* This report was based on the fact that three cars were stolen by joy-riding teenagers, compared to 1996 when only one car was stolen.

| | |
|---|---|
| | Small Sample |
| | Unrepresentative Sample |
| | Biased Methodology |
| | Bad Base Line |
| | Suppressed Evidence |
| | Gambler's Fallacy |

Explain your answer:

## FALLACIES OF COMPARISON

Frequently the evidence for an inference depends upon the making of some comparison or other. In such cases, evaluating the inference depends upon assessing the merits of the comparison. In general, a good comparison assimilates things which are alike in relevant ways and does not gloss over relevant differences. The general strategy for critiquing an argument based on a faulty comparison consists of pointing out a relevant difference between the items compared. When an argument depends on comparing things which are not relevantly alike some sort of fallacy of comparison has been committed.

Note that this is a two-step procedure. First, it has to be established that there is a difference between the items compared. Second, and more important, the relevance of the difference to the point of the comparison needs to be established. Overlooking the second step in particular results in a common misapplication of this criticism: One often hears by way of objection, "Your argument is like comparing apples and oranges." Notice that to criticize an argument as akin to comparing apples with oranges is to make a comparison of one's own. The point of the comparison *being made in* such a criticism is that the comparison *being criticized* is misleading. Well, let's suppose that the argument being criticized does make a comparison which really is comparable to a comparison between apples and oranges. Let's suppose, in other words, that the argument compares items which can be distinguished in some way. But is such a comparison necessarily misleading? Is a comparison between apples and oranges necessarily misleading? Not if you're trying to sort the fruit out from the vegetables.

The important point here is this: First of all, there are no two items in the universe so different from each other that they cannot be compared in some way and for some purpose. Apples and oranges, for example, have quite a few important things in common, and can therefore be usefully and accurately compared for many purposes. But there are also limitations to any comparison between two distinct items. The risks inherent in both arguing on the basis of comparisons and criticizing such arguments are exactly the same. One wants to avoid overestimating the significance of both the common points and the distinctions between the items compared.

## QUESTIONABLE CLASSIFICATION

Many arguments turn on how things are grouped together in categories. For example in Chapter 2 we considered an issue over whether a music video was in the category of "pornography." When an argument depends on grouping things together which do not belong together the fallacy of questionable classification has been committed. Look around the neighborhood and count the houses and cars. Do you have any trouble deciding which is which? Not likely. But an interesting case in constitutional law called even this seemingly obvious classification into question. It seems that police officers had observed a certain vehicle parked for several days during which time individuals and small groups of people were also observed coming and going to and from the vehicle. Suspecting possible drug activity, the police investigated further and indeed found the occupant of the vehicle had drugs in his possession. The occupant was arrested and brought to trial on drug charges. The hitch for the prosecution was that the police had not obtained a search warrant before moving to investigate the vehicle. Why would that be necessary? Police don't need a search warrant to inspect a motor vehicle. But it turned out that the occupant lived in the vehicle, a motor home, and it was argued that since the vehicle was the occupant's place of residence, it should be covered by the Fourth Amendment provision which protects "the right of the people to be secure in their *houses* . . ." against unreasonable search and seizure. Who was right? Is a motor home to be classified as a house or a motor vehicle? The point is there is no simple answer that will work here.

## FALLACY OF COMPOSITION

A special kind of ambiguity is frequently involved in our references to groups of individuals or things. It is not always clear whether the members of the group are being referred to individually or collectively. This can result in one or the other of two common informal fallacies. The fallacy of composition consists in incorrectly inferring characteristics of the group as a collective whole from characteristics of its individual parts or members. For example, a man observes that every member of a local club is wealthy and therefore infers that the club itself must be wealthy. Not necessarily. The confusion results from assuming that what is true of the part must also be true of the whole. In fact, the whole represents something different from simply the sum or combination of its parts. Of course it is sometimes true that a collective whole has the characteristics of its individual members. It may be the case, for example, that a series of good lectures is a good series of lectures. But there is no generally reliable equation here. For example, a program of short pieces of music can be a very long program. A team of highly efficient workers may nonetheless be hopelessly inefficient as a team.

## FALLACY OF DIVISION

The fallacy of division works in the opposite direction, incorrectly inferring characteristics of the individual parts or members of a group from characteristics of the group as a collective whole. Observing that a club is wealthy, a man infers that each club member must be wealthy or that a particular member must be wealthy. But just as a property of the part need not imply a property of the whole, so a property of the whole need not imply a property of the part. That a book is a masterpiece doesn't mean that each chapter is one; that an orchestra is outstanding doesn't imply that each member is an outstanding musician. Again, it is sometimes the case that the individual parts or members of a group have some of the characteristics of the group as a whole, but again not always. A million-dollar inventory, for example, might be made up out of a great many 5- and 10-cent items.

## QUESTIONABLE ANALOGY

Arguments based on analogies were extensively discussed in Chapter 7 as a kind of inductive reasoning. From that discussion you'll recall that an analogy is an elaborate comparison, or a comparison based on multiple points of similarity, and that an argument by analogy essentially infers that if things are alike in some respects, they are probably alike in other ways as well. You'll recall from Chapter 7 that evaluating an argument by analogy is a matter of adding up the relevant similarities and differences between the items compared in the analogy. If we find that the argument is based on similarities which are irrelevant to the conclusion or that it glosses over relevant differences, then we may reasonably object that the argument is based on a questionable, false, or even a misleading analogy. An important area in which to be on the alert for this sort of fallacy is the area of foreign policy. Because this is an area in which the relevant political circumstances are always very complex and at the same time an area where the "lessons of history" weigh heavily, there is a tendency to think in terms of historical precedent, in terms of comparisons between the current crisis or situation and some historical period or turning point (e.g., the Great Depression, the Vietnam War). The risk inherent in such thinking is based simply on the complexity and historical uniqueness of each and every new crisis.

## EXERCISE Fallacies of Comparison

1. Each of the following examples contains (or points out) at least one major fallacy of comparison. For each example pick the fallacy category (or categories) that best explains the problem. Then use your choices to explain your diagnosis of the flaws in the reasoning.
   a. Colleges should start paying students for getting high grades. After all, business handsomely rewards its top people with bonuses and commissions, and everybody can see the beneficial effect of that practice on worker productivity.

| | |
|---|---|
| | Questionable Classification |
| | Composition |
| | Division |
| | Questionable Analogy |

Explain your answer:

______

______

______

______

   b. "Can the universe think about itself? We know that at least one part of it can: we ourselves. Is it not reasonable to conclude the whole can?" —Jose Silva[2]

| | |
|---|---|
| | Questionable Classification |
| | Composition |
| | Division |
| | Questionable Analogy |

Explain your answer:

______

______

______

______

c. So you're new love connection's a Yale man, is he? Well then, I'm sure he'll consider himself too good for the likes of me. The whole snooty institution considers itself too good for me. They turned down my application for admission.

| | |
|---|---|
| | Questionable Classification |
| | Composition |
| | Division |
| | Questionable Analogy |

Explain your answer:

d. Adding a health tax to tobacco products is unfair to the tobacco industry. We are like any other legitimate business in this country. We sell a legal product to willing buyers in a free market, and we pay a fair share into the public purse through various forms of taxation. If tax revenue is to be raised to support Medicare, let the burden be shared across the board.

| | |
|---|---|
| | Questionable Classification |
| | Composition |
| | Division |
| | Questionable Analogy |

Explain your answer:

## FALLACIES OF CAUSAL REASONING

Frequently an issue will turn in some important way upon correctly accounting for the cause of something. But reasoning about causes and effects is tricky, as we explained in Chapter 7. You'll recall that causal relationships are never directly observable, but must be inferred inductively. From the discussion of causal reasoning in Chapter 7 we can derive a number of fallacies which can be understood as failing to meet one or more of the standards and criteria of good inductive reasoning.

Superstitions provide the most obvious cases of this kind of fallacious thinking, as for example when a basketball coach refuses to change his "lucky" socks in an attempt to influence the outcome of the game. But there are a number of more subtle pitfalls of causal reasoning to be aware of.

### CONFUSING CORRELATIONS WITH CAUSES

One of the most common kinds of evidence for a causal connection is a statistical correlation between two phenomena. For example, medical scientists knew for some time of a statistical correlation between cigarette smoking and lung cancer: The incidence of lung cancer in the smoking population was higher than in the nonsmoking population. Such a correlation is genuinely relevant inductive evidence for a causal connection between lung cancer and smoking. The problem is that by itself it is inconclusive. It suggests, but does not establish, the causal link. For several decades the tobacco industry was successful in eluding the implications—and liabilities—of the causal connection between smoking and cancer on the basis of this distinction between correlations and causes. That's how real and significant a distinction it is. Some people may find this hard to accept, and may even be inclined to wonder why we should not, as a society, have been able to move earlier and more decisively against the tobacco industry to establish antismoking policies. Notice, however, that there is also a strong statistical correlation between the incidence of lung cancer and age. Yet it would be misleading to suggest that age causes lung cancer, or that lung cancer causes aging. So, isolating the causal factor does indeed require further scientific evidence.

### OVERLOOKING A COMMON CAUSE

Two phenomena may be so closely connected that one of them seems to be the cause of the other, though both are really results of some additional, less obvious factor. Suppose a person suffers from both depression and alcoholism. Does the drinking cause the depression or the depression cause the drinking? Or could it be that the depression and the drinking sustain each other causally? Perhaps so. But one shouldn't overlook the further possibility that there is some additional underlying cause of both the depression and the drinking, for example a biochemical imbalance or a profound emotional disturbance. The fallacy of overlooking a common cause, then, consists of failing to recognize that two seemingly related events may not be causally related at all, but rather are effects of a common cause.

## POST HOC

A similar fallacy consists in inferring a causal connection from temporal contiguity. In other words, it is a fallacy to infer that one thing is the cause of another simply because it is preceded by it in time. For example, someone observes that crime among youth has increased in the United States since the arrival of punk rock from England, and concludes, therefore, that punk rock is causing an increase in juvenile crime. Or someone observes that every war in this century has followed the election of a Democratic president, concluding therefore that the Democrats caused those wars. This kind of reasoning came to be known in Latin as *post hoc ergo propter hoc,* which means literally, "after this, therefore because of this."

## CAUSAL OVERSIMPLIFICATION

The fallacy of causal oversimplification consists of assuming that what merely contributes causally to a phenomenon fully explains it. For example, intense debates are waged regularly over the wisdom of increased taxation as a means of balancing the federal budget. Opponents of such measures frequently point to the predictable negative effects that taxation will have on the vitality of the consumer economy, while proponents of such measures stress the effects on real disposable income of the increasing debt burden on the economy as a whole. It is likely that both sides have a point, but it is at least as likely that both sides are in effect oversimplifying the economic equation in a number of ways. Clearly tax policy is not the only causal factor which affects the consumer economy. But neither is public indebtedness the only such causal factor. Both factors, and numerous others, are involved and influence each other in a great many ways.

## SLIPPERY SLOPE

A specific kind of causal fallacy consists of objecting to something on the grounds of the unwarranted assumption that it will inevitably lead to some evil

consequence which will lead to some even more evil consequence which in turn will lead "on down the slippery slope" to some ultimately disastrous consequence. For example, it is commonly argued that marijuana is a dangerous drug which inevitably leads to experimentation with harder drugs and eventually to hard drug abuse and addiction. Frequently the alleged slippery slope is supported by further fallacious causal inferences such as pointing out that a high percentage of admitted heroin addicts testify to having tried marijuana early in their drug experience. But there is in fact no slippery slope here, as can easily be established by pointing out that numerous people, who at one time or another have tried or used marijuana, have never experimented with harder drugs, much less become addicted to them, and have moderated or given up their use of marijuana.

A variation on slippery slope reasoning takes the form of posing the rhetorical question "Where do you draw the line?" This of course has the effect of suggesting that there is no location for the line to be drawn. For example, some people are moved by arguments like this one:

> If you permit the withdrawal of life support from terminally ill patients, where do you draw the line between this form of "mercy killing" and the convenient disposal of one's sick and burdensome elders, or the "euthanasia" of the mentally or physically or racially "defective"?

Here it is merely assumed that we can't clearly distinguish between cases of "passive euthanasia" (the withholding of extraordinary measures that would forestall or postpone death) and "active euthanasia" (the taking of measures that would hasten death or bring death about), or between euthanasia done to alleviate the pointless suffering of the terminal patient and euthanasia done for selfish reasons or with deliberate disregard for the interests of the patient.

Now it is easy to see that such distinctions *are* possible, since they have just been made. It is not much harder to see that they are relevant distinctions. Indeed the argument presumes the relevance of such distinctions; otherwise why assume or suggest that they can't be made? Thus an effective strategy for exposing this sort of slippery slope reasoning: Simply draw the relevant distinctions. It is, however, important to recognize that in some contexts the question "Where do you draw the line?" rhetorical though it is, makes a good point. These are contexts—and there *are* some very important ones—in which some fundamental principle is at stake which would be irreparably compromised if a certain exception to it were allowed to pass.

A special case of slippery slope reasoning in the political context was the so-called domino theory, whose influence can be seen in discussions of United States foreign policy pretty much throughout the cold war period. During the Vietnam period the argument ran that if South Vietnam "falls" to the communists, then it will, like the lead domino in a chain of dominoes, bring down Laos, which will topple Cambodia, and so on throughout Southeast Asia and eventually throughout the world until the communists will eventually be at our very borders. The argument, refitted for Central American duty, was a Reagan administration favorite. But the argument's basic analogy is questionable. Political regimes, their stabilities and instabilities, and their interdependencies, are much more complex than can adequately be understood by means of a comparison to a row of standing domino tiles. It is, after all, the political complexities whose causal relationships are at stake here. To be fair to the argument, it should be pointed out that fundamental political changes frequently have impacts reaching far beyond the national borders within which they occur. There is some truth in the idea that political events in one country influence political events in others. For example, the French Revolution was inspired in part by the American Revolution. But this is only one of many factors involved, whose causal significance varies from situation to situation and depends upon a host of other variables.

## EXERCISE | Fallacies of Causal Reasoning

1. Each of the following examples contains (or points out) at least one major fallacy of causal reasoning. For each example pick the fallacy category or categories that best explains the problem. Then use your choices to explain your diagnosis of the flaws in the reasoning.
   a. Argument against raising cigarette taxes: "Taxing cigarettes encourages interstate traffickers in stolen cigarettes by opening up a whole new and very profitable market for them. A vote for this measure is a vote for increased crime. Vote 'NO.' Vote against the smugglers and traffickers and black marketers."

| | |
|---|---|
| | Correlations as Causes |
| | Common Cause |
| | Post Hoc |
| | Causal Oversimplification |
| | Slippery Slope |

Explain your answer:

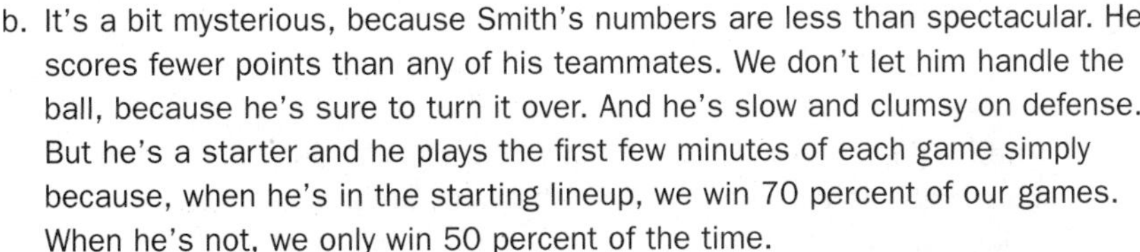

   b. It's a bit mysterious, because Smith's numbers are less than spectacular. He scores fewer points than any of his teammates. We don't let him handle the ball, because he's sure to turn it over. And he's slow and clumsy on defense. But he's a starter and he plays the first few minutes of each game simply because, when he's in the starting lineup, we win 70 percent of our games. When he's not, we only win 50 percent of the time.

(continued)

| | |
|---|---|
| | Correlations as Causes |
| | Common Cause |
| | Post Hoc |
| | Causal Oversimplification |
| | Slippery Slope |

Explain your answer:

c. From *Playboy* magazine: "Is adultery bad for your health? The chances of having a heart attack while making love are infinitesimal, but if you do have one, the chances are you'll have it with your mistress and not your wife. A study of 34 cardiac patients who died during intercourse revealed that 29 of the 34 were having an extramarital affair."

| | |
|---|---|
| | Correlations as Causes |
| | Common Cause |
| | Post Hoc |
| | Causal Oversimplification |
| | Slippery Slope |

Explain your answer:

d. I knew a guy who was so influenced by statistics, numbers ruled his entire life! One time he found out that over 80 percent of all automobile accidents happen to people within 5 miles of where they live. So he moved!

| | |
|---|---|
| | Correlations as Causes |
| | Common Cause |
| | Post Hoc |
| | Causal Oversimplification |
| | Slippery Slope |

Explain your answer:

e. "Whatever you do, DO NOT DESTROY THIS LETTER! Send it out to five of your friends. Mildred Wimplebush of Detroit destroyed her copy of this letter and a week later she died of a stroke. Henry Hinklefrump of El Segundo lost his copy of the letter and was fired within a month. Marlena Gorwangle of Missoula broke her ankle in a freak accident while tossing a salad only days after throwing her copy away."

| | |
|---|---|
| | Correlations as Causes |
| | Common Cause |
| | Post Hoc |
| | Causal Oversimplification |
| | Slippery Slope |

Explain your answer:

## UNWARRANTED ASSUMPTIONS

The slippery slope fallacy also illustrates another general problem area in the handling of evidence: introducing premises which are merely assumed to be the case, but which are both important enough to the argument and controversial enough to call for independent verification.

## FALSE DILEMMA

Another example of this sort occurs when an argument depends upon the presentation of what is merely assumed or misleadingly represented as an exhaustive range of alternatives. Such an argument, called a false dilemma, erroneously reduces the number of possible alternatives on an issue. The strategy best suited to exposing instances of this fallacy is to articulate a specific alternative which is left out of the range of alternatives presented in the premise. For example, a bank commits a false dilemma when it suggests: "The Logical Alternative to the Stock Market: Madison Savings and Loan." There are of course numerous other investment options.

False dilemma is one of the most powerfully persuasive of the common informal fallacies. This is due to the fact that it assumes the deductively valid dilemma form (see Chapter 6). Dilemma is the logical strategy of proving a point by showing that it is implied by each of two alternatives, at least one of which must be true. A false dilemma fallacy gives itself a running start by being deductively valid. If it's really true that there are only two possibilities and each of them entails some conclusion, we are logically forced to accept the conclusion. Accordingly, attacking the fallacy of false dilemma is a simple matter of falsifying one or more of its premises, usually the disjunction which says that there are only two possibilities. Bear in mind that the fallacy of false dilemma also appeals psychologically to the natural human tendency to prefer simplicity, to see things in terms of pairs of mutually exclusive alternatives, or as it is sometimes said, in black and white. This rare combination of formal logical and psychological persuasive power makes it an all-time favorite of political pundits and speechwriters. The fallacy is almost guaranteed to appear in any electoral contest in which there are two leading contestants. Here for example is a nicely matched pair of false dilemma arguments from the 1984 presidential campaign, starting with the challenger, Walter Mondale:

> Our choice is between two futures, between a Reagan future and a better future. It is a choice between expediency and excellence. It is a choice between social Darwinism and social decency. It is a choice between salesmanship and leadership.

And now here's the incumbent and election winner, President Ronald Reagan:

> The truth is, Americans must choose between two drastically different points of view. One puts its faith in the pipedreamers and margin scribblers of Washington; the other believes in the collective wisdom of the American people. Our opponents believe the solutions to our nation's problems lie in the psychiatrist's notes or in a social worker's file or in a bureaucrat's budget. We believe in the working man's toil, the businessman's enterprise, and the clergyman's counsel.

## THE ONLY GAME IN TOWN

A closely related fallacy, in this case a perversion of the concept of explanatory power as discussed in Chapter 7, consists of concluding that some explanation or solution holds simply because no one can think of a better one. For example, filmmaker Spike Lee once argued that AIDS originated as a genocidal attack on gays and black people. His argument seemed to rest largely on the idea that there are some peculiarities about the course of the AIDS epidemic for which there is no better explanation. "All of sudden, a disease appears out of nowhere that nobody has a cure for, and it's specifically targeted at gays and minorities. . . . So now it's a national priority. Exactly like drugs became when they escaped the urban centers into white suburbia. . . . The mystery disease, yeah, about as mysterious as 'genocide.' " To call this an *interesting* hypothesis would be fair enough. Worth investigating, sure. It's true that the origins of the HIV virus and its introduction into the human population remain a mystery. But as it stands, the "genocidal plot run amok" hypothesis is, well . . . hypothetical. It's an empirical hypothesis, too. This means there should be some hard evidence out there somewhere to confirm it, if it's true. But one thing that does not count as confirming evidence is the absence of any better explanations. Philosopher Elliot Sober calls this fallacy the "only game in town fallacy," and since we can't think of a better name for it, well. . . . Incidentally, as it turns out in this particular case there are a number of alternative "theories" of the origins of the HIV virus, some of them at least as plausible as the "genocidal plot run amok" hypothesis. So, in the final analysis, Lee's hypothesis is not the only game in town.

## BEGGING THE QUESTION

Here is a little story that illustrates the fallacy of begging the question. Three thieves have stolen seven bars of gold. The thief in the middle hands two bars of gold to the thief on the left and two bars of gold to the thief on the right and says, "I'm keeping three for myself." The thief on the left asks, "Why do you get to keep three for yourself, when we each only get two?" The thief in the middle says, "because I'm the leader of this outfit." The thief on the right asks, "What makes you the leader of this outfit?" to which the thief in the middle responds, "I've got the most bars of gold." The fallacy of begging the question occurs when the arguer assumes what is at issue, or when the conclusion or some statement presupposing the conclusion is introduced as a premise. This is sometimes called "circular reasoning," since its point of origin (the premise) is identical with its terminus (the conclusion). Such arguments are objectionable because the premise is just as questionable as the conclusion it is intended to support (hence the name "begging the question"). A classical example from the history of philosophy of religion goes like this: "We must believe in God's existence because it is taught in the Holy Scriptures, and conversely, we must believe in the Holy Scriptures because they have come from God." As seventeenth century philosopher and mathematician Rene Descartes pointed out about this still popular piece of reasoning, it is pretty clear that no reason for the conclusion has been offered besides the conclusion itself, hence, "this reasoning cannot be proposed to unbelievers because they would judge it to be circular." What makes this fallacy particularly tricky to deal with is that arguers are rarely so clumsy as to appeal to a premise which is *obviously* the same as the conclusion. More frequently the question-begging premise is a subtle rewording of the conclusion or the conclusion is presupposed by the premise in a way even the arguer may fail to appreciate. The strategy one frequently needs to pursue in order to effectively diagnose and expose question-begging therefore involves sensitive use of paraphrase. If the premise and the conclusion can be paraphrased into each other without significant loss of meaning, then we have a plausible case of begging the question.

## INVINCIBLE IGNORANCE

A related fallacy, which we'll call invincible ignorance, consists of refusing to give due consideration to evidence which conflicts with what one is already committed to believing. For example in the accompanying Peanuts episodes Snoopy commits this fallacy twice.

"Peanuts," by Charles M. Schulz. From *Charlie Brown's Cyclopedia,* 1975. Reprinted by permission of UFS, Inc.

In the first instance, Snoopy dismisses Lucy's testimony as ignorant; and later he dismisses the evidence of her research on the basis of the far-fetched assumption of a massive cover-up. In each case, there appears to be no reason for dismissing the information other than that it conflicts with the hypothesis he is initially, and as it seems, inflexibly committed to. In what might be called a definitive case of "sleeping dogmatism," Snoopy has closed his mind on this point, which now seems no longer to be open to question or challenge from any quarter.

## AD IGNORANTIAM

The fallacy of arguing ad ignorantiam (Latin for "arguing from ignorance)" consists in treating the absence of evidence for (or against) a claim as proof of its falsity (or truth). The fallacy is a perversion of the concept of "burden of proof" and legitimate presumption discussed in Chapter 7. Essentially it consists in misplacing the burden of proof. Understandably, many examples of this fallacy have to do with the unknown and the supernatural. For example, there is an argument for the existence of extraterrestrial intelligent life which goes like this: Because the universe is infinitely large, it is impossible to prove conclusively that the only intelligent life that exists is on the planet earth, and so we should assume that extraterrestrial intelligent life exists.

### EXERCISE | Unwarranted Assumptions

1. Each of the following examples contains (or points out) at least one major fallacy involving unwarranted assumptions. For each example pick the fallacy category (or categories) that best explains the problem. Then use your choices to explain your diagnosis of the flaws in the reasoning.
   a. In spite of the objections of the Associated Students and the Faculty Senate, we are moving ahead to implement the new tuition fees recommended by the committee. We have to do *something* and we have to do it *immediately* to restore our reputation as a leading undergraduate educational institution. No one has come forward with a better alternative.

| | |
|---|---|
| | False Dilemma |
| | Only Game in Town |
| | Begging the Question |
| | Invincible Ignorance |
| | Ad Ignorantium |

(continued)

Explain your answer:

b. A real miracle is something that demonstrably does occur but which cannot be scientifically explained. Now we formed a prayer circle over sister Sadie and her T-cell count has returned to normal and she no longer tests positive for HIV. The doctors have confirmed what the labwork shows but they can't seem to agree on an explanation. We believe God has sent the virus from her body.

| | |
|---|---|
| | False Dilemma |
| | Only Game in Town |
| | Begging the Question |
| | Invincible Ignorance |
| | Ad Ignorantium |

Explain your answer:

c. By the time you have wisely purchased this tome (book, for those of you in Rio Linda, California) most critics will have undoubtedly savaged it. In many cases, their reviews will have been written before the book was published. How do I know this? Because I do. —Rush Limbaugh[3]

| | |
|---|---|
| | False Dilemma |
| | Only Game in Town |
| | Begging the Question |
| | Invincible Ignorance |
| | Ad Ignorantium |

Explain your answer:

d. We must believe in the existence of God because it is written in the Holy Scriptures, and conversely, we must believe in the Holy Scriptures because they come from God. —Rene Descartes[4]

| | |
|---|---|
| | False Dilemma |
| | Only Game in Town |
| | Begging the Question |
| | Invincible Ignorance |
| | Ad Ignorantium |

Explain your answer:

e. Everything in this book is right and you must be prepared to confront that reality. You can no longer be an honest liberal after reading this entire masterpiece. Throughout the book you will be challenged, because you will actually be persuaded to the conservative point of view. Whether you can admit this in the end will be a true test of your mettle as a human being. —Rush Limbaugh[5]

| | |
|---|---|
| | False Dilemma |
| | Only Game in Town |
| | Begging the Question |
| | Invincible Ignorance |
| | Ad Ignorantium |

(continued)

Explain your answer:

________________________________________

________________________________________

________________________________________

## SOME ADDITIONAL INFORMAL STRATEGIES FOR CRITICIZING ARGUMENTS

Remember that in evaluating arguments, in assessing their soundness or cogency, you are trying to assess the strength or validity of the connection between the conclusion and the premises offered as support, and the truth or acceptability of the supporting premises. In addition to the tools you have so far, there are a number of important informal strategies of argument evaluation worth mentioning.

### CHECKING FOR CONSISTENCY

One of the most powerful notions for both formal and informal argument evaluation is consistency. (Remember the crucial role it plays in determining deductive validity.) Inconsistency is always a sign of something wrong. So it is always a good idea to check the arguments you come across for both internal consistency and consistency with what has already been established. For example, if there is a genuine inconsistency among the premises of an argument, then although you may not know which of the premises is false, you know they can't all be true. Again, if a premise, or the conclusion for that matter, is inconsistent with something you have good independent reason to believe is true, you have also therefore got good reason to doubt the argument's soundness or cogency. This is an especially useful device for getting your bearings in areas where the facts remain in dispute and good, hard, incontrovertible evidence is hard to come by.

Consistency is also a powerful tool for assessing the soundness of evaluative arguments. Indeed in the sphere of ethics and public policy it is frequently invoked as a basic moral principle: that like cases should be treated alike. Thus, sometimes a policy or position can be effectively criticized as a violation of this basic principle, that is, as a case of inconsistency. This is what is meant by the term "double standard." Bear in mind, however, that cases which seem to be alike are sometimes different from each other in subtle, hard to recognize, but nonetheless important and relevant ways. Thus, challenging the consistency of a policy is not the same thing as demonstrating that the policy is in fact inconsistent. It can, however, shift the burden of proof onto the advocate of the policy to draw a significant distinction between the apparently similar cases which policy refuses to recognize as such.

This strategy can also be applied in a global way to assess the overall consistency of a body of beliefs or set of conclusions. If one argues for conclusions which are genuinely inconsistent with each other, again, one may not yet know which of them is incorrect, but they can't all be. And so the arguments which support them can't all be cogent.

## TRACING IMPLICATIONS

Remember also that positions and arguments tend to have further implications. Without knowing for certain that a claim is correct or that an argument is sound or cogent it is often an effective strategy to treat it hypothetically, that is, to assume that the claim is true, or that the argument is sound or cogent, and trace out its further implications. If a claim or an argument leads by implication to further conclusions which there is good reason to reject, then there is good reason to doubt the claim or the argument.

This strategy, which has traditionally been known by its Latin name *reductio ad absurdum* (which means "to reduce to absurdity"), can be effectively used as a powerful general strategy of argument in its own right. In this strategy, one merely assumes that the conclusion one wants to establish is false. One then traces the implications of that assumption, hoping to find that it leads to some conclusion which there is good reason to reject, whereupon one also finds good reason to reject the original assumption. This is sometimes referred to as the "method of indirect proof."

## A FINAL WORD OF CAUTION

By now it should be pretty clear that evaluating arguments, particularly in informal terms, can be a pretty messy business. You can expect to encounter a fair number of arguments which can quite clearly be faulted in one way or another, and occasionally you'll find an argument which is pretty clearly impeccable. But a great many arguments are neither clearly fallacious nor clearly not. In such cases, you should consider your criticisms to be essentially contestable, and therefore you should also recognize the need to supply arguments in support of them, to deal with arguments against them, and perhaps to change your mind. In other words, assessing arguments, like verifying value judgments, takes you into areas where knowing how to construct and evaluate arguments becomes more and more important.

## ADDITIONAL EXERCISES

1. At the beginning of this chapter there is a cartoon in which a bunch of dubious "irrefutable" evidence of a UFO landing is presented. Which particular fallacies are illustrated by the cartoon?

2. At the beginning of the section on fallacies of comparison there is a cartoon about the topic of reproductive rights. Do you think there's anything fallacious about the pig's argument? Explain any criticisms you would offer in detail. Do

you think there's anything fallacious or objectionable about the fact that the cartoonist has put the argument into the mouth of a pig?

**3.** Here's another wonderful example of fallacious reasoning composed and drawn by the great satirist Jules Feiffer. The relevant background information is this: *Time* magazine once published a controversial story about the career of Israeli leader Ariel Sharon, who brought a libel suit against the magazine, which frightened a good many working journalists into some rather extravagant defenses of *Time* magazine in particular and journalistic practice and the freedom of speech in general. In this cartoon, Feiffer takes a satirical look at such defensive journalism. How many fallacies can you find in the columnist's argument? We count no less that seven distinct fallacious moves and at least eleven distinctly applicable fallacy categories.

**4.** In the eleventh frame of the Peanuts cartoon shown on page 328, to illustrate the fallacy of invincible ignorance, Lucy makes reference to medical history. See if you can explain why her argument is *not* an example of the fallacy of ad ignorantiam.

**5.** Imagine that you're a contestant on a game show, and you're given a choice between whatever is hidden behind one of three doors. You're told that behind one door is a brand new luxury sports car; behind each of the other two doors is a goat. You pick Door #1, and the game show host, who knows what's behind all of them, opens Door #3, revealing a goat. He then asks if you want to change your selection to Door #2.

a. Would you switch? Should you switch? On what basis would you decide?

b. Marilyn vos Savant publishes a column entitled "Ask Marilyn" in a widely distributed Sunday newspaper magazine. In her self-promotional introduction she proclaims that she is "listed in the Guinness Book of World Records Hall of Fame for *Highest IQ.*" In one of her columns she answered the question posed in the game show example as follows:

> Yes [you should switch]. The first door has a 1/3 chance of winning, but the second has a 2/3 chance.

A number of mathematicians wrote in to point out that Marilyn's reasoning was fallacious. Can you explain why?

c. One of the mathematicians wrote, "If one door is shown to be a loser, that information changes the probability of either remaining choice to 1/2." Marilyn defended her position as follows:

> My original answer is correct. But first let me explain why your answer is wrong. The winning odds of 1/3 on the first choice can't go up to 1/2 just because the host opens a losing door. To illustrate this, let's say we play a shell game. You look away, and I put a pea under one of three shells. Then I ask you to put your finger on a shell. The odds that your choice contains a pea are 1/3, agreed? Then, I simply lift up an empty shell from the remaining two. As I can (and will) do this regardless of what you've chosen, we've learned nothing to allow us to revise the odds on the shell under your finger.
>
> The benefits of switching are readily proved by playing through the six games that exhaust all the possibilities. For the first three games, you choose No. 1 and switch each time; for the second three games, you choose No. 1 and "stay" each time, and the host always opens a loser. Here are the results (each row is a game):

| Door #1 | Door #2 | Door #3 |
|---|---|---|
| **CAR** | goat | goat |
| (Switch and you lose) | | |
| goat | **CAR** | goat |
| (Switch and you win) | | |
| goat | goat | **CAR** |
| (Switch and you win) | | |
| **CAR** | goat | goat |
| (Stay put and you win) | | |
| goat | **CAR** | goat |
| (Stay put and you lose) | | |
| goat | goat | **CAR** |
| (Stay put and you lose) | | |

> When you switch, you win two out of three times and lose one time in three; but when you don't switch, you only win one in three times and lose two in three. Try it yourself.

What is wrong with Marilyn's "proof"?

**6.** Once again, with your study partner, take turns critically examining the following examples in terms of the informal fallacy categories you have learned so far, including those covered in the previous chapter, and testing your critical assessments for clarity and fairness. One of you can play the role of finding and explaining the flaw in the argument, while the other challenges and tests the diagnosis by trying to defend the argument against the proposed criticism. Take turns as you work your way through the following examples. Don't forget, a given argument can have more than one thing wrong with it. If you arrive at a consensus criticism, move on to the next example.

a. Should we not assume that just as the eye, the hand, the foot, and in general each part of the body clearly has its own proper function, so man too has some function over and above the function of his parts? —Aristotle[6]
b. From a letter to the editor: "Two terms of Democratic leadership in the White House have seen a drop in inflation and in unemployment, with modest but steady overall growth in the economy. No sooner has that leadership been replaced by a Republican, but interest rates and inflation begin to rise, the stock market turns sharply down and signs of depression abound. What further evidence do you need to conclude that Democrats are good and Republicans are bad for the economy?"
c. The Ayatollah Khomeini speaking in defense of state executions of those convicted of adultery, prostitution, or homosexuality: "If your finger suffers from gangrene, what do you do? Let the whole hand and then the body become filled with gangrene, or cut the finger off? . . . Corruption, corruption. We have to eliminate corruption."[7]
d. Suppose a survey shows that more than half of all college students with below-average grades smoke pot, while, by contrast, only 20 percent of nonsmokers have below-average grades. On the basis of these data, one person concludes that pot smoking causes students to get lower grades. Another person concludes that getting lower grades causes students to smoke pot. What do you make of this disagreement?
e. According to Associated Press reporters covering the 1988 presidential campaign of Vice President George Bush, the candidate endorsed the controversial key recommendation of the president's AIDS commission the day after its final report was submitted to the White House. At the time, President Reagan remained uncommitted regarding the recommendation that AIDS victims should have federal protection from discrimination on the job, in schools and elsewhere. "I think it is needed . . . to lay to rest some of the fears," Bush said, embracing the recommendation. But he added that Reagan "did the right thing" in withholding judgment. "How can the White House be asked to take an instant position?" he asked. When it was pointed out that Bush, himself, was doing just that, the vice president said Reagan "just saw this thing yesterday. He's not running for president. I've got a different role here. I want to say what I think."
f. According to folk wisdom in many cultures, redheaded people tend to be a bit temperamental. An Israeli researcher believes that there may be something to the ancient prejudice. At the Honolulu conference, psychiatrist Michael Bar of Israel's Shalvata Psychiatric Center reported a study showing that redheaded children are three or four times more likely than others to develop 'hyperactive syndrome'—whose symptoms include over-excitability, short

attention span, and feelings of frustration, and usually, excessive aggressiveness. Bar arrives at his conclusion after matching the behavior of 45 redheaded boys and girls between the ages of six and twelve against that of a control group of nonredheaded kids."[8]

g. "Before he took $B_{15}$ [her husband] could barely get up for his meals because of a severe heart condition," said Jayne Link, a 51-year-old Glen Cove, New York widow. "Two weeks after he started taking the vitamin pill he was completely changed." Then Bill stopped taking the vitamin. Three months later he was dead—victim of a fifth heart attack. . . . Now Mrs. Link takes $B_{15}$ herself for arthritis. "I take it constantly, three 50 milligram tablets a day," she said. "I have a slipped disc in addition to the arthritis. I tried everything under the sun to relieve the pain. But nothing else has worked."[9]

h. Are interior decorators necessary? Yes. . . . Since one cannot set one's own broken leg one relies on a doctor. Without a formidable knowledge of legal intricacies one depends on a barrister. Likewise, unless the individual is well versed in the home furnishing field the services of an interior decorator are a distinct advantage. —Helen-Janet Bonelli[10]

i. ***Ron:*** Smoking pot definitely leads to heroin addiction.
***Jon:*** That's ridiculous! What's your evidence?
***Ron:*** Figures don't lie. A report by the U.S. Commission on Narcotics on a study of two thousand narcotics addicts in a prison shows that well over two-thirds smoked marijuana before using heroin.

j. Since more suicides occur during the Christmas season than at any other time of the year, something about Christmas must lead people to take their lives.

k. Egyptian President Anwar Sadat was assassinated immediately after he began to crack down on political dissidents. Proof enough that one of those dissident groups was behind Sadat's murder.

l. Perhaps intimidated by flak from Capitol Hill, the Social Security Advisory Council has backed away from a proposal to increase the maximum pay subject to Social Security taxation from $14,000 to $24,000 to keep the plan on a pay-as-you-go basis. Instead it has recommended shifting the cost of Medicare to the general fund. The proposal, if adopted, would begin the process of transferring Social Security into an out-and-out welfare program. Once we start in that direction, where do we stop?[11]

m. The federal bail-out of big companies such as Chrysler and Pan American is wrong because the government makes no effort to rescue small businesses that are failing.

n. At the 1992 National Religious Broadcasters convention in Washington, D.C., an Israel Solidarity Rally was sponsored by the Christians' Israel Public Action Campaign (Cipac), whose director, Richard Hellman, suggested that the poor state of the U.S. economy, President Bush's attack of nausea during his state dinner with the Japanese prime minister, and storm damage to his house in Kennebunkport, Maine, were all signs from God. According to Hellman: "I did point out certain interesting coincidences. One day the President said there were a thousand lobbyists up on the Hill speaking out on behalf of loan guarantees for Israel (as if those of us who were up there were somehow doing something that was illegal) and it was very shortly after that that his house was blown in. And the fact that one day the U.S. strongly condemned Israel in the U.N., (in language more harsh than was used against Iraq), and the very next day we witness the quite literally terrifying view of our President stricken, many of us thought almost as though dead, before our very eyes in the paper and on television. One might say these are just coincidences. But I think that if it were I, and I were leading a nation that had gone through the worst quarter economically in 30 years, I would start to wonder if there was something more I could do. What more might I do for my nation, including what more might I do to bless Israel, so that my nation in turn would be blessed?"

o. Rush Limbaugh on abortion: "Right to choose what? Can a woman choose to steal using her own body? Of course not. Can she choose to do drugs? No. Not according to the law. Can she legally choose to be a prostitute? Again, no, which establishes, as does the drug example, that there is precedent for society determining what a woman can and can't do with her body. Look at it in another, and admittedly provocative, way: What if a man claimed the right to rape using the same principle found in the theory that it is his body and he has the right to choose? Well, it's nonsense, and it is nonsense for a woman, or any citizen, to assert such a right as well."

p. Letter to the Editor: "I was most disappointed with your paper for publishing that article about Madonna's book *Sex* in your 'Teen Life' section. I feel that the article is encouraging teens to buy and view sordid material on the basis that it is only 'fantasy.' Perhaps we need to remind ourselves that Ted Bundy's career started by viewing soft-core pornography, escalated to hard-core and then, when 'fantasy' was not enough, he decided that only the real thing would do."

q. Letter to the Editor: "Extinction is nothing new. It happened to the dinosaurs and God only knows how many other species. There's no use wringing our hands (or spending a lot of money) trying to stop something that's not in our power to prevent."

r. Opinion page editors have a time-honored way of assessing their own performance in reflecting community standards: If they receive a roughly equal number of letters accusing them of liberal and conservative bias, they figure they're hitting the mark.

s. In 1989 Judith Wallerstein published a longitudinal study of 131 children whose parents had divorced in 1971, claiming that almost half had experienced serious long-term psychological problems that interfered with their love and work lives. This summer she released an update based on twenty-six of these young adults, all of whom had been 2–6 years old when their parents separated. They had been extremely vulnerable to drug and alcohol abuse as teens, she reported, and were still plagued in their 20s and 30s by unstable relationships with their fathers, low educational achievement and severe anxieties about commitment.

But there is good reason to worry about the massive publicity accorded Wallerstein's work. Her estimates of the risks of divorce are more than twice as high as those of any other reputable researcher in the field. Her insistence that the problems she finds were caused by the divorce itself, rather than by pre-existing problems in the marriage, represents an oversimplified notion of cause and effect repudiated by most social scientists and contradicted by her own evidence.

Wallerstein studied sixty Marin County couples, mostly white and affluent, who divorced in 1971. Her sample was drawn from families referred to her clinic because they were already experiencing adjustment problems. Indeed, participants were recruited by the offer of counseling in exchange for commitment to a long-term study. This in itself casts serious doubt on the applicability of Wallerstein's findings. The people most likely to be attracted to an offer of long-term counseling and most likely to stick with it over many years are obviously those most likely to feel they need it. And after twenty-five years in a study about the effects of divorce, the children are unlikely to consider any alternative explanations of the difficulties they have had in their lives.

Wallerstein admits that only one-third of the families she worked with were assessed as having "adequate psychological functioning" *prior* to divorce. Half the parents had chronic depression, severe neurotic difficulties or "long-standing problems controlling their rage or sexual impulses." Nearly a quarter of the couples reported that there had been violence in their marriages. It is thus likely that many of the problems since experienced by their children stemmed from the parents' bad marriages rather than their divorces, and would not have been averted had the couples stayed together. Other researchers studying children who do poorly after divorce have found that behavior problems were often already evident eight to twelve years *before* the divorce took place, suggesting that both the maladjustment and divorce were symptoms of more deep-rooted family and parenting issues.[12]

t. Bill Clinton's recent troubles [the Monica Lewinski sex scandal] may have diminished him in the eyes of some Americans, but opinion polls show that most of us actually couldn't care less. Even though most think he hasn't been entirely honest, Clinton's approval rating is at an all-time high. What exactly does that mean?

Looking more closely, the polls also show that Clinton's numbers went down only while his denials were carefully worded. "The allegations I have seen are untrue" certainly sounds like there might be something we don't know yet. However, once his denials became absolute, the approval ratings began to increase, rising dramatically after a State of the Union address that refused even to acknowledge the scandal's existence.

The number of people who believe that illicit sex took place has remained fairly stable. So Clinton hasn't changed anybody's mind, though he has changed the way they *feel* about what they think. The only logical conclusion: we really don't mind when politicians lie. The only thing we *do* mind is when they do it unconvincingly. —Bob Harris[13]

7. Find examples of your own in the public media of the informal fallacies discussed in this chapter. For each example, give a brief but careful explanation of the fallacies you find in it.

8. Remember that a given argument can have more than one thing wrong with it. With that in mind, go back over the examples in the Additional Exercises section of Chapters 9 and 10. Give a brief and careful explanation of any additional fallacies you can find using the fallacy categories developed in this chapter.

## GLOSSARY

**ad ignorantiam** fallacy of inferring a statement from the absence of evidence or lack of proof of its opposite
**bad base line** fallacy of statistical inference based on an inappropriate basis of comparison
**begging the question** fallacy of assuming or presupposing one's conclusion as a premise
**biased methodology** any methodology, such as a loaded question, which distorts a statistical study
**causal oversimplification** variety of causal fallacy in which significant causal factors or variables are overlooked
**circular reasoning** another name for "begging the question"
**common cause** variety of causal fallacy in which one of two effects of some common cause is taken to cause the other
**composition** fallacy of inferring characteristics of the whole from characteristics of the parts
**correlation** an observed or established statistical regularity, often fallaciously thought to establish a causal connection
**division** fallacy of inferring characteristics of a part from characteristics of the whole
**false dilemma** fallacy of underestimating or underrepresenting the number of possible alternative positions on a given issue
**gambler's fallacy** any of a variety of fallacies of inductive reasoning having to do with estimating or beating the odds, often based on the use of past outcomes to predict the future outcome of chance events
**implications** claims which may be legitimately inferred from a given claim
**indirect proof** argumentative strategy of assuming the negation of some hypothesis and deriving from that assumption a clearly false or self-contradictory implication which then provides a reason to overturn the original assumption
**invincible ignorance** fallacy of refusing to give due consideration to evidence which conflicts with what one is already committed to believing
**post hoc** variety of causal fallacy in which order of events in time is taken to establish a cause-and-effect relationship
**reductio ad absurdam** use of the method of indirect proof to refute an opposing position

**slippery slope** fallacy consisting of objecting to something on the grounds that it will lead, by dubious causal reasoning, to some unacceptable set of consequences
**small sample** fallacy of statistical inference consisting of overestimating the statistical significance of evidence drawn from a small number of cases
**suppressed evidence** persuasive strategy consisting of covering up available evidence which conflicts with an intended conclusion
**unrepresentative sample** fallacy of statistical inference in which the sample underrepresents the variety of relevant variables in the population

## NOTES

[1] Samm Sinclair Baker, *The Permissible Lie* (New York: World, 1968), p. 16.

[2] Jose Silva, *The Silva Mind Control Method* (New York: Pocket Books, 1978), p. 116.

[3] Rush Limbaugh, *The Way Things Ought to Be* (New York: Simon & Schuster, 1992), p. ix.

[4] Rene Descartes, "Letter of Dedication," *Meditations on First Philosophy.*

[5] Limbaugh, *The Way Things Ought to Be,* p. x.

[6] Aristotle, *Nicomachean Ethics,* trans. Martin Ostwald (Indianapolis: Bobbs-Merrill, 1962), p. 16.

[7] Quoted in *Time,* October 22, 1979, p. 57.

[8] *Time,* September 12, 1977, p. 97.

[9] *Globe,* September 11, 1979, p. 22.

[10] Helen-Janet Bonelli, *The Status Merchants: The Trade of Interior Decoration* (Cranbury, N.J.: Barnes, 1972), p. 36.

[11] "A Quick About-Face," *New York Daily News,* January 21, 1975, p. 37.

[12] Adapted from Stephanie Coontz, "Divorcing Reality," *The Nation,* November 17, 1997.

[13] Bob Harris, "Fornigate, Part II: Politics Is a Confidence Game," *Sonoma County Independent,* February 12, 1998, p. 5.

# PART FOUR Applications

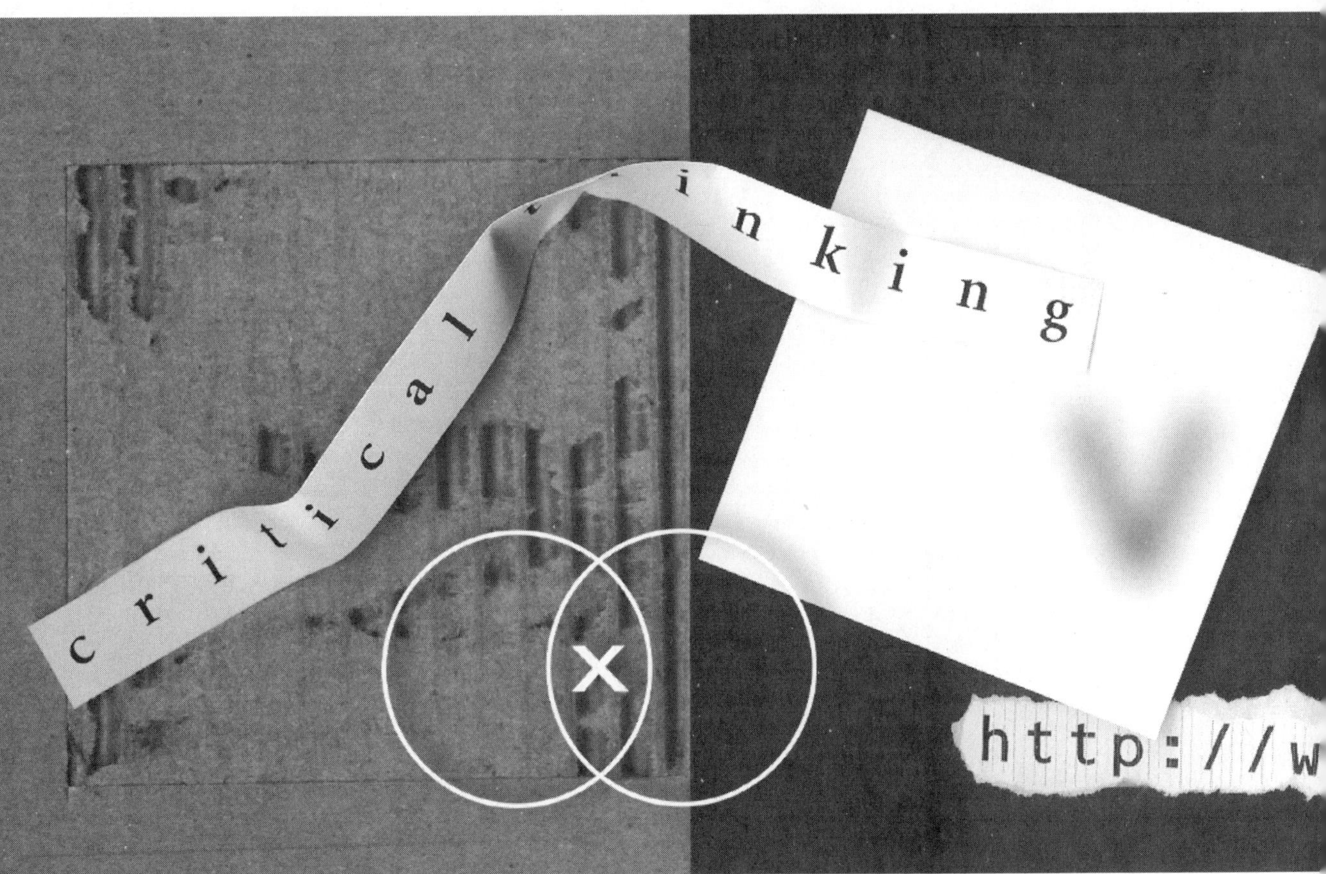

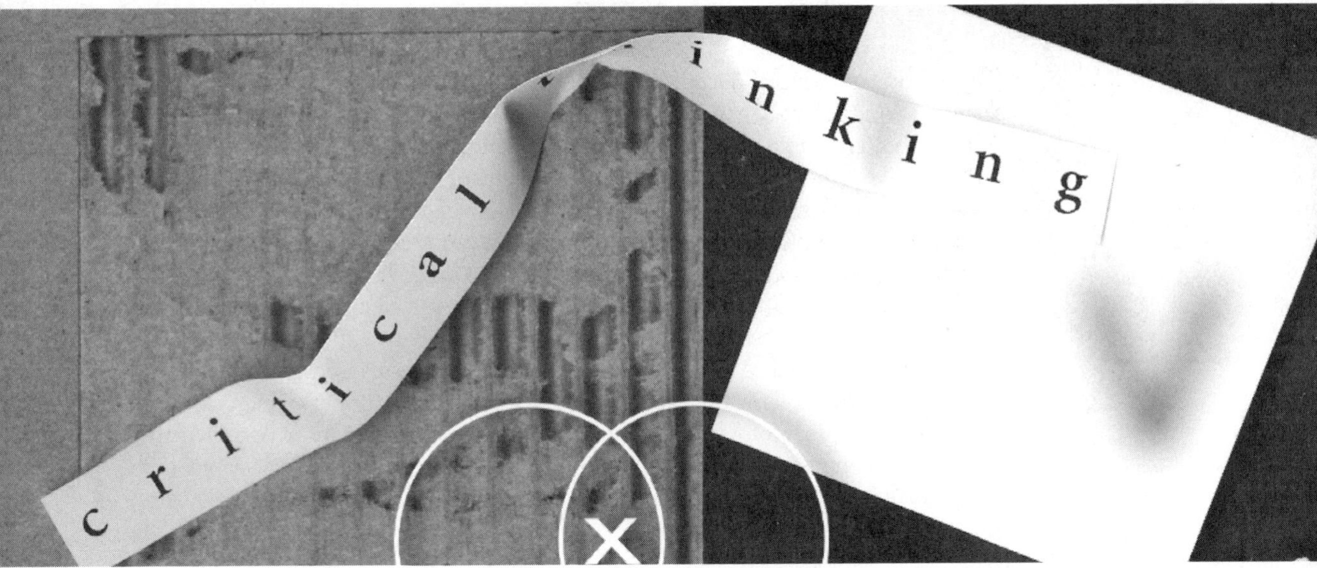


# CHAPTER 12 Research and the Media

A standing assignment in the critical thinking classes of the authors of this book is to carry out a sustained project involving research, argument identification, argument analysis, argument evaluation, argument design, and written composition focused on some significant issue of the student's choice. Once an appropriate issue has been selected, an early stage of the project involves research. Research essentially means finding out something we don't already know. In researching an issue we need to gain access to reliable information relevant to our topic, and most important, since our topic is the subject of debate and disagreement among reasonable people, we need to gain access to arguments of a reasonably high standard representing the range of opinion on our topic.

We live in what has come to be known as the Age of Information. Among the many meanings this label carries with it is reference to our unprecedented access to information. Individually and collectively we presently can gather, collect, store, sort, process, transmit, and receive more information more quickly than at any previous time in human history. This is both a blessing and a curse for research. Obviously the fact that information is so readily available is useful to research. But in an information-rich environment like ours, it's easy to get lost, distracted, and overwhelmed by the sheer volume of information available.

Over the last several decades we have seen profound changes in the way research is conducted. A generation ago (when the authors of this book were in college) to do research one went to the card catalog in the college library. The information and the arguments were in books (or periodicals) which were in the library and listed in the card catalog. And you just went there, looked them up by subject, found them in the stacks, and took them home and read them. Today the library is still the first and best place to go to do research. But now the information and the arguments are in all kinds of media—not just print—and all over the place—not necessarily housed in the actual library building. Today librarians are even more crucial as assistants to the research process than they were a generation ago. They are the college's experts in using new and increasingly powerful information technologies to sift through the mountains of information available on most any issue. The best piece of general research advice we have to offer is to consult one of your college reference librarians. Make sure you have your issue well and clearly defined.

## THE INFORMATION ENVIRONMENT

The Age of Information has made do-it-yourself research an easy undertaking, undoubtedly a good thing in and of itself. Yet at the same time the Age of Information has raised some "quality control issues" for the do-it-yourself researcher. When so much information is so readily available, how can we be sure that the information we're getting is reliable? How do we find among the arguments in wide circulation those that represent the full spectrum of opinion with the highest standard of reasoning? A critical thinking course is an appropriate forum for exploring these issues. And so, we turn now to the information environment and the mass media.

## THE MASS MEDIA

In our Chapter 2 discussion of language, we confined our attention to verbal meaning: to words and expressions made up out of words. But words and sentences are not the only meaningful things we encounter in the information environment. There are all sorts of meaningful items all around. Graphic material too is meaningful. Think for a minute of logos, or the logo-like

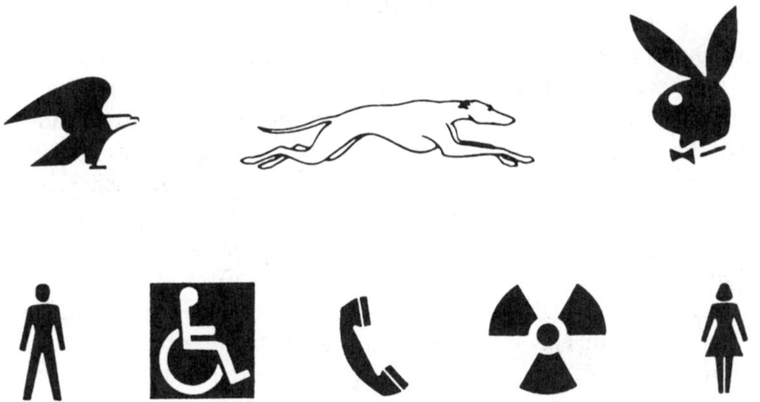

international symbols used in airports and so on to indicate where the baggage claim area and the telephones and the rest rooms are located. Then there is non-verbal audio material: foghorns, car horns, sirens, dial tones, the doorbell, music.

And all of these forms of meaningful material—words, graphics, and sound—are to be found in all sorts of complicated meaningful combinations, both static and in motion, throughout the information environment. Photographs, billboards, bumper stickers, T-shirt designs, the Yellow Pages, radio jingles, the Top Forty, music videos, Muzak, movies, television ads, the half-time show at the Super Bowl, and so on.

A lot of these "messages" are sent to us unsolicited, like junk mail, as a result of what have come to be known as "mass media." In Chapter 2 we suggested that the most basic and essential function of language is interpersonal coordination, or more simply, communication. And we distinguished five more narrowly focused functions under this general heading (Informative, Expressive, Directive, Persuasive, and Performative). All of these functions can be seen to operate in relatively simple settings such as direct face-to-face communication, one-on-one or in small groups. However, it is also interesting to look at the means we have evolved for extending the reach and broadening the scope of communication beyond the limitations of such settings. Over the course of human history we have developed an impressive array of strategies, techniques, and technologies to communicate across great gulfs of time and space and to communicate with massive audiences. These techniques and technologies are what we call "media of communication." For example, writing was developed as a technique for communicating with audiences outside of one's own immediate presence. And print was developed as a technology for distributing written communication to much larger audiences than one could write to individually. As we approach the third millennium, new communications technologies continue to burst upon the scene. But let us now focus on one medium of communication which has been pretty dominant for the last fifty years: television, as a good example of how mass media function in general.

## TELEVISION

Though the technology was already emerging in the 1920s, television really came into its own after World War II. During the 1950s, television quickly became the dominant communications medium in American society and throughout the industrialized world. Viewed as a technology and an information medium, television has always had immense functional potential for human society. It is an immensely flexible medium, able to accommodate information in a wide range of forms, from spoken word, to music, to moving visual imagery, to graphic text, and simultaneously in all manner of combinations. Once programmed, its messages engage the human perceiving subject simultaneously through multiple sense modalities, thus giving television unusually high power to attract and hold attention. With the enhancement of satellite transmission and reception technology, fiber optics and cable, television makes possible the instantaneous transmission and reception of huge quantities of audio-visual information on a global basis. Now an international audience of almost any size can witness a significant event, say an international summit meeting or the Olympic Games, as it is occurring. All of this makes possible a degree of social organization and coordination, on a planetary level, never before possible.

### TELEVISION'S IMPACT ON THOUGHT AND BEHAVIOR

Television's educational potential is likewise immense. Due to television's flexibility almost any subject whatever can be televised in some fashion and conveniently made available to an audience virtually anywhere. And it will accommodate virtually any audio or visual mode of presentation, from typographic, to didactic, to dramatic, to musical, easily and again in virtually any imaginable combination. This makes television probably *the* most flexible and powerful vehicle yet devised for the presentation and reinforcement of instruction at almost any level of sophistication and development, from preschool pre-literacy to the very most advanced. No one questions television's capacity to attract and hold the attention of human observers. And now, with the enhancement of widely available videotape technology, television program material itself, like literature, is open to quite detailed study and analysis on the part not just of the producer, which was always the case, but also the viewer.

Empirical studies confirm the highly plausible idea of a connection between television and the formation of patterns of human thought and behavior: For example, research conducted by James Bryan at Northwestern University has demonstrated that children who watched a five-minute videotape in which the characters donate their prize-winning certificates to charity were influenced by the segment to later do the same. Other researchers have replicated Bryan's work. They have found that children who watch videotapes of people sharing money and candy are also influenced to share. Similarly, in one of a series of studies using *Mr. Rogers' Neighborhood*—a children's television program stressing cooperation, sharing, and friendship—a group of researchers under directors Aletha Huston and Lynette Friedrich-Cofer found that the show, in conjunction with role-playing techniques, succeeded in producing more instances of empathy and helpfulness among children who watched the show than among those who watched shows unrelated to positive social behavior. Programs such as *Lassie, I Love Lucy, The Brady Bunch,* and *Father Knows Best* have been studied in Australia. Segments were designated as either "high" or "neutral" in positive social values. Children who watched "high" segments—which stressed concern for others, sympathy, and task persistence—were found to be more helpful and cooperative after four weeks of such viewing than children who watched the "neutral" segments of these programs. The results of these studies are consistent with a report issued by the National Institute for Mental Health in May 1982 of a consensus among most of the research community that violence on television does lead to aggressive behavior by children and teenagers who watch the programs. Fewer studies have been conducted to discover what, if any, effect television has on the adult viewer. One conducted by Rod Gurney at UCLA studied 183 married couples to see what would happen if husbands were assigned certain shows to watch. After only seven consecutive evenings, the wives (who were the observer-reporters, and who, of course, didn't know what programs the husbands were watching) found that the husbands viewing highly "helpful" programs showed less "hurtful" behavior toward family members. All of this raises a very puzzling question: Why is it, then, that television has over the course of its history, on the whole and with only a few notable exceptions, done such a lousy job in the service of society's pressing educational needs? Consider this brief letter to the writer of an advice column:

> A woman writes that her niece's three-year-old child saw a dog lying in the street after it had been hit by a car. When the niece used the incident to warn her child about the dangers of running out into the street, the child replied "Oh, no! Momma, Wonder Woman would fly down and stop the car."[1]

The fact that the episode recounted involves the impressionable mind of a preschooler speaks volumes about the actual impact of television on how we think and see the world. It is true that as we mature we realize that there is no Wonder Woman to rescue us from life's perils; we grow out of that television fantasy, at least as a literal representation of real life. But television remains a central and deeply influential part of the education process that makes adults out of children. How and what we think, what we value, what role models we follow, what we aspire to, how we view ourselves, other people, and the world—all are influenced by the messages that television programs transmit to viewers. And the portrait of the world television ultimately supplies us is only somewhat less obvious in its distortions and in the inappropriateness of the values it embodies than the world of Wonder Woman.

The question remains how to reconcile television's powerful potential as a teaching tool with the abysmal social lessons it generally teaches. In order to understand television and its role and impact in our culture more deeply we need to view television not only as a technology and an information medium but also as an industry and an institution.

We've all heard the expression "brought to you through the courtesy of . . ." many times on television. Here we are encouraged to understand television as a free entertainment and information service. Entertainment and information is delivered to us free of charge and this service is paid for by Procter and Gamble. From the vantage point of members of the audience (the vantage point most of us occupy) this is no doubt a comfortable way to understand television's institutional role. However it completely misrepresents the economics of the industry. From within the television industry such a description makes no sense at all. Why in the world would Procter and Gamble want to pour money into providing a free entertainment and information service for millions of people? What Procter and Gamble are paying for of course is public attention. What's really going on is that *we* (the audience) are being brought to *them* (the sponsor) by CBS. Viewed in these terms, television's primary function in our culture has been as a tool for harvesting public attention for sale in the public attention market. Television is a commercial medium functioning primarily to assemble audiences and sell them to advertisers. A corollary is that the primary function of television programming and its production is to gather up an audience and hold that audience in place and to maintain in that audience a receptive attitude for the advertiser's message, to maintain what is known in the industry as "buying mood."

This explains first of all why television programming is almost 100 percent entertainment. Even television news and public affairs programming is presented as entertainment, a topic to which we will be returning shortly. Entertainment provides the audience a form of immediate gratification requiring minimal expenditure of energy. Thus it perfectly suits the purpose of holding the audience at tranquil attention. The question remains, however, why does television entertainment embody what is on the whole such an unrealistic portrait of society and inappropriate set of values?

## TELEVISION'S REALITY WARP

George Gerbner, dean of the University of Pennsylvania's Annenberg School of Communications, is perhaps the nation's leading authority on the social impact of television. For some twenty years, from 1967 to 1987, he and his assistants videotaped and thoroughly analyzed some four thousand prime-time programs involving more than sixteen thousand characters. They then drew up multiple-choice questionnaires that offered correct answers about the world at large along with answers that represented what Gerbner saw as misrepresentations and biases of the world according to television. These questions were posed to a wide sampling of citizens of all ages, educational backgrounds, and socioeconomic strata. In every survey the Annenberg team found that heavy viewers of television (those watching more than four hours a day), who make up about one-third of the population, typically chose the television-influenced answers, whereas light viewers (those watching fewer than two hours a day) selected the answers corresponding more closely to actual life. Here's a summary of some of the dimensions of television's warped representation of reality as of 1987:[2]

**Gender:**

1. Male prime-time characters outnumbered females by three to one.
2. Women were usually depicted as weak, passive satellites to powerful, effective men.
3. TV males generally played a variety of roles, whereas females were portrayed as lovers or mothers.
4. Less the 20 percent of TV's married women with children worked outside the home. In real life more than 50 percent did.

**Conclusions:** Television's distortions reinforced stereotypical attitudes and sexism. An Annenberg survey showed that heavy viewers were far more likely than light ones to feel that women should stay at home and leave the running of the country to men.

**Age:**

1. People over 65 were generally underrepresented on TV.
2. Old people were typically portrayed as silly, stubborn, sexually inactive, and eccentric.

**Conclusions:** Again stereotypes were reinforced. Heavy viewers tended to believe that the elderly make up a smaller portion of the population today than two decades previously. In fact old people were and are the fastest-growing age group. Heavy viewers also believed old people to be less healthy today than twenty years previously, whereas the opposite was and continues to be the truth: Old people as a group continue to enjoy healthier lives.

**Race:**

1. The overwhelming number of television blacks were portrayed as employed in subservient, supporting roles.
2. Blacks rarely were portrayed as doing interesting and important things.
3. Blacks were typically presented as accepting minority status as inevitable and even deserved.

**Conclusions:** TV's distortion of blacks reinforced stereotypes and racism. This conclusion was supported by Annenberg surveys that included questions like "Should white people have the right to keep blacks out of their neighborhoods?" and "Should there be laws against marriages between blacks and whites?" Heavy viewers answered "Yes" to these questions far more frequently than light viewers.

**Work:**

1. Only 6 percent to 10 percent of television characters held blue-collar or service jobs, whereas 60 percent of the real workforce were employed in such jobs.
2. TV overrepresented and glamorized the elite occupations (e.g., law, medicine, entertainment, and athletics).

3. TV neglected to portray the occupations that most young people would end up in (e.g., small business and factory work).

**Conclusions:** Heavy viewers generally overstated the proportions of American workers who are physicians, lawyers, entertainers, or athletes. By glamorizing elite occupations, TV set up unrealistic expectations. Doctors and lawyers often find they can't measure up to the idealized image TV projects of them, and young people's occupational aspirations are channeled in unrealistic directions. The problem is especially frustrating for adolescent girls, who are given two conflicting views: the woman as homebody versus the woman as glamorous professional.

**Health:**

1. TV characters survived almost entirely on junk food and consumed alcohol fifteen times as often as water.
2. Despite such a punishing diet, video characters remained slim, healthy, and beautiful.
3. Health professionals typically were portrayed as infallible.
4. TV may be the single most pervasive source of health information.

**Conclusions:** The Annenberg investigators found that heavy TV watchers ate more, drank more, and exercised less than light viewers and had unflinching faith in the curative powers of medical science. TV's idealized image of medical people coupled with its complacency about unhealthy lifestyles left both patients and doctors vulnerable to disappointment, frustration, and even litigation.

**Crime:**

1. On TV, crime raged about ten times more than in real life.
2. Some 55 percent of TV's prime-time characters were involved in violent incidents at least once a week versus less than 1 percent in real life.
3. Video violence imparts lessons in social power: It shows who can do what to whom and get away with it. Usually those at the bottom of the power ladder are portrayed as not getting away with what a white, middle-class American male can.

**Conclusions:** Television breeds fear of victimization. In all demographic groups in every class of neighborhood, heavy viewers overestimated the statistical chances of violence in their own lives. They also harbored an exaggerated distrust of strangers—what Gerbner calls the "mean world syndrome." Forty-six percent of heavy viewers living in cities rated their fear of crime "very serious" as opposed to 26 percent of light viewers. The fear is especially acute among TV's most common victims: women, the elderly, nonwhites, foreigners, and poor citizens. In short, TV gets people to think of themselves as victims.

Among other things, this study belies the glib idea that TV is simply a reflection of the way things are. In many important respects, it is not. Why, then, does Hollywood offer what it does?

Remember that television's primary institutional function has been to assemble audiences for sale to advertisers. Given the high cost of television advertising time, literally hundreds of thousands of dollars for thirty seconds of network prime-time, it makes very good sense now to ask what sort of audiences advertisers want to reach with their messages. Indeed, the television and advertising industries are jointly obsessed with demographics, or various ways of measuring audiences. Prime-time sponsors want to reach the audience that buys most of the consumer products advertised on the tube. This audience happens to be white, middle-class, mostly female, between the ages of eighteen and forty-nine. These are the family-formation and career-building years during which household disposable income and consumer activity reach their peak. Observers like Gerbner believe that TV's scenes and fictional characters are tailored to what programmers perceive to be either this audience's expectations or what advertisers would like this audience's expectations to be. In short, TV creates a world for its best consumers.

Television does more than distort reality; it goes a long way to determine it. If social arrangements are portrayed repetitively in a certain way, and these portrayals are transmitted on a massive scale to the public at large, who come to accept them as realistic, and begin to follow them as patterns and to expect others to follow them as patterns, then social reality comes more and more into line with the televised portrait in certain areas and respects. Life begins to imitate art. In this way television becomes a powerful transmitter of ideology.

"Ideology" refers to the shared assumptions, doctrines, and ways of thinking in terms of which society defines itself. It is often conveyed through symbolic imagery. Such imagery is visible not only throughout television programming, but even more prominently in the carefully composed ads interspersed throughout it. Consider, for example the images of domestic family life in terms of which all sorts of household products are promoted, or the image Ford used in a recent television commercial of a committed and enthusiastic multiracial workforce in an automobile assembly plant—where "Quality Is Job One!"

Ideology is also spread by means of myths, which are stories that teach, explain, and justify the practices and institutions of a given society to people in that society. The "rags to riches" myth, for example, teaches that even the poorest of us can become wealthy and powerful. Myths deal with what is most important to us: love, death, violence, sex, work, success, failure, and so on; and they have a profound impact on consciousness, often influencing our thoughts and actions in subtle and unperceived ways. They manifest themselves most prominently in the plots, the story lines, of television programming, and in the themes and patterns which one finds repeated again and again in plot after plot and story after story.

TV sitcoms, for example, typically present problems which conveniently get resolved within an allotted time, usually thirty minutes. Crime dramas also present situations involving conflict which arrives at resolution at the end of the hour. These generally use a plot formula in which good is pitted against evil. The regular characters are the "good guys" and are associated with conventional morality and law and order. Intruders are evil, thus mirroring and promoting fear of outsiders and fostering group adhesion. The resolution is always in favor of the "good guys," which reinforces a commitment to conventional morality and faith in the system.

We're accustomed to thinking that ideology is transmitted by an elaborate apparatus or set of rituals, for example military pomp and parades, religious rites, political speeches, heady lectures given in university classes, and so on. It is true that ideology is passed on to the masses in these ways. But the centrality of the electronic media in our society has endowed them with the traditional functions of ritual and myth in the transmission of ideology. Watching television is itself a ritual, governed chiefly by the rhythm of television programming, which together with the content of that programming is determined for the immense mass of the viewing audience by an exceedingly tight little group. About one hundred people in Hollywood produce more than 95 percent of all network programming and thereby essentially determine what most Americans will see. Even more important, they thereby effectively determine what most Americans have available as nationally shared experience and vocabulary. In the words of George Gerbner:

> Television is a hidden curriculum for all people. . . . You can turn the set off, but you still live in a world in which vast numbers of people don't turn it off. If you don't get it through the "box" you get it through them.[3]

There have been a few changes in the years since Gerbner's results were published. In recent years a number of highly successful television series *(Hill Street Blues, L.A. Law, Wiseguy, Northern Exposure, NYPD Blue)* have abandoned the conflict/resolution plot formula in favor of one in which conflicts remain unresolved, and carry over from one week to the next, overlapping each other in what are called "arcs." Some of the more traditional myths and ideological themes have been lampooned and certain alternative and even oppositional values have been displayed *(The Simpsons, Beavis and Butthead)* and some traditional taboos, for example against the sympathetic portrayal of gay and lesbian characters in prime-time *(Ellen)*, have been broken. These developments are, however, quite consistent with Gerbner's general findings and with the general account of television's primary institutional role and function, as previously described. "Arcs," for example, serve to reinforce regular patterns of viewing, establishing a more reliable and predictable audience share for a given show on a weekly basis, while shows like *Ellen* delivered a significantly large and demographically desirable new audience: gays and lesbians.

## ADVERTISING

If television's primary function has been to assemble audiences and hold them at tranquil attention for the receipt of the advertiser's message, our discussion of television leads naturally into a discussion of advertising itself. Let us continue to apply our strategy of functional analysis to advertising. What goals or purposes can you identify as served by advertising? We can see right away that advertising performs at least two functions: Looked at from the point of view of the consumer, advertising provides information about available goods and services relevant to making choices in the marketplace. Looked at from the point of view of the advertiser, advertising is designed to motivate and direct consumer behavior, in other words, to persuade consumers to purchase one product rather than another. Perhaps you can identify other functions that advertising performs. If so, can you see ways in which the functions relate to each other? Which functions seem basic? Of the two mentioned so far, the second is arguably the most basic, since it is the function for which advertising is *produced and paid for.* Moreover notice that the two functions mentioned so far are not always compatible. The goal of motivating consumer behavior is not always best served by providing the information the consumer needs to make an informed choice in his own best interests. Awareness of this fact is extremely useful in coming to understand perhaps the two most remarkable peculiarities about advertising as a category of communication.

First is the prevalence in advertising of deceptive techniques, practices, and devices (see Chapter 9). In their attempts to persuade, advertisers often obfuscate, misrepresent, and even lie. This is not, of course, to say that *all* advertising is essentially misleading or dishonest. But, to put the matter tactfully, neither is the widespread use of deception, and con artistry, in advertising accidental.

Second is the strategic attempt to distract critical attention and appeal to emotion. In addition to its efforts to baffle and confuse the consumer's reasoning, advertising also frequently attempts to override reasoning by appealing to emotion. Since the advertiser naturally wants to maximize the consumer's inclination toward the purchase, regardless of the evidence he may have to bring to bear on the consumer's rational deliberations, advertisers frequently resort to psychological appeals. Ads that rely primarily on pitches to wealth, status, power, prestige, security, sex, masculinity, femininity, acceptance, approval, and so on, are offering to sell more than just the product. We wish to be more powerful than we are, to have more prestige than we do, to be more masculine or more feminine, to get more and better sex, and so on. And if we do not in fact wish for these things, the ads are designed and function to encourage us to. Such ads, in short, are calculated to appeal to, and in many cases to engender, a sense of psychological dissatisfaction.

## SEX IN ADVERTISING

Perhaps the best example of such appeals is the increasingly explicit and pervasive use of sexual pitches in ads. Consider the sexual innuendo pulsating in this ad for men's cologne:

*Scene:* An artist's skylit studio. A young man lies nude, the bedsheets in disarray. He awakens to find a tender note on his pillow. the phone rings and he gets up to answer it.

*Woman's Voice:* "You snore."

*Artist [smiling]:* "And you steal the covers."

***More cozy patter between the two. Then a husky-voiced announcer intones:***

"Paco Rabanne. A cologne for men. What is remembered is up to you."

While sex has always been used to sell products, it has never before been used as explicitly in advertising as it is today. And the sexual pitches are by no means confined to products like cologne. The California Avocado Commission supplements its "Love Food from California" recipe ads with a campaign featuring leggy actress Angie Dickinson, sprawled across two pages of some eighteen national magazines to promote the avocado's nutritional value. The copy reads "Would this body lie to you?" Not to be outdone, Dannon Yogurt recently ran an ad featuring a bikini-clad beauty and the message "More nonsense is written on dieting than any other subject—except possibly sex."

Many references to sex in advertising are rather subtle. A reference to sex may be veiled, or implied, or suggested through the use of visual or verbal metaphor, or conveyed symbolically. For example, an ad from the widely circulated Newport cigarette "Alive with Pleasure" campaign features a woman riding the handlebars of a bicycle driven by a man. The main strut of the bike wheel stands vertically beneath her body. Such an image, though it admits of an innocent interpretation, is nevertheless also sexually suggestive. Similarly the ad for the Gold Council below is based on the photographic image of a woman drinking water but is also strongly suggestive of oral sex:

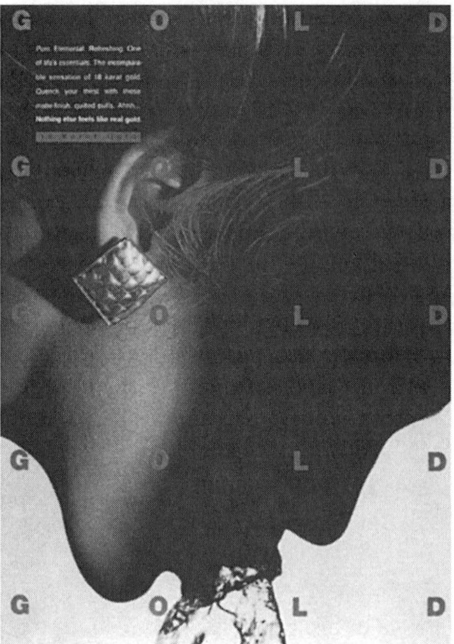


## SUBLIMINAL ADVERTISING

We can't leave the subject of sex in advertising without discussing, at least briefly, the notion of subliminals. A great many consumers are convinced that advertisers regularly employ techniques designed to communicate messages beneath the level of conscious awareness. These messages, many of them of a sexual nature, are supposedly beamed directly into the subconscious where they then go to work on our motivations, and all of this evades our awareness. Author Wilson Bryan Key, perhaps the best known writer on the subject of subliminals, claims:

> It is virtually impossible to pick up a newspaper or magazine, turn on a radio or television set, read a promotional pamphlet or the telephone book, shop through a supermarket without having your subconscious purposely massaged by some monstrously clever artist, photographer, writer or technician.[4]

This is an intriguing idea, and one that appeals to something rather basic in our nature as believers. Yet many of those who have seriously investigated the subject remain skeptical. The debate over subliminals goes back to the late 1950s when an advertising consultant named James Vicary published reports of an experiment in which the words "Eat Popcorn" and "Drink Coke" were repeatedly flashed on movie screens for only a small fraction of a second, well below the threshold of conscious perception. Vicary claimed that Coke sales and popcorn sales increased by 18 percent and 58 percent respectively. Initially these reported findings were taken seriously. So seriously that the Federal Communications Commission and the National Association of Broadcasters, as well as agencies in Australia and Great Britain, formulated policies to ban such techniques. In the years since these results were originally published numerous attempts to verify or replicate them have failed. Eventually, in a 1962 interview with *Advertising Age,* Vicary admitted that the original study was essentially a promotional stunt intended to boost his own struggling business as a marketing consultant. Still, belief in subliminals persists among consumers who take themselves to be market-savvy skeptics. This persistent belief is often supported by arguments which themselves ought to make us skeptical. Psychologist Anthony Pratkanis of the University of California at Santa Cruz writes:

> Instead of the scientific method, those accused of subliminal persuasion (mostly advertisers) are subjected to what can be termed the "witch test." During the Middle Ages, one common test of witchcraft was to tie and bind the accused and throw her into a pond. If she floats, she is a witch. If she drowns, then her innocence is affirmed. Protestations by the accused were taken as further signs of guilt. How do we know that subliminals work and that advertisers use them? As Key notes, advertisers spend a considerable amount of money on communications that contain subliminal messages. Why would they spend such vast sums if subliminal persuasion is ineffective? The fact that these subliminal messages cannot be readily identified or seen and that the advertisers deny their use further demonstrates the craftiness of the advertiser. It appears that the only way that advertisers can prove their innocence, by the logic of the witch test, is to go out of business at the bottom of the pond.[5]

Pratkanis goes on to point out the unfortunate consequences of clinging to the myth of subliminals:

> We live in an age of propaganda; the average American will see approximately seven million advertisements in a lifetime. We provide our citizens with very little education concerning the nature of these persuasive processes. . . . Perhaps the saddest aspect of the

> subliminal affair is that it distracts our attention from more substantive issues. By looking for subliminal influences, we may ignore more powerful, blatant influence tactics employed by advertisers and sales agents.[6]

Though there is much wisdom in Pratkanis's skeptical view, we don't want to represent it as absolutely the last word on the subject. There may yet be reason to wonder about advertising strategies designed to manipulate attention and influence awareness levels in viewers so as to advance an idea while viewer attention is distracted. After all, attention is a variable and subject to differing degrees of concentration and control, as well as to diffusion, distraction, and misdirection. It is therefore possible to deliberately deceive a human perceiver. Think of stage magic, for instance. Might there not be advertising strategies based on similar principles? Here, for example, is an advertising image we find frankly puzzling. What do you think? Can you find a hidden message in this picture? If so do you think it's an example of subliminal advertising?

Courtesy of Round Table Pizza, Inc.

*Hint: Not all subliminal advertising is sexual. Look closely at the part of the logo that looks like a set of medieval heraldic banners.*

The vast array of deceptive and manipulative advertising devices is a subject in itself worthy of an entire book. We would recommend Jeffrey Schrank's *Snap, Crackle and Popular Taste* to anyone interested in pursuing this subject in greater depth.

## NEWS MEDIA

Perhaps the most disturbing of the detectable effects of the nexus of television and advertising is the impact it has apparently had upon journalism, upon the news as it is gathered, reported, and interpreted in our society. Neil Postman, professor of communications at New York University and a media analyst who has taken considerable interest in critical thinking, notes in his book *Amusing Ourselves to Death: Public Discourse in the Age of Show Business* that news and public affairs programming on television has degenerated almost entirely into entertainment, and that more traditional print journalism is being dragged along in the same direction. One look at a typical national or local newscast will quickly confirm Postman's observations that television news consists almost entirely of discontinuous fragments presented in an essentially entertaining format and that it effectively trivializes most of what it touches. In case this assessment sounds uninformed or too harsh, Postman goes on to quote from Robert MacNeil, former executive editor and co-anchor of the *MacNeil-Lehrer News Hour* who writes that the essential idea in television news production is:

> to keep everything brief, not to strain the attention of anyone but instead to provide constant stimulation through variety, novelty, action, and movement. You are required to pay attention to no concept, no character, and no problem for more than a few seconds at a time. [The assumptions controlling the production are] that bite-sized is best, that complexity must be avoided, that nuances are dispensable, that qualifications impede the simple message, that visual stimulation is a substitute for thought, and that verbal precision is an anachronism.

Of course, there are occasional exceptions to this general rule: Once in a while a probing documentary, or serious dramatic presentation (such as the telecast of Stephen Spielberg's movie *Schindler's List*) or a genuine piece of tough investigative journalism on *60 Minutes.* But, such exceptions tend to prove the rule.

Assuming this account to be a fair assessment of the general trend in television journalism, what evidence is there of a similar tendency in journalism as a whole? Postman notes the emergence of *USA Today* and its rapid rise in its first two years of publication to the position of the nation's third largest daily newspaper. Its stories are strikingly short, frequently no longer than a single paragraph, approximating the level of demand on reader attention typical of television. Its design is colorful and emphasizes graphics over verbal text. It is even sold on the streets through dispensers which resemble television sets. The successful *USA Today* format has begun to penetrate the approach of more traditional dailies, chiefly local and regional dailies, particularly as they have become absorbed into larger organizations like the New York Times Company and undergone editorial and management changes. Now we turn to some additional evidence of an even more interesting sort.

## NEWSWORTHINESS

Since 1976, students of communications studies at Sonoma State University have conducted an annual national research project called Project Censored to explore and publicize significant underreported news stories. Each year, researchers in a seminar on mass media select twenty-five stories from a list of several hundred stories nominated by journalists, educators, librarians, and the general public as stories of national significance that failed to get due coverage in the mainstream of both print and broadcast journalism. These stories are then reviewed by a panel of professional journalists and media analysts to determine the ten best censored stories of the year.

In 1985, the top ten included the massive secret aerial war being waged under U.S. Defense Department supervision against the civilian population of El Salvador, officially a U.S. ally in Central America, a siege involving the heaviest aerial bombardment ever seen in the Western Hemisphere; well-documented studies of over half a million tons of hazardous waste, including radioactive wastes and nerve gas, produced by the American military establishment and thus exempt from Environmental Protection Agency regulation; and something the news media must certainly have been aware of, a virtual explosion of media mergers paving the way for an international information monopoly.

In 1986, the top ten included stories on high-level efforts to restrict the flow of information by eliminating, classifying, and privatizing government documents; a new official government "disinformation" program permitting the government to release deliberately false, incomplete, and misleading information; organized official harassment of political opponents of Reagan administration policies in Central America; and a story that eventually, about a year later, did hit the big time: Contragate.

In 1987, the top ten included further information on the growing media monopoly, indicating that the number of corporations controlling over half of the media business in the U.S. had dropped from fifty (in 1983) to twenty-nine; the CIA/Contra/Drug connection; and the role of George Bush in the Iranian arms deal.

In the years 1988 through 1996, the top ten list of stories has included new evidence (from the diaries of Oliver North) linking George Bush to the Iran-contra scandal from its start (1990), exposing a history of questionable activities on Bush's part dating from his role as a CIA "asset" in 1963 to his presidential election campaign's connection with a network of Nazi and fascist affiliates (1988), and exposing the Bush family's elaborate array of conflicts of interest (1991); an expose of the Pentagon's secret billion-dollar "Black Budget," which continues to shield massive military spending from public scrutiny even in the post–cold war period (1990 and 1992); documentation of the number of U.S. casualties and the level of civilian damage caused in the Gulf War (1991); analysis of the costs of the savings and loan bailout and of the distribution of those costs, an investigation linking the CIA and organized crime with the savings and loan crisis, as well as coverage of a similar financial crisis looming in the banking industry (1990); and a story the media must certainly have been fully aware of, the deterioration of traditional hard-nosed American journalism due to the wholesale sellout of the American free press to conglomerate corporate interests (1989 and 1992, see more on this one below).

All of these stories were, of course, reported in American media sources. The point is that they received nowhere near the attention they each inherently deserved in mainstream media coverage. They were essentially marginalized, a fact that can hardly be accounted for in terms of the unavailability of information. Nor can the marginalization of coverage of such stories be accounted for in terms of the traditional understanding of the journalist's "watchdog" function, for these are precisely the kind of stories that watchdog journalism would be expected to seize upon. Nor can the media's silence on these issues be accounted for in terms of limitations on mainstream time and space. This last point is demonstrated by comparison with a parallel list of the top ten "junk food news" stories of the year.

Junk food journalism creates "news" out of sensationalized trivia. In 1984 the biggest junk food news story of the year was literally a junk food item: Clara Peller's "where's the beef?" ad campaign, to which the mainstream media devoted the equivalent of over $100 million worth of free publicity. In 1985 top honors went to another junk food item: the introduction of a new soft-drink formula, the "new, old, classic, and cherry Coke" story. Just how big was that story? It was so big that a year later Coca-Cola took out full-page ads commemorating the media event which read in part:

> On April 22, 1985, the American public witnessed an event so important, it was covered in every newspaper, and on every TV newscast from Bangor to Big Sur!

In 1986 precious hours and pages of mainstream media attention were devoted to such crucial items as the seventy-fifth anniversary of the Oreo Cookie, the fifteenth anniversary of Walt Disney World, and Imelda Marcos's three thousand pairs of shoes. In 1987, with the nation's economy, administration, and foreign policy all in ruinous disarray, the mainstream media spent months focused on the saga of Jim and Tammy Bakker, on the basis of a seven-year-old, fifteen-minute tryst. In 1992 public attention was massively diverted by Johnny Carson's final days as host of the *Tonight Show,* the U.S. Olympic basketball "Dream Team," the election of the Elvis stamp, and the domestic problems of Mia Farrow and Woody Allen and the Prince and Princess of Wales.

All of this raises the important question: How is the "newsworthiness" of a story determined? The resources of all news organizations, even the really big ones, are finite. There are only so many reporters to send out on assignment. There are only so many camera crews. A news organization, whether in print or broadcasting, must allocate a finite quantity of space or time to the news of the day. There is always much more going on in the world, in the nation, in a city, on any given day than can be covered in the news section of the daily paper or in a half-hour newscast. Decisions have to be made as to what is worth covering, and how much coverage a given story deserves, as well as how prominent the coverage should be. What eventually gets reported as news reflects the judgments of newsworthiness made by those who report and edit it? What are the factors that influence these judgments? What factors ought to influence them?

In theory these judgments *ought* properly to reflect the role of a free press in a democratic society. In theory a democracy is a system of government in which the power is held collectively by the people and distributed equally among them as citizens. Thomas Jefferson theorized that in order for a democracy to work, the citizens need to be adequately informed in order to exercise power wisely. Furthermore they need a forum in which ideas can freely compete with one another for public support in vigorous and open debate. In addition they need an effective means of monitoring those in government who are entrusted with decision-making authority, so as to keep them honest and accountable. And they need means of organizing effectively among themselves so as to achieve and exercise power. A free press is therefore guaranteed under the First Amendment in the Bill of Rights in order to meet these needs.

Not surprisingly, the behavior of the press is frequently explained and defended, when it comes under attack, by appeal to this theoretical framework. Thus columnist Anthony Lewis writes in response to charges that the press has become "too adversarial" in its relations with government officials and too powerful and independent for its own good:

> The press is protected by the 1st Amendment not for its own sake but to enable a free political system to operate. In the end the concern is not for the reporter or the editor but

> for the citizen. . . . What's at stake when we speak of Freedom of the Press is the freedom to perform a function on behalf of the polity. . . . By enabling the public to assert meaningful control over the political process the press performs a crucial function in effecting the societal purpose of the 1st Amendment. Therefore a cantankerous press, an obstinate press, a ubiquitous press must be suffered by those in authority in order to preserve the even greater values of freedom of expression, and the right of the people to know.

But evidently some of the factors which influence judgments of newsworthiness are at odds with this traditional and idealistic conception of journalism's democratic watchdog function. One important factor we have already mentioned. Television's primary function as a device for harvesting tranquilized public attention for sale to advertisers explains the predominance of entertainment values in television programming generally and so also in television news. We will have more to say about this as an influential factor shortly. But by itself this only partly explains the behavior of the press as a whole.

## CONCENTRATED CORPORATE CONTROL

Another factor has to do with the corporate nature and concentration of ownership of the news media. As A. J. Liebling said, "Freedom of the press is guaranteed only to those who own one." But owning a newspaper is no longer as simple and straightforward as it was in Benjamin Franklin's day, when the First Amendment was written. Getting into business as a newspaper publisher can no longer be usefully compared to setting up shop as a silversmith. Nowadays the news business is big business. Very big. During the industrial expansion of the nineteenth century, so-called "economies of scale" took effect in many areas of enterprise, including journalism. This meant that the capital costs of acquiring, maintaining, and operating a large industrialized printing press, and the associated need to reach a more and more massive audience, rose by several orders of magnitude. In this business climate large and powerful business entities have been able to survive and flourish and have come increasingly to dominate the news business, while local, small independent operations have become increasingly marginalized. As these trends have progressed, concentration of ownership and control has become a fact of life not only within the newspaper industry, where newspaper chains have gobbled up local independents, but across the entire spectrum of communications. These trends have been studied and documented by media scholar Ben Bagdikian, a Pulitzer Prize–winning journalist and former dean of the University of California Graduate School of Journalism. In a 1989 update of this study he writes:

> A handful of mammoth private organizations have begun to dominate the world's mass media. Most of them confidently announce that by the 1990s they—five to ten corporate giants—will control most of the world's important newspapers, magazines, books, broadcast stations, movies, recordings and videocassettes. Moreover, each of these planetary corporations plans to gather under its control every step in the information process, from creation of "the product" to all the various means by which modern technology delivers media messages to the public. "The product" is news, information, ideas, entertainment and popular culture; the public is the whole world.[7]

How does the corporate nature of ownership affect the behavior of the news media? One of the most profound yet subtle things that happens is that individual judgment gets subordinated to the needs and agenda of the organization. A business organization, a corporation for example, behaves according to its own inherent logic, which derives from its survival imperatives, such as the need to generate surplus value (the profit imperative) and the need to expand (the growth imperative) and the need to win (the competitive imperative). Individual professional survival and success within such an organization is tied to one's contribution to the organization's survival and success. As a journalist one's judgments of newsworthiness come to reflect the needs of the organization within which one is employed. These needs are not essentially incompatible with the requirements of a healthy democratic process, but they are certainly not identical and don't always coincide with them either. And of course it remains true that organizations doing business in a democracy must maintain at least the appearances of good corporate citizenship in order to succeed. Thus quotes like the one above from Anthony Lewis. But where the news organization's business imperatives diverge from or conflict with the ideals of journalism in democratic theory, often enough the result is so much the worse for news judgment and for democracy.

## ECONOMY, EFFICIENCY, SPACE, AND TIME

The news media operate under the economic and technological constraints that typify other mass-production processes. As a result efficiency of operations emerges as a key value in news judgment. To appreciate this we need only consider the mountain of material made available to a news medium (primarily by its wire services) and the daily scramble to reduce it to usable size.

Editors work within such structural constraints as the size of the "news hole." What is the "news hole"? Well, start with the total number of column inches in the entire paper. Some of these column inches are already committed to certain regular features: the editorial column, letters to the editor, regular syndicated columns, the classified ads, the funnies, the sports and entertainment sections, the stock quotations. A good portion of what's left is sold as advertising space. Add all that up and what's left is the "news hole." The editor's job then is not so much one of making the newspaper conform to the stories of the day as it is one of fitting the stories of the day into the space allotted.

Decisions about which stories to run and how much coverage to give them occur under constant and intense deadline pressure. Editors regularly make split-second decisions regarding comparative newsworthiness, whether of facts to be included in a story that might be too long or of stories competing for limited space or time. The same applies to decisions about the relative prominence given to individual stories. Will they go on the front page or in a less important place? Will they be given a couple of paragraphs or several columns? These decisions are made with little time for deliberation. In fact, editors never see all the stories of the day before they make their decisions. Efficiency of operations dictates an editorial decision-making process that begins well before editors know what all the news reports will look like. Among other things this means that the later the news the less chance it generally has of being included. On a given day an editor may scan five times more words in five times more individual stories than there is space for. On a large metropolitan daily (circulation over 350,000) an editor may see ten times more words and seven times more stories than we will ever see. This sort of pressure is even more intense in television news.

## RATINGS AND DEMOGRAPHICS

A television station makes money by servicing advertisers—by assembling the audience the advertiser wishes to address with commercial messages. The same is true with radio. Exceptions must be made for "public" television and radio, which depend on viewer or listener support for a portion of their operating budgets. But even in public broadcasting the influence of corporate "underwriting" (a euphemism for advertising) is unmistakable and significant. A newspaper or magazine makes money in several ways. It sells subscriptions, it sells individual copies, and it also sells advertising space. The influence of advertising is pervasive throughout the news media. But it is only one aspect of the broader category of "market forces" which shape news judgment.

Audience size is an obvious and central market consideration. Audience size is directly related to the survival and success of a news organization whose revenue is derived from subscriptions or single copy sales. Audience size is indirectly, but no less importantly, related to the survival and success of a news organization whose support derives from advertising, for the obvious reason that advertisers are interested in reaching large audiences—generally speaking, the larger the better. Where several news organizations compete for the same audience, as for example happens when several television stations broadcast within the same city or geographical area, we speak of a "media market" and of "market share." Performance is measured according to how large a percentage of the total potential audience a given organization attracts. Such measurements are called "ratings" and they are one of the bases upon which advertising "rates" are set. The larger the market and the greater the market share, the more attractive and valuable the service is as a vehicle for advertising, and therefore the higher the rate the organization can charge to carry the advertiser's message.

How do considerations of audience size affect news judgment? To take a rather obvious example, consider the amount of coverage devoted to Great Britain's royal family. Since Great Britain is still a constitutional monarchy the argument can be made that in Great Britain the royal family's marital problems are legitimately newsworthy because they have potentially far-reaching constitutional implications. But this can't be used to explain the extent of the coverage in America. The explanation is rather simple and straightforward. When Princess Diana's face is on the cover of *People* magazine, single-copy sales shoot up dramatically, even since her death. The simple fact is that celebrity sells magazines. So celebrities, dead or alive, get coverage.

Advertisers are interested not only in the size of the audience they reach with their messages. They are also interested in many other variables about the audience. They are interested in those characteristics, such as age, gender, occupation, average annual disposable income, and so on, which are relevant to marketing and marketing strategy. Advertisers are more interested in reaching an audience of likely consumers of their products and less interested in reaching audiences unlikely to consume them. The manufacturer of shaving cream wants to reach an audience of men. The manufacturer of tampons is more interested in reaching an audience of women. The manufacturers of disposable diapers want to reach households with young children rather than an audience of college-aged singles or elderly retirees. Airlines want to reach travelers. Jenny Craig wants to reach people who are insecure about their weight and body image. And so on. As a consequence, audiences are carefully analyzed according to characteristics and differences which pertain to marketing strategy. Such measurements are called audience "demographics." To illustrate just how detailed these measurements can be, *Time* magazine's advertising rate card includes a "Student/Educator" rate (an advertiser may buy space in just those copies sent to readers who have subscribed at the "student/educator" subscription rate); a rate for "High Income ZIP Code Areas" (an advertiser may buy space in those copies which are to be delivered to subscribers living in high income communities); and a rate for "Ultra High Income Professional/Managerial Households." Needless to say, these and other specialized services to the advertiser come at a substantial price. And just as with increased market share, improved demographics also contribute to the success of the organization.

How do audience demographics affect news judgment? Well, different audience segments are interested in different kinds of stories. Those stories judged likely to appeal to the broadest range of the most profitable demographic categories are likely also to be judged more newsworthy than less demographically attractive stories. Stories primarily of interest to disenfranchised inner-city communities with relatively little significant purchasing power are less frequently and less prominently covered regardless of their inherent newsworthiness than stories primarily of interest to wealthier communities. The riots which broke out in West Los Angeles following the announcement of the verdicts in the Rodney King beating case became instant national news, attracting live remote network coverage, in part because such an urban uprising is of interest not simply to those living in the immediate vicinity of the violence. But when, two weeks later, rival gangs the Crips and the Bloods signed a truce and issued a joint manifesto pledging to exercise a peaceful leadership role in rebuilding and revitalizing inner-city neighborhoods as well as ridding them of drug traffic and violence, through programs of tree planting, cleanup, painting and lighting, and so on, the story got no coverage at all in the mainstream press. (Only Arsenio Hall seemed interested in bringing a discussion of these proposals to a wider audience through the medium of his late-night variety and talk show.)

## DRAMA

Television, including television news, is part of the entertainment industry. This helps to explain the importance of narrativity (over information). A narrative is a composition that tells a story. Stories are entertaining. They have drama and emotional appeal. Straight information by comparison comes across as "dry and lifeless." Material which lends itself to narrative treatment is therefore generally more likely to receive coverage than material which does not. Thus, for example, the tendency to focus on the personal and especially the scandalous, often at the expense of attention to policy issues, in political coverage. It also helps explain the media's fascination with trauma and disaster. Generally speaking, the more dramatic the story the better. Trauma and disaster make for high drama. Note how frequently disaster coverage is composed and constructed to heighten drama by amplifying an event's dramatic dimensions. In sudden unexpected disasters like the bombings of the World Trade Center in 1993 and the Alfred P. Murrah Federal Building in Oklahoma City in 1996 there is the element of *surprise,* a powerful dramatic device. Small wonder that earthquakes, hurricanes, plane wrecks, terrorist attacks, and the like make such gripping news. An equally powerful dramatic device is *suspense.* Again note how frequently coverage is composed and constructed so as to build suspense. For example, almost exactly a year after the 1992 Los Angeles riots, which had broken out in response to the acquittal of police officers accused of using excessive force in the beating of Rodney King, four of these same officers were again on trial, this time in federal court, accused of deliberately violating Rodney King's civil rights. As the trial reached its conclusion and the jury began its deliberations, coverage of the case naturally intensified. It also intensified its focus on the possibility of more rioting and the readiness of the police and national guard to respond to that eventuality.

## TECHNOLOGY AND THE VISUAL

In the television age a similar emphasis on the visual has emerged. This is easy to understand given television's crucial visual dimension. An event or story with visual impact makes better television material and hence better television news material than one which lacks a powerful visual dimension. The space shuttle disaster for example, or the collapse of sections of the San Francisco Bay Bridge and the Cypress Freeway in the Loma Prieta earthquake, were extremely powerful visually. So powerful that a single short video clip of a few seconds in duration can be used over and over again and continue to attract and hold viewer interest. It would be quite difficult to achieve the same effect with a story about, say, a cancer cluster and the gradual buildup of groundwater pollution.

Evolving technology with all its capabilities and limitations has played a remarkably strong and central role in shaping news coverage throughout the history of television. The "action-cam" or minicam is a good example. When it first appeared as a regular tool of TV news coverage around 1975, this portable, hand-held camera was hailed by many news directors as the device that would free journalism from the dreary "talking heads" era. But the short history of the action-cam reveals a somewhat different pattern. Because no one can predict when a story will actually break, much of the so-called on-the-scene coverage consists of prearranged, choreographed, and cliched "photo opportunities," or reporters standing at the scene in the aftermath of some significant event.

But more important, it is the action-cam itself and not the intrinsic value of the day's stories that often sets the nightly news agenda. Here's how Walter Jacobson, co-anchor of WBBM-TV's successful newscast in Chicago, described the process in 1982:

> The whole newscast is dictated by what the action-cam can do. We put stories on the air that are not worth anything. . . . Examples? All right. A 22-year-old man and his girlfriend are in a boat on Lake Michigan near the shore. It's a windy day and their boat capsizes. They're all right, but the Coast Guard tows the boat in. We pick up the Coast Guard call on our squawk box. We send an action-cam crew racing out to the lake. And we do a live shot: "Patrol boat bringing in sunken boat at this moment!" My feeling is, what the hell does the story mean? It doesn't help the viewer get through the city's system. It doesn't help him exercise his franchise as a voter. It doesn't really tell him anything he needs to know. It drives me nuts.[8]

Technology has of course changed considerably in the intervening years. But its role in shaping the news is still strong. Helicopter-based camera crews originally deployed to cover traffic conditions in the Los Angeles area accidentally resulted in some dramatic airborne news footage of high-speed car chases which have now become a regular feature of television news. What was most interesting and revealing about these stories—which in some cases ran at six and again at eleven and were also used to promote both the evening and late-night newscasts—was that they were not really about the fugitive, his alleged crime, or the disposition of his case. The typical story is that the Chopper Five camera crew had obtained some great footage of a car chase. This small but embarrassing craze in California local coverage went on until eventually the chopper-based camera crews began getting in the way of police helicopters. Here again though we can see technology driving news judgment.

Taken together, all of the above factors add up to a pattern of distortion in news coverage which reflects not so much the personal agendas of reporters and editors but the organizational imperatives of the news industry. The significance of this pattern goes deeper than the question of efficient use of time and resources. It goes to the heart of the mission and function of the news. This was one of the lessons of the NBC/GM fiasco in 1992 and 1993, a scandal which eventually led to the resignation of several top officials at NBC including then head of the News Division, Michael Gartner. NBC News admitted that its November 17, 1992, *Dateline NBC* exposé of dangerous design flaws in General Motors pickup trucks was produced by means of a rigged "crash test" involving mounted detonators designed to trigger a fiery explosion on impact. Our perceptions and understandings of our society's problems and prospects reflect the information we have access to. To the extent that we rely on news media for this information our perceptions and understandings of our society and its affairs depend on their performance. Where that performance is distorted and flawed, so will be our understanding. When the mission and function of the news are completely compromised, the integrity of journalism as a profession is destroyed.

## ANALYSIS AND INTERPRETATION

As important as what gets coverage and what doesn't is the "spin" that's put on what does. "Spin" is newspeak for "interpretation," an essential characteristic of all news. News is always presented in narrative form, as a "story." Journalism is essentially a kind of story-telling. And it is impossible to tell a story without engaging in interpretation. As you reflect on this, notice that the news is not presented to us as raw uninterpreted information. It is analyzed and interpreted for us, by reporters, editors, news analysts, commentators, pundits. And these interpretations play a very deep and significant role in shaping our understandings of the news and of the events covered in the news. So important are these interpretations in the scheme of things that people who are in the news a lot often hire expert specialists (media consultants—called "spin doctors") to help with "spin control." As consumers of news it's equally important that we try to understand spin and learn how to handle it critically.

### OBJECTIVITY, NEUTRALITY, BALANCE, AND BIAS

It would be nice if there were a simple way to identify and critique the interpretive dimensions of the news. Unfortunately there isn't. The tool most widely used for this purpose in recent discussions of press performance is the concept of "bias." But the concept of bias is not yet well enough defined to be of any practical use. To appreciate this consider how the concept is used by rival media watch organizations. On the one hand the group Fairness and Accuracy in Reporting (FAIR) publishes a bimonthly newsletter entitled *Extra* "in an effort to correct bias and imbalance" in national media coverage. Typically this consists in criticisms of the press as biased against the left side of the political spectrum. The editors of *Extra* have published a book entitled *Unreliable Sources: A Guide to Detecting Bias in News Media.* On the other hand the Media Research Center (MRC) publishes a monthly newsletter entitled *MediaWatch* to expose and correct what they take to be a pervasive liberal bias in national media coverage. The editors of *MediaWatch* have also published a book. Theirs is entitled *That's the Way It Is(n't): A Reference Guide to Media Bias.*

The term "bias" is used extensively throughout the media criticism published by both groups, but is not defined by either. It is not too difficult to extrapolate what either group means by the term "bias" from the criticism each group publishes. "Biased coverage" means something like "coverage which departs from professional standards or norms of objectivity, or balance, and neutrality." But the fact that they regularly attack the very same coverage, one group claiming that the coverage is biased in one direction while the other claims that the coverage is biased in the opposite direction, poses the problem of what independent standards or norms we can appeal to in order to identify and measure the direction and degree of "bias." It begins to look like each group measures press performance according to its own set of standards, and "bias" ends up meaning "a spin we disagree with." Professional journalists find this sort of disagreement convenient. Editors even use it to show how *un*biased their coverage is, based on the theory that if you're getting criticized from both directions you must be pretty well balanced.

Where can we look to find independent professional standards or norms of objectivity, or neutrality, or balance? Just as with judgments of newsworthiness we might begin with the role of a free press in a democratic society. As we noted earlier, one of the central functions of a free press in a democratic society is to provide the citizens a forum in which ideas can freely compete with one another for public support in vigorous and open debate. From this we can begin to see how professional standards of objectivity, neutrality, and balance might be derived and also how they have evolved.

One way to facilitate an open forum is for the press to accommodate a wide variety of partisan voices, each free to articulate and advocate its own position on the issues of the day as vigorously as it can and in whatever terms it chooses. Suppose every city had as many newspapers as there are significant distinct perspectives—a conservative newspaper, a liberal newspaper, a libertarian newspaper, a socialist newspaper, a communist newspaper, a radical feminist newspaper, a labor newspaper, a fundamentalist Christian newspaper, and so on. On this supposition the society would have an opportunity to witness and to participate in vigorous and open debate and all ideas would have access to the arena of debate. We could speak of a "free marketplace of ideas." In some ways this reflects what the American press was like in the early post-colonial period and well into the nineteenth century. The number of newspapers per capita was much higher than it is now and the variety of viewpoints represented in those newspapers was also wider. Notice that there's no need in such circumstances to criticize a given newspaper for having a conservative bias (or a liberal bias or a feminist bias or whatever). One would expect a given newspaper to stand for something, and other newspapers to stand for something else. Newspapers are expected to advocate ideas—to argue against each other, and so "bias" is not a problem.

As we noted earlier, the news business has come a long way since Ben Franklin's day. As large corporate entities have come increasingly to dominate the news business, while small independent operations have become increasingly marginalized, as more and more massive audiences have been assembled nationally and now globally with the advent of new global communications technologies, the model of a contentious marketplace of ideas animated by numerous distinctive partisan voices arguing against each other has gradually been replaced by a blander and more monolithic model in which the press seems to speak with a single voice. It hardly matters whether one is watching Dan Rather or Peter Jennings or Jim Lehrer or Bernard Shaw. The coverage becomes more and more indistinguishable. As these trends have progressed, a new set of professional values has arisen in journalism. Coverage is now evaluated in terms of "objectivity," "balance," and "neutrality." The voice of the press must now be "objective," "balanced," "neutral," or at least *appear* to be. In terms of democratic theory, these news values, to the extent they can be clarified at all, are degenerate. They are much less suitable to the functions of a free press in a democratic society than the earlier model in which the problem of bias doesn't even arise.

**OBJECTIVITY** Objectivity has been honored as a news value by American journalists ever since Adolph S. Ochs took on the languishing *New York Times* in 1896 and sought to rid it of any signs of bias on the part of his reporters, his editors, or himself. As a news value, objectivity is derived from the subjective/objective dichotomy. What is "subjective" is inner and private, and may vary from person to person. What is "objective" is what's "out there" and public, available to other perceivers. Thus any event which takes place in front of several witnesses may be experienced differently by each of the witnesses. The event is "objective," but the experience of it is "subjective." To be absolutely objective a reporter would have to refrain completely from commenting on or interpreting or introducing any private subjective element into a report of the event, and simply "let the facts speak for themselves." This understanding of objectivity is what underlies the distinction between editorializing and straight reporting, which is supposed to be reflected in the difference between the editorial and opinion pages of the newspaper and the news sections.

The problem with this is that understood in this way, absolute objectivity is unattainable. Strictly speaking it is impossible to report anything without introducing at least some subjective interpretive elements. The facts don't "speak for themselves," which is why there are reporters in the first place. Consider for example how an event might be reported. Suppose that you are witness to a convenience store robbery. You're standing in the check-out line when all of a sudden you become aware that three people ahead of you is someone with a gun and the clerk is filling a shopping bag with cash. The next few seconds seem to take forever, but you try to observe as much and as unobtrusively as possible. Now the police have arrived and you're about to be interviewed as a witness. What are "the facts"? What was the gunman wearing? It was a pro-sports windbreaker. Green. You're certain about this. So are all the other witnesses. Shall we say that this is a fact? Perhaps so. Are you being "objective"? Or does your account contain elements of your private experience of the event? Well, obviously your account contains elements of your private experience of the event. So do the accounts given by each of the other witnesses. So does any report of any event. That's the point. You can't get rid of the subjective element. And so, if the interpretive element is identified with the subjective, you can't get rid of the interpretive element either. Was the jacket the gunman was wearing a Celtics jacket or a Jets jacket? Suppose you thought it was a Celtics jacket, but two other witnesses thought it was a Jets jacket. Now a subjective element in your account comes front and center, because it has come into conflict with some equally subjective element in some other witness's account.

One of the lessons we can learn from this is that the best that can be achieved in reporting is *relative* objectivity. All reporting involves at least some subjective interpretive elements, and these are inevitably subject to challenge and criticism as not being completely objective. This should not be taken as cause for alarm because, as we pointed out a moment ago, in this strict and absolute sense, objectivity is unattainable. However, there is another equally important lesson to consider: What passes for objectivity is what goes unchallenged. This *should* be taken as cause for alarm because it indicates the misleading dimensions of the ideal of objectivity itself—the ways in which (ostensible) objectivity as a news value results in distortions in news coverage and in our understandings of news coverage. Where there is no disagreement, or where disagreement is effectively suppressed, we may get the *impression* of objectivity. When Peter Jennings, Tom Brokaw, and Dan Rather all report the same story in much the same terms on a given day, we may get the impression that the substance of these reports is objectively the case simply from the fact that the reports don't substantially differ. We may fail to notice, and thus also to critically evaluate, the interpretive elements of the coverage where they coincide and reinforce each other simply because they coincide and reinforce each other. We may think we're getting the story straight, with no spin at all. More likely, what we're getting is the "establishment spin," which is arguably the most subtle and dangerous spin of all.

In addition to this general danger, some of the specific things reporters and editors do in the name of objectivity have the effect of distorting coverage and interfering with the press's mission of facilitating vigorous and open debate among an informed citizenry. For instance, "objective" reporting tends to foster mere *acquaintance with* things, rather than *understanding of* them. For example we may be acquainted with the parliamentary system of government; that is, we've heard of it. It's the kind of government they have in some countries like, um, Britain and Canada, right? At the same time, we may have little or no knowledge about how a parliamentary system of government operates: what makes it different from a democratic republic; how, when, and where it originated; and so on. Thus we have acquaintance with the parliamentary system but not very much understanding of it. Acquaintance with things tends to be concrete and descriptive and, most important, superficial. To move along the continuum of ways of knowing from mere acquaintance toward deeper understanding requires that items of information be placed in a meaningful context, related to other items of information which are necessary in order to grasp their significance. And this requires interpretation.

In the routine practice of journalism as it has evolved, the sort of reporting required to facilitate in-depth understanding is taken to violate the norm of objectivity. Accordingly, for most reporters the truthful reporting of, say, a speech lies in its being accurate regarding the spelling of the speaker's name, what the speaker said, the size of the audience, the audience's responses, and other descriptive details. The reporter is not expected to comment on the reasonableness or truthfulness of the speaker's assertions, even if she has relevant knowledge, even if she knows for certain that the speaker is wrong about this or that factual matter, even if she knows for certain that the speaker is plain lying through his teeth. If the speaker's assertions have been publicly contradicted, the reporter may report that, but otherwise the reporter is expected to keep her own input out. Otherwise the reporter is not being "objective."[9]

By permission of Johnny Hart and Creators Syndicate, Inc.

**BALANCE** Earlier we spoke of a "free marketplace of ideas," in which partisans of any and all positions might participate. In introducing this idea we mentioned no regulations at all. The marketplace was not only unrestricted with regard to access, it was unregulated entirely. You can imagine how under these circumstances certain ideas and orientations might gain an advantage over others. Suppose the partisans of one position are able to shout louder than their opponents, or have a more powerful PA system, or simply outnumber them seven to one, or are better at debate and oratory. Their position will enjoy an advantage, and the other position will be at a disadvantage in the competition for public support. The concept of "balance" has evolved in an attempt to ensure "fairness in the marketplace of ideas," to make it so that none of the ideas or positions contending for public support be placed at an "unfair" disadvantage. The concept of balance can be seen operating in such regulations as the "equal time rules" and the "Fairness Doctrine," incorporated by Congress into the Communications Act. These regulations require that broadcasters make available reasonable opportunity for the discussion of conflicting views on issues of public importance, and that they do so fairly, so that for example if a broadcaster allows one candidate for office to make a statement, other qualified opponents must be granted equal time.

At first glance, the concept of balance seems to make pretty good sense as a means of ensuring fairness in the marketplace of ideas. For example, consider how we might go about setting up a format for a series of presidential debates. What rules will we propose? What rules do we think the participants might reasonably be expected to agree to? What rules do we imagine the listening and viewing audience will understand and appreciate as fair and reasonable? Well, first we might try to identify variables of the format which might confer an advantage to one or another of the participants, for example, length of speaking time. It would be pretty obviously unbalanced and unfair to allow one candidate twice as much speaking time as the other. Thus ordinarily a debate format will require participants to speak and to respond to each other in equal measured intervals. That's balance. And fairness too. Similarly, speaking order can be advantageous or disadvantageous. Someone gets to speak first; someone gets the last word. There are of course advantages (and hence, disadvantages) to each of these positions in the order of presentation. But again it's possible to distribute these advantages in a balanced and equitable way, for instance by alternating positions in the speaking order from time to time.

In a bipartisan debate and where such variables are easy to quantify (as speaking time is), balance is also fairly easy to conceptualize and to measure. In actual practice though things are not quite so simple. What do you do when there are five candidates for office? What about when there are fifteen candidates? What about when some of the candidates represent established parties in the political mainstream and others represent less well established political movements and agendas? We give the Democrats and the Republicans equal time. That's easy. What about the Libertarian Party? Shouldn't they get equal time? What about the Green Party, the Peace and Freedom Party, the Natural Law Party? Should time be allotted on a strictly equal basis, or in proportion to the number of voters registered in a given party? (Maybe the "fringe" parties should get *more* exposure than the two mainstream parties, because just being out there on the fringes is already a disadvantage.) Things get even messier when an independent "third(?) party candidate" like Ross Perot shows up. Even if the concept of balance is still coherent in theory, we can begin to see how difficult it can get to apply it in practice.

This shows the crucial limitation of balance as a news value and as a tool in critiquing news coverage. It invites oversimplification. Though it is a fairly workable idea if what is being covered is a routine electoral contest solidly within the framework and tradition of the two-party system, it becomes crude and clumsy in application to more subtle and complex issues and stories. Suppose what is being covered is something like the savings and loan bailout or welfare reform. It doesn't make any sense to treat this as a bipartisan story or issue. Indeed as this or any other similar story unfolds it is next to impossible to predict how many significant sides there may be to consider. Nor does it make sense to simply treat all sides equally as a matter of principle. Some perspectives on the issue are going to merit greater attention than others. Some for example are going to be better informed than others. Some are likely to be more impartial, detached, and disinterested than others. Deciding which perspectives to include in the coverage, which ones to feature, which ones to lead with, which ones to present for contrast, and how to prioritize them, these are all matters of complex editorial and journalistic judgment. This is not to say that there are no principles appropriate to evaluating or guiding such judgment. It's just that they can't be reduced to some simplistic notion of balance.

**NEUTRALITY** Some commentators like to use the term "neutrality" to describe the standard according to which they measure press performance. What people mean by "neutrality" seems to have more to do with the journalist's attitudes and professional posture than with what the journalist actually says in reporting the story. What they seem to have in mind might best be described as a sort of "Neutrality Principle" understood to function as part of the "professional ethics of journalism." The Neutrality Principle would go something like this: As a human being, and as a citizen, the journalist may be expected to have interests in and views about the stories she covers. But as a professional journalist she is expected to keep these out of play. To allow them to come into play would be unprofessional. To allow one's personal views and interests to enter into one's work as a reporter or editor would be to abuse the power one has as a member of the press to influence public opinion. To use one's position as a professional journalist in order to advance a personal political agenda would, according to the Neutrality Principle, destroy one's professional neutrality, compromise the integrity of the profession, and erode public trust in the press.

As fine as this may sound in principle, as a news value it's arguably even more confusing and misleading than objectivity and balance. First of all, like the concept of balance, it oversimplifies things. Sometimes some of the personal interests and views of the working journalist play a perfectly appropriate and even central role in the journalist's work. For example, suppose an American journalist goes abroad to cover some significant conflict like the pro-democracy demonstrations in Beijing's Tienanmen Square, and in the course of covering the story gets arrested and roughed up by government agents. Or suppose a journalist is taken as a hostage and held for forty days and forty nights somewhere in Beirut. Or suppose a camera crew traveling with a platoon in combat gets captured and taken prisoner along with a number of soldiers. Naturally the journalist will have some personal interest in and views about being arrested and roughed up or taken hostage or held as a prisoner of war, and not just about being so treated as an individual human being but about being so treated in one's professional capacity as a member of the foreign press. Here it would make very little sense to separate the personal from the professional or to insist on such a separation on the part of the working journalist. After all, this is all part of the story. In fact, the actual personal experience of journalists in such circumstances, down to the minute details of their treatment at the hands of their captors, becomes absolutely central to the story.

Even more important, the concept of neutrality in journalism completely misses the point of concern about journalistic spin. The real danger is not that the personal views of individual journalists will be insidiously imposed on the vulnerable reader. There are so many individuals with such a wide range of differing views working in the profession of journalism, that if they were all to freely express their personal views in their coverage, these views would just cancel each other out. Or more accurately, they would reestablish and reinvigorate the "free and unregulated marketplace of ideas" model of journalism we spoke of earlier. We should give the vulnerable reader (ourselves) enough credit to be able to deal intelligently with the kind of diversity of opinion which would be reflected in press coverage if all the journalists just spoke their minds. The real danger is that the views and the agendas of large and powerful institutions—like the government and its various agencies, and the corporations and powerful lobbies, and the mass media organizations themselves—will insinuate themselves into and through the coverage, and come to dominate the coverage, compromising and overwhelming the judgment of individual working journalists in the process. The real danger once again is establishment spin.

In the last analysis, what's wrong with all three of the concepts we've been discussing here is that they each place the onus on the media themselves to, in one way or another, eliminate spin from news coverage. But, as we said earlier, spin is inherent and inevitable; it goes with the territory. We expect too much from the media if we expect them to do our job of critically informing ourselves. We must take the responsibility as readers, listeners, and viewers for critically evaluating the news coverage we absorb. To do this, we need to be able to identify the spin and to ask intelligent questions about it. Questions like "Whose interests are best served by spinning the story in this particular way?" and "What other possible interpretations of events are plausible?" and "Is spinning the story in this particular way likely to move us closer to, or further from, the truth?" To do this, we need also to be aware of the forces that influence news coverage. The same institutional forces (mentioned earlier as influencing judgments of newsworthiness) also influence spin. Market forces, ratings, demographics, the public relations agendas of powerful advertising interests, and other organizational imperatives play a considerable role in determining the analysis and interpretation of the news. No treatment of this topic would be complete, however, without a discussion of news sources and the ways they "use" media for propaganda purposes.

## SOURCES

Powerful, authoritative people are the primary sources of news. To get some idea of the predominance of high public officials as news sources, consider an analysis conducted of the origin of 2,850 domestic and foreign stories that appeared in the *New York Times* and the *Washington Post.* Seventy-eight percent of the stories had public officials as their sources.[10]

By far, the single most valuable public official news source is the president. As George E. Reedy, press secretary to President Lyndon Johnson, pointed out:

> There is no other official of the government who can make a headline story merely by releasing a routine list of his daily activities. There is no other official of the government who can be certain of universal newspaper play by merely releasing a picture of a quiet dinner with boyhood friends. There is no other official who can attract public attention merely by granting an interview consisting of reflections, no matter how banal or mundane, on social trends in fields where he has no expertise and in which his concepts are totally irrelevant to his function as a public servant.[11]

High public officials and those associated with them can always be counted on to supply authoritative and newsworthy information. As a result journalists develop a kind of institutionalized relationship with the most regular sources. There is a regular White House press corps. Similarly reporters are regularly assigned to cover such "beats" as the Pentagon, the United Nations, the Senate and House of Representatives, the Supreme Court. Beat reporters get to know their sources quite well, and develop close working relationships with them. The White House press secretary for example will know many of the members of the White House press corps and be on a mutual first-name basis with them. As a working journalist the cultivation of such close, friendly, working relationships with highly placed sources is an essential means to professional survival and success. For a reporter working in Washington to "lose access" to a source would be a professional setback not only for the individual reporter but for the news organization she represents. Sources understand this all too well. They understand that this provides a powerful set of levers with which to achieve spin control.

No administration in American history has understood these things more deeply or exploited them more effectively than the administration of Ronald Reagan. It is for this reason (not for his command of the English language) that Reagan became known as "the Great Communicator." To this day, there is still a great deal that we can usefully learn about spin control, about the capacity of powerful news sources to override independent journalistic analysis and interpretive judgment in order to influence the news. A few examples from the Reagan years that follow will serve to illustrate the point.

A good example of this occurred in the winter of 1981 when Libyan leader Muammar Quaddafi reportedly sent a "hit team" to the United States to assassinate President Reagan and other high officials in the U.S. government. Even though there was no hard evidence for the suspected plot, the press ran it as a working story, primarily because administration officials, including the president himself, gave it importance and credibility. Running with the story, television and newspapers variously relied on "informed" and "reliable"—though rarely identified—sources at home and abroad to keep this dramatic and sensational story on the front burner of news coverage for at least a month. As a result, between November 25 and Christmas Day, 1981, viewers were told that:

1. The number of hit men being sought was three (ABC), five (CBS), six (ABC), ten (ABC, CBS), twelve (CBS), and thirteen (NBC).
2. The would-be assassins had entered the United States from Canada (ABC, CBS), were in Mexico (NBC).
3. Carlos "the Jackal" was a possible hit team member (CBS, NBC).
4. The personal habits of various hit team members involved wearing cowboy boots and Adidas jogging shoes and smoking English cigarettes.
5. The hit team was composed of three Libyans (ABC, NBC), three Iranians (CBS, NBC), two Iranians (ABC), one East German (NBC, CBS, ABC), one Palestinian (ABC, CBS, NBC), and one Lebanese (ABC, CBS, NBC).
6. One hit team member visited Phoenix, Arizona (ABC).

All this information came from off-camera interviews with sources—"officials," "security officials," "Capitol Hill sources"—unwilling to be identified and thus were introduced by such phrases as "It has been learned . . ." "Sources say . . ." "ABC has learned . . ." and the like. On the evening news of November 26, ABC anchor Frank Reynolds announced it was known that Libyan agents were in this country to assassinate the highest officials of the U.S. government. Neither Reagan, nor CIA Director William Casey, nor Secretary of State Alexander Haig had confirmed this. In fact, William Webster, the head of the FBI, told ABC's Sam Donaldson on January 3, 1982, "We've never confirmed any hard evidence about a hit team inside the United States."[12] And ABC senior correspondent John Scali, who first broadcast reports about the Libyan plot on ABC, insists, "No one ever told me there was hard evidence."[13]

In fact, the only thing the press knew for sure was that security around Reagan and his top aides had been increased and that Reagan had been briefed about a possible plot. That the expressed concern of administration officials was well founded was strictly the opinion of the press. It's entirely possible that Muammar Quaddafi exploited the American press's reliance on "official sources" for information and on television's penchant for the sensational to influence events in the United States. At least that was the way *Time* magazine's David Halevy tried to explain away the growing embarrassment to the press in having run so hard and so far with the story. Halevy was able to check a number of purported hit team names on a Tel Aviv–based computer system listing fifty-five thousand to sixty thousand terrorists and came up empty. His conclusions:

> While the threat was perceived as serious, too few in the American media looked at the possibilities of Quaddafi playing a disinformation game. Send squads to Europe. Send Libyans to the North American continent. Just get the word out. Quaddafi is no madman—he's a shrewd Bedouin who understands the demands of his society, and also how Western society works. Take that supposed voice intercept of Quaddafi threatening Reagan's life. In the Middle East, everybody who ever makes a phone call assumes the call can be intercepted by somebody.[14]

Even more likely, however, is that the episode resulted as part of a disinformation campaign orchestrated by the Reagan administration itself in order to stir up public sentiment against an "official enemy." What is meant by this odd word "disinformation"? "Disinformation" is a technical term in the intelligence community meaning not merely false information, but misleading information—misplaced, irrelevant, fragmentary, and superficial information designed to foster the illusion of understanding while actually leading the recipient astray. Halevy's research is, if anything, even more consistent with the hypothesis of a U.S.-directed campaign than with his own arabesque speculations, which amount in the end to more of the usual and predictable mainstream fare of Quaddafi-bashing.

It may be difficult for us to believe, even in these cynical post-Watergate and Contragate times, that the U.S. government would play such dirty tricks on its own people, that it would subvert the free press, and that committed professional journalists would go along with it. But consider this more recent series of developments in U.S./Libyan affairs: On October 8, 1986, Bernard Kalb, a prominent career journalist (the *New York Times,* CBS, NBC), called a press conference to announce his resignation from the position he then held in the U.S. State Department as the nation's principal foreign policy public relations officer. What were the events that led up to Kalb's resignation? On April 14, 1986, U.S. warplanes bombed Libya in retaliation for what the Reagan administration said was Quaddafi's sponsorship of international terrorism. The Reagan administration continued to attempt to mobilize world opinion in opposition to Libya and Quaddafi by means of what was later exposed as a disinformation campaign, designed to confuse world public opinion and mislead the media. Word was put out that Quaddafi was still supporting terrorism and that another U.S. military "retaliation" was in the works. On August 25 the *Wall Street Journal* reported that "The U.S. and Libya are on a collision course." The story was picked up by the networks and other major media. As the story gained momentum, numerous official briefing officers passed along information—always attributed to anonymous sources like "senior White House officials"—confirming the *Journal*'s story. Then, on October 2 the *Washington Post* published excerpts from an earlier White House memo written by President Reagan's national security advisor, Admiral John Poindexter, which advised a strategy that "combines real and illusionary events—through a disinformation program—with the basic goal of making Quaddafi think that there is a high degree of internal opposition to him within Libya, that his key trusted aides are disloyal, and that the U.S. is about to move against him militarily." This revelation put Kalb in a moral bind. We may presume that Kalb was not privy to the memo prior to its publication, and that he, like many other official briefing officers, was passing along what he thought to be authoritative and responsible information in good faith. That is, until he learned of the memo, at which point he promptly resigned.[15]

This episode demonstrates the extent to which reliance on high officials for information results in managed news; that is, news that the sources cut to fit their own purposes. Because more news occurs than a journalist could begin to cover, news people must rely on surrogate observers—on "briefings"—to acquaint themselves with the day's events. But these sources are continually deciding what information to provide; what details to stress, downplay, or suppress; and when the story should be given to the press, if at all. By the account of journalist Richard Rorchler, "Scores of American newspapers give their readers no hint that the 'news' they are reading has been 'generated', 'leaked', provided not by journalistic legwork and thought but by a government handout which is 'not for attribution.'"[16]

The Reagan administration, again more than any other in American history (with the possible exceptions of the Kennedy and Clinton administrations), understood the importance of imagery, especially visual imagery, in the television age. The Reagan White House team became famous and even ruefully admired within Washington press circles for the care and skill with which they were able to orchestrate the president's public appearances. They developed presidential public appearances into what have now come to be known as "photo-ops" (photo opportunities). The Reagan public relations team's accomplishments and exploits are chronicled by investigative journalist Mark Hertsgaard in his book *On Bended Knee: The Press and the Reagan Presidency.* He writes of a typical case:

> The news media and especially the television networks loved good pictures of the Commander-in-Chief, and the more the better; it was the visual equivalent of "good copy." After Reagan visited the demilitarized zone separating North and South Korea in November 1983 (fresh from his triumph in Grenada), the evening news shows, newspapers and newsweeklies across the country were filled with inspiring photos of the Leader of the Free World, dressed in a flak jacket, staring down the Communists through field glasses. As was their habit whenever Reagan made a foreign trip, [Deputy Chief of Staff] Deaver and his

> aides visited the site in advance, accompanied by representatives of the major networks, to plan the media event down to the smallest detail. "I saw the toe marks for him," Andrea Mitchell of NBC later recalled. . . . "When he didn't stand on his toe mark he was signaled by one of the advance men to move over into the sunshine."[17]

The Reagan team truly appreciated the wisdom in the old saying "One picture is worth a thousand words." In the television age especially this is a powerful insight. As Sam Donaldson of ABC put it, a simple truth about television is that "the eye always predominates over the ear when there is a fundamental clash between the two." Asked about this, Reagan's spin doctors agreed wholeheartedly and one even offered an example:

> Exactly. Oh, exactly. In the 1984 campaign the Defense Department and the Air Force continually wanted us to do a rollout on the B-1 bomber. And of course one of the negatives on Reagan was that he was more likely to get us into a war, so I was always shying away from military kinds of events. But jobs were just as important during the campaign in California, and the B-1 accounted for something like 40,000 jobs in southern California, so I agreed to do a stop at the Rockwell plant in Palmdale. But I said, across the B-1 I want the biggest sign you can make saying "Prepared for Peace." So you never really saw the B-1. All you saw was the President with this big sign behind him.[18]

Taking our cue from these masters of spin control, we repeat, one picture *is* worth a thousand words. The picture mentioned above (and shown below) did indeed appear in newspapers throughout California and across the nation just days before Reagan won reelection in what the news media called a "landslide." Notice how closely the Rockwell corporate logo resembles the Aldermasten peace symbol used in so many antiwar demonstrations.

## THE INTERNET AND THE WORLD WIDE WEB

When the first edition of this book was published in the 1980s, the Internet was not much more than an obscure and geeky experiment. The World Wide Web didn't even exist. Now, it has become the world's largest and fastest growing computer and communications network, a development that has already brought big changes in information access in general, and which promises to bring more and perhaps even bigger changes to come, especially in the practice of research and education. The Internet and World Wide Web are the result of a major revolution in computer technology—and one rather large accident. The revolution was the development of the "personal computer," replacing earlier generations of room-sized mainframe computers and putting computing power onto the individual desks of people at their offices and in their homes. The rather large accident is the Internet itself, which happened as a result of a U.S. Defense Department attempt to construct a computer network that could survive nuclear attack. The idea was to build a network with no center, so that it could continue to function even if any particular portion of it got knocked out. In brief (there are a great many detailed books on the subject now available), the Internet is now a vast and evolving, decentralized network of networks of computers to which individual users may connect, using a personal computer and a telephone line, in order to post or retrieve information.

In many cases, connecting to the Internet seems to be free of charge. We stress "seems to be," because there are always costs involved. But in many cases, these costs are absorbed by some institution, such as a college or university, or a corporation where one works. If you are fortunately situated in an institution which provides Internet access, chances are you can connect "for free." Most people who access the Internet ("users"), however, must connect through an Internet service provider ("ISP"), which functions like the telephone company or cable television service provider, collecting a fee for access privileges. Once connected to the Net, you can gain access to information stored on computers that are literally situated all over the world. And, with a few additional tools and steps, you can also publish/disseminate information to the whole world via the Internet.

It's little wonder that there is so much excitement surrounding the Internet. This is very impressive technology. It literally opens up a "world of information" on any imaginable subject from astronomy to Zen. The world's great libraries can be accessed; government files and databases, too. Detailed up-to-the-minute weather information, celebrity gossip, sports scores, and stock quotations from any part of the world can be obtained, and on and on. So vast and dynamic is this information environment that it has spawned a hugely profitable new industry devoted to maintaining updated Internet databases and constructing "search engines" to assist people with their Internet research.

When you first begin to explore the Internet (or "browse,") and when you get good at it, ("surfing"), one of the things you'll notice fairly quickly is that just about anyone with a computer can publish on the Internet and thereby reach an indefinitely large global audience. Many Internet enthusiasts point to this as an indication of the Internet's democratizing potential. By effectively eliminating barriers to publication, the Internet seems to enhance freedom of speech and expression and freedom of access to information, yet at the same time to raise some of those quality control issues discussed at the beginning of this chapter. If you look up some information about the human genome project in the *New England Journal of Medicine* or the *Journal of the American Medical Association,* you can be confident in the reliability of the information. Why? Because these and other reputable scientific and academic journals are very careful about what they put into their pages. They also use rigorous "peer review" processes designed to maintain high standards of accuracy and integrity. There is no editorial board that is in charge of screening Web pages. Anybody, even crackpots and hustlers, can put up a Web page. And not only can they put up a Web page, but they can also make it look as "professional" as an official Harvard University Web page. Indeed, this is exactly what members of the Heaven's Gate community (discussed in Chapter 1) were doing to support themselves and raise money before they committed mass suicide. So, Internet surfers need to beware: Although the Internet is a great information resource, the "garbage-to-good-stuff" ratio is way higher on the Internet than in the Expanded Academic Index.

## ADDITIONAL EXERCISES

**1.** Use the following chart to record and rate the coverage of an entire local newscast with respect to (1) order of stories, (2) subject of story, (3) time given to each story (in seconds), (4) the depth of the coverage, or the extent to which the coverage merely acquaints you superficially with or gives you in-depth understanding of the subject (on a 10-point scale), (5) the visual impact (on a 10-point scale), the dramatic impact (on a 10-point scale) and (7) inherent newsworthiness of each story (on a 10-point scale).

| | Subject | Time | Depth | Visual Impact | Drama | Newsworthiness |
|---|---|---|---|---|---|---|
| 1 | | | | | | |
| 2 | | | | | | |
| 3 | | | | | | |
| 4 | | | | | | |
| 5 | | | | | | |
| 6 | | | | | | |
| 7 | | | | | | |
| 8 | | | | | | |
| 9 | | | | | | |
| 10 | | | | | | |
| 11 | | | | | | |
| 12 | | | | | | |

Based on your analysis, rate the overall newscast. Do a comparative analysis of the newscast on a rival channel. Now compare these with the front or main news section of your daily newspaper. (Instead of story order, look at position. Is the story on the front page or on page 10? Instead of time, look at the amount of space given to each story. This can be measured in column inches.)

2. Here's a little research project. Find out who owns the news media in your service area. On the basis of your findings, see if you can project how the news coverage of current local issues might be affected. Test your projections by following the coverage of some current local issue or story.

3. Follow one story of national or international significance for a period of a week in one or more of the major metropolitan or national dailies, such as the *New York Times,* the *Washington Post,* the *Los Angeles Times,* the *Wall Street Journal.* Identify the sources of authoritative attribution. Who are the people, in other words, that the reporters quote or refer to in order to establish facts? What significant patterns, if any, do you notice? What significance do you attach to such patterns?

4. A metaphor is a figure of speech in which things which are unlike each other in some respects are compared to each other or understood in terms of each other. News reporters and commentators make extensive use of metaphors. For example, elections are typically covered as "races," more specifically, "horse races." Military strategy is often discussed in sports metaphors like "game plan." And vice versa. Sports coverage is full of military metaphors like "blitz," "field general," and "the long bomb." So here's a little exercise in metaphor sensitivity: Take the lead story from today's front page and list every metaphor you can find. How do these metaphors affect the "spin"? What other metaphors can you think of that would convey the story? How would switching metaphors affect the accuracy with which the story is conveyed?

## GLOSSARY

**demographics** measurements of audience characteristics that pertain to marketing strategy
**ideology** shared assumptions, doctrines, and ways of thinking in the terms in which society defines itself
**newsworthiness** the estimated news value of a given story or item of information
**ratings** measurements of how large a share of the total potential audience is attracted by a given program or programming service
**spin** interpretation; the attempt to influence the public's interpretation
**subliminal** below the threshold of conscious awareness, sometimes thought to apply to certain forms of communication or strategies of advertising

## NOTES

[1] Dorothy Singer and Jerome Singer, "Today's Lesson Will Be Mork and the Fonz," *TV Guide,* June 12, 1982, p. 35.

[2] George Gerbner, "Television: Modern Mythmaker," *Media and Values,* Summer/Fall, 1987.

[3] Ibid.

[4] Wilson Bryan Key, *Subliminal Seduction* (New York: New American Library, 1972), p. 11.

[5] Anthony Pratkanis, "The Cargo-Cult Science of Subliminal Persuasion," *Skeptical Inquirer* 16, Spring 1992, pp. 260–272.

[6] Ibid., p. 270.

[7] Ben Bagdikian, "Lords of the Global Village," *The Nation,* June 12, 1989.

[8] Quoted in Ron Powers, "Now! Live on the Action Cam! A Reporter Talking!" *TV Guide,* June 19, 1982, p. 22.

[9] See Bernard Roscho, *Newsmaking* (Chicago: University of Chicago Press, 1975), pp. 13–14.

[10] Leon V. Sigal, *Reporters and Officials: The Organization and Politics of Newsmaking* (Lexington, Mass.: Heath, 1973).

[11] George E. Reedy, *The Twilight of the Presidency* (New York: Mentor Books, 1971), pp. 101–102.

[12] Quoted in John Weisman, "Why American TV Is Vulnerable to Foreign Propaganda," *TV Guide,* June 12, 1982, p. 12.

[13] Ibid.

[14] Ibid., p. 121.

[15] See Conrad Fink, *Media Ethics: In the Newsroom and Beyond* (New York: McGraw-Hill, 1988), pp. 241–243.

[16] Richard Rorchler, "Managing the News," *Commonwealth,* March 22, 1963, p. 659.

[17] Mark Hertsgaard, *On Bended Knee: The Press and the Reagan Presidency* (New York: Farrar, Straus and Giroux, 1988), pp. 24–25.

[18] Ibid, p. 25–26.

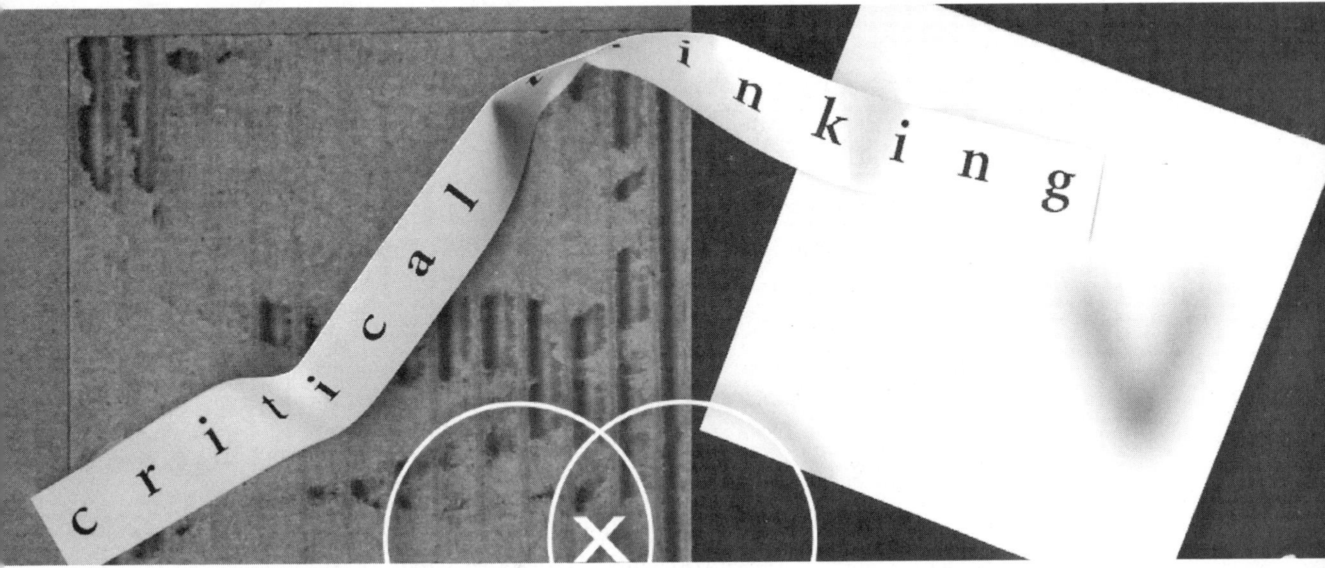


# CHAPTER 13 Reading for the Argument

Good writing, and this includes argumentative writing, functions on many levels. Which is to say that there's a lot—and a lot of *different kinds of things*—to pay attention to in a good piece of writing. For example, you could read a passage for the rhythm, or the rhyme, or the imaginative power of its metaphors. There are many important appreciable features, or things to "read for" in a good piece of writing. In critical thinking, the most important thing to read for is the argument. As critical thinkers what we try to concentrate on above all else when we read, and especially when we read a piece of argumentative writing, is the argument it presents. And since arguments are essentially tools of persuasion, argument analysis and argument evaluation should both be well developed and fully integrated into "reading for the argument." Many find it useful to have a structured strategy to follow in "reading for the argument." Here, then, is a seven-step structured strategy, offered with the following hint in advance: In some cases you may find it more useful to omit or to reverse the order of certain steps, or to work back and forth between them.

## SEVEN-STEP STRATEGY

1. Clarify meaning.
2. Identify conclusion and premises.
3. Cast the argument.
4. Fill in the missing premises.
5. Evaluate the argument for soundness and/or cogency.
6. Check for informal fallacies.
7. Overall evaluation.

Steps 1–4: **Analysis**
Steps 4–7: **Evaluation**

### STEP 1: CLARIFY MEANING

Start by reading a passage all the way through once, trying to get a feel for the argument as a whole. Even if you happen to disagree with the position advanced, try not to allow your disagreement to distract you. Along the way if you encounter words that you don't understand consult a dictionary. Don't simply *assume* that you understand a passage which contains unfamiliar vocabulary items. Make sure by looking the words up. As you read, pay attention to language function and be alert especially for the persuasive function of language. (See Chapter 2.)

### STEP 2: IDENTIFY CONCLUSION AND PREMISES

If you detect the persuasive function of language in what you're reading, look for relationships of support among the claims. Be alert for argument indicators like:

**Conclusion signals:** thus, therefore, consequently, it follows that (and so forth)

**Area premise signals:** since, because, for, insofar as (and so forth)

**Specific premise signals:** first, second, third; for one thing, for another (and so forth)

Also try to orient yourself to the issue. What issue or question or problem or controversy is the author addressing herself to? This may help you to get a better or quicker handle on the argument's conclusion. Similarly, to locate premises in the absence of signals, ask yourself: Why should I accept the conclusion as true? What basis does the arguer give for drawing the conclusion? (See Chapter 3.)

### STEP 3: CAST THE ARGUMENT

If it seems useful, for instance if the argument is relatively complex, produce a graphic map or "casting" of the argument. (See Chapter 4.)

## STEP 4: FILL IN MISSING PREMISES

Make sure that all of the argument's crucial claims and embedded sub-arguments are fully and explicitly articulated. (See Chapter 5.)

## STEP 5: EVALUATE FOR SOUNDNESS AND/OR COGENCY

Start with the main argument. The main argument consists of the thesis and the premises which most directly support it. First determine what kind of an argument it is. (See Chapters 6 and 7.) Depending on whether it is a deductive or an inductive argument, apply the appropriate criteria and standards to determine its strength. Deductive arguments should be checked for validity by seeing whether accepting the premises and denying the conclusion is self-contradictory. Further tests for deductive validity include constructing Venn diagrams (for categorical syllogisms) and truth tables (for arguments involving truth functional compound premises). Inductive arguments should be assessed for strength according to the type of inductive reasoning involved. (See Chapter 7.) Continue to work your way through whatever additional layers of premise support there may be until you arrive at the argument's most basic premises. Depending upon what kinds of claim are asserted in these basic premises, you can then make an assessment of their defensibility. (See Chapter 8.)

## STEP 6: CHECK FOR INFORMAL FALLACIES

Pay close attention to the strategies which the argument employs. Does it try to make its point on the basis of a comparison or analogy? Does it depend heavily on criticizing an opposing position? Does it involve a causal hypothesis? Use your insights into the argument's strategies to guide your search for possible weaknesses. Is the comparison a good one? Is the argument's representation of the opposing position fair? And so on. Be alert for possible ambiguity and abuse of rhetorical features of language, and check the relevance of the support to what is supported. Also check for consistency among the claims made in an argument, between those claims and other things you have good reason to believe, and between the positions involved in a system of beliefs; and don't forget to trace the implications of a thesis or argument. (See Chapters 9, 10, and 11.)

## STEP 7: OVERALL EVALUATION

Having completed the preceding steps, you are now in a position to give the argument an overall assessment. Does it have force? If so, how much? Are you ready to go with the argument on balance, or against it? Has the arguer won you over? To answer questions like these, return to your criticisms, especially to Steps 5 and 6. Are the argument's essential premises so flawed that they provide little or no support for the conclusion? Or are there flaws contained in premises that are not essential to the claim? In a very short argument, it's rarely necessary to ask questions like these, for the judgments made in Step 6 will dictate the overall evaluation. But a complicated argument poses the same problem of overall judgment that the intelligent voter faces when voting. Inevitably there are reasons that argue for a vote and reasons that argue against it. Your job and ours is to decide whether, when all things are considered, we should endorse one candidate rather than another. Similarly, a long, sophisticated argument may offer many reasons for advancing its claim, some fair and legitimate and others unfair and illegitimate. We must decide which reasons are legitimate and whether they are sufficient to endorse the claim.

Rendering an overall evaluation is an important part of the evaluative process, for—if nothing else—it keeps critical thinking from becoming a bloodless, abstract exercise. It allows you to decide whether or not to believe, to endorse, and possibly to act on a claim. It also gives you an opportunity, which you should take, to show how the argument could be improved. Finally, it allows you to clarify your own beliefs as you respond to the argument in a creative and constructive way, and perhaps most important of all, to study and reflect critically on your own beliefs and procedures.

## THE SEVEN-STEP STRATEGY APPLIED

With these preliminary remarks behind us, let's now see how the seven-step strategy can be applied to argumentative essays. We want to start with an example in which the authors assign high priority to strength of argument and clarity of presentation. So we have selected as our first example a piece of legal reasoning, an excerpt from an important judicial opinion which is both clearly articulated and forcefully argued. Here is an excerpt from the decision of the United States Supreme Court in the case of *Wyman* v. *James*. It concerns an issue of constitutional interpretation. The question that came before the Court in this case was whether the right to be secure against unreasonable search and seizure, guaranteed under the Fourth Amendment, is violated by a practice of a state welfare agency requiring periodic official visits in the homes of welfare recipients as a condition of eligibility for welfare benefits. The opinion of the majority was written by Justice Harry A. Blackmun:

> This appeal presents the issue whether a beneficiary of the program for Aid to Families with Dependent Children (AFDC) may refuse a home visit by the caseworker without risking the termination of benefits.
>
> The New York State and city social services commissioners appeal from a judgment and decree of a divided three-judge District Court. . . .
>
> The district court majority held that a mother receiving AFDC relief may refuse, without forfeiting her right to that relief, the periodic home visit which the cited New York statutes and regulations prescribe as a condition for the continuance of assistance under the program. The beneficiary's thesis, and that of the District Court majority, is that home visitation is a search and, when not consented to or when not supported by a warrant based on probable cause, violates the beneficiary's 4th and 14th Amendment rights. . . .
>
> When a case involves a home and some type of official intrusion into that home, as this case appears to do, an immediate and natural reaction is one of concern about 4th

Amendment rights and the protection which that Amendment is intended to afford. Its emphasis indeed is upon one of the most precious aspects of personal security in the home: "The right of the people to be secure in their persons, houses, papers, and effects. . . ." This Court has characterized that right as "basic to a free society. . . ." And over the years the Court consistently has been most protective of the privacy of the dwelling. . . .

This natural and quite proper protective attitude, however, is not a factor in this case, for the seemingly obvious and simple reason that we are not concerned here with any search by the New York social service agency in the 4th Amendment meaning of that term. It is true that the governing statute and regulations appear to make mandatory the initial home visit and the subsequent periodic "contacts" (which may include home visits) for the inception and continuance of aid. It is also true that the caseworker's posture in the home visit is, perhaps, in a sense, both rehabilitative and investigative. But this latter aspect, we think, is given too broad a character and far more emphasis than it deserves if it is equated with a search in the criminal law context. We note, too, that the visitation in itself is not forced or compelled, and that the beneficiary's denial of permission is not a criminal act. If consent to the visitation is withheld, no visitation takes place. The aid then never begins or merely ceases, as the case may be. There is no entry of the home and there is no search.

If however, we were to assume that a caseworker's home visit, before or subsequent to the beneficiary's initial qualification for benefits, somehow (perhaps because the average beneficiary might feel she is in no position to refuse consent to the visit), and despite its interview nature, does possess some of the characteristics of a search in the traditional sense, we nevertheless conclude that does not fall within the 4th Amendment's proscription. This is because it does not descend to the level of unreasonableness. It is unreasonableness which is the 4th Amendment's standard.

There are a number of factors that compel us to conclude that the home visit proposed for Mrs. James is not unreasonable.

The public's interest in this particular segment of the area of assistance to the unfortunate is protection and aid for the dependent child whose family requires such aid for the child. . . . The dependent child's needs are paramount, and only with hesitancy would we relegate those needs, in the scale of comparative values, to a position secondary to what the mother claims as her rights.

The agency, with tax funds provided from federal as well as from state sources, is fulfilling a public trust. The State, working through its qualified welfare agency, has appropriate and paramount interest and concern in seeing and assuring that the intended and proper objects of that tax-produced assistance are the ones who benefit from the aid it dispenses. . . .

One who dispenses purely private charity naturally has an interest in and expects to know how his charitable funds are utilized and put to work. The public, when it is the provider, rightly expects the same.

### Step 1: Clarify Meaning

Many of the crucial terms in this passage are subject to rather precise definition. An important preliminary to clarifying the meanings involved in this passage would be the Fourth Amendment itself. The Fourth Amendment to the Constitution reads:

The right of the people to be secure in their persons, houses, papers, and effects, against unreasonable searches and seizures, shall not be violated, and no warrants shall issue, but upon probable cause, supported by oath or affirmation, and particularly describing the place to be searched, and the persons or things to be seized.

In common vernacular this means that the government cannot search or seize a person or a person's house or private property without a warrant, and that a warrant must be obtained from a judge on the basis of sworn testimony that there is reason to suspect that something criminal is going on. "Probable cause" means "reason to suspect that something criminal is going on." There is one crucial term whose vagueness we should notice right away as a matter of central importance not only to the argument but to the issue. The term "unreasonable" is vague.

**Step 2: Identify Conclusion and Premises**

Remember that one good way to find the thesis of an extended argument is to orient yourself to the issue to which the argument is addressed. In this case the issue can be formulated with a good deal of precision: Does the practice of the New York State welfare agency requiring periodic official visits in the homes of welfare recipients as a condition of eligibility for welfare benefits violate the welfare recipient's right to be secure against unreasonable search and seizure, as guaranteed under the Fourth Amendment? Once the issue has been formulated in this way, it is quite clear what the thesis of the passage is:

The New York State welfare agency practice does not violate the Fourth Amendment.

There are two main lines of argument offered in support of the thesis. One is based on the point that the practice of the welfare agency does not constitute a search. The other is based on two main points: that (even if it *does* constitute a search) the practice of the welfare agency is not unreasonable; and the Fourth Amendment is concerned only with *unreasonable* searches.

**Step 3: Cast the Argument**

This appeal presents the issue whether a beneficiary of the program for Aid to Families with Dependent children (AFDC) may refuse a home visit by the caseworker without risking the termination of benefits.

The New York State and city social services commissioners appeal from a judgment and decree of a divided three-judge District Court. . . .

The district court majority held that a mother receiving AFDC relief may refuse, without forfeiting her right to that relief, the periodic home visit which the cited New York statutes and regulations prescribe as a condition for the continuance of assistance under the program. The beneficiary's thesis, and that of the District Court majority, is that home visitation is a search and, when not consented to or when not supported by a warrant based on probable cause, violates the beneficiary's 4th and 14th Amendment rights. . . .

[When a case involves a home and some type of official intrusion into that home, as this case appears to do, an immediate and natural reaction is one of concern about 4th Amendment rights and the protection which that Amendment is intended to afford. ①] [Its emphasis indeed is upon one of the most precious aspects of personal security in the home: (2) ] "The right of the people to be secure in their persons, houses, papers, and effects. . . ." [This Court has characterized that right as "basic to a free society. . . ." (3) ] [And over the years the Court consistently has been most protective of the privacy of the dwelling. . . . (4) ]

[This natural and quite proper protective attitude, however, is not a factor in this case, (5) ] *for the seemingly obvious and simple reason that* [we are not concerned here with any search by the New York social service agency in the 4th Amendment meaning of that term. (6) ] *It is true that* [the governing statute and regulations appear to make mandatory the initial home visit and the subsequent periodic "contacts" (which may include home visits) for the inception and continuance of aid. (7) ] *It is also true that* [the caseworker's posture in the home visit is, perhaps, in a sense, {both rehabilitative and} investigative. (8) ] *But* [this latter aspect, we think, is given too broad a character and far more emphasis than it deserves if it is equated with a search in the criminal law context. (9) ] *We note, too, that* [the visitation in itself is not forced or compelled, (10) ] *and that* [the beneficiary's denial of permission is not a criminal act (11) ]. [If consent to the visitation is withheld, no visitation takes place. (12) ] [The aid then never begins or merely ceases, (13) ] as the case may be. There is no entry of the home and there is no search.

If however, we were to assume that a caseworker's home visit, before or subsequent to the beneficiary's initial qualification for benefits, somehow (perhaps because the average beneficiary might feel she is in no position to refuse consent to the visit), and despite its interview nature, does possess some of the characteristics of a search in the traditional sense, *we nevertheless conclude* [that does not fall within the 4th Amendment's proscription. (5)[1]] *This is because* [it does not descend to the level of unreasonableness. (14) ] [It is unreasonableness which is the 4th Amendment's standard. (15) ]

There are *a number of factors that compel us to conclude* that the home visit proposed for Mrs. James is not unreasonable. [The public's interest in this particular segment of the area of assistance to the unfortunate is protection and aid for the dependent child whose family requires such aid for the child. . . . (16) ] [The dependent child's needs are paramount, (17) ] *and* [only with hesitancy would we relegate those needs, in the scale of comparative values, to a position secondary to what the mother claims as her rights. (18) ]

[The agency, with tax funds provided from federal as well as from state sources, is fulfilling a public trust. (19) ] [The State, working through its qualified welfare agency, has appropriate and paramount interest and concern in seeing and assuring that the intended and proper objects of that tax-produced assistance are the ones who benefit from the aid it dispenses. . . . (20) ]

[One who dispenses purely private charity naturally has an interest in and expects to know how his charitable funds are utilized and put to work. (21) ] [The public, when it is the provider, rightly expects the same. (22) ]

The first three paragraphs give important background information on the history of the case which, though it helps orient us to the issue, is not part of the argument. Paragraph four, however, contains claims which, though they too are part of the background, are also relevant to the argument's thesis. The author acknowledges them as weighing against the thesis. Thus we would cast them as concession claims. We find the thesis stated at the beginning of paragraph five followed by the first main premise, and restated again in paragraph six, followed by the two other main premises. Thus the main argument can be cast as follows:

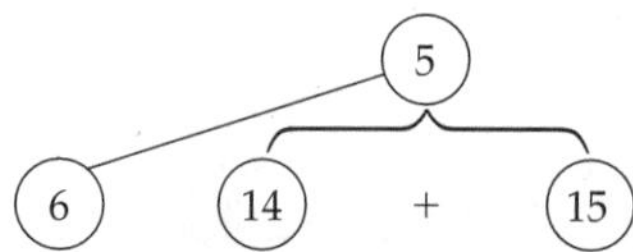


The beginning of paragraph six "If we were to assume . . . we nevertheless conclude" indicates that claim 6 functions independently as support for the thesis, whereas claims 14 and 15 function together interdependently in support of the thesis. The remaining claims relate to claims 6 and 14:

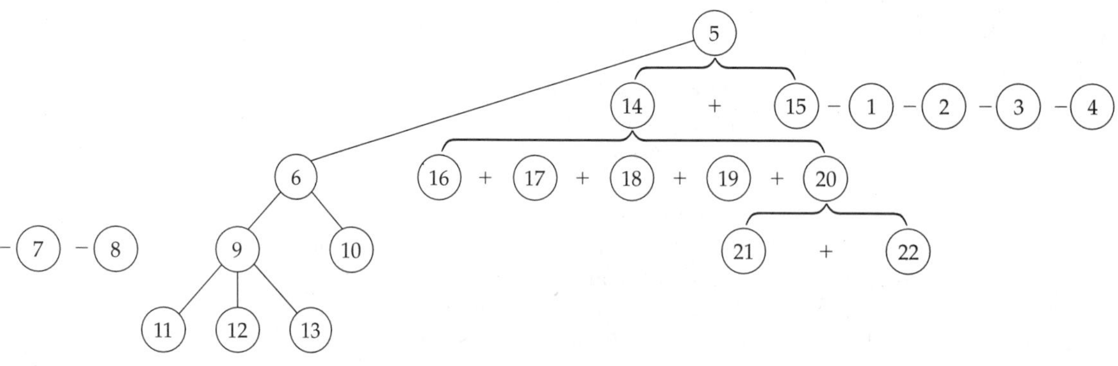


**Step 4: Fill in Missing Premises**

The inference from 9 to 6 is incomplete, and so is the inference from 16, 17, 18, 19, and 20 to 14. Two premises need to be added to the inference from 9 to 6:

a: The investigative aspect of the home visit should neither be given too broad a character nor be overemphasized.

b: The Fourth Amendment sense of the term "search" is confined to the criminal law context.

The inference from 16, 17, 18, 19, and 20 to 14 seems to depend on the additional premise:

c: A policy or practice for which there are good reasons is not unreasonable.

Thus, the argument may finally be cast:

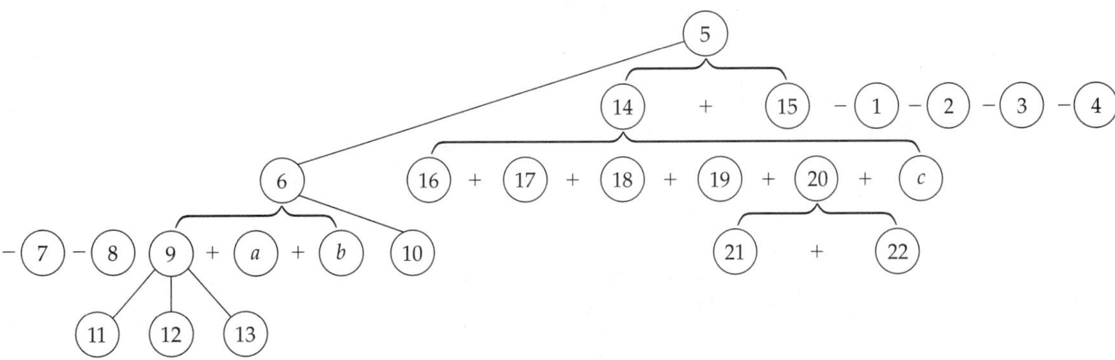

**Step 5: Evaluate for Soundness and/or Cogency**
The main argument seems clearly to be intended to function deductively; and indeed, based on a "literal" reading of the Fourth Amendment, the argument seems also to be valid. So we can move immediately to the next layer of support, to the arguments offered in support of claims 6, 14, and 15. One of the strengths of this passage is the degree to which the author has made clear where the main premises stand in need of support, and the lengths to which the passage goes in attempting to supply the needed support.

Of the three main premises—6, 14, and 15—the most vulnerable seems to be claim 6: that the welfare agency practice does not constitute a search. The author acknowledges some six separate considerations that might be thought to weigh against it. Its acceptability depends on premises 9, 10, 11, and 12, as well as unexpressed premises *a* and *b*. Premise 9 makes an interpretive claim which, especially in view of the points which the author concedes as weighing against main point 6, must be regarded as open to serious challenge. Premise 9 is left unsupported, and in the context of an issue concerning the interpretation of the Fourth Amendment, this might well be regarded as question-begging (see Step 6). Without 9, unexpressed premise *a,* that the investigative aspect of the welfare agency visit should neither be too broadly construed nor overemphasized, would be reduced to a vague truism of little use to the argument. And unexpressed premise *b,* like premise 9, makes an interpretive claim which in the context of this issue needs independent support. Support for 6 also comes from 10, 11, 12, and 13. Though 11, 12, and 13 are probably acceptable as accurate accounts of the official consequences for the welfare recipient of refusal of consent to the visit, they do not make a very convincing case for 10, that the visit is not compelled. Indeed, the author acknowledges the weakness here when he says in making the transition to the second line of argument, "the average beneficiary might feel she is in no position to refuse consent to the visit."

Main premise 15 is little more than a verbatim quotation from the text of the Fourth Amendment itself. Thus it is hard to imagine how it might be objected to in any substantive way. Nevertheless, it does bring one crucial vague element to the center of attention: the term "unreasonable." The acceptability of main premise 14, that the visit prescribed for Mrs. James is not unreasonable, and consequently the cogency of the entire second line of argument turns on the question of what is meant by "unreasonable." This is never made explicit in the passage. However, the support which is offered for 14 seems to imply the understanding of "unreasonable" which is formulated in unexpressed premise *c.* If we assume for the moment that claims 16 through 20 do constitute good reason for the state agency's practice of conducting mandatory home visits, we can see once again how important it is to fill in missing premises, for now it becomes apparent that, with main point 6 in trouble, the entire argument hinges on the acceptability of unexpressed premise *c.* So what about the unexpressed premise? Initially it seems a perfectly plausible idea. However, on closer inspection a serious question might be raised to challenge it: Is it not possible that a policy or practice for which there are good reasons is nevertheless still an unreasonable policy or practice on balance, because there are overriding and even more compelling reasons for objecting to it? For example, let's suppose that we could find one or two very good reasons to raise taxes by 200 percent. Does this mean that it would be "reasonable" to do so? Not if there are even better reasons for not doing it.

Now let us return to premises 16 through 20. Here we find the reasons for the welfare agency practice spelled out. The agency is charged with a responsibility to look after the welfare of a dependent child and to monitor the disbursement of public funds. Suppose we accept these both as legitimate public concerns for which the agency has properly been made responsible—even without the additional support offered in the form of the analogy between public assistance and private charity (premises 21 and 22). But this may still be a bit of a red herring, because what they constitute good reason for is *some* policy or practice designed to discover cases of child abuse and neglect and cases of welfare fraud, but not necessarily *this* one: a practice which, in addition to raising the privacy issue, also seems to go against the constitutionally guaranteed presumption of innocence. Is there no way for the welfare agency to fulfill its legitimate public responsibilities other than by means of a practice which raises such serious issues of constitutional principle? These, it might be argued, constitute overriding reasons for reforming the agency policy, in spite of the legitimacy of the reasons which underlie it. Notice how this brings us around once again to the acceptability of unexpressed premise *c.*

**Step 6: Check for Informal Fallacies**

This passage is relatively free of fallacies, as one would naturally expect of a ranking member of the judiciary, which maintains very high standards in the area of argumentation. Nevertheless, as we already indicated in Step 5, it is possible to challenge several of the argument's elements.

In premise 9 we are asked to accept that the admittedly investigative posture of the welfare caseworker in the home of the recipient is "too broadly construed" and "overemphasized" if we think of it as like a criminal search. Notice that this premise therefore makes an interpretive claim. It interprets the welfare caseworker's visit. Now, that's not by itself an objectionable thing. But remember what's at issue in this case. What's at issue is whether or not the visit constitutes a Fourth Amendment violation. So the question of how the caseworker's visit is to be interpreted or understood is absolutely central to the issue. Thus to simply assume, without independent support, that the visit can't be construed as a search amounts to assuming, again without independent support, that it isn't covered by the Fourth Amendment. But that's what's at issue. Consequently, premise 9 can be faulted as a case of question-begging.

Similarly, unexpressed premise *b* makes an interpretive claim which in the context of this issue requires independent support. Unexpressed premise *b* tells us that the Fourth Amendment sense of the term "search" is confined to the criminal law context. Here what is interpreted is not the caseworker's visit, but the Fourth Amendment. Again, this isn't by itself an objectionable thing. After all, the case calls upon the Supreme Court to do precisely that: interpret the Fourth Amendment. Specifically, the Court is asked to determine whether the Fourth Amendment's protection extends to cover cases like that of Mrs. James. If we now assume for a moment that the visit prescribed for Mrs. James is not a criminal search, we can see again that the question of whether the Fourth Amendment extends beyond the criminal law context is precisely what's at issue. Consequently, to assume without independent support that it doesn't extend beyond the criminal law context simply begs the question.

We should be cautious in making these criticisms, however. We should bear in mind that there is a considerable body of literature from which powerful arguments could be constructed to support something like premise *b*. In other words, we should not presume that we have blown the Supreme Court's argument out of the water just yet. And we should not overlook the fact that the Court recognizes a certain vulnerability in this first line of argument, and that, as a consequence the Court attaches greater weight to the second line of argument.

There remains the matter of the possible red herring in support of main premise 14. But we feel that this should not be separated from the question of the acceptability of unexpressed premise *c*. And that's too deep an issue to be dismissed as a mere fallacious inference. So we'll come back to it in Step 7.

**Step 7: Overall Evaluation**

Though there are a number of flaws in this argument and though some may feel that ultimately it fails to secure its thesis, we must recognize its overall respectability as an argument. It is generally very clear and forcefully argued, again as one would naturally expect it to be.

Moreover, the points at which it is most vulnerable to challenge or objection are fairly and accurately represented as such to the reader. And some of these are subject to additional support. For example, the assumption that the Fourth Amendment sense of the term "search" is confined to the context of criminal law, to which we objected as a case of question-begging, could no doubt be supported. Such support might take the form of a survey of relevant legal precedent: For example, if the Fourth Amendment has always, or traditionally, been interpreted as confined to or rooted in the criminal law context, this would be relevant (though not by itself decisive) support.

We should also recognize certain specific strengths in the second and most important line of argument. First of all, the main inference from 14 and 15 to the thesis is deductively valid. If both of its premises are acceptable, that puts the thesis beyond question. Similarly, with the addition of unexpressed premise *c*, the sub-argument in support of 14 is deductively valid. If its several premises are acceptable, then main point 14 is also established beyond question.

The problems that arise for the argument turn out, in the final analysis, to be rather subtle and deep ones. This highlights an important point about argument analysis and evaluation. When we're dealing with issues of depth and substance, as we are in this case, we cannot expect to arrive at complete and final closure of the issue, at least not very often. Notice how this important insight is recognized in the structure and procedures of the Supreme Court. The Court is made up of nine justices in part because it is recognized that the issues which come before the Court will predictably admit of persistent disagreement among reasonable people. This means that one cannot expect to arrive at complete and final closure of the issues, at least not very often. This is one reason why the majority presents its decision as an "opinion," and why there is also in the typical case at least one dissenting "opinion" presented as well. Yet this hardly means that there is no point to constructing, analyzing, and evaluating arguments about such issues. This is also recognized in the structure and procedures of the Court, for that is precisely what the Court does: argument analysis, argument evaluation, and argument construction. Perhaps it would be nice if we could use these methods to arrive at complete and final closure of all of the deep issues that divide people, but the point of these activities and methods is not lost when we fail to reach that goal (which is most of the time). The point of these activities and methods is that they are essential to the pursuit of truth and the accumulation of wisdom in these areas. Even when the issue remains open, as we think it does in this case, what the exercise of analyzing and evaluating the arguments does is deepen the discussion and deepen our understanding and appreciation of the depths and complexities of the issue.

## ADDITIONAL EXERCISES

Here are some additional arguments for analysis and evaluation:

**1.** Most Americans . . . will argue that technology is neutral, that any technology is merely a benign instrument, a tool, and depending upon the hands into which it falls, it may be used one way or another. [So] the argument goes that television is merely a window or a conduit through which any perception, any argument or reality may pass. It therefore has the potential to be enlightening to people who watch it and is potentially useful to democratic processes. —Jerry Mander[2]

**2.** These assumptions about television, as about other technologies, are totally wrong. If you once accept the principle of an army—a collection of military technologies and people to run them—all gathered together for the purpose of fighting, overpowering, killing and winning, then it is obvious that the supervisors of armies will be the sort of people who desire to fight, over-power, kill and win, and who are good at these assignments: generals. . . . If you accept the existence of automobiles, you also accept the existence of roads laid upon the landscape, oil to run the cars, and huge institutions to find the oil, pump it and distribute it. In addition you accept a sped-up style of life and the movement of humans through the terrain at speeds that make it impossible to pay attention to whatever is growing there. Humans who use cars sit in fixed positions for long hours following a narrow strip of gray pavement, with eyes fixed forward, engaged in the task of driving. . . . Slowly they evolve into car-people.

If you accept nuclear power plants, you also accept a techno-scientific-industrial-military elite. Without these people in charge, you could not have nuclear power. You and I getting together with a few friends could not make use of nuclear power. We could not build such a plant, nor could we . . . handle or store the radioactive waste products which remain dangerous to life for thousands of years. The wastes, in turn, determine that *future* societies will have to maintain a technological capacity to deal with the problem and the military capability to protect the wastes. . . .

If you accept mass production, you accept that a small number of people will supervise the daily existence of a much larger number of people. You accept that human beings will spend long hours, every day, engaged in repetitive work, while suppressing any desires for experience or activity beyond this work. . . . With mass production, you also accept that huge numbers of identical items will need to be efficiently distributed to huge numbers of people, and that institutions such as advertising will arise to do this. . . .

If you accept the existence of advertising, you accept a system designed to persuade and to dominate minds by interfering in people's thinking patterns. You also accept that the system will be used by the sorts of people who like to influence people and are good at it. . . .

In all of these instances, the basic form of the institution and the technology determines its interaction with the world, the way it will be used, the kind of people who will use it, and to what ends. And so it is with television.

Far from being "neutral," television itself predetermines who shall use it, how they will use it, what effects it will have on individual lives, and, if it continues to be widely used, what sorts of political forms will inevitably emerge. —Jerry Mander[3]

**3.** As the nation heard with sorrow the news of the deplorable shooting spree at abortion facilities in Brookline, the question is asked: Why? Why this sudden rise of violence in this arena?

I have been intricately involved in the antiabortion movement for more than a decade. I have led thousands of people in peaceful antiabortion activism via Operation Rescue. Hence, I enjoy a perspective few have. So I submit these answers to the question "Why?"

Enemies of the babies and the anti-abortion movement will argue that the conviction that abortion is murder, and the call to take nonviolent direct action to save children from death, inevitably leads to the use of lethal force. This argument is ludicrous—unless one is prepared to argue that Gandhi's nonviolent civil disobedience in India during the 1930s led to the murder of British officials; or that Dr. Martin Luther King's nonviolent civil disobedience led to the violent actions that accompanied the civil rights movement in the United States during the 1960s.

So why, then, this recent violent outburst? Law enforcement officials need look no further than *Roe* v. *Wade;* abortion providers need look no further than their own instruments of death; and Congress and the president need look no further than the Freedom of Access to Clinic Entrances Act to understand the roots of the shootings.

The Supreme Court's attempt to overthrow Law (capital "L") in order to legalize and legitimize murder has led to the inevitable—a disregard of or contempt for law. I say the court's attempt, for the court can no more overturn Law and legalize murder than it can overturn the law of gravity. God's immutable commandment "Thou shalt not murder" has forever made murder illegal. The court's lawlessness is breeding lawlessness. The court cannot betray the foundation of law and civilization—the Ten Commandments—and then expect a people to act "lawful" and "civilized."

Let us look at the abortion industry itself. Abortion is murder. And just as segregation and the accompanying violence possess the seeds for further violence, likewise it appears that the Law of sowing and reaping is being visited upon the abortion industry. A society cannot expect to tear 35 million innocent babies from their mothers' wombs without reaping horrifying consequences. Was it perhaps inevitable that the violent abortion industry should itself reap a portion of what it has so flagrantly and callously sown?

Now to Congress and the judiciary. Similar to the civil rights activists, antiabortion activists have often been brutalized at the hands of police and then subjected to vulgar injustices in sundry courts of law. Add to this the Freedom of Access to Clinic Entrances Act, which turns peaceful antiabortion activists into federal felons, and perhaps one can understand the frustration and anger that is growing in Americans.

The abortion industry can partly blame itself for the recent shootings. It clamored for harsh treatment of peaceful antiabortion activists, and it usually got it. Now it has to deal with an emerging violent fringe. John F. Kennedy stated, "Those who make peaceful revolution impossible will make violent revolution inevitable." One would think the pro-choice crowd would belatedly heed the late president's warning, but they haven't. They're urging an all too political Justice Department to launch a witch hunt into the lives of peaceful antiabortion activists and leaders. Make no mistake—what the pro-choice people want is to pressure law enforcement and the courts to intimidate anyone who condemns abortion as murder. Their recent public relations scam is to blame all anti-abortion people for the shootings. And they will not be content until they have crushed all dissent against abortion. We must not allow them to cause us to cower in silence.

To those of you who support the recent shootings or herald John Salvi as a hero, I ask you: Has God authorized one person to be policeman, judge, jury, and executioner? Is it logical to leap from nonviolent life-saving activities to lethal force? Read your history! Remember the principles of Calvin, Knox, and Cromwell concerning lower magistrates. Are you likening John Salvi and company to Knox or Cromwell? Are you calling for revolution? Please consider these questions before calling someone who walks into a clinic and starts randomly shooting people a hero.

So what can be done to curtail this trend? First, the Freedom of Access to Clinic Entrances Act should be repealed immediately. This oppressive law is an outrage. The crushing weight of the federal government punishing peaceful protesters is the kind of thing we would expect in Communist China against political dissidents.

Second, the courts must stop abusing antiabortion activists. We must be accorded the same tolerance and leniency that every politically correct protester receives nationwide, i.e., small fines, two days in jail, charges dismissed, etc.

Finally, and this is most urgent, child killing must be brought to an immediate end. Whether the Supreme Court declares the personhood and inalienable right to life of preborn children or the Constitution is amended or the president signs an emancipation proclamation for children or Congress outlaws abortion outright, we must bring a swift end to the murder of innocent children. —Randall Terry (founder of Operation Rescue)[4]

**4.** You know, whether we like it or not, in ways that are mostly positive, the world's economies are more and more interconnected and interdependent. Today, an economic crisis anywhere can affect economies everywhere. Recent months have brought serious financial problems to Thailand, Indonesia, South Korea, and beyond.

Now, why should Americans be concerned about this? First, these countries are our customers. If they sink into recession, they won't be able to buy the goods we'd like to sell them. Second, they're also our competitors. So if their currencies lose their value and go down, then the price of their goods will drop, flooding our market and others with much cheaper goods, which makes it a lot tougher for our people to compete. And, finally, they are our strategic partners. Their stability bolsters our security.

The American economy remains sound and strong, and I want to keep it that way. But because the turmoil in Asia will have an impact on all the world's economies, including ours, making that negative impact as small as possible is the right thing to do for America—and the right thing to do for a safer world.

Our policy is clear: No nation can recover if it does not reform itself. But when nations are willing to undertake serious economic reform, we should help them do it. So I call on Congress to renew America's commitment to the International Monetary Fund. —President William Jefferson Clinton[5]

**5.** President Clinton's proposed drug-control budget will cost America $16 billion. This is the largest federal anti-drug expenditure in our nation's history, up from

$1 billion in 1980. When all is said and done, it is a continuation of failed policies and an exercise in deceit.

As the first president of the post–World War II baby-boomer generation, President Clinton should have some insight into drugs and human behavior—many of his peers, his largest contributors and the staff around him have had some experience with illegal drugs. It is obvious that few of them are addicts or criminals, and they shouldn't be thrown in jail or forced to submit to testing. And it is also obvious that after more than 25 years and hundreds of billions of dollars squandered on interdiction and punishment—in California, more state money is now spent on incarceration than on higher education—the "war on drugs" is wasteful and socially destructive.

It is disappointing that Clinton has chosen to take part in this hypocrisy. The real problem is the war itself and the unwillingness, or inability, to look for new options. In fairness, this year's drug strategy put forth by Gen. Barry McCaffrey is softer in tone than those issued by the first drug czar, William Bennett. There's even a nod to education, treatment and compassion.

But beneath the rhetoric, *the federal government is still waging war on citizens,* 70 million of whom have used illegal drugs. Though voters in both California and Arizona have taken their disapproval of the nation's drug policies to the voting booths, the Clinton administration continues to pour funds into a campaign that is cowardly and dishonest, and is starting to become comparable to the ugly government excesses of the McCarthy and Vietnam eras.

Our challenge as individuals, communities and a nation is not to eradicate drugs—an impossible task that flies in the face of the history of human experience—but to learn how to live with their presence so that they cause the least possible harm and generate the greatest possible benefit. There is no denying that a small percentage of those who use drugs also abuse them, but we can deal more effectively with drug abuse only if we are open and honest in talking about drugs and considering all the options.

How can that be done? For openers, heed the election results in California and Arizona, where voters demonstrated that they are ready and willing to adopt more pragmatic policies. Voters are fed up with the drug war, and they have begun to show it. They've lost faith. They want a saner drug policy, not old rhetoric and new prisons.

Start with the truth. When it's pointed out that "almost three-quarters of drug users are employed," take that as evidence that most drug users are responsible citizens, students and employees—not as a justification for a drug-testing witch hunt. There is little reason to keep pretending that there is no difference between responsible and irresponsible use of drugs, legal or illegal.

Respect the science. Nearly every independent commission assigned to examine the evidence on marijuana and marijuana policy—including a National Academy of Sciences committee—has concluded that marijuana poses fewer dangers to individuals and our society than either alcohol or tobacco and should be decriminalized. Similarly, virtually every expert scientific advisory body ever created to study drug abuse agrees that making sterile syringes available to injection-drug users stems the spread of HIV without increasing drug abuse. The

U.S. is essentially alone among advanced industrialized nations in not making access to sterile syringes a central component of its HIV-prevention efforts.

Act pragmatically, not ideologically. Drug treatment can work if given half a chance. But drug treatment is a matter of different strokes for different folks. Twelve-step programs and therapeutic communities are what some people need to put drug problems behind them. When it comes to heroin addiction, there is scant disagreement among scientists: Methadone works best. But someone has to take the lead in fighting the stigma associated with this form of treatment and making it readily available to those who need it.

Use common sense. Everything we know about addiction tells us that the choices are not solely between drug abuse and complete abstinence. When people reduce their drug intake, or restrict their use to particular times and places, or consume drugs in less dangerous ways and forms, all these represent steps in the right direction. It's called harm reduction. A negative drug test is not necessarily the desired end point of successful drug treatment. Far more important are improvements in health, employment and responsible living—even if one's urine is not clean.

Finally, remember the bottom line. American citizens have a right to insist that government officials stop tossing their money down the drain on programs that do nothing. It's time to skewer the sacred cows of the drug war: interdiction efforts that do nothing to protect homes and communities; DARE drug-education programs that cost hundreds of millions of dollars but don't educate or otherwise prevent drug abuse; federal- and state-prison cells for tens of thousands of nonviolent drug offenders; asset-forfeiture programs that enrich police departments and divert police priorities from focusing on violent and other predatory criminal activity.

By criminalizing a basic human behavior, we have done nothing but allow vast criminal enterprises not only to flourish but to take over the governments of nations like Mexico and Colombia while imprisoning 400,000 people in the U.S. Now, Clinton proposes to escalate the war. The facts are clear: People take drugs no matter what the government says or does. Real leadership requires the courage and honesty to recognize that the war on drugs, like the war in Vietnam, is cruel, wrong, and unwinnable. —Jann S. Wenner and Ethan A. Nadelman[6]

## NOTES

[1] This is a reiteration of claim 5 (the thesis of the argument).

[2] Jerry Mander, *Four Arguments for the Elimination of Television* (New York: Quill, 1978), p. 43.

[3] Ibid., pp. 43–45.

[4] Randall Terry, quoted in *Boston Globe,* January 9, 1995.

[5] President William Jefferson Clinton, "The State of the Union," January 27, 1998.

[6] Jann S. Wenner and Ethan A. Nadelman, *Rolling Stone,* no. 758, April 17, 1997.

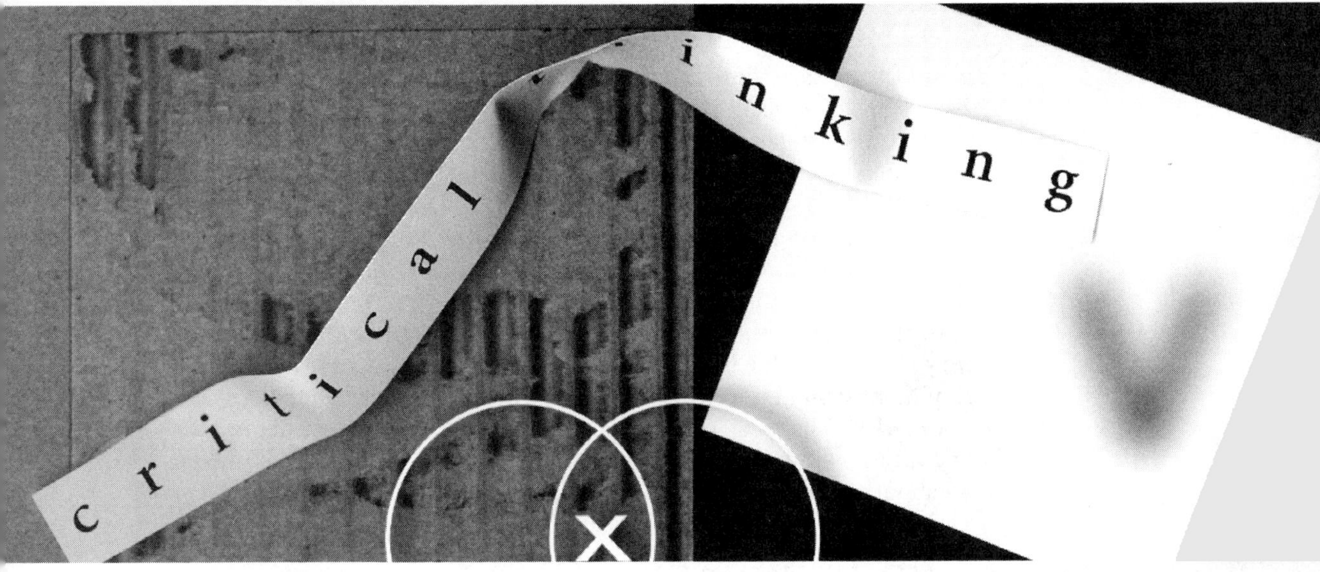


# CHAPTER 14 Writing Argumentative Essays

As you make your way through college, you will have many occasions to express yourself. Probably there is no single expressive activity you will be called upon to do more often in your coursework than write. And the kind of thing you will be called upon to write more often than not will be an argumentative essay. This chapter is intended to help you write good argumentative essays. It not only shows you what argumentative essays consist of but also gives you strategies for writing them that are based on the critical thinking skills you have acquired.

You might wonder why the essay is so central to education. There are so many kinds of writing: fiction, biography, poetry, jokes, news reports, letters, screenplays, ad copy, and so forth. Why always an essay? Probably the best short answer is that the essay's elements and format are basic to so many practical applications and other kinds of writing. Indeed, a good many instances of the kinds of writing just mentioned—fiction, biography, humor, news reports, letters, ad copy—are influenced by the essay. In editorial pieces, in art criticism, in business reports, in scholarly papers, in political speeches, in corporate memos, just about anywhere you care to look, you'll see the elements and organizational format of the essay cropping up. This means that learning how to write essays gives you one of education's most useful tools.

Perhaps this explanation doesn't go deep enough. What makes the essay so important in so many areas? The answer is that the essay is so flexible a framework and so well suited to the related and essential human tasks of exploring and communicating ideas. We stress the fact that the essay is suited to *both* these tasks, not just to the task of communicating. Writing is at least as much a process of discovering what one thinks as it is a matter of composing the results of prior thinking. Thus the importance and value of the essay is not merely as a format for the presentation of the results of your explorations, a sort of literary mold into which you pour your thoughts when they're ready to go to market. The essay has an even more basic value as an organizational framework for finding out or figuring out what one thinks—what one has to say—about a subject.[1]

## ARGUMENT AND PERSUASION

Rhetoric is the classical discipline devoted to the general study of expressive discourse. Indeed, the term "rhetoric" derives ultimately from the Greek expression for "I say." Classical rhetoric distinguishes four forms of discourse under which all kinds of writing could be classified: narrative or "story-telling"; description, or telling how something looks, sounds, feels, tastes, or smells; exposition, the setting forth or clarification of facts and ideas; and finally, persuasion, intended to induce readers to accept the opinion of the writer or speaker.

Of these four categories, rhetoric's main traditional concern has been the development and systematic refinement of skills, techniques, and strategies of persuasion. Historically, rhetoric's traditional emphasis on persuasion arose in ancient Greece. In the developing political context of the city-states, citizens found it increasingly important to learn how to make effective and persuasive presentations in the assemblies and law-courts, the principal institutions of self-government, where the laws were made and interpreted.

There is, then, a deep historical connection in rhetoric between persuasion and argument. Argumentative essays, though they may employ narrative, descriptive, and expository discourse, fall into the persuasive category. This is because argument is essentially a persuasive device. It is aimed at *rational* persuasion—persuasion by appeal to reason.

But as you are already well aware, argument and persuasion are not identical. Nor do they always go hand in hand. A rational approach may fail to persuade; and it is possible to be persuasive without being very rational. A perfectly cogent argument may well turn out to be less persuasive than some blatant fallacy. The central aim of the argumentative essay is to be rationally persuasive. The best argumentative essays combine a good argument with a persuasive presentation.

But before we can usefully address this as a goal, we have to have a writing project. The first questions you will need to ask as a writer are: "What do I want to write about?" and "What do I want to say about it?" These questions correspond to two essential preliminary steps in the writing process: selecting—and focusing—a subject; and formulating a thesis about it.

## THE ISSUE STATEMENT

The introduction of your essay should orient your reader to your topic. It should clearly indicate what is within the scope of your inquiry. Every essay relates to some topic. The topic is the area of concern or interest. In argumentative writing the topic will be an issue, that is some topic about which reasonable people may disagree. "Education in the United States," "the electoral process," "drugs," "feminism," "the penal system," "religion," and "conflict between the generations" all represent topics that are ripe for argumentative exploration. The first job of the argumentative writer, then, is to decide on some such topic. Often instructors do this for students. When instructors assign you a topic your job of formulating a thesis is simplified. But sometimes they leave the choice up to you. Faced with no topical limitations, students sometimes falter; they can't formulate a thesis because they can't settle on a topic or even select a subject area that they wish to write about.

Have you ever noticed how much longer it takes to make a decision and place an order in a restaurant with a huge menu than it does in a restaurant with only three choices? Whatever one winds up choosing, there are *so many things one will not get to eat.* Baffled by an overabundance of options, we frequently don't know what we want—and sometimes even start to wonder if we were hungry at all! When the array of options is unlimited, as it is in a free-choice assignment, we might wonder what it is that we really want to address ourselves to. But don't forget: It's not as if you have a shortage of interests, or of opinions about interesting and controversial topics. And it's not as if you have to write about all of them at once. All you have to do is choose one. Here are four things you can do when stymied by a free-choice assignment.

*First, you can select something that you are familiar with and about which you would like to learn more.* Perhaps you've had a health course and learned something about vitamin therapy in the treatment of disease. If you want to learn more, why not make vitamin therapy your subject? Or maybe you recently read a newspaper article entitled "The American Indian: The Forgotten Minority." You remember being moved by the piece and wishing that you had the time to explore the plight of American Indians further. Here again is a possible subject. Or perhaps one of your outstanding gripes with colleges is the weight that admissions officers sometimes place on standardized tests. If you want to learn more about the pros and cons of such testing, make it the subject of your paper.

*Second, you can choose a subject that you know nothing about but would like to investigate.* A good place to begin is with terms you encountered once and glossed over, such as "supply-side economics," "circadian rhythms," "the big bang theory," "astral plains," or "cybernetics." Such terms are potential subjects for essays. Subjects you'd like to learn something about can originate in conversations.

A few years ago a student did an essay on what some experts on organizational psychology and management term "Theory Z," which is a way of approaching and structuring work that was then new to the United States but had been common throughout Japan for decades. When asked how he had decided on such an unusual subject, the student explained that some time earlier he had struck up a conversation with a passenger on a flight from San Francisco to Los Angeles. As it happened, the exchange turned to the subject of work and young people's attitudes toward it. The passenger thought that the Japanese approach to work organization might be more appealing to young American workers and help improve U.S. productivity. The flight ended before the passenger could explain very much about this approach. The student didn't think much more about the encounter until, a few months later, he was asked to write a free-choice essay. Recalling the conversation, he discovered his subject.

*Third, you can skim newspapers, magazines, and other periodicals for possible subjects.* A good newspaper (and sometimes even a poor one) is a treasure trove of subjects. Daily columns, commentaries, and editorials abound with information about current events, science, medicine, the arts, sports, religion, and education. In fact, brief news reports often inspire a subject. Another enterprising student once chanced upon an item explaining that the Food and Drug Administration had banned for sale in the United States an intrauterine device called the Dalkon Shield. A few weeks later the student came across another item concerning the export of the Dalkon Shield for sale abroad. She found this odd and began to wonder how many other products that were banned in the United States were being shipped overseas for sale. "Why not write an essay on this subject?" she thought. She did, and was it an eyepopper!

*Fourth, you can consult the library for a subject of interest.* Because the card catalogs contain information on every subject, merely perusing them should yield a clutch of ideas. Better yet, cruise the Internet!

Once you have found a subject area you may find that it contains a great many possible topics. "Write a five-hundred-word essay on advertising," your English professor might tell you. Faced with such an assignment, you could be confused. "What *about* advertising?" you wonder. Your instincts rightly tell you that advertising is far too broad and unwieldy a subject to be handled in a mere five hundred words. The problem you perceive is analogous to the overabundance of options mentioned just a moment ago. Therefore you may feel the need to select among the possible topics contained within a given subject area and to focus it so that it can be managed within the prescribed length.

This problem of focusing is one which will continue to crop up again and again from time to time as you go. As you focus on a particular subject area within the endless array of possible subject areas, you begin to see the complexities, the numerous topics, involved in it. As you focus more narrowly on a particular topic within a subject area, you may again come to see further complexities embedded within it, you may begin to notice how many different aspects it has. In any case, at the outset of your essay you will need to indicate to your readers what they may expect to find contained within the scope of your essay.

### BALANCE

Since you're writing about an issue, a topic about which reasonable people may disagree, initially your statement of the issue should be "balanced." This means not prejudiced either in favor of or against any of the positions that a reasonable person might be inclined to hold about the topic. You don't want to alienate any of your potential readers before they have a chance to consider your argument in its totality. One of the best ways to achieve this is to make a relatively clear distinction between your issue statement, in which you bring your topic into focus for your reader, and your thesis statement, in which you tell your reader where you stand on the issue. If you can present the issue in a balanced way, this tells your reader that you understand that there is room for reasonable disagreement on the matter, and that you are capable of understanding positions that may differ from your own in a respectful way.

## THE THESIS STATEMENT

Every argument has a point or conclusion, which in an argumentative essay usually is termed the "thesis." The thesis is the argumentative essay's main idea; that is, the main point being advanced. Thus formulating a thesis statement is an essential early step in the writing process. The thesis statement gives the essay its purpose and direction, without which it would be little more than a random collection of sentences and paragraphs.

Think of your thesis as your topic plus your attitude toward it or opinion about it. Being aware of your attitude toward your topic may help you decide what you have to say about it. For example, you may be *fearful* of the impact of three landmark decisions; *critical* of the use of ambiguity to sell aspirin, toothpaste, and mouthwash; or *convinced* of the significant effects of advertising costs on the retail prices of alcoholic and nonalcoholic beverages.

It is important to stress at this point that saying anything substantial enough to warrant an essay involves taking risks. To write an entire essay in defense of a thesis that no one would dispute is too safe. It amounts to a waste of your own and your reader's time and attention. "Millions of Americans smoke cigarettes" for example is an assertion so uncontroversial and so easily verified that the need—and certainly the wisdom—of constructing an essay to demonstrate its truth is precluded.

On the other hand, nor should you *confine* yourself in your thesis to assertions about your own attitudes and experience, your own inner life. Suppose that the topic you have selected is the impact on consumers of three landmark decisions in consumer law, and that your attitude is that you are fearful that progress made in consumer protection during the past decade will be undone. Your thesis should of course express your attitude. But it should do more than merely state that you have this attitude.

Suppose others have a different attitude. (Indeed, you pretty much have to suppose this. Otherwise you're not taking enough of a risk.) Having read your thesis they now challenge you to defend it, and you point out, "My thesis is merely that *I* am fearful that progress made in consumer protection during the past decade will be undone." This is another way of playing it safe. Indeed, it amounts to a retreat from the issue.

Your thesis is determined by your attitude but it is not *about* your attitude. Remember, the aim of an argumentative essay is to be rationally persuasive. You *are* trying to win your reader over. This involves taking risks. One of the risks is the risk of being mistaken. After all, this is precisely why you are looking for good reasons to support your position, isn't it?

After writing your thesis statement it's a good idea to check it for clarity and accuracy. Does it clearly communicate what you have to say? A good way to check your statement is to have somebody else read it back to you, while you listen to it critically. Or have someone read it and then paraphrase it back to you. Ask the person, "What do you think I'm trying to demonstrate in my essay?" If the reply corresponds with your purpose, you have a well-focused thesis statement. If it doesn't, then back to the drawing board!

## ARGUMENT DESIGN

In general, good argument design flows from a clear and detailed understanding of both the thesis and the issue to which the thesis responds. Depending upon the precise nature of the issue with which one is concerned, and of the sub-issues involved in it, and of the claim one is defending as one's thesis, different argument design strategies will be more or less viable and promising. The kind of argument we might need to design in order to effectively support and defend a value judgment may not work very well to support and defend a causal hypothesis. One general principle for argument design therefore is simply to study your issue closely and analytically, letting your insights into its character and complexities guide you to a deeper awareness of the strengths and vulnerabilities of your position. (See especially Chapter 2 and Chapter 8.)

## ORGANIZATIONAL APPROACHES

The familiar general essay format—introduction, body, conclusion—is extremely flexible as to length, topical focus, and so on. And it will accommodate a wide variety of more specific organizational strategies or approaches which may prove to be more or less appropriate to some particular argument on a given topic. We will discuss four of the most common of these: (1) the inductive approach, (2) the pro-and-con approach, (3) the cause-and-effect approach, and (4) the analysis-of-alternatives approach. These and other organizational plans can be used individually or in combination with each other depending primarily on this first general principle of argument design.

## INDUCTIVE APPROACH

Suppose that you want to make your main argument deductively valid, but you can't find any premises for your main argument that are "self-evident." So you structure your main argument as a deduction and then turn to the matter of supporting your main premises. Again suppose you want to make your arguments in support of your main premises deductively valid, but you can't find any useful premises that are "self-evident." At some point you might consider proceeding inductively. An inductive approach is especially useful when your purpose is to convince the audience of a rather controversial assertion and the evidence you have to present is, though not absolutely conclusive, less controversial than the thesis. Presenting the body of evidence first helps you turn audience attention to the evidence, which is allowed to speak for itself. Ideally, having seen the evidence, members of the audience will change their minds or will at least be more receptive to your controversial conclusion.

For example, suppose your purpose is to convince a skeptical audience that Americans are not as well fed as they think they are. Using the inductive approach you might structure your essay as follows:

**Fact 1** According to the most recent information, 20 percent to 50 percent of Americans run some risk of not meeting the U.S. recommended daily allowance for at least one or more of the vitamins C, A, $B_1$ (thiamine), $B_2$ (riboflavin), and folic acid.

**Fact 2** Although the diets of most Americans may be richer in minerals than they were fifty years ago, our intake of such minerals as iron and calcium still is likely to be insufficient.

**Fact 3** Many people today, young and old, are dieting and skipping meals. As a result they may be eliminating foods that contain many vitamins, including C, E, and B-complex.

**Conclusion** These facts point to an unmistakable conclusion: There are serious gaps in our national diet, most frequently because of poor eating habits.

## PRO-AND-CON APPROACH

Notice that the preceding example presents a "closed case" for your contention. Here is an alternative strategy based on a more dialectical, "balance-of-considerations" approach: The pro-and-con essay attempts to reach a balanced conclusion by treating an issue as an open question worth thinking about. In it the arguer usually begins by discussing the pros and cons of an issue. The discussion serves as a basis for a balanced conclusion to emerge as a compromise position. This format, then, consists of (1) the confirmation of an idea, (2) the objection to the idea, and (3) the thesis as a compromise arrived at by balancing considerations. This approach has special audience appeal because it flatters their intelligence and sense of fair play and speaks well of the writer's thoughtfulness and impartiality. Here's an example:

**Confirmation** Undoubtedly the United States enjoys one of the highest standards of living and is the largest producer of food products in the world. Our agricultural and industrial resources understandably make many Americans and non-Americans alike consider us the best-fed people on earth.

**Objection** Current evidence suggests that we are far from realizing the nutritional promise of our bountiful resources. For one thing 20 percent to 50 percent of us run some risk of not meeting the U.S. recommended daily allowance.

**Conclusion** Calling ourselves the best-fed people on earth is misleading. Rather, we appear to be potentially the best-fed people on earth. Whether we realize our potential depends largely on whether we can close the gaps in our national diet by improving our eating habits.

## CAUSE-AND-EFFECT APPROACH

The cause-and-effect essay is especially appropriate obviously for discussing issues which involve some question of causality. One way to do this is to present the major causes in chronological order, as in treating some historical event. Another is to arrange the causes in order of importance. Often writers of a cause-and-effect essay have in mind some remedy, which they present after they have discussed the causal conditions underlying a problem. In that event the writer's purpose is twofold: (1) to make the audience aware of the causes and (2) to make it accept the proposed solution. The cause-and-effect essay, then, often follow this structure: statement of problem, various causes, proposed solution. Here's an example:

**Statement of Problem** It is commonly thought that Americans are the best-fed people on earth. Yet current evidence indicates that there are serious gaps in our national diet.

**First Major Cause** The deficiencies in our national diet are attributable to several factors. Perhaps the most important is poor eating habits.

**Second Major Cause** Lack of education is another reason for the deficiencies in our national diet. Although public school curricula inevitably include a "health" component, very little of it is devoted to the study of proper nutrition.

**Third Major Cause** Still another factor that explains our nutritional deficiencies is the medical profession's traditional ignorance of or lack of interest in proper nutrition. Historically doctors have spent little time impressing on patients the link between poor diet and ill health.

**Conclusion Proposal** Undoubtedly we Americans have the potential for being the best-fed people on earth. But until we change our eating habits, schools start instructing students in proper nutrition, and health professionals begin reinforcing this instruction, we stand little chance of realizing our potential.

## ANALYSIS-OF-ALTERNATIVES APPROACH

Often the purpose of an essay is to make the audience accept one of several alternatives. This is accomplished by structuring the presentation according to options. Thus the essay that analyzes alternatives tries to make the audience accept one option as preferable by examining and eliminating other less desirable options. This strategy is especially useful in making the audience accept the "lesser of the evils" or an untried approach. For example:

**Thesis** The eating habits of elementary schoolchildren can be improved in many ways.

**First Alternative** One way is for the U.S. government to exercise tighter control over the school lunch program. Undoubtedly this approach will invite a full-scale social debate about the proper role of government in relation to business and consumers.

**Second Alternative** Another approach is for schools to prohibit the sale of junk food on campus. Where this has been tried, it has met widespread opposition from children, parents, and, of course, the junk food industry.

**Third Alternative** A third alternative is to make nutrition a basic and continuing part of a child's education. This approach has the advantage of being far less controversial than either of the other two. More important, it respects the autonomy of individuals by equipping them to make informed food choices but not restricting their choices. Perhaps most important, this approach stands the best chance of getting students to eat properly outside school and to develop sound eating habits for life.

# APPRECIATING YOUR OPPONENT'S POSITION

Because your thesis responds to an issue, and because issues are by definition topics about which reasonable people may disagree, your thesis will tend to be relatively controversial. A second general principle for argument design flows from this, and from the fact that in arguing for your thesis, you are essentially trying to be persuasive, to win your audience over. Try to identify premises that are less controversial, less subject to debate, than your thesis. In other words, try to find "common ground" on which to base your argument for your thesis.

This second general principle of argument design suggests some further ideas about argument construction. The medieval philosopher and theologian Thomas Aquinas once remarked that when you want to convert someone to your view, you go over to where he is standing, take him by the hand (mentally speaking), and guide him to where you want him to go. You don't stand across the room and shout at him. You don't call him nasty names. You don't order him to come over to where you are. You start where he is, and work from that position. To put it another way: When you think that someone is wrong, and you disagree with her, you should first try to figure out in what ways she is right. This is not as paradoxical as it sounds. Suppose you're firmly convinced of some particular position on a complex and controversial subject like the death penalty. Are you absolutely certain that you're 100 percent correct? Can you be absolutely certain that someone who disagrees with you is entirely wrong in everything she might have to say? Wouldn't it be wiser to thoughtfully consider what your opponent might have to say, and to concede as much as you honestly can? Then when you go on to offer criticisms of your opponent's position, you can reasonably expect her to be given thoughtful consideration as well. After all, think how you would react as a reader to a criticism of your position. If the criticism starts out by identifying your position as out-to-lunch, you're not likely to be very receptive, are you? You'd be much more open to a criticism which began by stating your position in a way that you would yourself state it, recognizing its intuitive plausibility, or its explanatory power, or the weight of evidence in its favor, or whatever strengths it may have. Thus, when you oppose a position and undertake to criticize it you enhance your chances of being persuasive if you can state that position in a way that would fully satisfy someone who holds it—even more so if you can make out a better case for it than the proponent herself can.

## ANTICIPATING OBJECTIONS

Just as you should be aware of the possibility that your opponent's position may embody certain strengths, you should be aware of the possibility that your own position may have certain weaknesses—weaknesses which very likely will be more apparent to your opponent than to you. Thus an additional strategic advantage for the writer of an argumentative essay flows from making a genuine attempt to appreciate the opponent's position. Your opponent's position affords you a much better vantage point from which to troubleshoot your own position and argument—to make yourself aware of points at which your argument stands in need of additional support, or of needed qualifications and refinements of the thesis itself.

## AUDIENCE AWARENESS

Let's now return to the central aim of the argumentative essay—to be rationally persuasive. The best argumentative essays combine a good argument with a persuasive presentation. And one of the keys to a persuasive presentation is awareness of one's readership. If your essay has been assigned as part of a class, your immediate readership is your instructor or your instructor's teaching assistant. But even in such circumstances it's worth thinking beyond the limits of the assignment and the class. Imagine yourself as writing for a "real world" readership outside of the academic setting. Many of your instructors (especially the good ones) will appreciate and encourage this sort of imaginative approach on your part for a number of reasons. First of all, if you imagine yourself writing for a "real world" readership, in effect you're practicing and developing skills for which you will no doubt find useful applications outside your immediate academic setting (and your instructors like to feel that they are helping you prepare yourself for a successful life after graduation). Secondly, if you imagine yourself writing for a "real world" readership—as opposed to simply doing homework for a grade—chances are that what you write will be more interesting and rewarding to read (and believe it or not, your instructors really do prefer to read interesting and rewarding compositions). So try to imagine writing for some readership other than your instructor.

Now, if you are imagining a readership beyond your instructor, imagine that you were going to stand up before them as an audience and address them orally. In other words, think of your readership as real people, not just disembodied pairs of eyes. One of the scariest things about public speaking is that you get to see the evidence of the impression your words are making on your audience as you speak them. For example, your instructor gets to see how many of her students are nodding off or reading their physics assignment while she's delivering her lecture. Have you ever wondered what makes a stand-up comic funny? Certainly mannerisms, temperament, delivery, timing, and a sense of the tragic and absurd all contribute. But one of the most important ingredients is audience awareness. Without a particular audience response—laughter—a comic "dies." So stand-up comics have to study their audiences, learning as much as they can about their audience members' ages, social and educational backgrounds, sexual and racial characteristics, their biases, inhibitions, fears, and so on. All of this will influence the comic's choice of words, dialect, and points of reference. Most often stand-up comics have to accomplish this on the fly, in the moment, while they're doing the jokes, which helps explain how tricky it is to draw and walk that thin line between being funny and being offensive, between good humor and bad taste. When comics overstep the line, chances are it's because they have ignored or misjudged their audience.

There is a lesson in this for the writer of an argumentative essay. For the comic, winning over the audience means getting them to laugh. For the writer of an argumentative essay it means getting your readers to agree with you, or at least to sympathetically enter into your way of thinking. Success depends largely on how well each has shaped the material to suit the audience or readership. Shaping an argument to suit your readership requires the same kind of audience study that the comic makes. Keep in mind the values, prejudices, and basic assumptions of the people you want to influence. Also be aware of their educational, economic, and social backgrounds; their ages; their occupations; and their feelings about current issues. Here is an inventory of key areas to think about when analyzing your audience or readership:

1. *Age:* How old are the members of my audience? What effect, if any, will their ages have on their reception of what I'm trying to say?
2. *Values:* What is important to my audience—family, job, school, neighborhood, religion, country? What are their fundamental ideals—being successful, getting married, realizing their potential, ensuring law and order, guaranteeing civil liberties, establishing international harmony?
3. *Economics:* Is my audience wealthy, middle-class, poor, or a cross-section? Are they currently employed, unemployed, training for employment?
4. *Social Status:* From which social group does my audience come? What's important to this group? What references will they identify with?
5. *Intellectual Background:* What does my audience know about my subject? What can I take for granted that they will know? Which words can I expect them to understand; which ones should I make sure to explain?
6. *Expectations:* What will my audience be expecting of my essay? Why will they be reading it? What will they be looking for?
7. *Attitude:* What can I assume will be my audience's attitude toward my topic? Will they likely be sympathetic, hostile, or indifferent?

Let's imagine a case in which we put this to work. Suppose that you are a member of a student group that has been selected to meet with a committee of professors and administrators who are considering a new policy to award academic credit for work experience. You have been chosen to argue the case in favor of such a policy. And so now you will want to do an audience inventory in preparing your case.

First, the members of your audience will be mostly middle-aged, from thirty-five to fifty-five. Second, they probably never received any such credit when they were in school and some of them may never have been associated with any institution that gave such credit. Third, they will be intelligent, well-educated people who see themselves as open-minded, reasonable, and flexible. Fourth, they will be concerned about the institution's academic integrity and reputation. Fifth, they will be naturally concerned about the "nuts and bolts" of administrative implementation of any such policy. (Will *any* kind of work experience count for credit? If not, what conditions should be met to warrant credit?) Sixth, they will be sensitive to the opinions of alumni, the board of trustees, and parents, all of whose financial and moral support the school needs.

Armed with this kind of commonsense information about your audience, you can give your argument form and character, and also assume an appropriate posture or "persona."[2] In rhetoric the term "persona" refers to the role or identity assumed by a writer or speaker. In arguing your case before a group of professors and administrators, you will want to appear thoughtful, intelligent, serious, and mature. But suppose you were addressing a student audience. While your argumentative purpose remains the same—to win assent for the granting of academic credit for work experience—you might be more effective if you struck a different pose, let's say of an angry young person who sees elements of elitism and a fundamental injustice in the traditional policy of giving academic credit only for coursework. You might heighten this image by projecting yourself as a youthful progressive locked in combat with academic traditionalists out of step with the times. There is nothing in and of itself objectionable about considering your audience and working hard to strike a pose calculated to win them over, assuming of course that there's more to your case than mere posturing—that you have a genuinely defensible position and a worthy argument to present.

## OUTLINING

As you build your case you will want to ensure that your argument hangs together and that your thesis is convincingly and legitimately supported. An excellent device for testing the web of logical relationships in your essay—as well as for guiding and controlling the work of composition—is an outline. But many student writers (and nonstudent writers, for that matter) don't fully exploit the outline, a very powerful tool for structuring an essay. Often the outline goes no further than:

I. Introduction
   A. My issue statement
   B. My thesis statement
II. Body
   A. Reasons in favor of my position
   B. My objections to the other side
III. Conclusion

A minimal outline such as this is of very little use in thinking things through and building a strong argument and a quality composition. To get the most out of your outline you will want to go into much greater depth and detail, especially as regards the argument you are building. Break item II down further. What are the reasons in favor of your position? And how are those reasons related to each other? What evidence supports those reasons? What are your objections to the opposing position? And what objections can you anticipate coming from the opposing side? How will you respond to such objections? Be specific. Make sure to define key terms and concepts, and any terms that are ambiguous. Be conscious of the need to support your claims with facts, and to illustrate your points with examples. All of this material needs to be placed in some order so that your reader can follow your train of thought through your composition. The main function of outlining is to allow you to think through these structural details of the argument, as they relate to the organization of the composition, without at the same time having to work out all of the nuances of wording and presentation that will eventually go into the finished composition.

Here is one additional observation that further points up the value of outlining. Sometimes in the course of outlining you will find that your argument is taking you in some unplanned and unanticipated directions, suggesting maybe a different approach or thesis than the one you had originally undertaken to defend. If this happens, don't necessarily resist. Perhaps what's happening is that you are discovering things about the argument and the issue that are important. Let the reasoning carry you where it wants to go. There's nothing wrong with adjusting your thesis in accordance with the best reasoning you find yourself able to develop.

## WRITING THE ESSAY

Now that you are satisfied with your outline, it's time to start writing the essay. Actually, to be precise, you're already well under way in the writing process. But you will need to compose the results of your work in the form of a finished essay, and in the process, turn fragmentary sketches of your ideas into complete sentences and paragraphs, make smooth transitions, and so on. Essays of any length consist of a beginning, a development, and an ending.

### BEGINNING THE ESSAY

Many writers find beginning the most challenging moment in writing. It is helpful to bear in mind what you are doing as a writer in beginning an essay. Your primary tasks at the beginning of an essay are to orient your reader and motivate your reader's interest. Your issue statement and thesis statement are important elements in the introductory section of your essay. Their primary function is to orient your reader. Here are five strategies you can use to motivate reader interest:

1. *Indicate your feelings about the topic.* Illustration from a paper opposing pornography: "Rarely do we consider it politically interesting whether men and women find pleasure in performing their duties as citizens, parents, and spouses; or, on the other hand, whether they derive pleasure from watching their laws and customs ridiculed on stages, in films, or in books. Nor do we consider it politically relevant whether the relations between men and women are depicted in terms of an eroticism separated from love and calculated to undercut the family. Nevertheless, much of the obscenity from which so many of us derive pleasure today is expressly political."
2. *Relate your topic to something current or well known.* Illustration from a paper dealing with the evolution of the term "competition": "In the winter

of 1982, two monumental antitrust cases came to an end. In the first, AT&T (American Telephone and Telegraph) agreed to divest itself of a score of subsidiaries; in the second, the Justice Department dropped its suit against IBM (International Business Machines). Some heralded these events as a great victory for the free enterprise system. Others deplored them as a defeat for free enterprise at the hands of big business. Whether one sees these cases as good or bad for free enterprise depends very much on one's definition of *competition,* a concept whose current meaning does not always parallel its eighteenth century classical formulation."

3. *Challenge a generally held assumption about your topic.* Illustration from a paper on the virtues of not voting: "In the last presidential election, at least half of those eligible did not vote. These nonvoters faced the combined scorn of political parties, schoolteachers, chambers of commerce, the League of Women Voters, and sundry high-minded civic groups and individuals. In upcoming elections we can expect to see these same forces again heroically trying to 'get out the vote.' Yet the notion that 'getting out the vote' makes for better election results is not nonpartisan, patriotic, or logical."
4. *Show something paradoxical (puzzling) about your topic.* Illustration from a paper on the deficiencies in textbooks: "Textbooks certainly are among the most influential factors in an individual's intellectual, cultural, and social development. Yet, though they are called 'educational,' textbooks often teach little. Although they are thought 'liberalizing,' they sometimes inculcate narrow-mindedness and intolerance. Though they are viewed as disseminating American values, they sometimes work to undermine them. Yes, textbooks are influential, but not always in a positive way."
5. *State a few striking facts or statistics related to your topic.* Illustration from a paper dealing with the overconsumption of medical drugs in the United States: "The volume of drug business in the U.S. has grown by a factor of one hundred during the twentieth century. Twenty thousand tons of aspirin are consumed per year, about 225 tablets per person. Central-nervous-system agents are the fastest-growing sector of the pharmaceutical market, now making up 31 percent of total sales. Dependence on prescribed tranquilizers has risen about 290 percent since 1962. Medicalized addiction has outpaced all self-chosen forms of creating a sense of well-being, such as marijuana or alcohol."

## DEVELOPING THE ESSAY

In developing your essay you will be arguing your thesis, using the material you have gathered to make your points. Your thesis statement and your outline together contain your whole developmental strategy. If you've done a good job of formulating your thesis statement and of outlining your essay, developing the essay should be a fairly straightforward process of following your own earlier leads. Let your thesis statement guide the order of presentation. If your thesis contains divisions, you can take up points in the order indicated in your thesis statement. For example, if the thesis statement is:

> It's high time that laws were passed to restrict the advertiser's use of ambiguity to sell aspirin, toothpaste, and mouthwash.

the essay could take up ambiguity in selling aspirin, then in toothpaste, then in mouthwash. Or if the thesis statement is:

> Often overlooked in the retail prices of alcoholic and nonalcoholic beverages are the hidden costs of advertising.

the essay might take up the hidden costs of advertising in the price structure of alcoholic and then in nonalcoholic beverages. Let your organizational structure guide your order of presentation. In inductive essays the reasons are usually presented in order of importance. In a pro-and-con essay the confirmation of an idea is followed by an objection to that idea, which then is followed by a balanced view. In a cause-and-effect essay causes and effects are arranged either in chronological order or in order of importance. And in an analysis-of-alternatives essay alternatives typically are presented in order of the most common, most popular, or best-known first.

## ENDING THE ESSAY

The conclusion of your paper should reinforce your thesis, tie your paper together, and gracefully relinquish your reader's attention. (Think of your essay not as a "thing" which you hand in, but rather as a communicative interaction, a relational activity between two people, you and your reader. In this context, you play a role rather like leading a dance. Think of your reader as your dancing partner. Your reader has accepted your invitation and has followed you through your arrangement of ideas. Now it is time for you to take your leave. You will want to do so in a way which enhances, rather than detracts from, the experience of your reader.) Here are three strategies for ending the argumentative essay:

1. *Put a "new spin" on your thesis.* Rather than merely repeat your thesis, put it into perspective. Draw out some important further implication of it, something for the reader to "take away." Illustration: "In their editorial decisions, communication methods, and marketing devices, the media contribute dramatically to our individual and collective anxiety. For those in print and electronic journalism to ignore or minimize this psychological impact or glibly subordinate it to some lofty mission guaranteed by the Constitution seems irresponsible. To be sure, we need an unfettered press. But we also need a citizenry that is self-confident, optimistic, and panic free."
2. *Encapsulate your argument.* Assist your reader in digesting and retaining the substance and complexity of your thesis and its development and demonstration. Illustration: "'Getting out the vote,' then, does not necessarily make for better election results. On the contrary it is always partisan,

for a calm and dignified effort benefits the party in power and a frenetic one benefits the party out of power. It is no more patriotic than the time-honored American attitude of 'a plague on both your houses.' Nor is it logical. Since a successful 'getting out the vote' campaign generates votes from the poorly informed, uninformed, misinformed, and the downright indifferent and ignorant, it undercuts the votes of the intelligent electorate. No, let's not get out the vote; let's get out the *informed* vote."

3. *Tie your paper to something further.* Use the occasion of the ending to invite your reader to think on. Indicate an agenda that your paper has helped to determine. Illustration: "When classical capitalists such as Adam Smith talked about competition, they did so in a social and economic atmosphere quite different from today's. Whereas the economy of the industrial revolution was characterized by a comparatively free and open market system, the economy of the twentieth century is made up of relatively few enormous holding companies that can secretly fix prices, eliminate smaller companies, and monopolize an industry. Ironically, through intense competition such corporate giants have reached a point at which they can now make a mockery of the classical doctrine of competition. The challenge that lies ahead for society and government is to redefine competition in such a way that the classical notion is integrated into present-day realities. As the AT&T and IBM cases well illustrate, this is no mean undertaking."

## NOTES

[1] See V. A. Howard and J. H. Barton, *Thinking on Paper* (New York: Morrow, 1986).

[2] "Persona" comes from the Latin word for the masks worn by actors in ancient classical drama to immediately delineate their roles for the audience. Accordingly, a smiling mask signaled a comic character, and a sorrowful mask, a tragic character.

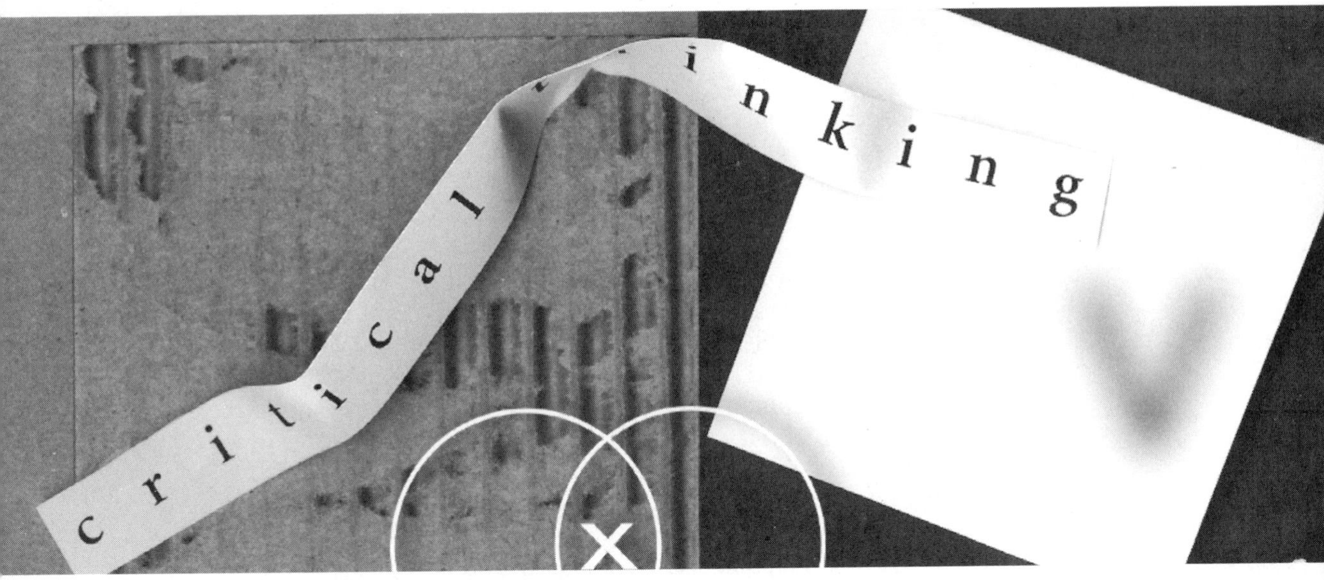


# CHAPTER 15 Solving Problems

In our approach to critical thinking so far our primary focus has been on issues and arguments. By now you should be comfortable with recognizing, analyzing, and evaluating relatively lengthy arguments about issues, as well as with composing your own in the form of argumentative essays. But this may seem to some readers a too limited focus for critical thinking. After all, not all of us are destined to devote our lives to the study and discussion of controversial issues. Many of us will write nothing other than personal correspondence and shopping lists after we exit college. Yet each and every one of us will have decisions to make and problems to solve throughout our lives. Does critical thinking have anything to offer outside the limited range of its application to social and political issues? The answer to this question is decidedly yes. So let's take a look at some of the dimensions of everyday decision making and problem solving from the perspective of critical thinking.

## IDENTIFYING THE PROBLEM

Problems come in an extremely wide variety of shapes, sizes, and kinds. And so the specific strategies and skills one needs to be an effective problem-solver are equally diverse. Solving problems in mathematics requires mathematical skills. Solving writing problems requires verbal skills. The specific strategies and skills you'd need to overcome writer's block probably won't take you very far in balancing the household budget. And budget-balancing skills are not the specific skills you need to resolve a conflict between two sets of in-laws over Thanksgiving dinner plans.

What critical thinking has to offer for making decisions and solving problems generally in everyday situations is quite useful, but it is also very basic and abstract. Accordingly it should not be regarded as sufficient *by itself* for solving actual particular problems. The first basic abstraction of critical thinking for problem solving is that solving any particular problem calls for specific skills, strategies, and insights appropriate to the kind and specific details of the problem one is facing. This is a good example of the kind of knowledge which is important and useful, but not sufficient by itself, for solving problems.

On the other hand, nor are the specific skills and strategies appropriate to a given problem sufficient *by themselves* for solving it. In addition, these skills and strategies need to be intelligently and effectively applied. Thus, in general, solving particular problems effectively draws heavily upon the skills, strategies, and dispositions of critical thinking, in addition to whatever more specific skills and strategies may be required. Let's discuss some of these ideas in relation to a typical everyday problem.

### AN EVERYDAY PROBLEM

Eric is halfway to campus, with just enough time to make it to his 9 o'clock class, where an important midterm exam is scheduled, when he realizes that he left his essay assignment, due in his 10 o'clock class, on his dresser. Should he go back to his room and get it? Should he keep going? If he goes back to his room to get it, he'll be at least fifteen minutes late for the exam in his 9 o'clock class, and he can't afford to risk taking that much time out of an important exam. But he can't afford to be late to his 10 o'clock class either. The instructor always takes attendance at the beginning of class, and one more absence or tardy will cost Eric a full grade point. Nor can he afford to show up without his assignment. He's scheduled to present the essay orally in today's class.

"What a hassle!" Eric thinks. "Now I'm spending all my energy wrestling with this problem instead of going over the material for the midterm like I planned. My concentration is blown and I'll bomb out on the exam and I still won't be prepared for my 10 o'clock class. Maybe I should just quit school!"

Then a thought occurs to him. "Wait a minute. Today is Tuesday, so my roommate is still at home, and he'll be coming in for his 10 o'clock lab. I'll just cut past the gym. There's a pay phone. It'll take two extra minutes to give him a call. Maybe he'll be able to swing by and meet me on his way in and drop the essay off."

## CORE SKILLS

Compressed into this small scenario, we can see a number of typical moments in the process of confronting a problem and arriving at a solution—moments from which we may abstract core skills basic to all problem solving: awareness, analysis, evaluation, and generation. In this context, it is important that these *not* be understood as discreet procedural steps to be followed in serial order in the process of solving problems. Indeed, they are inseparable aspects of what should be understood as an integrated—and flexible—process. As we shall see, in actual practice these aspects of problem solving interpenetrate each other. Awareness of a problem involves analysis, analysis in turn involves the evaluation of strategies and options, which involves or presupposes the generation of strategies and options, which involves or presupposes awareness of the problem.

## AWARENESS

There is a close connection between awareness and effectiveness at solving problems. It's a truism that awareness is a necessary first step in virtually all problem solving. Problems may occasionally evaporate but they almost never "fix themselves." Problem solving begins with an awareness that a problem exists. For instance, Eric only begins to work on his problem when he realizes that he left his essay assignment on his dresser. Had he not recognized the existence of the problem it would have gone unattended to until eventually he did recognize its existence.

A number of corollaries follow immediately from this. Any of the common obstacles to critical thinking, discussed in Chapter 1, which block awareness of the existence of a problem also stand in the way of solving it. Thus, it is of the first importance that one be aware of the common obstacles to critical thinking such as egocentricity, ethnocentricity, self-deception, and so on, and be on guard against them in order to become a more effective problem-solver. The old maxim about identifying and tackling small problems early, before they have a chance to grow into larger crises, also deserves mention in this connection.

Moreover, awareness plays an important role in Eric's progress toward a solution to his problem. His awareness of what day it is and of his roommate's routine, his awareness of his own whereabouts and of the locations of campus phones, all help him to identify a course of action which promises a way out of his problem. In general, maximizing awareness of oneself and one's circumstances enhances problem-solving ability.

### SHARPENING OBSERVATION SKILLS

Some years ago ABC television produced a program about a blind sports enthusiast, a fan of the Los Angeles Lakers who, in spite of his handicap, was able not only to follow the action of a game in progress, but to give accurate and sophisticated play-by-play commentary from courtside. It is worth dwelling on this to appreciate the remarkable difficulty of this individual's accomplishments. Basketball is an extremely complex and fast-moving sport, particularly when played at the professional level. Describing the play-by-play action of the game often strains the abilities of seasoned professional sportscasters who can not only *see* the game, but whose grasp of the action is facilitated by a wide range of visual cues including the scoreboard, the uniforms of each of the players and officials, the large numerals and names on the players' uniforms to assist in their identification, the painted areas of the court, and so on.

How could a blind person even begin to understand the game, much less appreciate its subtleties and nuances? There is, of course, a courtside announcer, who identifies crucial plays and players over the public address system. But that is the smallest part of the story. The real answer lies in the degree to which this man had cultivated and sharpened observation skills in his other senses. For example, since each player has a distinctive style, gait, and set of moves, he was able to identify players by the squeak of their shoes on the court, the force and frequency with which they dribble the ball, and so on, and to follow the ball, as it is dribbled, passed, and shot. He is able to identify, and even determine the mood of, the officials by the sound of their whistles. The crowd's reactions to the game are also full of useful information. In short, he had become acutely aware of the myriad sounds of the game, and he used these to construct, if not the actual visual experience of the game, something almost as rich or maybe even richer in relevant detail.

This is, as is frequently remarked, one of the most profound lessons that people with disabilities have to teach: the degree to which observation skills can be cultivated, sharpened, and refined. The importance of this for problem solving can't be overemphasized. It's no accident that detectives such as Sherlock Holmes and Lt. Columbo, the essence of whose characters is their problem-solving ability, are portrayed as having remarkable powers of observation. Of course Holmes and Columbo are fictional characters. But there is a real lesson in the way they are drawn—a lesson for all "real-world" problem-solvers. They notice what ordinarily goes overlooked, and this is one of the main mechanisms whereby they gather and identify the relevant information which enables them to solve the mystery of the moment.

## PROBLEM FINDING

Perhaps you've heard the old saying that one shouldn't go looking for trouble—it will find you anyway. There's a common and understandable attitude toward problems associated with this: Problems are to be avoided as far as possible. Nevertheless there is a very good case to be made for investing energy in *finding* problems. Studies of effective problem solving often focus on the creative and problem-solving efforts of successful thinkers in the arts, the humanities, and the sciences. Such studies have shown that a common factor among the most creative thinkers and successful problem-solvers is that they have selected very good problems to devote their energies to: intriguing problems with significant and far-reaching implications, and so on. The great British philosopher Bertrand Russell once remarked on the value of stocking the mind with a store of puzzles. The more difficult, the better. They make great exercise materials for the mind. And working on them often leads to interesting and worthwhile discoveries, valuable ideas which might otherwise never have occurred to anyone. If you can't find any really good problems to work on, you might try making some up.

This, too, is part of maximizing one's awareness: awareness of life's abundant mystery. Some writers have called this "cultivating a sense of wonder." Good problem-solvers are not only keen observers, they are good at wondering and asking questions about what they observe. Questions like: Why is a tree trunk round? How come a flag is made of cloth? Why do fish have scales? Why do children ask questions like these? And why do grown-ups react the way they do?

## ANALYSIS

Suppose we are aware of the existence of a problem. A second important element in effective problem solving is the analysis of the problem, coming to terms with it. What precisely is the problem? How should we describe or represent it? What precisely does the problem consist of? What sort of problem is it? Is it a calculation problem? A problem involving interpersonal dynamics? A mysterious mechanical problem requiring a diagnosis?

### DEFINING THE PROBLEM

In becoming aware of the existence of the problem we have already begun to come to terms with it, because obviously we have to be able to describe the problem of whose existence we are becoming aware in some way or another. Thus for example, when Eric realizes that he has a problem, he realizes at the same time a good deal of what the problem consists of. He is immediately aware of a number of the problem's characteristics. He realizes that he left his essay assignment on his dresser, that it is due in his 10 o'clock class, that he is already halfway to campus, and that he has just enough time to make it to his 9 o'clock class, where an important midterm exam is scheduled.

### CLARIFYING THE PROBLEM

But Eric's analysis of his problem doesn't stop there. In fact the analysis of the problem continues throughout the course of solving it. Each of the problem's characteristics has certain further implications. For example, the fact that Eric is halfway to campus entails that returning to his room will triple his remaining travel time. Thus as Eric proceeds to analyze his problem, he clarifies its various dimensions by drawing inferences. By now you're already quite familiar with the wide range of inferential possibilities. The importance of drawing and assessing inferences in coming to terms with oneself and one's circumstances, in this case with one's problems, should come as no surprise.

### CLARIFYING AVAILABLE INFORMATION

The same applies to observations made in the course of analyzing and solving the problem. Let's return for a moment to the case of the blind sports fan. For most of us, the sound of a basketball game at courtside, were we temporarily deprived of sight, would be an incomprehensible cacophony of squeaks, thumps, grunts, and undifferentiated crowd noise. But a more acute observer can gather from these sounds that Magic Johnson has the ball at the top of the key, has not given up his dribble yet, that Byron Scott has just set a pick for him to the left of the free-throw line, while Kareem is coming around the base line to set a low post on the right side. How is so much information discerned in these sounds? By reasoning about them, by drawing inferences from and about them based on observed patterns and relationships of similarity and difference. For example, if the sound of the bouncing ball and the squeaking shoes is moving from right to left, that means that the Lakers have possession. If the squeaking passes to the left ahead of the bouncing, and the bouncing is heard at a relatively constant rate, that means that one of the guards is advancing the ball deliberately and will be setting up the half-court offense. If the squeaking is faster than normal and we hear only one bounce, that indicates a fast break.

Earlier in this chapter we indicated that the aspects of problem solving interpenetrate each other. This is part of what we meant. Here we can see how the analysis of sensory experience "informs" awareness—literally gives form to it, makes "information" out of it. It also brings into focus an important range of core analytical problem-solving skills: discerning patterns and relationships.

## RECOGNIZING PATTERNS AND RELATIONSHIPS

A New Yorker, on first visiting San Francisco, takes a bus tour of Golden Gate Park and immediately thinks of Central Park. A new pop song appears on the radio, and listeners immediately recognize the artist as Sting. An art appraiser examines a canvas and exposes a hitherto undetected forgery of Picasso, and almost as an afterthought, identifies the hand of the forger.

Recognizing patterns and relationships, similarities and differences, is something we each do constantly. Patterns and relationships are present and discernible not only in human artifice, but throughout nature. Indeed, pattern is the indispensable guide to the adaptation of any intelligent organism to its environment. Pattern recognition is so basic and central to intelligence and to all intelligent activity that it is impossible to imagine what intelligent life would be like if such "analytical acts of awareness" weren't possible. Accordingly, a pattern which runs throughout all of human inquiry, from the most "primitive" to the most advanced and scientific, is the search for and discovery of pattern.

What you learned in Chapters 6, 7, and 8 about making and verifying observations, about formulating and testing hypotheses, and about drawing and assessing deductive and inductive inferences applies here to understanding how intelligent beings seek and discern patterns and relationships. In fact, a very reasonable and insightful way to understand the techniques and standards of reasoning that you've been studying throughout this course would be simply as aspects of intelligence, as ways that intelligence goes about seeking and discerning patterns and relationships.

But though the seeking and discerning of patterns and relationships is as natural for humans as breathing, we don't always do it as effectively as we might. Sometimes this is because we aren't seeking in the appropriate way. This is another area in which awareness of the barriers to critical thinking, discussed in Chapter 1, becomes important.

Let's consider how the limitations of a person's culture and worldview can inhibit the ability to discern patterns. People raised in a technological society sometimes find it hard to understand how so-called "primitive" peoples could have figured out regularities about the environment which high-tech teams of scientists work on for years, at great expense, and still haven't figured out. And yet, if anything, so-called "primitive" cultures frequently achieve a more sophisticated and accurate grasp of significant—not to mention "useful"—patterns in nature, particularly the "larger" ones, than do technological cultures like our own. With all of our science and technology, how can this be?

It is highly plausible to suppose that people who are used to and surrounded by technology tend to look for patterns typical of the surrounding technology. For example, they may expect to see regularities at intervals that fall within a certain limited range. They may not expect to wait a hundred and fifty years for the pattern to emerge. Thus, for example, naturalists schooled in modern scientific methods frequently remark how important is the virtue of *patience* in observation. To gather useful information about the natural environment, it is frequently necessary to wait and wait and watch and wait some more and watch some more until a pattern eventually becomes evident. Pre-technological peoples would not find this sort of observation of the natural environment extraordinary at all, least of all extraordinarily patient. Indeed, constant, close, and detailed attention to the natural environment has an easily understandable tendency to "tune the observer in" to the environment's natural rhythms, however fast or slow they may be.

## EVALUATION AND GENERATION

Let's rejoin Eric on his way to school. You remember that Eric has begun to analyze his problem. He realizes that he left his essay assignment on his dresser, that it is due in his 10 o'clock class, that he is already halfway to campus, and that he has just enough time to make it to his 9 o'clock class, where an important midterm exam is scheduled. And he has begun to trace the implications of these features of his situation. He knows for example, that the fact that he's halfway to campus entails that returning to his room will triple his remaining travel time. As Eric's analysis of his problem progresses, it begins more and more apparently to involve evaluation—evaluation of options, evaluation of consequences, evaluation of the analysis itself—and at the same time to generate new information, new options, and even new problem-solving strategies.

### EVALUATING OPTIONS

Returning to his room to retrieve his essay assignment is probably one of the first optional courses of action that occurs to Eric. But following this option would triple his remaining travel time, and that would make him late for his midterm exam, and that would be an unacceptable consequence. This means that returning to his room is not an adequate option. And this is one of the dimensions of the problem, as Eric now understands it.

## EVALUATING CONSEQUENCES

Here we can clearly see a number of the aspects typically involved in evaluating optional courses of action. Each optional course of action is going to have associated with it a number of consequences, some of them perhaps certain, some relatively less certain, but probable to one degree or another. Of these consequences some will be more desirable and some less desirable in relation to one's operative goals. So evaluating an optional course of action will involve identifying and determining the relative likelihood and desirability of its consequences. This will involve reasoning inductively about causes and probabilities, and it will also involve being clear about our goals. Again we can see how the various aspects of problem solving interpenetrate each other.

Other optional courses of action are similarly evaluated. One option would be to keep on going, take the midterm in the 9 o'clock class, and then return to his room for the essay. But this option would make him late for his 10 o'clock class, where attendance is taken promptly, and that would cost Eric a full grade point, which would be an unacceptable consequence. This means that returning to his room between classes is not an adequate option.

Another option would be to go to his 10 o'clock class without the essay assignment. But this option would leave Eric unprepared to perform as scheduled, and that would be an unacceptable consequence, which means that this is not an adequate option either.

## EVALUATING THE ANALYSIS

So far Eric's analysis of his problem has led him to a dead end. None of the options he can think of would adequately solve the problem. Now he's becoming frustrated with the problem and with his efforts to solve it, so frustrated that he even begins to consider a relatively self-destructive option: "Maybe I should just quit school!"

What Eric needs to do is to generate some new options. So far Eric has evaluated only the options that immediately occur to him, as "direct remedies" to the situation, so to speak. But in Eric's frustration we can already see him beginning to evaluate something else. Though he is not fully aware of it, he is beginning to turn his efforts in a creative and constructive direction. He is dissatisfied with his problem-solving process, and has begun to evaluate his analysis of the problem so far.

## CHALLENGING ASSUMPTIONS

Consider the following old Chinese puzzle: A man is taking a bushel of apples, a sheep, and a tiger to market when he comes to a wide river. There is a small raft which he can use to cross, so long as he takes only one item with him at a time (otherwise the raft will sink). The problem is that if he leaves the apples and the sheep alone together, the sheep will eat the apples; but if he leaves the sheep and the tiger alone together, the tiger will eat the sheep. How can he get himself, the apples, the sheep, and the tiger all to the other side of the river?

Let's approach this as methodically as we can. The man cannot begin by taking the bushel of apples, because that would leave the tiger alone with the sheep. Nor can he begin by taking the tiger, because that would leave the sheep alone with the apples. Suppose he takes the sheep, leaving the tiger and the apples. So far, so good. Now he returns for another load.

Suppose he takes the apples on his second trip. He cannot leave the apples alone with the sheep while he returns to get the tiger. Suppose he takes the tiger on his second trip. But neither can he leave the tiger alone with the sheep while he returns for the apples. Hmmm! Now what?

Suppose he takes the sheep back with him on his return trip. Aha! Now we have a solution. It no longer matters whether he takes the tiger or the apples on his second trip, as long as he takes the sheep back with him when he returns for his third trip. Suppose that on his second trip he has taken the apples. Now he returns for the tiger, taking the sheep with him on the return trip. He leaves the sheep and returns across the river with the tiger. He leaves the tiger alone with the apples again, and returns one last time for the sheep.

What stands in the way of a solution to this puzzle is a particular tacit assumption. The assumption is that taking any one of the items back across the river to the point of origin is not an option. This is a perfectly natural assumption. Given that the man's goal is to get all three items across the river, taking any item back in the other direction understandably seems counterproductive. Nevertheless, it is only when this assumption is suspended that a solution to the problem emerges.

This example illustrates a frequent obstacle in solving problems. Quite often, progress toward a solution hinges on identifying and suspending some tacit assumption in terms of which the problem is initially understood or defined. Here is another example:

Try to link up the following arrangement of nine dots using only four straight lines, without raising your pencil from the paper:

○ ○ ○

○ ○ ○

○ ○ ○

Hard, isn't it? A great many people approach this puzzle on the basis of a tacit assumption that the lines may not extend beyond the area defined by the nine dots. As long as this assumption is in effect, it is impossible to link all nine dots using only four straight lines without raising the pencil from the paper. However, as soon as this assumption is identified and suspended, the problem can be reconceptualized, new options become available, and a solution emerges:

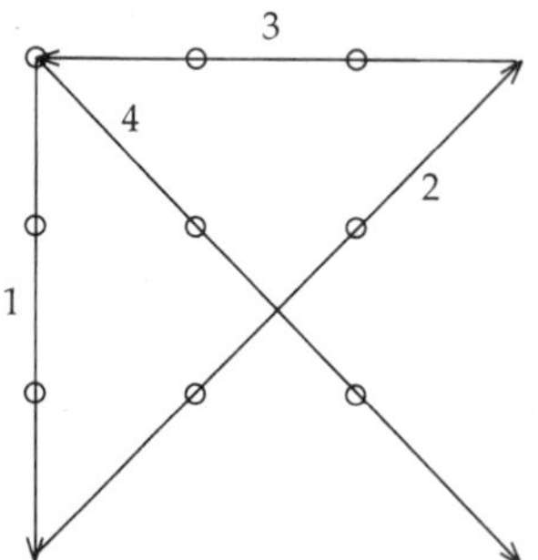


## REDEFINING THE PROBLEM

As we have just seen, challenging assumptions facilitates a redefinition or reconceptualization of the problem, which frequently brings new options into focus. In the example of the Chinese puzzle, the solution depends upon a reconceptualization of the problem as one of finding a sequence of moves which avoids sacrificing one of the pieces, rather than as one of moving all of the pieces forward without sacrifice. And this depends upon identifying and suspending the assumption that moving any piece backward is not an option. Some writers have called this sort of approach to problem solving "lateral thinking."

Some of the most dramatic examples of successful redefinition of the problem, through the identification and challenge of tacit assumptions, are to be found in the history of science. For example, Copernicus eventually succeeded in explaining the observed motion of the planets, where his predecessors had failed, by identifying and challenging the tacit assumption with which his predecessors had begun, and through which they had conceptualized the problem of accounting for planetary motion: that the planets revolved around the earth.

## EVALUATING STRATEGIES

Redefining a problem can also help us evaluate problem-solving strategies by helping us discover a simpler or more efficient route to the solution. Consider the mathematical problem: "What is 3/7 of 1/3?" When the problem is represented in this way, the most likely method of calculation would be to multiply the two fractions together, arriving at the result "3/21," then simplifying the result to arrive at "1/7." But suppose the problem had been represented as "What is 1/3 of 3/7?" A much simpler procedure now suggests itself: Simply divide the numerator.

We can see that Eric also successfully redefines his problem. Initially he conceives of the problem as an impossible time-management dilemma in which his only available options are blocked or unacceptable. He cannot return to his room to get his paper. That will in effect triple his remaining travel time to school, and he cannot afford to be late for his exam. But neither can he afford to be late for his next class, or to appear there without his paper, but there is no time between classes to return home for it. Eventually, however, Eric reconceptualizes the problem as one of coordinating his resources, and thus a new option emerges. He has a potential collaborator, his roommate, and he has a means of quickly reaching his roommate without losing too much time or causing serious inconvenience.

## EVALUATING AND GENERATING INFORMATION

Earlier we remarked how detectives such as Sherlock Holmes and Lt. Columbo are portrayed as having remarkable powers of observation, how they tend to notice what ordinarily goes overlooked, which enables them to solve the mystery of the moment. The inspector arrives at the scene of the crime, and orders that nothing be disturbed so that the investigative team can gather information. The room is full of information. Yet it's not that the investigative team records each and every detail. There are no doubt infinitely many details to be noted. The information is recorded selectively. Some relatively obvious piece of information—the fact that the room, like all the other rooms in the motel, is decorated in loud and tacky floral print wallpaper—may be unimportant, while some seemingly insignificant detail—the position of the hands of victim's smashed watch—may be crucial. Thus, two of the most important problem-solving skills are evaluating available information and using it to generate new information.

The most important difference between important and unimportant information is relevance. If the tacky wallpaper is an unimportant piece of information, that's because it doesn't help the investigators solve the crime. The position of the hands of the victim's smashed watch is valuable information, however, because it is relevant to solving the crime. It helps establish the time at which the crime was committed. Here the relevance and value of the information is as a means of generating new information which is also relevant and valuable.

The tricky thing about relevance however, as mentioned in Chapter 10, is that things can seem relevant which aren't, and seemingly irrelevant things can likewise be relevant. In other words "relevance" is sometimes misleading. Consider, for example, the following puzzle:

> A bus leaves Los Angeles bound for San Francisco. Three hours later a bus leaves San Francisco bound for Los Angeles. The buses are traveling at the same rate of speed. Which of the buses will be nearer to San Francisco when they meet?

What do you make of this? People frequently spend quite a bit of time trying to work out some algebraic formula for the solution to this puzzle. "Let's see. . . . Three hours, minus *x* divided by the same rate of speed equals ? ? ?" But this is all a waste of time. The speed information and the information about the difference in departure time, though it *seems* relevant, is all irrelevant to the problem. The relevant information is contained in the seemingly insignificant words "when they meet." When they meet the buses will be equidistant from San Francisco.

There are of course reasons why the irrelevant information in the puzzle seems relevant. We naturally tend to assume that any quantitative information given in what looks like a math problem will be relevant to solving that problem. But, however reasonable this is as a general rule, it's not always true. Many mathematical problems contain irrelevant as well as relevant quantitative information. Also we should not be too quick to assume that what looks like a math problem (because it contains quantitative information) really is one. In other words, we should not be too quick to adopt a problem-solving strategy based on the assumed relevance of certain available information. An appropriate safeguard in this kind of situation is to clarify the problem.

## MORE PROBLEM-SOLVING STRATEGIES

We have just seen how identifying and challenging assumptions can lead to a fruitful redefinition or reconceptualization of a problem, and thus to the generation of new options and strategies in the pursuit of a solution. This constitutes one very effective problem-solving strategy. The most effective problem-solvers among us generally have a fairly large repertoire of problem-solving strategies to draw upon, and are always open and on the lookout for new such strategies to explore. Here are a few additional problem-solving strategies you can use.

### BREAKING A PROBLEM DOWN INTO SUB-PROBLEMS

Problems which may seem insurmountable due to their size or degree of complexity can often be overcome by breaking them down into more manageable sub-problems. Goals whose distance may make them seem unreachable can often be reached by setting a series of intermediate goals. As ancient Chinese wisdom has it, the longest journey begins with the first step. (That's how this book was written, by the way: chapter by chapter, section by section, step by step.)

Here's a simple example of this strategy in application. Suppose you're the student assistant in charge of maintaining the collection in the Political Science Department Reading Room. For the past year there has been no student assistant. As a result the collection is all mixed up and a full inventory is in order. The storage capacity of the existing shelf space is already stretched by the collection, but additional shelving for the periodicals has been ordered. You've been assigned the task of conducting the inventory and reorganizing the collection. How do you go about it? You could start by locating all the periodicals in the collection, organize them chronologically and by title, list them and arrange them in the new shelving, and then compare your list with the card catalog to identify any missing items. This would create a small amount of space on the existing shelves which could be consolidated. Then you could begin working through the collection of books, one shelf at a time.

### WORKING BACKWARD

Some problems are easier to solve if one imaginatively works one's way back from where one wants to wind up to where one is at the moment. This is often an effective way of solving scheduling problems, for instance. Knowing that the deadline is six weeks away, one can often budget the available time more effectively by estimating the time needed to complete the last step, and then the next to last step, and so on back to the beginning. This is often a very good way of avoiding other sorts of problems which would result from inadequate planning.

This strategy comes in handy in other ways, too. Consider, for example, standard reading comprehension tests. Usually these consist of a passage of prose and a set of questions about the passage. One of the best test-taking strategies for this kind of examination is to read the questions first, and then read the passage with the questions in mind.

## USING ANALOGOUS PROBLEMS

Earlier, we mentioned what a wide variety of shapes, sizes, and kinds of problems there are, and that solving any particular problem calls for specific skills, strategies, and insights appropriate to the particular problem being faced. But few problems are so unique that they are totally unlike every other problem. In fact, often the best way of figuring out what specific skills, strategies, and insights would be appropriate to a particular problem is to try to remember or imagine a similar problem or a related problem.

For example, suppose you are in charge of organizing the annual Ping-Pong tournament. You have a room with four Ping-Pong tables in it, and 208 individual entrants. You are trying to work out the schedule of matches, assuming an hour per match, for a single-elimination tournament (a player is eliminated after losing once). How many hours will the tournament take?

This is not an easy problem, is it? One relatively easy way to approach it, however, would be to ask: How did we schedule the matches in last year's tournament? Are there more or fewer entrants this year? And so on.

Another approach would be to break the problem down into more manageable sub-problems, such as: How many matches will be required to determine the winner? And then, how many hours, assuming one hour per match and four simultaneous matches, will it take to complete the required number of matches? Each of these sub-problems can be assimilated to a familiar sort of math problem.

Let's take the first sub-problem: How many matches will be required to determine the winner? Suppose we had enough tables for all of the entrants to play in the first round. That would be 104 matches in the first round (208 entrants, matched one on one). At the end of the first round, the field would be cut in half, to 104 entrants. Round two would then require an additional fifty-two matches (104 entrants, matched one on one). At the end of round two, the field would be cut to twenty-six. In round three, an additional thirteen matches would cut the field to thirteen. In round four an additional six matches would eliminate six more entrants, leaving a field of seven. In round five an additional three matches would eliminate three more entrants, leaving a field of four, which would leave three more matches: two semi-finals and one final match. Now we simply add the number of matches in each round, for a total of 207 matches.

Sometimes remembering or imagining analogous problems can be an effective way of discovering or formulating a simple general rule or principle or algorithm for arriving at a solution. Let's take the first sub-problem again. How many matches will be required to determine the winner? Let's imagine an analogous, but much simpler problem. Suppose only two people had entered the tournament. Obviously only one match would be required to determine the winner. Now suppose three people had entered the tournament. In this case two matches would be required to determine the winner. Now suppose four people had entered. In this case we'd need three matches. It's beginning to look like the number of matches required to determine the winner is equal to the number of entrants minus one: in this case 207 matches.

## MYTHS ABOUT PROBLEM SOLVING

Before we leave the subject of solving problems it is worth dwelling briefly on and dispelling two of the myths or common misconceptions which frequently mystify and obstruct the process.

### PROBLEM SOLVING IS INEFFABLE

Probably the most common myth about problem solving is that the process is ineffable, that nothing useful or illuminating can be said to facilitate the development of skill at solving problems. As we have seen, solving problems often depends on thinking about them in new and creative ways. It is also true that creativity cannot be fully programmed in terms of procedural steps. But this does not mean that problem solving is a form of magic.

A related myth is that the solution to a problem "emerges automatically" as a result of simply assembling all the "relevant data." One problem with this idea is that frequently we do have all the "relevant data," but we are approaching the problem in such a way that its relevance is obscured. Some psychologists refer to this as the problem of "access to inert knowledge."

For example, consider the following problem: You have two 5-gallon cans full of water, and a 15-gallon tub. How can you put all the water into the tub and still be able to tell which water came from which can? One solution to this problem would be to freeze the water in one of the cans. The knowledge needed to arrive at this solution, namely that freezing water is easily accomplished and that frozen water can easily be distinguished from water in the liquid state, is already present presumably in most people. But the fact that this solution to the problem does not immediately occur to most people shows that this knowledge is not automatically brought to bear on the problem.

Though we may not always be aware of what it is that "triggered" a particular breakthrough, though we may not always be aware of the nature of the mental processes involved, there is nothing "automatic" about problem solving. Nor is problem solving accomplished passively. Problem solving is an active process. This doesn't mean that it is never a good idea to put a problem aside, or to "sleep on it." But it would be misleading, to say the least, to think that the solution to the problem is produced by *not* working on it. It's much more reasonable to suppose that the mind continues to work on the problem in subconscious ways and that this work is greatly facilitated by the conscious work already invested in the problem.

## ALL PROBLEMS ARE SOLUBLE

It's tempting for many of us to believe that there are no absolutely insoluble problems, that if we think about a problem long enough, and hard enough, and in the right kinds of ways, sooner or later we're bound to arrive at a solution to it. There's nothing essentially wrong with maintaining an optimistic attitude in the face of difficulty. No doubt it's better to presume that problems are soluble than to presume that they're insoluble. Nevertheless, on the basis of examples we have already looked at, it is relatively easy to generate truly insoluble problems.

For example: Try to link all nine dots using only four straight lines, which do not extend beyond the area defined by the nine dots, without raising the pencil from the paper:

o o o

o o o

o o o

There just isn't any solution to *this* problem. The problem is in effect defined in terms of contradictory requirements.

As we learned earlier, the recognition of a problem's insolubility, or that one is approaching it as an insoluble problem, is sometimes very important. Persistent optimism in the face of a problem which is defined in terms of contradictory requirements frequently stands as the main obstacle in the way of any real progress. Recognizing the insolubility of the problem is what leads us toward a fruitful redefinition, toward a reconceptualization of a similar problem which we *can* solve.

Some real-world problems are very much like this. For example, there may be no way to resolve certain disputes so that all parties are completely satisfied. Suppose twin brothers each claim the exclusive right to inherit the family property. The best we can hope for in such a situation is to arrive at some compromise. But any compromise will necessarily fall short of satisfying both parties completely. Recognition of this fact may be necessary before any compromise can be seriously considered.

A related misconception is that there must be some single solution superior to all other alternatives for every problem. On the contrary, there are quite a few problematic situations in which several alternative solutions present themselves, each of which brings certain advantages as well as certain drawbacks.

Suppose you are trying to book air travel home from school for the holidays. There are no nonstop direct flights to your city. Your alternatives are to fly through Denver, changing planes and airlines with a two-hour layover, leaving at 9 A.M. and arriving finally at 6 P.M.; or to take a single flight at slightly higher fare with stops in St. Louis and Chicago, leaving at 3 P.M. and arriving finally at 9 P.M. Neither of these alternatives is clearly superior overall, though each is clearly superior to the other in certain respects. This, however, is not the sort of problem which can be better resolved by redefinition. Redefining the problem is not going to generate any new travel options.

## ADDITIONAL EXERCISES

**1.** Here's an exercise for sharpening your observation skills: For each of the following familiar items (a) identify three features or properties including one which you've never noticed before and (b) using the techniques of functional analysis described in Chapter 2, explain what functions each of these properties might serve.

| Item | Feature or property | Function |
|---|---|---|
| Styrofoam coffee cup | Made of Styrofoam | Does not conduct heat, keeps coffee hot, hand comfortable |
| | Flat bottom | Stability when left unsupported |
| | Conical shape | Fits hand, nested storage when empty |
| A brick | | |
| | | |
| | | |
| A nickel | | |
| | | |
| | | |
| A pencil | | |
| | | |
| | | |

| Item | Feature or property | Function |
|---|---|---|
| A sock | | |
| | | |
| | | |
| A textbook | | |
| | | |
| | | |

**2.** Identify at least three properties shared by each of the following pairs, and at least one point of difference between the members of each pair:

| Items | Shared properties | Differences |
|---|---|---|
| An orange and a lemon | | |
| | | |
| | | |
| A family and a nation | | |
| | | |
| | | |
| A vein and a garden hose | | |
| | | |
| | | |
| A square and a rectangle | | |
| | | |
| | | |
| The numbers 7 and 9 | | |
| | | |
| | | |
| A textbook and a comic book | | |
| | | |
| | | |

**3.** Identify at least three ways in which the following pairs of things differ, and at least one point of similarity:

| Items | Differences | Similarities |
|---|---|---|
| Verbs and nouns | | |
| | | |
| | | |
| Religion and science | | |
| | | |
| | | |
| Science and art | | |
| | | |
| | | |
| Republicans and Democrats | | |
| | | |
| | | |
| The numbers 36 and 35 | | |
| | | |
| | | |

**4.** Here's an exercise in pattern recognition. See if you can think how concepts relate to each other. Complete the following analogies, and explain the connection you see in each case.

**Example:** Robin is to Bird as Chevrolet is to ________ .

To complete the analogy: (1) think how the first concept (Robin) relates to the second concept (Bird). In this case the most plausible answer is that Robin is a species of Bird. (2) Try to find a fourth concept which stands in an analogous relationship to the third. In this case Chevrolet would be a "species" of *Car* or *Automobile.*

a. Chinese is to Asian as Protestant is to ________ .
b. Rule is to Game as Law is to ________ .
c. Artery is to Blood as Nerve is to ________ .
d. Heat is to Energy as Push is to ________ .

**5.** Sometimes there's more than one way to complete an analogy. Here are a couple of extra tricky analogies to try. In each case, see how many different ways you can think of to complete the analogy, and explain the various connections.

e. Who would you say was the First Lady of Great Britain when Margaret Thatcher was prime minister? (i.e., Hillary Clinton is to the United States as ________ was to Great Britain in the Thatcher years.)
f. Who would you say is America's counterpart to Gandhi? (i.e., ________ is to America as Gandhi was to India.)

**6.** The following three problems are designed to give you practice in challenging assumptions. If you cannot initially solve them, try to identify, and challenge, your assumptions.

a. You're a gardener. Your employer asks you to plant four olive trees so that each one is exactly the same distance from each of the others. How would you arrange the trees?
b. A man works in a tall office building. Each morning he enters the elevator on the ground floor, presses the button to the ninth floor, exits, and then walks up to the fourteenth floor. At night he enters the elevator on the fourteenth floor and gets out on the ground floor. Account for his behavior.

**7.** Consider the following puzzles and scenarios using the techniques and strategies mentioned in this chapter, and any additional strategies you can devise on your own. Can you solve any of the puzzles? Explain how you arrive at your solution. What are the problems involved in each scenario? What possible options can you formulate that would solve these problems? What are the advantages and drawbacks of the options you can devise?

a. Forty years ago, in a certain land, the popular and democratically elected regime was overthrown in a bloody coup and replaced by a tyrannical military oligarchy. Many families were driven into exile, and their land expropriated by the ruling families. In the intervening forty years, peasant families were allowed to work the land in exchange for subsistence wages under increasingly intolerable circumstances until finally they have risen up and overthrown the oligarchy and driven the tyrannical ruling families out of the land. Now, however, members and descendants of families originally driven into exile by the military dictators have returned to claim what they regard as their land.
b. The doctor has prescribed thirty pills. The prescription says, "Take 1 every 30 minutes." How long does the prescription last?
c. You're a member of a committee that must decide the best place to locate a town dump for burning the town's rubbish. In descending order of importance, list the factors that you would consider in arriving at your decision. Be prepared to account for your priorities.
d. You're placed in charge of interviewing students for the position of tutor in critical thinking. If you could ask each applicant no more than three questions, what would those questions be, and why?
e. You have black socks and blue socks in a drawer. You mustn't wake your roommate, and since it is dark, you cannot see the colors of the socks as

you take them out of the drawer. But you do know that the ratio of black socks to blue socks is 5/6. How many socks must you take out in order to be sure that you have a matched pair?

f. You're away from home for your first year at college. You've met the most gorgeous and delightful member of the opposite sex, who has accepted your invitation to join you and your family for Thanksgiving dinner. Meanwhile, your Great Aunt Ethel has sent you one of her usual birthday gifts: a horrible shirt that she thinks you will look cute in but which makes you look like Mickey Mouse. Your parents have just told you that your Great Aunt Ethel will be joining the family for Thanksgiving dinner, and that she asked how much you liked the birthday gift. What should you wear for the occasion?

g. You buy one hundred shares of stock in Amalgamated Conglomerates Unlimited at $50 per share. A year later you sell the stock at $75 per share. A year later you buy the same shares of ACU back for $8,500 and eventually sell them for $90 per share. How much money did you make? Explain two distinct methods of calculating your earnings.

h. Scene: the Annual Halloween Exotic/Erotic Masqued Costume Extravaganza for Truth-Tellers and Liars. A man and a woman are dancing. One says to the other "I'm a man." "That's nice, I'm a woman," replies the other. At least one of the two is lying. Which is the man and which is the woman? Explain.

# ANSWERS TO EXERCISES

## CHAPTER 1

### FREEWRITING—PAGE 7

Answers will vary.

## CHAPTER 2

### FUNCTIONS OF LANGUAGE—PAGE 29

Answers will vary.

### LANGUAGE FUNCTIONS—PAGE 33

| Example | Inf. | Ex. | Dir. | Pers. | Perf. |
|---|---|---|---|---|---|
| The suspect left the scene driving a green convertible with out-of-state plates. | X | | | | |
| Follow Highway 12 west to Madrone Road, take Madrone to Arnold Drive, then turn left and drive 2 miles 'til you see the golf course. | | | X | | |
| We must all hang together or most assuredly, we shall all hang separately. —Ben Franklin (to other signers of the Declaration of Independence) | | | | X | |
| Baseball umpire: "You're out!" | | | | | X |
| Teenage moviegoer after seeing *Star Wars:* "Awesome!" | | X | | | |
| And God said, "Let there be light;" And there was light. —Genesis 1:3 | | | | | X |
| Combine 2 cups water and 1 tablespoon butter and bring to a boil. Stir in rice and spice mix, reduce heat and simmer for 10 minutes. | | | X | | |
| "How 'bout those Dallas Cowboys cheerleaders, ya know what I'm sayin'?!" | | X | | | |
| Noticing that it was 5 minutes past bedtime, Mrs. Cleaver said, "Okay Beaver, let's close the book now and go to bed." | | | X | | |
| For answers to these exercises and other similar exercises, click on the Language Functions button in the Critical Thinking tutorial. | | | X | | |

### AMBIGUITY AND VAGUENESS—PAGE 39

*Headline: Rappers continue to get bad rap in the press.*

Ambiguous. "Rappers" refers to people who perform "rap music;" "rap" in "bad rap" means "reputation."

. *How do reasonable people come to hold unreasonable beliefs?*

Vague. Both "reasonable" and "unreasonable" have indefinite extensions.

*Headline: "Drunk Gets Nine Months in Violin Case"*

Ambiguous. The preposition "in" is ambiguous. In one conventional usage the sentence of nine months jail time was handed down in the case of the violin. In another conventional usage the drunk is sentenced to confinement in a violin case for a period of nine months.

*The streets are perfectly safe here in New York City. It's the muggers you have to watch out for.*

Ambiguous. This one's a bit tricky. Both "streets" and "safe" contribute to the ambiguity. "Streets" could refer to the pavement, or to the social environment that one finds there. "Safe" could refer to the driving conditions or to the incidence of crime.

*Random urinalysis for drugs in safety-sensitive job categories does not constitute an unreasonable search.*

Vague. Both "safety sensitive" and "unreasonable" have indefinite extensions.

*A man walks up to the Zen Buddhist hot dog vendor and says, "Make me one with everything."*

Ambiguous. "One with everything" refers to a hot dog with all the trimmings. And it also refers in Zen Buddhist practice to a condition of unity with all of creation.

*Nuclear energy is just as natural as any other fuel, and cleaner than many already in use.*

Vague. Both "natural" and "clean" have indefinite extensions. What's vague about "many" is that the specific fuels referred to are not identified. So, it is impossible to know the basis of comparison.

*Can you explain the humor in Victor Borge's remark about "finding something missing?"*

Ambiguous. One way to explain the ambiguity would be to point out that the colloquialism "finding something missing" means "discovering that something is missing," while the word "find" conventionally implies that what you found is no longer missing.

*According to the Supreme Court, flag burning is protected under the First Amendment as an instance of political speech.*

Neither vague nor ambiguous. By itself, the concept of "political speech" is vague, leaving questions like whether or not flag burning is or is not, in the extension of the term, open to argument. But this sentence answers that question clearly and definitively.

*For answers to these and other similar exercises, click on the Ambiguity/Vagueness button in the Critical Thinking tutorial.*

Vague. The word "similar" has an indefinite extension.

## DEFINITIONS—PAGE 49

1. Answers will vary.
2. Answers will vary.

3. "Reason," p. 6; "Critical," p. 8; "Autonomy," p. 9; "Define," p. 40; "Ostensive," p. 41; "Synonymy," p. 41; "Etymology," p. 41; "Stipulate," p. 42.
4. Answers will vary.
5. Answers will vary.
6. Answers will vary.
7. Classify the following definitions.

| Example | Func. | Osten. | Syn. | Etym. | Stip. | Pers. | Ess. | Meta. |
|---|---|---|---|---|---|---|---|---|
| For purposes of financial aid eligibility, a "full-time student" shall be defined as a student enrolled in twelve or more units per semester. | | | | | X | | | |
| Octad: a group or sequence of eight, from the Greek word *okto* for "eight." | | | | X | | | | |
| Philosophy? Oh yeah, that's the stuff written by Plato and Aristotle and Descartes and those guys. | | X | | | | | | |
| Floppy disk: A small magnetically coated piece of plastic used to store electronic information. | X | | | | | | | |
| The blues ain't nothin' but a good man feelin' bad. | | | | | | | | X |
| That's not music. Real music by definition has rhythm *and* melody. | | | | | | X | | |
| Art is anything that humans do or make for reasons other than survival or reproduction. | | | | | | | X | |
| "Augur" means "predict." | | | X | | | | | |

8. Critique the following "essential definitions."

| Example | Broad | Narrow | Neg. | Figrtv. | Circ. | Expl. |
|---|---|---|---|---|---|---|
| "Pornography" is any pictorial display of human sexuality or nudity. | X | X | | | | |
| "Philosophy" is the study of the classical Greek works of Plato and Aristotle. | | X | | | | |

| Example | Broad | Narrow | Neg. | Figrtv. | Circ. | Expl. |
|---|---|---|---|---|---|---|
| "Rape" is forcing a woman to have sex against her will. | | X | | | | |
| "Circular": Of or pertaining to a circle; the property of circularity. | | | | | X | |
| "Alimony" is when two people make a mistake and one of them continues to pay for it. | | | | X | | |
| A "definition" is an explanation of the meaning of a term. | | | | | | The definition is correct. |
| Jazz: "The music of unemployment." —Frank Zappa | | | | X | | |
| Economics is the science which treats of the phenomena arising out of the economic activities of men in society. — J. M. Keynes | | | | | X | |

## ISSUES AND DISPUTES—PAGE 58

| Example | Verbal | Factual | Eval. | Interp. |
|---|---|---|---|---|
| Don King: Boxing is a great sport! It requires excellent physical skills and conditioning and mental toughness.<br>Larry King: Come on, Don. Boxing is nothing but a barbaric spectacle: two brutes beating each other senseless. | | | X | |
| Newt: Nuclear weapons have been effective in keeping the peace ever since World War II.<br>Noam: Not if you count the wars in Korea, Vietnam, Nicaragua, the Middle East, and the Persian Gulf. | | | | X |
| Tommy and Timmy are identical twins. Tommy says, "I'm Timmy's older brother." Timmy says, "No, we're the same age." | X | | | |
| Did O. J. Simpson kill Ronald Goldman and Nicole Brown Simpson? | | X | | |
| Did the prosecution in the criminal trial establish O. J. Simpson's guilt "beyond a reasonable doubt"? | | | X | |
| Were the verdicts in the O. J. Simpson criminal and civil trials "just"? | | | X | |

| Example | Verbal | Factual | Eval. | Interp. |
|---|---|---|---|---|
| Brad has an old car. One day he replaces one of its defective parts. The next day he replaces another. Before the year is out, Brad has replaced every part in the entire car. Is Brad's car the same car he had before he began changing parts? | X | | | |
| A bad peace is even worse than war. —Tacitus<br>The most disadvantageous peace is better than the most just war. —Erasmus | | | X | |
| Gene: That example where Tacitus and Erasmus seem to be disagreeing about peace is just a verbal dispute. They just mean different things by the word "peace."<br>Jean: No I think they have a factual dispute. They really disagree about history. | | | | X |
| Phil told his brother Fred, "When I die I'll leave you all my money." A week later he changed his mind and decided to leave all his money to his wife instead. So Phil wrote in his will, "I leave all my money to my next of kin" (his wife). Unknown to Phil, his wife had just died in a car accident. The day after he made out his will Phil himself died, and his money went to his next of kin—his brother Fred. Did Phil keep his promise to his brother Fred or didn't he? | X | | | |

## CHAPTER 3

### ARGUMENT IDENTIFICATION—PAGE 71

| Example | Arg. | Not. | Undec. |
|---|---|---|---|
| ". . . a principle I established for myself early in the game: I wanted to get paid for my work, but I didn't want to work for pay." —Leonard Cohen, poet | | X | |
| I object to lotteries, because they're biased in favor of lucky people. | X | | |
| The most serious issue facing journalism education today is the blurring of the distinctions between advertising, public relations, and journalism itself. | | X | |
| "Even the most productive writers are expert dawdlers, doers of unnecessary errands, seekers of interruptions—trials to their wives and husbands, associates, and themselves. They sharpen well-pointed pencils and go out to buy more blank paper, rearrange their office, wander through libraries and bookstores, | | | |

(continued)

| Example | Arg. | Not. | Undec. |
|---|---|---|---|
| change words, walk, drive, make unnecessary calls, nap, day dream, and try not 'consciously' to think about what they are going to write so they can think subconsciously about it." —Donald M. Murray, in "Write before Writing" | | | X |
| "They're going to feed you," said Roosta, "into the Total Perspective Vortex!" Zaphod had never heard of this. He believed that he had heard of all the fun things in the Galaxy, so he assumed that the Total Perspective Vortex was not fun." —Douglas Adams, in *The Restaurant at the End of the Universe.* | | | X |
| "Willy Loman never made a lot of money. His name was never in the paper. He's not the finest character that ever lived. But he's a human being, and a terrible thing is happening to him. So attention must be paid. He's not to be allowed to fall into his grave like an old dog. Attention, attention must be paid to such a person . . ." —Arthur Miller, in *Death of a Salesman* | X | | |

## SIGNALS—PAGE 78

1. Two out of three people interviewed preferred Zest to another soap. *Therefore,* Zest is the best soap available.
2. In the next century more and more people will turn to solar energy to heat their homes *because* the price of gas and oil will become prohibitive for most consumers *and* the price of installing solar panels will decline.
3. People who smoke cigarettes should be forced to pay for their own health insurance *since* they know smoking is bad for their health, *and* they have no right to expect others to pay for their addictions.
4. It's no wonder that government aid to the poor fails. Poor people can't manage their money. *(Not an argument. The passage presumes agreement that government aid to the poor fails and offers to explain why.)*
5. Even though spanking has immediate punitive and (for the parent) anger-releasing effects, parents should not spank their children, *for* spanking gives children the message that inflicting pain on others is an appropriate means of changing their behavior. *Furthermore,* spanking trains children to submit to the arbitrary rules of authority figures who have the power to harm them. We ought not to give our children those messages. Rather, we should train them to either make appropriate behavioral choices or to expect to deal with the related natural and logical consequences of their behavior.
6. Public schools generally avoid investigation of debatable issues and instead stress rote recall of isolated facts, which teaches students to unquestioningly absorb given information on demand so that they can regurgitate it

in its entirety during testing situations. Although students are generally not allowed to question it, much of what is presented as accurate information is indeed controversial. But citizens need to develop decision making skills regarding debatable issues in order to truly participate in a democracy. *It follows then that* public schools ought to change their educational priorities in order to better prepare students to become informed, responsible members of our democracy.

7. Ever since the injury to Jerry Rice, the 49er running game has been under pressure to produce. But *since* their won/lost record is best in the NFL west, *we must conclude that* the loss of Rice, while damaging to their overall offense, has not been devastating.
8. Late night radio talk show host: "I've heard more heart attacks happen on Monday than on any other day of the week, probably because Mondays mark a return to those stressful work situations for so many of you. *So,* let's all call in sick this Monday, ok, folks, *because* we don't want any of you to check out on us."
9. The answers to these exercises are programmed into our Critical Thinking tutorial. *So,* if you want to check and see how you're doing, you should click on the Argument Identification button.

## INCOMPLETELY STATED ARGUMENTS—PAGE 81

1. I'm sorry, but you may stay in the country only if you have a current visa; and your visa has expired.
   *Therefore, you may not stay in the country.*
2. God has all the virtues, and benevolence is certainly a virtue.
   *Therefore, God is benevolent.*
3. Either the battery in the remote control is dead or the set's unplugged, but the set is plugged in.
   *Therefore, the battery in the remote control is dead.*
4. All mammals suckle their young, and all primates are mammals, and orangutans are primates.
   *Therefore, orangutans suckle their young.*
5. Software is written by humans, and humans make mistakes.
   *Therefore, software will contain mistakes.*
6. Legislation that can't be enforced is useless, and there's no way to enforce censorship over the Internet.
   *Therefore, Internet censorship legislation is useless.*
7. All propaganda is dangerous. Therefore network news is dangerous
   *because network news is propaganda.*
8. UCLA will play in the Rose Bowl, because the Pac 10 champion always plays in the Rose Bowl,
   *and UCLA will win the Pac 10 championship.*

9. Everything with any commercial potential eventually gets absorbed into the corporate world, so the Internet will eventually get absorbed into the corporate world.
   *because the Internet has commercial potential.*

10. Hip-hop is a fad, so it will surely fade,
    *because all fads fade.*

## CHAPTER 4

### THESIS IDENTIFICATION—PAGE 93

1. Capital punishment is meted out to some groups in society more than to others. Minority groups are hit hardest by this imbalance of justice. In addition, wealthy people seldom receive the death penalty because they can afford better counsel. All the people executed in the United States in 1964 were represented by court appointed attorneys. Finally, the death penalty can wrongfully execute an innocent person. There are documented cases of this happening.

   | | |
   |---|---|
   | Topic | *Capital punishment* |
   | Author Attitude | *Concerned about injustice in the administration of the death penalty* |
   | Thesis | *Capital punishment is not administered equitably.* |

2. We have seen hunting rifles used to kill a president, Martin Luther King Jr., and numerous others. It is said that these and other guns would not kill if there were not people to shoot them. By the same token, people would rarely kill if they lacked the weapons to do so. There exists, however, an even more pressing threat to our lives than the sniper or assassin. African Americans, after centuries of exploitation, are openly rebellious. Given the weapons, young African Americans could ignite the bloodiest revolution in this country since the Civil War. The Los Angeles riots may have been merely a glimpse of what's ahead. On the other side are white racists arming in fear. And don't forget the militant right-wingers, survivalists, and even religious cults storing up arsenals in anticipation of Armageddon.

   | | |
   |---|---|
   | Topic | *Gun control* |
   | Author Attitude | *Concerned about risks of readily available firearms* |
   | Thesis | *Uncontrolled access to guns constitutes a grave social danger.* |

3. This weekend, the city of Indianapolis is hosting approximately 500,000 people to create a two-day saturnalia out of the annual celebration of grease, gasoline, and death.

   The stands inside the Indy Speedway will be filled on Monday with hundreds or thousands of real racing fans. I can't help but think of them as vultures who come to watch the 500-mile race on the highway of death to nowhere, hoping that the monotony of watching cars flick by at speeds in excess of 190 mph will be relieved by mechanical—and human—catastrophe.

   The beltway around Indianapolis is staked with grim white crosses, mute reminders to travelers of the fatal consequences of a too-heavy foot on the accelerator.

Watching the race from the Indy grandstand is little like watching hyperactive hamsters tread a cage wheel. The cars fly by like brightly painted, berserk vacuum cleaners sucking the ground.

| | |
|---|---|
| Topic | *The Indianapolis 500* |
| Author Attitude | *Generally disgusted* |
| Thesis | *The Indianapolis 500 is a generally disgusting, morbid spectacle.* |

**4.** Feminists have long complained that playing with dolls is one way of convincing impressionable little girls that they may only be mothers or housewives. . . But doll playing may have even more serious consequences for little girls than that. Do girls find out about gravity and distance and shapes and sizes by playing with dolls? Probably not.

A curious boy, if his parents are tolerant, will have taken apart a number of household and play objects by the time he is ten, and, if his parents are lucky, he may even have put them back together again. In all this he is learning things that will be useful in physics and math.

Sports is another source of math-related concepts for children which tends to favor boys. Getting to first base on a not-very-well-hit grounder is a lesson in line, speed, and distance. Intercepting a football thrown through the air requires some rapid, intuitive eye calculations based on the ball's direction, speed, and trajectory.

| | |
|---|---|
| Topic | *Childhhood gender-role-playing and its effects on education* |
| Author Attitude | *Critical of* |
| Thesis | *Childhood gender-role-playing has harmful effects on the education of girls.* |

## BASIC CASTING—PAGE 100

| | |
|---|---|
| *Since* [it is only a matter of time before space-based missile defense technology becomes obsolete ①], *and since* [the funds earmarked for the development of such technology are sorely needed elsewhere ②], [we should abandon the Star Wars program ③]. | ③ ← ① + ② |
| [The Star Wars program is our only realistic option for national defense in the nuclear age ①]. [Any defense program which relies on nuclear deterrence raises the risk of nuclear war ②], and [that is not a realistic option for national defense ③]. [The Star Wars program is the only option yet proposed which does not rely on nuclear deterrence ④]. | ① ← ② + ③ + ④ |
| [President Bush promised no new taxes ①]. *But* [in his first term of office, he compromised with the Congress over tax hikes ②]. [*Such behavior clearly amounts to* a betrayal of the public trust ③]. | ③ ← ① + ② |

## CASTING SUB-ARGUMENTS—PAGE 104

| | |
|---|---|
| [President Bush promised no new taxes ①]. *But* in his first term of office he compromised with the Congress over tax hikes ②]. But *since* [such behavior clearly amounts to a betrayal of the public trust ③], [President Bush did not deserve to be re-elected for a second term ④]. | 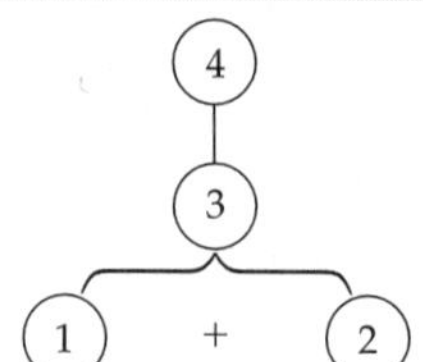 |
| A recent five-year study at a major electronics company indicates that getting fired may have a lot to do with overreaching ①]. [Among 2,000 technical, sales and management employees who were followed during their first five years with the company, the 173 people who eventually were fired started out with much higher expectations of advancement than either the 200 people who left voluntarily or the people who remained ②]. [On a questionnaire given during their first week on the job, more than half of the people who were fired within the first two years ranked themselves among the top 5% of typical people in their job category ③]. [Only 38% of those who stayed with the company ranked themselves that highly ④]. —Berkeley Rice | 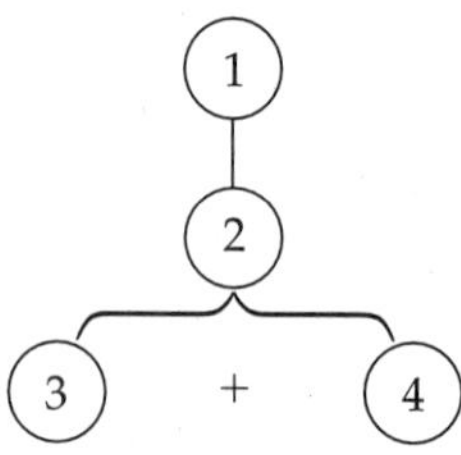 |
| [We must stop treating juveniles differently from adult offenders ①]. [Justice demands it ②]. [Justice implies that people should be treated equally ③]. *Besides,* [the social effects of pampering juvenile offenders has sinister social consequences ④]. [The record shows that juveniles who have been treated leniently for offenses have subsequently committed serious crimes ⑤]. | 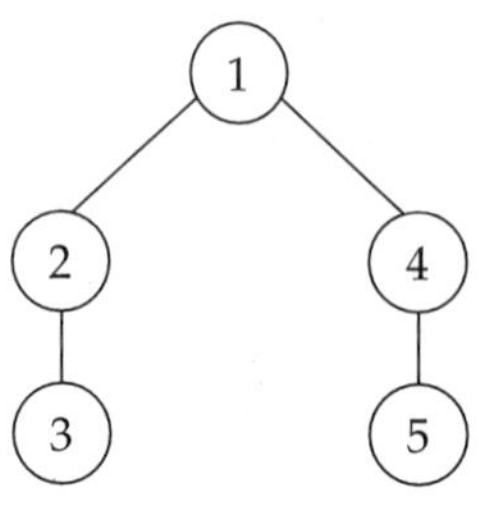 |

## CASTING UNEXPRESSED PREMISES AND CONCLUSIONS—PAGE 107

| | |
|---|---|
| I'm sorry, but [you may stay in the country only if you have a current visa ①], *and* [your visa has expired ②]. | a: You may not stay in the country. 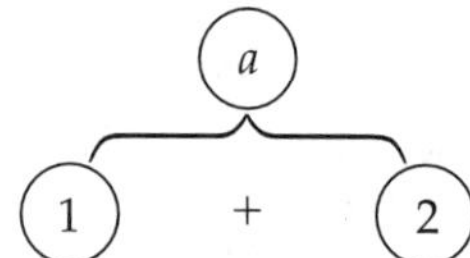 |

| | |
|---|---|
| [God has all the virtues ①], *and* [benevolence is certainly a virtue ②]. | a: God is benevolent.<br>a ← ① + ② |
| [Either the battery in the remote control is dead or the set's unplugged ①], *but* [the set is plugged in ②]. | a: The battery in the remote control is dead.<br>a ← ① + ② |
| [All mammals suckle their young ①], *and* [all primates are mammals ②], *and* [orangutans are primates ③]. | a: Orangutans suckle their young.<br>b: Orangutans are mammals.<br>a ← ① + b; b ← ② + ③ |

## CHAPTER 5

### COMPLETENESS AND THE "WHAT IF" STRATEGY—PAGE 123

| | Enth | Complete |
|---|---|---|
| Because prisons do not rehabilitate inmates, they are an ineffective form of punishment for criminal behavior. | X | |
| The United States should develop solar energy on a widespread basis because it must become energy-independent. | X | |
| Abortion involves the taking of a life. Therefore, it should be discouraged. | X | |
| Jane's probably married. She's wearing a wedding ring. | X | |
| God has all the virtues. Therefore, God is benevolent. | X | |
| Men are not innately superior to women. If they were they wouldn't establish caste systems to ensure their preferred positions, and they wouldn't work so hard to maintain these systems. But obviously men do both. | | X |

## RELEVANCE AND THE TOPIC COVERAGE STRATEGY—PAGE 124

1. People who were born at exactly the same time often have vastly different life histories and personalities. Therefore, astrology is not a reliable, predictive system.

| | |
|---|---|
| | People who believe in astrology are superstitious. |
| X | If astrology were a reliable predictive system, people born at exactly the same time would not have vastly different life histories and personalities. |
| | No two people are born at exactly the same time. |

2. Since no human system of justice is infallible, and capital punishment imposes an irreversible penalty, capital punishment is an unacceptable form of punishment.

| | |
|---|---|
| | No form of punishment which imposes an irreversible penalty is acceptable. |
| | If we could perfect a system of justice so that no mistaken convictions could possibly occur, then capital punishment would be acceptable. |
| X | No form of punishment which imposes an irreversible penalty is acceptable within a fallible system of justice. |

## PLAUSIBILITY—PAGE 126

Answers will vary.

## FILLING IN MISSING PREMISES—PAGE 130

1. Answers will vary.
2. Select the best reconstructed premise from the alternatives offered for each of the following arguments:
   a. Some of these people can't be golfers. They're not carrying clubs.

| | |
|---|---|
| | Some golfers are carrying clubs. |
| | Everyone carrying clubs is a golfer. |
| X | All golfers carry clubs. |

b. If capital punishment isn't a deterrent to crime, then why has the rate of violent crimes increased since capital punishment was outlawed?

| | |
|---|---|
| | Because the rate of violent crime has increased since capital punishment was outlawed, it must be a deterrent to crime. |
| | An increase in the rate of crime following the abolition of a punishment proves that the punishment is a crime deterrent. |
| X | An increase in the rate of crime following the abolition of a punishment usually indicates that the punishment is a crime deterrent. |

c. Constitutionally, only the House of Representatives may initiate a money-raising bill. Thus, when the Senate drafted the recent tax bill, it acted unconstitutionally. Therefore, the proposed tax bill should not be made law.

| | |
|---|---|
| | Any bill the Senate drafts should not be made law. |
| X | Any bill that originates unconstitutionally should not be made law. |
| | Any tax bill originating in the Senate should not be made law. |

# CHAPTER 6

## DEDUCTIVE AND INDUCTIVE ARGUMENTS—PAGE 149

| | Ded. | Ind. |
|---|---|---|
| Since tests proved that it took at least 2.3 seconds to operate the bolt of the rifle, Oswald obviously could not have fired three times—hitting Kennedy twice and Connally once—in 5.6 seconds or less. | X | |
| At bottom, I did not believe I had touched that man. The law of probabilities decreed me guiltless of his blood. For in all my small experience with guns, I had never hit anything I had tried to hit, and I knew I had done my best to hit him. —Mark Twain | | X |
| All of the leading economic indicators point toward further improvement in the economy. You can count on an improved third quarter. | | X |
| During an interview with the school paper, Coach Danforth was quoted as saying, "I think it's safe to assume that Jason Israel will be our starting point guard next year. Both of our starting guards are graduating this spring and no one else on the team has Jason's speed and ball-handling skills." | | X |

| | Ded. | Ind. |
|---|---|---|
| The answers to many of the exercise sets in this book so far have been in the Critical Thinking tutorial. Chances are, the answers to this exercise set will be in the Critical Thinking tutorial as well. | | X |

## THE CONCEPT OF DEDUCTIVE VALIDITY—PAGE 153

| True | False | |
|---|---|---|
| X | | A deductively valid argument can have a false conclusion. |

| True | False | |
|---|---|---|
| X | | A deductively valid argument can have false premises. |

| True | False | |
|---|---|---|
| | X | One cannot tell whether a deductive argument is valid without knowing whether its premises are actually true. |

| True | False | |
|---|---|---|
| X | | A deductively valid argument can have false premises and a true conclusion. |

| True | False | |
|---|---|---|
| | X | If a deductive argument is cogent, it may still be invalid. Explain or give an example. |

## TESTING FOR DEDUCTIVE VALIDITY—PAGE 155

| | V | Inv |
|---|---|---|
| Some entertainers abuse drugs, and all comedians are entertainers, so it stands to reason that some comedians are drug abusers. | | X |
| Some college professors support the idea of a faculty union, an idea supported by many socialists. So at least some college professors must be socialists. | | X |
| Everyone knows that whales live in the sea, and anything that lives in the sea is a fish. Therefore whales must be fish. | X | |
| All artists are creative people. Some artists live in poverty. Therefore, some creative people live in poverty. | X | |
| All of the justices on the Supreme Court are lawyers, and all members of the prestigious Washington Law Club are lawyers, so at least some of the Supreme Court justices are members of the Washington Law Club. | | X |

## THE SCENARIO METHOD—PAGE 155

Answers will vary.

## FORMAL ANALOGIES—PAGE 159

Answers will vary.

## TRANSLATING CATEGORICAL STATEMENTS INTO STANDARD FORM—PAGE 163

| | | | |
|---|---|---|---|
| All computer hardware has a short shelf life. | C = Computer hardware | S = Things with short shelf life | All C's are S's |
| Some of my beliefs are false. | B = My beliefs | F = Things which are false | Some B's are F's. |
| One major corporation is Microsoft. | C = Major corporations | M = Microsoft | All M's are C's |
| Some of the members of Heaven's Gate were reasonable people. | M = Members of Heaven's Gate | R = Reasonable people | Some M's are R's. |
| Any discipline has rules, or at least regularities of some kind. | D = Disciplines | R = Things with rules or regularities | All D's are R's. |
| El Niño is the cause of some of these abnormal weather patterns. | A = These abnormal weather patterns | N = Things caused by El Niño | Some A's are N's. |
| I like action movies. | A = Action movies | L = Things I like | All A's are L's. |
| San Francisco is a city in California. | S = San Francisco | C = Cities in California | All S's are C's. |
| My favorite actress is a Gemini. | F = My favorite actress | G = Geminis | All F's are G's. |
| Answers to these exercises can be found in the Critical Thinking tutorial under Categorical Logic. | A = Answers to these exercises | C = Things that can be found in the Critical Thinking tutorial under Categorical Logic | All A's are C's. |
| Dogs love trucks. | D = Dogs | L = Lovers of trucks | All D's are L's. |

## VENN DIAGRAMS—PAGE 174

1.

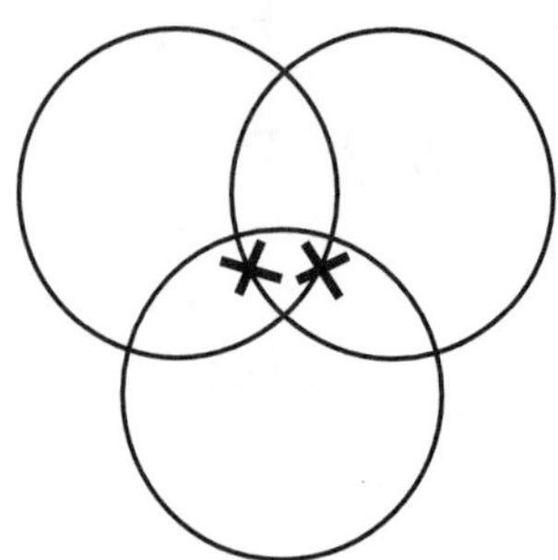

Invalid

2.

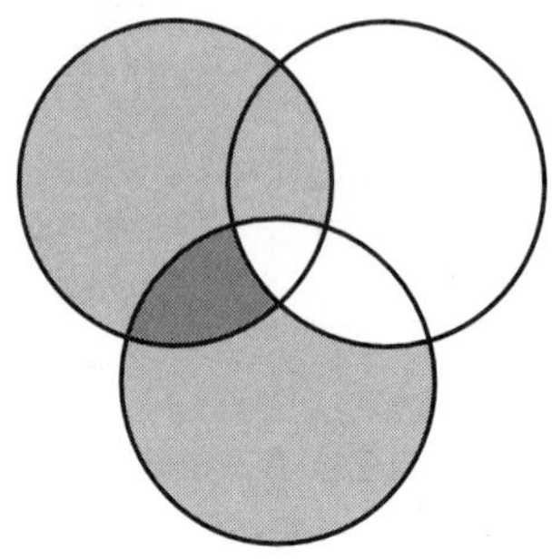

Valid

3.

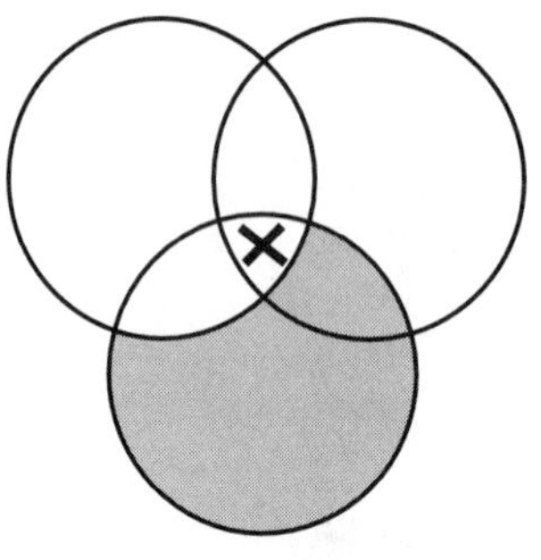

Valid

4.

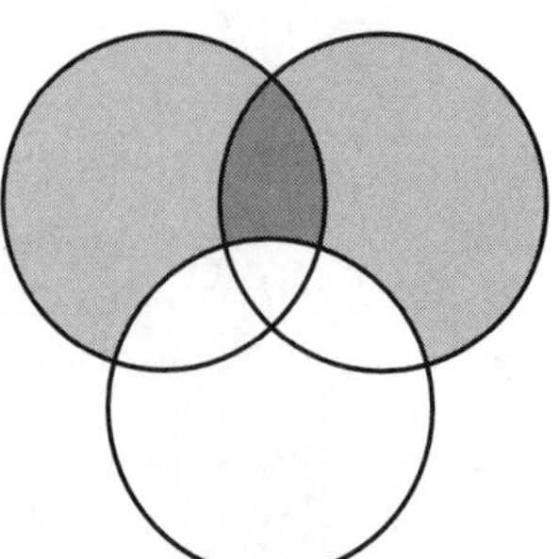

Invalid

## USING TRUTH TABLES TO TEST FOR VALIDITY—PAGE 187

1. **a.** Thesis: Astrology is not correct.
   Form: Modus Tollens
   Valid
   See truth table on page 184

   **b.** Thesis: We should depend on the predictions in the horoscope.
   Form: Denying the Antecedent
   Invalid
   See truth table on page 185
2. Answers will vary.

## CHAPTER 7

## INDUCTIVE GENERALIZATIONS—PAGE 198

1. *Middle*—Contrary to current media claims, our schools appear to be doing a superb job of teaching our children to read. A leading news magazine recently tabulated the results of the thousands of responses it received to the survey it published in its May issue. Readers from every state in the Union responded. Ninety percent of the respondents believed that their school-aged children's reading skills were good to excellent. Eight percent more believed that their children's reading skills were at least adequate. Less than one percent felt that their children were developing less than adequate reading skills. (One percent of the respondents failed to answer this question.)
   *Strongest*—In all of the studies that have been done over the past thirty years concerning the relationship between standardized test performance and success in school—involving several hundred thousand school age subjects from a variety of ethnic, regional, and socio-economic backgrounds—I.Q. (Intelligence Quotient) tests have been shown to be the single most reliable predictor of success in school. Therefore, if one scores high on I.Q. tests, one will probably perform well in school.
   *Weakest*—An hour in a hot tub will probably impair a man's fertility for up to six weeks. According to one study, three men who sat in a hot tub with water heated to 102.4° F—most health clubs heat theirs to 104° F—showed reductions in the number and penetrating capacity of their sperm cells. In samples taken thirty-six hours later, the damage was present, but the most dramatic effects did not show up until four weeks later. This indicated that even immature sperm cells had been harmed by the high heat. (It takes about seven weeks for a newly created sperm cell to mature and pass through a system of storage ducts.) Seven weeks after their dip in the hot tub, their sperm returned to normal.
2. Answers will vary.

## ARGUMENT BY ANALOGY—PAGE 201

1. An explanatory analogy in which the target is rhythm and the analogue is other organizational units of space (five blocks as opposed to 6,737 steps) and time (ten minutes as opposed to 600 seconds).
2. See pages 205–206.
3. An argumentative analogy in which the target is social security, and the analogue is a pyramid scheme.
4. See pages 207–209.

## PLAUSIBILITY AND EXPLANATORY POWER—PAGE 215

Answers will vary.

| Plausibility | Explanatory Power | |
|---|---|---|
| 7 | 7 | The assassination was carried out by aliens from outer space. |

## TESTING HYPOTHESES—PAGE 207

Answers will vary.

# CHAPTER 8

## NECESSARY TRUTHS AND CONTINGENT STATEMENTS—PAGE 235

| | NT | SC | CON |
|---|---|---|---|
| A rectangle has four sides. | X | | |
| Abortion is murder. | | | X |
| Murder is wrong. | X | | |
| Either we go out for burgers, or we order a pizza. | | | X |
| Either she's married, or she's not married. | X | | |
| She's either married or engaged. | | | X |
| Wherever you go, there you are. | X | | |
| White is a color. | X | | |
| The White House is white. | | | X |
| All arguments have to start somewhere. | X | | |

# CHAPTER 9

## FALLACIES OF AMBIGUITY—PAGE 253

a. Airplanes are used for getting high. And airplanes are perfectly legal. Drugs are used for getting high. So, they should be legal, too. —*Equivocation on the word "high"*

b. I passed nobody on the road. Therefore, nobody is slower than I am. —Lewis Carroll —*Amphiboly. "Nobody" is first used as an object, then as the subject.*

c. Look! The notice on his office door says, "Back Soon." But, I've been waiting here for over an hour and a half! —*Equivocation based on the ambiguous temporal reference of "soon"*

## FALLACIES OF LANGUAGE—PAGE 266

a. Look! The notice on his office door says, "Back Soon." But, I've been waiting here for over an hour and a half! —*Equivocation based on the ambiguous temporal reference of "soon." The vagueness of "soon" is also exploited.*

b. "It's not a pay raise. It is a pay equalization concept."—U.S. Senator Ted Stevens explaining a Congressional measure to increase the compensation of members of the U.S. Congress —*Best answer: Phantom distinction followed by a euphemism*

c. "Have you just lost your mind, or were you born nuts?" —*Complex question that presupposes you are "nuts"*

# CHAPTER 10

## AD HOMINEM APPEALS—PAGE 279

a. No man can know anything about pregnancy and childbirth, because no man can ever go through the experience. So, no man is qualified to render an opinion about abortion. —*Poisoning the well*

b. How can you believe anything that this bimbo has to say? Can't you see that she has everything to gain by implicating the President in this scandal? Look, she's sold her story to *Hard Copy!* — *"Bimbo" is an abusive ad hominem.*

c. Letter to the Editor: "I was profoundly dismayed by the badgering of witnesses during the hearings by Senator D. 'Mo' Cratic. Doesn't he realize that such criticism reflects badly on the president? If we can't expect the members of our own party to support the president in a time of crisis, just who can we turn to?" —*Circumstantial ad hominem*

d. I can't vote for the man, because I remember some years ago in his law practice, he defended that wacko Unabomber guy. —*Guilt by association*

## APPEALS TO AUTHORITY / PSEUDO-AUTHORITY—PAGE 287

Student explanations will vary.

a. We are, quite bluntly, broke. We don't have the money to sustain the dreams and experiments of liberalism any longer. We have a $400 billion a year budget deficit and a $4 trillion debt. The economist Walter Williams points out that with the money we've spent on poverty programs since the 1960s, we could have bought the entire assets of every Fortune 500 company and virtually every acre of U.S. farmland.—Rush Limbaugh —*Division of expert opinion*

b. Letter to the Editor responding to the question, "Do you care about preserving the local July 4th fireworks display?": "Not celebrate the 4th of July with fireworks? What would John Adams—having been the very first to advocate (the very day after independence was declared) that the birth of our nation ought to be "celebrated by succeeding generations as the great anniversary festival"—say? What would our founding fathers—who planted the seeds of liberty and Christianity on a wilderness shore (not for themselves only, but for their children and their children's children)—say?" —*Tradition*

c. Turns out roughing up punks ain't really necessary, on account of most guys and gals hurt *themselves* by not getting enough calcium. So, reach out for three glasses of milk a day. Your body will thank you, especially if we don't have to tell you again. —Ad sponsored by the National Fluid Milk Processor Promotion Board, featuring actors Jimmy Smits and Dennis Franz of *NYPD Blue* who posed menacingly with glasses of milk in their hands and milk on their mustaches —*Irrelevant expertise (testimonial)*

d. Owner of a San Francisco restaurant, reacting against a proposed truth-in-advertising ordinance requiring restaurant owners to identify food prepared off the premises and then frozen: "Three-quarters or seven-eighths of the people who come into my place. . . don't give a good goddamn." —*Popularity*

e. Letter to the Editor: "I was profoundly dismayed by the badgering of witnesses during the hearings by Senator D. 'Mo' Cratic. Doesn't he realize that such criticism reflects badly on the president? If we can't expect the members of our own party to support the president in a time of crisis, just who can we turn to?" —*Provincialism (Appeal to loyalty)*

## DIVERSIONS AND EMOTIONAL APPEALS—PAGE 294

a. And the Lord God commanded man, saying, "You may eat freely of every tree of the garden; but the tree of the knowledge of good and evil you shall not eat, for in the day that you eat of it, you shall die." —Genesis 2: 16–17 —*Appeal to fear or force*

**b.** Precisely what is Nixon accused of doing. . . that his predecessors didn't do many times over? The break-in and wiretapping at the Watergate? Just how different was that from the bugging of Barry Goldwater's apartment during the 1964 presidential campaign? —Victor Lasky —*Two wrongs*

**c.** [The fight for the Equal Rights Amendment in Iowa] is about a socialist, antifamily political movement that encourages women to leave their husbands, kill their children, practice witchcraft, destroy capitalism, and become lesbians. —Televangelist and former candidate for U.S. president Pat Robertson —*Straw Person*

**d.** Turns out roughing up punks ain't really necessary, on account of most guys and gals hurt *themselves* by not getting enough calcium. So, reach out for three glasses of milk a day. Your body will thank you, especially if we don't have to tell you again. —Ad sponsored by the National Fluid Milk Processor Promotion Board, featuring actors Jimmy Smits and Dennis Franz of *NYPD Blue* posed menacingly with glasses of milk in their hands and milk in their mustaches. —*Appeal to fear or force*

## CHAPTER 11

### FALLACIES OF STATISTICAL INFERENCE—PAGE 312

**a.** My last three blind dates have been bombs. This one's bound to be better! —*Gamblers' fallacy*

**b.** A poll is being conducted to find out what students think of their college newspaper. A sample is taken in the cafeteria on a Tuesday between 8 A.M. and noon. Every fifth person who enters the cafeteria is asked his or her opinion. The results find that 72 percent of the students are highly critical of the newspaper. The student government decides to use these results to revamp the editorial board. —*Unrepresentative sample that was limited to students whose class schedules permitted them to go to the cafeteria on Tuesday mornings*

**c.** Professor Smith, wishing to improve his teaching, decides to poll his physics class. He commissions a questionnaire from one of his colleagues (in statistics) that satisfies all the criteria of a sound polling instrument. He calls each member of his class individually into his office and asks them to complete the questionnaire. What is wrong with his polling methods? —*Biased methodology. He was administering the questionnaire individually to current students who found themselves in the professor's office, which would tend to be intimidating and would possibly diminish the candidness of responses.*

**d.** Survey question: "Whom do you think the U.S. should support in the Middle East: The Israelis or the Arab states?" —*Biased methodology. The question excludes the option of neutrality.*

e. In 1997, the small town of Sulphur Springs experienced a 200 percent increase in felony auto theft, according to the *Sulphur Springs Weekly Standard.* This report was based on the fact that three cars were stolen by joyriding teenagers, compared to 1996, when only one car was stolen. —*Bad baseline*

## FALLACIES OF COMPARISON—PAGE 318

a. Colleges should start paying students for getting high grades. After all, business handsomely rewards its top people with bonuses and commissions, and everybody can see the beneficial effect of that practice on worker productivity. —*Questionable analogy*

b. Can the universe think about itself? We know that at least one part of it can: we ourselves. Is it not reasonable to conclude the whole can? —José Silva —*Fallacy of composition*

c. So, you're new love connection's a Yale man, is he? Well then, I'm sure he'll consider himself too good for the likes of me. The whole snooty institution considers itself too good for me. They turned down my application for admission. —*Division*

d. Adding a health tax to tobacco products is unfair to the tobacco industry. We're like any other legitimate business in this country. We sell a legal product to willing buyers in a free market, and we pay a fair share into the public purse through various forms of taxation. If tax revenue is to be raised to support Medicare, let the burden be shared across the board. —*Either questionable classification or questionable analogy depending on how much emphasis is placed on the work "like"*

## FALLACIES OF CAUSAL REASONING—PAGE 323

a. Argument against raising cigarette taxes: "Taxing cigarettes encourages interstate traffickers in stolen cigarettes by opening up a whole new and very profitable market for them. A vote for this measure is a vote for increased crime. Vote 'NO.' Vote against the smugglers and traffickers and black marketeers." —*Causal oversimplification, which in this context is used to support a straw person argument*

b. It's a bit mysterious, because Smith's numbers are less than spectacular. He scores fewer points than any of his teammates. We don't let him handle the ball, because he's sure to turn it over. And he's slow and clumsy on defense. But, he's a starter, and he plays the first few minutes of each game simply because—when he's in the starting lineup—we win 70 percent of our games. When he's not, we only win 50 percent of the time. —*Correlations as causes*

c. From *Playboy* magazine: "Is adultery bad for your health? The chances of having a heart attack while making love are infinitessimal, but if you do have one, the chances are, you'll have it with your mistress and not your wife. A study of thiry-four cardiac patients who died during intercourse revealed that twenty-nine of the thirty-four were having an extramarital affair." —*Causal oversimplification*

**d.** I knew a guy who was so influenced by statistics. Numbers ruled his entire life! One time, he found out that over 80 percent of all automobile accidents happen to people within five miles of where they live. So he moved! —*A joke, based on overlooking a common cause*

**e.** Whatever you do, DO NOT DESTROY THIS LETTER! Send it out to five of your friends. Mildred Wimplebush of Detroit destroyed her copy of this letter, and a week later, she died of a stroke. Henry Hinklefrump of El Segundo lost his copy of the letter and was fired within a month. Marlena Gorwangle of Missoula broke her ankle in a freak accident while tossing a salad only days after throwing her copy away. —*Post hoc*

## UNWARRANTED ASSUMPTIONS—PAGE 329

**a.** In spite of the objections of the Associated Students and the Faculty Senate, we are moving ahead to implement the new tuition fees recommended by the committee. We have to do *something*—and we have to do it *immediately*—to restore our reputation as a leading undergraduate educational institution. No one has come forward with a better alternative. —*The only game in town; also, false dilemma between doing nothing at all and doing this now*

**b.** A real miracle is something that demonstrably does occur but that cannot be scientifically explained. Now, we formed a prayer circle over Sister Sadie and her T-cell count has returned to normal, and she no longer tests positive for HIV. The doctors have confirmed what the labwork shows, but they can't seem to agree on an explanation. We believe God has sent the virus from her body. —*Ad ignorantiam; also, only game in town*

**c.** By the time you have wisely purchased this tome (book, for those of you in Rio Linda, California), most critics will have undoubtedly savaged it. In many cases, their reviews will have been written before the book was published. How do I know this? Because I do. —Rush Limbaugh —*Invincible ignorance*

**e.** We must believe in the existence of God, because it is written in the Holy scriptures, and conversely, we must believe in the Holy Scriptures, because they come from God." —Rene Descartes —*Begging the question*

**d.** Everything in this book is right, and you must be prepared to confront that reality. You can no longer be an honest liberal after reading this entire masterpiece. Throughout the book you will be challenged, because you will actually be persuaded to the conservative point of view. Whether you can admit this in the end will be a true test of your mettle as a human being. —Rush Limbaugh —*Invincible ignorance*

# INDEX